"Many many happy returns
With all my very best wishes
to d. father from Son
London 8th May 1949.

THE WHITE HOUSE PAPERS
VOLUME II

THE
WHITE HOUSE
PAPERS

of

Harry L. Hopkins

An intimate history by

ROBERT E. SHERWOOD

VOLUME II

JANUARY 1942—JULY 1945

EYRE & SPOTTISWOODE
LONDON

This book, first published in 1949, is produced in full conformity with the Authorized Economy Standards and is made and printed in Great Britain for Eyre & Spottiswoode (Publishers) Ltd. 15 Bedford Street, London, W.C.2., by The Stanhope Press Ltd., Rochester

CONTENTS

OF VOLUME II

Chapter   *Page*

PART IV

1942—*The Narrow Margin*

XXIII.	WINTER OF DISASTER	495
XXIV.	THE DECISION TO ATTACK	523
XXV.	THE MOLOTOV VISITS	548
XXVI.	THE DECISION IS CHANGED	585
XXVII.	THE TURNING-POINT	615

PART V

1943—*The Second Front*

XXVIII.	THE CASABLANCA CONFERENCE	665
XXIX.	THE POLITICAL FRONT	695
XXX.	TRIDENT AND QUADRANT	723
XXXI.	CAIRO, TEHERAN, AND OVERLORD	755

PART VI

1944-45—*Victory and Death*

XXXII.	THE FOURTH TERM	801
XXXIII.	BEGINNINGS OF DISSENSION	824
XXXIV.	THE YALTA CONFERENCE	842
XXXV.	THE TERRIFIC HEADACHE	860
XXXVI.	THE LAST MISSION	872
XXXVII.	CONCLUSION	907

OPERATION CODE NAMES	925
NOTES	929
INDEX	955

LIST OF ILLUSTRATIONS

Notes by Hopkins during a meeting at No. 10 Downing Street in April, 1942, when agreement was first reached on the opening of a second front in northern France (*see page* 540).   *facing page*   548

President Roosevelt's sketches of a landing craft, drawn on the eve of Mr. Molotov's visit to Washington in May, 1942 (*see page* 558).   565

Message to General Marshall and Admiral King, drafted jointly by President Roosevelt and Harry Hopkins on July 20, 1942, revealing their anxiety about the situation on the Russian Front. The marginal initials were added by Hopkins to indicate the author of each section (*see page* 591).   *facing page*   596

Joint draft by President Roosevelt and Harry Hopkins of a telegram to General Marshall on July 30, 1942, dealing with the situation in the Middle East brought about by the fall of Tobruk (*see page* 598).   *between pages* 604–5

Message (to Joint Chiefs of Staff) drafted jointly by President Roosevelt and Harry Hopkins, showing their concern over the situation at Guadalcanal (*see pages* 622–623).   *facing page*   613

Harry Hopkins, President Roosevelt and General George S. Patton lunching in the open air during a visit from Casablanca to American troops of the Fifth Army (*see page* 682).   *facing page*   692

The famous photograph of Generals Giraud and de Gaulle about to shake hands at the Casablanca Conference, and a page from Hopkins's notes describing the way in which it was brought about (*see page* 690).   *between pages* 700–1

The Vichy broadcast reporting General Marshall's dismissal. Comments by General Marshall and President Roosevelt (*see page* 758).   *facing page*   709

Marshal Stalin, President Roosevelt and Mr. Winston Churchill, with their chief advisers, at the Teheran Conference.   *facing page*   788

Memorandum to the Prime Minister prepared by President Roosevelt and Harry Hopkins regarding revised decisions on China following the Teheran Conference (*see page* 792).   *facing page*   805

Note from President Roosevelt to Robert E. Sherwood, written after the Fourth Term Campaign in November, 1944.   *facing page*   820

Stalin, Roosevelt, Churchill and Molotov lunching at Yalta—the Prime Minister showing a strong taste for caviar.   *facing page*   837

Harry Hopkins's note to the President, written during the final meeting at Yalta, suggesting a solution to the deadlock on reparations (*see page* 851).   *facing page*   852

Mrs. Anna Boettiger (the President's daughter), Section Officer Sarah Oliver (daughter of the Prime Minister), President Roosevelt, Mr. Churchill and Harry Hopkins on board the U.S.S. *Quincy* on Great Bitter Lake after the Yalta Conference (*see page* 858).   *facing page*   869

PART IV

1942—THE NARROW MARGIN

CHAPTER XXIII

WINTER OF DISASTER

WITHIN a month after the announcement that the great coalition had been formed, there were alarming evidences that it was about to be knocked to pieces by the blows delivered by the reinforced Germans in Africa and the staggering procession of Japanese conquests southward and westward. The manifold accomplishments of the Arcadia Conference appeared to be so many melancholy scraps of paper and the relationship of Roosevelt and Churchill was subjected to strains which would have overtaxed to the breaking-point the patience of smaller men. The accumulation of calamities provided a severe test in adversity for the American people—and, be it said, they met it admirably. For the British, the ordeal was far worse. This was their third wartime winter: in the first, they had been lulled by the illusions of the Phony War—in the second, they had been inspired to endure the Blitz by the glory of fighting alone—and now, with 750 million Russian, American, and Chinese allies fighting on their side, they were compelled to confront some of the most humiliating and inexplicable disasters in their entire history. Similarly, the Chinese had been fighting alone against Japan for four and a half years—and now the sudden acquisition of powerful Allies put them in much worse peril than ever.

The underrated Japanese forces shattered all previous Allied appraisals and calculations, and did so with such bewildering speed that the pins on the walls of the map rooms in Washington and London were usually far out of date. Reinforcements would be rushed to some threatened point, but even the radio messages to the isolated commanders announcing that reinforcements were on the way failed to arrive before the enemy did.

The area of Japanese conquest in the months following Pearl Harbour was an opened fan, with its handle in Tokyo, its radii more than three thousand miles in length, spreading eastward to the mid-Pacific, southward to the coast of Australia, and westward to the coast of India. It was probably the quickest conquest of a major empire that the world has ever seen.

Fortunately for the American people, they could be only dimly aware of the significance of this area which was so remote and unknown and full of unpronounceable names. But one did not need to be a military expert to see that the Japanese were possessing themselves of incalculably rich resources and of bases from which to make further advances in almost any direction that they might choose. The problem of preventing such further advances was bad enough by itself; but the problem of driving the Japanese out of the positions they had seized seemed too terrible to contemplate.

The most dreadful of all prospects, which came perilously close to realization, was that of a German break-through into the Middle East and a Japanese march through India, which would have enabled the two powerful Axis partners to join up and pool resources. This, of course, did not happen; but there were many moments in subsequent months when the 'best-informed sources' would not dare to bet against it.

During the two weeks while Hopkins was in the Navy Hospital following the Arcadia Conference, Rommel turned suddenly to the counter-attack, and the depressing story of reversal in Libya was beginning to be retold; the Japanese advanced to the tip of the Malay Peninsula, from which they could start the siege of Singapore, they effectively bombed Rangoon, the port of entry for the Burma Road, they landed on Borneo, Celebes, New Guinea, New Britain, and the Solomon Islands, from which they could threaten the lifeline between the United States and Australia.

Hopkins was very much worried about public morale. He was afraid that the flood of bad news would produce a resurgence of isolationist sentiment. He anticipated malicious cries of 'We told you so!' He favoured the creation of a counterpart of the British Ministry of Information which would counteract attacks on the Government at home and conduct the propaganda campaign abroad.

On January 24 he drove from the hospital to the White House for an evening with the President, and subsequently noted:

> I dined with the President alone tonight and he gave me a dispatch from Churchill covering the agreements on raw materials, shipping, and the distribution of munitions of war, and asked me to prepare an answer for him.
>
> This morning the various comments about the Justice Roberts Pearl Harbour report are coming out.
>
> One of the ironical and interesting things about these reports are the criticisms that come from the Senators who opposed every move to prepare for war, and of all the people who shouldn't have anything to say about Pearl Harbours these Senators like ... [*Note.*—There followed some caustic remarks about personalities which I have felt, regretfully, should be deleted.]
>
> It is perfectly clear that the President is going to have to go through just what Lincoln had to go through with this Senate Committee on the war and I fancy he is going to do it with the same imperturbability as did Lincoln.
>
> He is going to have many of the same problems that Lincoln had with generals and admirals whose records look awfully good, but who well may turn out to be the McClellans of this war. The only difference between Lincoln and Roosevelt is that I think Roosevelt will act much faster in replacing these fellows.

This war can't be won with . . . men who are thinking only about retiring to farms somewhere and who won't take great and bold risks, and Roosevelt has got a whole hatful of them in the Army and Navy that will have to be liquidated before we really get on with our fighting.

Fortunately he has got in King, Marshall, and Arnold three people who really like to fight.

The cables were coming in at great length from the A.B.D.A. Area, and each one deepened the discouragement. Admiral Hart was making no secret to Wavell and to the Dutch authorities of his conviction that he was not the man for this job—despite the fact that he had been for a long time conspicuous among high-ranking American officers in warning against the tendency to underrate Japanese military strength.

Hopkins noted further:

The President is disturbed about Admiral Hart and has a feeling that he is too old adequately to carry out the responsibilities that were given to him, and I fancy before long there will be a change in our naval command in the Far West.

The President is amazingly calm about the war; pleased at the news of our destroyers having got into action in the Far East; talked at great length about a device he is working on to get tanks ashore and discussed ways and means of bombing Japan.

(The 'ways and means' referred to here included the launching of Army medium bombers from Navy carriers, as was done three months later in the Doolittle raid.)

Roosevelt was not greatly worried about public morale. He was cool to the suggestion of a Government information service. If he had been inclined to shilly-shally before Pearl Harbour, and to shirk leadership, he was now in time of disaster exercising the functions of Commander-in-Chief with all the confidence and courage and imagination that he possessed in such abundance. It may be said that the American people were following his leadership, or that he was merely reflecting the people's spirit; either way, he was right in refusing to become alarmed about public morale, and Hopkins was wrong. The people needed no hypodermic stimuli other than the daily doses of bad news that they were absorbing.

There was fortunately a minimum of crying over the milk spilled at Pearl Harbour. The swift destruction of the ultramodern *Prince of Wales* showed what would have happened had the antiquated battleships of the Pacific fleet attempted to operate in the enormous area controlled by Japanese air power west of the international date line and north of the equator. Roosevelt said in February: 'The only way we could use those ships if we had them now would be for convoy duty in case the Japs ever started using capital ships to break the lifeline to Australia.' This, however, never happened, because American and Australian air power was established and maintained over that lifeline, and the Japanese were reluctant to risk their own battleships within its range. American weakness in these days could not be attributed to what happened at Pearl Harbour, where the enemy could have done far more serious damage had he attacked the vital installations of the base itself rather than the defensively huddled battleships: the weakness was the obvious result of years of puerile self-delusion which had manifested itself in such errors of calculation as the refusal to appropriate funds even for dredging the harbour at Guam.

General Marshall stated the case accurately and poignantly when he said: 'The Army used to have all the time in the world and no money; now we've got all the money and no time.'

The feeling of Americans was that the blame for the present situation was so widely distributed, from the top to the bottom of our national structure, that there wasn't much sense wasting any further time on recrimination. Much the same feeling had prevailed in Britain after Dunkirk and had produced the great rallying under Churchill. But Dunkirk was by now ancient history to the British people, who felt they had rendered full expiation for their previous sins of complacency. Now they were capable of angry protest against their Government.

When Churchill arrived home in London he found to his surprise that he was being attacked in the Press and Parliament for having overstayed his leave in Washington; he was being charged, in effect, with spending too much time surveying the great forest while paying insufficient attention to the toppling trees.

On January 27 the Prime Minister faced his critics in the House of Commons at the start of a three-day debate. In the course of a very long speech, he said:

> It is because things have gone badly and worse is to come that I demand a Vote of Confidence. . . . No one need be mealy-mouthed in debate, and no one should be chicken-hearted in voting. . . . Everyone in these rough times must do what he thinks is his duty.

His vote of confidence was 464 to 1. Beaverbrook cabled Hopkins that in all of Churchill's colourful life he had never achieved a triumph comparable to this one and that he was now 'established in authority and power exceeding all that has gone before'.

Hopkins cabled his hearty congratulations to Churchill, saying that the speech he had given and the magnificent victory that he had won in the House of Commons would prove to be tremendously heartening to all of the United Nations. Roosevelt also sent his congratulations, adding that 'there was also one vote in opposition to us', a reference to the solitary vote cast by Jeannette Rankin in the House of Representatives against a declaration of war the day after Pearl Harbour. In this same cable Roosevelt told Churchill that he had been informed that Admiral Hart would like to be relieved of his combat command, and he suggested the Dutch Admiral Helfrich as replacement. The President said that the combined organization which had been formed during the Arcadia Conference was working very smoothly and efficiently and, while there were many cases in which the Australian, New Zealand, and Dutch authorities should be consulted, such discussions should not be permitted to delay the taking of decisions in critical matters by the Anglo-American combined staff. Roosevelt undertook to work out and maintain close and intimate relationships with the military missions representing the Australian, New Zealand, and Netherlands Governments in Washington in regard to policies for the war in the South-West Pacific.

This was the cable in which Roosevelt told Churchill, as previously quoted: 'It is fun to be in the same decade with you.'

Churchill replied immediately that these matters would be taken up with the War Cabinet. He added: 'Thank you so much for all your kindness. . . . You can rest assured that you and I will have no disagreements.'

When Hopkins returned to the White House from hospital he was on the following regimen:

Alutropin (Campball Products Co.)—teaspoonful, ten (10) minutes before each meal (without water).

Amino-acid powder (Mead Johnson) and Hepavex Compound (Lilly) —teaspoonful each in ounce of tomato juice five (5) minutes before meals.

Dry diet—no fluids with meals. (All fluids to be taken between meals. To rest fifteen minutes before meals and one hour after meals. Diet to be adjusted so that most calories given at breakfast and luncheon.)

V-caps (Abbott)—one capsule with each meal.

Haliver oil with Vitamin 'D' (Abbott)—one capsule with breakfast.

Calcium bluconate (Abbott)—one tablet with each meal.

Liver extract (Lederle)—5 c.c. intramuscularly every other day for two weeks.

Appella powder, when required.

Roosevelt told Churchill at the end of another long cable: 'Harry is much better, but I am trying to confine him to barracks until he learns to take care of himself.'

It seemed to me at the time that Hopkins was not particularly rigorous in following the regimen, but his health did improve considerably, and I felt that this was due more to the inspiring spectacle provided by Roosevelt in action under pressure than to any amino-acid powder or liver-extract injections.

Aside from the thrills derived from the gallantry of the fight put up by the American-Filipino force on Bataan—and such thrills were always choked with the awareness that these brave men were doomed—the only source of good news was the Russian Front. The Red Army, continuing its amazing counter-attacks, drove the snowbound, frost-bitten Germans out of many of their advance positions. Even these successes were considered only temporary, however, for the belief persisted that the Russians were dependent on their traditional ally, General Winter, and that with the coming of spring the dread march of German conquest would be resumed. An Anglo-American intelligence appraisal of the prospects stated elegantly but grimly:

> The uncertainty which shrouds this facet of the general world situation causes the consideration of factors which are contradictory among themselves. The state of affairs most likely to produce a negotiated Russo-German settlement would be one where neither side envisioned a quick and sweeping victory. Such a situation might range from a true balance of forces to a definite German ascendancy.

More intelligence came from the British military mission in Moscow, telling of talks with Stalin and a visit by General Mason Macfarlane to the Russian Front:

> In reply to questions as to the prospects of a Second Front being opened in Europe, Stalin was told that although this could not be accomplished in the near future, one of the purposes of the present campaign in Libya was to obtain bases from which an attack on Italy could be launched. Stalin said that the Germans still possessed greatly superior strength in tanks and would undoubtedly resume their offensives against the Russians in the spring. He was asked for his views on the possibility of an attack by the Japanese on the Russians in the Far East and he said that he would 'regard this without enthusiasm'. He believed that the Japanese would attack the Soviet Union before the spring. If they did not, time would be given to reinforce the Russian armies in Siberia and bring them back to full strength, and Stalin would then consider resuming conversations on the advisability of the Soviet Union joining the war against Japan.

This British report stated that 'the Red Army was in a bad way in the autumn, but its tail is now up', and that there was a general feeling of confidence in Moscow, and high morale. In private conversations Stalin expressed a degree of confidence which 'struck a more sober note'. He said that Russian strength might be so increased during the rest of this year and the Germans might be so badly shaken that there was a possibility of ending the war in 1942.

Laurence Steinhardt was appointed Ambassador to Turkey to conduct the immensely important negotiations in that strategic though neutral country, and Admiral William H. Standley became the new American Ambassador to the Soviet Union. An old friend of Roosevelt's, Standley had been one of the President's most rugged supporters in the long battle for aid for the Allies before Pearl Harbour.

Hopkins wrote to General Marshall asking that Colonel Faymonville be given the rank of general so that he might be able to operate on a higher level when dealing with the Russians on questions of Lend-Lease. Hopkins added: 'The Russian fighting front is undoubtedly weakening Germany far more than all the theatres of war put together. There is a real possibility that the Russians may smash them during the next year.' Marshall immediately complied with the request for Faymonville's promotion.

In mid-January Roosevelt wrote to Admiral Land saying:

> I am still terribly disturbed about the fact that an adequate number of ships are not available for Russia. . . . This Government has made a firm pledge to Russia and we simply cannot go back on it. . . . You simply must find some ships that can be diverted at once for this Russian business.

Roosevelt cabled Stalin a statement of the numbers of fighter planes, bombers, and medium and light tanks for shipment during January and February, and said: 'Although we are at present having our troubles in the war with Japan, we are sending reinforcements to the Pacific which I believe will be sufficient to stop the Japanese advance. We are prepared for some more setbacks, however.' He assured Stalin that there would be no relaxation of efforts to keep the shipments going to the Soviet Union.

To this Stalin replied:

> I have received your message informing me of consignments of armaments from the United States for January and February.
>
> I would like to emphasize the fact that at the present moment, when the peoples of the Soviet Union and its army are exerting all their powers to thrust back, by their determined offensive, Hitler's troops, the fulfilment of American deliveries, including tanks and aeroplanes, is of the utmost importance for our common cause, for our further successes.

Stalin always gave evidence of very considerable respect for Roosevelt, but Soviet propaganda at that time was expressing scant admiration for the character of the American or British contribution to the total war effort. Indeed, the estimates of the fighting qualities of American troops as broadcast

B

by Moscow did not seem to be very much higher than Hitler's, which have been quoted in a previous chapter. A marked change in the nature of this propaganda was brought about in a curious way. The twenty-fourth anniversary of the foundation of the Red Army was to be celebrated on February 23, and in preparation for that event the Tass News Agency was collecting expressions of tribute and salute from various eminent personages throughout the United Nations. It occurred to some workers in the embryonic psychological warfare agency in Washington that it would be a fine idea to include General MacArthur in this greeting to our Russian allies. MacArthur had by then become a tremendous figure as the only commander in the Pacific who had been able to stop the Japanese advance at any point. The idea was suggested to officers in the War Department, who scornfully refused to put through a cable from an obscure civilian agency to Corregidor requesting that General MacArthur take time from other duties to pay tribute to the Red Army. However, a short daily file of world news was then being sent through Navy communications to MacArthur's headquarters for the beleagured men there and on Bataan, and the enterprising psychological warriors, without authorization from anyone, tacked on to that a message to the general calling his attention to the forthcoming anniversary. MacArthur immediately replied with the following:

> The world situation at the present time indicates that the hopes of civilization rest on the worthy banners of the courageous Russian Army. During my lifetime I have participated in a number of wars and have witnessed others, as well as studying in great detail the campaigns of outstanding leaders of the past. In none have I observed such effective resistance to the heaviest blows of a hitherto undefeated enemy, followed by a smashing counter-attack which is driving the enemy back to his own land. The scale and grandeur of this effort marks it as the greatest military achievement in all history.

This message from MacArthur was turned over to the Tass Agency and transmitted to the Soviet authorities, who broadcast it to the entire world as coming from the heroic and brilliant American general who commanded the valiant forces in the epic struggle for freedom in the Philippines. From then on, the Russian propagandists were much more favourably disposed toward American fighting men.

The whole task of getting supplies to Russia—and to Britain, and for operations in Africa and the Middle East—was gravely complicated by new developments in the Battle of the Atlantic. In mid-January, Germany took the offensive against the United States. U-boats were the only weapons available for this purpose, but they were now weapons of terrible effectiveness and the defences against them were inexcusably inadequate. The submarines came in within sight of the glow that arose from Broadway, sinking ships within a few hundred yards of the East Coast. The results are told in awful tables of losses during that winter of disaster. In two months the U-boats sank 132 ships in the Western Atlantic. The meaning of these losses has been graphically demonstrated in a quotation by Professor Morison from a Navy Training Manual:

> The massacre enjoyed by the U-boats along our Atlantic Coast in 1942 was as much a national disaster as if saboteurs had destroyed half a dozen of our biggest war plants. . . . If a submarine sinks two 6,000-ton ships and one 3,000-ton tanker, here is a typical account of what we have totally lost: 42 tanks, 8 six-inch howitzers, 88 twenty-five-pound guns, 40 two-pound guns, 24 armoured cars, 50 Bren carriers, 5,210 tons of ammunition, 600 rifles, 428 tons of tank supplies, 2,000 tons of stores, and 1,000 tanks of gasoline. Suppose the three ships had made port and the cargoes were dispersed. In order to knock out the same amount of equipment by air bombing, the enemy would have to make three thousand successful bombing sorties.

The ships moving along the Atlantic Coast at night, although showing no lights themselves, passed between the waiting submarines and the glare of lights from the shore and therefore presented easy targets. Morison has written,

> Miami and its luxurious suburbs threw up six miles of neon-light glow, against which the southbound shipping that hugged the reefs to avoid the Gulf Stream was silhouetted. Ships were sunk and seamen drowned in order that the citizenry might enjoy business and pleasure as usual.

After three months of this massacre, the military authorities ordered the lights dimmed in coastal areas—it was called 'the brown-out'—and 'squawks went up all the way from Atlantic City to Southern Florida that *the tourist season would be ruined*'.

Since the defence of shipping in American coastal waters was obviously the responsibility of the U.S. Navy, Churchill was anxious to know what measures were being taken, aside from curtailment of neon signs. Roosevelt cabled on February 6: 'This matter is being given urgent consideration by Stark, King, and me.' But it took many months for this urgent consideration to produce results.

Roosevelt was greatly annoyed with the Navy for paying insufficient attention to the Battle of the Atlantic, and he remained so for a considerable time. Incidentally, his extreme partiality for the Navy was not always the advantage to that service that it was supposed to be; he was continually asking the admirals embarrassing questions based on his knowledge of naval matters, whereas he left the generals to shift pretty much for themselves. More than once harassed officers in the Navy Department were heard to mutter: 'I wish to God he'd get absorbed in the *Army* for a change!'

In the February 6 cable referred to above Roosevelt confirmed the substitution of Helfrich for Hart in the A.B.D.A. Area. Churchill replied at length, expressing the belief that the Combined Chiefs of Staff machinery, 'ponderous and complicated though it was bound to be, is functioning smoothly and well. I even think we may plume ourselves a little having brought it all into action so soon.' Churchill went on to talk of Chinese troops in Burma and of the French situation, saying: 'The Vichy attitude described by you and manifesting itself in many ways is rotten. They have certainly been helping Rommel with supplies. . . . The Libyan setback has been both a shock and a disappointment.' He mentioned British plans to occupy Vichy-controlled Madagascar before the Japanese could get there. He commented on a new Lend-Lease agreement—which will be discussed later in this chapter—and concluded: 'I trust Harry is improving. Please give him my regards. You would like an American film I saw last night, *The Remarkable Andrew*. It stirs one's dander.'

The reference to the 'Vichy attitude' in Churchill's cable proves that this sore subject was again a factor, but Roosevelt's reply indicated that Hull was away from Washington and there was no disagreement as to the desirability of taking a sharper tone toward Pétain.

Roosevelt cabled Churchill on February 10 that he had received information from many sources—and it had been confirmed by Pétain and Darlan in admissions they had made to Leahy—that the French had been shipping trucks and food supplies to Tunis for the use of the German and Italian forces in North Africa. The President had therefore sent a message to Pétain which was, in substance, as follows:

> The American Government has information that the French Government has entered into some arrangement with the Axis Powers providing for the use of French ships for the transportation of supplies and possibly war material to Tunis for delivery to the enemy forces in Libya. There can be no possible justification under the terms of the Armistice for the shipment of war materials or other direct aid to the Axis Powers and without official assurances from the Vichy Government that no military aid will go forward to the Axis in any theatre of war and that French ships will not be used in the furtherance of their aggression, Admiral Leahy will be instructed to return immediately to the United States for consultation as to our future policy.

Shortly after that Hopkins, Rosenman, and I were having dinner with the President in the Study, and there was talk of the forthcoming trials in Riom,

France, where the Vichy Government was to charge Blum, Daladier and others of the Third Republic with failure to prepare France for war. It had been announced that the trials would be secret, with no representatives of the world Press admitted. Rosenman said: 'I certainly want to read the full records of those hearings after this war is over.' Roosevelt thought about that for a moment, then asked that the telephone be brought to him; the telephone was on his desk with a cord so long it could be carried to him wherever he was sitting. He called Sumner Welles and said: 'Send a cable to Bill Leahy asking him to tell Pétain that I want to get full transcripts of those Riom trials from day to day.'

Roosevelt did not care to wait until the end of the war to read this interesting material.

I do not know whether or not it was a direct result of this message, but Pétain changed his mind about keeping the trials secret, and the Press was admitted. The courageous and eloquent statements of defendants were thus made known to the French people and the world, and did more than anything that had happened since June, 1940, to stimulate the spirit of resistance in France and to discredit the Vichy Government. So effective was this defence of the Third Republic that the German masters of Vichy ordered that the proceedings at Riom be stopped.

The question of French aid to Rommel in Africa produced a considerable amount of bickering correspondence, and Ambassador Leahy again became so disgusted with the Vichy attitude that he asked to be recalled. Two months later he was recalled to become Chief of Staff to the Commander-in-Chief.

Returning to Churchill's cable of February 7.

The Prime Minister said that seventy per cent of the British troops that had fought in Malaya had been evacuated successfully across the strait to Singapore. With the reinforcements that had arrived, there were the equivalent of four divisions for the defence of the great base. A hundred Hurricane fighter planes had also arrived to strengthen the air force, but the bombardment of the airfields reduced their operations materially. However, Churchill said: 'The Japanese have to cross a broad moat before attacking a strong fortified and still mobile force. Tobruk was held for six months under these conditions, so I have good confidence. Every day that Singapore holds out gives Wavell time to get a strong grip on Sumatra and Java.'

That was on February 7. It was the start of one of the worst weeks of the war.

On February 9 the Japanese began to stream across the 'broad moat' of the Strait of Johore. On the same day the huge liner *Normandie* burned at her dock in New York City, indicating that the long arm of the German saboteur had reached to West 49th Street.

On February 12 the German cruisers *Scharnhorst*, *Gneisenau*, and *Prinz Eugen* escaped from Brest on the French coast, passed through the English Channel and reached German ports, damaged but still navigable.

On February 15 Singapore surrendered with apparently no real battle having been fought in its defence.

For Churchill, the Naval Person, the escape of the cruisers was an 'annoying incident', but no major misfortune, since these dangerous ships constituted less of a menace in German ports than they had in French ones; to Churchill, the imperialist, the fall of Singapore constituted, as he said, 'the greatest disaster to British arms which our history records'. The British people as a whole evidently did not agree with these relative estimates. They regarded Singapore with a certain detachment. The painfully sorry showing made by British colonial officials and officers in the Far East was a matter of rage and disgust to the London man in the street who had been taking punishment for going on two years; he now felt sure that Colonel Blimp, the flabby, bird-brained creature who appeared in Low's cartoons, was no caricature. But when German warships, that were constantly under surveillance, managed to steam right under the guns of Dover and through everything that the Royal Navy and the R.A.F. could throw at them, then, it was assumed, there must be tragic incompetence right at home. Thus, the 'annoying incident' had undoubtedly done more damage even that the 'greatest disaster' to the confidence and to the pride of the average Englishman.

Churchill, who had won his greatest Parliamentary triumph a scant three weeks before, now faced the worst predicament of his career as Prime Minister. He made a broadcast speech in which he attributed the whole series of misfortunes in the Far East to the fact that America's shield of sea power had been 'dashed to the ground' at Pearl Harbour. There were numerous expressions of irritation at this statement in Washington, as though Churchill were attempting to escape censure by blaming it all on the U.S. Navy, but it did not bother Roosevelt at all. He merely remarked: 'Winston had to say *something*.'

The day after the fall of Singapore, Hopkins noted:

> Last evening the President and I had dinner and talked at great length about the immediate steps which should be taken by our Army and Navy.
>
> This memorandum is the result of our talk. There were many implications in the conversation, of course, which are not in the memorandum. The memorandum itself is not inclusive.

LIST OF PRIORITIES—A

1. United States to take primary responsibility for reinforcing the Netherlands East Indies, Australia, and New Zealand. The men, material,

and munitions to leave the United States prior to March 31. Supporting supplies of men and material to compensate for attrition rate to follow regularly. The force to include the men and material that the Joint Chiefs of Staff consider necessary.

2. In addition to convoy, the Navy to strike with every means available in that area the supply lines of concentration points of the Japs. The Navy to provide in Australia such naval base material as is required.

3. Every effort made to hold Java as well as defending with all means available all further advances of the Japanese. Hold the island of Timor. [Note.—The Japanese landed on Timor, within striking distance of Australia, only four days later.]

4. The British to make such supplementary assistance as they have available in this area in ships and manpower.

5. The British to take the primary responsibility for reinforcing Burma immediately and defending Rangoon. The United States to provide such supplementary aid as is available.

6. The United States to continue to take the primary responsibility for military assistance to China in terms of material, but confining that material for the present to the urgent munitions of war such as aircraft, ammunition, high-octane gasoline, and such other weapons of war as can be utilized when they reach the Chinese Army. The volunteer air force now in Rangoon to be considered part of American support of Chiang Kai-shek.

7. Intensification of the campaign against submarines in the Atlantic, including the great extension of the use of smaller ships.

8. The Russian Protocol, the supplies to the Middle East, the Persian Gulf, the United Kingdom and to selected South American countries.

9. The reinforcement of Hawaii. The increase in our attacking force on the Atlantic Seaboard to 100,000 men and the preparation of shipping for their purposes. The British to increase their special forces from 55,000 to 100,000 men.

10. Carry out the proposed plans for bomber squadrons in England.

11. The strengthening of the Atlantic Ferry Service.

12. Put up in the very top production priorities for the machine tools, the equipment and facilities required for the production of high-octane gasoline plants, of all combat aircraft of the Army and Navy and merchant ships.

LIST OF PRIORITIES—B

1. The complete occupation by American forces in Iceland and the reaching of our objective in the North of Ireland.

2. A complete plan for striking force in Alaska and the Aleutian Islands and pushing that plan as far as possible prior to July 1.

3. The induction and enlistment of ——— hundred thousand men for the Army and the Navy and the provision of training and equipment for these men.

Roosevelt then sent Churchill a cable which was so warmly friendly and sympathetic that I hestitate to attempt to make the paraphrase required by the security authorities. He said that the defeats suffered at Singapore and elsewhere had given the 'back-seat drivers a field day', but he knew that the Prime Minister would be of good heart, secure in the assurance that he was supported by the confidence of the great masses of the British people, and would never cease to look forward to the main task of fighting and winning the war. Churchill replied that he was deeply grateful for this 'warmhearted message'. He said that he had 'found it difficult to keep my eye on the ball' during these days of personal stress. He said he had made some changes in the British Cabinet, including the appointment of Oliver Lyttelton to the newly created post of Minister of Production from which Beaverbrook had been compelled to resign because of ill health. Churchill said that he was grieved at the temporary loss of Beaverbrook from the British Government and added, 'I know you will realise what friends we are and how helpful his driving power will be when he has recovered his health.'

In Roosevelt's cable he had promised to talk about the escape of the German cruisers in his radio speech which had been announced for February 23. It was in celebration of Washington's Birthday, but February 22 fell on a Sunday that year and Roosevelt had recently departed from his long-established practice of giving his speeches on Sunday evenings (when the radio audience was largest) because of complaints from church leaders that he was reducing attendance at Sunday-evening services. Roosevelt did not fulfil his promise to Churchill. He dictated several lengthy explanations of why it was better for the German cruisers to have removed themselves from Brest, but they all sounded lame. For no matter how elaborate the explanations, he could not answer the really persistent question: 'Why weren't those ships sunk in the Channel?' Instead, Roosevelt dwelt largely upon purely American misfortunes and promised that 'soon we and not our enemies will have the offensive'. Whenever criticism was being concentrated on the British Roosevelt was wonderfully skilful and graceful in directing it elsewhere. In this speech he even went back to Valley Forge:

> For eight years General Washington and his Continental Army were faced continually with formidable odds and recurring defeats. Supplies and equipment were lacking. In a sense, every winter was a Valley Forge. Throughout the Thirteen States there existed Fifth Columnists— selfish men, jealous men, fearful men, who proclaimed that Washington's cause was hopeless, that he should ask for a negotiated peace.

And he ended with the famous words: 'Tyranny, like hell, is not easily conquered', which Tom Paine had written on a drumhead in 1776.

Churchill cabled: 'Warmest congratulations on your heartening declaration.'

When Roosevelt finished his broadcast in the White House basement that night we went upstairs to the Oval Study for a drink, and word came from California that while the President was speaking a Japanese submarine had surfaced off the coast near Santa Barbara and had fired some shells at a ranch. This was merely a demonstration—a minor 'insult'—which resulted in no casualties and only negligible damage. It was one of the instances, previously alluded to, when the enemy attempted to nullify the propaganda effect of a Roosevelt speech by some spectacular, headline-gathering operation; but it taught Roosevelt a lesson never again to have speeches announced more than two or three days ahead of time.

Some twenty-four hours after the attack by submarine there was another disturbance in Southern California which provided the nation with some welcome comedy relief in the midst of all the far-flung tragedy. An air-raid alarm went off in the vicinity of Los Angeles which brought the Pursuit Interceptor Command into action and caused the anti-aircraft artillery barrage to be opened up. Two versions of this episode were given out to the Press, one by the Secretary of the Navy and the other by the Secretary of War. Knox said that wide reconnaissance indicated that no airplanes whatsoever had been over Los Angeles at the time of the alarm. Stimson stated that the available details indicated the presence of unidentified airplanes, perhaps as many as fifteen of them. He read a telegram from the West Coast which said that these planes 'may be some from commercial sources operated by enemy agents for the purpose of spreading alarm, disclosing position of anti-aircraft positions or effectiveness of black-outs'. All that could be said for certain by either the War or Navy Department was that 1,430 rounds of ammunition had been fired by the anti-aircraft batteries, no planes had been shot down, no bombs dropped, no casualties. In fact—this was precisely the kind of top-level snafu best calculated to delight the American people. As if the Army and Navy did not have trouble enough with this one, the very next night two air-raid alarms went off in Washington, which caused the President to write sharply to the War Department asking who had the responsibility for setting off air-raid alarms and who had the responsibility for explaining these occurrences to the Press. From then on the air menace to the continental United States diminished.

There was some hopeful news from MacArthur in this last week of February. On February 22 he reported that for the first time a surface vessel, the *Coast Farmer*, had run the blockade and got through to Mindanao in the Philippines with a cargo of balanced rations and ammunition. He said: 'She had no difficulty getting through. The thinness of the enemy's coverage is such that it can readily be pierced along many routes, including direct westward passage from Honolulu. I have secure bases for reception in Mindanao and the Visayas.'

In another dispatch that day MacArthur reported indications that the Japanese had been so badly mauled during the Bataan fighting that there was the possibility that the American forces had gained the respite they so desperately needed. As MacArthur expressed it, 'with his present forces, the enemy appears to be unable to make the attack required to destroy me'. He requested that none of the encouraging material contained in this dispatch be given any publicity at this time.

Three days later the troops on Bataan even managed to launch a drive and advance five miles through the malarial jungle-choked hills.

Yet this was the time when Roosevelt had to make the indescribably difficult decision to order MacArthur to leave his men on Bataan and Corregidor and embark in a PT boat on the perilous attempt to reach Australia.

By February 23 it had become obviously impossible for Wavell to continue even the pretence of exercising command of the A.B.D.A. Area, and he was ordered by the Combined Chiefs of Staff to dissolve his headquarters on Java and turn over responsibility for defence of that rich, populous, and strategically vital island to the Dutch. On the same day that these fateful orders were dispatched to Wavell, Hopkins received a long and pitiful cable from H. J. Van Mook, Lieutenant-Governor of the Netherlands East Indies. Van Mook had left Washington only three weeks previously to return to his post in Java, writing to Hopkins as he left: 'I feel sure that the conduct of the war and the general policy towards the Far East are safe in your hands'; in words of desperation he now begged that there be no decision to abandon the fight in the A.B.D.A. Area. He gave details of means by which he believed that Java could be defended, particularly by the ferrying of fighter planes on the U.S. aircraft carrier *Langley*. This cable ended with the words: 'For God's sake take the strong and active decisions and don't stop sending materials and men pending deliberations as time factor more pressing than ever.'

Hopkins replied that it was the determination of all the authorities in Washington to support the fighting in Java with all available means including any fighter aircraft that could possibly be dispatched. He said that there was no disposition to abandon the fight to hold Java—in fact, the very contrary was the case. These were wishful words, but they were not, unfortunately, based on the dreadful realities of the situation.

Two days later the *Langley* was sunk in the Battle of the Java Sea. So were most of the ships of the Allied fleet in those waters, including the cruiser *Houston*, on which Roosevelt had cruised so often on salt-water holidays.

There was now neither sea power nor air power available to stop the Japanese landings on Java, and the island surrendered a week later. Now, it seemed, the north coast of Australia was completely exposed to the enemy.

The day after the surrender of Java the Japanese took Rangoon, and thus choked off access by sea to the Burma Road. The situation in the words of the Australian Foreign Minister, Dr. Herbert Evatt, was 'practically desperate'. The Rising Sun had indeed risen: the gigantic fan was now almost fully unfolded, and it covered territory, land, and sea, the security of which had previously depended largely upon the power of the British Empire. This traditional power was now frail indeed east of Suez, and none too sure of its chances of survival even in the Middle East. Roosevelt was consequently put in a position such as no previous President of the United States had ever occupied or dreamed of occupying. Hundreds of millions of people on the other side of the earth looked to him for deliverance or protection. He was considered, as the Chinese Foreign Minister said in a letter to Hopkins, 'the Commander-in-Chief of the United Nations . . . the one hope of mankind'. It was a position which imposed inconceivable responsibility—and it added many complications in his dealings with Winston Churchill, that proud and imperious man whom someone once described with rare accuracy as 'half American and all English'.

Even in the heat of battle it was impossible to avoid arrangements affecting the postwar world, and here the President and Prime Minister were on most difficult common ground. I have mentioned the Lend-Lease Agreement which Churchill discussed in his long cable of February 7, just before the series of calamities culminating in the fall of Singapore. This Agreement had been under discussion for some time and was of very considerable importance in laying 'the foundations upon which we may create after the war a system of enlarged production, exchange and consumption of goods for the satisfaction of human needs in our country, in the British Commonwealth, and in all other countries which are willing to join in this great effort'.

Churchill reported that the majority of the British Cabinet felt that it would be a great mistake to consider any proposals for the abandonment after the war of imperial preference in return for Lend-Lease aid from the United States. (It will be recalled that, at the Atlantic Conference, Churchill himself had confessed to a lack of enthusiasm for the system of imperial preference set up under the Ottawa Agreements.) The Cabinet majority felt that any discussion of such a 'barter' deal would provoke unpleasant debates in Parliament and throughout the Dominions; it would provide welcome material for the enemy propagandists who were constantly harping on the theme that the rich and greedy United States was using the war emergency as a means of seizing control of the entire British Empire. The negotiations relative to this Lend-Lease Agreement had been conducted by the State Department in communication with the Foreign Office, but Churchill expressed the hope that the President would take a personal hand in the matter and deal directly with him. The President did so.

A reply to the Prime Minister, drafted by the State Department, was couched in the usual formal terms, but Roosevelt rejected this and wrote a cable in his own intensely personal and considerate manner. He told Churchill: 'I understand something of the nice relationships which are required by your constitution for dealings between your Home Government and the Dominions.' He said that nothing could be further from his mind than an attempt to use Lend-Lease as a trading weapon over the principle of imperial preference. He urged that there be 'bold, forthright and comprehensive discussions looking forward to the construction of what you so aptly call "a free, fertile economic policy for the post-war world".' He expressed the belief that developments 'which neither of us dreams of will be subjects of the most serious consideration in the not-too-distant future. So nothing should be excluded from the discussions.' He did not want any agreements to be hedged with qualifications or footnotes which would give 'to our enemies the impression that we are overly cautious'. He said that it had been and remained the determination of the United States 'to approach the whole subject of Lend-Lease in a manner that will avoid the terrible pitfalls of the First World War'.

In his Washington's Birthday speech Roosevelt gave clear statement of his own attitude toward the scope of the Atlantic Charter:

> We of the United Nations are agreed on certain broad principles in the kind of peace we seek. The Atlantic Charter applies not only to the parts of the world that border the Atlantic, but to the whole world; disarmament of aggressors, self-determination of nations and peoples, and . . . freedom of speech, freedom of religion, freedom from want, and freedom from fear.

Every word of this, of course, was notice to the peoples of the far Pacific and East Asia that their interests and rights were of no less concern than those of the peoples of Europe or the Western Hemisphere. It was intended as an answer to the currently formidable Japanese propaganda, but it served to confirm Roosevelt's position as 'the one hope'.

The Australian Government demanded that their divisions in the Middle East be returned to their homeland for its defence. These troops could ill be spared nor could the shipping for their transport. Churchill begged that at least one Australian division be diverted to Burma. Prime Minister John Curtin, the head of Australia's Labour Government, refused this point blank.

Churchill appealed to Roosevelt to intervene, and the President then cabled

Curtin asking him, 'in the interests of our whole war effort in the Far East', to reconsider the decision to move the First Australian Division to Australia. He pointed out that, in addition to all of the American troops and forces now *en route*, a further 27,000 men, fully equipped in every respect, were to be sent from the United States to Australia. He pointed out that the Americans were better able to reinforce the Allied right flank in the war against Japan—this right flank being represented now by Australia and New Caledonia—whereas the left flank in Burma and India must be the responsibility of Great Britain. It was on this left flank that the veteran Australian division was most sorely needed.

Curtin agreed to this, but events were moving so swiftly that before any troops could be sent from Suez, Rangoon had fallen and access to Southern Burma was denied. Some Australian troops were consequently diverted to Ceylon, the last sea base that was left in the Indian Ocean.

However, more trouble flared up between the Dominion Government and London over Churchill's appointment of Richard G. Casey, Australian Minister in Washington, as member of the War Cabinet and Minister of State in the Middle East. The disputes over this led Roosevelt later to dispatch a cable in which he paid Churchill the compliment of speaking plainly:

> The publicity from the Casey business disturbs me greatly. . . . It is particularly disturbing to learn from the newspapers that you, on the one hand, feel compelled to discuss this matter publicly in Parliament, while Curtin, on the other hand, may have decided to issue a detailed White Paper. It would be desirable all round if any way can be found to avoid all further public discussion of this which, it seems to me, plays right into the hands of our enemies. I realize that the Casey appointment is only an incident. The more important issue is the basic relationship of Australia to Great Britain. I sense in this country a growing feeling of impatience at what publicly appears to be a rather strained relationship at this critical time between the United Kingdom and Australia. . . . I say this to you because I myself feel greatly responsible for the turn of events. I still consider the decision to send Casey to the Middle East is a wise one and I told him quite frankly that I hoped he would take this job because of his knowledge of the American and Australian as well as the British angles in the Middle East area.

It was this 'strained relationship', and the desperate predicament of Australia that caused it, which influenced the orders to MacArthur. Roosevelt knew full well that the departure of MacArthur from Corregidor would be a grievous blow to the heroic men of his command and thus to the whole United States. It was ordering the captain to be the first to leave the sinking ship. But Roosevelt had to weigh these considerations against the fact that no move he could make would be so well calculated to bolster the morale of the people of Australia and New Zealand. He made his serious decision at a conference with Hopkins, Marshall and King in the White House late in the afternoon of Sunday, February 22—which was the day before the orders went to Wavell to dissolve the A.B.D.A. command—but the news did not come out until MacArthur arrived in Australia three weeks later. During those three weeks a sense of panic was developing throughout the entire South-West Pacific area, for it seemed that all the ambitious attempts to establish unified command, or any command at all, had collapsed. When the news of MacArthur did come out Americans had to accept the chilling realization that the troops who were continuing resistance anywhere in the Philippine Islands had been written off. On April 9 the forces on Bataan surrendered and on May 5 General Jonathan M. Wainwright on Corregidor made the final surrender of all American-Filipino forces still in action.

While awaiting news of the passage of MacArthur to Australia, Roosevelt sent a long cable to Churchill setting forth the results of the current deliberations of the Chiefs of Staff. It stated: 'The U.S. agrees that the Pacific situation is now very grave', and then went on to give in detail the effects of this in every quarter of the globe, from Iceland to Ceylon, and the measures to be be taken to meet the crisis. (One of the most vitally important spots on earth was New Caledonia, on the lifeline to Australia, which was held by the Free French; there was no talk of restoring *that* to Vichy sovereignty.)

Following this long cable, which was obviously prepared by the Chiefs of Staff, Roosevelt sent another long one of his own giving his purely personal views of 'the complexity of the present operational command set-up to which is added equal complexity in the political set-up'. He said: 'Since our meetings in January the excellent arrangements established then have become largely obsolescent in relation to the whole South-West Pacific area', and he offered the following main suggestions for the Prime Minister's consideration:

1. The United States will assume responsibility for all operations in the Pacific area. Decisions governing this area will be made in Washington by the U.S. Joint Chiefs of Staff in consultation with an advisory council on operational matters composed of representatives of Australia, New Zealand, the Netherlands East Indies, China and possibly Canada. The supreme command will be American, and the main objective will be to regain the offensive. (Roosevelt cited as one example the offensive in a north-westerly direction from the main southern bases—and, as will be seen in a later chapter, this plan was developed as an actual alternative to the invasion of the continent of Europe.)

2. The area of British responsibility will extend from Singapore to the Persian Gulf and the Red Sea and include Libya and the Mediterranean area.

But it is assumed that the Operation GYMNAST, the landings in North-West Africa, has been temporarily shelved.

3. The North and South Atlantic, and the Western European continent, will form the area of joint British-American responsibility, with details of command to be worked out later as required. Roosevelt said that he was becoming 'more and more interested in plans for the establishment of a new front on the European continent this summer'. He said that such a front provided the shortest distance from the United States for supply lines of any possible front anywhere in the world, and while the development of it would undoubtedly involve heavy losses, he considered that these could be compensated by at least equal losses for the Germans and 'by compelling Hitler to divert heavy forces of all kinds from the Russian front'. He emphasized the necessity of maintaining the delivery of all possible aid to the Soviet Union.

Roosevelt added that the grand strategy governing operations in all areas would continue to be the subject of study and decisions by the Joint Chiefs of Staff and that the various Boards on munitions, raw materials and shipping would continue their functions subject to the joint approval of the President and the Prime Minister.

Churchill cabled general agreement to this, summing up: 'I feel that your proposals as I have ventured to elaborate and interpret them will achieve the double purpose, namely (a) integrity of executive and operational action, and (b) opportunity of reasonable consultation for those whose fortunes are involved.' He believed that division of responsibility should not extend to determination of naval strategy, saying: 'Nothing must prevent the United States and British Navies from working to a common strategy from Alaska to Capetown.' He suggested that a Pacific Council be set up in Washington as well as in London for 'those whose fortunes are involved'—namely, China, Australia, New Zealand, and the Netherlands.

It was impossible for the harassed Chiefs of Staff with all their charts and compasses to draw any enduring line of demarcation between one theatre and another in the Far East, for the war was no respecter of man-made frontiers nor even of the natural obstacles imposed by Divine Providence. The Japanese surge on land through Burma, and a series of devastating blows to British naval units and shipping in the Bay of Bengal, brought India into the zone of war, and although this tremendous problem was one for which Roosevelt wanted to have no responsibility, it was deposited on him and remained with him for a long time.

On March 10, the day before Churchill announced the Cripps mission, Roosevelt wrote the Former Naval Person a long cable on the Indian problem. He said: 'Of course this is a subject which all of you good people know far more about than I do and I have felt much diffidence in making any suggestions concerning it.' He said that he had tried to consider it from the point of view of history and had gone back to the inception of the United States Government with the hope that this might provide 'a new thought' for India.

Roosevelt then wrote that during the American Revolution the Thirteen Colonies had set themselves up as separate sovereignties under a temporary government with a Continental Congress, which he described as 'a body of ill-defined powers and large inefficiencies'. Following the war, a stopgap Government was formed under the Articles of Confederation, and this continued until real union was achieved under the Constitution in 1789. Roosevelt suggested a somewhat similar process for India: the setting-up of a Government to be 'headed by a small group representative of different religions and geographies, occupations and castes; it would be representative of the existing British Provinces and the Council of Princes and would be recognized as a temporary Dominion Government'. This representative group would be charged with the duty of considering the structure of the permanent Government of India, such consideration to extend 'for a period of five or six years, or at least until a year after the end of the present war'. In the meantime, it would exercise executive and administrative authority over public services, such as finances, railways, telegraphs, etc. Roosevelt wrote: 'Perhaps some such method, with its analogy to the problems and travails of the United States from 1783 to 1789, might cause the people of India to forget past hard feelings, and to become more loyal to the British Empire, and to emphasize the danger of domination by the Japanese, and the advantages of peaceful evolution as contrasted with revolutionary chaos.' Roosevelt added that this was, of course, 'none of my business' and 'for the love of Heaven do not bring me into this, though I do want to be of help'. He expressed the hope that the move toward the achievement of self-government for India would originate in London and would be made in such a way that the people of India would have no grounds for criticism that it was 'being made grudgingly or by compulsion'.

It is probable that the only part of that cable with which Churchill agreed was Roosevelt's admission that it is 'none of my business'. Hopkins said a long time later that he did not think that any suggestions from the President to the Prime Minister in the entire war were so wrathfully received as those relating to solution of the Indian problem. As one of Churchill's closest and most affectionate associates has said to me, 'The President might have known that India was one subject on which Winston would never move a yard. It was indeed one subject on which the normal, broad-minded, good-humoured, give-and-take attitude which prevailed between the two statesmen was stopped cold. It may be said that Churchill would see the Empire in ruins and himself buried under them before he would concede the right of any American, however great and illustrious a friend, to make any suggestions as to what he should do about India. It may be added that, four years later, the Labour Government in Britain made a proposal to the Indian leaders which, Sumner Welles has written, was 'almost identical in principle with the suggestions made by President Roosevelt in 1942'.

After the fall of Singapore, Roosevelt had cabled Churchill his impression that the visit of Chiang Kai-shek to Burma and India 'will be useful'. It is doubtful that Churchill agreed with this, either, or that Roosevelt himself subsequently felt so confident of the results of the visit. The Generalissimo had gone presumably to put some anti-Japanese fighting spirit into the Burmese and Indian peoples, to tell them from the point of view of one who had been battling the Japanese for many years what a cruel mockery was their propaganda of 'Asia for the Asiatics'. This was a desperately urgent matter, for Gandhi was telling his people not to resist Japanese aggression if and when it came, and there seemed dreadful likelihood that the Japanese would be able to march through India at will and thus gain access to the Middle East and establish the dreaded link with the Germans.

Chiang Kai-shek met with Gandhi and evidently exerted no influence whatsoever on the Mahatma's determination to accord the Japanese the same treatment that he had for so long accorded the British. Indeed, it is possible that Gandhi was the one who exerted the greater influence. Chiang later quoted him as saying: 'They [the British and Americans] never voluntarily treat us Indians as equals; why, they do not even admit your country to their staff talks.' That was a home thrust for the Generalissimo, who was bound to resent the fact that China was considered as no more than a 'consultant' by the Combined Chiefs of Staff.

The Chinese Foreign Minister, T. V. Soong, was working all this time in Washington with great persistence and tortured patience to secure and expedite aid to China. When it seemed evident that the Burma Road might be cut off, he gave Averell Harriman a map showing an alternate land route by way of the Persian Gulf and Soviet territory. Harriman sent this map to the President with the following outline:

> The route marked in red follows the Iranian Railway for 840 miles from the Persian Gulf to the Caspian Sea—by boat about 200 miles on the Caspian Sea to the terminus of the Russian railroad—about 2,000 miles over the Russian-Turkestan Railway to Sargiopol near the Chinese border—and from this point over the motor road used by the Russians to get supplies to China, some 2,000 miles to Chungking. The total distance is upwards of 5,000 miles.

Soong felt that a lifeline by air from Assam, in North-East India, into China, would be far more effective in meeting the emergency needs. He wrote to Roosevelt:

G

Miraculously enough that new lifeline is conveniently at hand. From Sadiya, the terminus of the Indian Railways, to Kunming or Suifu [the centre of land and water communications in Szechuan] is only 550 or 700 miles respectively, flying over comparatively level stretches.

This route covered some of the most terrible, murderous terrain to be found anywhere on earth; presumably the 'comparatively level stretches' referred to the air strips at the start and the finish.

On February 9 General Joseph W. Stilwell paid a farewell visit to Hopkins before leaving to take command of the American and Chinese forces in Burma. Hopkins assured him that the President wished to do everything possible to further the success of his efforts. Stilwell agreed that the air route to China should be inaugurated regardless of the ability to keep open the Burma Road, but he was evidently not greatly worried about his own supply problem, for the huge liner *Normandie*, on which more than two thousand men were then working for her quick conversion to war purposes, was to be used for the transport of troops and material to Stilwell's command. Hardly had the General left the White House before he heard that the *Normandie* was on fire, which was only the first of a long series of bitter discouragements for this rugged, fearless, tactless American soldier.

The same day Roosevelt sent a cable to Chiang Kai-shek telling him that the air ferry service by way of Africa and India to China was being increased rapidly and giving definite assurance that this supply route to China would be maintained even though there were further setbacks in Burma.

Thus was inaugurated the air service over 'The Hump' into China, on which many thousands of missions were flown in the next three and a half years and thousands of brave young men gave their lives. It could not begin to supply, as General Marshall has written, 'China's most critical needs [which] were in trucks and rolling stock, artillery, tanks, and other heavy equipment'. But it was the only route there was. It represented far more in the expenditure of effort and courage than it could produce in tangible results.

The Generalissimo returned to Chungking after his trip through Burma and cabled the President a profoundly depressing report saying that 'I have never seen anything in all my lifelong military experience to compare with the deplorable confusion, unpreparedness and degradation'. In this message and in an accompanying cable to Soong, Chiang Kai-shek was bitterly critical of the British performance in Burma and of the attitude of both the British and the Russians toward the direction of the overall strategy of the war. He urged Soong to have 'a frank heart-to-heart talk with the President ... who has consistently shown himself to be the one great friend of China'.

The 'heart-to-heart talks' were held with Hopkins, and after them Soong wrote him this letter:

I have given a great deal of thought to our talks of the last two days, and your desire to lift the plane of our efforts beyond the material difficulties of the day, to the necessity of close and lasting political and ideological associations between our two countries. After graduating from an American school and returning to China a quarter of a century ago to embark on the vicissitudes of politics, I have been a consistent advocate of this very idea. The Generalissimo's appointment of myself as Foreign Minister was directed to that end, and you can unhesitatingly count on me as your loyal collaborator.

Both you and I serve the President who is the one hope of mankind. You sustain him day by day. . . .

I am doing my utmost to keep the Generalissimo informed accurately of the situation at this end, with all its difficulties. On the other hand, I am doing my best to keep the President informed of the grim realities of our situation. . . .

I think your suggestion of associating the United States and China in periodic conversations with Great Britain and Russia holds great possibilities, and will be particularly conducive to better mutual understanding beyond our own narrow interests.

And I think if you could accept the invitation of the Generalissimo to visit Chungking, you will be opening a new chapter in Sino-American history. If you desire, I shall be glad to accompany you.

I feel I did not succeed in putting across to you our desperate need for planes and artillery as the mainspring of the Generalissimo's anxiety. We are in the 57th month of our war, embattled in Burma, and on us may soon be turned once again the full fury of the Japanese army, fresh from its recent laurels. This is not mere speculation on the part of London. On April 16 a friend in Chungking in whose objective judgment I have great faith cabled me that the Japanese threaten to attack the most important strategic centres: 'The situation looks ominous. I personally believe that in May or June the Japanese will attack Changsha and Hengyang (in Hunan Province) and at the same time attack Sian (in Honan Province).'

As you know, we have but little artillery and planes left. Our economic situation is bad. It is true our request for planes and artillery is modest by British or Russian standards, but they will be the only essential weapons that stand between us and the enemy.

We have tried for a year to abide by the established procedure, but we have come to the conclusion that we need a simple and direct procedure of participation in the technical sub-committees which examine and determine the requirements and allocations.

None but we ourselves can explain properly our needs. It could not be done by American officers, not only because they do not have sufficient knowledge of our situation, but on political grounds such a procedure would be misunderstood by our people. I know you have real difficulties on your end, but certainly some workable method may be found.

With this participation in the procedure of allocation, and with the larger conversations envisaged by you, we may be filling some of the gaps in wholehearted collaboration at this crisis of the war and at this most critical moment for China.

The charge was sometimes made that Hopkins was 'in Churchill's hip pocket' and was therefore constantly influencing the President to ignore the war against Japan and concentrate on Europe. Actually, the records prove that Hopkins was a tireless agitator for the interests of the Far Eastern theatres. When the Pacific War Council was organized, on April 1, Dr. Evatt of Australia (who was then in Washington) telegraphed:

After most careful consideration Australia has come to the conclusion that it is essential to success of Council scheme that chairman should be the President or his deputy and further that such deputy should be Harry Hopkins.

Of the organization of this Council, Hopkins wrote, on April 1:

The President and I have been discussing for some time the question of a Pacific War Council. The Army and Navy never had much enthusiasm for it, because they were afraid it would require too much of the time of the military people, and they fundamentally dislike any advice on strategic problems from political sources, a prejudice of theirs with which I have become sympathetic.

On the other hand, it was essential that there be an opportunity for the various countries in the Pacific to find a common meeting-ground.

While in Hyde Park on this past week-end I told the President that I thought the matter must be decided affirmatively, and he readily agreed and asked me to prepare a public statement to announce the formation of the Council, which I did in the notes that are attached.

Halifax yesterday urged the State Department to invite a representative of India, apparently feeling that it might help with the negotiations going on in India. However, the President disagreed with this because, of course, India has nothing to do with our Pacific front. [Note.—Australia was also originally opposed to the inclusion of India.]

The first meeting of the Council was held at 11.45 today and not much happened. The President outlined the problems in the whole Pacific Area, but kept away from the tough tactics which are now in progress. It is perfectly clear, however, that this body wants to talk about military strategy and the distribution of munitions. How it is coming out I don't know.

The original Council consisted of the President, Hopkins, Lord Halifax, Dr. Soong, Dr. Evatt, Alexander Loudon (for the Netherlands), Hume Wrong (for Canada), and Walter Nash (for New Zealand). Both India and the Philippines were added to the Council later.

President Quezon had been evacuated from Corregidor at the same time as General MacArthur, and when he arrived in Washington as head of a Government in Exile he and Hopkins established a close relationship. Hopkins wrote to Roosevelt:

President Quezon of the Philippines came to see me yesterday morning to express the hope that he could become a member of the Pacific War Council.

He stated that the fact that he was a member would be known to every Filipino at an early date and would greatly hearten his people. He thinks that the Philippines have as much at stake as any of the commonwealths and, furthermore, guerrilla fighting is still going on in many parts of the Philippine Islands and will continue.

He told me that, while he had been advised by members of his Cabinet and by General MacArthur to come to the United States, he felt he was making no contribution here and told me that he was somewhat inclined to return to Australia at an early date.

He thought, however, that his membership on the Pacific War Council, together with some visits which he has in mind to American communities that have a substantial number of Filipinos and to South American countries, which he wants to visit on his own, would give him adequate reasons for remaining indefinitely.

Quezon subsequently wrote to Hopkins:

I shall never forget, as long as I live, the part that you have taken in securing for my Government the recognition which the President of the United States has accorded us in making the Government of the Commonwealth of the Philippines a member of the United Nations and giving me a seat in the Pacific War Council.

With assurances of my heartfelt gratitude . . .

In view of Hopkins's unique position in relationship to Roosevelt, and his exceptional powers as chairman of the Munitions Assignment Board, he might well have become an object of abomination to all the leaders of the various contending national factions and the representatives of the various services—as he did with so many government officials and politicians who felt that he was always giving priority to the interests of somebody else, beginning with his own, and who poured on him the resentment that they did not dare to direct at the President. It is all the more remarkable that, among the various interests represented in the Pacific War Council, and in the Combined Chiefs of Staff, and with Churchill and Stalin and representatives of the European nations who dealt with him, including the Free French, Hopkins was respected and trusted and liked.

His position with the Congress and the Press remained, however, unchanged. Along toward the end of March he was ill again—he had to spend five days in the hospital—and he had time to catch up on his reading about himself. For instance—Hugh S. Johnson again raised the cry that 'nobody ever elected Mr. Hopkins to any office'—as if a President were compelled by the Constitution to put the names of his friends and confidants on the ballot together with his own. Johnson added: 'Many of the delays, false starts, bad selections of leaders and subsequent blunderings in getting our production machinery attuned for war over the past two and a half years are attributable directly to Mr. Hopkins and his palace janissariat of men of similar mind.'

(It can be said that at this time the 'janissariat' consisted primarily of Stimson, Knox, Marshall, King, and Arnold—also Welles, Patterson, Forrestal, McCloy, Lovett, and General Burns.)

Another news item: Representative John W. Taber addressed a meeting of the Women's National Republican Club on March 16, the day before MacArthur landed in Australia. According to the *New York Herald Tribune*, Taber told the ladies that 'everyone in Washington with the exception of the President of the United States and a certain group that he has surrounded himself with is doing his best to put the defence programme across'. Taber put Hopkins at the head of the 'certain group' and asked: 'How much longer must he [Hopkins] with his proven incompetence have the major "say" in our defence programme and its operations? How much longer shall his incompetence interfere with our doing our part?' But the time had long passed when Hopkins could be bothered by such fulminations from Capitol Hill: there was a war on, and he was in it, and however dismaying the immediate circumstances might be he knew in his heart that he was doing a damned good job in his ultimate life's work, which was reducing the burden on President Roosevelt.

CHAPTER XXIV

THE DECISION TO ATTACK

THE first meeting of the Pacific War Council was held on the morning of April 1, against the background of seemingly unmitigated disaster in the Far East. That was a Wednesday. After lunch that day, the President met with Secretaries Stimson and Knox, Generals Marshall and Arnold, Admiral King, and Hopkins. That night and the next night the President and Hopkins dined together, and the next day they lunched with General Marshall, then went for a drive to see how the construction on the new Naval Hospital (Roosevelt's pride) was getting along out in Bethesda, Maryland. That night they dined together alone again, and at 4.30 the next morning (Saturday, April 4) Hopkins and Marshall took off for London to propose the invasion of the Continent of Europe.

In his long cable to Churchill of March 9, Roosevelt had spoken of 'plans for establishment of a new front on the European Continent', adding: 'I am becoming more and more interested in the establishment of the new front this summer.'

On March 14, Hopkins wrote the following memorandum to the President:

MATTERS OF IMMEDIATE MILITARY CONCERN

1. Australia. To be sure we have enough forces there to hold Australia, New Caledonia, Fiji, and New Zealand. Believe Army should be pressed on this point, particularly as to air. We must not underrate the Japs' air strength.

2. China. We must keep that line to China open and get it going. Believe Army needs to be jogged on this regularly. The second phase of the Chinese business is to get a springboard from which to bomb Japan itself. For morale reasons this is extremely important and the sooner it can be done the better.

3. England. I believe Arnold's plan in England should be pressed home. There is nothing to lose. The bridgehead does not need to be established unless air superiority is complete. I doubt if any single thing is as important as getting some sort of a front this summer against Germany. This will have to be worked out very carefully between you and Marshall in the first instance, and you and Churchill in the second. I don't think there is any time to be lost, because if we are going to do it plans need to be made at once.

4. Russia. Increase if possible our supplies to Russia. The Protocol

runs out in June. Believe it would be wise to have another conference
here as soon as possible to cover supplies after July 1.

5. Real priorities for machine tools must be given merchant ships and
combat planes. Should reaffirm to people concerned, namely Land and
Stimson, that you want the planes and the ships in 1942.

At this time, a definite plan for invasion of Northern France was being
made by the War Plans Division, of which Eisenhower had recently become
Chief. It involved direct assault across the Channel at its narrowest point to
the French Coast between Calais and Le Havre, east of the Seine—as opposed
to the Normandy area west of the Seine to the Cotentin Peninsula where the
landings were made two years later. The beachheads were to be further
extended to the eastward beyond Dunkirk to Ostand and Zeebrugge on the
Belgian Coast.

The basic military argument for invasion of the Continent as stated in a
memorandum from Marshall to the President was as follows:

> Western Europe has been selected as the theatre in which to stage the
> first great offensive of the United Powers because:
>
> It is the only place in which a powerful offensive can be prepared and
> executed by the United Powers in the near future. In any other locality
> the building up of the required forces would be much more slowly
> accomplished due to sea distances. Moreover, in other localities the
> enemy is protected against invasion by natural obstacles and poor com-
> munications leading toward the seat of the hostile power, or by elabor-
> ately organized and distant outposts. Time would be required to reduce
> these and to make the attack effective.
>
> It is the only place where the vital air superiority over the hostile land
> areas preliminary to a major attack can be staged by the United Powers.
> This is due to the existence of a network of landing fields in England and
> the fact that at no other place could massed British air power be employed
> for such an operation.
>
> It is the only place in which the bulk of the British ground forces can
> be committed to a general offensive in co-operating with United States
> forces. It is impossible, in view of the shipping situation, to transfer the
> bulk of the British forces to any distant region, and the protection of the
> British islands would hold the bulk of the divisions in England.
>
> The United States can concentrate and use larger forces in Western
> Europe than in any other place, due to sea distances and the existence
> in England of base facilities.
>
> The bulk of the combat forces of the United States, United Kingdom,
> and Russia can be applied simultaneously only against Germany, and
> then only if we attack in time. We cannot concentrate against Japan.

Successful attack in this area will afford the maximum of support to the Russian Front.

It will be seen that the desirability of meeting the Russian demands for a Second Front was the last in the priority list of arguments in favour of the proposal. However, this consideration weighed heavily with Hopkins, as it did with Beaverbrook, who was in Washington at the end of March and early April following his temporary retirement from the British Government.

The invasion plan was originally known as ROUNDUP and eventually OVERLORD. The main operation, involving thirty American and eighteen British divisions, was planned to take place in the spring of 1943. The code name BOLERO was applied to the enormous preliminary process of building up the required forces and supplies in the British Isles.

Provision was made for a more limited operation, known as SLEDGE-HAMMER to take place about September 15, 1942. Speaking of SLEDGEHAM-MER, the plan stated:

> This Limited Operation Would Be Justified Only in Case
> (1) The Situation on the Russian Front Becomes Desperate, i.e. the success of German arms becomes so complete as to threaten the imminent collapse of Russian resistance unless the pressure is relieved by an attack from the west by British and American troops. In this case the attack should be considered as a sacrifice in the common good.
>
> (2) The German Situation in Western Europe Becomes Critically Weakened.

In the event that the operation was undertaken as a purely desperate, emergency measure to relieve pressure on the Russian Front, it was clearly foreseen that it might involve the loss of most of the troops involved.

A further and more enduring justification for SLEDGEHAMMER was later added: It might be employed to seize a bridgehead on the Continent *and hold it* until such time as sufficient American forces were available for the major drive through France into the heart of Germany. The most favourable bridgehead would undoubtedly have been the Cotentin Peninsula, including the port of Cherbourg.

Roosevelt was inclined to be leary of a trans-Channel frontal attack. He was still in favour of GYMNAST, the North African operation which had been planned at the Arcadia Conference and then shelved because of the need for diverting ships to the Pacific and the Indian Ocean plus the severe tonnage losses in the Western Atlantic. However, he was persuaded of the desirability of BOLERO-ROUNDUP by Stimson, Marshall, and Hopkins. Roosevelt also attached great importance to the political importance of this in relation to Russia.

He approved it at the April 1 meeting in the White House and told Hopkins and Marshall to go at once to London and present it to the Prime Minister and his Chiefs of Staff. Hopkins sent a jubilant cable to Churchill: 'Will be seeing you soon, so please start the fire.' (This was another of the frequent references to the temperature at Chequers.)

Roosevelt cabled Churchill:

> Having completed a survey of the immediate as well as the long-range military problems which face the United Nations, I have reached certain conclusions of such vital importance that I want the whole picture to be presented to you and to ask for your approval thereon. All of it is dependent on the complete co-operation of our two countries. Therefore, Harry and General Marshall will leave soon for London to inform you of the salient points. When I have heard from you after your talks with Harry and Marshall, I propose to ask Stalin to send immediately two special representatives. It is my hope that the Russians will greet these plans with enthusiasm. I want them to be identified as the plans of the United Nations and I think they can be worked out in full accord with the trends of British and American public opinion.

The Hopkins-Marshall mission which left from Baltimore in the early morning of April 4 was given the code name 'Modicum', and the members of the party bore the following aliases: Mr. Harry Hopkins—Mr. A. H. Hones; General G. C. Marshall—Mr. C. G. Mell; Commander James R. Fulton—Mr. A. L. Foss; Colonel H. A. Craig—Mr. J. H. Case; Lieutenant-Colonel A. C. Wedemeyer—Mr. J. E. White.

Commander Fulton was a Navy doctor assigned by Ross McIntire to attempt to take care of Hopkins. Wedemeyer, who was then with Eisenhower on Marshall's brilliant planning staff, became Commander of American Forces in the Chinese theatre two years later.

One odd feature of this mission was that Hopkins was given some editorial credit for it. The *Richmond* (Virginia) *News Leader* uttered these surprisingly kind words:

> Harry Hopkins's record in administering relief during the depression years did not impress the nation, but Harry Hopkins's work during the war will be found of a different and higher level. The plain truth is that Hopkins is an ill man. He knows it. Frequently he has to slip away from the White House for a day or two and get blood transfusions. Then he comes back and, though he scarcely is able to keep on his feet, he is deep in his duties as chief of lease-lend. At that post, believe it or not, he is displaying much sagacity. Those who most deserve his support are getting it wholeheartedly.
>
> Now Hopkins has gone once more to London—this time by bomber

and doubtless on the 'straight-away'. That is a severe ordeal for a man in perfect health and with flesh enough to keep him from feeling the extreme cold of a flight at more than 20,000 feet. Often strong men have to take oxygen as they speed through the cold, thin air four or five miles above the sea. To Hopkins, thin and bloodless as he is, the flight must have been literally so many hours in hell. . . .

You may not like his former administration and you may not have forgotten the bitterness of his tongue during the days when he was dictator of relief expenditures; but you have to take off your hat to him now for as fine a display of persistent, day-by-day courage as this war has offered in America.

Although Hopkins had previously made the severe transatlantic flight by bomber (B-24) as well as the terrible round trip in a PBY to Archangel, on this trip he enjoyed comparative luxury. The Modicum party had an entire Pan-American Clipper all to itself. The first stop was Bermuda, where they were delayed for two pleasant days over Easter Sunday. At the request of the Governor, Lord Knollys, Marshall read the lesson in church. Hopkins attended a children's party, admired the Easter lilies, and slept a great deal. Both he and Marshall inspected the enormous work being done by the U.S. Army at one end of this lovely island and the Navy at the other end to convert it into a great landplane, seaplane, and submarine base.

Hopkins also asked a great many questions about the use of Pan-American Clippers for carrying civilian airmail. For more than a year he had been fussing and stewing almost constantly about civilian use of passenger and cargo space in commercial transport planes. A month before he had written the following angry note to Lovett in the War Department:

I noticed in the paper the other day that the New York Giants were flown to Havana and back in two or three transport planes.

Who authorizes such a trip as this, wearing out engines and burning high-octane gasoline?

From now on he never stopped agitating to remove all civilian airmail from the Clippers. A month later he cabled to Harriman:

The President is issuing some new instructions with a view to removing the chit-chat mail from the commercial aircraft. Evidently there are some people who think that it is important that these commercial planes should be used to tell each other how Aunt Bessie is progressing with her lumbago. If you are feeling well enough I hope you will keep on raising hell about this at your end, because it is all a lot of damned nonsense.

Marshall and Hopkins flew directly from Bermuda to Scotland, and arrived in London on the morning of Wednesday, April 8.

Following are Hopkins's notes on their first sessions at No. 10 Downing Street:

> Marshall and Hopkins with Prime Minister at 10 Downing Street, 4-6 p.m. Marshall presented in broad outlines our proposals to the Prime Minister. It was perfectly clear that the Prime Minister was well aware of the proposals which we were going to make, because he stated they had them under careful consideration for many weeks and were prepared to go ahead, implying that they would go ahead without us. He made it, however, perfectly clear to me that he did not treat the proposals as seriously as either the facts warranted or as did the United States. On the other hand, he indicated that he had told the Chiefs of Staff that, in spite of all the difficulties, he (Churchill) was prepared to go along. He repeated the several objections that had obviously been made to him by the Chiefs of Staff, all of which we had heard in Washington before coming to England. Marshall was more optimistic about the interview than I was. He thought that Churchill went a long way and he (Marshall) expected far more resistance than he got. Churchill reviewed the whole military situation, which was none too optimistic, particularly in the Indian Ocean. He also expressed a good deal of criticism of Auchinleck; said he had had pretty acrimonious correspondence with him by cable. Churchill as ever is pressing his commanders for action, and they in turn indicate that they never have enough supplies. It is more of the old story. He told us that the Singapore business was a mess and he feels that the whole thing was very badly handled and that there is no explanation of the lack of resistance on the part of the British. He simply thinks they folded up and let him and the British Army down very badly.

> At dinner at 10 Downing Street: Churchill, Marshall, Attlee, General Brooke and Hopkins. Eden came in after dinner. We dined at 10 Downing Street as the guests of the Prime Minister, but the conversation was in the main social. Churchill, displaying his talents as a military historian, spent most of the evening discussing the Civil War and the (First) World War and never really came to grips with our main business, although General Brooke got into it enough to indicate that he had a great many misgivings about our proposal. Brooke made an unfavourable impression on Marshall, who thinks that although he may be a good fighting man, he hasn't got Dill's brains. While at dinner, Churchill got word from the Bomber Command they were sending 350 bombers over Germany tonight.

The following day Hopkins cabled Roosevelt that he and Marshall had presented the proposals in full to Churchill, whose response was sympathetic. It seemed that the outlook was hopeful for agreement right down the line.

Hopkins added: 'The Prime Minister has just sent for me for a discussion of India.' He promised to telephone or cable the President further about this. The discussions that day were described by Hopkins as follows:

In conference with the Prime Minister in the Cabinet Room at 10 Downing Street, 10.30 to 12. Prime Minister read me a dispatch which he had just received from the Governor-General of India indicating that Cripps had presented a new proposal to Nehru without consultation with the Governor-General, but presumably with the assistance of Louis Johnson. The gist of this proposal was that an Indian would on paper at any rate be given charge of the Defence Ministry. The Commander-in-Chief of the British Forces would have powers and duties substantially comparable to those in the original British proposal. The Governor-General's dispatch indicated that he and Cripps could have got Nehru's agreement to the original proposal had not Cripps and Johnson worked out this new arrangement. It was perfectly clear that the Governor-General was irritated with the whole business and laid great stress on the fact that Johnson acts and talks as though he were sent to India as Roosevelt's personal representative to mediate in the Indian crisis. It is apparent that this new proposal, which is known as the Cripps-Johnson proposal, might well be turned down by the British Cabinet which is meeting at 12 today, in which case Roosevelt would be in the embarrassing position of having ostensibly made a proposal which the British Government rejected. I told the Prime Minister that Johnson's original mission to India had nothing whatever to do with the British proposals and that I was very sure that he was not acting as the representative of the President in mediating the Indian business. That I believed Cripps was using Johnson for his own ends, Cripps being very anxious to bring Roosevelt's name into the picture. That it was to Cripps's interest to get Roosevelt identified with his proposals. I told Mr. Churchill of the President's instructions to me, namely that he would not be drawn into the Indian business except at the personal request of the Prime Minister, and then only if he had an assurance both from India and Britain that any plan that he worked out would be acceptable, and that he (Roosevelt) was unwilling to be put into a situation before the world in which he undertook to moderate between the conflicting forces and then have these forces turn down his proposals. Churchill at once wrote in longhand a cable to the Viceroy stating that he was sure Johnson was not acting as personal representative of the President in negotiations between the Indian Congress and Cripps.

It was clear that Churchill did not wish at this time to bring the United States into what he calls a constitutional question, and he is unhappy at the turn the Press has taken, namely that public opinion in America and Roosevelt in particular can handle this matter over the head of the British Government.

The Prime Minister also discussed at some length the naval situation in the Indian Ocean. While he was there his secretary brought in a memorandum to say that the *Hermes*, a small aircraft carrier, has just been sunk. He stated that the British Fleet in the Indian Ocean was badly outgunned by the Japanese naval forces; that the Japanese had complete air superiority as evidenced by the sinking of two cruisers, which, incidentally, were attacked by sixty Japanese fighters each one carrying a 500-lb. bomb and in the attack the two cruisers both sank within fifteen minutes. He showed me the dispatches received this morning from the Commander-in-Chief, Indian Fleet, stating that he was going to withdraw his major forces to East African ports; that he could not risk battle; and that he would leave behind a fast striking force to harass the enemy. He told me, too, that Ceylon has just been attacked by air a second time, but that he has not learned as yet what the effect of this air attack is. The Commander-in-Chief's dispatch this morning was quite discouraging and, while Ceylon can undoubtedly put up a good fight because of its heavy shore batteries and some aircraft, it was clear that the Prime Minister is not too hopeful about it.

This led to a discussion of the co-operation between our Fleet and the British naval forces in the Far East. Churchill feels, and I gather he expresses the point of view of the Admiralty, that there is no real joint planning of naval strategy in the Far East and in the Pacific and Indian Oceans. He asserted that, while the Admiralty kept our Navy informed of everything, consultation ended here and that our naval responses were that 'we have the matter in hand'. Churchill is obviously disturbed at this and would like to see the same kind of joint planning of naval tactics and strategy as goes on between our two armies. He was not critical of our various actions in the Pacific, but rather expressed the belief that we were in the war together; that our two fleets were acting as though they were two totally independent forces; and he thought this was not conducive to victory.

He showed me the maps of Rommel's advances in Libya where the patrol forces on both sides are in contact. He said that Auchinleck felt that he was not ready to conduct the major offensive until May, but that Rommel's advance might force the fighting there sooner. He thinks Auchinleck is pretty well prepared, and that Rommel will have trouble in breaking through. I gather that he is quite impatient with Auchinleck, but nevertheless considers Auchinleck a first-rate fighting man.

I then discussed again with the Prime Minister the purposes of General

Marshall's and my visit to England and impressed upon him the serious weight which the President and Marshall gave to our proposals; and I made it very plain that our military leaders had, after canvassing the whole situation, made up their minds that this plan was the one of all considered that was by far the most advantageous from a strategic point of view. I impressed as strongly as I could on Churchill that he should not agree to this proposal on any assumption that we do not mean business, nor should he assume that in all probability it will not require the use of ground forces. I told him that the President and Marshall were prepared to throw our ground forces in and that he did not wish an agreement on the basis that in all probability the ground forces would never be used. I said this to him because, in conversations the previous day, I sensed that his advisers had told him that the ground attack would never be made, at least for nearly a year. I particularly stressed the impossibility of immobilizing large numbers of our troops indefinitely, and that the disposition of the United States was to take great risks to relieve the Russian front. Churchill took this very seriously and led me to believe that he didn't fully take in before the seriousness of our proposals. He told me that he would send a message by Eden, with whom I am lunching, relative to the Indian business, and asked me to return at six o'clock tonight to continue conversations.

Lunch at the Foreign Office with Eden, Lyttelton, and Harriman. I outlined our proposal to Eden and Lyttelton today. Both of them responded very favourably and the only reservation was the timing. They think that as early in 1942 as possible is the time. It is their opinion that the Chiefs of Staff are going to come to a meeting of minds with Marshall. We discussed the Persian Gulf as a supply route to Russia, but that does not seem too encouraging. I told Lyttelton I thought he ought to make a new effort to open that route up. Eden showed me a paper that had apparently been prepared by the soldiers about supplies to Russia after July 1. The memorandum clearly indicated that some of the military people here aren't too anxious to get supplies to Russia and that we have got to overcome a good deal of resistance. I also told Eden the President's position about signing the treaty with Russia, making it perfectly clear that the President did not approve of this action. I told Eden the President could not, of course, prevent them from signing it, but in the last analysis it was a decision the British must make and that no useful purpose could be served by exploring it further with the Russians. I impressed on Eden as strongly as I could the President's belief that our main proposal here should take the heat off Russia's diplomatic demands upon England.

Marshall conferred at length with the British Chiefs of Staff, including

Lord Louis Mountbatten, who had become Chief of Combined Operations, the mysterious organization which conducted the spectacular Commando raids and provided the laboratory for experiments in the techniques of amphibious warfare. Mountbatten, an adventurous and imaginative officer, was somewhat addicted to freakish schemes involving all manner of weird contraptions—one of them was a form of landing-craft made out of shatter-proof ice—but the work of Combined Operations produced much that proved valuable. In a war of this nature no innovation seemed too fantastic to be unworthy of consideration.

Incidentally, as an item of extreme interest in the history of the Second Front, shortly after this Marshall-Hopkins visit Churchill sent the following directive to Mountbatten:

PIERS FOR USE ON BEACHES

C.C.O. or DEPUTY.

They must float up and down with the tide. The anchor problem must be mastered. Let me have the best solution worked out. Don't argue the matter. The difficulties will argue for themselves.

W. S. C.
30.5.42.

This was one of the first references to the artificial harbours—known as 'Mulberries' and 'Gooseberries'—which two years later were towed across the Channel to the Normandy beaches. American officers who knew the whole story of these amazing developments gave Churchill a very large share of the credit for their origination.

Hopkins also conferred with Attlee and Ernest Bevin on the immeasurably complex requirements of manpower, and with Lord Leathers, Minister of War Transport, on the shipping situation, particularly the calamitous losses of tankers on the U.S. Atlantic Coast. Harriman was involved in all of these discussions, but Winant was in Washington at the time. The American Minister in London then was H. Freeman Matthews, later director of the State Department's Office of European Affairs.

On April 11 Hopkins cabled Roosevelt that the discussions with the Former Naval Person and the British Chiefs of Staff were progressing very satisfactorily and that he was about to meet with Lord Leathers to discuss the shipping problem in all its manifold implications. He said that all in the British Government were very much disappointed by the turn of events in India, but they believed that they had made a fair offer and every effort to reach agreement. It seemed apparent that it would be futile for Cripps to conduct any further negotiations. Hopkins added: 'Although I am not allowed to talk about the weather, I can tell you that my heavy underwear is itching like the devil. Please have a telephone message sent to Diana that General Marshall has got me well under control.'

That same day Hopkins received a copy of the following cable which Roosevelt had sent to Stalin:

It is unfortunate that geographical distance makes it practically impossible for you and me to meet at this time. Such a meeting of minds in personal conversation would be greatly useful to the conduct of the war against Hitlerism. Perhaps if things go as well as we hope, you and I could spend a few days together next summer near our common border off Alaska. But, in the meantime, I regard it as of the utmost military importance that we have the nearest possible approach to an exchange of views.

I have in mind very important military proposal involving the utilization of our armed forces in a manner to relieve your critical western front. This objective carries great weight with me.

Therefore, I wish you would consider sending Mr. Molotov and a General upon whom you rely to Washington in the immediate future. Time is of the essence if we are to help in an important way. We will furnish them with a good transport plane so that they should be able to make the round trip in two weeks.

I do not want by such a trip to go over the head of my friend, Mr. Litvinov, in any way, as he will understand, but we can gain time by the visit I propose.

I suggest this procedure not only because of the secrecy, which is so essential, but because I need your advice before we determine with finality the strategic course of our common military action.

I have sent Hopkins to London relative to this proposal.

The American people are thrilled by the magnificent fighting of your armed forces and we want to help you in the destruction of Hitler's armies and material more than we are doing now.

I send you my sincere regards.

This cable reflected what Hopkins had told Eden of 'The President's belief that our main proposal here should take the heat off Russia's diplomatic demands upon England'. The demands were substantially the same as those which had been made shortly before Pearl Harbour and had caused Eden's trip to Moscow in December. Roosevelt obviously saw the urgency of diverting the attention of the Soviet Government from such embarrassing postwar political considerations by emphasizing the British and American determination to establish the Second Front in the west for which Communist propaganda had been clamouring since the German invasion of Russia.

D

Hopkins cabled Roosevelt the main points of his discussions with Leathers on the shipping crisis:

> In the period from January 12 to April 12 the shipping losses in the western part of the North Atlantic Ocean totalled 1,200,000 gross tons, more than half of this being tankers. The losses for the past week in the same area have been 150,000 tons, more than two thirds of which were tankers. The ships that we are losing, it seems to me, are far more important than their cargoes. Our need for ships during the next few months is going to be desperate.

Hopkins strongly recommended that none but the most vitally essential cargoes be shipped until adequate escorts could be provided for convoys. He said that he had intended to postpone discussions of these matters until his return to Washington, but the situation seemed so urgent that immediate action must be taken to cut the losses.

Even during this visit to London when attention was concentrated on the English Channel and Hitler's 'Fortress of Europe' that lay beyond it, Hopkins could not forget the endless plight of China and what General Marshall called its 'unparalleled logistical problems'. Word came that the Air Ferry Command had completed its first flight over the Hump. As Hopkins was leaving for a week-end at Chequers on Saturday he received a long cable from T. V. Soong which had been sent through the Chinese Ambassador in London, Dr. Wellington Koo. Soong suggested a new supply route by sea and land from the United States to China—and this must be rated the most fantastically difficult of all the various proposals. It involved, to begin with, extension of the shipping route around the North Cape of Norway, already as perilous as any of the lifelines of the war, for a distance of nearly 2,000 miles beyond Murmansk. Shipping must go through the Arctic Ocean, past Nova Zembla, to the Yenesei River in Northern Siberia; cargoes were to be transhipped to Soviet river vessels at Igarka, 500 miles up the Yenesei, and moved 1,100 miles south to Krasnoyarsk on the trans-Siberian Railway, from which point the transhipped material would travel 800 miles by rail to Sargiopol, and then another 2,000 miles by road to Chungking. Hopkins knew all too well that the mere fact that his friend Dr. Soong could seriously present such a proposal as this one was in itself sufficient proof of the desperateness of China's situation. He also knew that there was nothing now to be done about it except to make every effort to get more and more transport planes for the Ferry Command.

When Hopkins went out to Chequers on Saturday afternoon he had his first real look at the English countryside now that April was there. Experiencing something of the old lyrical impulse which had been so long suppressed within him, he later said: 'It's only when you see that country in spring that you begin to understand why the English have written the best goddam poetry in the world.' The usual gaiety and charm of a Chequers week-end was lacking this time, because Mrs. Churchill was ill with general exhaustion and Churchill himself was below normal in exuberance, the result of the fearful strain of the series of disasters which had by no means ended.

A cable arrived for Hopkins from Roosevelt saying that all possible efforts must be made to prevent a breakdown of the Cripps negotiations in India. The President asked that the following message be delivered immediately to Churchill:

I am unable regretfully to agree with the point of view you express in your message to me that American public opinion believes that negotiations have failed on general broad issues. The general impression here is quite the contrary. The almost universal feeling is that the dead-lock has been due to the unwillingness of the British Government to concede the right of self-government to the Indian people notwithstand-ing the Indians' willingness to entrust technical military and naval defence control to the competent British authorities. American public opinion cannot understand why, if the British Government is willing to permit component parts of India to secede from the British Empire after the war, it is not willing to permit them during the war to enjoy what is tanta-mount to self-government.

I know you will understand my reasons for placing this issue before you very frankly. If the current negotiations are allowed to collapse and if India were subsequently to be invaded successfully by the Japanese with attendant serious military defeats for the Allies, it would be hard to over-estimate the prejudicial effect of this on American public opinion. There-fore, is it not possible for you to postpone Cripps' departure on the ground that you have personally transmitted to him instructions to make final efforts to find some common ground of understanding? I gathered that last Thursday night agreement was almost reached. It appears to me that this agreement might yet be reached if you could authorize Cripps to say that he was empowered by you personally to resume negotiations as at that point with an understanding that minor concessions would be made by both sides.

It is still my feeling, as I have said before, that a solution can be found if the component groups in India could now be given an opportunity to set up a National Government similar in essence to our own form of government under the Articles of Confederation, with the understanding that after a period of trial and error the Indian people would then be enabled to decide upon their own form of constitution and their future relationship with the British Empire, as you have already promised them.

If you should make such an effort, and if then Cripps was still unable to achieve agreement, then American public opinion would be satisfied that at least the British Government has made a fair and real offer to the Indian people, upon whom the responsibility for failure of the negotiations would be clearly placed.

This cable reached Chequers at three o'clock Sunday morning, when the Prime Minister and Hopkins—the latter disobeying all instructions—were still sitting up talking. Its contents undoubtedly postponed any plans for going to bed for some time to come. Churchill set forth to Hopkins in detail, and probably with some vehemence, his answers to the President's arguments. Hopkins's scribbled notes on this can be summarized as follows:

Churchill refused to be responsible for a policy which would throw the whole subcontinent of India into utter confusion while the Japanese invader was at its gates. A Nationalist Government such as indicated by Roosevelt, first, would almost certainly demand the recall of all Indian troops from the Middle East and, second, would in Churchill's belief make an armistice with Japan on the basis of free transit for Japanese forces and supplies across India to Karachi. In return, the Japanese would give the Hindus the military support necessary to impose the Congress party's will upon the Moslems, the Princes, and the depressed classes. Churchill felt that any attempt to reopen the Indian constitutional issue in this way at this juncture would serve only to emphasize serious differences between Great Britain and the United States and thus do injury to the common cause. Far from helping the defence of India, it would make the task impossible.

It appears from Hopkins's notes that Churchill said that he personally was quite ready to retire to private life if that would do any good in assuaging American public opinion, but he felt certain that, regardless of whether or not he continued as Prime Minister, the Cabinet and Parliament would continue to assert the policy as he had stated it.

Hopkins, who loved to use the phrase 'meeting of minds', was by now convinced that the subcontinent of India was one area where the minds of Roosevelt and Churchill would never meet. He took the position that there was not much sense in burning up the transatlantic cables with more messages on this subject. Since the President's cable had been addressed to him for communication to Churchill, he felt that he should be the one to answer it. Early Sunday morning he tried to telephone the White House from Chequers, but was prevented from getting through by atmospheric conditions. Later he did manage to reach the President and explain that since Cripps had left India the day before, and explanations had been issued by both the British and Indian authorities, nothing more could be done about the matter at the present time. Evidently Hopkins told Roosevelt something about the reception of his cable at Chequers and the hour at which it had arrived, for the next day the President cabled this message to General Marshall:

> Please put Hopkins to bed and keep him there under twenty-four hour guard by Army or Marine Corps. Ask the King [George VI] for additional assistance if required on this job.

Marshall had his troubles obeying these orders. Although aided by Dr. Fulton and by General Robert A. McClure, Military Attaché at the American Embassy in London, he found it impossible to keep Hopkins under control. At the end of a long evening after a longer day, Marshall would send Hopkins to bed and then himself sit up with McClure and Wedemeyer to go over various matters. Later one of them would look into Hopkins's room to check up on him and find that he had disappeared through the separate entrance leading to the corridor; hours might pass before Hopkins returned to the suite. There were many Americans staying at Claridge's in those days, as always, and he could usually scare up a gin rummy game at almost any hour.

Dr. Fulton has written me an account of some of his troubles in the task of keeping Hopkins alive:

> Mr. Hopkins was a man of boundless energy, and during the trips on which I accompanied him he gave unstintingly of himself, without regard for his physical condition. It was extremely important that he get as much rest as possible, and my instructions from Admiral McIntire were to stay as close to him as was practical for me to do under the unusual circumstances involved, and to see that he received the necessary rest, medications, and preparations which had been prescribed for him by his consulting physicians.
>
> On several instances I believe my presence at his side, at prescribed hours for medication, caused Mr. Hopkins considerable annoyance. Frequently while in London he would become solicitous for my welfare and assure me that I should visit my naval medical colleagues for weekends and have outside interests and activities. . . .
>
> One particular prescribed preparation was, to say the least, not very palatable, and he preferred to take it in tomato juice. I would endeavour at every opportunity to stay with him until he took this preparation, because several times there was mute evidence that he had disposed of it in the bathroom in preference to taking it.
>
> If, as frequently happened, he was to dine out with his British colleagues or other diplomatic or military dignitaries, I would be sure that he had a small package with his necessary medications to take with him.

Almost invariably following such an evening out the intact package would be found on his dresser, in his bathroom, or in his dinner coat the next morning.

After the week-end at Chequers, Hopkins read a report from New York which alarmed him. It was a monitoring by the U.S. Government of the Paris radio, one of the more important and deceptive units in the Nazi propaganda machine. It said:

> Hopkins and Marshall have been conferring for nearly ten days in the British capital. According to the Anglo-American Information Services, Roosevelt's delegates have been entrusted with the commission of demanding that the British Government prepare an invasion of the Continent. Roosevelt is said to have given Hopkins and Marshall full power to provide all possible aid that England may need for an attempt at a second Narvik which will eventually become a second Dunkirk. In view of the reiterated announcements of an invasion of the Continent, launched for the purpose of aiding the Soviet armies which are living in expectation of a spring offensive, military circles in Berlin today made a statement which cannot be surpassed for clearness. The gist of this statement is that Germany can only once more confirm Hitler's proclamation inviting the British to come in the greatest possible numbers to Europe to measure themselves with the armed forces of the Reich. It is recalled in Berlin that the Fuehrer had made an offer to Britain to evacuate any part of the European continent to enable her to make an effective landing without difficulty.

There were so many elements of accuracy in this French broadcast, directed by Berlin, that one could jump to the jittery conclusion that the enemy must have had secret agents behind the arras at Chequers or a microphone under the green baize at Downing Street. However, this was only one of the more elementary propaganda tactics: an obvious piece of guesswork broadcast in the hope that it might provoke nervous replies which would reveal some part of the truth. It was as if a neurotically jealous husband were to say to a suspected rival: 'Don't think I don't know all about what's going on between you and my wife', on the chance that the rival will blanch and mutter: 'But how did you find out?' thereby betraying the sordid secret. It sounds silly, but it was tried time and again in this tough war, and even sometimes it worked. Actually, in this particular case, the Hopkins-Marshall visit to London was deliberately advertised—if anything, too much so—as a portent of an invasion. As *Time* magazine said in its first report of the mission: 'In the U.S. and Britain anxious millions forthwith believed what they wanted to be told; that their forces were about to take the offensive and open a second front in Europe.' Anxious millions in Russia, of course, were even more anxious to believe this. The London *Times*, normally well informed on the prevalent point of view on the upper levels of Whitehall, went pretty far in its editorial comment on the main subject under discussion, saying: 'There is mounting eagerness both in this country and in the U.S. to pass from defence to offence and to make 1942, not 1943 or 1944, the turning-point of the war.'

On Monday, April 13, Hopkins attended a meeting of the War Cabinet and the next day he cabled to Roosevelt:

> The serious naval situation which has been developing in the Indian Ocean requires your most urgent consideration. You will be readily aware of the implications of the fact that the Japanese have moved very powerful forces in that area.
>
> Tonight we will have a final meeting with the Defence Council and the Chiefs of Staff, and I am very confident of the outcome. Marshall, who has made a splendid impression here, has presented our case with moderation, but with great force. I believe we will achieve not only agreement in principle, but a real meeting of minds. Everyone here regrets that Admiral King could not also have been present.

The situation in the Indian Ocean was indeed so serious that, with British sea power virtually inoperative in the Bay of Bengal, the Japanese sank more than thirty ships, including an aircraft carrier and two heavy cruisers, within four days.

Roosevelt cabled Hopkins for the Former Naval Person that he had received a very despondent message from Chiang Kai-shek, and he believed it essential that despite the situation in the Indian Ocean there must be no curtailment in the supply of airplanes now on the way to General Stilwell for use in Burma.

He expressed the belief that the Japanese would not attempt to make a landing on Ceylon for several weeks and said he hoped that all shipping would be kept out of the Bay of Bengal and that British warships would remain for the time being 'under the umbrella of airplanes land-based in Southern India and Ceylon'. At the same time Roosevelt cabled Churchill: 'I appreciate quite fully the present lack of naval butter to cover the bread', which referred to the critical problem then facing the British of disposing enough ships for the defence of the Indian Ocean while at the same time maintaining the necessary strength of the Home Fleet for the security of the British Isles. Roosevelt proposed to use the U.S. aircraft carrier *Ranger* as a ferry boat to transport fighter planes for the maintenance of the air umbrella from India and Ceylon, and he sent units of the U.S. Navy, headed by the new battleship *Washington* and the aircraft carrier *Wasp*, to Scapa Flow to reinforce the Home Fleet both for the defence of Britain and the protection of the convoys around the North Cape to Russia.

On April 14 Roosevelt cabled Hopkins that Litvinov had called in to ask for fuller information about the import of the President's recent invitation to Stalin to send two personal representatives to Washington. In this cable, Roosevelt added that, although he had not yet received official confirmation from Leahy, it seemed true that Laval had returned to power in the Vichy Government.

That night at 10 o'clock Hopkins and Marshall met with the Defence Committee (Operations) of the War Cabinet. Present were Churchill, Attlee, Eden, Lyttelton, A. V. Alexander (First Lord of the Admiralty), Sir James Grigg (Secretary of State for War), Sir Archibald Sinclair (Secretary of State for Air), and the Chiefs of Staff—Pound, Brooke, Portal, Ismay, and Mountbatten.

Churchill opened this 'memorable meeting', as he called it, with all the grace and courtly flourish of which he was master. Speaking of the 'momentous proposal' which had been brought from the President by Mr. Hopkins and General Marshall he gave it his cordial and unhesitant acceptance, stating that it was in accord with the classic principles of war. However, he pointed out there was the problem immediately presented by the ominous possibility of a junction being achieved of the Germans advancing through the Middle East with the Japanese advancing through India. A substantial portion of the resources of Britain and America in men and material must be set aside to prevent this junction and the most vital points at which these resources could now be applied were in Burma and Ceylon and on and over the Indian Ocean.

Churchill said that the enormous preparations for the trans-Channel operations that would have to go forward in the United Kingdom would hardly escape the attention of the enemy, particularly in and around the ports of Southern England which were so readily accessible to German reconnaissance planes. However, this problem might well be overcome by obscuring the true objectives of the enterprise in a cloud of rumours. He said: 'With the whole coast of Europe from the North Cape to Bayonne [the French-Spanish border] open to us, we should contrive to deceive the enemy as to the weight, timing, method, and the direction of our attack.' Far from attempting to conceal the preparations for invasion, Churchill felt, some sort of public announcement should be made 'that our two nations are resolved to march forward into Europe together in a noble brotherhood of arms, in a great crusade for the liberation of the tormented peoples'.

General Marshall then spoke, expressing the great relief that he and Hopkins felt that agreement had been reached on basic principles for a frontal assault on the enemy in Northern France in 1943. In the meantime, he said, much would depend upon the development and intensification of the air offensive against Germany, and he also emphasized the desirability of repeated Commando-type raids all along the coast, not only for the purpose of harassing and confusing the enemy, but, even more importantly, to give our own troops combat experience. He foresaw no shortage of troops for the major operation, but he did believe there would be difficulty in making available the necessary shipping, naval escorts, landing-craft, and aircraft. However, these were problems to be faced in the United States, and he and Hopkins were confident they would be solved.

Marshall spoke at some length of the possibility that they might be compelled to launch the emergency operation, known as SLEDGEHAMMER, some time before the autumn of 1942. If this were necessary, he said, the American contribution in troops would necessarily be a modest one, since there was not enough shipping to transport a substantial force across the Atlantic within the next five months. He said that the President was opposed to any premature operation, involving such great risks, but that if such an operation were made necessary by developments on the Russian Front, American troops should take part in it to the fullest possible extent.

Marshall said that the Chiefs of Staff in Washington had made very careful calculations as to the measures that were necessary for holding the Alaska-Hawaii-Australia line in the Pacific and full provision for this had been made. He said that the U.S. Navy was now getting into position to attack the Japanese flank in the event of any further moves toward Australia. He spoke of the possibility of a Japanese attack on the Soviet Union, in which case the Americans would hope to make arrangements with the Russians to move the forces now based in Alaska into the Maritime Provinces of Siberia.

The next speaker at the memorable meeting was Sir Alan Brooke, Chief of the Imperial General Staff. He seconded the Prime Minister in welcoming the proposal for an offensive in Europe, but he also emphasized problems presented by the Japanese advances toward India. He pointed out that, if the Japanese were to gain unquestioned control of the Indian Ocean, the southern route to Russia would be cut, Turkey would be isolated, the Allies would lose the Middle Eastern oil supplies—which would go to the Germans—and the Germans would have ready access to the Black Sea and to the Russian rear in the Caucasus. The dreaded junction of the Axis partners would, of course, give both of them opportunity for the exchange of materials which they so greatly needed.

Churchill, Marshall, and Admiral Pound then discussed the naval problems in the Indian Ocean. The Prime Minister expressed confidence that these problems could be solved with American co-operation. He suggested that if the new U.S. battleship *North Carolina* were sent to Scapa Flow, the British ship *Duke of York* could be released to move to the Indian Ocean;

at least one ship of this power had to be kept at Scapa Flow in case the *Tirpitz*, sister ship of the *Bismarck*, were to come out from Trondheim, Norway. Marshall also expressed confidence that the two nations together could provide what was necessary for the Indian Ocean and other theatres and, at the same time, go right ahead with the main project.

It may be noted that the discussions at this meeting produced the contradictory circumstance of the American representatives constantly sticking to the main topic of the war against Germany while the British representatives were repeatedly bringing up reminders of the war against Japan. As he listened to the exchange of views Hopkins had been scratching notes and doodling on Downing Street notepaper. When it came his turn to speak he started off by saying that there was no question of doubt that American public opinion was generally in favour of an all-out effort against Japan. This sentiment had been intensified by the bitter ending of the gallant fight on Bataan Peninsula, and it would become more acute when General Wainwright was forced to surrender on Corregidor. However, Hopkins said, the President and the American military leaders and the American people were all agreed on one point: 'Our men must fight!' Obviously, Western Europe was the one place where the enemy could be fought most quickly and most decisively on land as well as on sea and in the air. Hopkins said that Americans did not want their men to be sent across oceans merely for purposes of sightseeing: they wanted to engage the enemy and finish the war.

Hopkins said very positively that once this decision was taken to go ahead with the trans-Channel Operation it could not be reversed, for the United States would consider this its major war effort. He said that of course the United States was fighting in its own interests, and the British were doing the same, but now the interests of the two nations coincided and they must fight together.

Attlee agreed that the time had come to take the initiative away from the enemy, and Eden emphasized the supreme political importance of a European offensive on the peoples of the occupied countries, on the Russians and even on the British people, who had become fed up after spending two and a half years on the defensive.

After further remarks by Air Chief Marshal Portal and Admiral Mountbatten, Churchill gave Hopkins assurance that the British Government and people would make their full and unreserved contribution to the success of this great enterprise.

The next day Hopkins cabled exultantly to Roosevelt that the British Government had agreed to the main American proposal, and Marshall cabled confirmation of this to the Secretary of War, saying that the Prime Minister 'declared in an impressive pronouncement his deep appreciation of the purpose and time of our visit'. The British Government, Marshall said, now intended to proceed immediately and energetically with all necessary preparations for the major operation. He added that he and Hopkins had lunched with the King and Queen that day and would dine that night with the King and the Prime Minister at 10 Downing Street.

The meetings with the royal family were of a purely social nature and Hopkins made no notes on them. However, one result was that Hopkins got the signature of King George VI on his short-snorter bill.

Confirmation came from Vichy that Laval was being restored to the position of Premier—an unmistakable evidence of further surrender by Pétain to the Germans. On April 15 all American residents of unoccupied France were asked by the U.S. Government to leave for home at the earliest moment, and Admiral Leahy was at last given his orders to report back to Washington 'for consultation'.

Hopkins cabled Roosevelt: 'How about nailing that wood pussy Laval to your barn door?' and Roosevelt replied: 'Your suggestion being studied, but consensus of opinion is that odour still too strong for family of nations.'

The American Embassy in London received from Washington a copy of a cable sent by Leahy:

It is, of course, difficult at Vichy accurately to gauge the reaction of the French public to the impending return of Laval to the Government of France. This is due to the fact that the great majority of the population of this provincial capital consists of Government officials. There seems, however, little doubt that Laval's return is extremely unpopular both with bourgeois elements and the great masses of the French people. On the other hand, in spite of the unpopularity of Laval there is no evidence, at least in Vichy, that the French people will at this time take positive or violent actions either against Laval or against the Vichy Government to demonstrate their dissatisfaction. While it is felt possible that there may be isolated incidents such as have already occurred in occupied France (where I have been reliably informed there were yesterday four or five attacks against members of the German Army, the most serious occurring at Caen), there appears to be in Vichy at the moment at least and possibly to a lesser extent elsewhere, a feeling that nothing can be done to prevent Laval's return. In Government circles we have heard from a number of people whose thorough dislike of Laval and his ideas cannot be doubted, the observation that while his return is to be deplored, he is at least a clever man who may perhaps obtain some concessions from the Germans and may at some future time be able to deceive them.

One of the arguments most often heard from people who believe Laval's return could not be prevented is that it is still too early for the French people to revolt against the Germans and their 'collaborationist' friends. The Russian Front, which the majority of French people consider is the key to the future of France, still remains a question-mark. In addition, the reverses of the British in the Indian Ocean and in Burma have created in French minds doubt as to British ability to hold their present position in the Near East. Therefore, runs their argument, any positive action taken against the authorities of occupation and their French collaborationist allies would be premature and would bring on terrible German reprisals. In spite of this apparent feeling of helplessness to prevent the return of Laval, should the Germans meet real reverses and find themselves in serious difficulty I believe there is little doubt that the majority of the people of France would be willing, if there seemed to be a possibility of success, to take action in some form or other against their cordially hated oppressors.

I hear the hope expressed from all quarters that the Allied Nations will be able to create some serious military diversion in Europe or North Africa by the dispatch of an expeditionary force. We are given to understand that the majority of the French people in the Occupied Zone are counting on this possibility, and from the Unoccupied Zone we receive a great number of letters and expressions of opinion upholding this view. I believe there is doubt that in the French mind the feeling exists that such a move is absolutely necessary and that it must be undertaken at an early date. Otherwise, they feel, Russia will be unable to hold and it will be too late. If it does not take place there is little doubt that among the anti-Axis elements, who are very considerable, there will be a feeling of profound disillusionment.

On the morning of Hopkins's last day in London he had a final meeting in Churchill's bedroom in the annexe to 10 Downing Street; Pound, Portal, and Ismay were also present. The Prime Minister, lying in bed, reviewed the whole war situation, urging that action be speeded up all down the line, saying 'the longer we wait, the hotter the water will become'. He hoped more planes could be rushed to India and the *North Carolina* to Scapa Flow.

Churchill, from his bed—which was usually a mass of pink, including its occupant—gave Hopkins the messages he wanted imparted to the President, and in spite of everything they were largely optimistic. Although, during the discussions of the past ten days, it had been obvious British policy to emphasize the grimmer aspects of the situation, Churchill was constitutionally unable to dwell for long on the possibility or even what appeared to others to be the actuality of defeat. He did not really believe that the Japanese would sweep through India and join up with the Germans. He evidently considered it more likely that they would turn around and concentrate on an attempt to knock China out of the war. He urged Hopkins to come back soon, for his visits always exerted a tonic effect in Westminster. While they were talking a message came from the Embassy saying that Leahy had just sent a secret report that Goering and his staff were at Serqueux near Forges les Eaux in the Seine Intérieur in France; Portal said the R.A.F. had received similar information and were investigating with a view to bombing the place.

Hopkins said a cheerful good-bye and he and Marshall flew to Northern Ireland for a brief visit to the American troops there. They had dinner and spent the night in a country house near Londonderry, since the local commanders felt that one of Hopkins's frail condition should be billeted in luxury; this weird episode has been amusingly described in Mrs. Marshall's delightful book, *Together*. The next morning Hopkins received a cable from Roosevelt relayed by Matthews at the Embassy in London through Army headquarters:

> This morning we have received reports indicating that Pétain has resigned, and although his place has nominally been taken by Darlan it is probable that Laval is in control. Welles and I both feel that there is some chance that orders from Laval will not be accepted by the French in North Africa. I therefore hope that you and Marshall will discus this changed situation with Mr. Churchill, who undoubtedly has further information. I ask that you discuss this whole subject with him, although I do not suggest revival of GYMNAST. I have some reason to believe that Orange battleships are now withdrawing eastward from the Bay of Bengal. We are progressing with the loading of the *Ranger*.

Matthews added to this cable that no confirmation had been received in London of the report of Pétain's resignation, but that Washington had officially announced the recall of Leahy.

While Marshall went about his inspection trip in Northern Ireland, Hopkins telephoned Downing Street, communicating the contents of this cable and saying that he felt it might be wise for him and Marshall to return to London, instead of flying back to the States, to await further developments of the French situation; it seemed possible that some sort of Allied expedition to North Africa might be launched immediately. Churchill agreed on this and Hopkins so cabled the President.

After lunch at the Army camp near Belfast, Hopkins and Marshall flew to Port Patrick, a little village on the West Coast of Scotland. General McClure had accompanied them from London, and in the small hotel in Port Patrick, Hopkins asked McClure to put through a telephone call to President Roosevelt. Anyone who has ever tried to use the telephone in a Scottish village knows that it is a considerable feat in itself to establish contact with some point as much as a dozen miles away. The effect on the local operator of a call to the White House in Washington is something utterly unimaginable. McClure was told to wait, then was put through to one supervisor after another, each of whom wanted to know who he was and why he desired to be put through to the President of the United States. McClure established his identity to the best of his ability, but he could not mention either Hopkins or Marshall, who by now had returned to the characters of Mr. Hones and Mr. Mell. At length McClure was told to hang up and wait. When he was called back to the telephone he heard a vaguely familiar voice—but it was no one in the White House; he had been put through to Commander Thompson at 10 Downing Street, and he managed to explain to him that 'the two friends who are with me' want to speak to the President. Thompson arranged matters in no time and Hopkins was was talking to Roosevelt, who told him to come on home without waiting for further bulletins from North Africa. In the meantime Scotland Yard had been alerted when McClure first made his remarkable call and its operatives closed in on the Port Patrick Hotel. Unfortunately, they made no arrests.

Hopkins and Marshall and Admiral Pound, who had joined them, took off on the Clipper that night from Stranraer, near Port Patrick, and they were in New York for lunch the next day.

On his last day in London Hopkins had received a letter from an English housewife, a Mrs. Martum of Newmarket, Suffolk, enclosing a cutting from the *Daily Express* which stated that 'It will not be long now before American bombs fall on Tokyo.' Mrs. Martum expressed the hope that this was right. She said: 'Lots of people in this country have the wind up about India. . . . We want no soft stuff with Germans or Japs. . . . Let's give it to them thick. . . . May God bless you all who are working so hard to save our dear countries, also our boys. . . . Let's have *action*, not words.'

Mrs. Martum got her wish in a hurry. While Hopkins and Marshall were flying home the news came from an almost incoherent Japanese broadcast of the Doolittle raid on Tokyo. This was only one, valiant, wildly adventurous shot at the enemy, which may have done negligible tangible damage to his power—but it was the first good news for the United Nations that had come from any non-Russian sector of war in many awful months. The men who risked and sacrificed their lives on this raid helped to accomplish as much as the winning of a great battle would have done in providing a badly needed lift of the heart for countless millions of discouraged people. It was a classic demonstration of the inestimable morale element in war which can turn fear of defeat into assurance of victory. Three weeks later came the Battle of the Coral Sea, which Admiral King has described as 'the first major engagement in naval history in which surface ships did not exchange a single shot' (there were more of them to come in the Pacific). This marked the beginning of the turning of the tide of Japanese conquest, although there were very few who could realize this at the time.

The whole atmosphere in Washington was changed. The gratification that Hopkins and Marshall had brought back with them from London was communicated from one department and war agency to another; there was a feeling, unfortunately not justified by the immediate facts, that we had passed from the defensive to the offensive phase of the war.

After Hopkins had made his first report at the White House, Roosevelt cabled Churchill that he was delighted with the agreement that had been reached in London. He said: 'Marshall and Hopkins have told me of the unanimity of opinion relative to our proposals [for the opening of a Second Front] and I greatly appreciate the messages you have sent me confirming this. I believe that the results of this decision will be very disheartening to Hitler. It may well be the wedge by which we shall accomplish his downfall.' Roosevelt expressed doubts that the dreaded junction of the Germans and Japanese would be accomplished. He said he was very pleased to have received a cordial message from Stalin announcing that Molotov and a Russian general were being sent to London and Washington. He added: 'I am frank to say that although we still have many mutual difficulties, I feel better now about the joint war situation than I have at any time in the past two years.'

Hopkins wrote to his old friend of relief days, Jacob Baker: 'I returned from England greatly encouraged about everything, but I think the whole business is going to take a lot of doing. I wish I were twenty-five years' younger.'

CHAPTER XXV

THE MOLOTOV VISITS

THE main work that now confronted Hopkins was the problem of supplies for the Soviet Union. The Germans were increasing the severity of their attacks against the route to Murmansk by submarine and by aircraft and surface craft based in Northern Norway. Here in these Arctic latitudes where there was perpetual daylight in summer there was no such thing as refuge under cover of night.

At the time when Hopkins left England there were fifteen ships in Iceland that had turned back from the Murmansk run; there were twenty-three more there that were waiting for convoys; there were twenty-one more Russian-bound ships half-way to Iceland that had to be re-routed to Loch Ewe in Scotland because of the congestion at Reykjavik. Thus, there were fifty-nine ships loaded with guns, planes, ammunition, oil, tanks, trucks, machinery, medical supplies, etc., for the Russians which were stalled and useless. In order to free some of these idle ships for some useful service their cargoes were unloaded in Scotland, which led to all manner of acrimonious charges from Moscow that the British were 'stealing' Lend-Lease material assigned to them. There was consequently an increasing effort to get the ships through at whatever cost—and the cost was awful. In the months of April, May, and June, eighty-four ships carrying 522,000 tons left U.S. ports for Murmansk. Forty-four of these, carrying 300,000 tons, got through. Of the remainder, seventeen discharged their cargoes in Scotland and twenty-three were sunk by the enemy or lost by shipwreck. Later, the losses became even worse; in one convoy twenty-two out of thirty-three ships were sunk. In addition to all other hazards on this route was the horror of the Arctic Ocean itself; the crews knew the terrible death by freezing that confronted even those who might survive the loss of their ships.

The route across the Pacific to Siberia was kept open after Pearl Harbour for Russian ships because of the Japanese desire to keep the Soviet Union out of their part of the war, but any bullet sent by that route had to travel half-way around the world before it could be fired at a German. The third route, via the Persian Gulf, became the most favourable after the opening of the Mediterranean in 1943 and the expansion of the port of Basra and the Iranian railroad by the 'forgotten men' of the Persian Gulf Command. In the meantime, however, a ship could make only two round trips a year on this route and the extremity of the bottleneck at the Basra end made it necessary to unload many cargoes at Karachi in India, where some goods were still piled up awaiting transhipment when the war ended.

Soon after Hopkins returned to the White House he cabled Churchill about

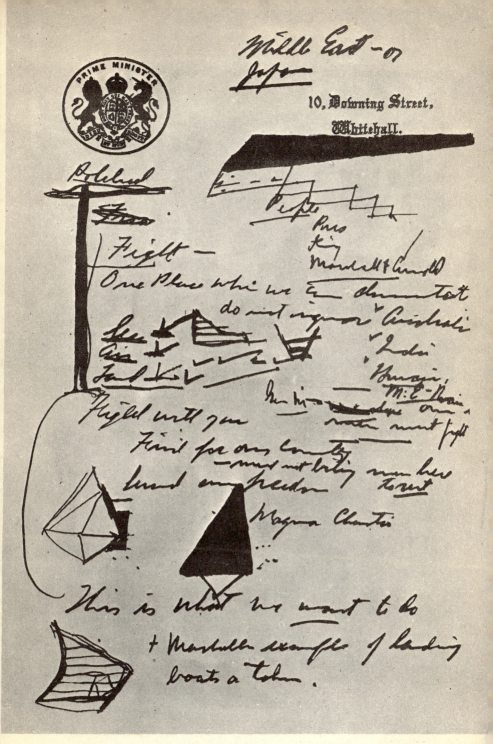

Notes by Hopkins during a meeting at No. 10 Downing Street in April, 1942, when agreement was first reached on the opening of a second front in northern France (*see page* 540).

the Murmansk convoy situation. Replies came from both Churchill and
Harriman, giving the official British view that, in consideration of the
enormous difficulties, a new understanding should be reached with the
Russians for reducing the promises of supplies to be delivered.

Roosevelt thereupon cabled the Prime Minister that the British and
American Naval Chiefs of Staff, Admirals Pound and King, had been discussing ways and means of breaking the log jam of ships loaded with cargoes
for Russia. Roosevelt expressed the belief that any unloading and reloading
of these ships in the British Isles would produce a 'very disquieting impression in Russia' and said that he hoped that, despite all risks, the proposed
convoys with additional escorts would be forced through to Murmansk.

Churchill replied to this: 'With very great respect what you suggest is
beyond our power to fulfil.' He pointed out that the convoy problem east
of Iceland was no mere matter of anti-submarine escort craft, but involved
major naval operations. He reported that two damaged British cruisers were
now immobilized at Murmansk and that he had just received word that the
new battleship *King George V* had collided with the destroyer *Punjabi*, which
was sunk, and her depth charges exploded, damaging the battleship.
Churchill added: 'I can assure you, Mr. President, we are absolutely extended'
and begged that they be pressed no further.

On May 4, Roosevelt sent the following cable to Stalin:

You will have been informed by Litvinov of the grave complications
we are having along the northern convoy route. However, I can assure
you that we will spare no effort to get off as many ships as possible.

I look forward to a meeting with Molotov. We shall make preparation
to provide immediate transportation for him the moment we know the
route he is to follow. I had hoped that he can stay with me at the White
House during his visit to Washington, but we can make available to him
a private house nearby if that is preferable.

I wish to express my appreciation for the cordial reception you have
extended to Admiral Standley of which I have been informed.

The reply from Stalin arrived ten days later:

I thank you for the message conveyed through Ambassador Litvinov.
I have already requested Prime Minister Churchill to contribute to the
speediest overcoming of certain difficulties in connection with the transportation and convoying of ships to the U.S.S.R. Since the delivery of
materials in May from the U.S.A. and England is of the utmost urgency,
I make a similar request to yourself, Mr. President.

The journey of Mr. Molotov to the U.S.A. and England must be postponed for a few days owing to uncertain weather conditions. It appears
that this journey can be made on a Soviet airplane both to England and

E

to the U.S.A. I would at the same time add that the Soviet Government considers that Mr. Molotov's journey should be accomplished without any publicity whatever till the return of Mr. Molotov to Moscow, as was done when Mr. Eden visited Moscow in December last.

In regard to the place of residence of Mr. Molotov during his sojourn in Washington, Mr. Molotov and I thank you for your kind suggestions.

Some indication of the magnitude and complexity of the shipping problem at this time can be found in the following memorandum which Hopkins sent to Lewis Douglas:

I wonder if I could see the statistical material which you get on a monthly basis which shows the efficiency of the turn-around.

Could I have the same thing that shows the relative efficiency of repair?

Incidentally, are our merchant-ship repair facilities used on a twenty-four-hour basis? Is there adequate personnel in these facilities? What inducement is there to the companies to finish the job with all possible speed? What are the general terms of contract? Is it on a cost-plus basis? What are the average hours worked by employees in merchant-ship repair yards? Are the facilities adequate or do the ships have to remain for a long period of time awaiting their turn?

Are you satisfied with the security of the stevedoring? Do we still permit enemy aliens to work on the docks and, if so, why? How many are there and in what ports? How adequate is the investigation machinery? Are you sure about the complete loyalty of some of the stevedoring managements? You know there have been charges that the Nazis are mixed up in these companies.

Do you think the docks are properly guarded and are these guards all military people or are there still private guards on some of these docks? Who investigates the loyalty of private guards?

Has an inquiry been made as to whether there are any stevedores or guards who were ever members of the Bund or the Christian Front, or similar organizations, the membership of which we may assume do not want us to win this war?

Douglas, it will be remembered, had resigned as Director of the Budget in 1934 largely because of his violent disagreements with the President over the whole philosophy of spending for relief. He had subsequently been outspoken in opposition to Roosevelt in the campaigns of 1936 and 1940. There was, therefore, every reason on the record why he and Hopkins should have disliked each other intensely. However, after the defeat of Wilkie, Douglas had asked for war service of any kind and Hopkins had been largely responsible for bringing him into a position of authority with Admiral Land in the

War Shipping Administration. All of the questions in the foregoing memorandum were not answered immediately; but they were answered ultimately.

In the performance of his limitless duties as 'Commander-in-Chief of the United Nations', Roosevelt could not entirely ignore the existence of domestic political affairs, much as he would have preferred to do so. Nineteen-forty-two was a Congressional election year and, while that was not a consideration which ranked high on the priorities list in the White House, it was a matter of life or death on Capitol Hill. The Senators and Representatives who faced hard fights for re-election knew that they could keep their records clean in so far as the war was concerned by voting loyally for all the vast appropriations that were required, and they did so; furthermore, an attitude of vigilance over expenditures was maintained through various media of investigation, notably the Truman Committee. However, seriously controversial political issues were created by measures which involved arbitrary interference with the civilian economy. The American people, who were so willing and proud to give whatever was required of them in blood and sweat, were loudly reluctant to cut down on their normal consumption of red meat and gasoline and their use of such essentials as electric toasters and elastic girdles. More than any other people on earth, Americans were addicted to the principle that you can eat your cake and have it; which was entirely understandable, for Americans have been assured from the cradle that 'there is always more cake where that came from'.

In the frantic weeks and months following Pearl Harbour, Roosevelt paid little attention to the question of controls on the civilian economy. As a convenient means of dodging the necessity of confronting this tough problem, he accepted the advice of those who said that everything could be settled on a purely voluntary basis. As a result of which, the spectre of inflation was beginning to haunt the land, and this was something that Roosevelt could clearly recognize with his keen memories of the First World War and its distressing aftermath. In a Message to Congress on April 27 and a Fireside Chat the following day he took cognizance of the dangerous situation and called for a seven-point programme:

(1) We must tax heavily, and in that process keep personal and corporate profits at a reasonable rate, the word 'reasonable' being defined at a low level.

(2) We must fix ceilings on the prices which consumers, retailers, wholesalers, and manufacturers pay for the things they buy; and ceilings on rents for dwellings in all areas affected by war industries.

(3) We must stabilize the remuneration received by individuals for their work.

(4) We must stabilize the prices received by growers for the products of their lands.

5) We must encourage all citizens to contribute to the cost of winning this war by purchasing war bonds with their earnings instead of using those earnings to buy articles which are not essential.

(6) We must ration all essential commodities of which there is a scarcity, so that they may be distributed fairly among consumers and not merely in accordance with financial ability to pay high prices for them.

(7) We must discourage credit and instalment buying, and encourage the paying off of debts, mortgages, and other obligations; for this promotes savings, retards excessive buying, and adds to the amount available to the creditors for the purchase of war bonds.

Before each of these seven points he used the words 'To keep the cost of living from spiralling upward. . . .' However, he did not really face up to the necessity of rigid rationing and price control; his generalizations were too broad and the Congressmen who were fearful of their constituents' wrath were able to evade the issue until Roosevelt presented it to them in precise and unmistakable terms four months later.

In his Fireside Chat, Roosevelt did have one passage of importance in indicating the direction of strategic policy:

In the Mediterranean area matters remain, on the surface, much as they were. But the situation there is receiving very careful attention.

Recently we have received news of a change in government in what we used to know as the Republic of France—a name dear to the hearts of all lovers of liberty—a name and an institution which we hope will soon be restored to full dignity.

Throughout the Nazi occupation of France we have hoped for the maintenance of a French Government which would strive to regain independence to re-establish the principles of 'liberty, equality, and fraternity', and to restore the historic culture of France. Our policy has been consistent from the very beginning. However, we are now concerned lest those who have recently come to power may seek to force the brave French people to submission to Nazi despotism.

The United Nations will take measures, if necessary, to prevent the use of French territory in any part of the world for military purposes by the Axis powers. The good people of France will readily understand that such action is essential for the United Nations to prevent assistance to the armies or navies or air forces of Germany, Italy, and Japan.

The overwhelming majority of the French people understand that the fight of the United Nations is fundamentally their fight, that our victory means the restoration of a free and independent France—and the saving of a France from the slavery which would be imposed upon her by her external enemies and her internal traitors.

We know how the French people really feel. We know that a deep-seated determination to obstruct every step in the Axis plan extends from occupied France through Vichy France to the people of their colonies in every ocean and on every continent.

These words, of course, were aimed directly at the French people—in metropolitan France, North and West Africa and, most specifically at the moment, the island of Madagascar. As Roosevelt spoke in this Fireside Chat about rationing and price control, he knew that a British force was on the way to seize the strategically vital French island off the East Coast of Africa. Madagascar was athwart the sea route from the Cape of Good Hope to Middle Eastern ports, including Basra, and to India. It would have been an enormous prize for the Japanese, and in view of the naval situation in the Indian Ocean at the time, there was too large a possibility that the Japanese might be able to take it. If they had landed forces on the island, the Vichy French authorities would presumably have yielded to them without a struggle as they had done in Indo-China. Therefore, the British move, which had been fully discussed between London and Washington and with Hopkins and Marshall at the recent conferences, was heartily approved by Roosevelt as a demonstration of the ability of the United Nations to get to some important point before the enemy did. On May 1 Churchill cabled Roosevelt the terms to be offered to the local Governor, providing the following guarantees: that the territory would remain a part of the French Empire, that those French-men on the island who wished to return to France would be repatriated as opportunity offered, that salaries and pensions of all officials who elected to co-operate would be continued, that trade would be restored and various economic benefits granted, etc. It was hoped that the Governor and other authorities would see the light of reason and offer no resistance to the British. The hope was in vain. Roosevelt expressed his approval of the measure in messages to Vichy as soon as news was flashed from the British commander that the forces were moving, but the old men of Vichy asserted the sacred 'honour' which impelled them to defend French sovereignty to the death against British, American or Free French forces, though not against Germans or Japanese. Admiral Darlan sent a message to the authorities on Madagascar:

Do not forget that the British betrayed us in Flanders, that they treacherously attacked us at Mers-el-Kebir, at Dakar and in Syria, that they are assassinating civilians in the home territory [by the bombing], and that they have sought to starve women and children in Djibouti.

As a result, the fighting on Madagascar went on for months.

Some time later highly interesting information was received from S. Pinkney Tuck, Counsellor of the American Embassy in Vichy, concerning the attitude of General Weygand, who had been in retirement in Cannes since his dismissal from command in North Africa six months previously. The information was indirect, for Weygand was under such strict surveillance that, as Tuck said: 'The General could not even blow his nose without it being heard in Vichy'; but General Strong, head of G-2 in the War Department, believed that the information had the ring of authenticity. These were Weygand's views as reported:

He believed that the Allies should land in *continental* France, preferably in the northern, German-occupied portion, rather than in North Africa. He said that the military and administrative structure which he had built up in North Africa had sadly deteriorated since his retirement—that the morale there was so poor that an American landing would be met with general apathy if not direct hostility. He felt strongly that fighting between Frenchmen and Americans should be avoided at any cost, for there had been already too much fighting between the British and French. Tuck said in his cable:

> On the other hand he [Weygand] believes that practically the whole French army in metropolitan France would not hesitate to give up its allegiance to a tottering Government of Vichy and come to the support of an American force landed in France itself. He considers it highly important that French patriots should at once formulate plans for the establishment of a provisional government which would be recognized immediately by the occupying forces and which would provide the necessary legal authority which would be psychologically indispensable at least to the officers of the French army.

In his April 28 speech, Roosevelt said:

> Our planes are helping the defence of French colonies today, and soon American Flying Fortresses will be fighting for the liberation of the darkened continent of Europe.

This referred to a subject over which there was some controversy between London and Washington. The British wanted American heavy bombers to be turned over to the R.A.F. and manned and operated by their own crews. The U.S. Air Force leaders—General Arnold, General Carl Spaatz, General Ira C. Eaker—wanted to get into action themselves, with American bombers manned by American crews under American command operating from bases in the United Kingdom.

Roosevelt cabled Churchill expressing his belief that all reserve American airplanes, except for a reasonable number held in the British Isles, should be removed from a reserve status, which was in effect a status of inactivity, and put into operation to maintain the maximum continuous combat competition with the enemy. He said: 'I think that the minimum number of planes consistent with security should be held in reserve and for operational training purposes and the maximum number should be applied in combat, and that United States pilots and crews should be assigned for the manning of American-made aircraft on the various combat fronts to a far greater extent than at present. I am sending General Arnold and Admiral Towers to London for discussion of the very important details of broad policy implied in this message.' Churchill replied to this in characteristic terms:

> We understand and respect the generous impulse which inspires the United States air force to engage American lives in the conflict at the earliest moment. God knows we have no right to claim undue priority in the ranks of honour. Let us each do our utmost. So may it be to the end.

Churchill went on to urge that Arnold and Towers proceed to London at the earliest possible moment. (Admiral John H. Towers was Chief of the Navy's Bureau of Aeronautics.) Despite the warm assurances at the start of Churchill's cable, the R.A.F. still wanted the bombers without the crews, and many further difficulties had to be overcome before the U.S. Eighth Air Force could start its historic operations from Britain during the following summer.

The problem of getting aircraft to the Soviet Union was much harder to solve. After the winter interlude of counter-attacks, the Russians now faced the spring and summer months of renewed German offensive, and their most pressing need was for fighter aircraft rather than bombers. Since there were no pursuit planes at that time with sufficient range to fly the Atlantic at any point, the grievous shipping problems were involved, although they could be reduced to a certain extent by assembling the planes in Africa and flying them into Russia by way of Iran. There was a far easier and more obvious route by way of Alaska to Siberia. Hopkins discussed this with General Eisenhower on May 1 and practical and comparatively simple plans were drawn up in the War Department by which the planes could be flown directly from aircraft factories all over the United States to Soviet fields in Siberia within a few days; yet this was one of the proposals on which the always suspicious Russians proved obdurate and, although they agreed 'in principle', it was a painfully long time before they would make the actual necessary arrangements for putting into operation the sensible delivery route by way of Fairbanks, Alaska.

One exchange of correspondence at this time showed how acute was the determination to disarm Russian suspicions of American motives: Hopkins received a suggestion that in view of 'the various strategic considerations which make Eastern Siberia a region of prime importance' the United States Government might well consider the desirability of introducing 'individuals of proven ability and discretion' (i.e. secret agents) into Siberia under the guise of Lend-Lease representatives. Hopkins rejected this suggestion, saying:

> I don't see how the Siberian business can work out by having a Lend-Lease person in that area. The whole question of air routes to Russia has been and is being thoroughly explored and I hesitate because of my relationship with the Russians to explore it in any other than the direct manner.

On May 1 Hitler and Mussolini had another of their meetings, this time near Salzburg, and again the world waited for the next big German offensive to start. It was surprisingly late this year. Churchill said:

> We now wait in what is a stormy lull, but still a lull, before the hurricane bursts again in full fury on the Russian Front. We cannot tell when it will begin; we have not so far seen any evidences of those great concentrations of German masses which usually precede their large-scale offensives. They may have been successfully concealed, or may not yet have been launched eastward. But it is now the tenth of May, and the days are passing. We send our salutations to the Russian armies, and we hope that the thousands of tanks and aeroplanes which have been carried to their aid from Britain and America will be a useful contribution to their own magnificently developed and reorganized munitions resources.

The consensus of opinion was that when the German drive did come it would move in a south-easterly direction toward the Middle East—either through the Caucasus, or through Turkey, or both. Turkey was one of the most important battlegrounds for economic and political warfare and, among neutral nations, by all odds the most favoured object for Lend-Lease aid. Hopkins received reports on the situation from his friend, Ambassador Steinhardt, in Ankara:

> I find no evidence that the Germans intend to attack Turkey in the immediate future. While they have prepared bases in the Balkans for that purpose, there are insufficient German troops at present available in Greece and Bulgaria to launch such an attack. In any event it would take them at least two weeks to move their troops into position. I think the critical moment for the Turks will be when the coming German offensive in Southern Russia either stalls or goes through to the Caucasus. On the happening of either of these two events the Germans will have to decide whether to try and go through the difficult terrain in Turkey or keep hammering at the Russians. It is most unlikely that either of these two conditions will exist before July or August.

I am convinced that in their present frame of mind the Turks will fight if they are attacked. . . .

While I believe the army will give a good account of itself if attacked, you must expect no such resistance as the Russians have offered, for the Turks possess no tanks and only a small obsolete air force which probably would not last more than two or three days against the Germans. Furthermore, they have very limited artillery. On the other hand, if they fall back into the mountains they should be able to make the going very tough for the Germans, particularly if by that time the R.A.F. and some British artillery come to their assistance.

As I telegraphed you to London the March shipments of Lend-Lease material and the new Lend-Lease procedure have had a marked effect on Turkish morale. The highest Government officials have gone out of their way during the past two weeks to tell me of their keen satisfaction with the increased shipments. The disappointment they felt earlier in the year has been completely dissipated. They are now contrasting the unfulfilled German promises of armament with our steadily increasing deliveries, so that I think that phase of the matter is now in good shape. I am very grateful to you for stepping up and speeding up these deliveries which have materially strengthened our position here.

The result of all this is that the Turks fear the Germans and ardently hope for an Anglo-American victory while at the same time they mistrust the Soviets and are doubtful that the United States and Great Britain will be able to restrain a victorious Soviet Union from taking the Straits away from them. It is difficult to predict just how far this situation may develop. I keep hoping that both the Turks and the Russians will have the good sense not to let the matter go any further than the mutual recriminations which have already taken place.

On May 12 Hopkins received a strictly unofficial message indicating that Churchill was considering the possibility of calling Lord Halifax back to London for service in the War Cabinet and as Leader of the House of Lords. His place as British Ambassador would be taken by Lord Beaverbrook. Hopkins discussed this proposal with the President and cabled Churchill that 'the idea of Max coming is of course agreeable and it is believed here that he could be extremely useful in the light of the problems which confront our two countries.' If this idea was pursued any further, I have seen no record of it, but it was highly interesting and significant to both Roosevelt and Hopkins at the time, because Beaverbrook had established himself publicly as well as privately as a vigorous, uncompromising advocate of the Second Front.

On April 23 he had come out flatfooted on this subject in a speech that he gave in New York. Even though Beaverbrook was no longer in the Government, his association with Churchill was known to be so close that his expression of opinion was widely interpreted as a statement of official British policy. However, it is my understanding that Beaverbrook had not cleared this speech with Churchill or anyone else in the British Government, but he had discussed it at length with the President and Hopkins in the White House. He thus had official though off-the-record American sanction for it. The naming of Beaverbrook as Britain's Ambassador following his statements would be, in effect, another form of commitment to the Second Front.

With the approach of Molotov's visit to Washington, plans for the great offensive in Europe occupied more and more attention in the White House, although Hopkins continued his close associations with Dr. Soong, President Quezon, and the Pacific War Council. In all preparations for amphibious warfare, then and for a long time thereafter, the biggest bottleneck was landing-craft. Roosevelt discussed this subject at great length with Hopkins and drew two sketches of a landing-craft which he had in mind. These sketches were drawn on a memorandum pad that someone had printed and inscribed 'From the desk of Franklin D. Roosevelt'. The President disliked these pads and rarely if ever used them again. I do not know what kind of craft he was illustrating in these sketches, or whether they provided any guidance to the naval architects. There was a protracted argument at the time over the design of the fifty-foot tank lighters. The production schedule called for the completion of six hundred of these within three months— and this requirement was made with the SLEDGEHAMMER operation in mind —but it took twice that long to do the job. 'Responsibility for this production lag', says the official record, 'could hardly be charged to industry or to the Government agencies supervising production. The chief difficulty was the failure of top officials responsible for strategic planning to anticipate the need for landing-craft in the North African campaign sufficiently far in advance.' It was also due to the Navy's reluctance to devote shipbuilding facilities and scarce materials to the construction of vessels to be used for essentially Army operations. In March, 1942, landing craft were tenth on the Navy's Shipbuilding Precedence List. By October, just before the North African landings, they had gone up to second place, preceded only by aircraft carriers, but the next month they dropped to twelfth place. General Marshall wrote that of all the problems of implementation of strategy faced at the Teheran Conference a year later 'the greatest by far was the critical shortage of landing-craft'.

In one of his frequent outbursts of impatience Hopkins said: 'Estimates can be made and agreed to by all the top experts and then decisions to go ahead are made by the President and the P.M. and all the generals and admirals and air marshals—and then, a few months later, somebody asks:

"Where are all those landing craft?" or "Whatever became of those medium bombers we promised to China?" and then you start investigating and it takes you weeks to find out that the orders have been deliberately stalled on the desk of some lieutenant commander or lieutenant colonel down on Constitution Avenue.'

Allowing for some slight elements of exaggeration, this was all too often the truth, particularly in 1942, when the President's production goals were still referred to derisively in the War and Navy Departments as 'the numbers racket'. There were many officers, pardonably sceptical concerning the extravagant programme that had come from the White House, who believed they could count only on the minimum of production and were consequently determined to fight or to connive, if need be, to keep that minimum for their own services.

In London, Molotov negotiated the treaty of Anglo-Soviet Alliance which was mainly a restatement of the military agreements made on July 12, 1941, and the principles of the Atlantic Charter as applied to the postwar world and particularly to any revival of the German menace.

On May 28 Churchill cabled Roosevelt a report of his talks with Molotov. Both the Prime Minister and Eden had been careful to avoid making any of the positive commitments that the Russians wanted regarding the establishment of a Second Front in 1942; they had limited themselves to discussion of the present state of the elaborate plans for BOLERO, SLEDGEHAMMER, and ROUNDUP, and had urged Molotov to stop again in London, when, they felt sure, it should be possible to talk more definitely about the future. (Meaning, of course, after they had been advised what the President said to him.) In this same cable Churchill said that Mountbatten was soon to arrive in Washington to inform the President and the Chiefs of Staff concerning certain difficulties that had arisen in the planning and to present a new suggestion (known as JUPITER) for a landing in the north of Norway through which a junction could be effected by land with the Russians, thereby greatly simplifying the task of getting supplies through to the Soviet Union. Churchill added: 'We must never let GYMNAST pass from our minds', and said that he and Molotov had made great progress in 'intimacy and good will'. This cable provided the first danger signal to Roosevelt and Hopkins, Marshall and King, that British thinking was beginning to veer toward diversionary operations far removed from the main point of frontal attack across the Channel.

Molotov arrived at the White House about four o'clock in the afternoon of Friday, May 29. He then met with the President, Hull, Hopkins, Ambassador Litvinov, and two interpreters, M. Pavlov and Samuel H. Cross, the latter Professor of Slavic Languages and Literature at Harvard University. The record of this first meeting, as written by Cross, is as follows:

After the customary introductions and greetings, Mr. Molotov presented Mr. Stalin's good wishes, which the President heartily reciprocated. To the President's inquiry as to Mr. Stalin's health, Mr. Molotov replied that, though his Chief had an exceptionally strong constitution, the events of the winter and spring had put him under heavy strain.

Mr. Molotov described his flight from Moscow to London and thence to Iceland, Labrador, and Washington as not especially unpleasant or wearing. His plane had flown from Moscow to London direct, over the front and Denmark, in about ten hours, but this was not particularly good time, as the same trip had been made before in seven and a half hours. He explained that his military adviser had broken his kneecap in an automobile accident in London, and was, thus, detained in England. Mr. Molotov consequently regretted that he would have to act as both diplomat and soldier. The President remarked that none present were military specialists, but that Mr. Molotov would have an opportunity next day to talk with General Marshall and Admiral King.

Mr. Molotov expressed his intention to discuss the military situation fully. He had covered it in detail with Mr. Churchill, who had not felt able to give any definite answer to the questions Mr. Molotov raised, but had suggested that Mr. Molotov should return through London after his conversations with the President, at which time a more concrete reply could be rendered in the light of the Washington discussions.

The President noted that we had information as to heavy Japanese naval concentrations in the Fuchia and Mariana Islands, but that we could not tell as yet whether they were directed against Australia, Hawaii, Alaska, or perhaps Kamchatka. Mr. Molotov said he was not informed about this, but he had no doubt the Japanese would do anything in their power to intimidate the Soviets.

To Mr. Molotov's remark that Hitler was the chief enemy, the President noted his agreement and mentioned his repeated statements to the Pacific Conference that we should remain on the defensive in the Pacific until the European front was cleared up. It had been difficult, he added, to put this view across, but, in his opinion, it was now accepted.

The President remarked that he had one or two points to raise which had been brought up by the State Department, and could be discussed by Mr. Molotov or between Mr. Litvinov and Secretary Hull, as seemed expedient.

The President then inquired what information Mr. Molotov had as to the Nazi treatment of Soviet prisoners of war. The Commissar replied that, from such data as Moscow received, not only from their own agents, but also from Polish and Czech sources, it was plain that the Russian prisoners were brutally and inhumanely handled. Direct reports to the effect had been received from some twenty-five Soviet prisoners who had escaped from Norway into Sweden. Mr. Molotov remarked that the Germans felt themselves bound by no rules, though the Soviets (he implied) were acting according to The Hague convention to the best of their ability.

The President expressed the hope that at least some arrangements might be made to exchange lists of names of prisoners of war. Mr. Molotov replied with emphasis that his Government was not disposed to negotiate any arrangement with the Germans which would give the latter the slightest pretext for claiming that they (the Germans) were observing any rules whatever, because the fact was they were not doing so. He showed no interest in the President's original suggestion. The President remarked that we had a similar problem in connection with our own nationals in Japanese captivity. While there was, for the moment, no official confirmation of radio reports of positive maltreatment, these prisoners were being fed on the Japanese army ration, which was starvation fare for any white man.

The President then had a memorandum on the state of Soviet-Turkish relations, which had become considerably less cordial than was previously the case. The memorandum expressed the willingness of our Government to co-operate in any way toward the improvement of these relations. Mr. Molotov replied succinctly that he was ready to discuss this matter.

The President also referred to the disturbances among the Kurds in Eastern Iran and expressed his hope that the trustful co-operation now existing between the Soviet and the Iranian authorities would continue and manifest itself hereafter as occasion might arise. Mr. Molotov said he was familiar with the situation and shared the President's hope.

In the course of conversation the President asked Mr. Molotov whether he had noted any intensification of reports on the deterioration of German domestic morale. Mr. Molotov admitted the increased frequency of such reports, but failed to comment on their significance.

The President described his plans for continuing the conversations and for receiving Mr. Molotov's staff and the flyers who brought him over. Mr. Molotov decided to spend Friday night at the White House, and ostensibly withdrew to rest, though between adjournment and dinner he took a walk with Mr. Litvinov, whom it had been decided not to include in the next day's conversations, to the Ambassador's obvious annoyance.

Hopkins's personal record of this same meeting was as follows:

Molotov and the President greeted each other very cordially, Molotov expressing his warm appreciation for the invitation to come to America and extending to the President the warm greetings of Stalin. It was pretty difficult to break the ice, although that did not seem to be due to any lack of cordiality and pleasantness on the part of Molotov.

The President had two or three memoranda on his desk which I had never heard of before, which were obviously given him by the Department of State, in which the Department was offering their good offices in alleged difficulties between the Russians and the Iranians on the one hand and the Russians and Turks on the other. I gathered Molotov was not much impressed. I at any rate so imagined, and in front of the President he raised the point that they thought they knew a good deal more about their relations with Iran and Turkey than we did. I confess I did not see in what way our good offices were to be executed.

The State Department also obviously wants Russia either to sign or adhere to the Geneva Convention of 1929 relative to the care and treatment of prisoners of war. This agreement requires that the adhering countries permit a neutral body, such as the International Red Cross, to inspect the prison camps. You don't have to know very much about Russia, or for that matter Germany, to know there isn't a snowball's chance in hell for either Russia or Germany to permit the International Red Cross really to inspect any prison camps. Molotov's final answer was that 'Why should we give the Germans the diplomatic advantage of pretending to adhere to international law. Germany might well say that they would agree and then not, of course, do anything about it because you couldn't trust them.'

Molotov indicated that it would be a mistake from a propaganda point of view to give Germany the chance to say that they were the people who upheld international law. He said that all the reports that Russia has of the treatment of Russian prisoners indicates that they are getting a very bad deal. Twenty-six prisoners recently escaped from Norwegian prison camps came back telling of starvation and beatings on the part of the Germans. I gather this is going to be a pretty difficult nut to crack for the State Department.

Hull later handed me the attached memorandum indicating the things he wanted taken up with Molotov while he is here. One of the interesting things about this is that none of these things has anything to do with the war on the Russian Front, although the first four are matters of considerable importance to us, but very little to the Russians unless we really mean business.

The President got into a discussion with Molotov about the Japanese. Molotov said the Japs are going to use every possible measure to prevent the movement of any divisions from Siberia to the German Front and he thought they were going to constantly threaten Siberia so that no troops could be moved.

The President told Molotov he thought the Japanese fleet might strike in any one of four directions—either at Australia and New Caledonia, or at Midway, Guam, and Hawaii, or at the Aleutian Islands, or, finally, at Kamchatka.

Molotov indicated that Kamchatka, while defended, was only lightly so, because they did not have the forces or the guns to spare to protect it adequately.

There was some discussion of the use of poison gas. Molotov said that they had evidence that the Germans were moving large amounts of gas to the Russian Front, although up to the present it had not been used.

The conference seemed to be getting nowhere rapidly and I suggested that Molotov might like to rest.

Litvinov acted extremely bored and cynical throughout the conference. He made every effort to get Molotov to stay at the Blair House tonight, but Molotov obviously wanted to stay at the White House at least one night, so he is put up in the room across the way.

I went in for a moment to talk to him after the conference and he asked that one of the girls he brought over as secretaries be permitted to come and that has been arranged.

Following is the memorandum handed to Hopkins by Hull:

A. The Establishment of an Airplane Ferrying Service From the United States to the Soviet Union Through Alaska and Siberia.

B. Establishment of a Civil Air Service between the United States and Vladivostok or Some Other Railway Point in Siberia Through Alaska.

C. The Establishment of a Civilian Air Service Between the United States and the Soviet Union Through Africa and the Middle East.

D. The Supply Route Over the Soviet Union to China.

E. Finland.

F. Economic Matters.

G. Iran.

H. Turkey.

I. Prisoners of War Convention—1919, Geneva.

The same group, with the exception of Hull, reassembled in the Oval Study at 7.40 for cocktails and dinner and conversation that lasted until midnight.

During the course of the evening, Roosevelt talked a great deal of his desire to start the process of disarmament after the war, maintaining arms only for the purpose of policing the world, particularly Germany and Japan, to make sure that they would not regain powers of aggression. It was his persistent belief that world economy could not recover if all nations, large and small, had to carry the burdens of heavy armament in order to survive. He said to Molotov what he said to many others during these war years: he believed that a peace could be established and guaranteed for at least twenty-five years, or as long as any of his and Stalin's and Churchill's generation could expect to live—which was what Roosevelt meant when he spoke of the 'foreseeable future'.

Professor Cross later noted:

> At the close of the conversation the President asked Mr. Molotov whether there were any Americans he particularly wanted to see, to which Mr. Molotov replied that he would, if possible, like to exchange greetings with ex-Ambassador Davies. Earlier in the evening he had spoken appreciatively of Admiral Standley, of whom the President remarked that he had chosen him because he was direct, frank, and simple. Mr. Molotov agreed that these were among the Admiral's conspicuous qualities.
>
> The whole evening's conversation, on Mr. Molotov's part, was marked by a somewhat unexpected frankness and amiability, which leads, not unnaturally, to the supposition that, since the Soviets want something very seriously, the word had gone out from Mr. Stalin to be somewhat more agreeable than is Mr. Molotov's custom.

Hopkins later told me—but this was not included in his written record—that Roosevelt was unusually uncomfortable and 'his style was cramped' in these meetings primarily because of the enormous language difficulty and the inevitable waits while each statement was translated, with additional delays while the two interpreters discussed shadings of meanings with one another. There was also the fact that in all of Roosevelt's manifold dealings with all kinds of people he had never before encountered anyone like Molotov. His relationship with the Kremlin from 1933 to 1939 had been through Litvinov, who, although qualifying as an old Bolshevik, had a Western kind of mind and an understanding of the ways of the world that Roosevelt knew. During the years 1939-41 of the Nazi-Soviet pact Roosevelt had few personal contacts with Ambassador Oumansky, leaving that tough proposition largely to Hull and Welles. However, Roosevelt was by no means appalled by the new and strange problem in human relations that Molotov presented. It offered a challenge which stimulated him to spare no effort to discover the common ground which, he was sure, must somewhere exist.

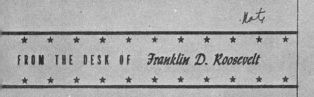

Note

THE WHITE HOUSE
WASHINGTON

May 13, 1942

MEMORANDUM

The President drew these two
views of a landing craft which he
has in mind.

This was preparatory to a
conference on landing craft which
he held recently.

H.L.H.

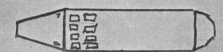

President Roosevelt's sketches of a landing craft, drawn on the eve
of Mr. Molotov's visit to Washington in May, 1942 (*see page* 558).

The next morning the President and Hopkins met with Molotov, General Marshall and Admiral King, and Pavlov and Cross. Hopkins wrote no personal record of this or of the two further meetings. Professor Cross's record was as follows:

After a brief private conference between the President and Mr. Molotov, conversations were resumed at 11 a.m. The President asked Admiral King whether there was any special news from the Pacific. The Admiral replied that there was nothing of importance save some momentary disagreement between General MacArthur and Admiral Nimitz as to an operation against the Solomon Islands. Admiral King thought this difference was due to a misunderstanding, since Admiral Nimitz had in mind a specific project for destruction of installations rather than anything like a permanent occupation.

Opening the general discussion, the President remarked to Admiral King and General Marshall that he first wished to place them *au courant* with the questions Mr. Molotov had raised, and he hoped that Mr. Molotov himself would then put the situation before them in detail. Mr. Molotov, the President continued, had just come from London, where he had been discussing with the British authorities the problem of a Second (invasion) Front in Western Europe. He had, the President added, been politely received, but had as yet obtained no positive commitment from the British. There was no doubt that on the Russian Front the Germans had enough superiority in aircraft and mechanized equipment to make the situation precarious. The Soviets wished the Anglo-American combination to land sufficient combat troops on the Continent to draw off forty German divisions from the Soviet Front. We appreciated, he continued, the difficulties of the situation and viewed the outlook as serious. We regarded it as our obligation to help the Soviets to the best of our ability, even if the extent of this aid was for the moment doubtful. That brought up the question, What we can do even if the prospects for permanent success might not be especially rosy? Most of our difficulties lay in the realm of ocean transport, and he would in this connection merely remark that getting any one convoy through to Murmansk was already a major naval operation. The President then suggested that Mr. Molotov should treat the subject in such detail as suited his convenience.

Mr. Molotov thereupon remarked that, though the problem of the Second Front was both military and political, it was predominantly political. There was an essential difference between the situation in 1942 and what it might be in 1943. In 1942 Hitler was the master of all Europe save a few minor countries. He was the chief enemy of everyone. To be sure, as was devoutly to be hoped, the Russians might hold and fight on

F

all through 1942. But it was only right to look at the darker side of the picture. On the basis of his continental dominance, Hitler might throw in such reinforcements in manpower and material that the Red Army might *not* be able to hold out against the Nazis. Such a development would produce a serious situation which we must face. The Soviet Front would become secondary, the Red Army would be weakened, and Hitler's strength would be correspondingly greater, since he would have at his disposal not only more troops, but also the foodstuffs and raw materials of the Ukraine and the oilwells of the Caucasus. In such circumstances the outlook would be much less favourable for all hands, and he would not pretend that such developments were all outside the range of possibility. The war would thus become tougher and longer. The merit of a new front in 1942 depended on the prospects of Hitler's further advantage, hence the establishment of such a front should not be postponed. The decisive element in the whole problem lay in the question, When are the prospects better for the United Nations—in 1942 or in 1943?

Amplifying his remarks, Mr. Molotov observed that the forces on the Soviet Front were large, and, objectively speaking, the balance in quantity of men, aviation, and mechanized equipment was slightly in Hitler's favour. Nevertheless, the Russians were reasonably certain they could hold out. This was the most optimistic prospect, and the Soviet morale was as yet unimpaired. But the main danger lay in the probability that Hitler would try to deal the Soviet Union a mighty crushing blow. If, then, Great Britain and the United States, as allies, were to create a new front and to draw off forty German divisions from the Soviet Front, the ratio of strength would be so altered that the Soviets could either beat Hitler this year or ensure beyond question his ultimate defeat.

Mr. Molotov therefore put this question frankly: Could we undertake such offensive action as would draw off forty German divisions, which would be, to tell the truth, distinctly second-rate outfits? If the answer should be in the affirmative, the war would be decided in 1942. If negative, the Soviets would fight on alone, doing their best, and no man would expect more from them than that. He had not, Mr. Molotov added, received any positive answer in London. Mr. Churchill had proposed that he should return through London on his homeward journey from Washington, and had promised Mr. Molotov a more concrete answer on his second visit. Mr. Molotov admitted he realized that the British would have to bear the brunt of the action if a Second Front were created, but he also was cognizant of the role the United States plays and what influence this country exerts in questions of major strategy. Without in any way minimizing the risks entailed by a Second Front action this summer, Mr. Molotov declared his Government wanted to know in frank terms what position we take on the question of a Second Front, and whether we were prepared to establish one. He requested a straight answer.

The difficulties, Mr. Molotov urged, would not be any less in 1943. The chances of success were actually better at present, while the Russians still have a solid front. 'If you postpone your decision', he said, 'you will have eventually to bear the brunt of the war, and if Hitler becomes the undisputed master of the Continent, next year will unquestionably be tougher than this one.'

The President then put to General Marshall the query whether developments were clear enough so that we could say to Mr. Stalin that we are preparing a Second Front. 'Yes,' replied the General. The President then authorized Mr. Molotov to inform Mr. Stalin that we expect the formation of a Second Front this year.

General Marshall added that we were making every effort to build up a situation in which the creation of a Second Front would be possible. As an officer, he appreciated how serious present conditions were, and the necessity of quick action. He had been greatly encouraged by the Russian resistance and counter-offensive on the Southern Front. Frankly speaking, we had the troops, all adequately trained; we had the munitions, the aviation, and the armoured divisions. The difficulties lay in transport, but the convoy problem was complicated by the necessity of sending tonnage to Murmansk, and the delivery of aircraft to the British Isles, where the heavier planes could be shipped by air under their own power, was limited by present deliveries to the Soviets.

Strategically the idea was, said General Marshall, to create as quickly as possible a situation on the Continent under which the Germans would be forced into an all-out air engagement, but they will not engage on this scale without the pressure of the presence of our troops on the ground. General Marshall added that, while Mr. Molotov based his considerations on the number of German divisions (forty) which the Soviets would like to see diverted from their front, what we had to base our own action on was the number of men we could ship across the Channel in order to provoke an all-out battle for the destruction of the German air force. The essential preliminary to a successful continental operation was to make the German aviation fight; we must therefore have an air battle.

The President then asked Admiral King to outline his point of view. The President observed that sending each convoy to Murmansk had become a three-dimensional naval engagement on account of providing defence not only against the lurking German major units (*Von Tirpitz, Scharnhorst, Gneisenau, Prinz Eugen*), but also against enemy submarines and aircraft. Admiral King concurred in the President's estimate of the situation. Getting convoys into Murmansk and Archangel was a major problem because of the heavy German units in Narvik and Trondhjem and the German air bases in Northern Norway. German reconnaissance planes shadowed our convoys from Iceland to Murmansk, and when a convoy approached they caused it to be attacked by both submarines and surface craft. This complex situation also rendered it necessary for large forces of the British Home Fleet to remain at sea to guard against attacks from heavy German ships which are stationed nearer to the convoy routes. Similarly, the United States Navy has had to reinforce the British Fleet with such heavy ships so that the British should have enough such ships on hand in order to maintain their convoying forces on the requisite level. At present we were running two convoys in opposite directions simultaneously, i.e. one would be leaving Murmansk as another left Iceland, so that the necessary cover could be provided in one operation.

Admiral King added it would be helpful if the Soviet air force could make additional efforts toward aiding the convoys, especially by air attacks on the German air and submarine bases at Narvik and Kirkenes, and remarked that such additional co-operation was justifiable by the importance to the United States and Great Britain of the safe arrival of munitions in Northern Russia. The situation was obviously complicated, the Admiral continued, by the southward drift of the polar ice, which limited the range of movement by the convoys. In one convoy due in Murmansk the previous day (Friday, May 29) we had lost five ships out of thirty-five, together with one destroyer, and other ships of the convoy had been damaged. To be sure, as the ice withdraws northward during the summer the convoys would have more room to manoeuvre in, but this advantage would be pretty well cancelled out by increased visibility during long summer days. The route by which ships could be put into Archangel during the summer was obviously longer, but we might even so gain something by increased freedom of movement.

The President then remarked to Mr. Molotov that we had in Khartum twenty-four bombers of the finest and heaviest type, and inquired what the Soviet attitude would be to having these bombers fly north to bomb the Roumanian oilfields and then go on to land at Rostov or somewhere in the neighbourhood. The President added that it did not seem expedient to turn these planes over to the Russians, as we do with the 200 pursuit planes supplied them monthly, but only for the reason that it took two months to train a bomber crew. Mr. Molotov said the whole idea was entirely acceptable, and, in fact, his Government would not mind an arrangement whereby Soviet bombers could shuttle back and forth across Germany to be serviced and rearmed in England.

The President also referred to the advisability of delivering fighter planes to the U.S.S.R. by air from Alaska to Siberia and then across the latter westward. Mr. Molotov objected, however, that, while this method would be appropriate for supplying the Soviet Far-Eastern Command, he doubted its efficacy or practicability for the delivery of planes to the Western Front because of the long distance involved and the difficulty of arranging for gasoline depots.

The conversation was then adjourned for lunch.

The gathering at lunch in the White House that day—Saturday, May 30 —was as follows: The President, Molotov, Litvinov, Vice-President Wallace, Hull, Marshall, King, Forrestal, Senator Connally, Congressman Bloom, the Soviet Military and Naval Attachés, General Burns, the President's Naval Aide, Hopkins, Pavlov, and Cross.

Cross has written:

The conversation during lunch was mainly desultory. The President described to Mr. Molotov the acquisition of the new Lincoln portrait, and commented upon the nearness of the Confederate lines to Washington during the early days of the Civil War. When Hitler was brought into the conversation, the President remarked that, after all, Mr. Molotov had seen and talked with Hitler more recently than anyone else present, and perhaps Mr. Molotov would be willing to communicate his impressions of the man. Mr. Molotov thought a moment, then remarked that, after all, in the world, it was possible to arrive at a common understanding with almost anyone. Obviously Hitler had been trying to create a good impression upon him. But he thought he had never met two more disagreeable people to deal with than Hitler and Ribbentrop. To the President's remark that Ribbentrop had formerly been in the champagne business, Mr. Molotov observed dryly that he had no doubt Ribbentrop was better in that line than in diplomacy. On being informed of Senator Connally's functions as Chairman of the Senate Foreign Affairs Committee, Mr. Molotov asked the Senator what he considered the most serious diplomatic problem now confronting the United States. When the Senator answered 'Vichy', Mr. Molotov remarked that there was nothing genuine about the Vichy Government, and that they were a nuisance.

At the close of lunch the President secured the general attention and spoke substantially as follows: He was glad to welcome our distinguished guest, whose nation was contributing so signally to the successful prosecution of the war. His conversations with Mr. Molotov had been friendly and frank. The President hoped they would lead to definite and salutary results. There was, however, one Russian whom he looked forward to meeting, and that was Mr. Stalin, whose masterly leadership was carrying his country through so serious a crisis. After a toast to Mr. Stalin, the President emphasized that this luncheon was entirely off the record, since no Press announcement of Mr. Molotov's visit would be released until after the Commissar's safe return to Moscow.

When the President had concluded his remarks Mr. Molotov rose and said he was happy to answer. His visit was unusual, and he had travelled unusual paths across the front and the ocean. His visit was going well and attaining its purpose. The enemy to be met was not only cruel and powerful, but was driven by a limitless appetite. Mr. Molotov wished to remind his hearers that the Soviet, by bitter experience, knew best what Hitler is. Hitler wanted more territory, and was becoming more insatiable day by day. The Red Army was doing its best, but we must reckon fully with all possible dangers. Mr. Molotov thanked the President for his generous toast to the great Soviet leader and general. President Roosevelt, he added, was popular in the Soviet Union because of his clear understanding of the interests of his people and the farsightedness with which he promoted these interests. He proposed the President's health, thanking him for his statesmanlike handling of the grave international problems with which he was confronted in his high office. Mr. Molotov added that his grateful acknowledgments were equally addressed to all members of the United States Government concerned with the prosecution of the war.

The President then asked Mr. Molotov if he would not give the guests a picture of the current military situation. Mr. Molotov then remarked that the present operations were the beginning of the summer offensive period for which Hitler had been preparing. Marshal Timoshenko had begun his Kharkov offensive as an offset to the German drive on the Kerch peninsula. This drive had resulted unfavourably for the Russians. The Soviets had originally possessed superiority of forces in the Eastern Crimea, but had used this superiority ineffectively because of the inefficiency of the local commander, General Kozlov, who had proved weak and had not, as a matter of fact, taken part in previous operations against the invading forces. A concentration of aviation and of armoured units, supported by Roumanian troops, had enabled the Germans to achieve a relatively easy success. This was regrettable, but there was no use in disguising the facts. The German drive in the Crimea necessitated speeding up by several days the opening of Marshal Timoshenko's Kharkov offensive. As far as personalities went, the Soviets had found that inexperienced officers and men were the least effective. For example, Marshal Timoshenko was the more dependable because he had had field experience since the beginning of the invasion, while Kozlov was an instance of the opposite state of affairs in both respects.

The Germans' easy success in the Crimea had rather surprised them, and had led to boastful German talk about new and secret weapons which they actually did not possess—a characteristic and usual form of German propaganda. The Soviet tactics used at Kharkov to encircle the city on the north and south had been at first very successful, and in the first three days netted 400 German tanks damaged or destroyed. This reverse had led the Germans to start the Izyum-Barvenkovo movement with six armoured divisions, infantry, and aviation. South-east of Kharkov the Soviet troops had opened out a salient which the Germans were now trying to even out, and were thereby seriously endangering the Soviet forces in the salient. Marshal Timoshenko commands the south-western front, while the southern front (Rostov-Voroshilovgrad) is commanded by General Malinovski under Timoshenko's supervision. Mr. Molotov reminded his audience that he had been away from Moscow two weeks, but he believed the situation was still serious, especially if the Red troops were cut off in the salient just mentioned. He would not undertake to speak positively on the outcome of the present struggle. The Germans might next concentrate on Moscow or Rostov, or even make an effort to penetrate the Caucasus along the line Novorossisk-Maikop-Baku. Success in this last effort would confer vast advantages upon Hitler, particularly with respect to oil. The morale of the Red Army was excellent, and its confidence in ultimate victory unimpaired. To a question by the President regarding guerilla operations, Mr. Molotov replied that the partisans were most active in the Moscow-Smolensk-Mozhaisk (Dorogobuzh) sector. They numbered 19,000 irregulars and parts of two-three cavalry divisions under General Belov. They were in absolute control of an egg-shaped area measuring some 60 kilometres east and west by 20-30 kilometres north and south. They were, however, less conspicuous in other areas.

At the close of lunch the President casually mentioned to Mr. Molotov that we had never got around to declaring war on Roumania, as it seemed something of a waste of effort. Mr. Molotov said that might be the case, but the Roumanians were fighting against the Soviets and causing some trouble by helping the Nazis. The President then turned to Senator Connally and Congressman Bloom with a query as to the probable attitude of their respective Committees toward a formal declaration of war upon Roumania. Their thought was that there would be no objection, whereupon the President suggested that appropriate action might take place during the coming week (of May 31). On taking leave of Mr. Molotov, Senator Connally assured him that the enemies of the U.S.S.R. were our enemies, a sentiment which Congressman Bloom emphatically shared.

After lunch the President returned to his study, where he received the officers and crew of Mr. Molotov's bomber and the members of the Commissar's clerical staff, who were presented by Mr. Litvinov. The President addressed a few words of cordial greeting to the group, congratulated the flyers, and expressed the hope that, now they had found the way, they would return again, bringing the Commissar with them once more.

The President handed Mr. Molotov a list of 8,000,000 tons of Lease-Lend material which we should produce during the year from July 1, 1942, but stated that we could ship only 4,100,000 tons of this total.

The group then broke up about 3.30 p.m.

During his stay in Washington, Molotov bore the code name of 'Mr. Brown'. His visit imposed a strain on Steve Early and on Byron Price, Director of the Office of Censorship, for, in accordance with Stalin's request, the presence of Mr. Brown in Washington could not be made known to the public. It was utterly impossible to keep the White House correspondents from finding out about it, and this was one occasion when Early and Price asked for voluntary censorship, and it was observed until the official announcement was released a week after Molotov's departure.

Evidently the Russian airplane which had brought Molotov blew a tyre, for the following note came to Hopkins from Colonel K. M. Walker:

Bolling Field is flying the airplane tyre off the Russian ship to Akron, Ohio, this afternoon.

The Chief Engineer of the Akron people will be on the job personally, and will work all tonight and tomorrow rebuilding the tyre, which they expect to have available to be flown back to Washington Tuesday morning.

Everything else about the ship is o.k. The Russians are well pleased with the service and co-operation they have been receiving.

There were no meetings with Molotov in the White House between Saturday lunch and Monday morning.

There was a meeting with the Chiefs of Staff on Sunday afternoon (General Arnold was at that time in London) which Hopkins described:

The President had a conference this afternoon for an hour with General Marshall, Admiral King and myself, in which we discussed the final statement the President would make to Molotov.

The President told General Marshall and Admiral King that he thought the matter was a little vague and the dangerous situation on the Russian Front required that he, the President, make a more specific answer to Molotov in regard to a second front.

The President read a draft of a cable which he had prepared to send to Churchill. Marshall thought that the use of the word 'August' was unfortunate and would arouse great resistance on the part of the British. I agreed with this.

There was then considerable discussion as to the Russian convoy by the northern route and the effect of the withdrawal of that route or, at any rate, a marked cutting down of the number of ships on the BOLERO operation.

I expressed the opinion that if the Russians could get those munitions which they could actually use in battle this year, such as tanks, airplanes, spare parts, guns and ammunition, that they probably would be quite satisfied if they had definite assurances of BOLERO in 1942.

Clearly the revision in our shipping to Archangel would provide more ships for BOLERO. By the same token, according to King, it would very substantially relieve the pressure on the British Home Fleet and make more destroyers available for the Atlantic convoy.

Marshall, I believe, thinks that BOLERO is inevitable some time in 1942 merely by the force of circumstance.

The President asked me if I would redraft the cable to the Former Naval Person and the final draft is the one that was sent.

(*Note.*—In the foregoing Hopkins seems to have made the mistake, which Roosevelt also did in some messages, of referring to BOLERO as the trans-Channel operation itself.)

Following is the cable to Churchill to which Hopkins referred:

I think that Molotov's visit has been a real success. We have got on a personal footing of candour and of friendship as well as can be managed through an interpreter. He will leave here in two or three days.

Molotov has clearly expressed his anxiety concerning the next four or five months. I think that this is sincere and that it is not put forward for the purpose or forcing our hand.

I am, therefore, more anxious than ever that BOLERO shall begin in August and continue as long as the weather permits.

After discussion with the Staffs, I believe that the German air forces cannot be destroyed unless they have been forced to take the air by preliminary or temporary actions by ground forces. If we can start this phase early in August we can produce one of the following results:

1. Divert German air forces from the Russian Front and attempt to destroy them.

2. If such air forces are not moved to the west, we can increase our operations with ground forces and determine on the establishment of permanent positions as our objective.

I am especially anxious that Molotov shall carry back some real results of his mission and give a favourable report to Stalin. I am inclined to believe that the Russians are a bit down in the mouth at present. Our Combined Staffs are now working on proposals to increase the shipping for BOLERO use by making large reductions of materials for Russia which we could not manufacture in any case before 1943. This should not diminish the supplies which the Russians could use in combat this summer, such as ammunition, guns, tanks or planes.

In this same cable Roosevelt suggested to Churchill that he would like to have a talk with Field Marshal Smuts, saying: 'I think it may be of help to him in his home problems to get a picture of the general situation from a fellow Dutchman like me.' He also acknowledged receipt of a set of the complete works of Winston Churchill, saying he was 'thrilled' by them and 'shall always cherish them'.

At this same meeting with Marshall and King, on May 31, there was also considerable discussion of the New Russian 'Protocol' (programme of Lend-Lease aid) which would go into effect July 1, at the expiration of the First Protocol, drawn up when Beaverbrook and Harriman were in Moscow nine months previously. The Staffs in Washington and London had been working out the details of the Second Protocol and had arrived at the schedule of 4,100,000 tons of shipments which Roosevelt had handed to Molotov after lunch the previous day. Now, in view of the critical shipping situation, it seemed that this programme must be cut down if any major transatlantic operation were to be undertaken in 1942. On this Hopkins wrote the following note:

The attached memorandum was written by the President at the conference with General Marshall and Admiral King this afternoon.

The memorandum indicates how the total number of tons of shipping to Russia might be cut down. The problem is how many ships this would release for BOLERO.

The President is very insistent, however, that all of the tough items of supply go through.

The President's memorandum:

Present Plan:

4,100,000 tons made up of

_____

1,800,000 Planes tanks guns
2,300,000 General supplies

New Plan:

1,800,000	Planes tanks guns
700,000	General supplies

2,500,000	tons

4,100,000
2,500,000

1,600,000 saving

The final meeting of the President, Molotov, and Hopkins was held at 10.30 on Monday morning, June 1, with Litvinov, Pavlov, and Cross the only others present. This is Cross's record:

The President opened the conversation by remarking that the Washington Press representatives knew about Mr. Molotov's visit, but had been very decent about making no reference to it. He suggested that, after Mr. Molotov's safe return to Moscow, the Soviet Government might simultaneously inform Messrs. Maisky and Litvinov of his arrival, and set an hour at which synchronized announcements of his visit might be released in London and Washington. Mr. Molotov accepted this suggestion.

On the basis of State Department memoranda, the President then went on to say he had a few points to mention, mostly for Mr. Litvinov's attention. We had, the President continued, reports from Finland that representative groups in that country wish to make peace with the Soviet Government. They could not, however, mobilize their strength to demonstrate to Finnish public opinion the possibility of peace unless something concrete were done by Moscow or Washington. These groups had asked the United States to ascertain a possible basis for peace, and the United States Government would proffer its good offices for this purpose if the Soviet Government wished to avail itself of them.

In the whole of Monday morning's conversation Mr. Molotov was much more gruff and assertive than in the previous interviews, perhaps for the purpose of playing the big shot in Mr. Litvinov's presence. In this case, at any rate, he immediately became terse and pressing. 'I should like to know,' he asked, 'whether these Finns are official.' 'No,' replied the President, 'they are merely a number of leaders of public opinion, but not the Finnish Government.' 'Do they want peace?' inquired Mr. Molotov. The President replied in the affirmative. 'Have they any special conditions in view?' Mr. Molotov asked. 'No,' said the President. 'They express no desires as to the basis on which peace should be concluded'?

'No,' answered the President, 'what they want is to show the Finnish people that peace is possible with safety to Finland.' Mr. Molotov then inquired whether these groups were able to represent Finland. The President replied that our information was confined to the statement that several such representative private groups existed. Mr. Molotov then observed that he would discuss the matter with Mr. Stalin.

The President next observed that postal connections and official travel between Washington and Kuibyshev were slow and difficult. We were running a plane service as far as Basra which we would be disposed to extend as far as Teheran if the Soviets would send down a connecting plane to that point, perhaps once a week. Mr. Molotov replied without hestitation that his Government would establish such a Kuibyshev-Teheran service, but at the start only once in two weeks. He directed Mr. Litvinov to carry on with the detailed arrangements.

The President then noted that, for substantially the same purpose we should like to organize a civilian air service from Washington to Nome, and then continue on to some convenient point at the east end of the Trans-Siberian, e.g. Petropavlovsk. The President remarked that it was immaterial whether the American planes flew over to Petropavlovsk, or whether the Soviets sent their own planes over to Nome. He also raised the point of organizing a civilian ferrying service for military planes from Nome to Siberia. Admiral Standley had already talked on this subject to Mr. Stalin, who had said he would study the question. Mr. Molotov observed that both these suggestions were under advisement, but he did not as yet know what decision had been reached.

The President remarked that he wished Mr. Molotov would take up one other matter with Mr. Stalin. We knew, he said, that there would be two kinds of post-war settlements: first, those among the United Nations and, second, arrangements for the reconstruction of the other nations with a view to ensuring a more stable form of peace. The President continued by saying that he had a new thought based on old experience. He believed that, instead of requiring interest on wartime advances, all the United Nations should work out a plan covering a long-term repayment of capital only. He hoped Mr. Molotov would discuss the point with Mr. Stalin for the purpose of exploring it without commitments. Mr. Molotov agreed to do so. The President observed that some such arrangement would facilitate matters for Great Britain, the Soviet Union, and the United States, and also prove helpful for other nations.

(At this point Mr. Hopkins inquired of the President whether the latter cared to discuss his project for setting up a special postwar fund under international trusteeship. This question was not translated to Mr. Molotov and thus did not figure in the discussion.)

On the President's previous suggestion Mr. Molotov commented that he thought Mr. Stalin would be interested, and promised that the proposal would be attentively studied. Both he and Mr. Stalin thoroughly appreciated the role played by the United States in the initiation of such proposals.

The President then recalled that he had already developed his ideas about disarming Germany and Japan, about control and inspection of their munitions industries to preclude surreptitious rearmament, about the future police activities of the four major nations, and about their role as guarantors of eventual peace. He had omitted one other point, viz. that there were, all over the world, many islands and colonial possessions which ought, for our own safety, to be taken away from weak nations. He suggested that Mr. Stalin might profitably consider the establishment of some form of international trusteeship over these islands and possessions.

In reply Mr. Molotov declared that he had considered and reported to Moscow the President's earlier proposals as to postwar organization. He had received an answer from Mr. Stalin, who was in full accord with the President's ideas on disarmament, inspection, and policing, with the participation of at least Great Britain, the United States, the Soviet Union, and possibly China. This idea had the full approval of the Soviet Government, which would support it fully. He had no doubt that the President's trusteeship principle would be equally well received in Moscow.

The President then pointed out that the acceptance of this principle would mean the abandonment of the mandate system. For example, after the last war the Japanese had received a mandate over the previously German islands in the Pacific, which they had fortified. These islands were small, but they ought not to be given to any one nation. The Japanese should, of course, be removed, but we did not want these islands, and neither the British nor the French ought to have them either. Perhaps the same procedure should be applied to the islands now held by the British. These islands obviously ought not to belong to any one nation, and their economy was substantially the same everywhere. The easiest and most practical way to handle the problem of these islands over a long period would be to put them under an international committee of three-five members.

The President then inquired of Mr. Litvinov whether he was ready to abandon the League of Nations. 'Anything for the common cause,' the Ambassador replied.

Turning to the question of colonial possessions, the President took as examples Indo-China, Siam, and the Malay States, or even the Dutch East Indies. The last-mentioned would some day be ready for self-government, and the Dutch know it. Each of these areas would require a different lapse of time before achieving readiness for self-government, but a palpable surge toward independence was there just the same, and the white nations thus could not hope to hold these areas as colonies in the long run. Generalissimo Chiang Kai-shek therefore had the idea that some form of interim international trusteeship would be the best mode of administering these territories until they were ready for self-government. They might, the President added, be ready for self-government in twenty years, during which the trustees might endeavour to accomplish what we accomplished in the Philippines in forty-two years. The Generalissimo, then, was thinking of the principle of trusteeship looking toward independence. The President hoped Mr. Molotov would discuss this suggestion with Mr. Stalin.

The Commissar expressed the opinion that this problem deserves serious allied attention, and it would certainly receive such attention in the U.S.S.R. For him it was obvious that any decision upon it would depend on the guarantees exercised by Great Britain, the Soviet Union, and the United States (with China, perhaps), coupled with such control functions as would prevent Germany and Japan from arming again to menace other nations with war. Starting from this principle, Mr. Molotov expressed his conviction that the President's proposals could be effectively worked out. The President said he expected no difficulties once peace was achieved.

The President then interjected that he had to entertain the Duke and Duchess of Windsor at lunch at twelve, but that he had one more point to discuss. Mr. Molotov also noted that he had another question to present.

The President then went on to say that on the previous day he had discussed questions of tonnage and shipping with the Chiefs of Staff. Every week we were building up troop and plane concentrations in England with a view to getting at the Germans from there as quickly as possible.

We were also shipping landing-craft. But the time-element involved depended on available ships. We hoped and expected to open a Second Front in 1942, but we could progress more rapidly only with more ships. The Chiefs of Staff had therefore suggested that, in order to speed up the opening of the Second Front, the Soviet Government, with this in mind, should reconsider the Lease-Lend list previously submitted, remembering that, of the 4,100,000 tons which were to be shipped during the year from July 1, 1942, only 1,800,000 tons are material ready to be used for military purposes on the Russian Front this summer. The rest was mostly raw materials and other items for the production of material which would not be ready for use this summer: 2,300,000 tons, in fact, represented items that would not be used for fighting at all. The President therefore

THE MOLOTOV VISITS 579

proposed that the Soviet Government consider reducing its Lease-Lend requirements from 4,100,000 tons to 2,500,000 tons. This reduction would release a large number of ships that we could divert to shipping to England munitions and equipment for the Second Front, and thus speed up the establishment of that front. Mr. Hopkins further emphasized that there would be no cut in the volume of tanks and ammunition being shipped. Everything that the Red Army could use in actual fighting would still go forward.

Mr. Molotov replied that, while he would report this suggestion at home, he hoped that such non-military supplies as metals and railroad material, which have a direct bearing on the solidity of the present front, would not be cut too much, as they also were in large degree essential. In checking over the Lease-Lend list, his Government would have to reckon with the degree in which any reduction on non-military items would impose restrictions on the Russian rear, e.g. on electric plants, railroads, and machinery production. These were, after all, comparatively vital, and he hoped these needs would not be lost from view. He remarked again that he had a couple of points for discussion.

The President repeated that we expected to set up a Second Front in 1942, but that every ship we could shift to the English run meant that the Second Front was so much the closer to being realized. After all, ships could not be in two places at once, and hence, every ton we could save out of the total of 4,100,000 tons would be so much to the good. The Soviets could not eat their cake and have it, too.

To this statement Mr. Molotov retorted with some emphasis that the Second Front would be stronger if the first front still stood fast, and inquired with what seemed deliberate sarcasm what would happen if the Soviets cut down their requirements and then no Second Front eventuated. Then, becoming still more insistent, he emphasized that he had brought the new treaty out of England. 'What answer,' he asked, 'shall I take back to London and Moscow on the general question that has been raised? What is the President's answer with respect to the Second Front?'

To this direct question the President answered that Mr. Molotov could say in London that, after all, the British were even now in personal consultation with our staff officers on questions of landing-craft, food, etc. We expected to establish a Second Front. General Arnold would arrive next day (Tuesday, June 2) from London, and with him Lord Mountbatten, Marshal Portal, and General Little, with whom it was planned to arrive at an agreement on the creation of a Second Front. Mr. Molotov should also say in London that we could proceed toward its creation with the more speed if the Soviet Government would make it possible for us to put more ships into the English service. Mr. Molotov, the President observed, would be back from New York either on Tuesday or Wednesday (June 2 or 3). After General Arnold had reported to General Marshall, the President hoped Mr. Molotov would discuss further arrangements with General Marshall.

The conversation thus ended with decreased tension on the Russian side. The President bade Mr. Molotov a cordial farewell, wished him a safe return home, and presented the Commissar with his photograph. The meeting broke up at about 12.10 p.m.

After that meeting Hopkins went with the President to Hyde Park, where they remained for three days. While at Hyde Park, Hopkins received the following memorandum from General Burns:

At a luncheon today at the Soviet Embassy, Mr. Litvinov and his distinguished guest pressed for an answer to the four requests which they said had been submitted to you on June 1.

They are as follows:

1. Sending of one caravan of ships monthly from the ports of America directly to Archangel under escort by U.S. naval ships.

2. Monthly supplies of fifty bombers B-25 by flight through Africa with their delivery at Basra or Teheran.

3. Delivery of 150 bombers Boston-3 to the ports of the Persian Gulf and their assembly there.

4. Delivery of 3,000 trucks monthly to the ports of the Persian Gulf and their assembly there.

The following information is submitted for a basis upon which to make a reply:

Item 1. No suggestion. This is a matter to be decided by the highest level.

Item 2. The proposed Protocol provides for a monthly quota of twelve B-25 bombers to be flown across Africa and to be delivered to the Russians at Basra or Teheran.

Item 3. The proposed Protocol provides for the delivery of 100 A-20's each month through October to the ports of the Persian Gulf and for their assembly there. After October, war developments will determine rate. (The A-20's are the equivalent of the Boston-3.)

Item 4. Our information is to the effect that 3,000 trucks per month could be shipped to the Persian Gulf and be assembled there.

Hopkins noted his reply on this as follows:

I talked to the President about General Burns's memorandum. I asked Burns if he would not see Molotov this evening and advise him formally, but not in writing, as follows:

In regard to No. 1, that we were acting jointly with the British Admiralty in regard to convoying merchant ships to Murmansk and that independent United States naval convoy could not be established, but that every effort would be made to get the ships through as long as possible. I told Burns to emphasize to Molotov the importance of air support from the Russians, both in attacking the airports from which Germany is operating and to give far more adequate air cover to the convoy coming in.

In regard to No. 2, I told Burns to tell Molotov that the commitment we made relative to bombers was final.

In regard to No. 3, the answer is the same as for No. 2.

In regard to No. 4, to tell Molotov that we could deliver 3,000 trucks monthly.

After his subsequent meeting with Molotov, Burns sent this information to Hopkins:

Mr. Molotov made no comment with reference to the rendering of more effective air support to the northern convoy route.

He seemed to desire a more definite answer to Request No. 1 (monthly U.S. convoy from America to Archangel). I repeated that my understanding is that while the President is most anxious to move the maximum amount of supplies to Russia, he does not feel that more specific commitments as to convoys can be made at this time.

Mr. Molotov asked me to thank the President for his prompt consideration of these four requests and for his decisions thereon. He said that while he had hoped they would be granted in full, he was deeply grateful for the help offered. He stated we could rest assured that all munitions supplied to the U.S.S.R. would be put to work against the Germans as promptly and effectively as possible, and that Russia could be relied upon to continue the war until victory is won. I told him I was sure the President and the country had that same feeling about Russia. He seemed to be very friendly and very appreciative of the efforts being made to assist his country.

Hopkins also noted while at Hyde Park:

Steve Early called me up at Hyde Park today and said that the President had asked the State Department to prepare a draft of a proposed public statement which would be made concurrently in Moscow and Washington when Molotov arrives in Moscow.

Steve said this was submitted to the Russians, who did not like it, and had in turn submitted their own proposed draft, which is attached.

I talked to General Marshall about this, and he felt that the sentence

G

THE WHITE HOUSE PAPERS

about the Second Front was too strong and urged that there be no reference to 1942. I called this particularly to the President's attention, but he,
nevertheless, wished to have it included, and the only amendment made
was the one recommended by Mr. Hull, namely, that his name be excluded from those participating in a military conference and a sentence
be added, which I drafted as follows:

'Mr. Cordell Hull, Secretary of State, joined in subsequent conversations on non-military matters.'

The reference to the Second Front which Molotov wrote and which
appeared in the public statement issued on June 11 was: 'In the course of the
conversations full understanding was reached with regard to the urgent
tasks of creating a Second Front in Europe in 1942.'

The exact meaning of those words and all the implications involved in
them provoked interminable and often violently acrimonious discussion for
a long time thereafter.

Hopkins later was given an Aide Memoire which the British authorities
had handed to Molotov on this subject. It said:

We are making preparations for a landing on the Continent in August
or September, 1942. As already explained, the main limiting factor to
the size of the landing force is the availability of special landing-craft.
Clearly, however, it would not further either the Russian cause or that
of the Allies as a whole if, for the sake of action at any price, we embarked on some operation which ended in disaster and gave the enemy
an opportunity for glorification at our discomfiture. It is impossible to
say in advance whether the situation will be such as to make this operation
feasible when the time comes. We can therefore give no promise in the
matter, but, provided that it appears sound and sensible, we shall not
hesitate to put our plans into effect.

After Molotov's departure, Hopkins wrote a letter about things in general
to Winant:

Molotov's visit went extremely well. He and the President got along
famously and I am sure that we at least bridged one more gap between
ourselves and Russia.

There is still a long way to go, but it must be done if there is ever to
be any real peace in the world. We simply cannot organize the world
between the British and ourselves without bringing the Russians in as
equal partners.

For that matter, if things go well with Chiang Kai-shek, I would
surely include the Chinese, too. The days of the policy of the 'white
man's burden' are over. Vast masses of people simply are not going to
tolerate it, and for the life of me I can't see why they should. We have left

little in our trail except misery and poverty for the people whom we have exploited.

I think the publicity release gives all I can tell you about the Second Front. I have a feeling some of the British are holding back a bit, but all in all it is moving as well as could be expected.

Our victory at Midway may turn out to have been a great one. So much so that it may change the whole strategy of the Pacific. After all, it is fun to win a victory once in a while. Nothing that I know of quite takes its place.

The new Lend-Lease Agreement with Russia, I think, also helps.

Lyttelton has made a fine impression here and I am sure he is going back greatly encouraged.

The visit of Oliver Lyttelton, who had replaced Beaverbrook as Minister of Production, resulted in the establishment of the Combined Production and Resources Board on June 9. The Combined Food Board also came into being at this time.

The Production Board should undoubtedly have been formed at the Arcadia Conference along with the Combined Chiefs of Staff and the Munitions Assignment Board. It had been considered impossible then, because neither the War Production Board in the United States nor the British Ministry of Production had begun to function. Although now launched with Lyttelton and Donald Nelson as its two members, it never exercised adequate co-ordinating authority. The main reasons for its failure have been recorded in *Industrial Mobilization for War*:

> Despite early efforts, CPRB did not engage in comprehensive production planning or in the long-term strategic planning of economic resources. The American and British production programmes for 1943 were not combined into a single integrated programme, adjusted to the strategic requirements of the war. CPRB's isolation from the sources of decision regarding production objectives, its failure to develop an effective organization, its deference to other agencies and its tardiness in asserting its jurisdiction, the inadequacy of programme planning by the agencies upon whom CPRB relied for forecasts of requirements, the delay of the Combined Chiefs of Staff in formulating strategic objectives for 1943—all these contributed to a result that saw adjustments in the American and British production programme for 1943 made by the appropriate national authorities in each case, rather than through combined machinery.

The trouble was that the 'appropriate national authorities' in the United States were not only Nelson and his associates in WPB, but also the procurement officers of the War and Navy Departments, with whom the civilians were engaged throughout the war in one of the many running battles of Washington.

After returning to the White House from Hyde Park, Roosevelt cabled Stalin that Molotov's visit had been a very satisfactory one and that he was anxiously awaiting the news of the Foreign Commissar's safe return to Moscow. At the same time he cabled Churchill: 'Molotov warmed up far more than I expected, and I feel sure that he now has a much better understanding of the situation than he had previously. I must confess that I view the Russian Front with great concern. However, our operations in the Pacific are going well, and I am certain that we are inflicting some severe losses on the Japanese fleet. Our aircraft are giving a very good account of themselves. I shall keep you informed about the outcome of the present battle [Midway] which is still indecisive, but we should know more about it before this day is over.'

These two cables from Roosevelt to Churchill and Stalin were sent on June 6, 1942, which was the date of the decisive Battle of Midway in the Pacific and also two years to the day before the real Second Front was at last opened in Northern France.

CHAPTER XXVI

THE DECISION IS CHANGED

THE Battle of Midway was, in the Pacific, what the Battle of Britain had been in stopping the Germans on the Channel and what Stalingrad was to become in the war on the Russian Front. It was, as Admiral King has written, 'the first decisive defeat suffered by the Japanese Navy in 350 years. Furthermore, it put an end to the long period of Japanese offensive action, and restored the balance of naval power in the Pacific.'

On that day, Hopkins wrote to Churchill:

This note will, I hope, reach you by the hand of Franklin Roosevelt, Jr., who is leaving today to join his destroyer.

From the last forty-eight hours we have had our minds on the Jap attack on Midway and Dutch Harbour. Our reports this morning are quite good. Whether the beating they have taken is going to force them to withdraw we do not know, but it rather appears so. When you add this to the Coral Sea business, it will change the relative value of our naval forces in our favour very substantially.

The Japs simply cannot stand the attrition and I am sure we can beat them down gradually in the air and on the sea until finally they must collapse. This does not mean there will not be bad news in the Pacific. I think there will be plenty of it, but I am sure their days of pushing around there with impunity are over.

The Molotov visit went off well. I liked him much better than I did in Moscow. Perhaps it was because he wasn't under the influence of Uncle Joe! At any rate, he and the President had very direct and straightforward conferences.

We are disturbed here about the Russian Front, and that anxiety is heightened by what appears to be a lack of clear understanding between us as to the precise military move that shall be made in the event the Russians get pushed around badly on their front.

The full implications of Arnold's visit are still being analysed here and I think probably the President will not come to grips with them for a day or two.

I confess that I am somewhat discouraged about our getting into the war in a manner that I think our military strength deserves, but I have always been an impatient person and I have no doubt that our time will come.

You have no idea of the thrill and encouragement which the Royal Air Force bombing has given to all of us here. Whatever happened to the list of cities marked for inevitable destruction? I imagine the Germans know all too well what they have to look forward to.

I am sure there are certain matters of high policy which you must come to grips with the President on, and he is hopeful that you can make a quick trip and I fancy will be cabling you about it at once.

Oliver is here and getting about his business quietly but effectively. He had lunch with the President yesterday and is off to Detroit today. He will get a chance to have some real talks with the President before he goes back.

I saw Mountbatten for a moment yesterday. The President is going to spend the evening with him next Tuesday.

Above all, I am ever so glad to learn of your good spirits and health. The timid souls here and in England, heartily joined, no doubt, by every Nazi-minded person in our two countries, would like to see you laying bricks in the countryside of Kent. I gathered when I was in England that you didn't want to do that for a while. I think it might be all right just after Laval's funeral.

Give my love to Clemmie and Mary. Why don't you bring Clemmie with you? She would be worth far more than all Brendan's propaganda pills.

On the night of May 30 the R.A.F. had put over its first 1,000-bomber raid on Cologne, a demonstration of power which gave a formidable boost to morale in the United Nations. General Arnold was with Churchill at Chequers that day, urging the case for U.S. bombing operations from Britain. Arnold quoted Churchill as saying: 'Your programme apparently will provide an aerial striking force equal to, or in some cases larger than, that provided and planned by us. Perhaps your programme is too ambitious. You are trying to do within a few months what we have been unable to accomplish in two or more years.' Churchill stuck to his argument that for the time being the United States should deliver heavy bombers without crews to the R.A.F. until full production could be reached and there would be more than enough for all. In the meantime, Churchill undoubtedly felt —although he was far too polite to say so—that the British were more competent to use the weapons than were their American allies.

Hopkins noted on that night of the Cologne raid:

The Prime Minister called me at 7 p.m. today, obviously from Chequers, where he was entertaining Winant, Harriman, Arnold, Somervell, and Eisenhower for the week-end.

The Prime Minister was obviously in good spirits and told me he was sending twice as many bombers that night over Germany as had ever gone before. He indicated the weather was good and he was very hopeful of the outcome. They were apparently planning to stay up all night to learn the results.

He also indicated that the battle in Africa was going well and said to me: 'I may see you very soon.'

Later, Arnold and Harriman called from England.

Arnold indicated he was coming home at once; that he felt his mission had been very successful and he, too, was very hopeful about the night's bombing operations.

Eisenhower and Somervell were then on a quick trip to London for discussion of problems of planning and supply. They returned to Washington a few days later, Arnold bringing with him Admiral Lord Louis Mountbatten, who conveyed to the U.S. Chiefs of Staff the disturbing impression that there might be some question of revision of the ROUNDUP-SLEDGEHAMMER agreements made by Marshall and Hopkins in London six weeks previously. It was believed in Washington that Mountbatten was expressing the attitude of the British Chiefs of Staff rather than his own.

Mountbatten had dinner with Roosevelt and Hopkins and then returned to London to report his conversation to the Prime Minister, after which he sent a summary of this report to the President, as follows:

> I was so very grateful to you for giving me the opportunity of such a long and interesting talk last Tuesday, and I did my best to convey all that you told me to the Prime Minister and the Chiefs of Staff. In order to make sure that I correctly conveyed your points I propose recapitulating here what I told the Prime Minister.
>
> I pointed out that you stressed the great need for American soldiers to be given an opportunity of fighting as soon as possible, and that you wished me to remind the Prime Minister of the agreement reached last time he was in Washington, that in the event of things going very badly for the Russians this summer a sacrifice landing would be carried out in France to assist them. I pointed out that no landing that we could carry out could draw off any troops, since there were some twenty-five German divisions already in France and landing-craft shortage prevented our putting ashore an adequate number. The chief German shortage lay in fighter aircraft and all our efforts were being bent towards provoking fighter battles in the west.
>
> I said that you had asked for an assurance that we would be ready to follow up a crack in German morale by landing in France this autumn and that I had given you an assurance that such an operation was being planned and was at present held at two months' notice.
>
> I pointed out that you did not wish to send a million soldiers to England and find, possibly, that a complete collapse of Russia had made

a frontal attack on France impossible. I said that you had asked whether we could not get a footing on the Continent some time this year, even as late as December, in which case you would give the highest possible priority to the production and shipping of landing-craft, equipment, and troops. The need for securing a port for supplying the troops under winter conditions made it clear that we should have to capture a port such as Cherbourg and hold a suitable line such as the Cherbourg Peninsula, possibly expanding across towards St. Nazaire and eventually holding the whole of Brittany.

I made a point that you were sure that, in any case, when the operation came off we should have to secure the Atlantic ports and not go rushing off in the direction of Germany until we were firmly established, unless German morale had really cracked.

I pointed out that you did not like our sending out divisions from England while American troops were still being sent in and that you suggested that we should leave about six divisions in England and that the corresponding six American divisions should be sent straight to fight in North Africa, either round the Cape to fight in Libya or straight into Morocco with a view to joining hands with the Army of the Nile and reopening the Mediterranean. In the latter connection, I told the P.M. how much you had been struck by his remark in a recent telegram: 'Do not lose sight of GYMNAST.'

This would mean that Dakar would fall into our hands without having to fight for it and I mentioned that you considered this important because the climate was not suitable for European soldiers to fight in.

As a result of the recent losses inflicted by the U.S. Fleet on the Japanese Fleet, particularly their aircraft carriers, there was a general desire to take the offensive from Australia, using the existing U.S. marine forces and combat shipping. General Marshall had suggested going for Timor and General MacArthur had telegraphed on his own suggesting making for Rabaul. I said that you and General Marshall were anxious that two British aircraft carriers with their destroyer screen should join the American naval forces in Australia to support these operations, and that there had also been a suggestion that the amphibious force which had assaulted Madagascar should be used for operations against the Japanese. . . .

I was so thrilled and heartened by all I saw in America, particularly by the American Army, which is forging ahead at a quite unbelievable rate.

(The deletions made in the above document before the final paragraph referred primarily to technical matters.)

There was an increasing conviction in Washington that the British were now inclined to dissuade the Americans from entertaining any ideas of engaging the Germans in force on land or in the air in 1942. This is what Hopkins meant when he wrote: 'I am somewhat discouraged about our getting into the war in a manner that I think our military strength deserves.' (He meant the European war, of course.) When it was made known that Churchill was about to embark on another trip to Washington, Marshall determined that the Prime Minister should be given an opportunity to observe for himself the quality of the U.S. Army and the advanced state of its training.

On June 9 Hopkins noted:

Ambassador Litvinov came to see me last night and told me the Russian Government had agreed to our flying bombers to Russia via Alaska and Siberia.

I told him that I would ask General Arnold to get in touch with him to work out all the plans for the route.

It seems to me this is one of the tangible results of Molotov's visit and I doubt very much if this would have been approved on any other basis.

I imagine the real reason the Russians approved our flying planes through Siberia is that in the event Japan attacks them we will already have organized a quick method of getting bombers to Vladivostok.

I later told General Arnold of Russia's agreement and he had agreed to get in touch with Ambassador Litvinov at once.

At that time, Japanese forces were landing on Kiska and Attu in the Aleutian Islands—the nearest advance they made to the North American continent—and Roosevelt cabled Stalin:

The situation in the Alaskan and North Pacific area is developing in such a way as to provide tangible evidence of intentions of Japanese preparations to conduct operations against the Siberian maritime provinces. We are prepared to come to your assistance with our air power in the event of such attacks if suitable landing-fields in Siberia can be made available to us. The operations of the Soviet Union and the United States must be carefully co-ordinated in order to carry out such operations.

I believe that an immediate exchange of detailed information concerning existing bases in the Alaskan and Siberian areas and the starting of secret staff talks between our joint navy, army, and air representatives are essential to our common security in order to meet this new danger from Japan. I am very happy to be told by Litvinov that you have given approval to the movement of our aircraft from Alaska through Siberia to your battlefronts against Germany. I propose that you and I designate representatives to meet in Moscow and Washington at once and that these representatives be empowered to make definite plans and initiate action which I consider to be a matter of great urgency.

A decisive battle was being joined in Libya between the advancing German forces under Rommel and the British under Auchinleck. Churchill, always interested in this theatre and almost always optimistic about it, advised Roosevelt that he expected 'considerable results' here, 'or even a complete decision'. Free French forces under General Joseph-Pierre Koenig covered themselves with glory and suffered heavy losses in the hopeless defence of Bir Hacheim which ended on June 10, leaving only the fortress of Tobruk between Rommel and Egypt. On this same day the Germans announced that the village of Lidice in Czechoslovakia was being levelled and its name 'extinguished', its men shot, its women put into concentration camps, its children distributed through 'appropriate educational institutions' in Germany—all in reprisal for the killing near this quiet village of Reinhardt Heidrich, deputy to Heinrich Himmler of the Gestapo. This act of calculated ferocity, advertised by the Germans themselves with such brazen cynicism, made it unnecessary for the Allies to invent propaganda to arouse the world's indignation and make certain that there would be the will to fight this war to the death. The barbaric fury and suicidal stupidity of the atrocities at Lidice were duplicated by the Germans throughout the conquered territories of the Soviet Union. Hatred was generated which in itself provided the strongest insurance against the possibility of the Russians making a separate peace.

The hopes and fears of the sorely tried Russian people were now concentrated on the beautiful Crimean seaport of Sevastopol which had been cut off and besieged for eight months. The Germans had been pounding it with dive-bombers, and on June 7 they launched all-out infantry and tank attacks in a determined effort to end the city's epic resistance before starting their major drive toward the Caucasus. It was evident that Sevastopol could not hold out much longer. The Russians were now more than ever in desperate need of nourishment for their faith in ultimate victory. The Soviet Government's propaganda to their own people had established the term 'Second Front' as the veritable talisman of deliverance.

On the evening of June 18 there was an Extraordinary Session of the Supreme Soviet of the U.S.S.R. held in the Kremlin for the purpose of ratifying the Alliance with Britain and welcoming Molotov home. The foreign correspondents in Moscow were invited to attend and to give to the world descriptions of this celebration of Anglo-American-Soviet solidarity. Molotov gave the principal speech, saying:

I cannot but associate myself with the words Mr. Eden spoke at the time of the signing of the Treaty: 'Never in the history of our two countries has our association been so close. Never have our mutual obligations in relation to the future been more perfect.' This is unquestionably a happy omen. . . .

Naturally, serious attention was given to the problems of the Second Front during the talks, both in London and Washington. The results of these talks can be seen from the identical Anglo-Soviet communiques. This has a great importance for the peoples of the Soviet Union, because the establishment of a Second Front in Europe would create insuperable difficulties for the Hitlerite armies on our front. Let us hope that our common enemy will soon feel on his own back the results of the ever-growing military co-operation of the three great powers.

Two days after this Extraordinary Session—at which Molotov expressed nothing more definite than his *hope* for a Second Front in 1942—Roosevelt and Hopkins at Hyde Park were discussing the possibility of collapse on the Russian Front and together they drafted a message to Marshall and King as follows:

On the assumption that the Russian Army will be hard pressed and retreating in July: that the German forces are in August (1) dangerously threatening Leningrad and Moscow and (2) have made a serious break through on the Southern Front threatening the Caucasus—

On the above assumptions—

At what point or points can:

A. American ground forces, prior to September 15, 1942—plan and execute an attack on German forces or in German-controlled areas which can compel withdrawal of German forces from the Russian Front.

B. British forces in the same area or in a different area, aid in the same objective.

Roosevelt added a note to this that Marshall was to come to the White House at eleven o'clock the following morning (Sunday) and was to be joined there by Sir Alan Brooke an hour later. The day before this message Churchill had arrived at Hyde Park and the British Chiefs of Staff in Washington. That Saturday night, June 20, the President and Prime Minister and Hopkins took the train to Washington and then spent Sunday morning, afternoon, and evening in conference with the Chiefs of Staff. On Monday morning Roosevelt, Churchill, and Hopkins met with Secretaries Stimson and Knox, then with Dr. Soong, and then with General Eisenhower and Mark Clark, who were about to leave for London and the newly formed European Theatre of Operations. After lunch, Hopkins went to New York to give a speech at Madison Square Garden at a Russian war relief rally in observance of the first anniversary of the German attack on the Soviet Union.

He said in this speech:

And what of our 3,000,000 trained ground troops with their modern mechanized equipment? I want to assure this audience that General Marshall, the great leader of this army, is not training these men to play tiddlywinks.

A second front? Yes, and if necessary a third and a fourth front, to pen the German Army in a ring of our offensive steel.

He spoke of Roosevelt in a way that may have sounded to some like phony platform sentimentality, but which represented Hopkins speaking strictly from the heart:

> The President, as no other American, knows and loves the trees and valleys of our country. He knows its mountains and hills and plains. He knows the factories and farms, the cities and towns and villages. He knows Maine and California, New York and Nebraska, and Idaho and Georgia. Above all, he knows the homes—miners' homes, farmers' homes, Negroes' homes, the homes of his friends in Hyde Park. While he loves the trees and hills and the valleys, above all else, he is devoted to the people who make up America.
>
> And tonight as he sits in the White House, talking to Mr. Churchill, planning the strategy of this gigantic struggle for freedom with his military advisers, you can be sure that the one thought above all others that guides him is his devotion to our people. He has confidence in us and knows that we trust in him. Never during these trying days and nights have I known him to falter once in his supreme assurance of victory. If he sleeps well at night, it is because of a deep and abiding faith in the righteousness of our cause. If he laughs, it is because he knows that wars are not won by being miserable.

There were a few men in authority—conspicuously Stimson and Marshall —who felt that too much of the strategic planning then going on in the White House was concerned with the third and fourth fronts mentioned by Hopkins and not enough with the second.

Churchill had stated his conception of the problems in writing to the President when they first met at Hyde Park. In this letter he said that all arrangements were proceeding to enable six or eight divisions to be landed on the coast of Northern France in September, 1942. But, though all preparations were being made, the British Government would not be in favour of undertaking a limited operation in 1942 if it were likely to lead to disaster. An unsuccessful operation, he argued, would not help the Russians, would expose the French population to Nazi vengeance, and would gravely delay the main operation in 1943. He expressed the view of the British Government that the Allies should not make any substantial landing in France in 1942 unless they were going to stay there. He said that the British military staffs had been unable to devise any plan for a landing in September, 1942, which had any chance of success. Churchill then went on to put a number of pointed questions. Had the American staffs devised such a plan? If so, what was it? What forces would be employed? At what points would they strike? What landing-craft and shipping were available? Who was the general who was prepared to command the enterprise? What British forces and assistance would be required? If there were a plan which offered a reasonable prospect of success, the British Government would welcome it and share to the full the risks and sacrifices which it involved. But if there was no plan which commanded the confidence of any responsible authority, and if no substantial landing could be made in France in September, 1942, could the Allies afford to stand idle in the Atlantic theatre during the whole of that year? Ought they not to be preparing some other operation, by which they might gain advantage and take some of the weight off Russia? It was in this setting, Churchill concluded, that the operation GYMNAST should be studied.

Here, then, was the argument that the proponents of the Second Front had feared: the revival of GYMNAST, the North African operation, instead of SLEDGEHAMMER, the trans-Channel assault in 1942. Stimson noted that Churchill had 'taken up GYMNAST, knowing full well, I am sure, that it was the President's great secret baby'. It may be said that neither Stimson nor Marshall had serious objection to the North African operation in itself; it was considered feasible and there were many strategic points in its favour; but mounting it and maintaining it would involve the diversion of such a vast amount of shipping as well as naval and air forces and troops to the Mediterranean area that the BOLERO build-up could not possibly be continued at a sufficient rate through the summer and autumn of 1942 and even through the following winter. Thus, if GYMNAST were decided on, adequate strength for a full-force invasion of the Continent could not be established in the United Kingdom in time for the spring of 1943.

This was the beginning of the protracted and often bitter dispute over the Second Front. Much has already been written on this extensive subject, and in most of it Churchill appears as the arch villain from the American and Russian points of view. Certainly, in this argument, he demonstrated to the limit his qualities of indomitability, or of pigheadedness, whichever word you prefer. He was accused by some of a cowardly fear of risking British lives—and that accusation was made by Stalin in brutally blunt words to Churchill's face. The charge of cowardice could hardly stand up against Churchill, who, in 1940, had deliberately risked the lives of the entire British population, including his own, when the United States was still 'neutral' and the Soviet Union was associated with the Germans in the Molotov-Ribbentrop pact; but there was no doubt about his reluctance to sacrifice British lives, and American lives, on the beaches of Northern France. He dramatized the possible cost of invasion in many lurid figures of speech; describing the Channel as a 'river of blood'—recalling the carnage of Passchendaele and the Somme in the First World War—describing his emotions as he stood in the House of Commons and looked about him 'at the faces that are not there', the faces of the generation that was lost in 1914-8.

In previous chapters I have underscored Churchill's repeated statements that, in the West, this would never be 'a war of vast armies, firing immense masses of shells at one another'. He had a healthy respect for the German ground forces. He knew that the British could never equal them numerically on land—and it was a long time before he developed any confidence in the 'battle-worthiness', as he called it, of the American infantry. He persisted in the belief that Germany could be defeated by the combination of superior sea and air power *plus superior wits*. He said time and again that a disastrous defeat suffered by the Allies on the French Coast would be 'the only way in which we could possibly lose this war'.

It has often been said that Churchill's advocacy of the 'soft underbelly' approach to Europe demonstrated his farsightedness—that he was motivated by the long-range purpose of keeping the Red Army out of the Danube Valley and the Balkans. In the opinion of some of the American authorities who were involved in the strategic discussions, this claim gave Churchill credit for too much prescience. He may have had such thoughts in mind in 1944, but certainly not in 1942; and one may ask, in this connection: If Anglo-American strength had been concentrated in Southern and South-Eastern Europe, what eventually would have stopped the Russians from marching into the Ruhr and Saar and even into Normandy? The American Chiefs of Staff believed that Churchill's strategic concepts were much more easily explained: he had an incurable predilection for 'eccentric operations', which had guided him in the First as well as the Second World War; he preferred operations which depended on surprise, deception, and speed, in terrain (for example, the Balkan valleys) where there was not sufficient room for huge ground forces to be deployed. He shrank from the conception of a frontal attack; indeed, it might be said that, in certain ways, he agreed with General MacArthur's (and Willie Keeler's) famous principle of 'Hit 'em where they ain't!'

Right or wrong—for better or worse—Churchill's arguments always made an appeal to Roosevelt, who was also interested in saving lives. One can only guess at the extent of the conflicts that went on in Roosevelt's mind and heart and soul when he had to decide whether to follow the advice of his own most trusted advisers (including Hopkins) or Churchill's warnings that the Channel would be a 'river of blood'.

When the discussions of June, 1942, shifted from Hyde Park to the White House, the situation had undergone a shocking change in Libya. Rommel had defeated and all but destroyed the British armoured forces in a tremendous tank battle. And on Sunday morning, June 21, the President handed the Prime Minister a slip of paper with the news that Tobruk had fallen. The year before Tobruk had withstood siege for thirty-three weeks. Now it had crumpled within a day before the first assault. This was a body blow for Churchill. It was another Singapore. It might well be far worse even than that catastophe in its total effect—for, with Tobruk gone, there was little left with which to stop Rommel from pushing on to Alexandria, Cairo— and beyond. The prospect of a German-Japanese junction now loomed larger than ever as a possibility or even probability, and remained so for weeks thereafter. Rommel did break through quickly into Egypt, pausing —only for breath, it seemed—before the precariously held lines at El Alamein.

This sudden turn disrupted the staff talks even before they could be started. The discussions in the White House on that Sunday continued through lunch and dinner and far into the night. Churchill poured out his matchless prose in opposition to the trans-Channel operation in 1942, and in favour of GYMNAST as a means of relieving the crisis in the Mediterranean. He was vigorously opposed by Marshall and Hopkins, and Roosevelt—for all that GYMNAST was 'his secret baby'—refused to depart from the previous agreement. Thus, there was no revision then of plans for BOLERO and ROUNDUP. —but concentration of attention was forcibly diverted from the Northern French coast to the Valley of the Nile. The situation there and on the southern end of the Russian Front, in General Marshall's words, 'threatened a complete collapse in the Middle East, the loss of the Suez Canal and the vital oil supply in the vicinity of Abadan. It was a very black hour.' The White House conferees were therefore desperately concerned with radical revisions of the shipping and allocation schedules to rush supplies, principally hundreds of Sherman tanks, around Africa to the Red Sea. Here was one of the occasions when Roosevelt had to make decisions, enormous in their implications and dangers, pretty much on snap judgment. Churchill said later: 'Nothing could have exceeded the delicacy and kindness of our American friends and Allies. They had no thought but to help.' Also, when he could view this tragic time with his normal humour, he confessed that he had then been the unhappiest Englishman in North America since General Burgoyne.

He read stories from London in the American papers stating that the House of Commons was demanding his immediate return 'to face his accusers', that this was his 'supreme political crisis as Prime Minister', etc., and his visit was cut to only six days. However, Marshall did not want him to get away without seeing some American infantry. Accordingly, Churchill spent June 24 in the South with Marshall. He later wrote that he was 'astonished at the mass production of divisions under General Marshall's organization and inspiration. But, of course, to make a fine professional Army on a great scale from wartime recruits requires at least two years, and better three.' He was most courteous and cordial in his expressions of enthusiasm for the exercises that he saw—but he was profoundly sceptical of the ability of American troops to compete with the Germans in ground warfare on a massive scale.

On his last day in Washington, June 25, Churchill lunched with the President, Prime Minister Mackenzie King of Canada, Hopkins, and the members of the Pacific War Council; Halifax, Soong, Quezon, Nash, Van Kleffens (of the Netherlands), Owen Dixon (Australia), and Leighton McCarthy (Canada). It seems that nothing of any great moment except some group photographs developed from this meeting. For obvious domestic political reasons, Hopkins was careful to keep out of the group photographs.

Later that day Hopkins noted:

> The Prime Minister and the President had not agreed upon any joint statement which the two of them would make upon Churchill's arrival in London.
>
> I went down to the doctor's room where the President was having his nose treated for sinus and he dictated the attached notes to me.
>
> I later redrafted this and gave it to the Prime Minister and the President that night when the three of us had dinner together. The final draft which appeared in the Press is attached.

This Press release, which was conspicuously lacking in news value, stated that the President and Prime Minister had 'covered very fully all of the major problems of the war', that 'the transportation of munitions of war and supplies still constitutes the major problem of the United Nations', that 'the coming operations . . . will divert German strength from the attack on Russia', and finally that 'the overall picture is more favourable to victory' than it had been in 1941.

One subject that came up during their first talks at Hyde Park was not mentioned in this Press release nor in any other public statement until four months after Roosevelt's death: the progress of experiments on the fission of uranium. 'This difficult and novel project', as Churchill then called it, was known by the British code name of 'Tube Alloys' and the American designation 'S-one'. Churchill later cabled Hopkins concerning the discussions at this time: 'My whole understanding was that everything was on the basis of fully sharing the results as equal partners. I have no record, but I shall be much surprised if the President's recollection does not square with this.'

Also during these June meetings Hopkins imparted to Roosevelt and Churchill the news that he was engaged to be married to Mrs. Louise Macy, whom he had met only recently when she applied for some sort of war service (she had been working as a nurse's aid in a New York hospital) and was given an introduction to him by mutual friends. Both the President and

In view of letter of yesterday) FDR
ask Marshall + King the following) FDR
I On the assumption that the
Russian army will be hard pressed
and retreating in July; that the
German forces are in August
dangerously threatening Leningrad
and Moscow and 2) have made a
serious break thru in the Southern
front threatening the Caucasus.
II On the further assumption
that American ground forces supported
by air — in a direct attack
on the German forces, with or without

British or Russian armistice —
Can force a withdrawal of German
forces from the Russian front ? —
On the above assumption
— At what point or fronts can :
A. American (sic)
ground forces, prior to Sept 15, 1942
on German forces on German soil
Also execute an attack which
can force withdrawal of German
by forces certainly lessen movement
forces from the Russian Front
B. British forces in the Dover area
(in a different area) aim in
the same objective,"

Marshall D Tom D H.H (H H H) Bradley

Message to General Marshall and Admiral King, drafted jointly by President
Roosevelt and Harry Hopkins on July 20, 1942, revealing their anxiety about
the situation on the Russian Front. The marginal initials were added by
Hopkins to indicate the author of each section (see page 591).

Prime Minister were delighted that their friend had found such happiness
—and Roosevelt immediately told the prospective bride that she would
find it easy to make herself at home in the White House.

On June 25 Churchill had a final dinner with Roosevelt and Hopkins and
then departed to 'face his accusers' in London. Hopkins accompanied him
to the airplane in Baltimore. Churchill took with him all the fervent best
wishes of his American associates for strength with which to meet this trial
—but he left behind him a growing sense of alarm that the Second Front
was not going to be established in 1942 or in 1943 either.

The disagreement at this stage gave evidence of becoming so acute that
the U.S. Chiefs of Staff seriously considered radical revision of the long
determined grand strategy of Germany first. MacArthur in Australia had
made his own plans for an offensive in the South-West Pacific. These were
co-ordinated with Navy plans in Washington into the conception of a major
offensive against the Japanese in 1942 and 1943 along the line of Eastern New
Guinea to the Admiralty Islands and up through the Celebes Sea to the west
of the Philippines to Camranh Bay in Indo-China and Hong Kong. This
would have involved committing the bulk of American ground forces to
fighting the war against Japan on the mainland of Asia in 1943—which would
have meant leaving the war against Germany in Europe to be fought out as
best they might by the Russians and British. Stimson has said that this drastic
plan was a 'bluff'—designed 'to bring the British into agreement with
BOLERO'. Roosevelt called it 'a red herring' and said that using it to force
British agreement was a little like threatening to 'take up your dishes and
go home'. There is, however, considerable difference of opinion as to this; the
Hopkins papers shed no light on it, but it is my impression that the plan was
far more than a bluff in General Marshall's mind and certainly in Admiral
King's. Indeed, the first step in it—the assault on Guadalcanal—was approved
on June 25, the last day of Churchill's short stay in Washington. One may
indulge in some pretty wild speculation as to the consequences had the plan
been followed through—including the thought that the first atomic bomb
might have fallen on Berlin instead of Hiroshima.

The details of this plan were, of course, well known to Dill and other
British representatives on the Combined Chiefs of Staff, who kept their own
Government informed about it. There is no indication that it was ever form-
ally offered as a serious proposal to the British.

In any case, the situation became so critical on the Russian Front and in
Egypt and in the Battle of the Atlantic early in July that a showdown was
enforced. Churchill had once said—it was in the speech that Hopkins had
seen him prepare at Chequers in February, 1941—that Hitler 'may tear great
provinces out of Russia; he may march to the Caspian; he may march to the
gates of India'. That prophecy was made four months before the Germans

H

attacked the Soviet Union. It seemed at the time to be the veriest oratorical fearmongering. But now it seemed horribly close to fulfilment.

With the fall of Sevastopol the storm of German offensive broke at last in full fury and the Wehrmacht swept eastward to Voronezh, Rostov, and across the Don in the advance that ended only in the streets of Stalingrad and the mountains of the Caucasus.

The desperateness of the situation in Egypt was set forth in a telegram to General Marshall that Roosevelt and Hopkins drafted on the morning of June 30 in the President's bedroom at Hyde Park. It was as follows:

> Are there any moves that we can make immediately that might favourably affect the situation in the Middle East? What is your personal opinion about the coming course of events there?
>
> On the assumption that the [Nile] Delta will be evacuated within ten days and the Canal blocked, I ask the following questions:
>
> 1. What assurances have we that the Canal will be really blocked? Do we know the specific plan? Could you talk to Dill about this at once? An effective blocking of the Canal is essential.
>
> 2. From what point or points would the British operate from Africa by air, land, and sea? Also from what point or points in Asia Minor?
>
> 3. What would Rommel's or Germany's next move be? Do you think it would be Cyprus and Syria? Is the objective the Mosul oilfields?
>
> 4. What British forces could be moved to these areas and what would be the probable strategic defence of the oilfields?
>
> 5. Will you give me your judgment on kind of air and land force in Syria that would tend to hold Turkey in line?
>
> 6. What consideration should be given to strong defence of Basra or Black Sea area?

Marshall's reply came back immediately. He said that the British could block the Suez Canal so effectively that it was estimated that six months would be required to reopen it—that the British would probably have to withdraw to the upper Nile region—that Rommel's primary objective was destruction of the British Army, next the occupation of Cyprus and Syria, and eventually the seizure of the Mosul and Basra area—also probable action to cut the American air-ferry route across Africa to the Middle East, the Soviet Union and the Far East. Marshall said that the defence of Syria and holding Turkey in line would require 'expansion far beyond our capacity' and, considering the defence of Basra, 'a major effort in this region would bleed us white'.

Marshall further stated that there were no moves that the United States could make immediately that could favourably affect the situation in Egypt. He gave the President the following appraisal of the situation:

Army G-2 estimates Rommel may reach Cairo in one week; Army Operations say two weeks and a minimum of another week to re-fit before further movement, which will probably be directed towards destruction of the remaining British forces. I feel that we need forty-eight hours more to judge the capacity of Auchinleck to meet the situation, as he is now in field command. Rommel is greatly extended and if checked by destruction of his supply bases and interruption of his supply lines, he would be in a difficult position.

Evidently the 'forty-eight hours' mentioned by Marshall did not yield any signs of encouragement, for on July 2 Marshall sent the following message to Hopkins:

In the event of a disaster in the Middle East it is believed to be important to the future conduct of the war that the United Nations present to the world a solid front. To this end it is suggested that the President guide public comment so as to indicate that the United Nations stand together in adversity as they ultimately will in victory.

Roosevelt had to make some very rapid and difficult decisions concerning diversion to the depleted British forces of Lend-Lease material that was in the Middle East *en route* to Turkey, Russia, and China. The most important items in this were bombers which could be used in hammering Rommel's supply lines and thus hamper the reinforcement of his far-extended army. When some heavy bombers that were destined for China were turned over to the British, Chiang Kai-shek made emphatic protest in Chungking to General Stilwell, who reported to the President as follows:

C.K.S. believes the President is sincere and feels these orders were given without his knowledge or consent. Feels that Allies do not regard China as part of Allied war effort. China has done her best for five years. Questions whether Allies are doing their best for China. If crisis exists in Libya a crisis also exists in China. He had assurances that Tenth Air Force was to operate in China and expected notification before any part of it was taken away. Now it appears that Allies have no interest in China theatre and he wants an answer yes or no to the question 'Do the Allies want the China theatre maintained?' Madame then added that pro-Japanese activity here was pronounced and the question was whether or not the United States wants China to make peace. Both C.K.S. and Madame were bitter about this matter and they were not mincing words when they asked for an unequivocal answer to the question as to whether or not the Allies were interested in maintaining the China war theatre.

Believe this matter of such importance that it should be presented by an officer who knows the background and the issues involved thoroughly.

I am returning General W. R. Gruber to the United States at once by air and request confirmation of this action. C.K.S. made an urgent plea that either I go myself or that I send a well-qualified officer and was obviously relieved to know that I was planning it. In my opinion the matter has reached a very serious stage.

Roosevelt immediately cabled the Generalissimo from Hyde Park as follows:

I have just received message forwarded to me by General Stilwell.

The rapid advance of the Axis forces in the Middle East suddenly confronted the United Nations with a most critical situation. This movement, if not stopped, will result in the severance of the air routes to India and China, and seriously interfere with if not interrupt our sea lanes to India. It is imperative that the Middle East be held. All reinforcements possible are being rushed to block the Axis advance.

The urgency of the situation demanded that any and all planes immediately available be dispatched to preserve our lines of communication to the China theatre. Accordingly the heavy bombers of the Tenth Air Force were ordered to the Middle East. The diversion of these planes is a temporary measure compelled by this sudden crisis. Upon arrival of sufficient air power to secure our lines of communication, the planes will be returned to the Tenth Air Force.

A decision has not been made as to the theatre in which the squadron of A-Twenty light bombers now departing from the United States will be used. This squadron has been ordered to await instructions at Khartoum. In the meantime the medium bombardment and pursuit echelon of the Tenth Air Force will continue in the support of your forces.

I reassure you that the United States and our Allies do regard China as a vital part of our common war effort and depend upon the maintenance of the China theatre as an urgent necessity for the defeat of our enemies.

On July 4 Churchill cabled mentioning that there were forty A-20 bombers (known as 'Bostons') which were then approaching Basra, headed for Russia. The Prime Minister asked if the President would feel inclined to suggest to Stalin that these forty bombers were desperately needed by the British. Churchill said: 'With Russia in the thick of the battle, this is a hard request, and I shall quite understand if you do not feel able to do as I ask.'

Roosevelt then cabled Stalin pointing out that the critical situation in Egypt directly affected the supply route through the Middle East to Russia. He mentioned Churchill's urgent request for the forty A-20 bombers for immediate use in the battle of Egypt and said: 'Since it is not possible for me to express judgment on this, due to the limited information available here, I am asking that you make the decision as to these bombers with the interests of our total war effort in mind.' Stalin replied that he had no objection to the transfer of these bombers to the British, whereupon Roosevelt notified Churchill of the transfer and then cabled Stalin an expression of his deep appreciation. He informed Stalin that he had arranged for immediate shipment of 115 additional medium tanks to Russia, complete with ammunition and spare parts.

A month later, when Churchill was in Moscow, he expressed his thanks to Stalin for the forty Bostons, and Stalin said: 'Those were American aircraft. It will be time enough to thank us when we give you some of our Russian bombers.'

Of the situation in the Battle of the Atlantic, Churchill cabled Roosevelt on July 14 that sinkings in the preceding seven days were close to 400,000 tons, 'a rate unexampled in this war or the last'. At this rate, even assuming that the President's high production goals for shipping were met (they were eventually surpassed), the sinkings would exceed the building of ships by two and a half to one.

The day following this grim announcement, Churchill sent Roosevelt for approval a copy of a very long cable that he proposed to send Stalin, setting forth the formidable naval problems encountered in getting convoys past Bear Island (between the North Cape of Norway and Spitzbergen) to Murmansk through the dangers presented by German U-boats, surface vessels, and aircraft. Churchill, who addressed Stalin as 'my comrade and friend', was offering the painful suggestion that convoys on this route must be suspended during the remaining summer period of perpetual daylight.

Roosevelt replied to this cable that he had consulted with Admiral King and had come to the reluctant conclusion that he must agree on the suspension of convoys to Murmansk for the time being. He said he thought that Churchill's message to Stalin was a good one. He asked the Prime Minister to consider the possibility that American railroad men should take over the operation of the route from the Persian Gulf to the Soviet Union, since all possible efforts must be made to develop this line of supply as an alternative to the Murmansk route.

On that same day, July 15, Roosevelt and Hopkins returned to Washington from Hyde Park and met with Marshall and King. It was on this occasion that Marshall, whose patience had been exhausted by the off-again-on-again status of the Second Front planning, offered most strongly the alternative plan for major American operations in the South-West Pacific. Out of these talks came Roosevelt's determination to settle the matter, and he cabled Churchill: 'Marshall, King, and Hopkins leaving for London at once.'

This was a very tense day in the White House. The U.S. Chiefs of Staff were in a 'fish or cut bait' mood. With the Russian and Chinese situations heavily in mind, it seemed that Allied unity was in immediate peril—and

Marshall was a soldier who had an extraordinary appreciation of the strategic necessity of Allied unity. Furthermore, he was responsible for the training of millions of men who could not meet Churchill's test of 'battle-worthiness' until they had been in battle. Roosevelt was certainly not in favour of 'getting tough' with Churchill, or subjecting him to any arbitrary threats—in fact, this was the occasion when the President made the remark about 'taking up your dishes'. He had every reason to be sympathetic with Churchill in the serious domestic political problems with which he was then involved. Following the disasters in Libya, there had been another and much more potent revolt in the House of Commons. Facing a Vote of Censure moved by Sir John Wardlaw-Milne, Churchill described the demands of his opponents in these scathing terms:

> The mover of this Vote of Censure has proposed that I should be stripped of my responsibilities for defence in order that some military figure or some other unnamed personage should assume the general conduct of the war, that he should have complete control of the Armed Forces of the Crown, that he should be the Chief of the Chiefs of the Staff, that he should nominate or dismiss the generals or the admirals, that he should always be ready to resign, that is to say, to match himself against his political colleagues, if colleagues they could be considered, if he did not get all he wanted, that he should have under him a Royal Duke as Commander-in-Chief of the Army, and finally, I presume, though this was not mentioned, that this unnamed personage should find an appendage in the Prime Minister to make the necessary explanations, excuses and apologies to Parliament when things go wrong, as they often do and often will. That is at any rate a policy. It is a system very different from the Parliamentary system under which we live. It might easily amount to or be converted into a dictatorship. I wish to make it perfectly clear that as far as I am concerned I shall take no part in such a system.

Such demands on the Prime Minister had an unpleasantly familiar ring in the President's ears. The same kind of criticism had been raised in the United States, although not with the same authority. Arthur Krock had written in the New York Times:

> Advocates of a joint Army-Navy general staff with a single head contend that the absence of such an establishment compels, as a substitute, the operation of a joint political-military command and lays directly upon the President in Washington, or Mr. Hopkins on his errand with the Chief of Staff of the Army, the responsibility to decide technical points of warfare for which neither has been trained.

Krock likened Hopkins's role to that of the 'political commissars' who accompanied the Russian armies on their invasion of Finland in the Winter War of 1939-40. However, neither Krock nor anyone else had been able to tell Roosevelt just how he might evade his own supreme responsibility as Commander-in-Chief without amending the Constitution. Thus, the American complaints about the conduct of the war carried little weight.

When it came to a division in the House of Commons on the Vote of Censure, Churchill was supported 473 to 25. Hopkins cabled him:

> We are delighted by today's action in the House of Commons. The military defeats you suffer are ours also and we will share together the certain victories to come, so I know you will be of good heart. More power to you. We are passing through some of the bad days of this war and no doubt there will be others. The timid and the faint-of-heart who run for cover with every setback will have no part in the winning of this war. Your own courage and tenacity and strength and everlasting confidence will bring your country through, and you know that the President does not quit.

Churchill replied: 'Thank you so much, my friend. I knew you and the President would be glad of this domestic victory.' Nevertheless, it was evident to both Roosevelt and Hopkins that the victory was not solid enough to satisfy the Prime Minister, whose powers of emotional endurance were now being tested to the limit after six months of mortification. This was a highly important consideration in the negotiations of far-reaching consequence which followed. It was further indication of the fact that the political element was always present in the determination of military decisions—a fact which had been foreseen by the framers of the Constitution of the United States.

On the evening of July 15 Hopkins had dinner as usual with Roosevelt and a long conversation afterward. He made careful notes during this conversation, quoting Roosevelt directly:

> I cannot agree that if it be impossible to develop BOLERO in 1942 that we should turn our faces away from Germany and toward Japan.
>
> In the first place I am not content with the British Cabinet position. I want to know what our men on the ground—Eisenhower, Spaatz, Clark, and Stark—think. Do they agree with the British Cabinet? Can you get a confidential report from them?
>
> Even though we must reluctantly agree to no SLEDGEHAMMER in 1942, I still think we should press forward vigorously for the 1943 enterprise. I see nothing in the message from England to indicate any luke-warmness on their part for the 1943 enterprise. I am somewhat disturbed about this readiness to give up 1942. Will they also give up 1943?

But my main point is that I do not believe we can wait until 1943 to strike at Germany. If we cannot strike at SLEDGEHAMMER, then we must take the second best—and that is not the Pacific. There we are conducting a successful holding war. Troops and air alone will not be decisive at once—it requires the increasing strength of our Navy—which takes time.

If SLEDGEHAMMER cannot be launched, then I wish a determination made while you are in London as to a specific and definite theatre where our ground and sea forces can operate against the German ground forces in 1942.

The theatres to be considered are North Africa and the Middle East.

GYMNAST has the great advantage of being a purely American enterprise; it would secure Western Africa and deny the ports to the enemy, it would offer the beginning of what should be the ultimate control of the Mediterranean—it is the shortest route to supply. The other theatre is the Middle East; here we would possibly have no resistance—we can use our forces either in Egypt or from the head of the Persian Gulf. Both Russia and England are sorely pressed in this area.

Either of the above operations will require a substantial reduction in BOLERO for the next three months. I am prepared to accept this.

Under any circumstances I wish BOLERO and ROUNDUP to remain an essential objective, even though it must be interrupted.

I am prepared to consider in event SLEDGEHAMMER is not mounted—an appropriate transfer of air and landing-craft to the South-West Pacific.

The conversation summarized in those notes led to the drafting of the final orders which Hopkins, Marshall, and King took with them to London, as follows:

July 16, 1942.

MEMORANDUM FOR

HON. HARRY L. HOPKINS
GENERAL MARSHALL
ADMIRAL KING

SUBJECT: Instructions for London Conference—July, 1942.

1. You will proceed immediately to London as my personal representatives for the purpose of consultation with appropriate British authorities on the conduct of the war.

2. The military and naval strategic changes have been so great since Mr. Churchill's visit to Washington that it became necessary to reach immediate agreement on joint operational plans between the British and ourselves along two lines:

TELEGRAM

The White House
Washington

June 30, 194·
12 A.M

On the assumption that, the Delta Alexandria that area will be evacuated within ten days and the Suez Canal is blocked, I ask the following questions —

1. What assurances have we that the canal will be really blocked. do we know the specific plans could you talk to Dill about this at once? An effective blocking of the canal is essential.

2. From what point or points would the British operate from Africa by air, land and sea? Also from what points in Asia Minor?

3. What would Rommel's or Germany's next move be? Do you think it would be Cyprus and Syria. Is the objective the Mosul Oil

Joint draft by President Roosevelt and
on July 30, 1942, dealing with the si
fall of T

TELEGRAM

The White House
Washington

Fields?

4. What British forces could be moved to these areas and what would be probable strategic defense of oilfields

5. Will you give me your judgement on kind of air and land force in Syria that would tend to hold Turkey in line?

6. What consideration should be given to strong defense of the Basra & Black Sea area?

Roosevelt

FDR

kins of a telegram to General Marshall
he Middle East brought about by the
age 598).

(a) Definite plans for the balance of 1942.

(b) Tentative plans for the year 1943 which, of course, will be subject to change in the light of occurrences in 1942, but which should be initiated at this time in all cases involving preparation in 1942 for operations in 1943.

3. (a) The common aim of the United Nations must be the defeat of the Axis Powers. There cannot be compromise on this point.

(b) We should concentrate our efforts and avoid dispersion.

(c) Absolute co-ordinatel use of British and American forces is essential.

(d) All available U.S. and British forces should be brought into action as quickly as they can be profitably used.

(e) It is of the highest importance that U.S. ground troops be brought into action against the enemy in 1942.

4. British and American material promises to Russia must be carried out in good faith. If the Persian route of delivery is used, preference must be given to combat material. This aid must continue as long as delivery is possible and Russia must be encouraged to continue resistance. Only complete collapse, which seems unthinkable, should alter this determination on our part.

5. In regard to 1942, you will carefully investigate the possibility of executing SLEDGEHAMMER. Such an operation would definitely sustain Russia this year. It might be the turning-point which would save Russia this year. SLEDGEHAMMER is of such grave importance that every reason calls for accomplishment of it. You should strongly urge immediate all-out preparations for it, that it be pushed with utmost vigour, and that it be executed whether or not Russian collapse becomes imminent. In the event Russian collapse becomes probable SLEDGEHAMMER becomes not merely advisable, but imperative. The principal objective of SLEDGE-HAMMER is the positive diversion of German air forces from the Russian Front.

6. Only if you are completely convinced that SLEDGEHAMMER is impossible of execution with reasonable chances of serving its intended purpose, inform me.

7. If SLEDGEHAMMER is finally and definitely out of the picture, I want you to consider the world situation as it exists at that time, and determine upon another place for U.S. troops to fight in 1942.

It is my present view of the world picture that:

(a) If Russia contains a large German force against her, ROUNDUP becomes possible in 1943, and plans for ROUNDUP should be immediately considered and preparations made for it.

(b) If Russia collapses and German air and ground forces are released, ROUNDUP may be impossible of fulfilment in 1943.

8. The Middle East should be held as strongly as possible whether Russia collapses or not. I want you to take into consideration the effect of losing the Middle East. Such loss means in series:

(1) Loss of Egypt and the Suez Canal.

(2) Loss of Syria.

(3) Loss of Mosul oil wells.

(4) Loss of the Persian Gulf through attacks from the north and west, together with access to all Persian Gulf oil.

(5) Joining hands between Germany and Japan and the probable loss of the Indian Ocean.

(6) The very important probability of German occupation of Tunis, Algiers, Morocco, Dakar and the cutting of the ferry route through Freetown and Liberia.

(7) Serious danger to all shipping in the South Atlantic and serious danger to Brazil and the whole of the East Coast of South America. I include in the above possibilities the use by the Germans of Spain, Portugal and their territories.

(8) You will determine the best methods of holding the Middle East. These methods include definitely either or both of the following:

(a) Sending aid and ground forces to the Persian Gulf, to Syria and to Egypt.

(b) A new operation in Morocco and Algiers intended to drive in against the back door of Rommel's armies. The attitude of French Colonial troops is still in doubt.

9. I am opposed to an American all-out effort in the Pacific against Japan with the view of her defeat as quickly as possible. It is of the utmost importance that we appreciate that defeat of Japan does not defeat Germany and that American concentration against Japan this year or in 1943 increases the chance of complete German domination of Europe and Africa. On the other hand, it is obvious that defeat of Germany, or the holding of Germany in 1942 or in 1943 means probable eventual defeat of Germany in the European and African theatres and in the Near East. Defeat of Germany means the defeat of Japan, probably without firing a shot or losing a life.

10. Please remember three cardinal principles—speed of decision on plans, unity of plans, attack combined with defence, but not defence alone. This affects the immediate objective of U.S. ground forces fighting against Germans in 1942.

11. I hope for total agreement within one week of your arrival.

(signed) FRANKLIN D. ROOSEVELT

Commander-in-Chief

The seemingly strange statement at the end of Paragraph 9 of the above document was an expression of belief that, after the conquest of Germany, Japan's surrender could be enforced without the need for an invasion of her home islands.

Of all the instructions given by Roosevelt to Hopkins and the Chiefs of Staff, the most important—and, indeed, the ultimate determining factor— was this: *U.S. ground forces must be put into position to fight German ground forces somewhere in 1942.*

In this, Roosevelt was thinking not only of the effect on the Russians if eight autumn and winter months were to pass with no substantial action by Anglo-American forces; he was thinking also of the effect of inaction on the spirit of the American and British people, who might well begin to feel bogged down in the deadly lethargy of another period of 'Phony War'.

The question of terminology for the various trans-Channel operations was clarified by Roosevelt as follows:

> The term 'Bolero' shall be used to designate the preparation for and movement of United States Forces into the European theatre, preparations for their reception therein and the production, assembly, transport, reception, and storage of equipment and supplies necessary for support of the United States Forces in operation against the European Continent.
>
> The term 'Sledgehammer' shall be used to designate an offensive operation of the British and American troops against the European Continent in 1942 to be carried out in case of German internal collapse or imminent Russian military collapse which necessitates an emergency attack in order to divert German forces from the Russian front.
>
> The term 'Roundup', or any other name which the Prime Minister may desire, shall be used to designate an offensive operation against German dominated Europe to be carried out by combined American and British forces in 1943 or later.

Roosevelt and Hopkins also contrived some code names for their own private use in cables—as follows: Marshall was 'Plog'; King, 'Barrett'; Eisenhower, 'Keuren'; Spaatz, 'Depew'; Clark, 'Robert'; Stark, 'Draiss'; Churchill, 'Moses Smith'; Cripps, 'Mrs. Johansen'; Portal, 'Rev. Wilson'; Brooke, 'Mr. Bee'.

Every one of these code names represented was taken from Hyde Park. Grace Tully has told me that William Plog was Mrs. James Roosevelt's superintendent for many years (he always called the President 'Mr. Franklin'), Depew was her chauffeur, Robert McGaughey was her butler and, as this is written, is still at Hyde Park. Moses Smith rented a farm on the place and was the moving spirit of the Franklin D. Roosevelt Home Club. Reverend Wilson was Rector of St. James Church, Christian Bee caretaker of Roosevelt's hilltop cottage, Barrett ran the farm, Van Curan (misspelled by Hopkins) worked with Plog, Draiss worked on roads and trees, Mrs. Johansen was a neighbour who ran a gas station and restaurant near Mrs. Roosevelt's cottage.

Hopkins, Marshall, and King flew from Washington in a Stratoliner on July 16. They were accompanied by Steve Early, who was to make a study of the British Information Services, but take no part in the strategic discussions. Also in the party were General Walter Bedell Smith (later Chief of Staff to Eisenhower and Ambassador to the Soviet Union), Colonel Hoyt S. Vandenberg, Dr. Fulton, and Colonel Frank McCarthy and Commander R. E. Libby, the last two being *aides* to Marshall and King.

Hopkins usually loved to go on trips. Despite his fear of flying, he was thrilled as any normal person would be by all the trappings of official mystery and high significance—the secret orders, the special passports, the drive (usually at dawn) in a White House car to the airport, the passage through saluting sentries to the carefully guarded olive-drab transport plane with its 'Destination Unknown' classification, etc. Then, at the other end, the landing at a blacked-out airfield, the greeting by quietly efficient officers who conducted the Very Important Person to a large Daimler limousine which bore on its windshield that inexpressibly impressive word 'PRIORITY'—and finally the welcome from a Prime Minister who considered him one of the half-dozen most influential individuals on the face of the earth. Few men could have been impervious to the excitement of all of this, and Hopkins was certainly never one of those few.

This time, however, he hated to go. He wanted to stay home and be married.

On arrival at Prestwick, in Scotland, it was found that the weather over England was too bad to permit flying on to London. Churchill had, therefore, provided a special train, and Commander Thompson was on hand to greet the distinguished visitors. He informed them of the Prime Minister's wish that the train stop near Chequers, so that they might proceed there directly and spend the week-end (it was Saturday, July 18) with him. However, that did not fit in with Marshall's and King's plans. Time being short, they wanted to get to London immediately and start their talks with Eisenhower, Clark, Spaatz, and Stark, as Roosevelt had directed, and then with the British Chiefs of Staff. So the train did not stop at Chequers. Shortly after their arrival at Claridge's, Churchill had Hopkins on the telephone, and the conversations then and subsequently must have been hot ones. Hopkins reported to Roosevelt: 'The Prime Minister threw the British Constitution at me with some vehemence. As you know, it is an unwritten document, so no serious damage was done. Winston is his old self and full of battle. Hopkins did his best over the telephone to try to persuade the Prime Minister that no rudeness had been intended, that Marshall and King had been expressly instructed by the President to meet first with Eisenhower—but his best was evidently not good enough, and Hopkins finally concluded that he must go to Chequers himself to try to absorb some of the wrath. He did so and peace was restored. Churchill had too much respect as well as affection for 'Lord Root of the Matter' to subject him to the protracted, and often calculated, rages which cowed others.

The whole mission of the Chiefs of Staff and Hopkins in London was a secret one—indeed, no public announcement of it was made until several weeks later—but it was extremely difficult for any of the hundreds of people who went about Claridge's to miss the fact that top-level conferences were in progress. With remarkable speed, sixteen rooms on the fourth floor of Claridge's were converted into a military headquarters, complete with message centre, scrambler telephones, safes for documents, and a U.S. sentry posted at every door (the sentry at Admiral King's room was, of course, a Marine).

On Monday, July 20, Hopkins made his first report to the President— but the only copy of this cable in his papers is such an awkward paraphrase that I have paraphrased it again, translating the code names:

> Our first conferences on Saturday were exclusively with our own people here. Eisenhower, Spaatz, and Clark are anxious to go ahead with SLEDGEHAMMER. Stark is lukewarm. Marshall and his staff worked all Saturday night on details. I spent Saturday and Sunday night at Chequers with Mr. Churchill, who is pretty restless and quite unhappy that we did not go to see him in the first place. However, all of this was cleared up over the week-end and he is now in the best of spirits. I had a long conference this morning with Marshall and King and we are going to push for SLEDGEHAMMER. We then went to the first formal conference at Downing Street. The whole field was thoroughly outlined, but there was no discussion of the merits of the various operations under consideration. We stayed there for lunch. This afternoon Marshall and King are conferring with Brooke, Portal, and others. We meet again at six, and then I am invited to dine with the Prime Minister. I would say that in general satisfactory progress is being made.

A different SLEDGEHAMMER was now being advanced: the seizure of the Cotentin Peninsula to be held as a bridgehead on the Continent until ROUND-UP could be mounted. This changed it from an emergency 'sacrifice' operation into a permanent gain. I am not clear just when the U.S. Chiefs of Staff decided on this—it had certainly been under consideration for months— but presumably the final planning was done by Marshall and Eisenhower in London. Also under consideration, but only as a pretty remote possibility, was the sending of American ground forces all the way around Africa either to reinforce the British in Egypt or, if Suez were lost, to oppose the Germans in Syria or the Persian Gulf area; Roosevelt had mentioned this in his orders to Hopkins, Marshall, and King.

If Hopkins felt somewhat optimistic on Monday afternoon, before the 'merits of the various operations' were discussed, forty-eight hours later he was writing, on a sheet of Downing Street notepaper, 'I feel damn depressed.' This was written as a note—to whom, I do not know, but probably Marshall —during a formal conference held on Wednesday afternoon, July 22. The meeting was opened by Marshall with the statement that the American Chiefs of Staff had now had three meetings with the British Chiefs of Staff and a point had been reached where it was necessary for the Americans to report to the President. In other words—the discussions had come to complete stalemate. Roosevelt was consequently informed that the British would not willingly go ahead with SLEDGEHAMMER. Furthermore, as Hopkins indicated, the U.S. Navy officers involved had been inclined to respect the British position from the strictly naval point of view; they considered that the representatives of the Royal Navy knew what they were talking about in pointing to the perils of weather that would beset a trans-Channel operation late in September or October when the Northern French Coast became a 'lee shore'. There was sufficient unanimity on the British side and a large enough fragment of doubt on the American side to make it impossible to push through the agreement for SLEDGEHAMMER.

Roosevelt then cabled Hopkins, Marshall, and King that he was not particularly surprised at the disappointing outcome of the London talks, and he agreed that mere acquiescence on the part of the British was not sufficient for the carrying out of plans of such magnitude. He therefore repeated the directive that he had given them before they left Washington—that some other operations involving American ground troops against the Germans in 1942 must be worked out. He suggested the following in order of priority: (1) A new form of offensive with Algeria and/or Morocco as targets; (2) the original North African operation (GYMNAST) carried out by American troops only in the first stages; (3) the operation into Northern Norway; (4) reinforcement of the British by American troops in Egypt for an offensive there; (5) American operations through Iran into the Caucasus.

Roosevelt added that intelligence had been received from the American Legation in Berne, Switzerland, indicating that plans were under way for substantial strengthening of the coast defences and air bases in French Morocco, and it was therefore essential that any contemplated Allied operations in this area should not be too long delayed. It was estimated (by the source of this information) that an Allied force of 150,000 could succeed in occupying all the French air bases in North Africa, those near Tunis being the most important. The French troops in Morocco would be most likely to join with the Allies, those in Tunis would be less likely. It was stated that although General Nogues could not be relied on in the beginning, a quick Allied success would probably win him over.

Having relayed this information, Roosevelt urged Hopkins, Marshall, and King to reach a decision with 'our friends' as quickly as possible.

This was the really conclusive order from the Commander-in-Chief. It was based on that one factor which Roosevelt considered so important: U.S. ground forces must be put into position to fight German ground forces somewhere in 1942.

The next day Hopkins cabled Roosevelt:

> I want you to know that Marshall and King pushed very hard for SLEDGEHAMMER. We are naturally disappointed, but good will prevails nevertheless. Now that the decision has been made we are hard at work on the next steps. I believe that our people will finally turn to an expanded GYMNAST, first, because of the difficulty of mixing our troops with the British in Egypt, and secondly because if we go to Syria we may not do any fighting there. Your message has been received, but it is important that you express your ideas on these matters by cable today. We are bothered by logistical problems, particularly escort vessels, but I have hope that it will be worked out today. It is my belief that we can give King some additional air and landing-craft in the Pacific. It is also my hope that you will consider putting some of our air squadrons into Russia. We will press for early decisions.

The next day, Roosevelt sent a longer and more detailed cable repeating that he favoured the launching of the North African operation in 1942, even though, as he frankly admitted, it involved the abandonment of ROUNDUP as the primary objective for the time being. He said he saw no reason why the transport problem could not be worked out so as to put 80,000 American infantry and air force personnel into the initial operation, using American forces then in the United Kingdom and others sent directly across the Atlantic from the United States. He believed that after the original bridgeheads and ports had been secured, the American forces should drive eastward from Algiers to Tunis, and that British forces should push southward from Morocco toward Dakar, so as to secure the bulge of Africa. He again emphasized that 'time is of the essence to forestall air concentrations by the Germans' which may affect the proposed operations.

On July 25 Hopkins cabled Roosevelt that there was a tendency in the discussions to postpone a final decision on GYMNAST until September 15. He strongly urged the President to name a date for GYMNAST not later than October 30, 1942, since the situation in Russia was so serious that delay was dangerous. He said: 'What I fear most is that if we do not now make a firm decision on GYMNAST and fix a reasonably early date there may be procrastinations and delay. Although I believe that the intention here is to mount the operation aggressively, unless the written language of the orders is precise there may be difficulties when it comes to carrying out the orders by the secondary personnel' (meaning, of course, that the whole project might become bogged down on desks in the Pentagon Building and the War Office in Whitehall).

Roosevelt immediately replied that plans should proceed at once for the GYMNAST landings not later than October 30. He asked Hopkins to tell the Prime Minister that he was delighted that the decision had finally been made and that orders were now 'full speed ahead'. He emphasized the need for absolute secrecy. He told Hopkins to come home immediately, adding: 'Tell Winston that not even he can stop that wedding. Give him my best.'

That evening Hopkins, Marshall, and King left for Prestwick, flew to Iceland, where they paused to inspect the installations and forces there, and arrived back in Washington on July 27. Three days later Hopkins and Louise Macy were married at noon in the Oval Study, with President Roosevelt acting as best man. The ceremony was performed by the Reverend Russell Clinchy, of Hartford, Connecticut. Present were: Mrs. Roosevelt, Hopkin's three sons and his daughter, members of Mrs. Macy's immediate family, General Marshall, Admiral King, Sam Rosenman, and the present biographer.

One might have thought that the hatred that dogged Harry Hopkins would have let up for a spell—but one would have been wrong. After his marriage, it became more virulent in its manifestations than ever. The first of these was the amazing story of the yacht, *My Kay IV*. Two weeks after the wedding Senator Prentiss M. Brown received the following letter from one of his constituents:

> Five men, all whose employment is contributing to war production, paused today at noon to discuss the discouraging newspaper headlines and expressed their sorrowful opinions of the task ahead. One man interrupted and related the following to us, emphasizing his distrust of administration sincerity and his discouragement.
>
> This is the story. A man by the name of Fruehauf—that name is well known in truck-trailer manufacturing circles—offered his yacht docked in Detroit to the Government. It was commandeered, but conversion for Naval use delayed. On inquiry, it was disclosed that conversion was delayed so that Harry Hopkins could and is reported to be now cruising the Great Lakes with his bride. Presumably, this yacht is being operated at the expense of taxpayers.

Message (to Joint Chiefs of Staff) drafted jointly by President Roosevelt and Harry Hopkins, showing their concern over the situation at Guadalcanal

(see pages 622–623).

That, in my opinion, is another example of 'acts' which are damaging morale and its companion, hopeless discouragement.

Of course, Mr. Hopkins's 'honeymoon' is no business of mine, but delaying conversion of a requisitioned yacht for his convenience and probable operation at the expense of taxpayers is my business.

Senator Brown referred this to Secretary Knox. Later a similar letter was received by Senator Millard E. Tydings—but this time it was said that Mr. Fruehauf was cruising with his family off New London when the yacht was forcibly seized by the Coast Guard and turned over to Hopkins and bride. (As if anyone were likely to do any pleasure cruising along the Atlantic Coast in those days!) Tydings also referred this to Knox. The rumour got into the New York Stock Exchange, whose members happily spread it far and wide. It became so persistent, despite frequent denials by busy officials, that the F.B.I. investigated it, as they did innumerable other demoralizing rumours in wartime. It seemed that a fifty-five-foot boat, owned by Roy Fruehauf of Detroit, had been purchased by the Coast Guard after some weeks of negotiation. When the actual requisition came through Fruehauf was on a fishing cruise on Lake Superior with his wife and two friends, but was permitted to finish his cruise and return in his own good time to Detroit, where the boat was turned over to the Coast Guard in an orderly manner. Then a special crew was put aboard and the boat ordered on a 'secret mission' to Amherstburg, on the Canadian side of Lake Erie, there to pick up some Canadian officials (one of whom, the rumour said, was Prime Minister Mackenzie King). It was then to proceed to a designated spot on the lake and transfer the officials to the vessel *City of Cleveland*, where they would meet with 'a personal representative of the President' (of course, Hopkins).

The F.B.I. learned that the Canadian officials were not of the top echelon —one of them being a fire chief. On board the *City of Cleveland* were members of the Federal Employees Association of Cleveland, on an excursion cruise, the highest ranking official among them being the chairman of their Recreation Committee. The boats did not meet as planned—the weather was too rough—so the Canadians were deposited in Cleveland, two of them seasick. Such were the facts concerning the *My Kay IV*. Just why there was any talk of a 'secret mission' was unexplained—but presumably someone had been talking big.

The F.B.I. reported as follows of its interview with Mr. Fruehauf:

He stated that some time after the boat was turned over, perhaps a week to the best of his knowledge, he received a telephone call from the Associated Press advising him that this agency had received a report from a Chicago representative that he had been forced to return to Detroit from his vacation cruise so that Mr. Hopkins could use the boat

I

on his honeymoon. He stated that he emphatically denied this story, but apparently was not believed, because he continued to receive telephone calls from the Associated Press and from other newspaper agencies. He stated that thereafter for several weeks he was besieged with calls from newspapermen, magazine publishers, and divers individuals in connection with this story which in the meantime had spread rapidly. Mr. Fruehauf advised that one of the most recent inquiries concerning this story came from Fulton Lewis, a news commentator connected with a Washington, D.C. radio broadcasting station. He stated that some of these sources even reported to him that the rumour was prevalent that he and his party had been forcibly ejected from their boat in Georgian Bay and were forced to make their own way back to civilization. He stated that he has since denied the story so many times until he feels that there is no one left who has not inquired about it at least once.

Hopkins and his bride actually spent their honeymoon on a small farm in Connecticut and he was back at work in Washington eleven days after the wedding. But the rumour of the *My Kay IV* continued in circulation for many weeks. In fact, three months later, on the eve of the North African landings, Hopkins was asking for legal advice as to whether there was anything he could do about this malicious lie; the answer was, 'probably not'. Nor could he do anything about the rumour, given wide publicity, that Mrs. Hopkins had received a wedding present of half a million dollars' worth of emeralds from Lord Beaverbrook as a mark of appreciation for her husband's service in giving Lend-Lease to the British. That one even went to the extent of an announcement by Representative Joseph W. Martin that proposals would be introduced for a Congressional investigation of the private and public activities of Harry Hopkins and the whole administration of Lend-Lease. Nothing, of course, ever came of this, since the smearers had too much sense to make the mistake of granting Hopkins his day in court.

CHAPTER XXVII

THE TURNING-POINT

IT is evident that even after Hopkins, Marshall, and King returned from London on July 27 there were further attempts to change the President's mind about the North African operation, the name of which had been changed for security reasons from GYMNAST to TORCH. Roosevelt, however, insisted that the decision had been made and must be carried through with expedition and vigour. This was one of the very few major military decisions of the war which Roosevelt made entirely on his own and over the protests of his highest-ranking advisers. Admiral Leahy had just been appointed to the unprecedented position of Chief of Staff to the Commander-in-Chief, and subsequently he became in effect Chairman of the Chiefs of Staff Committee. At this time, however, he had been out of touch with the progress of strategic planning; his return from Vichy was long delayed by the saddening illness and death of his wife.

On July 31 Churchill sent Roosevelt a cable which has considerable significance in the light of developments of the following year and a half. The Prime Minister pressed for a decision concerning the naming of the commanders for the various operations in prospect in the European theatre. He said: 'It would be agreeable to us if General Marshall were designated for Supreme Command of ROUNDUP and that in the meatime General Eisenhower should act as his deputy here.' This nomination of the most vehement proponent of the Second Front would hardly seem to indicate that Churchill was attempting to relegate the plan completely to the Files of Forgotten Things. Churchill suggested that Eisenhower should superintend the planning and organization of TORCH and that General Sir Harold Alexander should be in command of the task force from the British Isles and an American (who turned out later to be General George S. Patton) in command of the task force from the United States. This suggestion was made, of course, shortly before Churchill decided to place Alexander in supreme command of the British forces in Egypt.

Roosevelt was content to leave the question of supreme command of ROUNDUP in abeyance for the time being—and, as will be seen in later chapters, that turned out to be a very long time. He was now concerned primarily with the problem of how to explain to Stalin that there would be no Second Front in Northern France in 1942. Churchill planned a trip to the Middle East and suggested that he proceed on from there via Teheran to Moscow. On July 31 Stalin extended an invitation to the British Prime Minister and the Chief of the Imperial General Staff to come to the U.S.S.R. 'to consider jointly urgent questions of war against Hitler as a menace' which has 'just now reached a special degree of intensity'. Roosevelt cabled Churchill the following thoughts on the handling of the difficult negotiations:

It is essential for us to bear in mind our ally's personality and the very difficult and dangerous situation that he confronts. I think we should attempt to put ourselves in his place, for no one whose country has been invaded can be expected to approach the war from a world point of view. We should tell Stalin quite specifically, in the first place, that we have decided upon a course of action for 1942. Without advising him of the precise nature of our proposed operations, I think we should tell him without any qualification that they are going to be made.

I agree with you that we should run another northern convoy if there is any chance of success, despite the great risk which is involved. But I think that you should not raise any false hopes in Stalin relative to this.

The Russian need is urgent and immediate. I believe it would mean a great deal to the Russian people and their army if they were to know that units of our air force were fighting with them in a very direct manner. I am discussing this matter of putting air power directly on the Russian Front and I am hopeful that this can be done. I imagine that Stalin is in no mood to engage in strategic discussions of a theoretical nature and I am sure that, except for our major operation, the giving of our direct air support to the Russians on the southern end of their front is the enterprise that would suit Stalin best.

Although it had been planned that Churchill would conduct his talks in Moscow with no American representative present, after he had left London Harriman conceived the idea that it might be a good idea for him to go along and Roosevelt cabled him authority to do so with no special instructions. Accordingly, Harriman caught up with Churchill in the Middle East and flew with him to Moscow, where they arrived late in the afternoon on August 12. Despite his extensive travelling, Churchill was ready to plunge immediately into the conference at the Kremlin, scorning all suggestions that he might like to have a few hours' rest.

Harriman cabled to Roosevelt the following day as follows:

Last night the Prime Minister and I had an extended meeting with Stalin. Also present were Molotov, Voroshilov, and the British Ambassador. British and American strategic plans for the rest of 1942 and 1943 and their effect on the Russian military situation formed the centre of discussion.

It is my belief that, considering all the circumstances, the discussion could not have been better developed nor more satisfactory conclusions reached. Churchill explained the various possibilities of SLEDGEHAMMER and the reasons for its postponement in full detail and told of the plans for and proposed strength of the major trans-Channel operation.

At every point Stalin took issue with a degree of bluntness almost amounting to insult. He made such remarks as—that you cannot win wars if you are afraid of the Germans and unwilling to take risks. He ended this phase of the discussion by stating abruptly but with dignity that although he did not agree with the arguments he could not force us to action. He showed little interest in ROUNDUP, expressing the opinion that grave difficulties confronted it. Up to now, the atmosphere was tense, no agreement having been reached on any point.

Thereupon, Churchill described the bombing campaign against Germany and expressed the hope that participation by the U.S. Air Force would produce a substantial increase in this bombing. This produced the first agreement between the two men. Stalin took over the argument himself, saying that homes as well as factories should be destroyed. Churchill agreed that civilian morale constituted a military objective, but that the destruction of the homes of workers was only a by-product of near misses on factories. Now there began an easing of the tension and an increasing understanding of common purpose. Stalin and Churchill, between them, soon had destroyed most of Germany's important industrial centres.

With great adroitness, Churchill seized the opportunity presented by this friendlier interchange to bring the discussion back to the Second Front. He explained the TORCH decision and the tactics thereof. He emphasized the need for secrecy. He said he wished he had the same power that Stalin exercised over the Press, which further relieved the tension. Stalin expressed a great deal of concern over the political repercussions which might result from the TORCH operation.

Churchill drew a picture of a crocodile, pointing out that it was as well to strike the soft underbelly (the Mediterranean) as the snout (Northern France). He then brought the discussion back to the Russian Front, saying that you and he were exploring the possibility of sending an Allied air force to the southern end of the Russian Front after Rommel had been defeated in Egypt. He asked Stalin how he would receive such a suggestion and Stalin replied, briefly and simply: 'I would accept it gratefully.'

Thereafter, Stalin summed up the strategic advantages of TORCH, showing a masterful grasp of its implications. He asked specifically that the political angle be handled with the utmost delicacy and that it be launched at the earliest possible moment—earlier even than you have implied. He showed real enthusiasm for the operation.

After the conclusion of the three days of conference, Harriman returned to Washington, bringing with him the full details of all the talks. After the first two hours—which Churchill described as 'bleak and sombre'—the TORCH plan for landings at Casablanca, Oran, Algiers and, if possible, Bizerta, was presented, and Stalin made no secret of his intense immediate interest in it. He asked whether a date had been set, saying he would withdraw that question if it were embarrassing, but Churchill told him that it was to be October 1 at the latest. Stalin then asked would this bring Vichy France into the war on Germany's side—and would it bring in Spain—and where would the operation eventually lead? Churchill assured Stalin that the prime target was still the Continent in the west, and Harriman assured him that Roosevelt was in full agreement with the Prime Minister on the decisions reached.

Suddenly Stalin exclaimed: 'May God help this enterprise to succeed!' (The translation of this remark, as given by Churchill to Roosevelt, was: 'May God prosper this undertaking!') I have been told that it was by no means unusual for Stalin, who had been educated for a time in a religious seminary, to invoke the aid of the Deity.

Stalin expressed some doubts about the political soundness of the North African operation, but he was remarkably quick to name four outstanding military advantages:

It would take the German enemy in the rear.

It would provoke French and Germans to fight each other.

It would put Italy out of action.

It would make it all the more advisable for Spain to stay neutral.

After this meeting, which had lasted for three hours and forty minutes, Churchill and Harriman felt elated, as Harriman had stated in his cable. Both were enormously impressed at the intelligence of Stalin's instantaneous appreciation of TORCH. Churchill sent a long cable to Roosevelt confirming Harriman's and Roosevelt dictated a cable to the Prime Minister which Hopkins took down:

> The cordiality shown by Mr. Stalin and his understanding of our difficult problems make me very happy. Give him my warm regards and keep me advised of progress. I wish I could be with both of you, so that the party could be made complete.

On the second day of the meetings in Moscow, August 13, Churchill called on Molotov and had a short talk with him which was evidently less satisfactory—Molotov expressing the view that the North African operation was 'ambiguous' and reminding Churchill of the communiqué that had been issued after his visits to London and Washington two months previously.

At eleven o'clock that night there was another large meeting in the Kremlin, with Stalin, Molotov, Churchill, Harriman, Cadogan, General Wavell,

General Brooke, and Air Chief Marshall Sir Arthur Tedder. Stalin opened this meeting by handing copies of an *aide-mémoire* to Churchill and Harriman, as follows:

As the result of an exchange of views in Moscow which took place on the 12th August of this year, I ascertained that the Prime Minister of Great Britain, Mr. Churchill, considered the organization of the Second Front in Europe in 1942 to be impossible.

As is well known, the organization of a Second Front in Europe in 1942 was pre-decided during the sojourn of Molotov in London, and it found expression in the agreed Anglo-Soviet communiqué published on the 12th June last.

It is also known that the organization of a Second Front in Europe had as its object the withdrawal of German forces from the Eastern Front to the West, and the creation in the West of a serious base of resistance to to the German-Fascist forces and the affording of relief by this means to the situation of the Soviet forces on the Soviet-German Front in 1942.

It will be easily understood that the Soviet Command built their plan of summer and autumn operations calculating on the creation of a Second Front in Europe in 1942.

It is easy to grasp that the refusal of the Government of Great Britain to create a Second Front in 1942 in Europe inflicts a moral blow to the whole of the Soviet public opinion, which calculates on the creation of a Second Front, and that it complicates the situation of the Red Army at the front and prejudices the plan of the Soviet Command.

I am not referring to the fact that the difficulties arising for the Red Army as the result of the refusal to create a Second Front in 1942 will undoubtedly have to deteriorate the military situation of England and all the remaining Allies.

It appears to me and my colleagues that the most favourable conditions exist in 1942 for the creation of a Second Front in Europe, inasmuch as almost all the forces of the German army, and the best forces to boot, have been withdrawn to the Eastern Front, leaving in Europe an inconsiderable amount of forces and these of inferior quality. It is unknown whether the year of 1943 will offer conditions for the creation of a Second Front as favourable as 1942. We are of the opinion, therefore, that it is particularly in 1942 that the creation of a Second Front in Europe is possible and should be effected. I was, however, unfortunately unsuccessful in convincing Mr. Prime Minister of Great Britain hereof, while Mr. Harriman, the representative of the President of the United States, fully supported Mr. Prime Minister in the negotiations held in Moscow.

(*Signed*) J. STALIN.

From that point on, the visitors from the West encountered 'very rough sledding', as Harriman put it. The cordial atmosphere of the previous night's meeting had vanished. Stalin made it painfully clear that the Soviet Goverment took no interest in the TORCH operation. He spoke caustically of the failure of the Western Allies to deliver the promised supplies to the Soviet Union. He spoke of the tremendous sacrifices that were being made to hold 280 German divisions on the Eastern Front. He said that he thought it would not be too difficult for the British and Americans to land six or eight divisions on the Cherbourg Peninsula. Churchill described in great detail the perils of an operation across the English Channel, but Stalin was unimpressed. It was at this point that Stalin made the observation that if the British infantry would only fight the Germans as the Russians had done—and indeed as the R.A.F. had done—it would not be so frightened of them. Churchill said: 'I pardon that remark only on account of the bravery of the Russian troops.'

At one point, Harriman reported, Churchill became so voluble and so eloquent in his defence of Anglo-American policy, that the British interpreter, spellbound, forgot his own job of taking down every word and put aside his pencil the better to listen to the Prime Minister's oratory. Churchill did not overlook this lapse. He turned on the interpreter, scolding him vigorously, and then started to repeat everything he had said for the unhappy Civil Servant to write down and translate. During this diversion Stalin threw back his head and roared with laughter, saying to Churchill: 'I do not understand your words, but I like your spirit.' After that, the tension was reduced, but this meeting never became friendly. At the end Harriman asked about the plans for ferrying American aircraft across Siberia, and Stalin curtly dismissed this with the statement that 'Wars are not won with *plans*'.

The next day, Harriman made the following reply to Stalin's *aide-mémoire*:

> I have had an opportunity to study the memorandum of the 13th August you handed me last night, an identical copy of which you simultaneously gave to the Prime Minister. I have also had an opportunity to read the Prime Minister's *aide-mémoire* of the 14th August replying to your memorandum.
>
> I do not believe that any useful purpose would be served in comments by me additional to what the Prime Minister has said. I feel, however, that I must reaffirm his statement that no promise has been broken regarding the Second Front.

There was considerable puzzled speculation in the British delegation as to what had produced the dismaying reversal in Stalin's attitude as between the first night's session and the second. It was recalled that there had been a similar change from hot to cold when Eden had visited Moscow the previous year, and Harriman said that much the same technique had been used when he and Beaverbrook were there. The same technique was to be encountered on subsequent occasions and the most usual explanation of it was that when Stalin got really tough he was expressing the attitude of the mysterious Politburo rather than his own personal appraisal of the main issue.

On the evening of August 14 there was the usual state dinner in the Kremlin, which Harriman described in the following cable:

> Last night we dined in force at the Kremlin with all members of the Soviet General Staff as well as all members of the Defence Committee. Stalin seemed to be entirely oblivious of the unpleasant exchanges of the previous night. He was in the best of spirits and most cordial to the Prime Minister and myself. When Churchill arrived at the dinner, however, he still appeared somewhat annoyed by the rough treatment he had received, but he became more and more interested in his talks with Stalin as the evening progressed. The subjects of discussion ranged from theories of military tactics to post-war policies. Churchill talked in some detail about the air squadrons for the Southern Russian Front, which you and he have in mind.

Churchill left this function at 1.30 a.m. rather than wait to see a lengthy film, and Stalin accompanied him the long distance through corridors and down staircases to the main entrance of the Kremlin, where the two oddly met allies parted with a genial handshake.

At seven o'clock on the evening of August 15 Churchill went to the Kremlin for a final meeting with Stalin and came out of it more surprised than ever—for now the atmosphere of cordiality was completely restored and enthusiasm for the TORCH operation and its beneficial consequences was again running high. At the end of this session (to which Churchill had brought another interpreter) Stalin asked: 'Why not come over to my apartment in the Kremlin and have some drinks?' Although Churchill's airplane was to take off at dawn, he, of course, accepted this invitation and remained for seven hours, discussing all manner of subjects, including the possibility of a meeting between Stalin and President Roosevelt in Iceland. Churchill expressed the hope that Stalin would have occasion to visit England and assured him of 'a magnificent reception'. Stalin expressed his appreciaton of this invitation, but said that, at this particular time, receptions were not very important—all that mattered was victory. After this session, Churchill got home at 3.30 a.m., wrote and dispatched a long cable to Roosevelt, and at 4.30 started off for the nine-and-a-half-hour flight to Teheran. His stamina was extraordinary for a man of nearly sixty-eight or of any other age over twenty-one that one could mention. He reported to Roosevelt that the meetings had ended in an atmosphere of the greatest good will and that a personal relationship of real importance had been established.

Roosevelt cabled Stalin:

It is a matter of regret to me that I could not have joined with you and Mr. Churchill in the Conferences in Moscow. I am fully cognizant of the urgent requirements of the military situation, particularly in relation to your own Eastern Front. We have gained, I believe, a toehold in the South-West Pacific from which the Japanese will find it very difficult to dislodge us. We have had substantial naval losses there, but the advantage gained was worth the sacrifice and we are going to maintain hard pressure on the enemy.

I am very well aware that our real enemy is Germany and that we must bring our forces and our power against Hitler at the earliest possible moment. I can assure you that this will be done just as soon as it is humanly possible to arrange for the shipping. In the meantime, more than a thousand tanks will leave this country for Russia in August and other critical supplies, including aircraft, are being expedited.

Believe me when I tell you that we are coming as quickly and as powerfully as possibly we can. Americans understand that Russia is bearing the brunt of the fighting and the casualties this year and we are filled with admiration for the magnificent resistance you are putting up.

The 'toehold in the South-West Pacific' to which the President referred was on the beaches of Guadalcanal, Tulagi, and Florida Islands, where the Marines had landed on August 7. The chart of the Solomon Islands, forming a sort of spearhead which pointed north-west toward Japan, was now on the walls of all the map rooms in Washington, and it remained up for months and years as one of the greatest battlegrounds of American history. The capture and defence of these islands from Guadalcanal to Bougainville demanded extraordinary heroism and endurance by the ground forces and precariously based air forces, and the narrow channel known as 'The Slot' was the scene of recurrent naval actions which were fought in the manner of old-fashioned, bare-knuckled slugging. In the Hopkins papers is a message, handwritten by Roosevelt and himself, which was sent to all the Chiefs of Staff when the Japanese counter-attacks on Guadalcanal were most severe. It gives a good indication of the intensity of Roosevelt's feeling about this remote but desperately important area:

My anxiety about the South-West Pacific is to make sure that every possible weapon gets into that area to hold Guadalcanal. And that having held it in this crisis that munitions and planes and crews are on the way to take advantage of our success. We will soon find ourselves engaged in two active fronts and we must have adequate air support in both places even though it means delay in our other commitments, particularly to England. Our long-range plans could be set back for months if we fail to throw our full strength in our immediate and impending conflicts.

I wish therefore you would canvass over the week-end every possible temporary division of munitions which you will require for our active fronts and let me know what they are. Please also review the number and use of all combat planes now in the continental United States.

A month after the first landings in the Solomons MacArthur started to wrest the initiative away from the Japanese on New Guinea. Starting from defensive positions around Port Moresby—and with a hopelessly defensive state of mind prevailing in the troops there—MacArthur started to push back through the jungles and up the slopes and across the ridges of the Owen Stanley Range. Roosevelt was enthusiastic about this phenomenal campaign, in which the Air Force under General George C. Kenney played a brilliant part, acting not only as an attacking force, but as almost the sole train of supply and reinforcement for the ground troops. This was the start for MacArthur on the long road back to Manila. But it was far more than that in the war as a whole: the advances on New Guinea and in the Solomons, although relatively small in scale, marked the beginning of the offensive phase for the United Nations. Except for the back-and-forth drives in the Libyan Desert and the Russian winter counter-attacks, this was the first time that the arrows indicating advances on the daily newspapers' war maps started to point into enemy territory.

However, it was a long time before those arrows in the South-West Pacific could give much satisfaction. On September 7 three American heavy cruisers and an Australian cruiser were surprised and sunk in The Slot between Guadalcanal and Savo Island, and the position of the land forces was critical and terrible, with the Japanese largely in control of the sea communications.

On the Russian Front the great final historic test had come in the shattered streets of Stalingrad. Within a week after Churchill's departure from Moscow the Germans broke through across the Don to the Volga north of Stalingrad, thus cutting off all access to the city except by barges across the river from the east, and this hazardous line of communication was subject to constant attack by the Luftwaffe, which had command of the air, and it was soon also under artillery fire from German positions in the centre of the city itself. The southward drive of the German armies reached the foothills of the Caucasus by the eastern shore of the Black Sea before September 1.

On August 19 occurred the attack by Canadian forces supplemented by British Commandos and a few Americans on the French port of Dieppe. It was insisted that this should not be considered a Commando raid—or even a 'raid' of any kind—but a 'reconnaissance in force'. Whatever it may have accomplished in reconnaissance, or in losses inflicted on the Germans in the attendant air battle, it was a deplorable venture from the propaganda viewpoint, for it seemed to confirm all Hitler's boasts about the impregnability of the European Fortress and it put a fearful damper on the Russians' hopes for a Second Front.

During this summer Roosevelt had established his week-end retreat called Shangri-la in the Maryland hills about sixty miles north of Washington. This enabled him to get away from the White House at times when it was dangerous for him to travel even as far from base as Hyde Park. It was a simple woodland lodge with four bedrooms. There was a bathroom for the President and one for the guests with a door that couldn't be locked. There were other camp cottages for the secretaries, the telephone exchange, the Secret Service, etc., and a Marine training camp surrounding the place. There was one living- and dining-room. The staff consisted of Filipino sailors from the now idle yacht, *Potomac*, and the food was far better than that in the White House.

Roosevelt sat by the hour on the little screened porch with a fine view over the Catoctin Valley. He worked on his stamp collection, he played solitaire, and he wrote his name or his initials in books from his library. He had started doing this, he said, because people were always 'borrowing' books from the White House and not returning them—and Bennett Cerf, the waggish publisher, once ventured to ask him: 'Do you think, Mr. President, that people are *less* likely to steal books that have been autographed by you?' But he persisted in the belief that this was an effective precaution. He gave one of these books to me that August, 1942. (I have the accompanying note to prove I didn't steal it.) It was an old Book of Psalms that someone had sent him—it bore the name of Mrs. Herbert Lloyd Stoddard of Los Angeles, California. He had been through this book and marked certain passages— he wanted me to study them with a view to future speeches—and one that he marked was the last verse of the thirty-ninth psalm:

O spare me, that I may recover strength, before I go hence, and be no more.

On the week-ends at Shangri-la the dispatches came in and the President and Hopkins read them in the living-dining-room, which was also the only office, or on the porch, and wrote out and sent messages to Marshall and cables to Churchill, Stalin, or Chiang Kai-shek. Sometimes generals or admirals drove up from Washington on matters of pressing import, the veins on their temples distended with urgency, and I often thought that they must be annoyed by the calmness with which their Commander-in-Chief received them and their reports. On August 30 Harriman arrived there with his descriptions of the meeting of Churchill and Stalin in Moscow two weeks previously.

The situation in Stalingrad by then was so bad that, in the appreciations that came from G-2 in the War Department, the city could be written off as already lost to the Germans. Harriman, however, brought with him a sense of optimism. He thought the Russians could prevent the breakthrough which would have cut them off from the Caucasian oilfields and given the Germans a clear road into Iran and the Middle East. However, nobody could possibly have been optimistic enough to predict the cataclysmic reversal that was to take place at Stalingrad.

Harriman had stopped off at Teheran, which he described as a delightful spot, to study the problems of the supply route from Basra over the Iranian railroad into the Soviet Union. Stalin had emphasized the critical need of the Russians for motor trucks which he put on the same priority level with tanks, and the Iranian route seemed the best for such heavy equipment. Harriman was on familiar ground in considering railroad-building problems and when he rejoined Churchill in Cairo he made the proposal that U.S. Army engineers take over the responsibility of expanding the port facilities at Basra and the communications by rail and road through Iran to Trans-Caucasia. Some of the more conservative of the British officers viewed this with alarm, for it meant putting foreigners (i.e. Americans) in control of an essential line of Empire communications. Churchill asked: 'And in what *better* hands could it be?'

It was during this trip that Churchill made the important changes in the British command in Egypt, putting in Generals Alexander and Montgomery.

Harriman also reported Stalin's favourable response to the suggestion of British and American air forces operating in the Caucasus.

Roosevelt cabled Churchill that the United States was prepared to take over the Persian railroad and was developing plans for its operation. He said that he had heard that American Army officers had been encountering difficulties on this with their British opposite numbers. He said that he had received discouraging news that morning about the forthcoming Murmansk convoy and added: 'Of course I will do everything I can with Stalin if the decision is against our sending further convoys.' He said of the progressing preparations for the North African landings: 'We are in this together and I have great confidence in our success.'

There was continued correspondence between London and Washington about the planning of the TORCH operation. The British were dubious about the landings on the Moroccan coast because of the perils presented by the Atlantic Ocean surf—and there were authorities in Washington, including Secretary Stimson, who agreed with the British estimates of these hazards. On August 30 Roosevelt cabled Churchill:

I have considered carefully your cables in reference to the TORCH operation. It is my earnest desire to start the attack at the earliest possible moment. Time is of the essence and we are speeding up preparations vigorously.

I feel very strongly that the initial attacks must be made by an exclusively American ground force, supported by your naval and transport and air units. The operation should be undertaken on the assumption that the French will offer less resistance to us than they will to the British.

I would even go so far as to say I am reasonably sure a simultaneous landing by British and Americans would result in full resistance by all French in Africa, whereas an initial American landing without British ground forces offers a real chance that there would be no French resistance or only a token resistance.

Then your force can come in to the eastward. I realize full well that your landing must be made before the enemy can get there. It is our belief that German air and parachute troops cannot get to Algiers or Tunis in any large force for at least two weeks after initial attack. Meanwhile your troops would be ashore, we hope, without much opposition and would be moving eastward.

As to the place of the landings it seems to me that we must have a sure and permanent base on the North-West cost of Africa, because a single line of communication through the Straits is far too hazardous in the light of our limited joint resources.

I propose therefore that:

(a) American troops land simultaneously near Casablanca and near Oran.

(b) That they seek to establish road and rail communication with each other back of the mountains. The distance is little more than 300 miles. This gives to the enterprise a supply base in Morocco which is outside the Straits and can be used to reinforce and supply the operations in Algiers and Tunis.

The real problem seems to be that there is not enough cover and combat loadings for more than two landings. I realize it would be far better to have three with you handling the one to the eastward a week after we get in. To this end I think we should re-examine our resources and strip everything to the bone to make the third landing possible. We can give up the Russian convoy temporarily at that time and risk or hold up other merchant shipping. It is essential, of course, that all ships now assigned to Eisenhower for his two landings remain intact. Hence the eastward landing must be made on ships not now available to TORCH. I will explore this at our end. Can we not get an answer on this within forty-eight hours or less?

I want to emphasize, however, that under any circumstances one of our landings must be on the Atlantic.

The directive to the Commander-in-Chief of the operation should prescribe that the attack should be launched at the earliest practicable date. The date should be consistent with the preparation necessary for an operation with a fair chance of success and accordingly it should be determined by the Commander-in-Chief, but in no event later than October 30. I still would hope for October 14.

Churchill made the following reply:

We could not contest your wish if you so desire it to take upon the United States the whole burden, political and military, of the landings. Like you, I assign immense importance to the political aspect. I do not know what information you have of the mood and temper of Vichy and North Africa, but of course if you can get ashore at the necessary points without fighting or only token resistance, that is best of all. We cannot tell what are the chances of this.

Churchill said that it had always been agreed that this was to be primarily an American enterprise, but he made the point that it could not be represented as exclusively so, since it was hardly possible to disguise the presence of the British Navy. Churchill persisted in advocating that Algiers should be occupied simultaneously with Casablanca and Oran, saying that here was 'the most friendly and hopeful spot where the political reaction would be most decisive through North Africa', which proved to be the case.

In all the discussions preceding TORCH it was obvious that the eternally sore subject of de Gaulle and the Fighting French would again manifest itself. Roosevelt was obdurate on this point. He wrote: 'I consider it essential that de Gaulle be kept out of the picture and be permitted to have no information whatever, regardless of how irritated and irritating he may become.' In the subsequent protests over American policy on this there were further attacks on the State Department—repercussions of the 'so-called Free French' blunder; but this policy was attributable directly to Roosevelt himself and not to the State Department, and Churchill did not offer firm opposition to it. As Professor Langer has written:

Both at Dakar and in Syria, the British had employed Frenchmen to fight Frenchmen. These incidents had left a very bad and almost indelible impression. The French in North Africa were determined to oppose any repetition of this situation, and there can be no doubt that the use of Fighting French forces would have led to civil war.

In an effort to avoid bloodshed by making the strongest possible appeal to the minds and hearts of the French in North Africa, it was decided that the military forces on the TORCH operation should be accompanied for the first time by so-called 'psychological warfare teams', including civilians, to move in with the troops to disseminate anti-German, pro-Allied propaganda through every means available—the Press, radio, movie theatres, posters, etc. This novel phase was planned in London, largely by Sir Robert Bruce Lockhart, for the British, and James P. Warburg and Percy Winner, for the Americans. One instance of it: a radio transmitter was installed on the battleship *Texas*, tuned to the wavelength of Radio Maroc at Rabat, then under Vichy control. It broadcast from offshore while the landing-craft were moving in on D-Day, and the Moroccans were startled to hear the voice of President Roosevelt and renditions of the 'Marseillaise' apparently coming from their own local radio station, but actually from phonograph records on the *Texas*. From that time on there was no major Allied landing from Normandy to the Philippines that did not have a Psychological Warfare Division as part of the force.

At a meeting in London on the morning of September 22 Churchill, Eisenhower, and their staffs reviewed the whole TORCH prospect. Because of the expansion of the operation and the added shipping required for transport of men and material from the United Kingdom and the United States, Eisenhower made the decision that the date must be postponed to November 8. Following this meeting, Churchill informed Roosevelt that these shipping requirements would also probably compel the abandonment for that year of JUPITER, the landings in Northern Norway, which were almost constantly under consideration for three years, but which never took place. In the same cable Churchill informed Roosevelt of a new British operation which had then been ordered; this was known as LIGHTFOOT, and it was the drive by Generals Alexander and Montgomery from Egypt which was to begin with the memorable victory at El Alamein.

The postponement of the date for TORCH had considerable political significance in the United States; November 3 was election day, and it would have been obviously advantageous to Roosevelt to have this exciting news received before the voters went to the polls—but, as Roosevelt said at the time, this was a decision that rested with the responsible officer, Eisenhower, and not with the Democratic National Committee.

Roosevelt had to give a great deal of attention to the domestic political scene in this summer and fall of 1942. He hated it, but he couldn't escape it. The Congressional election was approaching and the partisan voices, temporarily stilled during the phase of national unity enforced by Pearl Harbour, were becoming more and more strident. They had plenty of targets for criticisms—more, in fact, than most of them knew about. The progress of production was in some important respects disappointing and in a few respects downright alarming. The war manpower situation was in a dreadful mess. There was even more than the usual bickering and backbiting between departments and agencies. In the battle of Washington, as on most of the real fighting fronts, this was the lowest point of the war. Worst of all was the failure of the Congress to do anything toward meeting the threat of inflation. The President's requests for higher taxes and more rigid controls on the civilian economy had been ignored or evaded by Congressmen afraid to face the voters, especially the farmers. Roosevelt himself was in a weak position politically, for millions of votes were lost by the shifting of manpower into the armed forces or to new centres of industry, while the farm vote largely stayed put.

Roosevelt was urged to take drastic action to stabilize farm prices, for which Congress was willing to provide a floor, but no ceiling. The principal force in this urging was Leon Henderson, Director of the Office of Price Administration and currently the centre for the storms of criticism and complaint. A public servant of exceptional ability, courage, and imperviousness, Henderson had an unfortunate flair for flamboyant publicity; he was often photographed dancing the rhumba and wearing funny hats, and that made him all the more unpopular with the conservative elements which always were strongest in the rural areas.

It was usual for the President to speak to the nation on Labour Day and Roosevelt decided that this was the occasion for decisive action against inflation. The preparation of that speech was ten days' work—at Shangri-la, the White House, and Hyde Park—and involved some arguments among Roosevelt's advisers. The President had the power to stabilize prices and wages by Executive Order without reference to Congress, and some of us believed that he should do just that immediately and not run the risk of hostile action or no action at all on Capitol Hill. There were unquestionably many Congressmen who fervently hoped that he would do it this way and thereby absolve them from all responsibility for decision on such a controversial issue. (It was an ironic fact that many of the Congressmen who were loudest in accusing Roosevelt of dictatorial ambitions were the most anxious to have him act like a dictator on all measures which might be unpopular with the people, but obviously valuable for the winning of the war.) Roosevelt himself was in favour of an arbitrary Executive Order to achieve stabilization, and his speech was at first written as a proclamation and explanation of that; but some of his advisers, notably Hopkins and Henderson, strongly recommended that he put the issue up to Congress in the form of an ultimatum—"You act before October 1 or I will'—and their arguments finally prevailed.

Roosevelt concluded his speech of September 7 with these words:

Battles are not won by soldiers or sailors who think first of their own personal safety. And wars are not won by people who are concerned primarily with their own comfort, their own convenience, their own pocket-books.

K

We Americans of today bear the gravest of responsibilities. All of the United Nations share them.

All of us here at home are being tested—for our fortitude, for our selfless devotion to our country and our cause.

This is the toughest war of all time. We need not leave it to historians of the future to answer the question whether we are tough enough to meet this unprecedented challenge. We can give that answer now. The answer is 'Yes'.

Roosevelt did not have much to say about the military situation in that speech. There was not much that he could say without informing the enemy of future plans.

Of the Eastern Front in Europe he said that the Russians 'are fighting not only bravely, but brilliantly' and 'will hold out'. This, of course, was during the bitterest phase of the Battle of Stalingrad.

Of the South-West Pacific: 'We must not overrate the importance of our successes in the Solomon Islands, though we may be proud of the skill with which these local operations were conducted.' Roosevelt spoke thus cautiously of a critical battle because he knew, as the public did not, of the severe naval losses we had sustained, and he was seeking to prepare the people for possible news that the Japanese had driven the Marines from the positions so precariously held on Guadalcanal.

Roosevelt said further:

In the Mediterranean and the Middle East Area the British, together with the South Africans, Australians, New Zealanders, Indian troops, and others of the United Nations, including ourselves, are fighting a desperate battle with the Germans and Italians. The Axis powers are fighting to gain control of that area, dominate the Mediterranean and Indian Ocean, and gain contact with the Japanese Navy. The battle is now joined. We are well aware of our danger, but we are hopeful of the outcome.

The European Area. Here the aim is an offensive against Germany. There are at least a dozen different points at which attack can be launched. You, of course, do not expect me to give details of future plans, but you can rest assured that preparations are being made here and in Britain toward this purpose. The power of Germany must be broken on the battlefields of Europe.

After this speech Roosevelt decided to take a trip around the country to see the Chrysler plant in Detroit (now making tanks), the Ford plant at Willow Run (B-24 Liberators), the Kaiser shipyards in Portland, Oregon, and the Higgins yards in New Orleans, the Boeing plant in Seattle (B-17

Flying Fortresses), and various army training camps, airfields, and naval stations. It was a good chance for the President to see a great deal of production and training progress—and he was one capable of understanding the essentials of what he saw—but the main purpose of the trip was, of course, for political influence on the Congress and on the Congressional elections.

Merriman Smith, of the United Press, has written of this trip in his book, *Thank You, Mr. President*, and emphasized the irritation caused by the secrecy surrounding all of Roosevelt's wartime journeys. It would seem to have been greatly overdone—especially on occasions such as this one, when the President was visible and often audible to millions of citizens over a route of some nine thousand miles. There were many stories at the time of workers who came home late for supper, explaining to their wives that 'President Roosevelt was at the plant', and, when the wives saw no mention of this important event in the local newspapers they accused their husbands of lying. Smith described one incident at the Kaiser shipyards:

After his daughter, Mrs. John Boettiger, had launched a ship—on the record and in full view of cameras—the President took over the meeting. There must have been twenty thousand people swarmed around a high ramp on which the President's open automobile was parked.

'You know,' he said to the people over the loudspeaker system, 'you know I am not supposed to be here today.'

The crowd laughed and the President joined in the merriment. Damned if I saw anything to laugh about. Here was the President of the United States making an important public appearance in front of twenty thousand people, yet the newspapers and radio stations had to play like they knew nothing about it.

Although three reporters whose normal duty was to send news to thousands of outlets around the world were standing only a few feet from him, the President went on with his joke:

'You are the possessors of a secret which even the newspapers of the United States don't know,' he told the shipworkers.

'I hope you will keep the secret, because I am under military and naval orders, and like the ship that we have just seen go overboard, my motions and movements are supposed to be secret.'

Roosevelt loved all this air of mystery. It was part of his nature to wear the mantle of military security like a small boy playing 'cops and robbers'. Furthermore, he loved to irritate the Press which had so often irritated him.

He returned to Washington on October 1, the deadline set for Congressional action, and the next day the Stabilization Act was sent to the White House and he signed it, expressing certainty that it would 'assist greatly in bringing the war to a successful conclusion' and 'will make the transition to peace conditions easier after the war'. The same day he sent for James F. Byrnes to leave the Supreme Court and assume the post of Director of Economic Stabilization which made him, in effect, Assistant President in charge of the home front. This relieved Roosevelt of a considerable amount of work and worry, and it consequently greatly reduced the accumulation on Hopkins's desk. Hopkins later laughed and said: 'Shortly after Jimmy Byrnes moved in I went to talk to him about something and he told me: "There's just one suggestion I want to make to you, Harry, and that is to keep the hell out of my business." He smiled very pleasantly when he said it, but by God he meant it and I'm going to keep the hell out.' It is improbable that Hopkins was entirely faithful in living up to this resolve.

In the elections on November 3 the Republicans gained forty-seven votes in the House, which was only nine short of a majority. They gained ten votes in the Senate. Roosevelt had only just escaped the overturn inflicted on Wilson in 1918, and he was now down to the narrowest margin of his entire Presidential career.

During September and October Wendell Willkie made the journey to Africa, the Middle East, the Soviet Union, and China which he described in his influential book, *One World*. He flew this enormous distance in an Army transport plane with, of course, Roosevelt's hearty approval; he was accompanied by Joseph Barnes, formerly foreign editor of the *New York Herald Tribune*, and Gardner Cowles, publisher of the *Des Moines Register and Tribune* and *Look* magazine. Because both Barnes and Cowles were then working for the Government in the Office of War Information, the former as Deputy Director of the Overseas Branch and the latter as Director of the Domestic Branch, there might have seemed to be a propaganda intent in their presence on the trip. But Willkie solicited and needed no official aid in that field. Cowles was a very close friend and ardent supporter of his, and Barnes spoke Russian and other languages fluently and had a background of distinguished service as correspondent in Moscow, Europe, and the Far East, and Willkie himself selected them as travelling companions.

Willkie's trip did an enormous amount of good and it also stirred up some trouble. In Moscow he heard very direct accusations that the British had 'stolen' American Lend-Lease material intended for Russia (this referred to the ships which were diverted from the Murmansk route to Scotland.) In Chungking Willkie heard the Generalissimo's expressions of bitterness against the Allies in general and Britain in particular and also against the American Ambassador, Clarence E. Gauss, and General Stilwell. The long feud between Stilwell and Chennault was then much in evidence.

From Moscow Willkie chided the Allies for failure to open a Second Front and from Chungking for failure to make an all-out effort in aid of China—two statements which caused Roosevelt to remark: 'You can't have it both ways.' (It might have been added that at this stage of the war it couldn't be had either way.) Shortly before Willkie returned to Washington via the North-West Passage from Siberia on October 14, Roosevelt let fall some remarks about 'typewriter strategists' at a Press conference, including an impish imitation of Willkie's pronunciation of some words, and Willkie consequently ended his mission of good will in a fury of rage at the President.

It is my belief that Roosevelt really regretted having yielded to the temptation, which so frequently seemed to afflict him at Press conferences, to indulge in unworthy wisecracks at Willkie's expense. He was talking off the record, but he had plenty of reason to know that his little quips would be given wide circulation by the correspondents present, many of whom were accurate reporters. There is no doubt in my mind that Roosevelt had far more admiration for Willkie than for any opponent he ever faced; he respected Willkie's enormous courage, if not his political acumen, and was profoundly and eternally grateful for Willkie's persistent battle against the isolationism of the Old Guard in the Republican party. Once I heard Hopkins make some slurring remark about Willkie and Roosevelt slapped him with as sharp a reproof as I ever heard him utter. He said: 'Don't ever say anything like that around here again. Don't even *think* it. You of all people ought to know that we might not have had Lend-Lease or Selective Service or a lot of other things if it hadn't been for Wendell Willkie. He was a godsend to this country when we needed him most.' The sceptical might suspect that Roosevelt's affectionate regard for Willkie was due at least in part to the fact that he had defeated him, but he had none of the same respect or regard for Herbert Hoover or Thomas E. Dewey, whom he also defeated.

When Willkie was in Chungking on his 'One World' trip he heard that there had been criticism of his previous statements in Moscow about the Second Front. He exploded to the Press that he had been commissioned by Roosevelt to do certain things, but he had not been limited by any instructions to any precise mission. 'When I speak for myself,' he said, 'I am Wendell Willkie, and I say what I damned please.' He obviously had not been thoroughly informed concerning the TORCH operation nor the situation in general. This was a circumstance that was incomprehensible to the Russians and the Chinese, and even to the British: that a statesman of the finesse of Roosevelt could authorize a globe-circling jaunt by any compatriot of Willkie's eminence without 'briefing' him thoroughly in advance so that he would know which points to emphasize and which to soft-pedal in all his statements, both public and private. But such was the case. Willkie was authorized to go on his own and 'say what I damned please', and he did.

Roosevelt was not greatly disturbed by Willkie's statements during his trip or the speeches that he made after his return. But Hopkins was fearful that Willkie was doing serious damage to the cause of Allied unity. He was particularly angered by the reports, which Willkie never made public but which were freely circulated, of the dinner in Moscow when Stalin had accused the British of 'stealing' Lend-Lease material. Hopkins knew all about this particular subject and, in fact, shared a considerable part of the responsibility for diverting some ships from the Murmansk route at times when the cost of getting convoys through was prohibitive. During October Harriman in London cabled Hopkins about three loaded ships then lying idle in Scotland awaiting a convoy to Murmansk. This was the time of the enormous diversion of shipping for the North African operation and the British wanted to unload these ships so that they could be used elsewhere. Hopkins replied to Harriman:

> It is essential in my belief that the three ships that you mention should be unloaded. We need every possible ship that is going through to Russia during the next two months. Although I realize that there may be compelling reasons for you and Stark to decide not to unload these ships —and we must, of course, accept your judgment on this point—I think you should tell Stark how very urgent are our needs for merchant ships here immediately. Douglas agrees with me on this. We have already advised Moscow about these matters and it seems to me to make no additional difficulty even if Maisky cables his Government. Under any circumstances, I think the ships should be unloaded.

There was a very heavy load of messages between Washington, London, and Moscow during these terribly tense and critical weeks of the fighting in Stalingrad and the Solomons, the immeasurably complex preparations for TORCH, and the build-up of British forces in the Middle East preparatory to the battle of El Alamein. Just before Roosevelt left for his swing around the country on September 17 he wrote a note to Admiral Leahy to make sure that Hopkins got all the cables:

> I am anxious to get the cables to me from the Prime Minister and other heads of government in various countries, and my replies to them, coordinated through Harry, because so much of them refer to civil things.
> I am asking him to see that all of the military aspects of these cables are referred to you and the Combined Chiefs of Staff, and he will co-ordinate them and give them to me for my approval.

When Roosevelt was in Seattle Churchill sent cables containing a message he proposed to send to Stalin relative to the cancelling of another convoy (PQ 19) to Murmansk and the proposal to establish a British-American strategic air force on the Russian flank in the Caucasus. The latter proposal had been originally discussed by Churchill and Stalin in August and approved by Roosevelt. The argument for the cancelling of PQ 19 was a powerful one; the preceding convoy to Murmansk had lost one ship out of three, but had required seventy-seven warships for escort duty. In view of the enormous naval requirements of the impending TORCH operation, it would be obviously impossible to assign anywhere near that number of warships for another convoy.

When Hopkins read these messages, he immediately cabled Churchill:

> The President is now at a distant point and your urgent messages are being relayed to him there. I very strongly urge you not to send Stalin the proposed message until you hear how the President feels about it. It seems very clear to me that the turning-point in the war may well depend on what is now said to Stalin and what firm commitments we are prepared to make to him. I shall do everything possible to assure prompt answer to your messages.

At the same time Hopkins cabled Harriman that 3,000 trucks were on the way to Russia by the southern route that month, that another 1,000 would undoubtedly be dispatched before the month ended, that he was trying to get the Persian railway problem unscrambled that afternoon, that he was taking up with General Arnold the question of delivering more transport planes to Russia by way of Siberia, etc. Hopkins sent a telegram to Roosevelt in the North-West as follows:

> I have just talked to Leahy, and our Chiefs of Staff are giving consideration to the Former Naval Person's cables to you today. Will meet with Leahy late this afternoon to send draft of reply for your consideration.
>
> I have no doubt there are compelling reasons for discontinuing the northern convoys for the balance of this year.
>
> In replying to the Former Naval Person relative to a wire to Stalin, I hope you will give full consideration to the importance of the proposal for a joint allied air force on the Caucasian Front. Churchill's previous proposal to do this only in the event of a victory in the Middle East seems to me to be totally inadequate. I believe the only thing that will do the trick is a firm commitment to put a token force on this winter and a real force on ready to make the fight next spring. Obviously our planes and manpower must come out of the BOLERO commitment. Our Chiefs of Staff are inclined to let the British do the Russian job, we reinforcing in the Middle East.
>
> Without having any opinion on the military necessities of this suggestion, I feel very strongly that from every other consideration it is essential that we join with the British rather than have the British carry that responsibility alone.
>
> I realize that any air force in the Caucasus would be almost a token

force between now and Christmas, but it surely could be built up with British co-operation to an effective fighting unit by next spring. It seems to me we must assume that Germany cannot break through the Caucasus this winter, and to make our plans accordingly. There are, of course, logistic problems involved in this of a serious nature. It seems to me they can be overcome in view of the great urgency of the situation.

If we must now tell Stalin that the convoys on the northern route must be discontinued, then it seems to me that it is almost imperative that we make a direct and firm offer to place our armed forces at his side in Russia against Germany. It is clear that the only armed force which we can get there is our air force and that the only place you can get any part of our force is further to cut in on air to England. This does not necessarily mean any reduction in the big bombers.

I do not, of course, suggest a diversion of any planes which are needed for special operations in the South-West Pacific or anywhere else. Indeed, I have a feeling that Bolero will have to supply them with additional reinforcements before we are through.

I hope you can take this up again with the Chiefs of Staff. I think that the Prime Minister's wire which he is asking you to endorse is going to be a terrible wet blanket at this particular time.

The most important thing that you could say to Stalin now is that England and the United States are going to send a joint air force to help fight Germany on the Caucasian Front.

You will hear from us late tonight.

From his train, *en route* from San Diego, California, to San Antonio, Texas, Roosevelt cabled Churchill that, whereas he was inclined to agree that the realities of the situation required cancellation of PQ 19, he did not feel that Stalin should be notified of this 'tough blow' to his hopes any sooner than was absolutely necessary. He spoke of progress being made in plans for the Allied air force in Trans-Caucasia, and said that perhaps it would be as well to wait to notify Stalin about PQ 19 until these plans were complete. Roosevelt added: 'I am having a great trip. Our war production is good, but it must be better. The morale of our forces is excellent and their training is far advanced.'

On October 5 Roosevelt, having returned to Washington, sent a cable to Churchill which indicated he had reconsidered the question of cancelling the convoy PQ 19:

Our greatest reliance today is the Russian Front, and we simply must find a way to help them directly aside from our diminishing supplies. It is my very strong feeling that we should make a firm commitment to put an air force into the Caucasus and that this operation should not be contingent on any other developments. . . . I feel most strongly that we should not tell Stalin that the PQ 19 convoy will not sail. I have talked with Admiral King about this and I would like to urge that we use a different technique in which the guiding factors are dispersion and evasion. We would thus let a convoy sail in successive groups comprising the fastest ships we have loaded and are now loading for Russia. Each of these groups would consist of two or three ships, to sail at intervals of twenty-four to forty-eight hours, supported by two or three escorts. We would have to take the risk of having them sail without the full naval covering support needed to protect a convoy from the battleship *Tirpitz* or the German heavy cruisers. In so far as air attack is concerned, we know that the longer nights will be of help and that in all probability the weather would not be against us every day.

It is my belief that we would thus stand a good chance of getting through as high a proportion of the ships as we did with PQ 18. I think it is better under any circumstances that we run this risk rather than endanger our whole relations with Russia at this time.

Please advise me when you are sending your message to Stalin and I shall immediately send him a similar message. I am certain, however, that both our messages should be phrased so as to leave a good taste in his mouth. Our Ambassador in Moscow has asked for permission to come home to deliver a very important message in person and I have some fears as to what that message might be.

General Marshall reported that it would be entirely possible to build up a group of U.S. heavy bombers in the Caucasus by the end of the year. Roosevelt then cabled Churchill suggesting that the United States should provide the heavy bombers for VELVET—the code name given the Caucasian operation—and that the British should provide the medium or light bombers and the fighter escorts.

On October 7 the following message was received by Roosevelt from Stalin:

As it is reported, the difficulties in the deliveries arise in the first place from the shortage of tonnage. In order to relieve the tonnage situation, the Soviet Government would be willing to agree to a certain curtailment of the deliveries of American war materials to the Soviet Union. We are willing to discard for the time being all of the deliveries of tanks, artillery, munitions, pistols, etc. But at the same time we are extremely in need of an increase in the deliveries of pursuit planes of modern type (such as 'Aircobra') and of securing to us under all conditions of certain other supplies. It should be borne in mind that the 'Kittyhawk' planes do not stand the fight against present German pursuits.

It would be well if the United States would in any case secure the following monthly supplies to us: 500 pursuit planes, from 8,000 to 10,000 trucks, 5,000 tons of aluminium, from 4,000 to 5,000 tons of explosives. In addition, it is essential to secure the delivery within twelve months of two million tons of grain (wheat) as well as such quantity as possible of fats, concentrated food, and canned meat. We could import a considerable amount of food via Vladivostok by Soviet ships, provided the United States agree to cede to the U.S.S.R. at least twenty to thirty ships to reinforce our merchant marine. All of this I already talked over with Mr. Willkie, confident that he will report it to you.

As to the situation at the front, you certainly know that during the recent months our situation in the south and especially in the region of Stalingrad has worsened due to the fact that we are short of planes, first of all pursuit planes. The Germans proved to have a great reserve of planes. The Germans have in the south at least a two to one superiority in the air, which deprives us of the possibility to cover our troops. The experience of the war has shown that the bravest armies become helpless if they are not protected from the blows from the air.

Roosevelt replied to Stalin that arrangements for the Allied air force in the Caucasus were being expedited—that he was trying to find additional planes and also additional merchant ships for the Russians to operate across the Pacific supply line to Vladivostok—that he had just ordered that a complete automobile tyre plant be made available for setting up in the Soviet Union—and that very substantial reinforcements were being sent to the Persian Gulf area to develop that route into Russia.

The President made no mention of the convoy PQ 19, which never sailed. The 'trickle method' was adopted, sending ships singly with no armed escort whatsoever, and this was continued with fair success until the descent of the long Arctic winter night made it possible to resume regular convoys.

While Ambassador Standley was *en route* from Moscow with the important message which Roosevelt awaited with some apprehension Hopkins cabled Harriman that 'None of us knows exactly why Standley is coming home'.

The message carried by Standley, however, proved to be substantially the same as the message dated October 7 quoted above. Roosevelt then cabled Stalin that he had received from the Ambassador a full report on the 'fighting qualities and strength of your. Army and the urgency of your need for supplies'. Stalin's brief acknowledgment of this message was delivered by Litvinov to Hopkins for the President. Hopkins was now more than ever 'Roosevelt's own, personal Foreign Office'.

On October 24 Churchill cabled Roosevelt that he was baffled and perplexed by the correspondence from Moscow—or, rather, the almost total lack of it. Two weeks previously he and the President had sent long, parallel messages to Stalin detailing the proposals for supplies and for the air force in the Caucasus. The only reply that Churchill had received consisted of two words, 'Thank you'. Churchill had sought to obtain further information through the British Ambassador in Moscow, Sir Archibald Clark Kerr, who had been able to gain nothing but evasive replies from Molotov's secretary. Churchill wondered what was going on inside the Soviet Union. Roosevelt cabled him:

> Having come to the conclusion that the Russians do not use speech for the same purposes that we do, I am not unduly disturbed about the responses or lack of them that we have received from Moscow.
>
> I feel very certain that the Russians are going to hold throughout this winter. We must be able to prove to Stalin that we have carried out obligations one hundred per cent and we must therefore proceed vigorously with our plans for supplying them and for setting up an air force to fight on their front.
>
> Nothing has been heard here about difficulties in arrangements for landing-fields on the Caucasus front, but I shall explore this immediately from this end.

The mysterious silence out of Moscow at that time was not due, as some alarmed authorities (not including Roosevelt or Churchill) then feared, to the possibility of a separate, negotiated Russo-German peace; it was the direct result of the historic circumstance of improvement in the situation at Stalingrad. The need for immediate help became less desperate day by day, and the Russians never did agree to the project for a British-American air force in the Caucasus. Some time later General Burns prepared a memorandum for Hopkins which is printed in full because it was an excellent statement of Hopkins's own views on the subject of relations with the Soviet Union:

> 1. There is nothing new or original in this paper. It is simply a summary of what is believed to be the consensus of best ideas.
>
> 2. We not only need Russia as a powerful fighting ally in order to defeat Germany, but eventually we will also need her in a similar role to defeat Japan. And finally, we need her as a real friend and customer in the post-war world.
>
> 3. *With reference to the importance of Russia in the defeat of Germany.*
>
> No arguments are necessary. She is as essential as the United Kingdom and the United States.
>
> 4. *With reference to the importance of Russia in the defeat of Japan.*
>
> It is generally conceded that the 'step-by-step' plan for reaching Tokyo by way of the Pacific Islands must be supplemented by large-scale bomb-

ing attacks based upon Asia which will have as their target the very heart of the Japanese Empire and the source of its strength.

This will require very substantial ground forces for the defence of bases, and in addition a large air force, together with its personnel, its ground installations, its planes, its gas, its spare parts, its ammunition, and all other supplies. An operating force of 1,000 bombers requires approximately 200,000 tons of supplies per month. This strength can hardly be placed in Asia without the assistance of Russia.

Even though we captured Burma, the capacity of the Burma Road is relatively negligible—perhaps 25,000 tons per month—and could not be made substantial for many, many months.

We could take into Asia only a negligible quantity of men and supplies by way of the Persian Gulf and the circuitous route to China to the north of the Himalayas—perhaps 10-20,000 tons per month. Of course, its capacity could be gradually increased, but its maximum probabilities are not great. Even this route goes through Russia.

We can hardly hope to reach the Chinese coast without the capture of Singapore and other strong points in that region, and such capture may be beyond our capabilities for a long while to come.

However, if Russia would join with us, we would not only have her forces to help us, but in addition, we could move men and supplies to Russia and through Russia to the eastward by way of the Trans-Siberian Railway to Eastern Asia. Furthermore, we could move some supplies—certainly planes and perhaps some ships—by way of Alaska and Siberia.

In other words, with Russia as an active and powerful ally, we should be able to bomb Japan effectively in the not too distant future. Without her, the time factor may be much longer. And we must remember that each month of this war will cost us many lives and billions of treasure.

Even though we cannot obtain the help of Russia as an active ally against Japan, it would be of great importance if she would assist us in getting men and supplies into China.

5. If it is accepted that Russian help is necessary to defeat both Germany and Japan, it is conversely true that the defeat of Russia by one or both of these countries might prevent us from defeating either Germany or Japan.

Such a defeat might occur if we do not help Russia to the limit, for her war with Germany has deprived her of a great part of her population, of her raw materials, of her industries, of her transportation, of her reserves, and of her food lands.

Such a defeat might also occur if Japan should now join Germany in the war on Russia. It seems, therefore, that it would be much more advantageous to our cause if a Russo-Japanese war could be postponed until Germany is defeated.

6. *With reference to our need for Russia as a real friend and customer in the post-war period.*

If the Allies are victorious, Russia will be one of the three most powerful countries in the world. For the future peace of the world, we should be real friends so that we can help shape world events in such a way as to provide security and prosperity.

Furthermore, Russia's post-war needs for the products of America will be simply overwhelming. She must not only rehabilitate her war losses in homes, industries, raw materials and farms, but she must provide the resources for the inevitable advances in her standards of living that will result from the war.

7. From the above, it seems evident that Soviet relationships are the most important to us of all countries, excepting only the United Kingdom. It seems also evident that we must be so helpful and friendly to her that she will not only battle through to the defeat of Germany and also give vital assistance in the defeat of Japan, but in addition willingly join with us in establishing a sound peace and mutually beneficial relations in the post-war world.

8. *Suggestions for improving relationships.*

(*a*) Arrange for a conference between the President and Mr. Stalin at some appropriate time and place.

(*b*) Establish a better spirit of 'Comrades-in-Arms' by sending General Marshall, Admiral King, and General Arnold or other appropriate military representatives to confer with corresponding Russian officials in Moscow or some other appropriate location and to discuss freely our plans, our capabilities, and our limitations.

(*c*) Do everything possible in a generous, but not lavish, way to help Russia by sending supplies to the limit of shipping possibilities and by sending forces to Russia to join with her in the fight against Germany.

(*d*) If at all feasible, arrange with Britain and Russia for an attack on Narvik and the Northern Norway coast to open up the Northern Supply Route to Russia and to deprive Germany of Swedish iron ore.

(*e*) Send to Russia an ambassador of top rank as to national standing, vision, ability, and willingness to serve the country first.

(*f*) In general, treat Russia as one of the three foremost powers in the world.

(*g*) Establish the general policy throughout all U.S. departments and agencies that Russia must be considered as a real friend and be treated accordingly, and that personnel must be assigned to Russian contacts that are loyal to this concept.

(*h*) Work to the general plan of assisting Russia to defeat Germany, of postponing a war between Japan and Russia until Germany is defeated, and of seeking Russian assistance at the proper time as an ally in the war with Japan. If this last cannot be achieved, then strive to obtain her agreement to assist in the transportation of supplies into China.

(*i*) Offer Russia very substantial credits on easy terms to finance her post-war rehabilitation and expansion.

(*j*) Agree to assist, in every proper and friendly way, to formulate a peace that will meet Russia's legitimate aspirations.

On the same day, October 24, that Churchill sent his message to Roosevelt confessing perplexity and bafflement, he sent another short cable that was full of the emotions of one who, having for long stared defeat in the face, now saw the first glimmer of victory. He said that the battle in Egypt had begun that evening at eight o'clock, London time, that the whole force of the Army would be engaged, and that a victory there would be fruitful for the main enterprise in Algeria and Morocco. The Prime Minister told the President, most movingly, that 'all the Sherman tanks you gave me on that dark Tobruk morning will play their part' in the battle now joined.

This was the first word of El Alamein which came to Roosevelt with his breakfast at Shangri-la; it was four months almost to the day after 'that dark Tobruk morning'. But it was impossible to be exultant, for those were indescribably nerve-racking days for everyone aware of the fact that great armadas carrying tens of thousands of men had sailed from the United Kingdom and the United States across the submarine-infested seas to North Africa. The TORCH operation was on and the possibilities for leakage in Washington could be (and were) so terrifying that it seemed inevitable the enemy would know all about it and would have ample time to take effective measures for combating it.

The Chinese Foreign Minister, T. V. Soong, had gone from Washington to Chungking in October, and on November 2 he cabled Hopkins asking if an airplane could be placed at the disposal of Madame Chiang Kai-shek, who, according to Soong, was seriously ill, and had been urged to go to the United States for treatment. Soong said that the Chinese Government intended to ask Owen Lattimore to accompany Madame in the event that the flight could be arranged and that she should enter a hospital immediately upon her arrival in the United States, deferring any official visits in Washington until after she had undergone treatment. Hopkins immediately cabled Soong that the President was greatly disturbed to hear of Madame's illness and that steps were being taken to make an airplane immediately available for her transportation from Chungking to New York.

The cabled correspondence about this complicated arrangement was carried on during the tense days preceding the TORCH landings.

Hopkins referred the matter to General Marshall, who, on November 5, advised him:

A stratoliner will go to Chengtu, China, via Karachi, arriving there on or before November 12, to bring Madame Chiang Kai-shek to this country. The plane should arrive in Washington about November 18, weather permitting.

A doctor and nurse will accompany the plane while Madame Chiang Kai-shek is aboard. The plane's capacity will permit a total of eight in the Madame's party. I will keep you advised of any further developments.

Soong thanked Hopkins for the rapid arrangements and said the Madame would be bringing her own doctor and nurse.

The final stages of preparation for TORCH involved a great deal of very careful word choosing for the various messages from the President to Pétain, Franco, General Antonio Carmona (President of Portugal), Yves Chatel (Governor-General of Algeria), the Sultan of Morocco, and the Bey of Tunis. These messages were to be flashed as the troops hit the beaches— and at the same instant every international radio transmitter in the United States and Britain would start broadcasting the same programme which had been in preparation for weeks. Every word of General Eisenhower's proclamations had been cabled back and forth between London and Washington and scrutinized and many words revised, for it was obvious that the slightest political slip could cost lives.

Most interesting of all was the drafting of the message to Pétain. I don't know who drafted this first, but when the text of it was cabled to Churchill he protested that it was 'much too kind'. The Prime Minister reminded the President that Pétain had 'used his reputation to do our cause injuries no lesser man could have done'. Roosevelt then took a good look at the message and what he did to it can be observed in an accompanying reproduction. The original draft started out:

> My dear old friend:
> I am sending this message to you *not only* as the Chef d'Etat of the United States to the Chef d'Etat of the Republic of France, *but also as one of your friends and comrades of the great days of 1918. May we both live to see France victorious again against the ancient enemy.*
> When your Government concluded, *of necessity*, the Armistice Convention in 1940, it was impossible for any of us to foresee the programme of systematic plunder which the German Reich would inflict on the French people.

The words that I have italicized were cut out by Roosevelt. At the end of the message he deleted a reference to 'the venerated hero of Verdun', and 'my warm regards' and the subscript, 'your friend'.

Pétain replied:

It is with stupour and sadness that I learned tonight of the aggression of your troops against North Africa.

I have read your message. You invoke pretexts which nothing justifies . . . France and her honour are at stake. We are attacked; we shall defend ourselves; this is the order I am giving.

Thus, for the 'honour' of the Vichy Government, was enacted the sordid spectacle of Frenchmen shooting at and killing Americans and Americans shooting at and killing Frenchmen. It was like a tragic misprint on the pages of history. Intense hostility to Britain had been expected in North Africa—at one time, it had even been planned to have British troops participating disguise their nationality by wearing American uniforms—but fortunately these fears proved to be greatly exaggerated. There was little if any difference in the reception accorded to the British as contrasted with American troops by the local populace. As it happened, by all odds the stiffest resistance was offered in Morocco to General Patton's Western Task Force, which was entirely American, in naval and air as well as ground forces. This action was the responsibility of General Nogues, one of the most dubious characters in the Vichy hierarchy, and by Admiral Michelier, whom Professor Morison has described as 'an honourable man'. There is considerable room for speculation as to whether either Nogues or Michelier would have ordered such determined resistance if the secret of the landings had been less well kept and both had been made aware of the strength of the forces that were moving in on Morocco and Algeria. Nogues took it to be merely another Commando raid, and French gunnery officers at Casablanca later testified they had no knowledge for hours of the nationality of the ships at which they were shooting. However, once resistance was offered, 'honour' dictated that it must continue until overcome by force. In three days of fighting the French suffered heavy losses in ships and in men; American losses were not as heavy, but they were deplorable because they were so unnecessary. Furthermore, the delay in landing caused by the resistance gave the U-boats time to assemble and do a considerable amount of damage.

At a White House conference some time later General T. T. Handy, Chief of the Operations Division of the War Department, expressed the opinion that TORCH was unquestionably the most complex operation in military history', and perhaps it still retains that distinction even after OVERLORD. General Marshall had firmly opposed it, and so had General Eisenhower, who is quoted as having described the day when the decision was made by Roosevelt as possibly the 'blackest day in history'. Yet, the decision having been made, it was carried out with extraordinary skill. Counting every mistake that was made in the military operations, it was a brilliant performance. The same could not be said for the concurrent and subsequent political conduct of affairs.

At noon on Sunday, November 8, a few hours after the landings, while there was still fighting at Algiers and Oran as well as on the Atlantic beaches, Secretary Hull suddenly summoned Press correspondents to the State Department for one of the most ill-advised conferences of the war. After all the criticism provoked by the St. Pierre-Miquelon episode, and continued off and on after that trivial episode, it was entirely understandable that Hull would wish to indulge in some gloating at the evidence that the Vichy policy had paid off in North Africa. But his public expressions of triumph were premature. The worst in criticism of Washington's policy was yet to come.

There have been all manner of charges brought in connection with 'the Darlan deal'; it has been said that secret arrangements had been made with him by Robert Murphy three weeks before TORCH and that Darlan's presence in Algiers on the night of November 7 was prearranged and not the surprise and embarrassment to Allied authorities that they pretended. I believe that if such charges were true the fact would have become evident long since, no matter how powerful or comprehensive the attempts to suppress it. If there are those who can accuse Roosevelt and Churchill of being capable of such duplicity—and there are those who can and do accuse them both of every form of perfidy—it is still virtually impossible to imagine Generals Eisenhower and Mark Clark and many other soldiers and sailors suddenly developing the exceptional talents as actors that the performance of this fabulous masquerade would have required. There was no previous deal with Darlan, but there was a degree of unaccountable miscalculation and misinformation which caused a subsequent deal with him to seem to be the only solution.

There may be reason to suspect that Darlan himself had at least an inkling of what was afoot and remained deliberately in Algiers, where he had gone to visit his critically ill son (there was no masquerade about this son's paralysis). According to Murphy, when the grim-visaged French admiral was awakened to receive the news that the Allied forces were moving in early in the morning of D-Day, Darlan turned purple, paced the floor for fifteen minutes, and exclaimed: 'I have known for a long time that the British were stupid, but I always believed the Americans were more intelligent. I begin to believe that you make as many mistakes as they do.' However, it is still possible that he was not taken totally by surprise. As soon as he was sure that this was a full-scale operation, he indicated a quick willingness to do business with the 'stupid' Allies, which represented a complete turning of his anti-British Vichy coat. The records show that within a few hours of his purpling before Murphy—still on the morning of D-Day—he telephoned Nogues in Morocco and ordered him to cease resistance—and it is most important to note that Nogues refused to obey this order.

Whatever Darlan's reasons for being in Algiers on that tremendous

L

occasion, he *was* there, and the consequences of his presence were almost sufficient to ruin Eisenhower's great career as supreme commander before it had even had time to get started.

When Murphy told Darlan that the Americans had brought the noble, gallant General Henri H. Giraud by submarine out of metropolitan France to be the new leader in North Africa, Darlan said: 'He is not your man, for politically he is a child. He is a good divisional commander, nothing more'. This must have come as an affront to Murphy, who had been responsible' for the secret communications with Giraud through General Charles Mast and Jacques Lemaigre-Dubreuil, who, according to Langer, 'long before the war had been prominent in French Fascist movements and might be regarded as a typical example of the French banker and big-business man who was not only ready but eager to play the Nazi game'. According to Murphy, Lemaigre-Dubreuil was a 'courageous, patriotic Frenchman, who hates the Germans and Italians with an intelligent implacability and favours the Allies'.

While Darlan was pacing the floor with Murphy in Algiers, and while Patton off the coast of Morocco was cursing the British and American short-wave radio stations for what seemed to him a premature broadcast of Roosevelt's recorded speech, Eisenhower was having his troubles in a session with Giraud on the Rock of Gibraltar—and the ultimate description of that heated interview can safely be left to Eisenhower himself. A tentative agreement with the proud French soldier was finally reached, and on Monday, the day after the landings, Giraud moved on to Algiers to assume political command of French North Africa. Darlan's estimate—'he is not your man'—proved lamentably correct. Eisenhower issued a public statement which he later regretted: 'It is expected that his [Giraud's] presence there will bring about a cessation of scattered resistance.' All that it did bring about among French colonial authorities was resistance to Giraud. As Roosevelt cabled Churchill two days later:

> In regard to de Gaulle, I have heretofore enjoyed a quiet satisfaction in leaving him in your hands. Apparently I have now acquired a similar problem in brother Giraud. I wholly agree that we must prevent rivalry between the French emigré factions and I have no objection to a de Gaulle emissary visiting Giraud in Algiers. We must remember there is also a catfight in progress between Giraud and Darlan, each claiming full military command of French forces in North and West Africa. The principal thought to be driven home to all three of these prima donnas is that the situation is today solely in the military field and that any decision by any one of them, or by all of them, is subject to review and approval by Eisenhower.

On the same day that cable was sent, November 11, Nogues in Morocco received another order from Darlan to cease fire and this time he obeyed, having fought for three days in defiance of the first order. Nogues's capitulation now may have been due to the fact that on this day the Germans marched into unoccupied France and the Vichy Government, under Pétain and Laval, no longer could maintain even the pretence of independent authority. (Nogues was also influenced by the fact that his remaining forces were by now completely surrounded and further resistance would only mean more French casualties, civilians as well as soldiers, and destruction of much of Casablanca.) In any case, it now seemed evident that Darlan was the only authority who could command the obedience of the French officers in North Africa—and that included Pierre Boisson, Governor of Dakar, and Admiral Jean Pierre Esteva, Governor of Tunisia. (Boisson, who was far from the Germans, did respect Darlan's authority, and the fortress of Dakar went to the Allies without the firing of a shot; Esteva, who was surrounded by Germans, chose to go on collaborating with them.) Therefore, Eisenhower and Clark, with the powerless Giraud on their hands, with long and tenuous lines of communication behind them and the rapid push into Tunisia ahead of them, made the only arrangement which seemed practical or even possible: the deal with Darlan. Eisenhower took full responsibility for this. Roosevelt quoted him as having said later, when they met in Casablanca: 'I believe in a theatre commander doing these things without referring them back to his home Government and then waiting for approval. If a mere General makes a mistake, he can be repudiated and kicked out and disgraced. But a Government cannot repudiate and kick out and disgrace itself—not, at any rate, in wartime.'

However, Eisenhower was not the prime target for the barrage of criticism laid down in the American and British Press and on the radio. Because Hull had been so importunate in claiming a substantial share of the credit for the success in North Africa, he and the State Department were given a huge and unfair share of the blame for a deal which seemed a sordid nullification of the principles for which the United Nations were supposed to be fighting. The widespread protests could be summed up in the statement: 'If we will make a deal with a Darlan in French territory, then presumably we will make one with a Goering in Germany or with a Matsuoka in Japan.'

Liberal opinion in the United States and Great Britain was understandably outraged, and Hull indignantly attributed all of it to 'ideological'—which meant 'Communist'—propaganda. However, in a message sent a few weeks later to Churchill, Stalin said:

It seems to me that the Americans used Darlan not badly in order to facilitate the occupation of Northern and Western Africa. The military diplomacy must be able to use for military purposes not only Darlan, but 'Even the Devil himself and his grandma'.

(Ambassador Maisky in translating this said it was an old and strong Russian proverb.)

On November 14 Roosevelt received a long cable from Eisenhower which I heard him read aloud to Hopkins. It was a remarkable statement of Eisenhower's reasons for the Darlan deal. Roosevelt was deeply impressed by it and, as he read it with the same superb distribution of emphasis that he used in his public speeches, he sounded as if he were making an eloquent plea for Eisenhower before the bar of history. While preparing this book I asked Eisenhower for permission to publish this message in its original form, and he freely granted such permission, but the Security authorities required that it could be published only in paraphrase. No paraphrase can do justice to Eisenhower's actual choice of words, but here is the substance of the message:

Existing French sentiment in North Africa does not even remotely resemble prior calculations and it is of utmost importance that no precipitate action be taken which will upset such equilibrium as we have been able to establish.

The name of Marshal Pétain is something to conjure with in North Africa. From highest to lowest, everyone attempts to create the impression that the shadow of the Marshal's figure dominates all his actions and, in fact, his very life. The military and naval leaders, as well as the civil governors, agree, that only one man has the obvious right to assume the mantle of Pétain and that man is Admiral Darlan. Even General Giraud clearly recognizes this overpowering consideration and he has modified his own ambitions and intentions accordingly. . . .

It must be understood that if we repudiate Darlan and attempt from the outside to dictate the personnel of the coalition to run North Africa, the following will be the consequences:

(a) French armed forces here will resist us passively and, in certain instances, actively.

(b) The hope of securing co-operation in this area will be lost at great cost to us in stagnation of operations and in requirements for additional troops.

(c) The opportunity for gaining some assistance from remaining French naval and military units in North Africa will disappear.

(d) The last glimmer of hope with respect to the Toulon Fleet will be gone.

(e) Admiral Esteva, in Tunis, will not co-operate and our hope of getting Tunisia quickly will not be attainable. Admittedly, Esteva may already be helpless, but there is still a chance of his being able to assist.

Admiral Cunningham and General Clark, together with my full staff, have assisted me in making what we consider to be the only possible workable arrangement designed to secure advantages and avoid disadvantages. No one who is not on the ground can have a clear appreciation of the complex currents of prejudice and feeling that influence the local situation. Also, it should be clear that General Giraud's earnest participation in this arrangement indicates the necessity for the agreements we have made.

In the event the British and U.S. Government, after analysis of this radio, are still dissatisfied with the nature of the agreement made, I suggest that a mission of selected U.S. and British representatives (including the Free French if deemed advisable) be dispatched immediately to Algiers, where they can be convinced in short order of the soundness of the moves which have been made.

Roosevelt attached great importance to Eisenhower's confession of astonishment at the situation as he found it in North Africa; it did 'not even remotely resemble prior calculations'. When the supreme commander of a major military operation makes an admission like that it indicates that there must have been something wrong with his Intelligence Service. This is all the more surprising since North Africa had not been enemy territory, into which secret agents could be introduced only with the utmost difficulty and at their own extreme peril, but was friendly territory with which the U.S. maintained diplomatic relations. Therefore, the headquarters of Robert Murphy in Algiers and all the American consulates in that area and in Spanish Morocco were centres of Intelligence with large staffs which included observers of undoubted competence as well as courage. Yet Eisenhower was astonished when the local French failed to hail Giraud as a conquering hero. This led to a display of political crudity which made the U.S. Government look ridiculously amateurish.

Roosevelt made no bones of his own attitude, publicly as well as privately. Two days after the Eisenhower cable the storm of criticism of the Darlan deal had reached such proportions that Hopkins, Rosenman, and I strongly urged the President to issue a statement to the Press. We had a draft of such a statement which had been prepared originally by Elmer Davis and Archibald MacLeish. When Roosevelt read it he made substantial revisions, all of them calculated to make the language tougher and more uncompromising. The statement as he issued it was as follows:

I have accepted General Eisenhower's political arrangements made for the time being in Northern and Western Africa.

I thoroughly understand and approve the feeling in the United States and Great Britain and among all the other United Nations that in view of the history of the past two years no permanent arrangement should be made with Admiral Darlan. People in the United Nations likewise would never understand the recognition of a reconstituting of the Vichy Government in France or in any French territory.

We are opposed to Frenchmen who support Hitler and the Axis. No one in our Army has any authority to discuss the future Government of France and the French Empire.

The future French Government will be established, not by any individual in Metropolitan France or overseas, but by the French people themselves after they have been set free by the victory of the United Nations.

The present temporary arrangement in North and West Africa is only a temporary expedient, justified solely by the stress of battle.

The present temporary arrangement has accomplished two military objectives. The first was to save American and British lives, and French lives on the other hand.

The second was the vital factor of time. The temporary arrangement has made it possible to avoid a 'mopping-up' period in Algiers and Morocco which might have taken a month or two to consummate. Such a period would have delayed the concentration for the attack from the West on Tunis, and we hope on Tripoli. . . .

Admiral Darlan's proclamation assisted in making a 'mopping-up' period unnecessary. Temporary arrangments made with Admiral Darlan apply, without exception, to the current local situation only.

I have requested the liberation of all persons in North Africa who have been imprisoned because they opposed the efforts of the Nazis to dominate the world, and I have asked for the abrogation of all laws and decrees insp red by Nazi governments or Nazi ideologists. Reports indicate that the French of North Africa are subordinating all political questions to the formation of a common front against the common enemy.

It will be noted how frequently Roosevelt inserted the word 'temporary' into that statement. This was a fact which certainly did not escape the attention of Darlan himself. He wrote a rather plaintive letter to Clark saying that Roosevelt's words tended to substantiate the view that 'I am only a lemon which the Americans will drop after they have squeezed it dry'. He expressed the hope that the U.S. Government would appreciate the difficulties of his position and 'not give Frenchmen the impression that the authority of the leader which has brought it [French Africa] back into the struggle is a diminished one'.

In addition to his statement to the Press, Roosevelt together with Hopkins drafted the following message to Eisenhower:

Marshall has shown me your dispatch giving your reasons for placing Darlan in charge of the civil administration of North Africa. I want you to know that I appreciate fully the difficulties of your military situation. I am therefore not disposed to in any way question the action you have taken. Indeed, you may be sure of my complete support of this and any other action you are required to take in carrying out your duties. You are on the ground and we here intend to support you fully in your difficult problems.

However, I think you should know and have in mind the following policies of this Government:

1. That we do not trust Darlan.

2. That it is impossible to keep a collaborator of Hitler and one whom we believe to be a Fascist in civil power any longer than is absolutely necessary.

3. His movements should be watched carefully and his communications supervised.

I have not consulted Churchill in regard to this message, but I am sending a copy of it to him at once and I am sure he will approve.

I want to add a personal note to you and Clark to tell you what great confidence we have in both of you and how satisfied we are with the progress of events. This message is not to be made public.

This message was written to make clear on the permanent record just how Roosevelt viewed this malodorous situation.

The whole Darlan deal, and the tremendous repercussions therefrom, provided much material for the de Gaulle propagandists who were broadcasting regularly from London and from Brazzaville in Equatorial Africa. It also inspired plenty of gleeful quips by Goebbels and his satellite broadcasters in Rome and Paris and throughout Europe. It seemed to confirm the impression that, while the Americans talked big about the principles of the Four Freedoms and the Atlantic Charter, they actually knew nothing about Europe and could be hoodwinked by any treacherous gangster who offered them collaboration.

I think I am justified in expressing the opinion that the British Foreign Office derived a certain private satisfaction from the embarrassment of the U.S. Government throughout the Darlan affair and its ridiculously protracted aftermath. The British could assume a very virtuous position of loyally supporting an Ally, but taking no direct responsibility for the Ally's political blunders. There was no doubt that, in the first place, Churchill and his colleagues were not happy about Roosevelt's insistence that the North African operation should be proclaimed an entirely American affair, even to the extent of putting American insignia on aircraft of the R.A.F. and American uniforms on British troops. It was obvious that the British, after their long, lonely struggle to keep alight the flame of European liberty, would hardly relish the spectacle of the Americans suddenly becoming the noble liberators of Europe. But the unfortunate developments in North Africa tended to change all that. Churchill made it clear to the House of Commons that 'neither military nor politically are we directly controlling the course of events'. He also made it clear that he gave his vigorous support to the decisions of President Roosevelt and of the generals in whom Roosevelt had reposed confidence. Churchill has subsequently stated in a letter to me that he had no previous knowledge of the negotiations with Admiral Darlan, but he would not have hesitated to deal with him, in the circumstances which befell Generals Eisenhower and Clark. In his messages to the President, however, Churchill urged strongly that the British and American Governments must find a means of reconciling the positions of Giraud and de Gaulle, so as to frustrate the taunting accusations of the enemy propagandists that each Ally had its own 'pet' Frenchman.

It was a time, indeed, when recriminations between the United Nations were not in order. It was a time when the news from all fronts was incredibly good.

The great British victory at El Alamein had been concluded just before the landings in North Africa, and approximately a week later the Red Army turned to the offensive at Stalingrad. On the night of November 12 the naval battle of Guadalcanal, which lasted twenty-four minutes and which Admiral King described as 'one of the most furious sea battles ever fought', shattered the last formidable Japanese attempt to drive American forces from their positions in the Solomons. In that brief but important action, two American admirals were killed—Norman Scott and Daniel Callaghan—the latter Roosevelt's former Naval Aide and great friend.

In a speech to the New York Herald-Tribune Forum on November 17, Roosevelt said:

> During the past two weeks we have had a great deal of good news and it would seem that the turning-point in this war has at last been reached. But this is no time for exultation. There is no time now for anything but fighting and working to win.

We tried to persuade the President to go further than that—to say something like 'the tide has definitely turned'—but he insisted on using the cautious subjunctive. I doubt that careful study of all the words that he spoke would reveal any statement about the progress of the war that could be termed even slightly overoptimistic. In this case, however, his caution was of no particular avail. The newspapers featured the one phrase, 'TURNING-POINT OF WAR REACHED SAYS F.D.R.'—and the public took that assurance as final.

Churchill, whose record on hopeful utterances was not quite equal to

Roosevelt's, was even more cautious at this time. He summed up the situation in his famous words, 'Now, this is not the end. It is not even the beginning of the end. But it is, perhaps, the end of the beginning.' In the same speech he made an even more famous statement: 'Let me, however, make this clear, in case there should be any mistake about it in any quarter. We mean to hold our own. I have not become the King's First Minister in order to preside over the liquidation of the British Empire.' Churchill had waited a long time for an opportunity to say just that. He had suffered and seethed when Roosevelt urged him to establish an independent, federated India, when Roosevelt proclaimed that the principles of the Atlantic Charter extended also to the Pacific and Indian Oceans and everywhere else on earth, when the Australian and New Zealand Governments insisted on withdrawing crack divisions from the Middle East; he had even consented now and then to refer to it as the British *Commonwealth*. But now, with the wine of victory coursing in his veins, he hurled at all and sundry, at friend as well as foe, the defiance that he never for one instant had abandoned: 'Here we are and here we stand, a veritable rock of salvation in this drifting world.'

On the evening of the day, November 9, that Churchill made this speech he had a conversation with Winant, Eden, and General 'Beedle' Smith which lasted, according to Smith's report to Marshall, 'the greater part of the night'. Churchill wanted Marshall, King, and Hopkins to return to London for another full-dress conference on future plans. He was reluctantly abandoning the idea of JUPITER, the Norwegian operation, and turning to the thought of getting Turkey into the war with her forty-five divisions of superior fighting men armed and equipped by the Allies for an invasion of the Balkans. According to Smith's report, Churchill appeared to be cooling on the ROUNDUP plan for Northern France, except as an ultimate deathblow against an opponent tottering and reeling from blows struck elsewhere (the soft underbelly).

Nevertheless, two weeks later Churchill was cabling Roosevelt in great concern over what appeared to be American abandonment of ROUNDUP in 1943. This, he said, 'would be a most grievous decision'. He said that TORCH could be considered no substitute for ROUNDUP. He conceded that it might not be possible to mass the necessary strength for an invasion of Northern France in 1943, but 'if so it becomes all the more important to make sure we do not miss 1944'. He repeated the hope that Hopkins, Marshall, and King would come to London or that he and his staff go to Washington.

Roosevelt replied as follows:

Of course we have no intention of abandoning the plans for ROUNDUP. It is impossible for anyone to say now whether or not we will be given the opportunity to strike across the Channel in 1943. But we must obviously grasp the opportunity if it comes. Determination as to the strength of the forces that we should apply to BOLERO in 1944 is a matter requiring our joint strategic considerations. My present thought is that we should build up our present striking force in the United Kingdom as rapidly as possible, this force to be available immediately in the event of a German collapse. We should build up a very large force for later use in the event of Germany remaining intact and assuming a defensive position.

The mounting of TORCH, according to the conclusions reached at the meeting last summer in London by the Combined Chiefs of Staff, postponed necessarily the assembling of the required forces in the British Isles. . . . The North African operations must naturally take precedence until we have provided adequately against situations which may possibly develop in Spanish Morocco or in Tunisia. We are much more heavily engaged in the South-West Pacific than I anticipated a few months ago. . . . I believe that we should arrange a military strategic conference between Russia, Great Britain, and the United States as soon as we have knocked the Germans out of Tunisia and secured the danger against any real threat from Spain. It is my hope that the military situation in North Africa will be such that we may hold this conference within a month or six weeks. . . . It is my strong feeling that we must sit down with the Russians round a table. My information is that this conference could be held in Cairo or in Moscow—that we could each be represented by a small group meeting in utmost secrecy—that any conclusions reached at this conference would of course be subject to approval by the three of us. I should in all probability send General Marshall to head up our delegation, but I presume that all of the three Services would be represented. . . . Please advise me what you think of this proposal as soon as you can.

On November 25, Roosevelt held a conference with Leahy, Marshall, King, Arnold, and Hopkins, the record of which was as follows:

The President first discussed the question of what operations should be undertaken as soon as the following have been accomplished in North Africa: first, a secure situation to the south and east of Spanish Morocco; and, second, the complete occupation of Tunisia. He asked General Marshall for his estimate of when Tunisia would be occupied.

General Marshall replied that, unless the Axis forces develop some unforeseen strength, he estimated that the occupation of Tunisia could be accomplished in from two to three weeks, provided that two divisions were sufficient to accomplish the task. He stated that if, on the other hand,

General Eisenhower found it necessary to commit four divisions for the purpose, the complete occupation would take somewhat longer because of the delay involved in assembling this number of troops.

The President then asked General Marshall for his estimate as to the time required for driving Axis forces from Tripoli.

General Marshall replied that, if we succeed in taking Tunisia, and barring the breakdown of General Alexander's forces due to over-extension, the Axis powers would find themselves in an impossible situation in Tripoli and would be forced to evacuate that area by what might be termed attrition.

The President then asked if any information had been received about the fortified position which he had been informed of about ten miles inside of the Tunisian border from Tripoli. He was informed that no reports had been received concerning this position. (A message will be sent to General Eisenhower, asking if any information is available on this subject.)

The President and General Marshall then discussed the possibilities of future operations. Action in Turkey was discussed, and it was agreed that there were many diplomatic questions involved, and that probably Turkey would not consider aligning herself with the United Nations until she had been given considerable armament and other munitions of war. In this connection, General Marshall stated that he felt that, if we were to strengthen the Turkish forces, it would be better to give them small arms and ammunition for their infantry units, but to have the heavier artillery and mechanized weapons manned by American troops.

General Marshall said that before any operations were decided on very careful consideration should be given to the cost of actually clearing the Mediterranean for sea traffic. He felt that the occupation of Sicily, Sardinia, and Crete would be necessary for this, and pointed out that a careful determination should be made of whether or not the large air and ground forces required for such a project could be justified, in view of the results to be expected.

The President then asked General Marshall what he considered to be the lines of action open to the Axis powers.

General Marshall replied that he considered that, in order of probability, their lines of action were as follows: first, occupation of Spain; second; a continued drive through the Caucasus; and, third, an attack against the British Isles.

There followed a discussion concerning the production programme. The President initiated this discussion by stating that the 82,000 combat airplane programme had his approval and must be carried out.

Admiral King and Admiral Leahy advised the President that Mr. Nelson had informed them that if this air programme was carried out many of the essential features of the naval programme could not be accomplished without some delay.

The President was of the opinion that the aircraft programme would not conflict with the Navy programme in any way.

The rest of this discussion was concerned with problems of production and allocation.

This same day Roosevelt cabled Stalin:

> We are going to drive the Germans out of Africa soon, I hope, and then we will give Mussolini's Fascists a taste of some real bombing. I feel sure that they will never stand up under that kind of pressure.
>
> We have hit the Japanese very hard in the Solomon Islands. We have probably broken the backbone of the power of their Fleet. They have still too many aircraft carriers to suit me, but soon we may well sink some more of them. . . . We are going to press our advantages in the South-West Pacific, and I am sure that we are destroying far more Japanese airplanes and sinking far more of their ships than they can build. I send you my warmest congratulations on the most encouraging news that we are receiving from the Stalingrad area.

Roosevelt did not include in this cable the information that the U.S. Navy in the Pacific was at that moment down to its last aircraft carrier and, during most of November, this lone survivor, the *Enterprise*, was damaged and out of action; but a tremendous force of new aircraft carriers was on the way.

Evidently Stalin had broken his long and apparently ominous silence to Churchill with a cable of congratulations on the developments in Egypt and in the TORCH area. On November 24 Churchill cabled Stalin his desire for a tripartite military staff conference—with emphasis on hopes of persuading Turkey to enter the war—and on December 2 Stalin's amiable and even cordial reply was relayed to the White House. Stalin said that he shared Churchill's views on the importance of developing personal relations—that he was grateful for measures taken to resume convoys to Murmansk, despite the difficulties presented by considerable naval operations in the Mediterranean—that he was in full agreement with Churchill and Roosevelt about Turkey and the arrangement of a Moscow conference on future military plans. He hoped that there was no change of mind 'in regard to your promise given in Moscow to establish a Second Front in Europe in 1943'. He said cautiously that the Russian counter-offensive in Stalingrad was so far successful partly because of weather conditions—fog and snow— which interfered with the operations of the Luftwaffe. He expressed the intention of the Russians to start a new offensive on the central front within the next few days.

In the midst of these cabled negotiations, Madame Chiang Kai-shek approached the United States, and Roosevelt sent Hopkins to New York as his representative to extend greetings. Hopkins wrote of this:

Madame Chiang Kai-shek was to arrive on Thursday, November 26, 1942 at Mitchell Field at 9 a.m. I had previously arranged that planes land only at military fields so there would be little probability of her entrance being discovered, because the Chinese were anxious to get her into the hospital before it became known. The plane actually arrived on Friday, November 27, 1942, at 2 p.m., and I met Madame Chiang Kai-shek and drove back to the Harkness Pavilion with her, where they had arranged for her to occupy all of the twelfth floor.

On the trip in she told me that she wanted to make it clear to the President she was here for no other purpose than medical treatment and rest. However, in the same breath she proceeded to raise many questions relating to China and the United States.

She first told me how greatly disturbed they were in China over negotiations between Japan and the United States immediately prior to Pearl Harbour. Everyone in China was afraid that we were going to sell them down the river and she, at any rate, believes that the intervention of a few of us here prevented that from happening and she expressed great gratitude to those of us in the Administration who urged that a firm line be taken with the Japs and that under no circumstances should the Chinese position be compromised.

She expressed more forcibly than I had heard anyone express it before her belief that the two wars against Germany and Japan can both be won, but that the way to do it is to put all our strength into defeating Japan. From what I could gather, she is perfectly willing we should take the pressure off Germany. I did not argue this point unduly with her beyond saying that I thought such a strategy was unfeasible. She seemed strangely uninterested in what our Navy was doing in the Solomon Islands and apparently confined her interest entirely to what we are doing in China proper. She laid great emphasis on keeping the Chinese population in the mood to fight. She felt that they had reached a very low ebb on two occasions; once, prior to Pearl Harbour and once on the collapse of Burma.

She is apparently quite critical of both the British and ourselves in relation to that enterprise, although she did not state so positively. She thinks Stilwell does not understand the Chinese people and that he made a tragic mistake in forcing Chiang Kai-shek to put one of his best divisions in Burma, where it was later lost. She said Chiang Kai-shek did this against his best judgment. . . . [Some words were garbled here]

It is pretty clear she does not like Stilwell and expressed the greatest admiration for Chennault. She spent a good deal of her time in explaining an article in *Life* magazine which attacked the British Government vigorously. She wanted me particularly to read that article as being her point of view.

I told her Mrs. Roosevelt wanted to see her and arranged for an appointment with Mrs. Roosevelt at the hospital the next morning. Inasmuch as the newspapers were bound to get hold of the story, it seemed best to get a news release issued immediately.

After this greeting, Hopkins joined the President at Hyde Park and then returned with him to Washington. For Roosevelt by now was convinced that the major strategic problems of the future could not be settled by the Combined Chiefs of Staff—there must be a face-to-face meeting of the President, the Prime Minister, and Stalin themselves. Hopkins influenced Roosevelt strongly along these lines. His own experience in Moscow had convinced him that there could be no really free discussion with the Russians, on a give-and-take basis, on anything less than the topmost level. Hopkins had been the first effective protagonist of a personal meeting of Roosevelt and Churchill; he was now the ardent protagonist of a meeting of the two of them with the great leader of the Soviet Union. Early in December Averell Harriman returned to London with Oliver Lyttleton, who had been in Washington attempting to straighten out the then enormously confused affairs of the Combined Production and Resources Board. (Nobody, it must be noted, ever succeeded fully in straightening them out.) Roosevelt conveyed messages to Churchill through Lyttleton—as he had indicated in a cable on November 25, previously quoted—and he gave Harriman the express assignment of discussing this proposed Big Three conference with Churchill and reporting back thereon, but not through State Department channels.

Churchill, agreeing to the proposal for a conference, wanted to include Eden in it because of Eden's vital position of authority as member of the War Cabinet as well as Foreign Secretary. But Roosevelt did not want to include Hull at this conference. He realized that if Eden attended it would be only proper that Hull should also be there; so he made it a firm condition that Eden be excluded.

On December 7 Harriman cabled Hopkins that he felt he had been 'thoroughly beaten up' after three talks with the Prime Minister on the arrangements for the forthcoming conference. However, Harriman said, Churchill had finally come to understand Roosevelt's point of view and had agreed to leave Eden out. He continued to insist that he must have his full secretariat and an adequate staff of cipher men to keep his map room going twenty-four hours a day. Churchill also wanted to bring along Lord Leathers because of the vital importance of the shipping factor in all planning.

In the preparations for this and other conferences there were often differences of opinion between Roosevelt and Churchill as to the number of *aides* that each would bring with him. Roosevelt, loving secrecy, and knowing that the more individuals who were made privy to the secret the more chance there was of it becoming public property, liked to travel with the smallest possible staff; Churchill, equally fond of secrecy, but more confident of the discretion of responsible officers, preferred to be accompanied at all important meetings by a large staff of experts.

In his cable to Hopkins Harriman said, 'Khartoum appears to be the most practical oasis', this location being considered at that time because of the continuing hope that Stalin would be able to join the conference. There are no records of cables in the Hopkins papers relative to the invitation to Stalin to meet with Roosevelt and Churchill at this time. Presumably messages relating to this were conveyed through Ambassador Litvinov. Notes written by Hopkins *en route* to Casablanca and included in the next chapter state that Stalin twice refused Roosevelt's 'urgent invitation' to a Big Three meeting, the reason for refusal being his constant concern with the immediate military situation on the Russian Front.

During the latter part of December there were very encouraging signs of the settlement of the always difficult French political situation. Following Roosevelt's 'temporary expediency' statement about the Darlan deal, de Gaulle had made various proposals to Admiral Stark in London looking toward the establishment of French unity and including the suggestion that he himself might go to Washington to discuss these proposals with the President. This suggestion, forwarded by Stark, was accepted and de Gaulle was to leave for Washington on or about Christmas Day. In the meantime, he sent his deputy, General d'Astier de la Vigerie, to Algiers to confer with Eisenhower and Giraud on plans for a new French National Committee to include both de Gaulle and Giraud, replacing the Darlan administration. Evidently these discussions proceeded satisfactorily and Roosevelt was hopeful that the North African political mess was about to be straightened out and that there was to be a final end to all the distasteful talk about the British and American Governments having their own 'pet' Frenchman. However, these hopes were shattered in a sudden, violent manner. On December 24 Darlan was assassinated. Rumours were immediately circulated in Algiers that this was part of a Royalist plot which involved threats of assassination of Eisenhower, Giraud, Murphy and others. Adherents of de Gaulle who had been of great aid to the Allies in the North African landings were accused of participation in this new plot and several of them were arrested and imprisoned. One of them was the brother of d'Astier de la Vigerie. On December 25 de

Gaulle had his luggage packed and, I believe, was on his way to the airport when he was informed that, in view of the consequences of Darlan's assassination, Churchill and Roosevelt had decided that the General's proposed visit to Washington should be cancelled. The beginnings of the achievement of French unity were thereby delayed for five months, during which some animosities deepened to an almost irreparable extent. It was a deplorable mischance.

On December 28 Marshall sent Hopkins the following letter:

DEAR HARRY,

Following in clear text are messages between General Eisenhower and myself concerning the proposed trip:

To General Eisenhower: December 23

Under consideration is plan for U.S. Chiefs of Staff to meet with British Chiefs of Staff in North Africa. Time of meeting will be in near future, but depends upon Tunisian and Spanish situation. Journey would be by air. It is desired that the meeting be held on land. Are there facilities for such a meeting in Fedalla or other detached places in Morocco?

It is proposed to keep the party small, but exact numbers have not been determined. My idea is that Patton will be charged specifically with insuring the necessary secrecy and protection. This would free you to give your entire attention to the battle in the East and to securing the Straits.

Some of the party, including myself, would visit your headquarters. Please give me your opinion on feasibility and practicability of holding meeting as indicated. Do not discuss any of this with British until clearance is given from here.

The President and Prime Minister will be in or join the party later.

To General Marshall: December 24

It is feasible and practicable to hold the meeting indicated in your message. The general area as mentioned is probably best suited and there are locations which will be satisfactory. We will have necessary information available for you when you require it.

To General Eisenhower: December 24

The code word for this project is 'Symbol'. There has been mentioned a hospital being built or prepared in the hills some sixty miles from Oran. Would this be suitable for our purpose? If so, how far is it from airfields? Is the Fedella Hotel, which I previously mentioned, clear of the town? Are there any surrounding buildings?

To General Marshall: December 26

Fedalla Hotel is not clear of town and there are buildings closely adjoining. It is also quite conspicuous from air and sea. Kitchen has been destroyed by shellfire. Hospital in vicinity of Oran is being investigated; details later. Will make further investigation of sites in vicinity of Fedalla where we are confident a suitable place can be found.

To General Marshall: December 28

Churchill's secretary arrived here yesterday with detailed information on the trip. Smith has sent him on reconnaisssance of Casablanca-Fedalla area accompanied by a selected officer of this headquarters. Casablanca-Fedalla area seems to be the only one considered desirable by British and Smith is familiar with facilities and requirements and is making preliminary arrangements based on information we now have as to Churchill's desires. Reconnaissance of area will be completed in about two days and report will be forwarded to you immediately.

Anticipate that security will be provided by Patton's forces and administrative and secretarial and stenographic personnel mainly from this headquarters where competent people are available. Adequate communications will be installed by anticipated date of trip.

On December 29, Eisenhower reported:

Reconnaissance by Churchill's secretary and Smith's representative has found a very suitable site for operation 'Symbol'. It consists of a hotel surrounded by a group of cxcellent villas situated five miles south of Casablanca and one mile inland. Area is detached and lends itself to segregation and can be guarded easily. Airfield is two miles distant, which is satisfactory for B-24's except in very rainy weather. If protracted spell of bad weather precedes Symbol, landing field at Marrakech, 120 miles distant, can be used and onward air carriage can be arranged.

Proposal is to set up two independent establishments, one American, one British, in two first-rate villas which have all essentials and are extremely well appointed in every way. That for President might have been made to order so far as lower floor appointments are concerned and will make movement from room to room easy.

Main group of assistants will live in hotel and in certain smaller villas adjacent. Offices and meals in hotel except for two independent establishments which will cater for themselves. Couriers, clerical personnel can be provided from here for American contingent.

Reconnaissance of Fedalla indicates that hotel there is unsuitably located and has suffered from bombardment. Brigadier Jacob, representing General Ismay, who made his side of reconnaissance agrees with scheme which he feels sure will be satisfactory to Churchill.

M

Please give us earliest possible information as to composition of United States parties and any special advance arrangements required. Smith understands generally what will be needed by American party.

On December 31 there was the usual New Year's Eve party for the family and old friends at the White House. At midnight, as always, the President raised a glass of champagne and proposed a toast to 'the United States of America', and this year he added 'and to United Nations victory'. During the evening a movie had been shown and there were very few of those present who had any idea as to the significance of its selection. It was Humphrey Bogart and Ingrid Bergman in *Casablanca*.

PART V

1943—THE SECOND FRONT

CHAPTER XXVIII

THE CASABLANCA CONFERENCE

ON January 7, 1943, Roosevelt delivered his annual State of the Union Speech to the 78th Congress which had been elected two months previously and in which his usually formidable majority had been all but wiped out. There were expectations that he would seize this opportunity to be tough and quarrelsome with the largely hostile legislators, but this was perhaps the most amiable and conciliatory speech he ever made to the Congress, at any rate since the end of the New Deal honeymoon. The newspapers reported that, during his forty-seven-minute address, he was interrupted forty-five times by applause and even occasional cheers. Although present on this occasion, I cannot vouch for the accuracy of those figures, but I do remember that at the end of the speech the President was given a loud and warm ovation by Republicans as well as Democrats.

Confidence was promoted by the very fact that Roosevelt devoted a large part of his speech to talking about the postwar world. He said:

> Victory in this war is the first and greatest goal before us. Victory in the peace is the next. That means striving toward the enlargement of the security of man here and throughout the world—and, finally, striving for the Fourth Freedom—Freedom from Fear.
>
> It is of little account for any of us to talk of essential human needs, of attaining security, if we run the risk of another World War in ten or twenty or fifty years. That is just plain common sense. Wars grow in size, in death and destruction, and in the inevitability of engulfing all nations, in inverse ratio to the shrinking size of the world as a result of the conquest of the air. I shudder to think of what will happen to humanity, including ourselves, if this war ends in an inconclusive peace, and another war breaks out when the babies of today have grown to fighting age.

As Roosevelt said those words he knew that one month previously at Stagg Field in Chicago the first self-maintaining nuclear chain reaction had been achieved—'the half-way mark on the road to the atomic bomb'.

During the long period of preparation of this speech we tried to persuade the President to say something like: 'It is within the realm of possibility that this 78th Congress may have the historic privilege of aiding in making of the peace'—which, of course, was a way of saying that the war might end before January 1, 1945. That would undoubtedly have brought the house down, but Roosevelt would not go that far in hopeful prophecy. He crossed out the last words and substituted, 'helping greatly to save the world from future fear'. In his analysis of the war situation, which was written with the collaboration of General Marshall, Roosevelt said: 'Great rains and appalling mud and very limited communications have delayed the final battles of Tunisia. The Axis is reinforcing its strong positions.' This provided the most important factor in all the military discussions at the Casablanca Conference. Recorded in the preceding chapter was General Marshall's estimate, of November 25, that the occupation of Tunisia would be accomplished in from two to three weeks '*unless the Axis forces develop some unforeseen strength*'. That development had certainly occurred. Hitler poured such numerous reinforcements by air and by sea across the narrow straits from Sicily that a major campaign was required, and in the end a major victory resulted.

Late in the evening of January 9 Roosevelt and Hopkins left the White House to travel by train to Miami. So complete was the secrecy surrounding this journey that the usual crew of Pullman porters, waiters and cooks was taken off the cars and the service on the train was rendered by the Filipino sailors from Shangri-la. Despite all precautions, the word was quickly passed around Washington that the President had gone off on an important trip; he was said to be heading for various destinations all the way from Siberia to Bagdad. The same rumours attended every one of his journeys during the war, and there were some pompous officials who made it their business to absent themselves from Washington when he did, leaving instructions with their secretaries to say to all telephone calls: 'Mr. So-and-so is out of the city at this time,' in a tone so mysterious that there would be excited whisperings that 'Mr. So-and-so is with the President's party'.

On this trip to Casablanca, Hopkins carried with him for the first and, so far as I know, the only time an unusual certificate of identification, as follows:

To whom it may concern   January 9, 1943.
      This is to certify that the bearer, Mr. Harry L. Hopkins, whose description appears below, is a member of the party of the President of the United States.

Age:	52
Height:	6 feet
Weight:	165 lb.
Hair:	Brown
Eyes:	Brown

                                          signed: Franklin D. Roosevelt
      Register No. 1

The journey from Miami to North Africa was made in a Pan American Boeing clipper, the crew of which, under the command of Captain Howard M. Cone, had been converted from civilian to naval status so that the aircraft operated under Navy orders. During the trip across the South Atlantic and after the arrival at Casablanca, Hopkins wrote some descriptive notes, as follows:

Monday evening, January 11, '43
Trinidad.

We left Miami at 6.05 this morning and landed here at 4.45 p.m., all this after two nights and a day on the train from Washington. Eleanor and Louise [Mrs. Roosevelt and Mrs. Hopkins] said good night at the rear door, and I must say that I didn't like the idea of leaving a little bit, only because Louise had been very unhappy all evening because of the political attacks on us.

(*Note*. This referred, of course, to the legends relative to the yacht, *My Kay IV*, and the Beaverbrook emeralds.)

Admiral Leahy—Admiral McIntire, the President's doctor, Captain McCrea, his Naval Aide—and a half-dozen Secret Service men, Arthur, his butler, two or three army officers, made up the party. Grace Tully was going along as far as Jacksonville.

To bed early and up late with a long, sleepy Sunday through the Carolinas and Georgia to Miami. We were called at 4.30 Monday morning. Knowing my airplane capacity, I ate nothing—found the President alone in his car and we laughed over the fact that this unbelievable trip was about to begin. I shall always feel that the reason the President wanted to meet Churchill in Africa was because he wanted to make a trip. He was tired of having other people, particularly myself, speak for him around the world. For political reasons he could not go to England, he wanted to see our troops, he was sick of people telling him that it was dangerous to ride in airplanes. He liked the drama of it. But above all, he wanted to make a trip.

(*Note*. I do not know what Hopkins meant by 'political reasons'. It seems improbable that, more than a year after Pearl Harbour, and nearly two years before the next election, Roosevelt should have been worrying about the Irish vote. On a later occasion, I believe, Hopkins advised the President against going to England, as he would have received a tremendous ovation and some Americans might have disapproved of that in wartime.)

The genesis of it was this. Last July, Marshall, King, and I went to London. I had told the President that there seemed to be no determination on the part of the Chiefs of Staff of either the U.S. or England to fight in 1942. This in spite of the fact that Marshall and I had gone to England in April '42 when the plan to cross the Channel was agreed upon. But it dragged—in spite of Marshall, and it was obvious that nothing was going to happen. The result of that trip was the landing in N. Africa in November 1942. On the assumption that we are going to drive the Germans out of Africa it became clear to me that there was no agreed-upon plan as to what to do next. We had to strike somewhere—across the Channel, at Sardinia, Sicily or through Turkey. But where?

Furthermore, I told the President that the next major strategic move should not be made without consultation with Stalin. Twice Stalin refused the urgent invitation of the President to meet with himself and Churchill. The Russian Front was too urgent. The next best thing was a meeting between Churchill, Roosevelt, and their respective staffs. And the President wanted to meet in Africa. Churchill agreed. The Army had found a safe place outside of Casablanca. And we are off to decide where we shall fight next. King, Marshall, and their *aides* are ahead of us by two days to iron out all possible differences in advance.

The President was carried on to the plane this morning in the dark— it taxied out of the harbour and long before sunrise took off with few people knowing the President was on his way to Africa. I sat with him, strapped in, as the plane rose from the water—and he acted like a sixteen-year-old, for he had done no flying since he was President. The trip was smooth, the President happy and interested. Dr. McIntire was worried about the President's bad heart—nothing happened—he slept for two hours after lunch. He asked the pilot to go over the Citadel in Haiti. We saw no ships and made a perfect landing at the Naval Base in Trinidad. The Admiral and General met us—took us for cocktails and dinner at an hotel run by the Navy. And at 9 to bed, for we are to be called at 4.15 a.m.

The next notes were written by Hopkins during the flight from Belem, Brazil, to Bathurst:

Tuesday evening, January 12—

And on the dot of 4.15 I was called after a good healthy sleep. Dr. McIntire told me that Leahy was running a fever and would have to be left behind. This is a tough break for him. I felt that he never had his heart in this trip and was going only because the President wanted him to. He doesn't seem to be unhappy at the idea of remaining in Trinidad till we get back.

We had a leisurely breakfast with Admiral Oldendorf and General Pratt—the President still treats it as a first-class holiday—he told some of his old favourite stories and seemed to be in no hurry to get off, though the Secret Service were having fits. We drove down to the dock in the dark, having seen but a handful of soldiers, and this visit will be exposed to the public only by a photograph taken by a Navy photographer at dinner.

The ship took to the air beautifully and the ride all the way to Belem
—we landed at 3.15 p.m.—was as smooth as glass. We flew though at
about 9,000 feet, and McIntire was quite disturbed about the President,
who appeared to be very pale at times. We flew over the Citadel in
Haiti—the wild wastelands of Honduras—hit the South American coast
and Dutch Guiana. We flew over acres of desolate jungle. Why anyone
should want to explore them is beyond me. The Amazon delta is a great
sight, with the river mouth widening out to a width of one hundred
miles—the equator cutting it in two. Belem is now a thriving Brazilian
port—about ten merchant ships—a coastguard cutter—and dozens of
small native fishing craft. We have established a Ferry Command post
there, and 250 American soldiers move all the bombers that go to Africa
to the next hop, Natal. The other day they put fifty-two planes through
in twenty-four hours.

We drove to the Officers' Quarters—and were given a first-class rum
drink—(I wangled two bottles and a cold turkey to take to Africa). Jonas
Ingram, who commands our operating fleet in the South Atlantic, was
there—a hearty, ribald, fighting Admiral that suits me. I saw four or
five officers that I knew in Washington. We left at six, getting off just at
dark.

Bathurst—W. Africa—
Wednesday evening, January 13, 1943—

They serve cocktails on this flying boat—everybody was feeling pretty
good, so we had one before dinner last night. But everyone was dog-
tired, so we turned in early. The President slept late, his first night on an
airplane, and woke up in the best of spirits. McCrea had an earache—
the heating system on the stove went out—I taught Ross McIntire gin-
rummy—talked to the President about our pending conference—read a
detective story—saw three escort vessels hunting something (I learned
later they thought we were out of gas)—and finally got dressed after
sighting land. A long, tiresome trip of eighteen and a half hours.

We landed in this big harbour at the mouth of the Gambia River—an
old slave post. The cruiser Memphis and one of our destroyers are in port.
Captain McCown met us—we took a trip around the harbour in a motor
whaleboat. The President was hoisted to the deck and one of the men
carrying him slipped as he stepped on to the cruiser and the President
landed on his rear. We had dinner with the Captain. This boat was built
for a flagship—the President has the Admiral's quarters and I have the
Captain's next door.

McIntire heard that we had to fly over mountains 13,000 feet to get
to our rendezvous with Churchill. Something will have to be done about
that in the morning, for the President can't stand that height

The final entry in these handwritten notes (Hopkins never had them typed) was made after the arrival at Casablanca.

Friday morning, January 15, 1943—
The sleeping was none too good on the *Memphis* Wednesday night, so I finished my detective story, only to find on the last page that I had read it before. We breakfasted together—the Secret Service seem to have our destination nicely balled up. McCrea had a good cigar and doesn't care —the President likes it—I think it is very funny that the President of the U.S. doesn't know where he is going to land in N. Africa. The height of the mountains seems to have shrunk during the night.

(*Note.*—The flight from Bathurst to Casablanca was made in an Army C-54 transport plane. There was a deviation from the straight route because Roosevelt wanted to have a look at Dakar, the fortress to which he had given so much attention during the past four years, and at the new French battle-ship *Richelieu* in the harbour there. After crossing the western rim of the Sahara Desert, the aircraft did fly over the Atlas Mountains, but, as Hopkins wrote, they had evidently 'shrunk', as the highest altitude attained was 11,500 feet.)

We got in a motor whaleboat to the dock (at Bathurst)—and a seven-teen-mile ride to the airfield. There we have about 250 men who service our bombers moving from Bathurst north or across Africa into Russia and China. There were about one dozen big bombers on the field. The soldiers had built a big ramp for the President and we took off in a Douglas C-54. The destination proved to be Casablanca—we went seven hours over desert that is hardly worth fighting for—we saw an American air-field used to move fighter planes to the battle areas—it is supplied entirely by air. We crossed the Atlas Mountains—great snow-capped peaks seemed incongruous after the desert. Then we suddenly came on the fertile fields of N. Africa—looking like the Garden of Eden should look and probably doesn't—camels—olive groves—oranges—wheat-fields—no cows—rain—miles of black earth. The President missed nothing. We landed at the airport about fifteen miles from Casablanca. The President's son Elliott was there to meet him. Much 'hush hush', and the President, Elliott, and I were hustled into a car blacked-out with mud to drive to our Villa. It is a lovely, modern, California bungalow—part of an hotel— taken over by the Army. The President, Elliott, and I are staying here.

Churchill has a house about fifty yards away. I went over to bring him back for a drink before dinner. He was in fine form, but looked older. We walked back—and the three of us had a long talk over the military situation. The British Eighth Army is attacking tonight.

(*Note.*—This was the attack at Buerat which led to the capture of Tripoli eight days later and the subsequent advance into Tunisia from the east.)

The two staffs are in the big hotel across the street, and just before dinner I found them all having a cocktail. The President invited the British and American Chiefs to dine with him and Churchill and Averell. Much good talk of war—and families—and the French. I went to bed at twelve, but I understand that the President and Churchill stayed up till two.

There was quite a family gathering in the President's villa, 'Dar es Saada', during the eight days at Casablanca. Aside from Lieutenant Colonel Elliott Roosevelt, there were Lieutenant Franklin D. Roosevelt, jun., U.S.N.R., who was serving on a destroyer with the Atlantic Fleet, Captain Randolph Churchill, of the British Special Service Brigade (Commandos), and Sergeant Robert Hopkins, whom Eisenhower had ordered out of a foxhole in Tunisia. There was some criticism in the American Press on the ground that there were many less fortunate soldiers and sailors overseas who did not get special leave and transportation for visits with their fathers, but Roosevelt paid no attention to this; when he travelled to theatres in which any of his sons were serving, he saw them.

As the most obvious immediate objective for consideration at Casablanca, Churchill repeated a paragraph from a message that he had sent to Roosevelt after the successful conclusion of TORCH and the Battle of El Alamein:

The paramount task before us is, first, to conquer the African shores of the Mediterranean and set up there the naval and air installations which are necessary to open an effective passage through it for military traffic; and secondly, using the bases on the African shore to strike at the under-belly of the Axis in effective strength and in the shortest time.

The Chiefs of Staff had been in session for three days prior to Roosevelt's arrival and had considered the various operations that might be launched after the final defeat of the Germans in Tunisia. The targets for attack which were considered included Sardinia, Sicily, Crete, Rhodes, the Dodecanese Islands, and the mainland of Greece. There was considerable argument before Roosevelt and Hopkins joined the Conference, and there was more argument thereafter, with Marshall still urging the invasion of Northern France in 1943. The U.S. Chiefs of Staff appear to have been by no means unanimous at this Conference: King as a sea-power man saw the enormous advantage of increased security in the Mediterranean, and Arnold as an air-power man could not fail to be tempted by the prospect of obtaining such advanced bases as Foggia in Italy. By Monday, January 18, four days after Roosevelt's arrival, the Combined Chiefs of Staff had agreed on the decision to attack Sicily, and this proposed operation was given the code name HUSKY. In

Marshall's words, this decision was made 'because we will have in North Africa a large number of troops available and because it will effect an economy in tonnage which is the major consideration. It is estimated that possession of the North coast of Africa and Sicily will release approximately 225 vessels which will facilitate operations in Burma, the Middle East, and the Pacific.' Not only would occupation of Sicily deprive the enemy of the base from which to attack Allied shipping in the Mediterranean at its narrowest point, it would give the Allies a base for the establishment of much broader air coverage for their shipping in the Mediterranean—their only base up to then having been lonely little Malta. Marshall said that another consideration in favour of the operation against Sicily was 'the possibility of eliminating Italy from the war'.

However, in so far as Hopkins was concerned, he was again disappointed and depressed by the further postponement of ROUNDUP; he was always solidly with Marshall in the conviction that there was no really adequate substitute for the opening of a Second Front in France. Plans were made at Casablanca for a large operation known as ANAKIM in Burma—a land offensive in the north for the purpose of re-opening the Burma Road and an amphibious operation in the south to recapture the port of Rangoon. Rabaul on the island of New Britain was named as the next main objective in the South Pacific—but this attack was never made, and Rabaul was one of the strongpoints that remained isolated in Japanese hands to the end of the war, its effectiveness nullified by surrounding operations.

The purpose of the Casablanca Conference had been almost entirely military, but Roosevelt and Churchill immediately became involved in the politics of the inescapable French situation. There had been another and even more violent outburst of criticism in the United States and Britain over the tendency to deal with the discredited men of Vichy. This criticism was all the more bitter because of the emphatic assurances given by Roosevelt in his 'temporary expediency' statement. Added to other powerful voices in the United States was that of Wendell Willkie, who had been persuaded by Stimson to tone down his protests during the Darlan period, but who was now ready to roar.

Before Darlan's assassination Murphy had sent a message to the State Department saying that Darlan felt that Marcel Peyrouton would be of great help to him in the government of North Africa, since Peyrouton had a reputation as an able administrator in that area, particularly in his knowledge of the many problems of the Arabs in Tunisia. Murphy therefore urged, in Darlan's behalf, that Peyrouton be given authorization and transportation to Algiers from Buenos Aires, where he was living in self-imposed exile. Hull approved this, and arrangements were accordingly made in a routine manner and, as Roosevelt later stated, without his knowledge. Peyrouton went to Rio de Janeiro to await transportation by air to Africa, and early in January Press correspondents discovered his presence there and the probable reasons for it. The newspapers presented the unsavoury details of Peyrouton's record as a particularly brutal Minister of the Interior in the Vichy Government. (He had later gone as Ambassador to Argentina, where his activities were also suspect.) Apparently the only good thing to be said for him was that he hated Laval, had been largely responsible for the overthrow of Laval in December, 1940, and had even recommended to Pétain that Laval be shot. When Laval returned to power in 1942 Peyrouton resigned his post as Ambassador, choosing to remain in Buenos Aires for obvious reasons.

When Sumner Welles learned of Peyrouton's presence in Rio he gave orders for the cancellation of his further passage, and when Hull learned of Welles's orders he overruled them, taking the position that the State Department should not assume responsibility for denying a request by Murphy which had been transmitted with the authority of General Eisenhower. (All cables out of North Africa were signed with Eisenhower's name.) So Peyrouton went on to Algiers, arriving there about the same time Roosevelt arrived at Casablanca. The outraged protests from the United States and Britain were plainly audible in the villa 'Dar es Saada'. St. Pierre and Miquelon were alive again.

On the first day of the Casablanca Conference, Roosevelt conferred with Churchill, Hopkins, Eisenhower, Murphy, and Harold Macmillan, whom Churchill had sent to Algiers after the TORCH operation to serve with Murphy as political adviser to General Eisenhower. After the first of these meetings, Roosevelt remarked to Hopkins: 'Ike seems jittery.' Eisenhower had ample reason to seem jittery. He had been suffering from a bad cold pretty steadily since coming to North Africa, and he had been forced to take to his bed with severe grippe just before the assemblage of 'Top Brass' was to descend on him at Casablanca. Although the initial operation under his command had been an inspiring success, he had subsequently seen the high hopes for quick victory in Tunisia frustrated; far worse than this for a good soldier was the bewildering political mess in which he found himself involved and for which he was so ill prepared.

As Butcher recorded in his diary, 'Eisenhower's neck is in a noose, and he knows it'. However, he stated his case to the President and Prime Minister with courage and candour. He made no attempt to disguise his ignorance of European politics, having spent most of the prewar years in the Philippines. He said that when the name of Peyrouton was mentioned to him by Darlan and Murphy he had no idea who the man was and no knowledge of his background, except that he had once been a successful official in Algiers, Tunisia, and Morocco. Eisenhower felt that this appointment should be checked with the State Department, which first said 'Yes' to it and then 'No' and finally 'Yes'. (Eisenhower, of course, did not know that the 'No' was from Welles and the final 'Yes' from Hull.) He defended his much-criticized action in imposing political censorship on North Africa on the ground that the de Gaullists were pouring hostile propaganda from their station in Brazzaville, and he did not want to advertise the conflict to the world by permitting the radio stations in Morocco or Algiers to talk back in this verbal war. (Years later, however, Eisenhower said to me that he believed this action had been a mistake—that 'censorship is never the answer'.)

It was on this occasion that Eisenhower made the previously quoted remark to Roosevelt that generals could make mistakes and be fired, but that governments could not. He was entirely ready to take the rap for whatever went wrong.

For a time there was some doubt whether Eisenhower would remain in supreme command for HUSKY. General Alexander, who outranked him, was now moving into Tunisia from the south with the victorious British forces under the field command of General Montgomery. Here was tough professional competition for Eisenhower at a moment when his own position was most insecure, and I believe he would not have been greatly surprised if he had been put under Alexander or transferred elsewhere. However, he was given the supreme command and a fourth star, which made him equal in rank to his subordinates, Alexander, Cunningham, and Tedder. In announcing this later to the House of Commons Churchill said: 'I have great confidence in General Eisenhower. I regard him as one of the finest men I have ever met.' What weighed most heavily with Churchill and Roosevelt in arriving at this decision, aside from Marshall's persistent faith in Eisenhower, was the tremendous admiration and affection for him of the British officers who had served with him, most importantly Admiral Cunningham, a fighting sailor who was held in very high esteem by the two Naval Persons. Thus, Eisenhower had achieved his first important victory in the merging of officers of two nations and three services into one effective and harmonious command. After Hopkins returned to Washington from Casablanca he told me that Eisenhower had said to Patton: 'I don't mind if one officer refers to another as that son of a bitch. He's entitled to his own opinion. But the instant I hear of any American officer referring to a brother officer as that *British* son of a bitch, out he goes.' Eisenhower maintained that basic policy with historic success all the way into Berlin, where he added the adjective 'Russian' to 'British'. His phenomenal and painful education of himself in the complex politics of Europe was perhaps the most brilliant of his great achievements.

Eisenhower left Casablanca on the second day of the Conference and flew back to Allied Force Headquarters in the centre of the arc of hills that make a beautiful amphitheatre of Algiers. He had promised Hopkins that he would promptly see Peyrouton and try to find out about him. The next day,

January 17, he sent a letter addressed to Hopkins 'somewhere in Africa' as follows:

DEAR HARRY:

I sent you a message today following a conference with Peyrouton, who just called at my office. He recited his past history to me, and one thing that struck me was that the day Laval returned to power, Peyrouton sent in his resignation as French Ambassador to Argentina. This may or may not be true, but it could easily be checked. He seems to be a realist, and the general views he expressed were contained in the telegram I sent you.

I cannot tell you how valuable it was to me to have the chance to talk to the President and yourself and to the Combined Chiefs of Staff, particularly General Marshall. There is no doubt that great good will came out of your meeting there, and I often regret that you people who are occupying the top positions cannot get together with greater frequency.

I am enclosing with this letter a short note to the President, which I request that you pass on to him if you think it an appropriate one.

If you can possibly get up here, I assure you of a warm welcome, and I will do all in my power to let you see everything that can be arranged within the time you may have.

With warm personal regard,

Cordially,
signed: IKE EISENHOWER

On January 16 Roosevelt sent the following cable to Hull:

General Giraud arrives here tomorrow, and Mr. Churchill and I have arranged that General de Gaulle shall be brought here on Monday. I feel sure that the British can be brought around to our point of view, and it appears that we must get a civilian into the administrative picture here. Apparently Giraud lacks administrative ability and the French Army officers will not recognize de Gaulle's authority. Since there are no French civilians readily available in this area, what would be your opinion of having Jean Monnet come here? It appears he has kept his skirts clear of political entanglements in recent years, and my impression of him is very favourable. I believe that Morgenthau knows and trusts Monnet. It had been my hope that we could avoid political discussions at this time, but I found on arrival that American and British newspapers have made such a mountain out of rather a small hill that I should not return to Washington without having achieved settlement of this matter. All well here, and I send you affectionate regards. I am particularly anxious that the mention of Monnet be kept completely secret, as everything will be spoiled if there is any leak.

The suggestion of the name of Monnet, which was made largely at Hopkins's instigation, did not find favour with Hull, who replied that from the information available to him he was not disposed to believe that Jean Monnet was the right man for the job. He said that Monnet had been identified with the banking firm of Lazard Frères, which was closely tied in with the de Gaulle organization in London, and Monnet had dealt extensively with Pleven, who acted as de Gaulle's adviser on foreign affairs. These associations, according to Hull, 'would clearly create doubts in a great many French minds'. Hull added that any Frenchman who received British and American endorsement in the North African situation must be of such quality that there could be no question as to 'his outstanding integrity and his loyalty to all the best elements of France'—and Hull certainly was not inclined to include the leaders of the Free French Movement among such elements.

Hull suggested as alternative candidates for Peyrouton's job Roger Cambon and Alexis Leger. However, Giraud convinced Roosevelt and Churchill that Peyrouton was the only man with experience enough to handle the immeasurably difficult situation, and his appointment as Governor-General of Algeria was announced on January 19. When Roosevelt was asked later if he had approved the sending of Peyrouton to North Africa he replied that he had not approved it or even known about it. Churchill also stated that he had known nothing of the transfer of Peyrouton from Argentina, but, in the light of what he learned at Casablanca, he found no fault with the step.

A month later Hopkins persuaded the President to authorize the sending of Monnet to North Africa to work with Giraud on handling the substantial Lend-Lease supplies for the equipping of the French Army. This was one of several occasions when Hopkins was successful in circumventing the State Department.

Roosevelt's statement in his message to Hull that de Gaulle would arrive 'Monday' proved overconfident. Anthony Eden was having plenty of trouble in London. On January 17, Eden handed de Gaulle the message from Churchill inviting him to Casablanca. 'When he had finished reading it,' Eden reported, 'he expressed no pleasure.' (One might observe that, in this sentence, Eden made a strong bid for the British and therefore world's understatement championship.) De Gaulle was offended because he had not been notified in advance of the impending Conference, as he had not been notified in advance of the landings in North Africa. Eden could hardly explain that both these circumstances had been due to Roosevelt's insistence that previous information to de Gaulle might jeopardize military security. This implied no disrespect for the general as a military man of honour. It reflected Roosevelt's belief that the de Gaulle organization contained a superabundance of Press agents.

De Gaulle told Eden and through him Churchill that he had sent Giraud several messages suggesting a meeting, but had received no favourable response. He said he would be glad to conduct 'simple and direct talks with Giraud', but not in 'the atmosphere of an exalted Allied forum'. He felt that such an atmosphere would suggest to the world the application of 'pressure' on the two French leaders.

Roosevelt became more and more irritated by de Gaulle's refusal to budge. If French political problems had constituted nothing more than 'a rather small hill', as he said in his message to Hull, he would have been only too glad to laugh off this situation and forget it, leaving de Gaulle to sulk in his tent on Carlton House Terrace, but Roosevelt knew what the criticism would be if he returned to Washington without having achieved any rapprochement between de Gaulle and Giraud. There were a great many jokes back and forth between the villas about getting the 'bridegroom' together with the 'bride', but the situation was essentially a serious one and everybody knew it. Roosevelt was uncomfortable and unhappy about the squabbles over French politics because the newspapers and columnists and radio commentators who were loudest in their denunciation of this manifestation of American policy were, for the most part, the most ardent supporters of Roosevelt's liberal policies, both foreign and domestic.

In the Hopkins papers is an unsigned memorandum dated December 24, 1942, the very day of Darlan's assassination, which seems to me an admirable statement of Roosevelt's fundamental point of view in dealing with the French problem:

The sovereignty of France rests with the French people. Only its expression was suspended by German occupation. The indispensable element for the restoration of France is the assurance of conditions making that expression possible when the time comes.

No French political authority can exist or be allowed to attempt to create itself outside of France. It is the duty of the United States and Great Britain to preserve for the people of France the right and opportunity to determine for themselves what government they will have, and the French people as well as the world must receive that solemn assurance.

The present dissensions are due to the concealed competition for future political power. De Gaulle seeks recognition by England and the United States on the basis of suppressed but assumed endorsement by the French people. Darlan will attempt to build a régime on the basis that he represents Pétain, the regularly constituted régime of France.

The sympathy of the French that expressed itself for de Gaulle, reflects not a choice of de Gaulle as the future head of the French Government, but the French anxiety to continue to *fight* Germany alongside of England

N

and the United States. They would, however, certainly resist a government, even if provisional, which would owe its initial authority to foreign
recognition. The basis of legitimacy which permitted Darlan to effectively
bring North Africa alongside the Allies, is due to the fact that he represented what was then the existing constituted authority of Vichy. He
was thus able to give orders which were followed by the local military
commanders and the local administration. Indeed, while as it has been
proved since, most responsible officials wanted at heart to co-operate
with America and Great Britain, their action had to be determined by an
order from the regular central authority. Men entrusted with authority
in an orderly society are not revolutionaries, and it is to be revolutionary
to act contrary to the orders of the central accepted authority. Admiral
Darlan gave the order that was wished for—but the order had to be
given. He alone could give it, not General Giraud at that time.

But now that this has been done, and that the various local commanders have sided with the Allies, it is important to prevent the use
which Darlan made of Pétain's authority from being developed into a
legitimacy recognized or fostered by the Allies. Such a development in
North Africa would be a denial of those conditions which alone will
enable the French people to give free expression to their sovereignty.

In those paragraphs may be found the basic reasons for Roosevelt's refusal
to recognize any provisional government of France whether headed by
de Gaulle or by anyone else. But the clash of personalities and the deplorable
tendency of the State Department to hold and repeatedly to assert old grudges
gave to these relationships qualities that were as unnecessary as they were
unhappy. Throughout the years of war, Roosevelt fluctuated considerably
in his attitude toward de Gaulle, and so did Churchill—but they seldom
fluctuated the same way at the same time.

On January 19 Hopkins dictated the following notes to Chief Ship's Clerk
Terry, who generally travelled with the President as a secretarial *aide*:

Had breakfast with General Arnold. He feels that the Southern Pacific
plans are too vague and that until we get Rabaul it is impossible to make
additional plans, and that material should not be tied up on any theoretical
assumption that we are going to get to Truk.

Arnold feels that in spite of the plan to open the Burma Road which
has been agreed upon here, he is very doubtful that this will be done, and
thinks that the only intelligent move immediately is to strengthen
Chennault's air force and get at the bombing of Japan as soon as possible.
Arnold tells me that he cannot tell exactly how this can be done until
he goes to China after this conference is over. He is sure, however, that
it can be accomplished. He tells me that General Bissell, the Air Force

commander in India, is very antagonistic to Chennault and that that complicates Chennault's supply line. Arnold is very confident, however, that the whole business can be worked out. He tells me that King is asking for airplanes in the South-West Pacific for which at the moment there are no airfields. On the other hand, he realizes we must be ready for any eventuality out there, and Arnold is sure that we can provide all the airplanes that are needed.

Arnold tells me that after the battle is over in Africa both the Germans and ourselves are going to be licking our wounds for a couple of months. After that, the air battle will be one between our bombers and the Italian fighters and anti-aircraft. Arnold tells me that the going is a little tougher here lately and that our losses have been heavier, but we still have knocked down about 1.8 Germans to 1 American. He tells me that he has worked out a satisfactory arrangement with the Middle East Air Command about the oncoming air battle in Tunisia.

Arnold insists that the targets from England are selected by the British, but he seemed to me to be a bit vague on this point, and I am sure that this needs to be settled definitively, so that the Admirals and the Navy can't continue to say that Arnold is picking out some soft targets and is not making an adequate attack on the submarine bases and factories making submarine supplies.

The Prime Minister told me he wanted to see me this morning. He had not yet heard from London about de Gaulle and seemed to be unhappy about the President's decision to close up the conference with the Chiefs of Staff here on Wednesday afternoon.

Had a call from Count Poniatowski, who is acting as General Giraud's civilian *aide*, who wanted to see me, but I sent for Harriman because I had learned that at one time he had been Harriman's brother-in-law.

I arranged with the President about the schedule for the rest of the week. The President agreed that we should close this up at a pretty early date and that he should review the troops on Thursday, have dinner with the Sultan on Friday, and get off to the south not later than Saturday morning.

Had a long talk with Count Poniatowski and Harriman. I did not tell him that de Gaulle had refused to come, because the President thinks that is British business and that they should acquaint Giraud of this fact. The Count told me what they proposed to say to de Gaulle in case he came down. It boils down that they are going to tell him that Giraud is going to be top-dog and that they will be glad to play with de Gaulle all around the world in a secondary capacity. He also told me the things he wanted to take up with the President, which included the adequate arming of the French Army, adjustment of exchange rates, the organization of a new French layout with Giraud in charge and de Gaulle No. 2 man, and then some other vague business about French sovereignty. I told him that there would be no trouble with the President about the arming of the French Army and the exchange rates, although I couldn't say what those rates would be, and I thought the President thought that Giraud should land on top, but as far as sovereignty is concerned, he is treading on very difficult ground, because the President stuck by his position that sovereignty rested exclusively with the French people, and that he would recognize no one, not even Giraud, as representing France. I told Harriman to see the President and tell him what had gone on at this conference, and I went over to see Churchill.

I found Churchill in bed and he told me that while the second raid on Berlin looked pretty good, the weather had been bad and he was not sure how much damage had been done. He told me that he was sure his forces attacking Tripolitania were much further along than they had anticipated and that that was very good. I asked him what was bothering him about winding up the business with the Chiefs of Staff on Wednesday and he told me that he didn't have anything specific in mind, that he thought the Chiefs of Staff were going to work out a pretty good agreement. He did tell me, however, that he intended to fly to Cairo as soon as the President left and work out the new Middle East Command with General Wilson in charge, and that he wanted to meet the President of Turkey perhaps in Cyprus, and push him pretty hard on the business of getting Turkey into the war, and giving us some adequate air bases, and to attack Roumanian oilfields. He told me he intended to take the line that Turkey should not wait until the last minute, but that if they were recalcitrant he would not hestitate to tell the Turks that in the event of their remaining out he could not undertake to control the Russians regarding the Dardanelles and that their position would be intolerable.

I arranged to have dinner with Harriman and Churchill tonight because the President and Elliott are dining with General Patton. The Prime Minister was anxious that the President not tell Giraud that de Gaulle had refused to show up, because he was hoping to get a message from de Gaulle any minute. He said he wanted to come to see the President around five or six o'clock tonight. I went back to the house and told the President that the Prime Minister did not want Giraud told.

I attended the conference between the President, Giraud, Murphy, Captain McCrea, Elliott, and Giraud's military *aide*, Captain Beaufre. The President laid out to Giraud in a masterful fashion his concept of French resistance, emphasizing the fighting. McCrea has made complete minutes of this meeting. I gained a very favourable impression of Giraud. I know he is a Royalist, and is probably a right-winger in all his economic views, but I have a feeling that he is willing to fight. He is about six feet, two inches, and a man of about 63 or 64. He has the appearance of health and vigour. He spoke with a good deal of modesty, but with confidence. Had a feeling that he had made up his mind that he was going to do whatever the President wanted in Africa. Apart from fighting in the war, it is impossible to tell whether or not he has political ambitions. He did not give me that impression, except when he stressed later, with great vigour, his determination to head the civil as well as the military areas in Africa.

Giraud speaks no English, but the President's French seemed to me to be better than usual, and Murphy, who did the interpreting, didn't have much to do. It was only when the President wanted to be perfectly sure that Giraud knew what he was saying on an important matter that he had Murphy interpret. Giraud laid out his problems, which his *aide* had previously told me, and the President settled them all to Giraud's complete satisfaction, but on the sovereignty point he was adamant, and insisted that Giraud, at the moment, act only as a representative in North Africa, and that he not in any sense speak for France, and that the understanding about all other French possessions should be worked out only when de Gaulle arrived. The President and Giraud then went out on the back porch and a flock of Army Photographers took pictures of them, and later of McCrea, Giraud's *aide*, and me, with the President and Giraud. On the whole I thought it was a very satisfactory conference and I am sure that Giraud and the President have mutual confidence in each other.

We had lunch with the President, Averell, Robert, and Elliott. I took a nap after lunch and then General Patton arrived to take Elliott and me downtown to do a little shopping. We went by the docks and saw the beaches on which our men landed at Casablanca and saw how the Navy knocked the hell out of the *Jean Bart*. A great convoy of ours was just steaming into sight. We saw the steel landing-fields for airports being loaded on the trains and American soldiers and sailors everywhere in the city. Shopping was pretty fruitless except for some rugs. I got back to the house about six o'clock and found the Prime Minister and his son, Randolph, talking to the President about this and that. I am going off to dinner with the Prime Minister, Averell, Randolph, and Robert in a few minutes.

Of the deliberations of the Combined Chiefs of Staff at Casablanca Churchill said, 'there never has been, in all of the inter-allied conferences I have known, anything like the prolonged professional examination of the whole scene of the world war in its military, its armament production, and its economic aspects'. Although the production situation was, of course,

682

far better than it had been at the first meeting in Washington a year before, there was one item of insufficiency on the gigantic list which seriously affected all the strategic calculations of the time—and that item was escort vessels. There were not enough destroyers and destroyer escorts to defend the convoys to Russia and to all the other far-flung theatres of war, and there were only two transports, the *Queen Mary* and the *Queen Elizabeth*, with sufficient speed to cross oceans without escort. After the war I asked a group of men who had been engaged in grappling with the production problems whether they could name any outstanding failures, the avoidance of which might have shortened the war; their answer was unanimous—the escort vessel programme.

On January 21 Roosevelt, Hopkins, Harriman, Murphy, and McIntire drove with Patton to Rabat, eighty-five miles north-east of Casablanca, for a visit to the American troops of the Fifth Army, in training there under General Clark's command. The Commander-in-Chief had lunch in the open air with some 20,000 soldiers. The menu: boiled ham, sweet potatoes, green string beans, fruit salad, bread, butter, jam, and coffee. I am indebted to Captain George Durno, former White House correspondent who accompanied the President on the Casablanca trip, for including in his official report the list of selections played by the 3rd Division Artillery Band during lunch that day: 'Chattanooga Choo Choo', 'Missouri Waltz', 'Naughty Marietta Waltz', 'Deep in the Heart of Texas', and 'Alexander's Ragtime Band'.

On that same day, which should have marked the wind-up of the Conference, the welcome news was received that Eden had at last prevailed with de Gaulle, and that the leader of the Fighting French would arrive in Casablanca on the morrow. After Hopkins returned from the trip to Rabat he received a note from Churchill suggesting a programme for the following day, which included this item:

> *Dinner.* At the White House (Dry, alas!); with the Sultan. After dinner, recovery from the effects of the above.

(Roosevelt's villa was always referred to by Churchill as the White House.) Hopkins later wrote the following note on the first meeting of Roosevelt and de Gaulle:

> The General arrived, cold and austere, accompanied by his *aide*, and for the first time met President Roosevelt.
>
> In the middle of the conference I noticed that the whole of the Secret Service detail was behind the curtain and above the gallery in the living-room and at all doors leading into the room, and I glimpsed a tommy gun in the hands of one. I left the conference and went out to talk to the

Secret Service to find out what it was all about, and found them all armed to the teeth with, perhaps, a dozen tommy guns among the group. I asked them what it was all about. They told me they could not take any chances on anything happening to the President. None of this hokus pokus had gone on when Giraud saw the President, and it was simply an indication of the atmosphere in which de Gaulle found himself at Casablanca. To me, the armed Secret Service was unbelievably funny, and nothing in Gilbert and Sullivan could have beaten it. Poor General de Gaulle, who probably did not know it, was covered by guns throughout his whole visit. To the best of my knowledge the Secret Service put on this little act on their own.

I attended all the meetings of the President and de Gaulle. Robert Murphy, I think, was always in attendance. There developed out of these meetings at Casablanca an apocryphal story which I think the President encouraged. The story was that at the first conference de Gaulle compared himself to Clemenceau, while at the next conference he indicated that Joan of Arc was perhaps more his prototype, and the President is alleged to have said to de Gaulle that he should make up his mind which one of these he was really like, because he surely could not be like both of them. This story is pure fiction ... although I heard the President tell the story, indicating that that was the kind of impression General de Gaulle made on him during the various conferences they held. Later, as the President told the story, I have no doubt it took on more authenticity and finally came to be accepted as a fact. Naturally, this story must have gotten back to General de Gaulle, as it was printed very widely in the American papers.

General William H. Wilbur, a Regular Army officer who had just been awarded a Congressional Medal of Honour by the President, wrote the following penetrating report on his own interview with de Gaulle:

January 23, 1943.
I called on General de Gaulle at his villa this afternoon at four o'clock. As we were both in the same class at the Ecole Supérieure de Guerre, we started on a friendly basis. He seemed inclined to unburden himself to me, and told me the entire situation.

He told me that before our arrival in Morocco, his forces were the only French Forces that had been fighting for the liberty of France; that they were the only elements that represented the true France; that without question the whole of the France that is willing to fight for its rights rested with people who were with him. He said that there had grown up the mystery of the Marshal and the mystery of La France Combattant, that these had become almost two religions. He said that the real Marshal

Pétain had died in 1925, and that the present Marshal was weak, was vain, and had the spirit and attitude of a grandfather.

He said that when Darlan came into power he represented the collaborationists. De Gaulle and his people could have no traffic with him. Darlan in his opinion had remained too long.

General Giraud did not in his present position, and could not in his present position, represent the Government of France, because he held a position by virtue of the vote of Nogues, Boisson, and Chatell, all of whom were representatives of the Vichy Government.

He said that he had offered General Giraud the command of the troops, but that General Giraud in his present position could not represent the true France. His thesis was that General Giraud should join the France Combattant, rather than that the Gaullists should join the present Government.

He said that it was perfectly possible that the United States might make the decision that he should be deprived of supplies and equipment, and that under such circumstances England and the others would have to agree to the United States' decision and that he, de Gaulle, would have to fold up.

He said that even if General Giraud succeeded in reaching France at the present time, he would find that the people would rise against him and that communism would result. I told him that as a friend of France I deplored the present situation, that it was of great importance that the French compose their differences now before the invasion of the Continent took place; that they must compose their differences before the peacetable was reached or that the French would find themselves in a very weak and poor position. I told him that I personally, and many Americans, were extremely sorry for the French, that we felt that the French people must be undergoing a very severe winter, that it was only by unity that we would reach them at the earliest possible date.

I stated that it seemed to me that General de Gaulle, who I knew had the real interest of France at heart, must be willing to withdraw from any position if no other way could be found to accomplish the union of those who wished to fight to liberate France. We discussed the situation of his adherents in Morocco. He is very anxious to have those individuals who wish to serve with his forces be permitted to join them. He asked for my address so that he could communicate with me further. I told him that many Gaullists had come to me with their stories. He asked me if any others came to see me, if I would tell them that I had seen him, that he had seen General Giraud, that they had not been able to compose their differences, but that he was sending a liaison officer to join Giraud.

I emphasized the necessity for calm and order in Morocco—and suggested that his adherents not only should not cause trouble, but should also do everything they could to help the American effort. He agreed to do that.

Hopkins dictated more notes to Terry on the afternoon of January 22

Had breakfast with Robert, who told me more of his experiences at the front. The President did not get up until ten, and I went in to talk to him about calling off the Press conference which was scheduled for twelve. It was perfectly clear that there was no meeting of the minds as to the exact statement that should be released. In view of the fact that de Gaulle was just arriving, it seemed to me that the wisest thing to do was to postpone the Press conference until we were ready to make a final statement. The President rather reluctantly agreed to this, but I told him that it was essential that we have a meeting of the minds with Churchill. The question of whether any reference to Stalin's having been invited must be decided, and a careful statement relative to the South-West Pacific ought to be included, and if the de Gaulle thing might be in the bag in another twenty-four hours, a much better statement on that could be made. The President told me to go over and see Churchill and tell him the conference was called off. I found Churchill in bed in his custom-ary pink robe, and having, of all things, a bottle of wine for breakfast. I asked him what he meant by that and he told me that he had a profound distaste on the one hand for skimmed milk, and no deep-rooted prejudice about wine, and that he had reconciled the conflict in favour of the latter. He commended it to me and said he had lived to be sixty-eight years old and was in the best of health, and had found that the advice of doctors, throughout his life, was usually wrong. At any rate, he had no intention of giving up alcoholic drink, mild or strong, now or later.

Churchill seemed to be relieved over the fact that the Press conference was not going to be held. We discussed the state of the conference for some time and he seemed satisfied with the outcome. I told him it seemed to me like a pretty feeble effort for two great countries in 1943. I told him, however, that I had watched this war develop for a long time now, and realized that the Chiefs of Staff may agree to do nothing today, but tomorrow, when the President puts the heat on, they will suddenly decide they can do a little more than they think they can at this conference. At any rate, everything seems to be settled from a military point of view. The Prime Minister told me that de Gaulle was definitely arriving at noon and that he hoped they would get somewhere.

Churchill said he wished the pictures were going to be taken later in the day, because he didn't look his best at twelve o'clock. He told me he could put on a very warlike look whenever he wanted to.

They set up for pictures in the rear of the President's villa and shot the Chiefs of Staff and *aides* with the President and the Prime Minister. They had a little difficulty getting a picture of the Prime Minister and the Chiefs of Staff alone, because nobody seems to know who makes up the Chiefs of Staff in the British and the U.S. Government, and I think there were two or three in that didn't belong there. The President gave a Medal of Honour to General Wilbur, and that was ground out for the benefit of the American people. Incidentally, Wilbur, who is a Regular Army officer, was passed over by the Army, and strange to say, passed over on the recommendation of General Patton. They cordially dislike each other, but Wilbur was the only man who spoke French fluently and who knew something about North Africa, so Patton agreed to bring him along, and since he has done such a magnificent job over here, of course they have had to promote him.

I lunched with Mountbatten and Averell, and Mountbatten told me a fantastic story about a non-sinkable ship made of ice which the British are working on, and he wants our co-operation. Mountbatten also believes very strongly that we should attack Sardinia rather than Sicily, because it can be done three months earlier, and he believes it is very important to keep the Germans on the run, once we can knock them out of Tunisia. Mountbatten claims all the younger officers in the British layout agree with this, but the big boys on the Chiefs of Staff have over-ruled their subordinates. Mountbatten told me that crossing the Channel was a hell of an enterprise. The Germans have armed to the teeth. He is working on a new explosive which he thinks the British have got, which would permit the explosive to be loaded into an antiquated submarine and banged up against a cliff fifty feet high, on the French coast, and the explosive can be so regulated as to permit them to blow a road right into France, which would be followed by his Commandos. He says he gets no more interest in this, however, than he does in his non-sinkable ship made of blocks of ice. Mountbatten always gives you the impression of being a courageous, resourceful, fighting man, but I fancy the British Chiefs of Staff push him around pretty much. At any rate, he cautioned us not to say anything to anybody about his urging the attack on Sardinia instead of Sicily.

The President had been lunching with Marshall and I came in on the tail end of that. Marshall was talking about the difficulties of not having Eisenhower a full General. He said it was difficult to do in view of the fact that Eisenhower's army is mired in the mud, and the President told General Marshall that he would not promote Eisenhower until there was some damn good reason for doing it, that he was going to make it a rule that promotions should go to people who had done some fighting, that while Eisenhower had done a good job, he hasn't knocked the Germans out of Tunisia. Marshall said he was cutting out all unnecessary overhead in Africa and was going to get his troops placed in a position where they could really fight. He thinks we should push the arming of the French as rapidly as we can so that they can take over some of our duties.

Later that afternoon Bob Murphy and Averell came in and discussed gossip about the lunch between de Gaulle and Giraud. Apparently de Gaulle spent the lunch telling Giraud that certain Frenchmen, notably Boisson and Nogues, should be thrown out of their jobs as Governors, and apparently they got down to no real discussion relating to the business of their getting together. De Gaulle, who had arrived at noon, had lunch and spent the afternoon with Giraud and his crowd, and was not going to see the Prime Minister until 6.30, which meant the President could not see de Gaulle until after the President's dinner that night with the Sultan.

The Sultan arrived at 7.40, which caused me to put on my black tie for the first time on this trip. He had expressed a desire to see the President alone prior to Churchill's arrival at eight, and he came loaded with presents—a gold dagger for the President, and some gold bracelets for Mrs. Roosevelt and a gold tiara which looked to me like the kind the girls wear in the circus, riding on white horses. I can just see Mrs. Roosevelt when she takes a look at this. The Sultan wore white silk robes. Apparently the etiquette prevents the drinking of liquor publicly, so we had nothing alcoholic either before, during or after dinner. I fortified myself an hour earlier, however. Also, no part of a pig could be eaten, and the Sultan didn't smoke. He had a young son there with a red fez on, which he kept on while eating. He was a kid about thirteen and seemed quite bright. At dinner I sat next to General Nogues, the Governor, who is the bird that de Gaulle wants pitched out of here. He has been the Resident Governor here for many years. He obviously likes it, because he lives in a big palace and is the big shot in this part of the world. I wouldn't trust him as far as I could spit. He didn't seem to me to be in a very easy frame of mind, because I imagine that he knows perfectly well that we may throw him out at any minute. Churchill was glum at dinner and seemed to be real bored. A smart British Marine walked in about the middle of the dinner with a dispatch, but I have a feeling Churchill cooked that up beforehand, because I saw the dispatch later and it certainly wasn't one that required the Prime Minister's attention at the dinner. Took some pictures after dinner. The President gave the Sultan his picture in a handsome silver frame, and a good time seemed to be had by all, except the Prime Minister.

The Prime Minister then told the President about his visit with de

Gaulle. He said he had handled de Gaulle pretty roughly and told him that he had to co-operate with us and Giraud, and suggested the President see de Gaulle at 10.30 in the morning. I told the President that would delay the whole business, and if he felt up to it, I hoped he would see de Gaulle tonight. The President agreed, and Bob Murphy went over to get de Gaulle, and Churchill went home.

The final full-dress meeting of Roosevelt, Churchill, and Hopkins with the Combined Chiefs of Staff—Marshall, King, Arnold, Somervell, Pound, Dill, Brooke, Portal, Mountbatten, and Ismay—was held on the afternoon of Saturday, January 23.

The Chiefs presented an eleven-page paper containing their proposals for the conduct of the war in 1943. It is interesting to note that as a result of eleven days of deliberations they gave top priority to 'security of sea communications'. This meant that they considered the Atlantic Ocean the most important battlefield of the war and that the shortage of escort vessels was the first need to be met.

Second on the priorities list—and closely involved with the first item—was 'assistance to Russia in relation to other commitments'.

Third on the list was 'Operations in the Mediterranean'—the plan for the capture of Sicily giving as the target day 'the favourable July moon', naming Eisenhower to be in supreme command with Alexander as his deputy and Cunningham and Tedder as naval and air commanders.

Fourth on the list was 'Operations in and from the United Kingdom' —provisions for the continued build-up of American forces (BOLERO) and for operations against the Channel Islands and another against the Cotentin Peninsula on August 1, 1943.

Fifth on the list was 'Pacific and Far East Theatre'—operations in the Aleutians, from Midway toward Truk and Guam, advances in the East Indies and the reconquest of Burma (ANAKIM).

The three final items on the list were provisions for a study of the Axis oil positions—for naval and air command in West Africa—and a provision that 'all matters connected with Turkey should be handled by the British'.

As Hopkins had told Churchill at breakfast, he had felt that the results at Casablanca represented 'a pretty feeble effort', but when he read this new document prepared by the Combined Chiefs of Staff he scribbled a pencilled note to General Sir John Dill as follows:

JACK,

I think this is a *very* good paper and damn good plan—so I am feeling much better.

HARRY.

It is not clear to me whether there was any serious contemplation at Casablanca of the extension of the Sicilian operation to the Italian mainland. Certainly, the plan to land at Salerno and take Naples and the Foggia air base was made before HUSKY was launched. General Mark Clark's Fifth Army was kept separate from the rest of the Allied force and trained for this specific purpose, and did not take part in the Sicilian battles.

Hopkins wrote the following notes on the events of the last day in Casablanca:

Sunday, January 24—

Up at 7 to get the communiqué—(official announcement of the conference which had been kept a total secret)—the telegram to Stalin—and one to the Generalissimo in final shape. Robert and Averell came in to breakfast—and then Bob Murphy, who had just been to see Giraud. Giraud was quite willing to co-operate with de Gaulle, but was unwilling to work under him. Bob told me that Macmillan thinks that de Gaulle is going to be difficult and insist on being top dog. Macmillan came in a moment later and told us that de Gaulle's proposition to Giraud is that 'he (de Gaulle) is to be Clemenceau and Giraud Foch'. I told him that the President would not stand for that, but might agree to a joint leadership of the two of them—with Giraud running Africa and de Gaulle the rest of the show.

(Note.—It was this remark by Macmillan that provided the genesis of the widely circulated Roosevelt anecdote previously mentioned by Hopkins. When Roosevelt heard what Macmillan had said about de Gaulle's proposal, he exclaimed: 'Yesterday he wanted to be Joan of Arc—and now he wants to be the somewhat more worldly Clemenceau.')

I left them in my room and went to see the President to tell him the news. He was none too happy about it, but I urged him not to disavow de Gaulle even though he was acting badly. Believing as I did and still do that Giraud and de Gaulle want to work together, I urged the President to be conciliatory and not beat de Gaulle too hard. If there is any beating to be done let Churchill do it, because the whole Free French Movement is financed by them. I told the President I thought we would get an agreement on a joint statement issued by de Gaulle and Giraud—and a picture of the two of them. Bob and I then told Macmillan that Churchill had to bring de Gaulle around.

Churchill had amended the communiqué and General Jacob brought it around and I revised it some more. I got the final draft at 11.15, which the President approved with slight modifications in language.

Giraud arrived at 11.30—de Gaulle was with Churchill by this time. Giraud wanted a confirmation on supplying his army, but the President referred him to Eisenhower. The conference went well. Giraud will play ball with de Gaulle. Giraud goes out, de Gaulle and his staff come in, de Gaulle calm and confident—I liked him—but *no* joint communiqué and Giraud must be under him. The President expressed his point of view in pretty powerful terms and made an urgent plea to de Gaulle to come to terms with Giraud to win the war and liberate France. The Secret Service called me up to tell me Churchill was outside. He was talking to Giraud, saying good-bye to him. Churchill walked in and I went after Giraud, believing that if the four of them could get into a room together we could get an agreement. This was nearly twelve o'clock and the Press conference was to be at that hour. The President was surprised at seeing Giraud, but took it in his stride. De Gaulle was a little bewildered. Churchill grunted. But the President went to work on them, with Churchill backing him up vigorously. De Gaulle finally agreed to a joint statement and before they could catch their breath the President suggested a photograph. By this time the garden was full of camera men and war correspondents who had been flown down (from Algiers) the day before.

I don't know who was the most surprised, the photographers or de Gaulle, when the four of them walked out—or rather the three of them because the President was carried to his chair. I confess they were a pretty solemn group—the cameras ground out the pictures. The President suggested de Gaulle and Giraud shake hands. They stood up and obliged; some of the camera men missed it and they did it again. Then the Frenchmen and their staffs left and Churchill and the President were left sitting together in the warm African sun—thousands of miles from home—to talk to the correspondents of war and the waging of war. It would be flashed around the world the moment a release date was fixed.

The President gave a background statement—not for quotation—but he chose his words very carefully and talked from notes. The only important addition to the communiqué was the President's statement that he and Churchill were determined to accept nothing less than unconditional surrender of Germany, Japan, and Italy. The President talked for about fifteen minutes. He told them of his visit to our troops and later agreed to be quoted on that. Churchill supplemented this with a masterly review of the military situation. He emphasized his personal friendship for the President and said the two of them were going to see the war through together. They have had no disagreements.

I talked after the conference to a number of newspapermen I had met in Washington, London, and Moscow. The fact that Churchill and Roosevelt were in Africa was a complete surprise.

At 1.15 we drove to Marrakesh—picnic lunch on the way. Everyone tired but relaxed. As the British had fixed up the lunch, we had plenty of

wine and Scotch. We were put up at the villa of the late Moses Taylor—
very pleasant. Our host was a young archaeologist named Pendar (Louise
had once rented his flat in Paris)—he was one of our secret agents in N.
Africa prior to the landings.

Averell, Randolph, Robert, and I went to visit a big fair—story-tellers
—dancers—snake-charmers—and 15,000 natives. Very colourful. The
great trading market was near—but nothing much to sell—though
thousands ever milling through. Dinner was good—army style—company aglow—much banter—Churchill at his best. The President tired.

After dinner we agreed on the draft to Stalin—Averell and I had re-
written it. I made a draft for the Generalissimo. They agreed and both
dispatches were put on the cables. At 2 a.m. we retired, leaving a call for 7.

Robert roomed with me—he is flying to Algiers with Averell early
in the morning.

The cables to Stalin and Chiang Kai-shek were lengthy reports on the
results of the Casablanca Conference, the message to Stalin being more
specific as to actual plans. In both cables much emphasis was placed for
obvious reasons on the importance of opening up the Mediterranean to
Allied shipping and thereby greatly facilitating the delivery of supplies to
the Persian Gulf for Russia, and to India for the Burmese operations and for
China.

Hopkins's next notes were written on arrival at Bathurst the following
afternoon, January 25:

Up early for breakfast—very cold—said good-bye—Churchill was up
and we talked a bit. Drove to the field with Robert and saw him fly off
to the front again. The big ramp was rolled up again and the President
pushed up on his wheelchair. Churchill had suddenly decided to drive
out to the field with us, wearing his ever flaming bathrobe, bedroom
slippers and the inevitable cigar. Churchill and I took one last walk
together—he is pleased by the conference—expressed great confidence
of victory—but warned of the hard road ahead.

We had an uneventful trip of eight hours to Bathurst—we skirted
the Atlas Mountains because McIntire did not want the President to fly
so high. Incidentally, Churchill has his paints and palette with him and
promises to paint the mountains from the tower in the villa. He told me
he was going to send it to the President as a remembrance of the conference. The President has a bad cough and looks very worn. When we got
to the *Memphis* he had a little fever. Everybody went to bed by nine. I
went to sleep reading a history of the Gambia River. The British can
have it.

Tuesday, January 26

Aboard the *Memphis*. Slept well and long. The President is still running a little fever—but it seems to be nothing very serious. I think the fishing we had planned is off. Ross says that he won't let the President go to Liberia unless the fever clears up. But I don't believe anyone can stop the President from going. Loafed all morning. All lunched together. Lord Swinton, the British High Commissioner, is coming aboard at four and —doctor or no doctor—the President is going to get on a tug and go up the Gambia.

That is the end of the Hopkins notes for this trip. Roosevelt did go up the Gambia on H.M.S. *Aimwell*, a seagoing tug that had been built at Bay City, Michigan, and transferred to the Royal Navy under Lend-Lease. At 7.10 the following morning the President made the four-hour flight to Liberia for lunch with President Edwin Barclay, then back to Bathurst for dinner, and at 11.30 that night took off on the flight across the South Atlantic to Natal, Brazil, where he met the next day with President Getulio Vargas. (A week later Brazil entered the war.)

On the day, January 31, that Roosevelt returned to Washington the Battle of Stalingrad ended with the capture of Field Marshal von Paulus and some sixteen of his generals, together with all that remained of the surrounded German forces. Now the road to victory appeared to many hopeful people to be a broad, smooth highway on which the traffic signs were all one-way— and the arguments about the phrase 'unconditional surrender' were already beginning and were to continue throughout the war and perhaps far into history.

There were many propaganda experts, both British and American, who believed that the utterance of these words would put the iron of desperate resistance into the Germans, Japanese, and Italians, and thereby needlessly prolong the war and increase its cost; there are some who still believe that it did so. These critics were not necessarily opposed to the principle of total defeat—but they considered it a disastrous mistake for the President to announce it publicly.

There were others who objected violently to the principle itself, and who, as this is written in 1948, are still attributing the world's postwar troubles to the enforcement of unconditional surrender on Germany. I can make no comment on this theory in this book.

I wrote Winston Churchill asking him if he had discussed the unconditional surrender statement with Roosevelt before the Press conference at Casablanca, and his reply was as follows:

I heard the words 'Unconditional Surrender' for the first time from the President's lips at the Conference. It must be remembered that at that

Harry Hopkins, President Roosevelt and General George S. Patton lunching in the open air during a visit from Casablanca to American troops of the Fifth Army (*see page* 682).

moment no one had a right to proclaim that Victory was assured. There-fore, Defiance was the note. I would not myself have used these words, but I immediately stood by the President and have frequently defended the decision. It is false to suggest that it prolonged the war. Negotiation with Hitler was impossible. He was a maniac with supreme power to play his hand out to the end, which he did; and so did we.

Roosevelt himself absolved Churchill from all responsibility for the state-ment. Indeed, he suggested that it was an unpremeditated one on his own part. He said: 'We had so much trouble getting those two French generals together that I thought to myself that this was as difficult as arranging the meeting of Grant and Lee—and then suddenly the Press conference was on, and Winston and I had had no time to prepare for it, and the thought popped into my mind that they had called Grant "Old Unconditional Surrender" and the next thing I knew I had said it.'

Roosevelt, for some reason, often liked to picture himself as a rather frivolous fellow who did not give sufficient attention to the consequences of chance remarks. In this explanation, indicating a spur-of-the-moment slip of the tongue, he certainly did considerably less than justice to himself. For this announcement of unconditional surrender was very deeply deliberated. Whether it was wise or foolish, whether it prolonged the war or shortened it—or even if it had no effect whatsoever on the duration (which seems possible)—it was a true statement of Roosevelt's considered policy, and he refused all suggestions that he retract the statement or soften it and continued refusal to the day of his death. In fact, he restated it a great many times.

Although Roosevelt implied that he went into the Press conference at Casablanca unprepared, Hopkins wrote in his description of the conference that Roosevelt consulted notes as he talked. The photographs of the con-ference show him holding several pages which had been carefully prepared in advance. Those pages contained the following paragraph:

The President and the Prime Minister, after a complete survey of the world war situation, are more than ever determined that peace can come to the world only by a total elimination of German and Japanese war power. This involves the simple formula of placing the objective of this war in terms of an unconditional surrender by Germany, Italy, and Japan. Unconditional surrender by them means a reasonable assurance of world peace for generations. Unconditional surrender means not the destruction of the German populace, nor of the Italian or Japanese populace, but does mean the destruction of a philosophy in Germany, Italy, and Japan which is based on the conquest and subjugation of other peoples.

What Roosevelt was saying was that there would be no negotiated peace,
o

no compromise with Nazism and Fascism, no 'escape clauses' provided by another Fourteen Points which could lead to another Hitler. (The ghost of Woodrow Wilson was again at his shoulder.) Roosevelt wanted this uncompromising purpose to be brought home to the American people and the Russians and the Chinese, and to the people of France and other occupied nations, and he wanted it brought home to the Germans—that neither by continuance or force nor by contrivance of a new spirit of sweet reasonableness could their present leaders gain for them a soft peace. He wanted to ensure that when the war was won it would stay won.

Undoubtedly his timing of the statement at Casablanca was attributable to the uproar over Darlan and Peyrouton and the liberal fears that this might indicate a willingness to make similar deals with a Goering in Germany or a Matsuoka in Japan.

It is a matter of record that the Italians and the Japanese were ready to accept unconditional surrender as soon as effective force was applied to their homelands. Whether they might have done so sooner, or whether the Germans might ever have done so, under any circumstances whatsoever, are matters for eternal speculation. One thing about Roosevelt's famous statement is certain, however—he had his eyes wide open when he made it.

CHAPTER XXIX

THE POLITICAL FRONT

WHEN Hopkins returned to Washington from Casablanca he found a formidable pile of clippings of newspaper attacks upon him and his wife. Added to the fantastic story of the Beaverbrook emeralds was a great deal of sensational material about the dinner for the Hopkinses given at the Hotel Carlton, on December 16, by Bernard M. Baruch. According to the various reports, there were from sixty to eighty guests present and Baruch paid anywhere from $10 to $40 per person. (I was one of the guests and can say that it was a large party, but I haven't the faintest idea what it cost.) Whatever the statistics, there was plenty of reason to regret the whole episode. The *American* magazine had just published an article by Hopkins with the title 'You and Your Family will be Mobilized', in which he wrote of the extreme toughness of the war, and the need for ever greater sacrifices on the part of the people. He said:

> Rationing and priorities far more widespread than at present will determine the kinds of food . . . we shall have and will affect every detail of our daily lives. Under total war our overall standard of living will be as low as it was at the bottom of the depression in 1932. . . . No family should object to meat rationing when they realize the beef and bacon they don't get is being served to their sons and brothers in the Army.

The newspapers had fun aplenty quoting those words together with the Carlton menu which ran from caviar and *pâté de foie gras* through beef alamode, corned beef in jelly and Virginia ham, to three kinds of ice cream, plus vintage champagne (imported). Naturally enough, the term 'Lucullan orgy' managed to creep into many of these accounts. Baruch gave this dinner as his wedding present to Hopkins and his bride. It was a generous, friendly gesture, made with no thought of possible political consequences, for there were comparable (and often far more lavish) parties being given then in Washington and in all other American cities. But this one involved the loathed name of Hopkins.

The enemy propagandists did not overlook the attacks on Hopkins. One Berlin broadcast stepped up the value of the Beaverbrook emeralds to five million dollars, adding: 'Although the White House issued sharp denial, various New York newspapers continue to express themselves sharply against such a case of corruption.'

Of course, Hopkins was long accustomed to vilification and had learned to disregard it—or, at any rate, to make a successful pretence of doing so.

He knew that the really savage attacks came from the Patterson-McCormick-Hearst newspapers and were therefore expressive of their hatred of Roosevelt and their temporarily frustrated isolationism. Ordinarily, he would have muttered 'to hell with them', and gone about his business. But now it was different. These attacks were directed at his wife as much as himself—and, in some scurrilous instances, even more so—and he was embittered and enraged and determined to fight back with suits for libel. He believed that citation of the manner in which all this material had been used by Goebbels would strengthen his case. Roosevelt talked him out of this, saying: 'This is a fight in which you would be licked before you could even get started. The whole proceedings would give them a glorious opportunity to pile on the smears—and, after what you would have to take, what earthly good would it do you to win a verdict and receive damages of one dollar?' Hopkins was very reluctant indeed to take this good advice, but he had to do so, as there were a great many subjects larger in importance than his own offended sensibilities to occupy his attention.

The completion of the gigantic Russian victory at Stalingrad changed the whole picture of the war and of the foreseeable future. With one battle—which, in duration and in the terrible casualties, had amounted to a major war in itself—Russia assumed the position as a great world power to which she had long been entitled by the character as well as the numbers of her people. Roosevelt knew that he must now look beyond the military campaigns of 1943 to the actual shape of things to come in the postwar world.

First, however, he had to look to some house-cleaning in his own Administration. There was more warfare in the War Production Board involving Donald Nelson and Charles E. Wilson, on one side, and Ferdinand Eberstadt, on the other. All three were distinguished businessmen, but they were giving a good imitation of traditional bureaucrats battling over jurisdictional frontiers. Eberstadt had the backing of the War and Navy Departments who had come to the conclusion that Nelson must go. The crisis came to a head shortly after Roosevelt's return from Casablanca and he reluctantly decided that he must intervene. He wrote to Bernard M. Baruch asking him to take over the Chairmanship of the War Production Board. Baruch was ill at the time and could not get to Washington for several days, and when he did arrive he learned that Roosevelt had changed his mind and that Nelson was to remain on the job. Nelson, having been informed of what was afoot, had suddenly taken bold, drastic action: he demanded and received Eberstadt's resignation and spread the story of the quarrel in the Press. I have heard and read many different versions of this episode. I do not know just what part Hopkins played in it, but it seems evident that he backed Nelson and persuaded the President to give him another chance. He also persuaded Nelson to delegate a very large amount of authority for the direction of W.P.B. to Wilson.

In Nelson's own account of this ruckus he quoted Roosevelt as saying:

> I wish the job could be accomplished without these head-on collisions. I believe that there are ways of manoeuvring so that head-on collisions can be avoided. It is my experience with businessmen in government that they always get into these battles, not alone with one another but with the heads of other Government agencies. They don't know how to administer the things they must administer as well as the politicians know how.

I am sure that is an accurate quotation. Roosevelt often talked, usually with amusement, of the difficulties of businessmen in adjusting themselves to the weird ways of government. This time he was certainly not amused—and he was even less amused a year and a half later when open strife developed between Nelson and Wilson on the eve of a national election. For the time being, however, peace prevailed in W.P.B. and production went forward at a remarkable rate.

On February 2 Churchill emerged from his talks with President Inonu of Turkey, and reported to Roosevelt that he thought this visit had been a great success. Despite Churchill's cheerfulness about his Turkish visit, Hopkins remarked a short time later that, in so far as he could learn, Inonu had been extremely agreeable and equally noncommittal. Churchill had proposed in his talks with Inonu—as he did in a public speech a few weeks later—that, as part of the United Nations world organization there should be established a Council of Europe and a Council of Asia. The former would come first, after the defeat of Germany and Italy, while Britain and the U.S. (and, Churchill thought, probably Russia) were applying their full, combined forces for the administration of punishment to 'the greedy, cruel Empire of Japan'. Most of Churchill's conversations with Inonu, however, had been concerned not with long-range prospects, but with the immediate desirability of getting Turkey into the war on the side of the United Nations. He and Roosevelt made further attempts to achieve that end at Cairo ten months later, but they met with no success until after the Yalta Conference, less than three months before Germany's unconditional surrender.

When Stalin received the message from the President and Prime Minister that they had despatched at the end of the Casablanca Conference he cabled Roosevelt as follows:

> Thank you for the information in your friendly joint message on the decision made at Casablanca in regard to operations to be carried out during the last nine months of 1943 by British and American armed

forces. It is my understanding that by the decisions you have taken you have set yourselves the task of crushing Germany by the opening of a Second Front in Europe in 1943 and I should be very obliged for information concerning the actual operations planned for this purpose and on the time scheduled for carrying them out.

I can give you assurance that the armed forces of the Soviet Union will do everything in their power to carry on offensive operations against Germany and her allies. But our troops are now tired and in need of rest and will be unable to continue the present offensive beyond the middle of February, and we intend, circumstances permitting, to wind up our winter campaign at that time.

This was not easy to answer. The situation in Tunisia was discouraging—and it was soon to become a great deal worse—and Eisenhower sent a long, detailed cable expressing the opinion that it would be dangerous to launch the Sicily operation as planned. If it were to be attempted too early, said Eisenhower, 'it is unlikely to succeed'.

When Churchill read that message he immediately cabled Hopkins stating his strong belief that the Sicilian operation could be launched in June and he said he considered it would be 'an awful thing' that for three months the Americans and British would be killing no German soldiers while the Russians were chasing around one hundred and eighty-five divisions. He said: 'If we had yielded to the fears of the professionals we should not have had any TORCH.' Churchill asked Hopkins to convey his felicitations to the President on a speech just delivered and to express his gratitude for certain references to himself.

The Roosevelt speech to which the Prime Minister referred was given on Lincoln's Birthday at the annual dinner of the White House Correspondents' Association. Roosevelt said:

I spent many hours in Casablanca with this young general [Eisenhower]—a descendant of Kansas pioneers. I know what a fine, tough job he has done and how carefully and skilfully he is directing the soldiers under him. I want to say to you tonight—and to him—that we have every confidence in his leadership. High tribute was paid to his qualities as a soldier when the British Government, through Mr. Churchill, took the lead at Casablanca in proposing him for the supreme command of the great Allied operations which are imminent.

Roosevelt was very careful in choosing his words on the subject of France:

In the years of the American and French Revolutions the fundamental principle guiding our democracies was established. The cornerstone of our whole democratic edifice was the principle that from the people and the people alone flows the authority of government.

It is one of our war aims, as expressed in the Atlantic Charter, that the conquered populations of today be again the masters of their destiny. There must be no doubt anywhere that it is the unalterable purpose of the United Nations to restore to conquered peoples their sacred rights.

French sovereignty rests with the people of France. Its expression has been temporarily suspended by German occupation. Once the triumphant armies of the United Nations have expelled the common foe, Frenchmen will be represented by a Government of their own popular choice.

It will be a free choice in every sense. No nation in all the world that is free to make a choice is going to set itself up under the Fascist form of government, or the Nazi form of government or the Japanese war lord form of government. Such forms are the offspring of seizure of power followed by the abridgement of freedom. Therefore, the United Nations can properly say of these forms of government two simple words: 'Never again.'

The right of self-determination included in the Atlantic Charter does not carry with it the right of any government to commit wholesale murder or the right to make slaves of its own people or of any other peoples in the world.

And the world can rest assured that this total war—this sacrifice of lives all over the globe—is not being carried on for the purpose or even with the remotest idea of keeping the Quislings or Lavals in power anywhere on this earth.

Of the war in the Pacific, Roosevelt said:

We do not expect to spend the time it would take to bring Japan to final defeat merely by inching our way forward from island to island across the vast expanse of the Pacific.

There are many roads which lead right to Tokyo. We shall neglect none of them.

He said that at Casablanca Churchill had offered to make a formal statement pledging that, after the defeat of Germany, all British Empire resources and manpower would be devoted to the final attack on Japan. 'I told him,' said Roosevelt, 'that no formal statement or agreement along these lines was in the least bit necessary—that the American people accept the word of a great English gentleman.'

In case anyone had failed to hear him first time, Roosevelt told the White House correspondents, and all the rest of the world, that 'the only terms on which we shall deal with any Axis government or any Axis factions are the terms proclaimed at Casablanca: "Unconditional Surrender".'"

It was now decided that Anthony Eden should make a visit to Washington to start the discussions of the postwar organization. He was due to make this trip immediately, but on February 18 Churchill was taken seriously ill. Hopkins immediately cabled him the expression of anxiety that was felt by so many millions of people, and Churchill replied that he might be indisposed for another week, but that the situation was well under control. He said that Eden's trip to the United States must be postponed because of this illness.

Churchill's doctors called him 'the world's worst patient' and he was described as 'restive and cantankerous and constantly calling for the forbidden cigars'. It was not until February 24 that it was announced that he was suffering from pneumonia, but on that day he again cabled Hopkkns that he was feeling definitely better now and 'so is Gandhi'. (This was a reference to one of Gandhi's most determined hunger strikes.) He asked Hopkins, as always, to present to the President his warmest regards.

During Churchill's illness he managed to give a great deal of attention to the subject of the atom bomb. There had been discussion of this vast subject at Casablanca, during which the Prime Minister expressed considerable concern because the previous Anglo-American co-operation and full exchange of information on research and experimentation seemed to have been ended. Hopkins promised to look into this matter on his return to Washington. On February 16 Churchill cabled Hopkins, saying: 'I should be very grateful for some news about this, as at present the American War Department is asking us to keep them informed of our experiments while refusing altogether any information about theirs.'

On February 24 Hopkins cabled Churchill:

> I have been making inquiries as a result of your request to me in regard to Tube Alloys. It would be of help to me to have Anderson send me a full memorandum by pouch of what he considers is the basis of the present misunderstanding. Since I gather the impression that our people here feel that no agreement has been breached, I should like particularly to have copies of any recorded conversations or references or memoranda which would reveal the nature of the misunderstanding.

From his sick-bed on February 27 Churchill sent Hopkins two long cables, one of them a complete record of all Anglo-American dealings since the first exchanges in 1940. He expressed the conviction that this record proved that, on grounds of fair play, he could justify his request for restoration of the policy of joint work in developing the joint resources of the two countries. He said: 'Urgent decisions about our programme both here and in Canada depend on the extent to which full collaboration between us is restored, and I must ask you to let me have a firm decision on United States policy in this matter very soon.'

Giraud to win the war and liberate France.
The secret service called me out to tell me
Churchill was outside. He was talking to Giraud
– saying good bye to him. Churchill walked
in and I went after Giraud believing
that if the four of them could get into
a room together we could get an agreement.
This was nearly twelve o'clock and the press
conference was to be at that hour. The President
was surprised at seeing Giraud but took it
in his stride. De Gaulle was a little
bewildered, Churchill grunted. But the
President went to work on them with
Churchill backing him up vigorously. De
Gaulle finally agreed to a joint statement
and before he could catch his breath, the
President suggested a photograph. By
this time the garden was full of
camera men and war correspondents who
had been flown down the day before.
        I don't know who was the
most surprised – the photographer or De Gaulle
when the four of them walked out – or rather
the three of them because the President was

...e Gaulle about to shake hands at the
...'s notes describing the way in which
... *page 690*).

It will be noted that Churchill was conducting this correspondence on the atomic project with Hopkins rather than with the President, and he continued to do so for many months thereafter. In a subsequent cable he said that if the full pooling of information on progress in nuclear fission were not resumed, then Britain would be compelled to go ahead separately in this work and that would be 'a sombre decision'. Hopkins talked to the President and Stimson about this and also to Vannevar Bush and Conant. The whole difficulty arose from the fact that, since the project had passed from the research phase to the actual design and manufacture of a weapon, control of it had passed from the hands of the civilian scientists into the War Department. Bush stated in a memorandum to Hopkins on March 31:

> The adopted policy is that information on this subject will be furnished to individuals, either in this country or Great Britain, who need it and can use it now in the furtherance of the war effort, but that, in the interests of security, information interchanged will be restricted to this definite objective.
>
> There is nothing new or unusual in such a policy. It is applied generally to military matters in this country and elsewhere. To step beyond it would mean to furnish information on secret military matters to individuals who wish it either because of general interest or because of its application to non-war or post-war matters. To do so would decrease security without advancing the war effort.

This, of course, was a sound position, but the British objection was that it gave the United States exclusive possession of all the fruits of joint research including the possible use of atomic energy for industrial purposes after the war.

The war news at this time was bad. In their first encounter with Rommel's forces in Tunisia, in mid-February, American troops were given a severe mauling at Faid and Kasserine Passes and had to abandon a lot of hard-won ground, including some airfields. Some people in Algeria were saying: 'The Germans will be back here within a week.' These local defeats were not as serious as that, but they were particularly discouraging because they seemed to confirm the impression that American infantrymen would require another year or more of intensive training before they could become a match for the Germans; however, the effects of Kasserine Pass proved salutary for, as 'Beedle' Smith put it: 'We needed to be given a bloody nose to knock some of the cockiness out of us.'

Hitler, who had refused to cut his losses by ordering withdrawal at Stalingrad, was now doing the same thing in Tunisia: he was still pouring in reinforcements and building up such strength that, when the campaign ended three months later, the German and Italian losses in killed and captured in Tunisia numbered some 350,000 men.

A few more than that, but probably very few, were successfully evacuated to Sicily. The enemy lost nearly 200,000 tons of material on land alone in this campaign, in addition to a great deal that was sunk at sea and shot down in the air. It was, in the end, a major victory—but at the time of Kasserine Pass it looked like a lamentable fiasco.

The Russians' offensive had ended, as Stalin predicted it would, by February 15, and the Germans then seized the initiative and recaptured Kharkov.

Stalin sent a message to Churchill, which, as always, was instantly relayed to Roosevelt. There is no copy of this in Hopkins's papers, but it evidently raised some embarrassing questions relative to tardiness in Tunisia and the opening of a Second Front in France. Roosevelt's reply to this, dispatched February 22, was as follows:

> It is a matter of regret to me as it is to you that the Anglo-American campaign in North Africa did not go ahead as planned. The schedule was interrupted by unexpectedly heavy rains that made transportation of our troops and supplies extremely difficult over the roads leading to the front lines from the distant landing ports. . . .
>
> The importance of a major effort on the continent of Europe at the earliest practicable date is fully understood by me. You may be assured that the American war effort will be projected to the European continent, to reduce the Axis forces opposing your heroic army, as soon as possible when transportation facilities can be provided following the successful conclusion of the North African campaign.

There were, however, more and more questions from Moscow and very few indications of cordiality. Among the latter was a comment by Stalin on the successful bombing of Nuremberg, Munich, Stuttgart, and Essen: 'From the bottom of my heart I welcome British aviation striking hard against German industrial centres.'

The prevailing tension was not lessened when, on March 8, Ambassador Standley was quoted as informing American newspaper correspondents in Moscow that Russia was getting American supplies in quantity, but was keeping the fact from the people and was leading them to believe that Russia was fighting unaided. In his book, *The Year of Stalingrad*, Alexander Werth has written that the Standley statement 'shocked and pained many Russians, who thought it callous and in poor taste'. The attitude of the White House toward the statement was somewhat similar, but Harriman reported from London:

Many of my friends here, both British and American, seniors and juniors, are secretly pleased at the way Standley spoke out in Moscow even if this was an indiscretion. The feeling is growing here that we will build trouble for the future if we allow ourselves to be kicked around by the Russians. As an example of this: Maisky has been conducting private talks with American journalists regarding the inadequacy of aid for Russia from the United States in addition to his public statements about the Second Front.

The interests and the enormous needs of China were also given sharp emphasis at this time. In the latter part of February Madame Chiang Kai-shek, now recovered from her illness, was a guest at the White House and made a very powerful speech on behalf of China's cause before a joint session of Congress, where the war in the Far East was always more popular than the war in Europe.

With her extraordinary charm and intellectual vigour she was both winning and persuasive as a propagandist, and the Combined Chiefs of Staff were alarmed that she would bring about a radical change in basic policy. But Roosevelt held to the 'Germany first' principle and the developments in Europe were making the logic of this principle appear all the more obvious.

After her departure from the White House, Hopkins wrote the following memorandum:

Mme Chiang Kai-shek asked me to see her Saturday afternoon and I had a talk of one and a half hours with her. While she said her conversations with the President had gone very well and she believed the conferences she would have with the President tomorrow would satisfactorily complete her talks, I sensed that she was not altogether happy about her visit. She was quite insistent about getting the planes for the new 15th Air Force in there on time and said to me: We do not want promises that are not fulfilled. The President has told me the planes will get there and he must not let me down with the Generalissimo.'

She then outlined her views at great length about the postwar world, the first burden of which was that we could be sure China would line up with us at the Peace Table. This is due to the fact that China has confidence in Roosevelt and his policy and is willing to make a commitment in advance because of that confidence.

She told me she thought some immediate move should be made to get the four great powers talking about the postwar affairs and that the President should be Chairman of that group.

She pressed me pretty hard to go to China; said she had a wire from the Generalissimo urging it. I told her that if Mrs. Roosevelt is going soon

I could see no purpose in my going; that I did not want to go unless there is a real reason for my doing so; that we knew already exactly what the Generalissimo wanted and that I was in sympathy with his views and would do everything I could to get them accomplished, because I thought they were right. She did not seem to be impressed by this argument. She looked tired and a little dispirited.

Sunday morning I told the President about my talk with Madame and her desire to get everything off her chest to him that day. The President obviously feels they have covered the businesses adequately, but I urged him to listen to her when he saw her later in the day and let her do the talking. I saw him again after his conference with Mme Chiang, which lasted from 4.00 to 5.30 Sunday afternoon, and he told me he had learned nothing new, but had given her every chance to tell her story and he seemed quite satisfied with the total sum of her visit here.

She is coming down again to spend a night or two before she leaves for China.

Dr. Soong told me privately that the Generalissimo did not want her to go to England and she told me she was going home as soon as her speaking engagements were over.

Anthony Eden arrived in Washington on March 12. According to a memorandum from John G. Winant to the President, Eden's mission was to be 'limited to the most effective method of preparing for meetings between the governments of all the United Nations to consider questions arising out of the war'. That would seem to be a rather broad limitation and was certainly treated as such, as the conversations with Eden, who was in the U.S. for more than two weeks, covered a vast variety of subjects in the political conduct of the war and in the construction of the hoped-for postwar world.

Shortly before Eden's arrival Roosevelt met with Welles and Hopkins, who made these notes:

We discussed the implications of Eden's visit at some length. The President told Welles he wanted to have his first meeting with Eden very informal and preferred that Welles not be present. He said that he would have dinner with Eden Saturday night alone with me.

I raised the question as to whether or not our Government was going to agree to the various set-ups which must be made within the United Nations to discuss various matters and whether or not the main committee should be made up of four members representing the British Empire, Russia, the United States, and China. The British are going to push for committees of seven or eight, which will include separate membership for Canada and Australia. I said I believe by this technique we would be constantly outvoted and that I thought we should put our foot down in

the very beginning in this Food Conference and insist on the main committee of four members only and let the British Government decide
whether they want their membership to come from England or Canada.
Both Welles and the President agreed to this. I told them I was sure
England was going to press this when Eden got here and I believe we
should be very firm about it.

The President then discussed at some length his notion of the postwar
shipping problem. We are going to have, by all odds, the largest merchant
marine in the world after the war. Our position with Great Britain will
be reversed.

I told him our control of shipping would be a powerful weapon at
the Peace Table and that we should not hesitate to use it. The President
said he was anxious to get into a discussion of communications and transportation between the United Nations as soon as this Food Conference
could get off the ground.

He got on his old subject of the manhandling of the news by the Press
and said he was going to try to work out some international news broadcasts which all of the United Nations would use, giving factual information and not coloured in any way, and that they would require the radio
stations in Germany, Japan, and Italy to use these international releases.
He also said under no circumstances should Germany, Italy, and Japan be
permitted to own or operate any commercial air lines.

I went to see Halifax an hour before dinner tonight and he told me he
was a little disturbed about Eden's proposal to go to the West Coast.
He thought in view of Mme Chiang's going there, many people might
think it was an attempt at counter-propaganda. He also felt he should not
go to the Middle West. I told him all problems of exactly what he would
do and where he should go could be left until he gets here, because any
arrangements can be made very quickly.

Roosevelt talked a great deal on that subject of a United Nations news
service. He believed there should be what he called 'Free Ports of Information' established at strategic points around the world, so that there would
be no area wherein the people could be denied access by totalitarian censorship to the same news that was available to all other people. He also believed
in a system of strategic bases—he gave as examples, Dakar, the tip of Tunisia,
and Formosa—which would be under United Nations control. This idea is
mentioned in some of Hopkins's memoranda of the Eden conversations
quoted subsequently. Roosevelt believed then, as he had believed when
Molotov visited Washington a year previously, that France and other
occupied countries in Europe should not have to bear the economic and
physical burden of rearmament after the war—that the burden of ensuring

postwar security should be borne by the nations that were of necessity already armed for combat purposes.

The first notes that Hopkins wrote after Eden's arrival were dated March 15, 1943, as follows:

The President, Mr. Eden and I dined last night and discussed, in great detail, the post-war geographical problems of Europe.

RUSSIA. Eden stated he thought Russia was our most difficult problem; that she undoubtedly had two different plans up her sleeve— one based on British-American co-operation with Russia and the other on the assumption that the U.S. would withdraw from all interest in European affairs after the war. Eden said he believed that Russia preferred and hoped for the former, because Stalin was not prepared to face the implications of Russia's control over European affairs, and England would probably be too weak to face Russia alone diplomatically. I asked him what he thought Russia's demands at the Peace Table would be. Eden said he thought they first would demand that the Baltic States be absorbed as states in the U.S.S.R. He felt Stalin would insist upon this for reasons of security and that he would make out a case that there had been a plebiscite in 1939 which indicated the desire of the Baltic States to join the U.S.S.R.

The President stated that he thought that this action on the part of Russia would meet with a good deal of resistance in the United States and England; that he realized that, realistically, the Russian armies would be in the Baltic States at the time of the downfall of Germany and none of us can force them to get out. He, the President, said he thought the United States would urge Russia not to take them into the U.S.S.R. without a new plebiscite, but agreed that they would have very close economic military arrangements with the Soviet pending a plebiscite.

Eden thought Stalin would not agree to this and would be insistent that we agree to the absorption of the Baltic States into the Soviet Union.

The President said he realized that we might have to agree to this, but if we did, then we should use it as a bargaining instrument in getting other concessions from Russia.

POLAND. Eden said he thought that Russia would demand very little territory of Poland, possibly up to the 'Curzon Line'. This would not affect Poland unduly from an economic point of view. Eden said he believed Stalin wanted a strong Poland, providing the right kind of people were running it and that (Russian) policy at the Peace Table would depend on this.

The President said it would be difficult to work out geographical boundaries on this basis, because, while there might be a liberal government in Poland at the time of the Peace Conference, they might well be thrown out within a year.

FINLAND. Eden thought that Russia would insist on the line which was drawn up at the end of the last war and he even thought this was reasonable and the President shared this point of view. Eden said that Stalin had told him he was going to insist on Hangoe for security reasons. The President said that with the emergence of air power this would not be necessary, but Eden reiterated that he was sure Stalin was going to insist on it. Both agreed that this would be a difficult matter to handle. Eden indicated that he thought there would be no trouble with Russia about the Straits, because, after all, it merely was a way of entrance from one locked sea into another. If Stalin really wanted to find a water route he would go after a new arrangement at the Suez Canal or Gibraltar. Stalin would surely demand Bessarabia. Both the President and Eden agreed that Russia should have Bessarabia, because it has been Russian territory during most of its history.

POLAND. Eden said that the Poles are being very difficult about their aspirations. He told a story of how the British Government wanted to turn a cruiser over to the Poles and Sikorsky insisted on naming it *The Lemburg* after the city over whose sovereignty Russia and Poland are bound to have a bitter fight. Eden stated that he told Sikorsky that naming this cruiser *The Lemburg*, would merely irritate the Russians and there was no earthly reason for giving it that name, because Lemburg is not a seaport. However, Sikorsky insisted and would not take the cruiser when the British refused to permit it to be named *Lemburg*. Eden said Sikorsky was forever meeting with the small states of the Balkans promoting Polish ambitions; that all this was known to the Russians, and Eden thinks Sikorsky is doing far more harm for Poland than good. Poland has very large ambitions after the war and Eden says that privately they say that Russia will be so weakened and Germany crushed that Poland will emerge as the most powerful state in that part of the world. Eden thinks this is completely unrealistic. Poland wants East Prussia and both the President and Eden agree that Poland should have it. Eden said that the Russians agree privately with this, but are not willing to tell this to the Poles, because they want to use it as a bargaining instrument at the Peace Table. Poland will want her original boundaries as they existed prior to the war. The President said that, after all, the big powers would have to decide what Poland should have and that he, the President, did not intend to go to the Peace Conference and bargain with Poland or the other small states; as far as Poland is concerned, the important thing is to set it up in a way that will help maintain the peace of the world.

The President said he thought we should make some arrangement to move the Prussians out of East Prussia the same way the Greeks were moved out of Turkey after the last war; while this is a harsh procedure, it is the only way to maintain peace, and that, in any circumstances, the Prussians cannot be trusted.

FINLAND. Eden said that the Finns were trying to use both Great Britain and the United States now to approach Russia about peace. He, Eden, thought the Russians would not deal with Finland in that round-about way, and Eden thinks that Stalin will not answer the note from the United States Government and that we should tell the Finns to talk direct to the Russians. Eden thinks Russia wants an independent Finland, but is going to insist on a line that will not threaten Leningrad. He, Eden, thinks the Finns must give way here. The President said he thought that probably Russia is not too anxious to make peace with Finland now because they are containing seven good divisions (German) in Finland which, if peace is declared, would move down on the Russian Front. The Russians, the President said, were containing these seven divisions with five inferior divisions at the present time. Both Eden and the President expressed the belief that the Finnish post-war problem would be difficult to arrange.

SERBIA. The President expressed his oft-repeated opinion that the Croats and Serbs had nothing in common and that it is ridiculous to try to force two such antagonistic peoples to live together under one Government. He, the President, thought that Serbia, itself, should be established by itself and the Croats put under a trusteeship. At this point Eden indicated his first obvious objection to the Trustee method which the President is going to propose for many states. Eden did not push it, but it was clear to me that the British Government have made up their minds that they are going to oppose this. Eden thought the President's opinion about the inability of the Croats and the Serbs to live together a little pessimistic and he, Eden, believed it could be done.

CZECHOSLOVAKIA, ROUMANIA, BULGARIA, TURKEY, GREECE. Both Eden and the President thought that none of these countries offered real difficulties from a geographical point of view.

AUSTRIA and HUNGARY. Both agreed that Austria and Hungary should be established as independent states. Eden said he thought Stalin would want to be pretty arbitrary about Hungary, because the Russians do not like the Hungarians, and that Stalin would be unwilling to give them any favours at the Peace Table.

GERMANY. Eden said that the most important thing we had to get a meeting of the minds on in regard to Germany was the question of whether we were going to be able to deal with Germany as a unit after

BULLETIN Oct 4

PARIS IN FRENCH AT 6:00 PM TO FRANCE:

TEXT- "GENERAL GEORGE C. MARSHALL, THE U.S. CHIEF OF STAFF,
HAS BEEN DISMISSED. PRESIDENT ROOSEVELT HAS TAKEN OVER HIS COMMAND.

"THIS OCCURRED TWO DAYS AGO, BUT HAS NOT YET BEEN COMMENTED
UPON IN WASHINGTON."

EH 10/5-4:11P

WAR DEPARTMENT
OFFICE CHIEF OF STAFF
WASHINGTON

Dear Harry;

Are you responsible
for pulling this fast
one on me?

G.C.M.

Dear George - duly
true in part - I am
now Chief of Staff
but you are President

F D R

The Vichy broadcast reporting General Marshall's dismissal. Comments by General Marshall and President Roosevelt (*see page 758*).

the war, disarming them, etc., and also for the peace, or whether we were going to insist that it be broken up into several independent states. Eden said that from the conferences he had had with the Russians he was sure that Stalin would not trust the Germans; that in his speech the other day when he said the Russian armies were going to stop at the German Border this was for propaganda purposes inside Germany (Eden believed); that he, Stalin, has a deep-seated distrust of the Germans and that he will insist that Germany be broken up into a number of states. The President said he hoped we would not use the methods discussed at Versailles and also promoted by Clemenceau to arbitrarily divide Germany, but thought that we should encourage the differences and ambitions that will spring up within Germany for a Separatists Movement and, in effect, approve of a division which represents German public opinion.

I asked what they would do if that spontaneous desire did not spring up and both the President and Eden agreed that, under any circumstances, Germany must be divided into several states, one of which must, over all circumstances, be Prussia. The Prussians cannot be permitted to dominate all Germany.

Eden said he believed that one of the reasons Stalin wanted a second front in Europe was political; that if Germany collapsed he had no desire, in Germany, to take the full responsibility for what would happen in Germany or the rest of Europe, and he believed it was a fixed matter of Russian foreign policy to have both British and United States troops heavily in Europe when the collapse comes. Eden expressed this purely as his private opinion and said that he was sure that in Russia a different view was held in some quarters, but, nevertheless, he thought he had stated Stalin's position.

We, then, discussed at some length, the political effect of our troops being in Italy as against France at the time of the collapse of Germany and, while both Eden and the President thought it would not be as advantageous, it was far better than not being there (on the Continent) at all.

I told the President it was important that we have the frankest kind of talk with Mr. Eden about potential differences in Europe and that, at the moment, I saw two: (1) The people of Serbia and Croatia and (2) the problem of what countries, free and otherwise, should be disarmed in Europe. I felt that from what Mr. Eden had said he would not believe in a disarmed Poland or France and I thought it would be very unfortunate if he went back to London without fully understanding the President's position in this, even if he did not fully agree and that he, Eden, should tell the President, frankly, what are his objections to the disarmament of

P

countries like France and Poland. The President reiterated to Eden what he had told Churchill, that after Germany is disarmed what is the reason for France having a big military establishment?

I suggested to Eden, in the light of this evening's conversation, that he articulate in his own mind the potential differences which the British and ourselves might have in Europe, and secondly, the differences which either or both of our countries might have with Russia in Europe and see if we could not come to grips with those, even though they would not be decided definitely at this conference. I suggested that we not explore anything beyond the European situation tonight and that we give two more evenings—one to the problems of the South-West Pacific and the Far East and a third evening to Africa. I said it was clear that in these latter two areas there were bound to be conflicts of opinion, but, nevertheless, I thought that we should exchange, with complete frankness, our points of view about such ticklish subjects as *HONG KONG, MALAYAN STRAITS, INDIA.*

I said I thought no useful purpose would be served at this stage of the war, and surely no useful purpose at the Peace Table, by Great Britain and ourselves having no knowledge of our differences of opinion. Both the President and Eden agreed to this and plans will be made for these conferences soon.

In the meantime, I suggested that Hull, Eden, and the President meet tomorrow for tea, and the President asked me to arrange it.

Eden and I left and went to the Carlton for some oysters and reviewed the evening's conference. Eden thought that some real progress was made, and he was surprised that he and the President seemed in as much agreement as they were about the European situation. He realized that the rest of the world might not be so easy to get a meeting of the minds on. Eden expressed his amazement at the President's intimate knowledge of the geographical boundaries of Europe and said that this knowledge would be of tremendous advantage in any conference.

On March 16 Hopkins wrote of a meeting with Litvinov:

I called to see the Ambassador this evening and asked him what he believed the Russian demands at the Peace Table would be. He said that they, of course, would want the Baltic States; that Russia considered them now part of the U.S.S.R.; that they had always been historically part of Russia, apart from the fact that they were essential to them for security reasons.

Litvinov said he thought Russia had no desire to occupy all of Finland and, indeed, would like to see a healthy, independent country there, but that Russia would insist on moving the line about to a point where the Russian armies were at the end of the Finnish War.

I asked him what about Hangoe and he said he had no idea how his Government would feel about that.

He said he thought Russia would agree to Poland having East Prussia, but that Russia would insist on what he called 'her territorial rights' on the Polish frontier. Said he did not anticipate any great difficulty with Poland about this, although he said Poland would make 'outrageous' demands. He felt that Great Britain and the United States should decide what was to be done about Poland and 'tell them' rather than ask them.

He said he assumed that everybody would agree that Russia should have Bessarabia.

I asked him about their ambitions in the Far East, and he was reluctant to discuss this in any way. He said he was sure Russia would like to see Germany dismembered; certainly Prussia should be cut off from the rest of Germany and probably two or three other additional states created.

In connection with the above interview, Eden told Hopkins of a talk he had had just before leaving London with Maisky, the Russian Ambassador there. Maisky, making it clear that he spoke for himself alone and not with any specific instructions from his Government, expressed the hope that Eden would make no definite commitments for detailed postwar settlements while in Washington. Eden gave assurance that the talks would be 'entirely exploratory'. Maisky, like Litvinov, expressed Russia's determination to absorb the Baltic States, and he also said that Germany should be broken up, but he did not exclude the possibility that its various parts might be joined in some sort of federal union. He said that Russia would certainly want reparations, not in money, but in kind. Maisky evidently expressed much the same views as regards Poland, Finland, and Roumania that Litvinov did, but he added that his Government desired the use of bases in these countries and would not look with favour on the re-establishment of the same kind of government as that which had existed in Poland before the war or which had the political colouration of the current Polish Government-in-Exile.

Maisky said that the Soviet Government was not enthusiastic about the proposal for a future federation of Europe. He believed that a federation including a number of small countries would have negligible significance, either from the military or the political point of view, although there might be some advantage in an economic federation. Eden disagreed on this, saying the very fact of the smallness of some of the countries made federation all the more desirable, politically and militarily as well as economically. He could point to the tragedies of Holland, Belgium, Luxembourg, and France in the spring of 1940, and to Yugoslavia and Greece in the spring of 1941, as instances of the disasters that resulted from a lack of agreement on military and political policy in advance of the German aggressions. Maisky saw the cogency of this argument and thought that his Government probably would

not oppose a Balkan federation, provided it excluded Roumania, nor a Scandinavian federation which excluded Finland. He described such arrangements as 'vegetarian'—meaning, presumably, innocuous. He also spoke of the possiblity of a Polish-Czech federation, saying that all such considerations depended on whether or not Poland was to have a Government friendly to the Soviet Union. He certainly did not believe that the small European nations should have the same voice as the big ones in the postwar organization—for example, Albania's vote should not be equal to Britain's.

On March 17 Hull, Eden, and Hopkins had tea with the President in his study, and Hopkins wrote:

> Hull said he hoped that we could find a way to avoid any longwinded trials of Hitler and his principal associates after the war; that he hoped we could find a way to get the ones that should be shot and do it quietly. He said he thought a public trial would be very bad; that we should settle with Hitler in the same way he would handle us if he were to do it.
>
> We discussed, for some time, the question of precisely what our procedure in Germany during the first six months after the collapse of Germany should be.
>
> I said I thought there was no understanding between Great Britain, Russia, and ourselves as to which armies would be where and what kind of administration should be developed. I said that unless we acted promptly and surely I believed one of two things would happen—either Germany will go Communist or an out-and-out anarchic state would set in; that, indeed, the same kind of thing might happen in any of the countries in Europe and Italy as well. I said I thought it required some kind of formal agreement and that the State Department should work out the plan with the British and the one agreed upon between the two of us should then be discussed with the Russians. The President agreed that this procedure should be followed. It will, obviously, be a much simpler matter if the British and American armies are heavily in France or Germany at the time of the collapse, but we should work out a plan in case Germany collapses before we get to France.
>
> Hull expressed his pleasure that Great Britain and the United States seemed to be getting closer together on the French question.
>
> The President discussed the importance of the United Nations holding certain strong points like Bizerta, Dakar and the Harbour of Formosa after the war. These should be held by the United Nations.

The next Hopkins notes are dated March 22, and describe a luncheon in the President's study at which Eden and Hull again were present:

> The President stated that he wanted no negotiated armistice after the collapse; that we should insist on total surrender with no commitments

to the enemy as to what we would or would not do after this action. The President stated that he doubted if a peace treaty should be signed for some time after the collapse of Germany and Japan.

Eden raised the question, in a delicate way, as to the President's Constitutional powers, during this interim while we are still technically at war with Germany, to agree to forming an independent Austria, as an example. The President replied that he thought he did have the power without reference to the United States Senate—at any rate, enough power to make the independence of Austria stick. It was clear from Eden's reply that he had some doubt about this.

After lunch he told me he thought it a matter of great importance because England, China, Russia, and the other United Nations wanted to be sure of the President's power to reach any agreement which would be binding prior to the actual signing of a peace treaty, which treaty, of course, would have to go to the Senate for confirmation.

We discussed the same situation with regard to East Prussia being turned over to Poland and the President's power to agree on a new eastern boundary line for Poland.

The President told Eden again that he did not like the idea of turning the Baltic States over to Russia and that she would lose a great deal of public opinion in this country if she insisted on this action. The President said he thought the old plebiscite was probably a fake and while he had no doubt that the Baltic States would vote to ally themselves with Russia, he thought Russia should take the trouble to go through the motions of getting that done, in the meantime having an agreement with Great Britain and the United States that Russia would control the foreign affairs and their finances until the new plebiscite could be taken. Eden again told the President that he thought Russia was going to be pretty insistent on the Baltic States.

Eden said he hoped the Japanese Mandated Islands would be turned over to us, preferably in outright ownership. The action would be approved by the United Nations. The President has always felt that these islands would be put under some kind of trusteeship, but it becomes clearer all the time that Eden thinks very little of a trusteeship and would rather have the full responsibility in the hands of one country.

Eden stated that in his conference with Hull this morning Hull had told him he thought Churchill had made a serious mistake in his speech yesterday by not mentioning China amongst the great powers. Both the President and Hull agreed on this point. The President told Eden he thought that China might become a very useful power in the Far East to help police Japan, and that he wanted to strengthen China in every possible way. Eden expressed a good deal of doubt about this on the

theory that he doubted very much if China could stabilize herself and may well have to go through a revolution after the war. He said he 'did not much like the idea of the Chinese running up and down the Pacific'. This was not further pursued, but from what Eden said it made me think the British are going to be pretty sticky about their former possessions in the Far East.

Eden is coming to the White House to spend the week-end and will be at lunch on Saturday.

I raised the question as to where our armed forces would be expected to be after the fall of Germany and, indeed, during the whole period of our policing the aggressor nations. The President said our armies, of course, would have to be in Germany and Italy and he assumed that the British and Russian troops would be there also. He said that so far as the other strong points of the world that had to be held were concerned, we should split up our troops—the British, for instance, would be in Tunisia or Bizerta and we would be in Dakar and, probably Formosa. Eden seemed to agree to this although he made no comment in regard to it except to say that he was glad to hear the President say our troops would be in Germany.

A large part of Eden's time while he was in Washington was devoted to discussion of the limitless problems of shipping. This subject was hardly within the scope of his department, but it was virtually impossible to consider any phase of the war without coming down to the present need for more and more transport. The American losses of material in Tunisia had greatly increased the demand for supplies in that theatre, and the shipping requirements for HUSKY were vast. Britain's food supply was so low that more stringent rationing had to be imposed.

On March 29 Hopkins cabled Harriman:

> Our shipbuilding programme fell behind by some forty-six ships in the first two months of this year, but Vickery is still hopeful that, in 1943, we will surpass the goal of eighteen million tons. We are now exploring every possible means of getting hold of additional ships but I believe there is no possibility of our being able to assign additional ships for the British import programme other than those which have been promised by Douglas. . . . Anthony's trip here has been good. Everyone likes him and we have made a thorough and frank exploration of everything with which the United Nations are concerned. He will return to London fully advised.

Hopkins also cabled Churchill that Eden's visit 'has been a great success'. The President directed Hopkins to organize a small committee to study the availability of shipping.

On March 27 there was a meeting of Roosevelt, Eden, Hull, Welles, Halifax, and William Strang, Assistant Under-Secretary of State in the Foreign Office, which Hopkins described as follows:

Hull raised the question of the sixty or seventy thousand Jews that are in Bulgaria and are threatened with extermination unless we could get them out and, very urgently, pressed Eden for an answer to the problem. Eden replied that the whole problem of the Jews in Europe is very difficult and that we should move very cautiously about offering to take all Jews out of a country like Bulgaria. If we do that, then the Jews of the world will be wanting us to make similar offers in Poland and Germany. Hitler might well take us up on any such offer and there simply are not enough ships and means of transportation in the world to handle them.

Eden said that the British were ready to take about sixty thousand more Jews to Palestine, but the problem of transportation, even from Bulgaria to Palestine, is extremely difficult. Furthermore, any such mass movement as that would be very dangerous to security because the Germans would be sure to attempt to put a number of their agents in the group. They have been pretty successful with this technique both in getting their agents into North and South America.

Eden said that the forthcoming conferences in Bermuda on the whole refugee problem must come to grips with this difficult situation.

Eden said he hoped that on our side we would not make too expansive promises which could not be delivered because of lack of shipping.

There was a general discussion about the organization of the United Nations after the war. 1. The President and Welles were very emphatic that the United States could not be a member of any independent regional body such as a European Council; they felt that all the United Nations should be members of one body for the purposes of recommending policy; that this body should be world-wide in scope. 2. That there would be under this body regional councils with similar advisory powers made up of the nations geographically located in the regions; but, finally, that the real decisions should be made by the United States, Great Britain, Russia, and China, who would be the powers for many years to come that would have to police the world.

The President was very insistent with Eden that China should be a member, although it was clear to me that Eden still was not convinced of the wisdom of the procedure. The President feels that China, in any serious conflict of policy with Russia, would undoubtedly line up on our side.

I said that Churchill's speech in which he advocated a purely European

Council of Nations, had a very unfortunate effect over here. Eden said he was sure Churchill had not meant to exclude the United States and that he rather felt that Churchill spoke on the spur of the moment and that he, Eden, agreed that the United Nations should be organized on a global basis.

The whole idea of the trusteeship of mandated islands, etc., was discussed and the President and Eden seemed to be much closer together than they were at the beginning of their conferences on this policy.

The President made it clear that he did not want a commitment made in advance that all those colonies in the Far East should go back to the countries which owned or controlled them prior to the war. He specifically mentioned Timor and Indo-China. He suggested that all the specific problems which Mr. Eden had raised in his visit here be referred to the State Department and they asked to start exploratory discussions with the British or with any other country in regard to all of them.

I said I thought it would have a very bad effect, both in England and the United States, if the world got the impression that the United States and England were, together, planning the future of the world without consulting anyone else. Eden agreed to this and said the British were conducting direct conferences on matters that concerned them and Russia and he assumed we would do the same thing.

That same day Hopkins received a cable from Churchill stating that the Australian Prime Minister was anxious that the Order of Knight Grand Cross of the Bath be conferred on General MacArthur. Churchill said: 'I cannot think that General Marshall or Admiral King would take it amiss that a junior like MacArthur should receive the G.C.B., as their position is so far above his, and I have the feeling that our gratitude to them must be expressed at a later date in the war. However, I am also told that Admiral Nimitz would have claims to receive equal decoration with General MacArthur. Is this really so?'

Hopkins replied:

It is felt here that high-ranking officers should not be given honours at this time. Decorations for bravery in combat are all right, but most people believe that the decorating should stop there. If, however, you decide to give a decoration to MacArthur, neither the world nor the war will come to an end any sooner and I doubt if Marshall, King, or Nimitz will lose any sleep because of it. The Tunisian news is great.

(Note.—The King conferred the G.C.B. on MacArthur and also on Eisenhower on May 26. The good news referred to by Hopkins was the breaking of the Mareth Line by the British Eighth Army and a wide American

advance in Central Tunisia. The Allies pushing from east and west in North
Africa were at last joining up.)

On March 29 Hopkins wrote his final note on the Eden visit, following a
dinner given by Cordell Hull at the Carlton Hotel:

> After dinner Eden and I sat up for a couple of hours reviewing the
> results of his trip. He, obviously, felt that from his point of view it had
> been altogether worth while, particularly from the point of view of his
> having had a chance to get well acquainted, first with the President and,
> second, with Hull. He told me he was going to invite Hull to come to
> England. While he found Hull a little difficult to talk to and obsessed
> with the problems of the Free French, nevertheless, he thought that he
> and Hull did see eye to eye on the major world problems.
>
> Eden said he had learned of the importance of Congress and particu-
> larly the Senate in any postwar discussions and he had not fully under-
> stood the working arrangement between the President and Congress.
> He found it pretty difficult to envision the wide separation of the powers
> of the executive and legislative branches.
>
> The President has once or twice urged the British to give up Hong
> Kong as a gesture of 'good will'. In fact, the President had suggested a
> number of similar gestures on the part of the British and Eden dryly
> remarked that he had not heard the President suggest any similar gestures
> on our own part.
>
> Eden, obviously, felt he got on extremely well with the President
> and I think this is true. The President liked Eden's frankness and admired
> his wide knowledge of world affairs.

Hopkins told Eden that he had asked Adolf Berle, Assistant Secretary of
State, about the questions of the President's constitutional powers that Eden
had raised. Berle's opinions were as follows:

> The recognition of a newly created state is a purely executive act and
> does not depend upon treaty or other executive action. If, after surrender
> and before a peace treaty, the President determines that a specific territory
> is so separated as to have become independent, he can recognize its
> existence by recognizing its Government, either provisionally or defini-
> tively, and by sending a minister or officer having diplomatic powers to
> represent the United States interests near its Government. No con-
> gressional action is needed in the first instance. Conceivably, when the
> post of minister was formalized, the Senate could decline to confirm a
> nominee to the post, or the Congress could decline appropriations to
> maintain it. But neither of these issues need be raised if the President
> chose to appoint an army officer or civilian representative as, say, High

Commissioner, with the rank and powers of a minister or ambassador; or if the State Department agreed to receive in Washington a delegate or diplomatic representative from that country.

Ultimately, of course, treaties of friendship, commerce, and so forth, would have to be negotiated, and they could be defeated in the Senate; but this is hardly likely, if sufficient time elapsed so that the new state was actually in existence.

The handling of the military forces of the United States could be so managed as to foster, in fact, the setting up of an independent state or states; for the military authorities could accept, deal with, and guide the organization of the local authorities to a point where they could be recognized as the Government of the country—assuming that the population of the country was prepared to accept such a Government.

In my judgment, the President could not enter into an agreement, in advance, with the Government of a third power—say, British—to take any of the foregoing steps, in a fashion which would bind his successors. He could merely make a pledge as to the policy he would carry out. A successor could decline to be bound by such an agreement, and the Government, as such, would not be bound. But—

In my judgment the President could, as commander-in-chief and under his war power, enter into military agreements in the nature of staff agreements, with the commander-in-chief of a third power as to military action and policy. Included in this could be an agreement for the handling of the military forces looking toward the creation of an independent state or states, especially if these were part of enemy or quasi-enemy territory. The precise binding quality of staff agreements has never been fully ascertained under our practice; but it is fairly arguable that agreements of this sort, so far as they related to military policy, are binding to a large extent even on a successor, since a commander-in-chief, having the power to lay and carry out campaigns, must be deemed to have the power necessary to make agreements reasonably appropriate to carrying out such campaigns. In this view, the President has the power, by military agreement, to create a situation in which all of the characteristics of an independent state will be created except that of recognition by this Government.

During Eden's visit there was a very considerable amount of spadework done on the organization of the United Nations. From this work there resulted the U.N.R.R.A. organization and the conferences at Moscow, Teheran, Bretton Woods, Dumbarton Oaks, Yalta, and finally San Francisco.

At a Press conference on March 30, after Eden's departure, Roosevelt spoke of the conversations in a very general way, emphasizing the fact

that they were purely 'exploratory', and that he hoped there would soon be similar conversations with the Russians. He said: 'If you want to be didactic and put it in terms of figures, I would say that so far . . . we are about ninety-five per cent together.' I asked Hopkins at the time what the other five per cent consisted of, and he replied: 'Mostly France'. Eden had stated the British view that they would greatly prefer to deal with one strong French authority, established in Algiers and representing all possible elements of French opinion. Roosevelt and Hull said that they preferred 'to keep the position fluid', and to deal with French individuals—for example, they wished to deal separately with the French authorities in the Pacific islands and with those in Martinique. Roosevelt persisted in his belief that no single French authority could be set up by the Allies, and recognized by them, without eventually incurring the bitter resentment of the people of metropolitan France itself. This was the margin of disagreement—but actually, at that time, the French political situation was improving. Jean Monnet had arrived in Algiers and was rendering considerable service to Giraud. Monnet was dedicated to the achievement of unity among the French factions, and the eventual French Committee of National Liberation owed much to his efforts. John J. McCloy, Assistant Secretary of War, made a visit to North Africa which was most helpful to Eisenhower and to the situation in general, for McCloy was one who believed that the time had come to put the Vichy policy away in the files as finished business and to concentrate our policy on strengthening the leaders of the French Resistance groups who were largely devoted to de Gaulle. Giraud took an increasingly firm pro-democracy, anti-Pétainist position and, advised by Monnet, publicly expressed his hopes for a union with de Gaulle. Months were to pass before this union was achieved, but progress toward it was being made.

I do not know to what extent Roosevelt and Eden considered the problems that would arise from the establishment of Allied military government in Italy, but this subject was certainly discussed at great length by Roosevelt and Hopkins shortly after Eden left. A long memorandum had been prepared by the State Department outlining its views as to the policy to be followed in Sicily and in any other parts of Italy which the Allies might occupy. Hopkins had a carbon copy of this memorandum and the revisions that he made in pencil and that Roosevelt made in ink on this copy provide eloquent testimony to the breadth of the differences of opinion that existed between the White House and its next-door neighbour to the westward on Pennsylvania Avenue. Following are two paragraphs which give the general idea:

State Department version:

On the basis of unconditional surrender the entire Fascist party leadership ('hierarchy') from local party secretaries to the top should be removed from any posts of Government.

The services of local technical and professional officials, although nominally party members, may be retained and the lower ranks of the existing political administration (executive, judicial, police, fiscal, public health, etc.) may be continued in the performance of their normal functions, responsible to the military administration, after the elimination of all of the political agents of the Fascist party.

Same paragraphs in Roosevelt-Hopkins version:

On the basis of unconditional surrender, the entire Fascist party membership from the highest to the lowest should be removed from any post of Government authority.

The services of local technical and professional officials, free from Fascist associations, can be used.

In another paragraph, the State Department said:

The prerogatives of the Crown should be considered as suspended. *The moral power of the Crown among the Italian people and the army may require some special treatment of this question as the situation develops.*

The words that I have italicized in the foregoing were cut out by Roosevelt, and provisions for an Italian Bill of Rights were substituted. Roosevelt wanted the prerogatives suspended—*period*—with no loopholes left for an exercise of the 'moral power' of the House of Savoy. Subsequent history, however, records the melancholy fact that he did not have his way on this point. Roosevelt later sent a message to Churchill saying:

I feel that in the initial stages of HUSKY we should avoid all risk of implications that would arise from any possible use of Italians in high positions such as Mayors of large towns and prefectures. I believe that it is highly preferable to remove any Italians from these positions, as they are all prominent Fascists. We should replace them with army officers for the time being and thus avoid stirring up Italian factions and producing repercussions at home.

Roosevelt certainly wanted to take all possible precautions against a repetition of the North African political blunders, but these precautions proved insufficient.

In considering the problems of Military Government in Italy, it was inevitable that Roosevelt and Hopkins should think of that brilliant, devoted, and tempestuous character, Fiorello LaGuardia.

There were hundreds and thousands of Mayors in the United States, and some of them, such as Kelly, Crump, Curley, and Hague, were of substantial political importance; but when you spoke of 'The Mayor' in the White House during the Franklin Roosevelt years you could be referring only to

the little Mayor of New York. Although LaGuardia was a singularly shrewd politician, he was a man of high honour and ferocious courage and independence. A sometime Republican, he had been a consistent supporter and champion of Roosevelt's policies throughout the New Deal and the battle against isolationism. When the Office of Civilian Defence was formed before Pearl Harbour, Roosevelt named LaGuardia to direct it. The Mayor was not very happy in that job and certainly not very successful. He did not like the word 'defence'—or 'civilian' either. He had served with distinction as a fighter pilot in the First World War and he wanted to serve actively and in uniform in this one. He was constantly begging his close friend, Hopkins, to help him to get into service, and the War Department was constantly turning down his applications. Hopkins felt certain that LaGuardia could be of tremendous help to Eisenhower in the Sicilian operation, and he urged the President to commission the Mayor and assign him to A.F.H.Q. in Algiers. LaGuardia had been broadcasting to Italy regularly over the short-wave transmitters, and it was learned later that these broadcasts were very effective as propaganda with the Italian people. Therefore, as an American general, or even colonel (LaGuardia would have settled for almost any rank), he could have gone to Italian soil as an acknowledged friend.

On March 17, after a talk with Roosevelt, LaGuardia wrote a longhand note to Hopkins which expressed his intense excitement:

DEAR HARRY,

I saw the Chief yesterday—and I am so happy that I can be of service to my country—besides cleaning the streets of N.Y.C. I expect to get my medical exam next week. The Chief indicated I could be commissioned right after I finish the Executive Budget in early April.

I am to be assigned to General Eisenhower's staff and am confident that I will be able to do a good job and be really useful.

After I am finished with the medicos, I will want to have a talk with you, to bring me up to date in certain matters with which you are familiar.

FIORELLO.

PS.—Writing this by hand, as I do not want office to know until last minute.

Subsequently it seemed to Hopkins all the more desirable that LaGuardia be given this assignment. There was considerable argument between London and Washington as to the political aspects of Eisenhower's command once the Allied forces had landed on Italian soil. The British wanted the civilian advisers, Macmillan and Murphy, to go along with the troops. The Americans insisted that Military Government in Italy should be exclusively military. The British thereupon assigned an experienced diplomat, Lord Rennell, who

had been commissioned major-general, to head the Civil Affairs Division on Eisenhower's staff. Hopkins wanted LaGuardia to be Rennell's 'opposite number'. Secretary Stimson, however, again refused to agree to this appointment.

In the middle of April, Roosevelt left for another tour of training camps and production centres and a visit with the President of Mexico. Hopkins sent him a telegram on April 19, begging him to intercede with Stimson in behalf of the 'Little Flower'. I do not know what Roosevelt did about this thereafter—but LaGuardia, to his infinite disappointment, never got into uniform, and the civil affairs job in Sicily was given to Charles Poletti, a former Lieutenant-Governor of New York. Hopkins could not quarrel with this excellent appointment, but he always felt that LaGuardia had been given a raw deal.

While the President was away on his trip, Hopkins was again the co-ordinating point for all cables into the White House—and there were plenty of them, from London, Chungking, Moscow, North Africa, and many other places. There was a pressing need for new decisions to be made in respect to South-East Asia and the Pacific as well as to the European and Mediterranean theatres. (The Middle East had at last faded into the background as a problem.) In the midst of all this, on April 22, Hopkins wrote a memorandum to his two *aides*, Dr. Lubin and Oscar Cox, as follows:

> I wish you two fellows would put your minds on the terminology to take the place of Social Security and similar words.
>
> I can remember the time when they changed all the names of the charity societies to Family Welfare Societies, and now I understand they are trying to get rid of these names.
>
> All this makes sense to me as we develop in our concept of the relation of people to Government. All terminology that connotes poverty, insecurity, etc., finds little favour with the American people.
>
> I don't think much of the 'Beveridge scheme' for America. I think what we have to provide is real security in terms of full employment. I don't mean to say that sickness insurance and old age should not be in this, but I don't think it can be the cornerstone of any American programme.
>
> Could you give me a digest of what our National Resources Board said in that long-winded tome of theirs. Get out the best things of that.

This was proof that Hopkins had not entirely changed his character; he was getting ready for the day when, the present world conflict having ended in total victory, he would resume his career as a fighter for the extension and amplification of the New Deal.

TRIDENT AND QUADRANT

AFTER the end of the Eden conferences in Washington, Churchill cabled asking Hopkins and General Marshall to join General Brooke and himself for a meeting with Eisenhower in North Africa, which the Prime Minister referred to as 'Torch Land'. On April 9 Churchill cabled Hopkins that he was greatly pleased to hear of a telephone call to Eden, then in Canada on the way home, indicating that it was agreed that the meeting should be held. The main purpose of the conference was to ensure that there would be no undue delays in the launching of the Sicilian operation and to determine the answer to the question, 'Where do we go from there?'

Hopkins replied that 'Anthony must have misunderstood me', and said that the President felt that the time for another meeting was not propitious until the situation in Tunisia was clarified. Churchill replied that he was greatly disappointed.

It was then decided that Churchill should come to Washington with his Chiefs of Staff for full-dress conferences in May. On May 2 he cabled Hopkins that he was well aware that the President was distracted by domestic affairs, particularly the coal crisis, and he suggested that on this occasion it might be well for him to stay at the British Embassy rather than at the White House. He confessed that he was disturbed by certain differences of opinion relative to future operations which seemed to exist beneath the surface; he did not specify what these differences were, but he did state his determination to bring them out into the open and settle them.

The coal crisis referred to was one of the recurrent eruptions of John L. Lewis. It compelled Roosevelt to issue an order to Harold Ickes, as Secretary of the Interior and Solid Fuels Administrator for War, to take over all the bituminous and anthracite mines and operate them under the U.S. flag and the protection of the U.S. Army. On May 2 Roosevelt made an extraordinary appeal over the radio to the miners to go back to work as a patriotic duty. But just as the President was being wheeled from his study to go down to the Oval Room on the ground floor of the White House where he made his broadcasts word came that the melodramatic Lewis had just announced that he had concluded an agreement with Ickes for the return of the miners to work in two days. Roosevelt gave the speech anyway.

At 4.15 on the afternoon of Friday, May 7, the U.S. II Corps and French troops broke into Bizerta in Tunisia, and five minutes later the British First Army entered Tunis. This was the real ending of this campaign, although there remained several days of mopping up and of gathering in the huge haul of prisoners, including Col. General Dietloff von Arnim, the German

commander, who had taken over when Rommel was recalled to fight again elsewhere.

On May 11 Hopkins went to Staten Island to meet Churchill, Beaverbrook and party of nearly a hundred, who had crossed on the *Queen Mary,* together with several thousand German and Italian prisoners of war. Hopkins then accompanied the guests to Washington for the two weeks' conference which bore the name TRIDENT and at which the date—May 1, 1944—for the Normandy invasion was at last definitely set.

Roosevelt would not hear of the suggestion that Churchill stay at the British Embassy throughout the conference, so the Prime Minister went straight to the White House, although he later spent two or three days at the Embassy. The week-end of May 15 was spent at Shangri-la. Roosevelt also invited Beaverbrook to Shangri-la, but Churchill and Beaverbrook were at the time having one of their clashes—I believe this one was over the old subject of imperial preference—and Beaverbrook concluded that his presence on the week-end might be an embarrassment; so he wrote a letter from the Wardman Park Hotel declining the invitation:

> MY DEAR MR. PRESIDENT,
>
> The prospect of spending three days with you has been a joyous vision.
>
> But some of the newspapers seek to associate me with the Prime Minister. And that always leads to complications for him in the British Parliament.
>
> So I will reluctantly acknowledge on that account that I must forgo the paths of pleasantness.
>
> Later on, I will ask if I may come to see you.

This letter was referred to Hopkins, who telephoned Beaverbrook, saying, with some indignation: 'The President of the United States is not in the habit of selecting his guests in deference to the sentiment of the British Press or any other Press.' Beaverbrook went to Shangri-la.

On the drive from the White House to the Catoctin Hills, the President's car passed as usual through the old town of Frederick, Maryland. Churchill saw the roadside signs advertising Barbara Fritchie candy, and asked about them. Roosevelt explained that Barbara Fritchie was a semi-legendary character of our Civil War about whom John Greenleaf Whittier had once written a poem. All the President could remember of it was:

> 'Shoot, if you must, this old grey head,
> But spare your country's flag, she said.'

Whereupon Churchill proceeded to recite the entire poem, stating afterward that he had not thought of it in at least thirty years. A little farther on he saw a road sign pointing to Gettysburg and asked him how far away that

was. It was, roughly, forty miles. He said: Why, this may have been the
very road by which Longstreet moved up', and then went on to review the
whole battle. A few days later Churchill was invited to speak again before
a joint session of Congress, and in that speech he compared the present status
of the Second World War—after Stalingrad and Tunisia—to the status of
the Civil War after Gettysburg. (This proved to be an amazingly accurate
estimate of the time that remained before victory.) Churchill's speech to the
Congress was so informative that Congressmen were louder than ever in
their complaints that: 'The only time we get to find out what's going on in
the war is when the British Prime Minister visits Washington and tells us.'

This TRIDENT conference represented by far the largest gathering of high-
ranking officials and officers that had yet taken place in the war. Here is a
list of the forty-eight guests at a luncheon in the White House on May 25:

British	*American*
The Prime Minister	The President
Lord Halifax	Mr. Stimson
Lord Cherwell	Colonel Knox
Admiral Pound	Mr. Harriman
General Brooke	Mr. Hopkins
Air Marshal Portal	Mr. Stettinius
Lieutenant-General Ismay	Admiral Leahy
Field-Marshal Dill	Admiral King
Admiral Noble	Admiral Wilson Brown
Air Marshal Welsh	Admiral Edwards
Lieutenant-General Macready	Admiral Cook
Field-Marshal Wavell	Admiral Horne
Admiral Somerville	Commander Long
Lord Moran	General Marshall
Brigadier Jacob	General McNarney
Brigadier Redman	General Somervell
Major-General Holmes	General Deane
Captain Lambe	General Wedemeyer
Brigadier Porter	General Street
Air Commodore Elliot	General Watson
Brigadier Kirkman	General Hall
Major-General Kirby	General Stilwell
Commodore Edwards	General Chennault
Major-General Cawthorne	

The most interesting names on this list were those of Wavell, Stilwell, and
Chennault. This was the first of the major conferences with representation of
field commanders from the war in the Far East. Churchill had brought

Q

Wavell from India by way of London, and Stilwell and Chennault had been summoned from China in an attempt to straighten out the persistent differences between them and between Stilwell and Chiang Kai-shek. After his unhappy observation of high-level goings-on in Washington, Stilwell wrote: 'The inevitable conclusion was that Churchill has Roosevelt in his pocket. That they are looking for an easy way, a short-cut for England, and no attention must be diverted from the Continent at any cost. The Limeys are not interested in the war in the Pacific, and with the President hypnotized they are sitting pretty.'

The bitterness of Stilwell, as commander of a neglected theatre, was understandable. As I have said in a previous chapter, officers of MacArthur's staff liked to say that 'Churchill has Roosevelt in his hip pocket', because of the priority given to the defeat of Germany. And once, in July, 1944, I heard a British commander in Italy complain about the neglect of *that* theatre because, as he put it, 'Churchill is mere putty in Roosevelt's hands'. It is probable that, with the exception of Eisenhower and Nimitz, there was no theatre commander in the war who did not feel that he was the most neglected, most abused, and most basely cheated of them all, and that if it hadn't been for Certain Sinister Influences in High Places *his* theatre would have been recognized as the decisive battleground and he would have been given top priority in the allocation of men and material. It is also probable that none had as much right to feel this way as did Stilwell. In the cases of Eisenhower and Nimitz, of course, they had no substantial grounds for complaint for they were given top priority and the record indicates that they knew how to use it to win and end the war.

Actually, despite Stilwell's hatred of the 'Limeys', there were many occasions in the recurrent disputes when Churchill was heartily on the same side with Stilwell in opposing policies advocated by the Generalissimo. At the time of the TRIDENT conference the Chinese demands were especially insistent and the problems of morale in the Far East were acute. A message from the Generalissimo to the President strongly supported Chennault's argument that all air transport tonnage into China during the next three months be devoted to aviation gasoline and supplies for a decisive air offensive from Chinese bases. Joseph Alsop, the columnist, who was later to go with Chennault to Chungking and to become his most effective personal propagandist, wrote to Hopkins:

> The Chinese are really frightened about the future for the first time in my experience. . . . You will recall that in my talks and communications with you, I have never to date said a word about the danger of internal collapse in China, but have stuck always to the straight military results to be expected from an air effort in that area. . . . Speaking perfectly cold-

bloodedly, I can tell you that T. V. [Soong] and the ablest people around him are downright terrified of what may happen if there is not some sort of immediate, fairly spectacular action to revive the spirits of the Chinese people and troops.

It was obvious that no 'spectacular action' could be accomplished immediately or even for many months on the ground in Burma, and since the building up of Chennault's Fourteenth Air Force was what the Generalissimo most desired, at the moment, Roosevelt's decision went against Stilwell. Furthermore, Roosevelt needed no urging from Churchill (and if he did need it, he did not get it) to concentrate his primary attention on the major operations on the continent of Europe. Now, at last, he was firm in his insistence on the massive invasion of Northern France, which was given its ultimate code name, OVERLORD, and detailed plans for which were ordered to be drawn in London immediately.

Hopkins wrote no extensive notes on this conference such as he had written at Casablanca—at any rate, there are none in his papers—but the specific decisions of the conference were recorded as follows:

An Operation to seize the Azores Islands:

The purpose of this was to provide another base in the Battle of the Atlantic against the U-boats and also to provide a new air base for the ferrying of bombers and for transport planes which would enable the saving of more than one hundred million gallons of high octane gasoline a year by shortening the route from the U.S. to Africa and the United Kingdom and eventually to the European continent. (I have seen no computation of the concomitant saving of ships, aircraft, and lives. But, because of this saving, the Azores operation was given the code name LIFEBELT.) The capture of the Azores was to be planned by the British Chiefs of Staff and mounted from the United Kingdom and carried out in midsummer. When the British Cabinet in London were informed of this proposal to seize the Azores they protested that no military attack should be decided upon until efforts had been made to get the concession of bases from the Portuguese Government by diplomatic negotiations. Churchill did not believe that there was the slightest fragment of a chance that the Portuguese Government would agree to permit the establishment of bases and that any request to them would only result in the strengthening of the defences of the islands. However, as it turned out, the diplomatic negotiations were conducted and by October 12, 1943, Churchill was able to announce that they had succeeded.

Combined Bomber Offensive from the United Kingdom:

The Chiefs of Staff approved the plan for a tremendous increase in the bombing of Germany and German-occupied Europe by the R.A.F. and the

U.S. Eighth Air Force. This offensive was planned in four phases, to reach its peak in April, 1944. Involved in it was the destruction of German strength in fighter planes.

Cross-Channel Operations:

As has been said, the date was fixed for May 1, 1944. The initial assault was to consist of nine divisions (two of them airborne) with twenty more divisions immediately available for movement into the bridgehead when it was secured. Four American and three British divisions were to be moved from the Mediterranean after November 1 for OVERLORD, and further American divisions were to be moved steadily from the U.S. at the rate of three to five per month.

Operations in the Mediterranean to eliminate Italy from the War:

Eisenhower was instructed to plan operations beyond HUSKY, provided HUSKY itself did not bring about Italian surrender, these plans to be reviewed later by the Combined Chiefs of Staff.

Bombing of Ploesti:

This was the attack by two hundred American bombers on the Roumanian oilfields which was carried out on August 1. It caused substantial damage, but at very heavy cost.

Operations in the Burma-China Theatre:

Although there was provision for 'vigorous and aggressive land and air operations at the end of the 1943 monsoon' in Burma, Stilwell did not get the American infantry divisions for which he was begging. Chennault's air operations were to be strengthened, and there were plans for small-scale amphibious operations on the Burmese west coast. Preparations were to continue for the eventual launching of ANAKIM, but these preparations were only 'administrative'—which meant they were to be made on paper, not loaded on ships.

Operations in the Pacific:

These included ejection of the Japanese from the Aleutians, seizure of the Marshall and Caroline Islands, seizure of the remaining Japanese positions in the Solomons, the Bismarck Archipelago, and New Guinea. There was also to be an intensification of the far-reaching campaign by U.S. submarines and raids against Japanese lines of communication by the aircraft carrier task forces which were now beginning to be built up in great strength.

Most important, the Chiefs of Staff could report that sufficient personnel and material were available for all proposed operations. No serious deficiencies were apparent—with the exception of steel for landing-craft construction. But that appeared to be a very large exception when the Teheran Conference assembled six months later.

A confident atmosphere prevailed during these TRIDENT meetings in Washington—it was the first of all the conferences that was held with tabulations of actual victories over Germany on the books—and hopes were high for the achievement of a better world in the future. During these days the first of the United Nations conferences (on food) assembled at Hot Springs, Virginia—the U.S. and British Governments announced the abandonment of 'extra-territorial rights' in China, an action of immense importance throughout the Far East—and the Soviet Government announced the dissolution of the Comintern, which was heralded as abandonment by the Russians of any plan they may have had to communize the world. After the end of the conference Churchill and Marshall flew to North Africa, where they were joined by Eden. On May 31 de Gaulle and Giraud announced their agreement on the formation of a French executive committee, consisting of themselves, General Georges Catroux, René Massigli, Jean Monnet, General Alphonse Georges, and André Philip, for the organization at last of a unified French Provisional Government-in-Exile.

In spite of all these manifestations of encouragement—or, possibly, because of them—British and American relations with the Soviet Union, which had been none too good for months, now became appreciably worse. Following Standley's outburst, it had been obvious that he must be recalled, but the selection of his successor was not an easy one for Roosevelt to make. He tried to persuade Joseph E. Davies to go back to his old job in Moscow, but the state of Davies's health made it impossible for him to accept the post. He strongly urged that Hopkins be made Ambassador to the Soviet Union; Roosevelt flatly rejected this suggestion, for he did not want Hopkins to be away from Washington for any length of time.

Davies agreed to make a brief trip to Moscow in May to convey to Stalin Roosevelt's suggestion that the two of them should meet and straighten matters out. It was Roosevelt's belief that he might be able to break the ice with Stalin more readily if Churchill were not present; with personal relations established a meeting of the Big Three could be held later on. After eleven hours with Stalin, Davies reported that his suggestion had at first evoked a great many suspicious questions concerning the purpose of this meeting, but Stalin became convinced that there was no purpose other than a friendly one and he agreed to meet Roosevelt on July 15, providing for a possible postponement of two weeks if developments on the Eastern Front compelled it. After Davies left Moscow, Stalin received copies of the full plans drawn up at the TRIDENT conference and he was evidently not impressed. In the latter part of June—I do not know the exact date—he sent Churchill a cable in which he reviewed at length all the assurances that had been given during the past thirteen months relative to the opening of a Second Front, and concluded with words which could be interpreted only as charges of deliberate bad faith by the Western Allies.

Churchill usually consulted Roosevelt on the text of any important cable that he was sending to Stalin and there was often a considerable amount of discussion back and forth between London and Washington on the precise choice of words. But now Churchill was evidently so angry that he sent off a scorching cable to which Roosevelt would never have agreed had he been given a chance to read it in advance. During this period of tension, Stalin recalled Litvinov from Washington, and Maisky from London. There was now an atmosphere alarmingly reminiscent of that which had preceded the Molotov-Ribbentrop Pact of August, 1939, and the fears of a separate Russo-German Armistice were revived. The Roosevelt-Stalin meeting was postponed indefinitely. It was fortunate that Hitler did not know how bad the relations were between the Allies at that moment, how close they were to the disruption which was his only hope of survival.

Hopkins had an unusual (for him) experience at this time: he was given some friendly publicity. Harold Ross, the brilliant but indescribable editor of *The New Yorker*, assigned one of his best men, Geoffrey T. Hellman, to do a profile of Hopkins, and Hellman paid several visits to the White House and persuaded Hopkins to talk freely about the old days at Grinnell, the welfare work in New York City, the passions and the hatreds of the New Deal era, and the peregrinations during the war. When Hopkins read this profile—which said that he resembled 'an animated piece of shredded wheat' —he wrote a note of appreciation to Hellman and remarked: 'I seem to turn out a mixture of a Baptist preacher and a race-track tout'. (He might say the same about this book if he had lived to read it.)

In 'Notes and Comment' in the July 3, 1943, issue of *The New Yorker*, E. B. White wrote the following:

We received a letter from the Writer's War Board the other day asking for a statement on 'The Meaning of Democracy'. It presumably is our duty to comply with such a request, and it is certainly our pleasure.

Surely the Board knows what democracy is. It is the line that forms on the right. It is the don't in don't shove. It is the hole in the stuffed shirt through which the sawdust slowly trickles; it is the dent in the high hat. Democracy is the recurrent suspicion that more than half of the people are right more than half of the time. It is the feeling of privacy in the voting booths, the feeling of communion in the libraries, the feeling of vitality everywhere. Democracy is a letter to the editor. Democracy is the score at the beginning of the ninth. It is an idea which hasn't been disproved yet, a song the words of which have not gone bad. It's the mustard on the hot dog and the cream in the rationed coffee. Democracy is a request from a War Board, in the middle of a morning in the middle of a war, wanting to know what democracy is.

Hopkins showed that to the President who read it and roared—as he always did when somebody told him a story that struck him as funny—'I LOVE it!'—with a sort of rising inflection on the word 'love'. Roosevelt read White's definition of democracy to various gatherings, adding to it: 'Them's my sentiments exactly.' He almost used this quotation in the speech that he gave at the end of July, but he was talked out of it on the ground that it might sound too frivolous, particularly to foreigners.

Beaverbrook remained in the U.S. for a month after Churchill had left, and before his return to England, at the end of June, he handed Hopkins a memorandum which bore the title 'Present and Future':

It was a year ago that the Prime Minister came to Washington to make the plans which have now culminated in the fall of all North Africa.

The dominant question then was whether to launch a Second Front. The decision, taken against the sombre background of defeat in Libya and impending retreat in Russia, was that the project was too ambitious, and that a lesser objective should be chosen—the clearance of the southern shore of the Mediterranean. Such a plan involved gambling on Russia's ability to stand, *for one more campaign*, on her own. In the event, Russia did hold fast, and North Africa succeeded. These two achievements have meant, for the British and Americans, that the spectre of defeat has been almost entirely banished.

It is against a new background of established confidence that fresh decisions have now to be taken. The odds have moved heavily in favour of the Allies—the wasting assets of the Luftwaffe, the damage to German industry from the air, the strain on German manpower, the development of American strength, the Russian offensive successes, the opening of the Mediterranean—cumulatively these advantages are impressive.

But for all that, in the West and in the East, the game is still 'all to play for'. The Russians are only back where they were this time last year. The Anglo-Americans are nowhere on the mainland of Europe.

This year, as last, the dominant question is the Second Front. For this reason: that so long as it is unattempted, there remains for Germany not only the chance, albeit an outside one, to knock out or mortally wound the Russian armies, but also time to prepare the defences of 'Festung Europa'.

Can *we* afford more time for preparation? The Germans have a most powerful army in the East. The Russians used up men and resources at a heavy rate last winter in an offensive which stopped short of its fullest aims. There is always the risk that Japan will stab in the back. It cannot be said that Moscow, Baku, or Leningrad are out of danger. It can still less

be said that we and the Americans could in any measurable space of time win without Russian assistance.

Can the Germans ignore the threat of a Second Front? They can and certainly will. To do otherwise would be to allow the initiative to slip finally from their grasp. They are likely to go even further. They will ignore or treat lightly any blow from the West which is not delivered against a vital point. Knowing that the primary object of a Second Front would be to divert troops from the East they will go almost to any lengths to prevent that occurring.

Add to these factors the change in the Anglo-American situation in the last year. Then there were strong grounds for saying that a Second Front would be nothing but a forlorn hope involving the risk of final disaster, and there was much truth in the contention that in a year we should be vastly stronger. Today, of the three major United Nations, we and the Russians are as strong as we shall ever be. Certainly American potential is still developing, and in a year's time the United States will be more powerfully armed. But can we afford the new delay? Even suppose that Germany leaves Russia alone, will she, given a 'year of calm' in which to organize for defence, grow much weaker? Can bombing alone make all the difference? We have the weapons now, and the men, and the Germans are uncertain of themselves, their calculations seriously upset. None of these facts can guarantee success for the launching of a major Second Front. They do go far to ensuring that its failure will not spell disaster.

Surely the inference is inescapable that the question today must be not whether but where to launch the Second Front. The preliminaries are over, brilliantly performed. If they do not prove to have been the curtain raiser, the conclusion will be hard to escape, in occupied Europe especially, that the main play is never destined for performance.

But the 'where' of the Second Front is all-important. To be more than a diversion the attack must come at a spot where success will bring an immediate *mortal* threat to the enemy. The Second Front can, if it is a real one, apparently fail and yet succeed. It can, if it is only a diversion, apparently succeed and yet in reality fail.

The invasion of Italy? It might prove a major psychological blow at the enemy, but it could not guarantee decisive results. It could be parried by redrawing the southern boundary of the Fortress of Europe at the Alps and Dolomites, fighting a delaying action meanwhile.

The invasion of Northern Norway? It would mean a link-up with the Russians, but again the decisive threat to Europe would be lacking.

A landing in Southern Greece? The passes northwards to the Balkans and the Danube valley could be held by small forces.

When any of these objectives had been achieved, the game, so far as the core of German Europe was the goal (and there can be no other) would still be 'all to play for'.

But two places of attack promise immediate results. A descent, through the Dardanelles, with Turkish connivance or assistance, on the Eastern Balkans, would lay open the whole Danubian plain and jeopardise all the German forces in Southern Russia. A landing in Northern France would point straight at Paris, at the Ruhr, and at the Rhine. If either plan succeeded the enemy would be exposed to an intolerable strain before he had time to conserve, perfect, and organise his defences.

There are factors, such as the exact shipping position, relative to the Second Front which may be unknown to the layman. There are two factors which the military will ignore at our peril. One is the danger to Russia, the other the danger of stalemate. There seems a real danger that we shall go on indefinitely sewing the last button on the last gaiter, and the risk is increased by the undoubted fact that a real Second Front will always entail big risks, always remain the most difficult operation in military warfare. But if we are not prepared to accept the risks, face the difficulties, suffer the casualties, then let us concentrate at once exclusively on the production of heavy bombers and think in terms of 1950.

Harriman accompanied Beaverbrook on his flight back to London, where they arrived June 30. Roosevelt had given Harriman messages to be delivered orally to Churchill relative to the proposal for an intimate meeting of the President with Stalin previous to any formal conference of the Big Three. Hopkins well knew how unenthusiastic the Prime Minister was about this proposal and laughed as he wished Harriman the best of luck in his mission. A few days later Roosevelt received a report from Harriman:

Max and I arrived late Wednesday afternoon after two nights on the plane with little sleep to find an invitation to dine with the Prime Minister that evening. Max was tired and would have preferred to go to bed. He was not, therefore, in too good a mood. The dinner was argumentative, and some of the fundamental disagreements between the two men came out. This type of argument with Max always upsets the Prime Minister.

Max left at midnight. I stayed to give the Prime Minister alone your several messages. The talk, which started with the proposed meeting, developed into a two-hour discussion on every subject—from de Gaulle to China to India to Poland, etc., coming back throughout the talk to Russia and the question of the meeting.

I have never had a better opportunity to be direct and frank and, as he has since been more friendly than ever, it is obvious that he accepted the

sincerity of my statements even though he did not always agree with them.

He firmly believes a three-cornered meeting is in the interest of the war, but he admitted that his viewpoint is coloured by considerations of the reaction in Great Britain. My main argument was based on the long view as against the immediate—(1) the value of the intimate understanding that in all probability would result from a *tête-à-tête*, impossible with three persons, and (2) the great importance of the favourable reaction of the American people to it and to your participation. I explained the difference in the public reaction in the United States to a personal meeting of two as compared with a three-cornered meeting on British soil in which it would appear that he, Churchill, had been the broker in the transaction.

There is no doubt in my mind as to his sincere desire and determination to back you up in anything that you finally decide to do and, although I must emphasize his disappointment if he is not present, I am satisfied he would accept it in good part and that it would in the long run improve rather than adversely affect your relations with him.

If a meeting of three were held reasonably soon after your first meeting alone, he recognizes, I believe, the logic of the historic sequence of the two *tête-à-tête* meetings culminating in the third with three present.

Whatever Churchill may have said to Harriman on this occasion indicative of sympathetic understanding and acceptance of Roosevelt's proposal, he certainly lost no time in doing everything he could to prevent the '*tête-à-tête*'. It was all very well for Churchill and Stalin to meet without Roosevelt, because it was then generally assumed that the President's infirmity made it impossible for him to travel such great distances. But it was obvious, in view of Churchill's record of readiness to take off for any given point at any given moment, that his non-attendance at a top-level conference in Alaska, Siberia or elsewhere, would be accepted by the British people as proof of the fact that he had not been invited, and the Prime Minister's prestige might suffer. Therefore, hardly had Harriman left 10 Downing Street in the early hours of the morning before Churchill was hard at work drafting a message to Roosevelt with a counter-proposal for a preliminary conference of the British, Russian, and American Foreign Secretaries (Eden, Molotov, and Hull or Welles) to smooth out various controversial points before any meeting of the Big Three, or any part thereof, should be held. Roosevelt was by now none too confident that he could persuade Stalin to meet with him in any event, and he agreed to Churchill's suggestion, which was then taken up with the Russians, who eventually accepted it.

On June 30 Roosevelt also made a proposal for a meeting between himself

and Chiang Kai-shek at 'some place midway between our two capitals', during the autumn. The palliative decisions taken at the TRIDENT conference had produced only a temporary calm in Chungking, and there was now more trouble over the question of command in the China-Burma-India theatre, and more disputes between the Generalissimo, Stilwell, and Chennault which had to be referred to Washington for settlement. Roosevelt told Hopkins to arrange a morning meeting of Leahy, Marshall, and Somervell. Of this meeting, which was held in the President's bedroom, Hopkins wrote:

The President indicated his very strong dissatisfaction with the way our whole show is running in China. He stated that Stilwell obviously hated the Chinese and that his cablegrams are sarcastic about the Chinese and this feeling is undoubtedly known to the Chinese and the Generalissimo. Furthermore, the President said that it is quite clear the Generalissimo does not like Stilwell.

General Marshall told of his difficulties and said he realized that Stilwell was indiscreet, but he is the only high-ranking officer we have that can speak Chinese, and that, while he, obviously, does not like Chinese officialdom, he has great regard for the Chinese people. . . .

What the President wants is to have an independent command from Stilwell, but Marshall resists this, and on good military grounds, primarily, that Chennault knows nothing about logistics, that he was for many years a paid employee of the Chinese Government and, hence, under the undue influence of the Generalissimo. Marshall admits that Chennault is probably a tactical genius and, as such, wants to encourage him.

Marshall has told me that his only serious difference of opinion with Hopkins in the entire war was over this issue as between Stilwell and Chennault. I cannot pretend to express any opinion as to the merits of this unpleasant dispute. Hopkins was unquestionably influenced by the eloquent pleadings that flooded in from Chennault and Alsop and also by innumerable communications from and with his friend T. V. Soong, and he was inclined to be critical of Stilwell's violent intransigence and therefore favourable to Chennault. Ideological considerations, which were later to become of so much importance in all arguments of the Chinese problem, did not enter into it at that time. Marshall and King were vehemently on the side of Stilwell, who had faith in the Chinese Communists as forming a stronger and more reliable fighting force against the Japanese. Hopkins was on the side of Chennault, who was close to the Fascist-tinted Kuomintang. Churchill favoured Stilwell, in so far as he was on any side at all. Stalin apparently was not greatly interested in either faction in China, believing that neither would be a potent fighting factor in this war. Roosevelt had high regard for both

Stilwell and Chennault, as fighting men, but his one overriding concern was to keep China in the war and to hold the friendship of the Chinese people for the United States, and he had those objectives in mind in every decision that he made. He believed that there was no chance that the Chinese Communists would surrender to the Japanese as long as Russia was in the war against the Axis, whereas there was always the possibility that the Kuomintang might make a separate peace. In any case, Chiang Kai-shek was head of the Government with which the U.S. Government must deal and the maintenance of good relations was difficult enough under the circumstances without the frequent disturbances created by Stilwell. Thus, whether or not Stilwell had the right on his side—and he certainly had a great deal of it—he was unquestionably a serious nuisance and there were many times when Roosevelt was on the verge of ordering his recall. Fortunately, in September, 1943, a semblance of harmony was established in Chungking, largely due to the efforts of Madame Chiang Kai-shek and her sister, Madame Kung, on Stilwell's behalf.

Roosevelt also had more domestic troubles during this summer. The 'Armistice' negotiated between Lewis and Ickes did not solve the coal crisis and there were further work stoppages. Congress passed the Smith-Connally Anti-Strike Bill. On June 25, Roosevelt vetoed it and immediately both the Senate and the House produced better than the two-thirds majority necessary to override his veto. This was the worst reversal Roosevelt ever had in his dealings with the Congress on social legislation. More than half the votes in the Senate for overriding the veto, and almost half of those in the House, were cast by Democrats, giving clear proof of the fact that on domestic issues of this nature the President could no longer control his own party.

On June 29, as the hazardous Sicilian expedition was about to embark and the tension with Moscow was most acute, Vice-President Wallace delivered his all too blatantly public blast against the Secretary of Commerce, Jesse H. Jones, charging that he had obstructed the efforts of the Board of Economic Warfare to build up stock piles of critical and strategic war materials in 1940, 1941, and even after Pearl Harbour. This was undoubtedly the worst of all the public brawls that marred the record of the Roosevelt Administration and it gave to the American people—not to mention the people of other United Nations—an alarming sense of disunity and blundering incompetence in very high places. Roosevelt was extremely angry at Wallace for this outburst and at Jones for the manner in which he snapped back. On July 15 Roosevelt dissolved the Board of Economic Warfare, of which Wallace was Chairman, and put its functions and various others connected with foreign economic matters, which had been in Jones's department, under the authority of Byrnes, whose title now was Director of the Office of War Mobilization. Those who were around the White

House at the time of this disagreeable incident felt there was now no chance that Roosevelt would support Wallace at the Democratic Convention in 1944.

On June 16 Roosevelt and Churchill jointly issued a statement which had been prepared a month before and held until the psychological moment when the success of the Sicilian operation was assured. It was a message to the Italian people, saying:

> The sole hope for Italian survival lies in honourable capitulation to the overwhelming power of the military forces of the United Nations. . . . All your interests and all your traditions have been betrayed by Nazi Germany and your own false and corrupt leaders: it is only by destroying both that a reconstituted Italy can hope to occupy a respected place in the family of European nations.

That statement was broadcast to Italy by all the available British and American radio transmitters, including some new ones that had been installed on the North Coast of Africa, and it was also delivered through millions of airplane leaflets. Three days after this a large force of American bombers made the first air raid on Rome, concentrating their accurate attack on the railroad yards through which the Germans had been sending reinforcements to the south. At the same time, it was announced that Hitler and Mussolini were meeting in Northern Italy; hearing this news, the outside world did not tremble at the thought 'Where will the monster strike next?' —it seeming more probable that they were discussing the best means of booking passage for Argentina. Sunday afternoon, July 25, Rosenman and I were with the President at Shangri-la, Hopkins having left that morning to go on a trip with General Arnold for some salmon fishing on the Restigouche in Canada. We had been working on a speech to be delivered the following Tuesday mainly for the purpose of trying to save the National Resources Planning Board from death at the hands of Congress; the N.R.P.B. was very dear to Roosevelt's heart, but to the conservative majority on Capitol Hill the very word 'plan' was considered a Communist invention and any planning board must be part of a plot to disrupt the capitalist system of free enterprise. Roosevelt made the point in this speech that we had *planned* the North African campaign more than a year ago and we had *planned* the Sicilian campaign more than six months ago, and it was none too soon to start planning for postwar reconversion; he presented for the first time the proposal for a G.I. Bill of Rights, the plan for which had been drawn by the N.R.P.B.

The President's speech was in virtually final form late in the afternoon of this quiet summer Sunday, when Steve Early telephoned from Washington to say he had just heard a news flash over the radio to the effect that Mussolini

had resigned. The announcement had been picked up from the Rome radio, which, of course, was at that time a highly unreliable source for any kind of news. The President seemed quite surprised, but not tremendously excited by this report, and said: 'I wonder how we could get any confirmation on that.' I thereupon telephoned to my associates in the O.W.I. short-wave broadcasting centre in New York and asked them what they knew about the story. They had heard it, all right, and had communicated with the B.B.C. authorities in London, who were inclined to believe it true; the O.W.I. people had subsequently been trying to get confirmation of it from the White House or any other official source in Washington, while the White House was now trying to get confirmation from *them*. I reported this to the President, and he said: 'Oh—we'll find out about it later.' We then resumed work on the speech, had a leisurely dinner, then drove back to Washington, arriving at the White House late in the evening, and the President went to his study to try and reach Churchill on the telephone. It was to me an amazing glimpse into Roosevelt's manner of life: for a matter of more than five hours all that the President of the United States heard of the downfall of the first of the Axis dictators was the chance report on a radio news flash from Steve Early and from what I had learned about the B.B.C. appraisal from my own office. One would have thought that during those hours dispatches would have been flashing constantly from and to all directions, even on the radio-equipped Secret Service cars during the drive back to Washington.

The next day the speech was substantially revised to meet the new developments. In it, Roosevelt said:

Our terms to Italy are still the same as our terms to Germany and Japan—'Unconditional Surrender'.
We will have no truck with Fascism in any way, shape, or manner. We will permit no vestige of Fascism to remain.

By then it became clear that the King of Italy had managed to remain on his throne throughout the palace revolution and had appointed Marshal Badoglio Prime Minister. The question immediately arose as to whether the Allies should treat with the new régime as a legitimate, non-Fascist Government, overlooking the fact that the king had accepted if not blessed the Mussolini régime throughout its disgraceful career and that Badoglio had been the Duce's commander-in-chief in the rape of Ethiopia. Again there were howls of protest from those who had been outraged by the measures of 'expediency' in North Africa and who believed that the last vestiges of the Vichy policy should have been buried with Darlan. The merest suggestion of recognition of the Badoglio Government brought down more and more opprobrium on the State Department, which by now was regarded in

liberal circles as the very citadel of reaction and of the policy of 'doing business' with the avowed enemy. However, the State Department was by no means the predominant policy-making instrument in consideration of the new situation in Italy. It was a matter of cold, hard military calculation. General Eisenhower and the Combined Chiefs of Staff were conscious of the enormous possible advantage of having any Italian Government, regardless of its political colouration, which would have the authority to deliver an immediate surrender. The question of immediacy was all-important, for the Allies wanted to move into Naples, Foggia, and Rome itself before the Germans could reinforce these points. Furthermore, and of much greater importance ultimately, was the factor of Winston Churchill's long-established conviction that constitutional monarchy was the strongest and most stable form of government for European states. Churchill was firmly in favour of the retention of the House of Savoy, just as he was later obdurate in his support of the restoration of the Greek King. In this connection, I was interested to read the following about the aftermath of the First World War in *The Gathering Storm*, the first volume of Churchill's tremendous memoirs of the Second World War:

> The prejudice of the Americans against monarchy, which Mr. Lloyd George made no attempt to counteract, had made it clear to the beaten [German] Empire that it would have better treatment from the Allies as a Republic than as a Monarchy. Wise policy would have crowned and fortified the Weimar Republic with a constitutional sovereign in the person of an infant grandson of the Kaiser, under a Council of Regency. Instead, a gaping void was opened in the national life of the German people. All the strong elements, military and feudal, which might have rallied to a constitutional monarchy and for its sake respected and sustained the new democratic and Parliamentary process, were for the time being unhinged. The Weimar Republic, with all its liberal trappings and blessings, was regarded as an imposition of the enemy.

That passage dispels any mystery as to Churchill's attitude in the settlement of both World Wars: he had been reared under a constitutional monarchy, he had served the Crown throughout his public career, and he had scant respect for the stability of the republican form of government as it had been tried in Europe. Certainly, in all of his subsequent dealings with Roosevelt, he made every attempt to avoid what he considered to be Lloyd George's serious mistake in accepting American opposition to the restoration of dethroned dynasties.

Shortly after the Italian surrender Hopkins wrote down his own views on this matter:

I have grave misgivings about both the king and Badoglio. Certainly neither of them, by any stretch of the imagination, can be considered to represent a democratic government.

It is very easy to recognize these people, but it is awfully hard to throw them overboard later.

I surely don't like the idea that these former enemies can change their minds when they know that they are going to get licked and come over to our side and get help in maintaining political power.

However, the prospect of removing Italy from the war without serious bloodshed—which meant possession of the air bases on the Italian mainland and elimination of the Italian Fleet as a threat to shipping in the Mediterranean—was so overwhelmingly tempting that long-term considerations of morality were apt to be shoved aside. It seemed a supreme opportunity for the attainment of objectives by political manoeuvring rather than force, and the psychological warriors in North Africa who had scored such a resounding success with their propaganda barrage against Mussolini now stepped up their attacks by radio broadcasts and leaflets. They started assuring the Italians that, if they were to surrender 'honourably', the Italian prisoners of war in British and American hands would be restored promptly to their homes—a promise that was obviously impossible to fulfil. When Churchill heard of this he was furious and he cabled Hopkins expressing his views on the 'anonymous and unauthoritative low-level propaganda pumped out by the machines'.

Churchill certainly did not object to the political manoeuvring, but he did object strenuously to the proffering of the olive branch on a silver platter.

In Badoglio's first public statement after the fall of Mussolini he indicated that Italy would not seek a separate peace with the Allies; he said, 'the war goes on', but he did not add '*positively*'. There was little doubt in the minds of either Roosevelt or Churchill that peace feelers would soon begin to emerge from Rome, unless the Badoglio régime were to be rapidly overthrown by German power and a puppet Quisling Government set up under Mussolini or any available Fascist. This presented a situation the handling of which, on a minute-to-minute basis, was a matter of overwhelming importance in its effect on relations with Russia, on the morale of Germany, the satellite states and even Japan—and, ultimately, on the whole future structure of world peace. It was obvious, therefore, that the time had come for another Roosevelt-Churchill conference, and arrangements were rapidly made for a meeting on the citadel of Quebec. As usual, the Chiefs of Staff assembled first to lay the groundwork for military discussion, arriving in Quebec on August 12. The following day the Prime Minister joined the President at Hyde Park for some preliminary conversations. *En route*, Churchill went far

out of the way to give his daughter, Lieutenant Mary Churchill, a look at Niagara Falls; he told assembled newspapermen that he had seen the Falls some thirty years before and that the principle of the thing still seemed to be about the same. Roosevelt arrived in Quebec for the conference, which bore the name QUADRANT, on August 17. In the President's party were Hopkins, Leahy, Early, Grace Tully, Louise Hackmeister, and Admiral Wilson Brown, who had succeeded McCrea as Naval Aide. Churchill was accompanied by Eden, Bracken, Leathers, and the usual large staff, and during subsequent days Hull, Stimson, and Knox arrived in Quebec and so did T. V. Soong, this being the first time that China was represented in these top-level deliberations, apart from the meeting of the Pacific Council.

This gathering came none too soon. Shortly after the conference started Roosevelt and Churchill sent the following message to Stalin:

> The British Ambassador in Madrid reported to us on August 15th that General Castellano, representing Badoglio, had arrived there bearing a letter of introduction from the British Minister at the Vatican. Castellano declared that he had authorization from Badoglio to state Italy's willingness to surrender unconditionally if she could thereupon join the Allies. This seems a firm offer, the British Minister at the Vatican having confirmed that Badoglio had stated in writing that he had given authorization to Castellano. We do not intend to enter into any bargain with Badoglio's Government for the purpose of inducing Italy to change sides. We recognize, on the other hand, many advantages in the acceleration of the campaign which might result. Our invasion of the mainland of Italy will begin probably before September 1st, and approximately a week later we shall make our full-scale landings at AVALANCHE [the Salerno Beachhead south of Naples]. It would seem likely that Badoglio's Government will not survive that long. There are one or more German armoured divisions outside Rome, and once they suspect that Badoglio is playing them false they would be able to overthrow him and set up another Fascist Government under Farinacci, for instance. Or, the Badoglio Government might collapse and plunge all of Italy into anarchy.

Therefore (this message continued), authorization had been sent to Eisenhower to send emissaries to meet with Castellano in Lisbon, which was evidently considered slightly more friendly ground than any point in Franco's Spain. This mission was entrusted to the tough-fibred 'Beedle' Smith, accompanied by Brigadier K. W. D. Strong, a British officer, who was G-2 on Eisenhower's staff. Castellano was undoubtedly aware of Roosevelt's statement about 'no truck with Fascism', and was at great pains to convince Smith and Strong that the new régime had purged itself of all elements of the old one. Speaking as a soldier, he gave full credit for Mussolini's over-

R

throw to the Italian high command. He said that sentiment against the Duce had increased in strength and determination in the Army throughout the long, humiliating series of Italian reverses in the field, beginning with the beatings administered by the surprising Greeks and continuing through to the loss of the last vestige of the Italian African Empire and of Sicily. The Army did not feel strong enough by itself to get rid of the inflated Duce, so a junta of three was formed to foment discontent within the Fascist machine. Count Grandi was enticed into the plot with the promise that if Mussolini fell he could save Fascism by becoming Mussolini's successor. However, as soon as Mussolini had been defeated in the Grand Council, the Army moved in and threw out Grandi and his accomplices. They regarded Grandi as half traitor and half dupe, and they despised Count Ciano as a man who had stabbed his father-in-law in the back. Castellano told Smith and Strong that the principal Italian desire was, first, for protection against the Germans during their present phase of defencelessness, and then an opportunity to join with the United Nations in fighting the Germans. Eisenhower's representatives said that all they were authorized to offer were terms for a military capitulation which must be accepted unconditionally, but they said that the Allies were prepared to give assistance and support to any Italian forces or individuals who would fight against the Germans or work to obstruct the German military effort.

Having completed the preliminary conversations with Castellano, Smith and Strong returned to Algiers and the Italian general returned to Rome. Responsibility for decisions as to further steps was then passed back to Quebec. Roosevelt and Churchill kept Stalin informed of every subsequent development, so that the Soviet Union would be in full agreement with all the terms of Italian surrender and would, indeed, participate in its acceptance.

Otherwise, on the political side, the principal accomplishments of the Quebec Conference were an Anglo-American agreement on the draft of a Four Power Declaration, to involve the Soviet Union and China, as well as the United Kingdom and the United States, for the establishment of an effective international organization—and an agreement to disagree on extending recognition to the French Committee of National Liberation in Algiers which, by now, was under the domination of de Gaulle.

In the military field, the principal decisions were the reaffirmation of the target date (May 1, 1944) for OVERLORD and the establishment of the South-East Asia Command under Mountbatten, with Stilwell as Deputy Supreme Allied Commander.

Churchill was by no means reconciled to the Normandy invasion nor to any other major operation in Western Europe. In accordance with the TRIDENT agreement three months previously, an outline plan for invasion had been drawn up in London, and implementation of it had started, but the

experiences of 1942 when decisions agreed to in April were reversed in July led the American Chiefs of Staff to fear that Quebec would end up with another reversed decision in favour of a diversionary 'eccentric operation' in the Mediterranean area against the soft underbelly. Churchill advanced his usual and always powerful warnings of the appalling casualties that might be suffered. He pointed again and again to the map of France, showing the tremendous logistical advantages enjoyed by the Germans, the quantity of supply lines running east and west, the roads and railroads built by the French in their own defensive plan to supply and reinforce the Belgian frontier and the Maginot Line from the Channel ports. However, the Air Force now had achieved the answer to this: the concentrated, unrelenting bombing of all German lines of communication which would disrupt the system of supply and restrict facility of manoeuvre. The combined bombing offensive was given the code name 'Operation POINTBLANK', and the Italian part of it was called 'Operation STRANGLE'. The ultimate story of the success of this huge and prolonged application of air power is written in the German records.

At Quebec the decision was made—for the first time, in so far as I know—to supplement the Normandy invasion with landings by American and newly armed French forces in the Toulon-Marseilles area of Southern France. This was an operation—it was known first as ANVIL and later as DRAGOON—against which Churchill fought implacably until within a few days of its accomplishment on August 15, 1944, whereupon he turned up aboard a British destroyer in the Mediterranean and, with apparent exultation, waved the victory sign to the astonished troops as they headed for the Riviera beaches.

As to the war against Japan: aside from the creation of the complicated and largely abortive (through no fault of its own) South East Asia Command, the Quebec Conference appears to have accomplished little, except the listing of a considerable number of individual operations, most of which never took place.

Quebec was unique among all the conferences up to that time in one vital respect: at last the Chiefs of the Naval Staffs could report that victory was being won in the war against the U-boats. Escort vessel production had been stepped up and the tide had at last turned in the Battle of the Atlantic. The Germans eventually found ways to overcome the Allied advantages in the defence of convoys—but they did not do so, fortunately, until it was too late.

Another piece of extremely favourable news that came out of Quebec was set forth in a message from Churchill and Roosevelt to Stalin:

Following the decisions taken at the TRIDENT Conference, the British Government entered into negotiations with the Government of Portugal

in order to obtain air bases and naval facilities in the Azores. In accordance with this, the British Ambassador in Lisbon invoked the alliance between England and Portugal which has lasted unbroken for 600 years, and invited the Portuguese Government to grant the desired facilities. Dr. Salazar was oppressed, of course, by fear of vengeful German bombing and of the possibility of attack on Portugal by Spanish forces. The British agreed to furnish him with fighter airplanes and anti-aircraft artillery which are now *en route*, and have informed Dr. Salazar that in the event of a Spanish attack, the Allies will immediately go to war with Spain and render fullest possible aid. Since neither of these contingencies seems probable, no precise military convention earmarking particular troops for this purpose has as yet been made. Dr. Salazar has now agreed that the British, with Portuguese collaboration, may start to make use of the Azores in the early part of October. As soon as the British are established on these islands and Salazar is relieved of anxieties, pressure will be brought to extend the use of the facilities by ships and aircraft of the United States.

The use of the Azores is of great importance in the war in the Atlantic. The German U-boats have now quit the North Atlantic, where our convoys have been running without loss since mid-May. The U-boats are concentrating more on the southern route. We shall be able to attack them with aircraft based in the Azores. In addition to which, the ferrying of United States heavy bombers to Europe and Africa will be greatly facilitated.

Hopkins had with him at the Quebec Conference a document headed, '*Russia's Position*', which was quoted from 'a very high-level United States military strategic estimate' (the source was otherwise unidentified). It contained the following:

Russia's post-war position in Europe will be a dominant one. With Germany crushed, there is no power in Europe to oppose her tremendous military forces. It is true that Great Britain is building up a position in the Mediterranean *vis-à-vis* Russia that she may find useful in balancing power in Europe. However, even here she may not be able to oppose Russia unless she is otherwise supported.

The conclusions from the foregoing are obvious. Since Russia is the decisive factor in the war, she must be given every assistance and every effort must be made to obtain her friendship. Likewise, since without question she will dominate Europe on the defeat of the Axis, it is even more essential to develop and maintain the most friendly relations with Russia.

Finally, the most important factor the United States has to consider in relation to Russia is the prosecution of the war in the Pacific. With Russia as an ally in the war against Japan, the war can be terminated in less time and at less expense in life and resources than if the reverse were the case. Should the war in the Pacific have to be carried on with an unfriendly or a negative attitude on the part of Russia, the difficulties will be immeasurably increased and operations might become abortive.

This estimate was obviously of great importance as indicating the policy which guided the making of decisions at Teheran and, much later, at Yalta.

Toward the end of the Quebec Conference, word was received from Stalin agreeing to a meeting of the Foreign Secretaries in Moscow, and this news was greeted enthusiastically, for it meant the beginning of the long-desired collaboration of the Big Three, as well as the easing of the dangerous tension that had existed between the Western Allies and the Soviet Union. The Germans had made their final attempt to launch an offensive against the Russians in the middle of July. This, it appeared, was no more than a propaganda demonstration to attempt to persuade the German people and the rest of the world that the Wehrmacht still retained some semblance of its former, fearsome striking power, but it petered out within a week, whereupon the Russians seized the initiative and never relinquished it.

Churchill accompanied Roosevelt back to the White House after the Quebec Conference and remained in Washington off and on for three weeks, during which time the British and Canadian troops landed on the Italian boot, General Clark's Fifth Army landed at Salerno, and Italy surrendered. On September 6 Churchill went to Cambridge, Massachusetts, to receive an honorary degree from Harvard University. This ceremony had been long planned and Roosevelt, a member of the Class of 1904, took a great deal of interest in it. He telephoned various suggestions to President Conant expressing the hope that there would be plenty of pageantry and colour in the ceremony. Conant conceived the idea that the Prime Minister should be outfitted with the scarlet academic robe of Oxford, from which he had received the LL.D. degree, rather than the austere American cap and gown. There were none of these robes in Cambridge or in Boston, but Conant finally located one at Princetown and borrowed it for the occasion.

In the speech that he gave at Harvard, Churchill made a statement that he would hardly have dared to make at any previous and less propitious moment in the war or, indeed, at any previous time since the Declaration of Independence. He said: 'This gift of a common tongue is a priceless inheritance, and it may well some day become the foundation of a common citizenship. I like to think of British and Americans moving about freely over each other's wide estates with hardly a sense of being foreigners to one another.'

He also said: 'The price of greatness is responsibility. If the people of the United States had continued in a mediocre station, struggling with the wilderness, absorbed in their own affairs, and a factor of no consequence in the movement of the world, they might have remained forgotten and undisturbed beyond their protecting oceans: but one cannot rise to be in many ways the leading community in the civilized world without being involved in its problems, without being convulsed by its agonies and inspired by its causes.' I doubt that Churchill ever made any important utterance on American soil during the war without the previous knowledge and approval of the President; in fact, he often consulted Roosevelt by telephone or cable before making his reports on the war situation to the House of Commons. He certainly talked to Roosevelt before suggesting even the remote possibility of 'common citizenship' and was assured by the President that the United States had advanced so far from its isolationist position that this would not outrage public opinion or provoke another Boston Tea Party.

After the Quebec Conference—and after practically every other conference in the war—Hopkins was in a state of utter depletion and had to go to the Naval Hospital for rest and revival. (His frequent visits to this hospital often impelled the critics of the Administration to ask why the taxpayers' penicillin should be wasted on the restoration of Hopkins.) One of the most interesting pieces of reading matter that now came to his sick-bed was a full-page feature from the *Chicago Sunday Tribune* with a huge coloured cartoon that showed Hopkins leering, and hovering over his shoulder was the sinister image of Grigoryi Efimovich Rasputin. In the accompanying article, Walter Tróhan (who was later to collaborate in the writing of *Jim Farley's Story*) achieved a remarkable effect in juxtaposition. He wrote: 'One evening in 1907 a tall, broad-shouldered peasant strode across the highly polished floor of the salon of Count Alexander Pavlovich Ignatiev. . . . He bowed clumsily to an ill-assorted circle of nobles, politicians, schemers, charlatans, adventurers, clergy, and dignitaries. . . . The ugly face, with a large pockmarked nose . . . the rough peasant clothes, unkempt brown hair, stringy brown beard gave him a wild appearance. . . . Rasputin went on to sway Russia by the power of his eye. Nicholas, the Czar of all the Russias, fell on his knees before this curious mixture of penitent and debauchee and called him a "Christ." The Czarina believed in him implicitly. For almost nine years this preacher of redemption through sin virtually ruled Russia. . . . His murder foreshadowed the end of the Romanoff dynasty and the collapse of the Russian empire in the World War.

'On a May day in 1933 a lean, gangly figure with thinning brown hair and dandruff made his way with his face twisted by a sardonic grin through an ill-assorted group of representatives, crackpots, senators, bums, governors,

job seekers, political leaders, and toadies . . . in the person of Harry Lloyd Hopkins, son of an Iowa harness-maker, Santa Claus had come to town. He emptied his hands of other people's money. This strange and contradictory figure spent on and on to sway a nation and then the world. The President of the United States brought him into his official family and then into his private family and poured his innermost thoughts into the spender's promi-nent ears. The wife of the President adopted his small child in all but name.'

Trohan quoted Representative Dewey Short of Missouri as having said in 'a message of extraordinary importance' to the House of Representatives: 'Would the followers of the Rasputin of the White House . . . and there are many in high and important places in our Government today . . . use this war as a smoke screen to saddle upon America a type of government and a kind of economy entirely foreign and contrary to those we have ever known?'

Hopkins wrote to Joseph E. Davies saying that he had never yet known a lawyer who would agree that *anything* was libellous, but he asked: 'Can't you dig up some bright, young men in your office who will tell me that these bastards can be sued for libel?' The Davies reply expressed the opinion that Hopkins would find it difficult to win a libel suit, because he occupied a public position and was, therefore, fair game for any kind of insult—so Hopkins merely pasted the Trohan article in his scrapbook.

This diversion came at the time of the Italian surrender, and two days thereafter Hopkins wrote to his brother-in-law, Captain Donald Duncan, who was then on the aircraft carrier *Essex* in the Pacific:

> The Italian show is fantastic, but none of us know yet just what all the implications are. For myself, I think we are in for some pretty rough fighting in Italy, particularly if the Germans really decide to try to hold the northern half. We have every reason to be hopeful that we are going to get the Italian fleet intact.
>
> Louise and I are hoping to get a house before the first of November and have a place of our own, which will suit me no end.

Hopkins's guess about the prospect of 'tough fighting in Italy' proved lamentably correct. The daring plan to take Rome with an American air-borne operation, synchronized with the Salerno landings, had been frustrated by German seizure of the Rome airfields—a development which seemed no more than momentarily disappointing at the time, but which resulted in the black winter at Cassino and the Anzio beachhead, the record of which has been told in the writings of Ernie Pyle, the drawings of Bill Mauldin, and the terrible casualty lists.

On September 20 Hopkins read a copy of the proposed agreement where-by Italy would be permitted to enter the war not as an 'ally' but as a 'co-

belligerent', and he wrote the following memorandum and sent it to the President:

> I hope you will not encourage Eisenhower to recognize Italy as a co-belligerent. This will put them in exactly the same status as the rest of our allies. Nor do I think there is enough evidence that Badoglio and the king can be trusted for us to arm any of their divisions. I should think that Eisenhower could quietly look the other way if some of the armistice terms are being violated, such as Italian naval ships being used to transport our troops, or Italian bombers from Sardinia fighting the Germans.
>
> Would it not be better in paragraph 2 to cut out the words 'to wage war against Germany' and substitute 'to assist us in the war'?
>
> I cannot see that a declaration of war by Badoglio gets us anywhere except a precipitated recognition of two men who have worked very closely with the Fascists in the past. I think we should get every possible advantage out of them, but I don't think we are under any obligation to them.
>
> I don't see why, if Eisenhower wants to use the Italian crews and Italian ships, he does not go ahead and do it, providing he thinks he can trust them. I simply hate to see this business formalized until we have had a much better look at Badoglio and the king. McFarlane, the British general's, report on them was certainly none too good.
>
> I would not throw out Badoglio, but recognitions would be an inevitable step. Could you not tell Eisenhower to keep on as he is for the present and make the decision in another week?

The news that Mr. and Mrs. Harry Hopkins had rented a house in Georgetown gave the Washington gossip columnists a welcome topic for their conjectural chatter. Was the controversial couple moving voluntarily or by request? Hopkins had lived in the White House for three and a half years, and since his marriage there had been more and more protests against his permanent-guest status, not only in the Press, but even in the halls of Congress. The merry-andrews of the capital were referring to the White House as 'that two-family flat'. There were ugly rumours, none of them carrying the weight of any authority whatsoever (authority, of course, was the last thing that the gossip columnists needed), concerning inter-family clashes upstairs at 1600 Pennsylvania Avenue. For obvious reasons, Hopkins and his wife had cherished the natural desire to have a home of their own where they could live and entertain their friends as they pleased, free from the circumscriptions which were inevitable in the Executive Mansion. Hopkins did not move into the Georgetown house until after his return from the Teheran Conference in December, and he spent very little time in it during the two years that remained of his life.

In its October issue the *American* magazine printed an article by Hopkins entitled 'We Can Win the War in 1945'. Hopkins, in the hospital, received a letter from a lady in Colorado who had two sons in the Service. She said:

> Mr. Hopkins, many of us feel that God is really the only one who can straighten out this appalling mess; and we are praying daily that he will hasten the end of this war. If God decides to end this war in 1943, no doubt he can and will do so, but it would surely be nice if he could have a little co-operation from you and the President and Winston. When you say 'in 1945', I am sure you don't mean 'by that time the election will be over', but don't you think most of the people will believe that is what you have in mind? . . . Every day this war continues, you and the President will become less popular. . . . I am not trying to tell you and the President what to do. I am only begging of you not to drag your feet; not to hold the boys back, for political or any other infamous reasons.

This was a letter to which Hopkins made immediate reply:

> You can be sure that I do not want the war to last an hour longer than necessary and nothing would please me more if we could have victory this year. I merely expressed my opinion that that is highly unlikely. There are friends of mine who believe that we may defeat Germany even by the end of this year. I happen not to share their view.
>
> One thing you can be sure of is that our military leaders want to end the war as soon as possible.
>
> My own feeling is that the war is progressing well and that the Allies are attacking with intelligence and vigour, but I believe that it cannot be done overnight.
>
> I have three boys in the armed forces and I surely understand how anyone feels who has sons in the army or navy. I am glad mine are there. I would not have them anywhere else, but I hope they get home safely.

Considerable annoyance was occasioned at this time by the publication of a photograph that had been taken during a Churchill visit to Hyde Park by a British Army officer, a member of the Prime Minister's official party. This was especially galling to Steve Early who had to take the violent and largely unanswerable protests of the American correspondents whenever British sources released news to which they had not been given access. (No American photographers had been permitted at Hyde Park on this particular occasion.) Hopkins sent a sharp cable to Brendan Bracken:

> One hell of a row has been raised here by publication of this picture and the President feels that there must be something done to put an end

to this sort of business. It serves to add to the already developing antagon-ism against Britain, since all the newspapers that get beat with a picture like this promptly find some way to take a crack at your country. This publication comes on top of the disclosure prematurely in London of the fact that Italy is determined to declare war on Germany, revealed in a dispatch from Reston to the *New York Times* passed by British censor-ship. . . . Altogether too many things of this type are happening in London. I believe you should give your most serious personal attention to this business and don't underrate for a moment the effect that this kind of thing is exerting on relations between our two countries. We are in the midst of fighting a tough war and why in God's world do we have to cope with such leaks? I put it mildly in saying that the highest circles here are irritated with this type of thing.

Bracken replied at length disclaiming all responsibility for the Hyde Park photograph and saying: 'We are just as much upset as you are by premature releases', and, 'knowing, as I do, that many publishers in the United States are eagerly searching about for any excuse to attack the President you may rely upon us to do everything in our power to prevent their getting any ammunition from Great Britain'.

At this time Beaverbrook returned to the Cabinet as Lord Privy Seal and Hopkins wrote to him: 'Needless to say, I am delighted you are back in the Government, although this will probably mean that I will hear none of your unrestrained conversation again.'

London papers printed the report that Hopkins would replace Winant as Ambassador—and that Winant would replace Frances Perkins as Secretary of Labour—and the *Chicago Tribune* printed the report from 'sources close to the State Department' that Hopkins might be made Ambassador to Russia. Following the previous report, Winant sent a cable to Hopkins which re-vealed poignantly the difficulties of his position:

During the past six months a situation has developed which has cut down my usefulness. I have had no business delegated to me as Ambas-sador that could not have been done by an efficient Foreign Service officer. I have been by-passed continuously. I have had no contacts with the Prime Minister except on two occasions when he invited me to meet with him so that he could bring me up to date on Anglo-American relations. Nine-tenths of the information I receive comes from British sources. Matters of serious importance relating to our foreign policy go to Mr. Churchill or Mr. Eden through other channels. Officials of the British Government have been friendly and frank with me but they are quick to appreciate when one in my position has been deprived of his authority.

Formerly, I saw a great deal of Brendan Bracken and usually met with him officially at least one and even three or four times a week. I have not seen him at all in the last six months except to meet him by chance in the street or shake hands with him at some function. I do not think he is any less friendly personally, but he happens to be quicker and more sensitive than most in gauging relationships.

There has been a whispering campaign in the past few months that I was to be relieved of my post and succeeded by Averell, and yesterday I read in the London papers that I am to be succeeded by you. Such reports would do no damage were it not for the fact that you and Averell have done a considerable part of the exchange of communications that normally should be done by the Ambassador.

I know that you have enough difficulties at home without worrying about my troubles. But this situation has begun to affect my job and I know you would want to help me. I think the President and Stettinius should know that no Ambassador can be an effective representative here in London unless he is given more information and more support than I am receiving.

Hopkins wrote a letter to Winant in which he said:

I know exactly how you feel about it and if I were in your shoes I would feel just the same.

There is, of course, nothing to the story of my becoming Ambassador to Great Britain and never any notion that Harriman would become Ambassador there. The President has repeatedly stated to me and others that he wanted you to stay there throughout the war and has always refused to consider replacing you when they had other jobs in mind for you here in America. I know the President not only has absolute confidence in you but feels you are doing the best job of any Ambassador to England. I am sure the country shares this view. I certainly do.

It looks to me as though the Russian offensive is not going to stop this winter, but that they are going to push it farther ahead, which, together with our increased bombing of Germany, is going to make it pretty tough on Hitler, and I do not see how he can stand it for more than another eight months.

I do wish I could see you to talk over all the implications of your cable which disturbed me a good deal. I know of no one who has made a greater contribution to the war than you have and that opinion is shared by all of your friends here.

Winant's complaints were based on far more than the awkward situation,

referred to in an earlier chapter, which resulted from Harriman's unusual position as Lend-Lease representative in London. Inadequacy of information from Washington to principal American representatives throughout the world was a far more serious matter. The British and the Soviet Foreign Offices, in peacetime as well as in war, were so enmeshed with the whole system of control of both political and military policy that the channels of communication were clearly established from the highest authorities in London and Moscow to every outpost thereof, so that the merest consul in the most remote office knew precisely what policy decisions were being made and what his instructions were for implementing them. The archaic and disjointed machinery of the State Department and the Foreign Service, however, was woefully unable to cope with the requirements of a global war in which the United States had suddenly assumed the position of a pre-eminent world power. There was, for one thing, the essential question of security, since most important policy decisions were linked directly or indirectly with military plans, and the State Department machinery was full of leaks as well as creaks. That is why both Roosevelt and Hopkins sent all of their vital messages through military communications instead of through the regular diplomatic channels which would have kept the State Department and the various embassies and legations informed as to the progress of the correspondence. In view of Winant's reference to the fact that Harriman in London often possessed information which had not been given to him, it should be noted that after Harriman became Ambassador to the Soviet Union in October he himself began to complain in cables to Hopkins that nobody was telling him anything and that he was put in the humiliating position of depending upon the Russian Foreign Office for news as to the latest decisions made by his own Government in Washington.

On September 25 Roosevelt announced the resignation of Sumner Welles as Under Secretary of State and the appointment of Edward R. Stettinius, jun., to that position. This marked the unhappy conclusion of the protracted conflict between Hull and Welles. It had at last reached a point at which even Roosevelt could no longer produce a semblance of pacification with temper-softening words. Roosevelt was very anxious to have Welles go to Moscow for the conference with Molotov and Eden, but the situation was impossible and Welles felt he had no course but to get out of Government service altogether. To the best of my knowledge, Hopkins wrote nothing about the Hull-Welles dispute and I never heard him comment on it one way or the other, although he frequently referred to its existence, as did many others in Washington. I know that he had very high respect for Welles and would rather deal with him than with anyone else in the State Department. Furthermore, it must be evident to those who have read thus far in this book that Hopkins was frequently in disagreement with Hull, particularly in the

interminable insistence on the sanctity of the Vichy policy which by now
had been extended into Italy to cover the arrangements of 'expediency' with
King Victor Emmanuel and Badoglio. However, in his memoirs, Hull has
written of Hopkins: 'I never had any friction, much less clashes, with him',
and this was certainly true of their relations, which, while never really warm,
were invariably courteous. Hopkins may have wished now and then that the
President would accept one of Hull's recurrent threats to resign and be done
with it, but he well knew why Roosevelt did not wish to lose a Secretary
of State whose prestige was so high and influence so strong with the United
States Senate. Here, again, Roosevelt was mindful of the ghost of Woodrow
Wilson, who had seen victory won on the battlefields only to be lost on
Capitol Hill when a minority of Senators proved able to raise an uproar
powerful enough to repudiate the President and the League of Nations.

Roosevelt's concept of his dependence on Hull was justified by the
enormous success of the Moscow Conference in October, and its consequent
profound effect on Congressional opinion. On November 5, as Hull was
returning from Moscow, the Senate approved by a vote of eighty-five to
five the Connally Resolution providing for postwar collaboration to secure
and maintain peace for the world and for the establishment of a general
international organization that might become a new League of Nations.
Incidentally, one of the five votes against this Resolution was cast by Hiram
Johnson, a member of the vociferous minority that had defeated Wilson in
1919. This new and decisive action by the Senate strengthened Roosevelt's
hand immeasurably as he embarked for the first conference of the Big Three
at Teheran. It served notice on the other United Nations that in the settlement
of the Second World War, as contrasted with the first one, the mortal Roosevelt had the backing of the Legislative branch which Wilson had so
disastrously lacked.

Stettinius, at Roosevelt's direction, made a determined effort to reorganize the State Department and bring it up to date. He drew up an enormous
and impressive chart with myriad boxes in orderly array. But he found out
that this rearrangement could produce no real change in the character of the
State Department as long as the occupants of the boxes, particularly on the
upper middle level of divisional chiefs, remained the same; and they did
remain the same, for these were the permanent career men who knew that
they would still be there when the Franklin Roosevelt Administration had
been replaced by another one, which might well be reactionary and iso-
lationsist in accordance with the inexorable ebb and flow of American
politics, and they were determined to keep their records clean of New Deal
or One World taints against that highly possible day. It would be unfair to
place the blame for this on the career men themselves. They were the
neglected, underpaid, and often much maligned creatures of circumstance.

Their point of view was reflective of that of the nation itself which had lived so long under the illusion of isolationism. The State Department, which should have been the vital instrument of our most important national policy, had been relegated to the status of the querulous maiden aunt whose sole function is to do all the worrying for the prosperous family over the endless importunities of the numerous poor relations living on the other side of the tracks.

CAIRO, TEHERAN, AND OVERLORD

PRIOR to the Quebec Conference, it had been generally assumed that the supreme command for OVERLORD would be British: for one thing, the huge operation was to be mounted in the United Kingdom and, for another, it was Britain's turn to take top rank, since the high command in North Africa, Sicily, and the first phases of the campaign on the Italian mainland had been entrusted by common agreement to the American Eisenhower. Churchill had promised the new post to Sir Alan Brooke, the Chief of the Imperial General Staff. However, it had become evident that, whereas in the original force for the securing of the beachhead the British troops would be about equal in strength if not superior to the Americans, in subsequent operations through France and into Germany the American forces would be steadily increased until they outnumbered the British by a ratio of approximately five to one. Therefore, Churchill agreed at Quebec that the supreme command should go to an American, and there was no question of doubt in his mind that this American should be General Marshall. Nor was there any doubt in Roosevelt's mind at that time that Marshall was the one man pre-eminently qualified to assume this awful responsibility and to push the tremendous enterprise through to triumph and this opinion was vociferously supported by both Stimson and Hopkins. There were considerations in this that went well beyond awareness of Marshall's capabilities as a great soldier: from Churchill's point of view Marshall's selection was important because of his enormous prestige with the British Cabinet and the British people, who might have had reservations about Eisenhower or any less celebrated American general—and from the point of view of Roosevelt, Stimson, and Hopkins, Marshall was the only one who could be trusted thoroughly to stick to the main objective without yielding to the persuasions and the blandishments of Churchill, with whom he would be in close and constant touch in his London headquarters. It must be borne in mind that at this time although Eisenhower had proved his ability as a great general there was still plenty of uncertainty as to whether he possessed the qualities of statesmanship required in the performance of this supreme assignment; there were still memories of the Mediterranean political messes.

Marshall was accordingly informed that he was to assume command, at the same time retaining his status as Chief of Staff, while Eisenhower would be recalled to Washington as Acting Chief of Staff; as Mrs. Marshall has written, they started surreptitiously to move their belongings out of the Chief of Staff's residence at Fort Myer. But then there started a hullabaloo which assumed fantastic proportions and which resulted as was so often the

case, in vicious newspaper and Congressional attacks on Hopkins. The appointment of Marshall to the supreme command of OVERLORD was vehemently opposed by Admiral King and General Arnold on the ground that Marshall could not be spared from his position as their colleague and, indeed, acknowledged leader in the Joint Chiefs of Staff. Admiral Leahy agreed with them on this, and said so when Roosevelt asked for his opinion, but he made no positive attempts to influence the President's decision. King, however, was by no means diffident in stating his opinion. He said: 'We have the winning combination here in Washington. Why break it up?' He said that if the proposed appointment went through, Marshall would be wearing 'two hats', one as Chief of Staff and the other as supreme commander. This was always productive of confusion and danger; for instance, as King pointed out, Stilwell was at the moment wearing 'five hats'—as Chief of Staff to the Generalissimo, as Deputy to Mountbatten, as supreme commander of the C.B.I. theatre, as field commander in Northern Burma, and as controller of the distribution of Lend-Lease to China, this last post being in some ways the most important and by all odds the most controversial of all. King pointed out, and so did Arnold, that neither Eisenhower nor anyone else who might be appointed Acting Chief of Staff could possibly have Marshall's extraordinary sense of the requirements of global war, his knowledge of land, sea, and air logistics, his balanced judgment as to the importance of one theatre or one ally or one arm of the service as opposed to another. Furthermore, if Eisenhower were to become Acting Chief of Staff the regrettable but real lack of cordiality which characterized the relationship between him and MacArthur could become a source of major embarrassments. So violent was the sentiment in the Navy and in the Air Force for keeping Marshall in Washington—and no doubt, in some of the upper echelons of the ground forces as well—that it inevitably erupted into print. An editorial appeared in the *Army and Navy Journal*, which was always described as 'unofficial, but authoritative'. It said that 'powerful influences would like to eliminate Marshall as Chief of Staff', adding that this action would shock the Army, the Congress, and the nation at large'. The implication was that Marshall was being forcibly removed by the politicians from the high post in which he had performed so faithfully and so brilliantly and was being literally kicked upstairs. General Pershing was impelled to write to Roosevelt, expressing his 'deep conviction that the suggested transfer of General Marshall would be a fundamental and very grave error in our military policy'. Roosevelt replied: 'You are absolutely right about George Marshall—and yet, I think you are wrong too! . . . I think it is only a fair thing to give George a chance in the field—and because of the nature of the job we shall still have the benefit of his strategical ability. The best way I can express it is to tell you that I want George to be the Pershing of the Second World War—and he cannot be that if we keep him here.' This letter was written on September 20, and

showed that Roosevelt had then made his decision on Marshall's appointment to OVERLORD. A few days later, the *Army and Navy Register*, which was also 'unofficial, but authoritative', came out with an editorial which was less openly indignant, but far more subtle than the one in the *Journal*. The *Register* stated that the opinion was held in 'some military circles' that 'the European Command would not be a promotion from his place as Chief of Staff of our Army, but only removal from Washington, where it is said that some concerned with strategy do not want him'. The *Register* did not specify directly who the 'some' might be, but it stated that Marshall was known 'to have had some differences over strategy' with Churchill and added: 'It is understood that Harry Hopkins prefers Lieutenant-General Brehon B. Somervell' for the post of Chief of Staff. With that, the uproar really started. Because Somervell was one of the many Army engineers who had been associated with Hopkins in W.P.A., the charge was immediately raised and shouted that this was all part of the New Deal plot to use the war emergency as a means of communizing America. A *Washington Times Herald* headline shouted, 'GLOBAL W.P.A. SEEN AIM IN MARSHALL "PLOT"', and an editorial on the same subject in the *Cheyenne Tribune* bore the heading 'HOPKINS'S SLIMY HAND'. It was charged in the House that Hopkins, backed by an oft-cited 'sinister' clique consisting of Justice Felix Frankfurter, Samuel I. Rosenman, and David K. Niles, was planning 'to turn the War Department into a global political organization', and that the activities of the men behind this plan were 'nothing less than treasonous'. It mattered little to any of the embittered isolationists that Frankfurter, Rosenman, and Niles had no more influence on the making of military decisions or plans or selections than did Fala, the President's Scottie; it mattered a great deal, however, that all three of them were Jews. Those same three names—and usually Henry Morgenthau's was added—were invariably linked by the isolationist Press with Hopkins (reared in the Methodist Church) as master-minds of the alien conspiracy against the American way of life.

The editorials in the *Army and Navy Journal* and the *Register* which had provoked the subsequently disgraceful uproar had undoubtedly been planted by someone in high authority in the War or Navy Department; I do not know who it was, and it makes little difference on the final record, but there was then and probably always will be the possibility of terrible dangers in the deliberate and irresponsible use of the malicious 'leak' as a political weapon. Hopkins wrote to a friend that it was 'amazing' that the story involving him and Somervell should have been cooked up—but it was not so amazing in view of the fact that whoever did the cooking wanted to create the maximum amount of public alarm and was smart enough to know that the best way to do that was to inject the fell name of Hopkins, the White House Rasputin.

Through all the hullabaloo Marshall himself said not a word, while Mrs. Marshall continued quietly to move the furniture from Fort Myer to the family home in Leesburg, Virginia, in anticipation of her husband's departure for his new post in London. Marshall most scrupulously refrained from making any attempt to influence Roosevelt's decision one way or the other, but those who knew him best have testified that never had he wanted anything so much in his whole career as to end it in the field in command of the decisive trans-Channel invasion which he had been the first to propose and for which he had been fighting with unflagging determination ever since he and Hopkins had travelled together to London in April 1942, when the United Nations' cause was at its lowest ebb. And Marshall knew that he had no friend more eager than Hopkins to see his wish fulfilled.

A light note in the midst of the unpleasant ruckus was struck by a monitoring of a Nazi propaganda broadcast from Paris which said: 'General George C. Marshall, the U.S. Chief of Staff, has been dismissed. President Roosevelt has taken over his command. This occurred two days ago, but has not yet been commented on in Washington.'

Marshall passed this on to Hopkins with the note: 'Dear Harry: Are you responsible for pulling this fast one on me? G. C. M.'

Hopkins showed this to Roosevelt, who then wrote in pencil on the same note: 'Dear George—Only true in part—I am now Chief of Staff, *but* you are President. F. D. R.'

Since Marshall was then a four-star general and, therefore, outranked by a British field-marshal, there were many suggestions that he be given the latter title which would have made a rather ridiculous combination with his own name—and in addition to that, both he and Roosevelt were opposed to the use of a title which had never existed in the U.S. Army. Stimson wrote a letter to Roosevelt urging that he ask Congress to confer on Marshall the rank of General of the Armies which was then held only by Pershing, this promotion to be made with Pershing's consent. Stimson wrote: 'I do not think we can safely postpone the date of his taking command beyond November first. The fatal delays and diversions which may sabotage Overlord will begin in the U.K. this autumn and nothing but his direct presence and influence will save us from them. No one dreads more than I do the loss of his influence in theatres other than the European theatres, but I hope that the rank and title which I have suggested will help to preserve that influence indirectly in those far-away theatres even if not directly. I have talked this matter over with Harry, and I think on most of these points he is in full sympathy with me.'

On September 26, after the 'Global W.P.A.' scareheads had begun to appear, Churchill cabled Hopkins expressing his concern about all the newspaper talk to the effect that Marshall was to become Supreme Com-

mander-in-Chief of all the forces in Western Europe. Churchill said that it was his understanding of the agreement at Quebec that while Marshall would be in a position to advise with the British Chiefs of Staff and the Combined Chiefs of Staff he would not be empowered to make decisions outside the sphere of OVERLORD. At the end of his cable, the Prime Minister asked Hopkins: 'Please let me know whether there is anything wrong with this message.' This was an embarrassing question for Roosevelt: in order to meet the trumped-up accusations that Marshall was being 'demoted' or 'kicked upstairs', the President wished to announce that Marshall's new post would be far more important and comprehensive than that of any mere theatre commander, and it was obviously desirable to have unified command for all operations against Germany, particularly in the strategic bombing offensive from bases in the United Kingdom, in Italy, and even in the Middle East. On September 30 Hopkins wrote the following note:

> The Prime Minister telephoned to say that he hoped that he and the President could make a joint statement at an early date relative to any changes in the Command.
>
> He stated that he was under considerable pressure to answer the newspaper reports and he seemed quite disturbed that he had had no reply to his cable to me.
>
> He thought that the statement should be timed after our next good success in Italy. While he did not say so, I imagine he might have preferred that the statement be made at the time of the fall of Rome.
>
> He said he was holding Eden in London until we get word from Stalin about the place of the Conference. He was, obviously, quite irritated that Stalin had delayed his answer for so long.

Two days later Hopkins cabled to Churchill:

> The hullabaloo in the newspapers over here about Marshall is dying out. The McCormick-Patterson Press inspired it for their own nefarious purposes. There is no basic change that I know of in the agreements reached at Quebec relative to Command. Our friend has your message on this same subject. He is away now, returning Monday, and will reply to you then. I think his feeling is that we should not permit the Press to stampede us into any premature announcements. Give Clemmie my love. See you in Rome.

It was generally assumed at this time, early in October, that the fall of Rome would rapidly follow that of Naples. Roosevelt, ordinarily so chary of making optimistic predictions, cabled Stalin on October 4: 'It looks as if American and British armies should be in Rome in another few weeks.'

On the same day Hopkins wrote the following memorandum for the President:

I feel very strongly that, from the point of view of organization, Marshall should have command of all the Allied forces, other than the Russian, attacking the Fortress of Germany.

It is essential that there be one strategic air force and that our bombers not be frozen either in England, Italy, or Africa. It is only human nature for a theatre commander to want to hang on to his airplanes. By the same token the disposition of the ground forces, the use of ships and landing-craft should be under a single commander.

I have talked to General Wedemeyer about this—who had previously been consulted by General Marshall. Wedemeyer feels that, from a military point of view, it is sound organization.

While we might have to give someone like Montgomery command of Overlord in order to satisfy the British, I think it would be wise for us to agree to that in order to get our main objective of Marshall's command over the whole business.

It seems to me that, above everything else, we want liquidity in our offensive in Europe against Germany and, whether we want it or not, the march of events, it seems to me, will undoubtedly require it.

It is simply impossible for anybody to know at what point or points we may need to change our emphasis and the force of our attack.

If Churchill would agree to such an organization, then I can see no difficulty about the early announcement of the change in commanders. Indeed, there would be every reason for doing it.

I believe there is a good chance of getting Churchill to agree to this.

Roosevelt subsequently cabled Churchill in much the same terms. He also informed Churchill that, although the Press had been beating its drums rather loudly about Marshall's appointment, the story by now was 'pretty much of a dead cat'. He said that if decisions were to be influenced by such Press campaigns, 'we will find ourselves with the newspapers running the war'. Commenting on the failure of the attempts to arrange the Foreign Secretaries' meeting at some point more accessible than Moscow, Roosevelt said to Churchill: 'The answer we got from Uncle Joe relative to the Moscow meeting was not unexpected, so it seems there is nothing to do but take the trip there, and we are organizing accordingly.' (Stalin was often referred to as 'Uncle Joe' or sometimes merely as 'U.J.' in the Roosevelt-Churchill cables.)

Behind Churchill's objections to the granting of all-inclusive authority to Marshall in the European war was his indefatigable determination to play his own strategic hand in the Eastern Mediterranean, the area that was now dearer to his heart than ever. Indeed, in the latter part of September,

Churchill had authorized General Sir Henry Maitland Wilson, commander in the Middle East, to launch expeditions which seized the Dodecanese Islands of Cos, Samos, and Leros in the Aegean Sea. The Germans then sent out sea and airborne forces and took these islands back; at Leros the British lost some 5,000 first-class troops, with four cruisers and seven destroyers either sunk or damaged. This surprising setback was shocking and humiliating at a time when the Germans appeared to have lost the power to capture the initiative anywhere. Churchill wanted to arrange an immediate meeting of Marshall, Eisenhower, and himself in Algiers to arrange more diversionary moves in the Mediterranean, and it appears from Hopkins's notes that some heated words were exchanged over the transatlantic telephone about the Dodecanese fiasco. Hopkins informed Churchill that there was no chance of Marshall's being sent to another meeting, and that any proposals for new moves could be handled by the Combined Chiefs of Staff. After one conversation, the security authorities in the War Department discreetly asked Hopkins to caution the Prime Minister against making too explicit statements in these telephone talks, to which so many people, including the enemy, might be listening.

Churchill had another source of worry in these days, which was of considerably less vital importance. Five United States Senators had made a world tour—through the United Kingdom, North Africa, the Middle East, India, China, Australia, Hawaii—and had come out of it with some very sour observations on the British Empire and the manner in which, according to their version of it, the British were using American Lend-Lease to promote their own political interests. Churchill sent Hopkins a very long cable containing a statement that he proposed to make in the House of Commons refuting the Senators' charges point by point. He asked Hopkins to show this statement to Roosevelt and to ascertain his views thereon—this being one of the many occasions when the Prime Minister relied on Hopkins's discretion as though the latter were his own Ambassador in dealing with the President. Hopkins promptly showed the cable to Roosevelt and then cabled Churchill: 'The inexorable events of the war are rapidly crowding the statements by the five Senators off the front pages and I therefore question whether you should feel inclined to say anything. Would it not be better to postpone your statement for a week or so, so as not to put yourself in the position of answering this backstage talk by the Senators?'

Churchill then telephoned Hopkins expressing gratitude for the advice from 'you and your friend', and when he was asked questions in the House of Commons a few days later about the five Senators he gracefully ducked the issue by saying: 'I have come to the conclusion that there would be no advantage in this Government taking part in this wordy warfare, especially at a time when British and United States Armies are engaged shoulder to

shoulder in battles taking place or impending on the Italian Front and when the Royal Air Force and the United States Eighth Air Force in a perfect brotherhood of arms are making heavy sacrifices in their attacks on Germany.' Following that statement, the 'wordy warfare' went with the wind on Capitol Hill and little more was heard of it.

Preparations were now going forward for the meetings with Chiang Kai-shek in Cairo and with Stalin in Teheran. This was no time for trivia. On November 10 Stimson wrote to Hopkins: 'I have reflected over our talk of yesterday and am putting on paper in this letter to you my reflections on the chance that they may be useful for you or the President. *In re* OVERLORD: My best estimate of the situation is that preparations are going all right. Provided there are no further diversions or delays, we shall be ready on the scheduled time. . . . The task for our Commander-in-Chief is to hold the situation firmly to the straight road which has been agreed to and which it is now on. He should tolerate no departures from the programme. . . . So the one prayer I make for the Commander-in-Chief is steadfastness—a very difficult virtue, but one more needed than any other in this particular problem. *The problem of command*: I believe that Marshall's command of Overlord is imperative for its success. To make it effective he should be there very soon. The success of Overlord is so much the most important thing in the world horizon that Marshall should take up that command in spite of all counter-reasons which I can envisage. . . . I anticipate that his European command will be extended in future to all auxiliary movements in Western Europe, even if that is not now agreed upon. No successor Chief of Staff should be appointed for the present, but that post should be carried on by an acting chief. I anticipate that Marshall's presence in London will strongly tend to prevent any interferences with Overlord even if they were attempted, and as to other theatres of operation we shall have to take our chances of carrying on along the present plans which have been pretty well laid out. Certainly they are in far better situation than they were two or three months ago. These are my views. Good luck!'

On November 13 the President sailed from Hampton Roads, Virginia, on the new battleship, U.S.S. *Iowa*, which was commanded by Roosevelt's former Naval *aide* and good friend, Captain John McCrea. Also travelling on the ship were Hopkins, Generals Marshall, Arnold, Watson, Somervell, and Handy, and Admirals Leahy, King, Brown, McIntire, and Cooke. There were some highly important discussions among the Chiefs of Staff aboard the *Iowa*; trained to anticipate and prepare for all kinds of trouble, they expected that Churchill would be ready to propose various alternatives to the Second Front in the forthcoming conferences, and that his array of arguments and persuasions might again divert Roosevelt from the main objective. It was their experience that, while the Prime Minister invariably

gave his most enthusiastic and eloquent approval to OVERLORD in principle, he steadfastly refused to accept it as a scheduled fact, preferring to believe that German power could be worn down by attrition to the point of collapse, whereupon the Anglo-American forces in the United Kingdom could perform a triumphal march from the Channel to Berlin with no more than a few snipers' bullets to annoy them. Whether or not these apprehensions were fully justified, they were so substantial that the U.S. Chiefs of Staff drew up papers looking toward compromise arrangements in the event that their British opposite numbers, dominated by the Prime Minister, should present a solid wall of resistance. They considered—and events proved that they were right—that the principal battle would be over the question of unified command over all European operations from the North Cape to the Golden Horn. In a memorandum to the President, signed by Leahy, the Joint Chiefs said:

> The necessity for unified command, in our opinion, is so urgent and compelling that, in spite of the fact that the bulk of the forces, both ground and air, will ultimately be American, we are willing to accept a British officer as overall commander for European operations provided the man named is Sir John Dill. This indicates the weight we give to the matter of undivided command and responsibility. Sir John Dill is well known to our officials and to the American public. He has worked on an intimate personal basis with the U.S. Chiefs of Staff since our entry into the war. We have the highest opinion of his integrity of character and singleness of purpose. He understands our organization, our characteristics, our viewpoint on many subjects, and our way of doing business.
>
> If the proposal outlined above is adopted—and it must be—then Eisenhower should remain in command in the Mediterranean. The question as to what individual should immediately command the cross-Channel phase of OVERLORD is a matter which can be discussed further.

In considering the foregoing document, it must be remembered that Leahy, King, and Arnold were all hoping that Roosevelt would not appoint Marshall to the field command, and that Marshall himself was taking no part in the discussion, although certainly supporting the naming of Dill.

On the second day out aboard the *Iowa* there was an extraordinary episode which caused the Navy's most ominous warning, 'THIS AIN'T NO DRILL!' to be shouted from the bridge. (The statement is generally entered in the log, if one survives, as, 'This is NOT a drill!'—but I believe that few sailors have ever said it that way in the heat of the moment.) Hopkins wrote a description of this episode, as follows:

> This afternoon the Captain arranged for an anti-aircraft drill. Three balloons are released—tied together—and the batteries of forties and

twenties let loose when the balloons reach a proper height and distance from the ship. The other method is for the five-inch battery to fire one shell—it explodes at perhaps 20,000 feet—then the other five-inch guns try to hit the ball of smoke left by the original explosion.

The President was wheeled from the luncheon table to the deck just outside his mess—Wilson, Brown, Ross McIntire, Pa Watson, and I went along. The firing began—it seemed pretty good to me, although the five-inch guns made a whale of a racket in spite of the cotton which all of us put in our ears.

We had just moved to the port side to see the five-inch guns fired the second time. Suddenly an officer from the bridge two decks above leaned over and yelled: 'It's the real thing! It's the real thing!' The President doesn't hear well anyway, and with his ears stuffed with cotton he had a hard time getting the officer's words, which I repeated to him several times before he understood. I asked him whether he wanted to go inside—he said: 'No—where is it?'

Just as I got to the starboard side to find out—everything fired at once at the wake of a torpedo about six hundred yards away—the firing lasted about thirty seconds. The wake went well astern.

It was a torpedo all right—but *not* from a German submarine. One of our destroyers had let loose a torpedo directly at the *Iowa*. The first the *Iowa* knew about it was a flash from the destroyer that a torpedo was moving toward the *Iowa*, and it was four or five minutes later that the message came that the torpedo was fired by our own escort.

The commander of the destroyer explained it as follows—the torpedo was in place, but with no primer attached—the torpedo must have been unloosed because of the heavy seas in some unaccountable fashion. But Admiral King and Captain McCrea thought this pretty thin. An investigation is afoot.

Can you imagine our own escort torpedoing an American battleship —the newest and biggest—with the President of the United States aboard—along with the Chief of Staff of the Army and the Chief of Naval Operations.

In view of the fact that there were twenty Army officers aboard, I doubt if the Navy will ever hear the last of it.

The records give the identity of the hapless destroyer from which the torpedo was accidentally fired, but I am not going to mention her name in these pages. Her skipper probably did not know who, if any, were the passengers aboard the *Iowa*. It was bad enough for him to know that one of his own torpedoes had been loosed toward the great ship and caused her to manoeuvre to avoid being hit. It would have been worse, of course, had

he been aware that the President of the United States was one of the possible victims. But had he known that the President's party included Admiral King, he would undoubtedly have attached the anchor to his neck and plunged himself to the bottom of the sea rather than live to face the awful consequences.

The *Iowa* arrived at Oran on November 20, where the President was met by Eisenhower and his staff and the three sons who were in that theatre, Elliott, Franklin D., jun., and Robert Hopkins. Roosevelt then flew to Tunis in the C-54 transport plane which had already been given the unofficial but enduring name, 'The Sacred Cow'. The next day, Sunday, he went for a tour of the Tunisian battlefields with Eisenhower, who did not realize at the time that he was being subjected to most searching scrutiny and appraisal. Roosevelt showed great interest in the site of ancient Carthage—which had once been subjected to unconditional surrender—and he wondered if any of the battles of the Punic Wars had been fought in the same places as the recent Tunisian campaign. He concluded that the Carthaginian armies had probably avoided these forbidding mountains which provided very bad terrain for elephants. Roosevelt, in his casual, seemingly offhand manner, also talked about the future—particularly OVERLORD. He said to Eisenhower: 'Ike, you and I know who was the Chief of Staff during the last years of the Civil War, but practically no one else knows, although the names of the field generals—Grant, of course, and Lee, and Jackson, Sherman, Sheridan, and the others—every schoolboy knows them. I hate to think that fifty years from now practically nobody will know who George Marshall was. That is one of the reasons why I want George to have the big Command—he is entitled to establish his place in history as a great general.' Roosevelt also told Eisenhower of the plan to bring him back to Washington as Acting Chief of Staff. It is probable that Eisenhower expressed to the President his total lack of enthusiasm for a career in the Pentagon Building, but he was a soldier, and he would go where he was sent. Later, Eisenhower was somewhat less certain that these decisions had been finally made, for Admiral King told him of his personal belief that Roosevelt would in the end refuse to move Marshall from his present position. However, King said that in the event he should be proved wrong about this he would certainly welcome Eisenhower to the councils of the Joint Chiefs of Staff.

When the Presidential party took off for the flight to Cairo late Sunday evening Eisenhower did not know what the future might hold for him, and he remained in ignorance for more than two weeks while the memorable conferences were taking place.

On the fourth and last day of the first Cairo Conference some forty-three American and British Press correspondents formed themselves into a committee, of which the able Cyrus L. Sulzberger of the *New York Times* was chairman, and signed a round robin letter to Hopkins which began:

The undersigned correspondents representing all Anglo-American and Dominion newspapers, agencies, and radio chains are addressing this to you as an influential friend of the Press.

We wish to express the strongest dissatisfaction with the manner in which we are being treated during the present important conferences. We demand that we be taken further into confidence of the authorities on an off-the-record basis and be given some idea of what everything is about in order to prepare our advance material.

We request a conference with yourself wherein we could present some of our problems to a person known to be our friend, of sufficient influence and energy to help us out, and of sufficient experience and understanding to be able to do so.

There followed specific requests, including one for a Press conference with the President, Prime Minister, and Generalissimo, and for another conference in the event that a Russian delegation might arrive in Cairo after the Chinese had departed. It was suspected that Stalin himself might appear, it not then being known, of course, that the British and American delegations were going on to Teheran to meet him there. (Andrei Vishinsky, Assistant Commissar for Foreign Affairs, was in Cairo at this time and conferred with Roosevelt and others, but took no part in the meetings relative to the war against Japan.)

Had Hopkins met the Press, there was not much he could have told them other than the agreements that were subsequently announced in the official communiqué. There was not much more that he could have told them even after V.J.-Day when the security bars were down. For while this first Cairo Conference had plenty in the way of 'colour'—the Pyramids, the Sphinx, and the extremely chic costumes of Madame Chiang Kai-shek, about which the correspondents could write much more skilfully than Hopkins could—its principal news value was the mere fact that it was held; aside from the declaration assuring the freedom and independence of Korea, the effect of these meetings on the progress of the war or on history was negligible.

The military talks produced a semblance of agreement on an expansion of the ANAKIM plan to drive the Japanese out of Burma and reopen the long-sealed land communications with China: there was to be a determined ground offensive in the north by Chinese, British, and newly assigned American troops under Stilwell's field command, coupled with large amphibious operations in the south directly under Mountbatten, who would have the benefit of strong units of the Royal Navy, especially aircraft carriers, which could now be diverted from service in the Mediterranean because of the surrender of the Italian Fleet. Chiang Kai-shek was particularly insistent on the necessity for the amphibious operation. From the records of the few

formal meetings involving the three nations, it would appear that the Generalissimo was usually reluctant to commit himself on specific details of plans, hedging each statement with reservations and qualifications; Stilwell, on the other hand, was not afflicted with any excessive cautiousness in stating his views as to precisely what was needed to ensure success in Burma. Of course, the language difficulties presented so many obstacles that only the larger generalities were sure of getting through. It was quite clear, however, that Chiang Kai-shek was not interested in the ground operations in the north, in which his own Chinese divisions would provide the bulk of the manpower, unless the British would agree to synchronize with them the major moves by land, sea, and air in the south to cut off the Japanese lines of supply and reinforcement, including the railroad that they had constructed from Bangkok to Rangoon. In one of his few positive statements appearing on the record, the Generalissimo said: 'Burma is the key to the whole campaign in Asia. After the enemy has been cleared out of Burma, his next stand would be in North China and, finally, in Manchuria. The loss of Burma would be a very serious matter to the Japanese and they would fight stubbornly and tenaciously to retain their hold on the country.' In all these discussions there persisted the question as to just how important was Burma as a front on which to engage the enemy—as compared with the various possible battlegrounds in the Pacific Ocean area—and this always led to the larger question: just how important was China itself as a front? There is no doubt that Roosevelt and the U.S. Chiefs considered the maintenance of the Chinese Front to be essential, and there is also no doubt that the Japanese were finally defeated by the attacks from the Pacific, with no decisive battle being fought anywhere on the mainland of Asia. The huge Japanese forces on the mainland were left stranded and largely unengaged, just as were those in the garrisons at Rabaul and Truk.

Churchill viewed the proposals for large operations in Burma with scant enthusiasm; he considered Burma solely as an outpost of the Empire, rather than as an area of strategic importance. He wanted to drive the Japanese out of it, not so much for the purpose of gaining access to China as to avenge a mortal insult to imperial prestige, and he did not relish the idea that the Americans or, more especially, the Chinese should have any share in the credit for its liberation. He always went along with the proposition that the supply route to China must be reopened in order to sustain Chinese morale and to keep this gigantic mass of humanity in the war, but it is apparent that he did this out of deference to Roosevelt's sentiments—or, perhaps, he thought of them as 'whims'—and not from any profound convictions of his own.

The most important objectives in South-East Asia, from Churchill's point of view, involved the re-establishment of British power in Singapore

and Hong Kong. This was by no means merely a matter of the advancement of imperial interests. It was based on strategic concepts with which, I believe, Admiral King and Admiral Nimitz were ultimately in agreement; it was the point of view of those who believed in winning the war against Japan primarily by sea power—destroying the Japanese lines of communication and subjecting the home islands to a strangling blockade. Generals Marshall and Arnold and, of course, MacArthur and Stilwell, disagreed with this point of view. They believed that total victory could not be achieved as long as there were substantial Japanese forces on the mainland of Asia, in China, Indo-China, Malaya, and Burma (and also the Philippines), which could continue to operate independently for a long time even after their lines of communication with the home islands had been cut.

However, it appears that at Cairo the U.S. Chiefs of Staff were united in approval of the full ANAKIM operation and Roosevelt supported that formula at these first meetings, for he was determined that this conference should be a success from the Chinese point of view. Here was certainly an instance of a sharp division between the British and the Americans on nationalistic lines. It had been intended that Mountbatten's South-East Asia Command could be organized on the same brotherly, bi-national basis as Eisenhower's, and this might have been possible if Mountbatten had been completely independent of control by his home Government. But that was obviously out of the question, for the decentralization which prevailed in the American military system, giving exceptional authority and freedom of decision to the theatre commander, did not obtain with the British. In Eisenhower's command, harmonious and wholehearted co-operation was possible because British and American objectives could be summed up in one word— 'Berlin'. In South-East Asia, on the other hand, the British and Americans were fighting two different wars for different purposes, and the Kuomintang Government of China was fighting a third war for purposes largely its own. I believe it may be said, without descending to a low level of chauvinism, that Roosevelt was the only one of the leaders in the entire war against Japan who adhered to the main military objective of destroying the enemy's power and compelling his surrender by the most direct means in the shortest possible time. Hopkins did not set down his views on this subject of Allied disunity in respect to the Far East, and the reader will have to take my word for it that I have given a faithful reflection of them. He could not ignore the fact that such disunity existed, nor could Roosevelt, Marshall, King, and Arnold, for there were too many emphatic and repeated reminders of it. Hopkins was certainly vehement in his denunciation of any American who by word or deed tended to aggravate it while the war was on, but he was also one who believed that the record is worse than valueless which, like the royal sundial, tells only of the 'shining hours' of sweetness and light.

Despite Churchill's obvious reluctance to commit considerable British forces to the proposed campaigns in Burma, Roosevelt at this time went down the line in supporting the view of Chiang Kai-shek, Stilwell, and possibly also of Mountbatten. Therefore, when the Generalissimo and Madame departed for Chungking on November 28 their hopes were high that at last China's demands were to be met with measures that were more than mere words. These hopes, however, were shortlived. The agreement at Cairo did not stick for more than ten days, and it was not until after American forces had started to strangle Japan from the Pacific, in the last six months of the war, that the first trucks started to roll over the Ledo or Stilwell Road from Burma into China. By then it was too late to matter much.

During these days at Cairo, Roosevelt had to spend many hours on the enormous mass of White House papers that had accumulated during his week at sea and been flown from Washington. Included in this were twenty-nine Congressional bills of which he signed twenty-seven and vetoed the other two. It was always necessary for the President to act on these bills within ten days—he could not delegate his authority to anyone in his absence—and this was the consideration which limited the scope of his travel. No previous President could have gone as far from Washington while Congress was in session as Roosevelt did, because only the development of the air transport (including the establishment of the intermediate bases) made it possible for documents to be delivered and returned within the ten-day period.

During these days at Cairo, Hopkins formed a friendship with Charles E. Bohlen, a young State Department career man who had been brought along by Harriman from the Embassy in Moscow because of his fluency in the Russian language. Hopkins asked him all manner of questions about the Soviet Union, and was surprised and impressed by the objectivity and lack of bias as well as by the considerable scholarship revealed in his answers. Hopkins told Bohlen in characteristic words of the low opinion he had formed of many of the Foreign Service men that he had encountered in his travels, describing them as 'cookie-pushers, pansies—and usually isolationists to boot'. Bohlen gave so vigorous and intelligent a defence of the State Department, and explanation of the hopeless handicaps under which its personnel often must work, that Hopkins subsequently persuaded the President to appoint Bohlen to a post in the White House where he would act as a liaison officer with the State Department, thereby filling a really long-felt want. From then on Bohlen's star was very much in the ascendant, and he later became Counsellor of the Department under Secretary Marshall.

On Thursday evening, November 26, Roosevelt was host at a Thanksgiving Dinner at his villa, the residence of Ambassador Alexander C. Kirk,

near the Pyramids of Giza some miles west of Cairo. The guests included the Prime Minister, his daughter Sarah, Eden, Winant, Steinhardt, and Elliott Roosevelt and Robert Hopkins. Roosevelt proposed Churchill's health, telling of the origin of the American Thanksgiving Day tradition, and of how this old custom was now being spread by American soldiers all over the world, and he expressed his particular delight that this year he could share the Thanksgiving celebration in company with his great friend, the Prime Minister. Evidently, at this point, he seemed to have reached the conclusion of his remarks, and Churchill arose to respond, but Roosevelt told him that he had not yet finished. He then went on to say that Thanksgiving was traditionally a family festival and that this year Britain and America formed one family which was more united than ever before. He was now really finished and, according to the official record, 'The Prime Minister responded in his usual masterful and inspiring manner'.

There was a meeting at Cairo of Roosevelt, Churchill, and the Combined Chiefs of Staff, Hopkins being the only other civilian present, at which a general survey was made of future European operations in anticipation of the forthcoming discussions with Stalin at Teheran. Churchill gave a lengthy résumé of the general situation, reviewing the long series of Allied successes in the Mediterranean, which, in recent weeks, had turned into a succession of disappointments on the Italian Front north of Naples and in the Dodecanese Islands. He urged that, despite the heavy German reinforcements that had been sent to the front in Italy, the Allied campaign there should be pushed more vigorously than ever with a view to capturing Rome at the earliest possible date—for 'whoever holds Rome holds the title deeds of Italy'. He placed particular emphasis on the assurance that he had in no way relaxed his zeal for OVERLORD, but he recommended that this major operation should not be such a 'tyrant' as to rule out every other activity in the Mediterranean. Among the various activities that he mentioned was the capture of the Island of Rhodes, which had been the ultimate objective of the recent ill-fated Dodecanese campaign. He said that when the Allies had reached the Pisa-Rimini Line north of Rome decisions could be taken as to whether the next move should be to the left (toward Southern France) or to the right (into the Balkans). The U.S. Chiefs of Staff had no doubt in their own minds as to just what all this signified. They felt certain that whenever the persistent Prime Minister started talking about Rhodes, or veering toward the 'right' from Northern Italy, he was resuming the advocacy of strategic diversions into South-Eastern Europe and away from Northern France. They prepared themselves for battles at Teheran in which the Americans and the Russians would form a united front.

Roosevelt's party on the trip to Teheran numbered approximately seventy, including the indispensable Filipino mess men from Shangri-la. On the

flight from Cairo of 1,310 miles the 'Sacred Cow' flew over the Suez Canal, Jerusalem, Bagdad, the Euphrates and Tigris Rivers, and the Iranian railroad which by now had become a vital link in the gigantic network of world supply lines.

At Teheran, Roosevelt, Hopkins, Leahy, Brown, and Major John Boettiger (the President's son-in-law) at first occupied quarters in the American Lega-tion as guests of the Minister, Louis G. Dreyfus. This Legation was at some distance from the compounds of the Russian and British Embassies, which were close together. Harriman told Roosevelt of Stalin's concern over the strong possibility that there were many enemy agents in the city and the distinguished visitors might be subjected to what was described as 'an un-happy incident'—a polite way, of course, of saying 'assassination'—while driving back and forth between their separated residences.

On the day after his arrival at Teheran—this was Sunday, November 28—Roosevelt agreed to accept Stalin's invitation to move to a villa in the Russian Embassy compound, where complete security could be enforced. It certainly was enforced, and the President and his party were never per-mitted to forget it, for the servants who made their beds and cleaned their rooms were all members of the highly efficient NKVD, the secret police, and expressive bulges were plainly discernible in the hip pockets under their neat white coats. It was a nervous time for Michael F. Reilly and his own White House secret service men, who were trained to suspect *everybody* and who did not like to admit into the President's presence anyone who was armed with as much as a gold toothpick.

Roosevelt arrived at his new quarters at three o'clock in the afternoon and fifteen minutes later Stalin came to call. This was the first meeting of the wartime leaders of the Soviet Union and the United States. Aside from the President and Marshal Stalin, the only two present at this meeting were the interpreters, Bohlen and Pavlov.

Roosevelt greeted Stalin with the statement: 'I am glad to see you. I have tried for a long time to bring this about.' Stalin, 'after suitable expres-sions of pleasure at meeting the President, said that he was to blame for the delay in this meeting; that he had been very occupied because of military matters'. Roosevelt asked Stalin how things were going on the Russian Front, and Stalin gave a realistic picture of the situation which was somewhat less favourable at the moment than the information then available to the Western Allies had indicated. Roosevelt said that among the main topics for discussion at Teheran were measures which would bring about the re-moval of thirty or forty German divisions from the Eastern Front and Stalin agreed that such a transfer would be most helpful. Roosevelt then said that, by the end of the war, the American-British merchant fleet would have achieved such proportions that it would be more than the two nations could

possibly need and he felt that some of these ships should be made available to the Soviet Union. To this, Stalin replied that an adequate merchant fleet would be of great value, not only to the Soviet Union, but for the development of relations between the Soviet Union and the United States after the war, which he hoped would be greatly expanded. He said that if equipment were sent to the Soviet Union from the United States a plentiful supply of the raw materials from that country could be made available to the United States.

There was considerable discussion of French affairs, during which Stalin surprised the President by expressing the opinion that it was Pétain rather than de Gaulle who represented 'the real physical France'. There was no doubt in Roosevelt's mind on this and subsequent occasions that Stalin considered the collaborationists more important than the fighters of the resistance movement in expressing French sentiments.

Mention of Indo-China brought the conversation around to the Far East, and Roosevelt told Stalin of his conversations with Chiang Kai-shek and the plans for offensive operations in Burma. Stalin expressed a low opinion of the fighting quality of Chinese troops, but said that this was the fault of their leaders. Roosevelt referred to one of his favourite topics, which was the education of the peoples of the Far Eastern colonial areas, such as Indo-China, Burma, Malaya, and the East Indies, in the arts of self-government; he pointed with pride to the American record in helping the people of the Philippines to prepare themselves for independence. He cautioned Stalin against bringing up the problems of India with Churchill, and Stalin agreed that this was undoubtedly a sore subject. Roosevelt said that reform in India should begin from the bottom and Stalin said that reform from the bottom would mean revolution.

This meeting lasted forty-five minutes, but, like all conferences with the Russians, most of the time was taken up in the arduous process of translation. At four o'clock Churchill and the Combined Chiefs of Staff arrived for the First Plenary Session of the Teheran Conference, which bore the exultant code name EUREKA. Also present at this first session were Hopkins, Eden, and Molotov—and it should be noted that throughout the Teheran Conference Hopkins acted, in effect, as Secretary of State in relationship to the two Foreign Ministers. Stalin's only Chief of Staff was Marshal Voroshilov, and Leahy and King represented the U.S. Joint Chiefs. Marshall and Arnold were not present; they had misunderstood the time of the meeting and had gone off on a sightseeing tour around Teheran.

Stalin and Churchill agreed that the President should take the chair at this first meeting, and he opened it by saying that he was glad to welcome the Russians as 'new members of the family circle' and to assure them that these conferences were always conducted as gatherings of friends with complete

frankness on all sides. He believed that the three nations represented would work together in close co-operation not only for the duration of the war, but for generations to come. Churchill said that here was represented the greatest concentration of power that the world had ever seen and that in the hands of those present was the happy future of mankind; he prayed that they might be worthy of this God-given opportunity. Stalin said that this fraternal meeting did indeed represent a great opportunity and it was up to those present to use wisely the power which their respective peoples had given them.

Roosevelt then expressed the American point of view toward the war. He had the impression that Stalin knew very little about the progress of the war against Japan and he therefore dealt with that subject first. He said, according to the record, 'that the United States was more directly affected by the war in the Pacific and that the United States forces were bearing the chief burden in that area, with, of course, help from Australian and British forces; the greater part of the U.S. naval establishment was in the Pacific and over a million men were being maintained there. He pointed out as evidence of the immense distances in the Pacific that one supply ship operating from the United States could make only three round trips a year. The allied strategy in the Pacific was based on the doctrine of attrition which was proving successful. We were sinking more Japanese tonnage than the Japanese were able to replace. He said that the Allies were moving forward through the southern islands and now through the islands to the east of Japan. On the north little more could be done, due to the distance between the Aleutian and Kurile Islands. On the west our one great objective was to keep China in the war, and for that purpose an expedition was in preparation to attack through North Burma and from Yunnan province. In this operation Anglo-British forces would operate in North Burma and Chinese forces from Yunnan. The entire operation would be under the command of Lord Louis Mountbatten. In addition, amphibious operations were planned south of Burma to attack the important Japanese bases and lines of communication in the vicinity of Bangkok. The President pointed out that although these operations extended over vast expanses of territory the number of ships and men allocated for the purpose was being held down to a minimum. He summed up the aims of these operations as follows: (1) to open the road to China and supply that country in order to keep it in the war, and (2), by opening the road to China and through increased use of transport planes to put ourselves in position to bomb Japan proper.

'The President then said he would turn to the most important theatre of the war in Europe. He said he wished to emphasize that for over one year and a half, in the last two or three conferences which he had had with the Prime Minister, all military plans had revolved around the question of

T

relieving the German pressure on the Soviet Front; that largely because of the difficulties of sea transport it had not been possible until Quebec to set a date for the cross-Channel operations. He pointed out that the English Channel was a disagreeable body of water and it was unsafe for military operations prior to the month of May, and that the plan adopted at Quebec involved an immense expedition and had been set at that time for May 1, 1944.'

At this point, Churchill interposed the remark that the British people had every reason in the past to be thankful that the English Channel was such a disagreeable body of water.

Roosevelt then went on to say that although he was not in favour of any secondary operations which might tend to delay the cross-Channel invasion, OVERLORD, he and the Prime Minister had been discussing possible future operations in Italy, the Adriatic and Aegean Seas, and from Turkey as a base in the event that the Turks might be induced to enter the war. The President also informed the Marshall of the plans for landings in Southern France.

Stalin then spoke of the war in the Pacific, making no bones of the fact that the Soviet Government welcomed all Anglo-American successes against the Japanese. He said that up to now the Russian forces had not been able to join in the war against Japan because of their heavy involvements with Germany. He explained that the Russian forces in Siberia were sufficient for purely defensive purposes, but that they would have to be increased three-fold before they could be strong enough to engage in offensive ground operations against the Japanese—and he added that when Germany was finally defeated the necessary Russian reinforcements could be sent to Eastern Siberia, and then, he said, 'We shall be able by our common front to beat Japan'. (This was the first assurance given to Roosevelt or Churchill to that important effect.) Stalin gave a detailed analysis of German strength on the Russian Front and described the difficulties encountered by the Red Army in advancing over recaptured terrain where the Germans had systematically destroyed all possible facilities for communication and supply. Referring to the Italian campaign, he said that great benefit had resulted from the freeing of the Mediterranean to Allied shipping, but he did not believe that further advances up the Peninsula would be of much avail, for the Alps presented 'an almost insuperable barrier, as the famous Russian General Suvorov discovered in his time'. He said the entry of Turkey into the war might be helpful in opening the way to the Balkans, but that the Balkans were far from the heart of Germany, and the only direct way of striking at that heart was through France.

Churchill gave assurance that both he and the President had long agreed as to the necessity of the cross-Channel operation, and that it was now planned to put one million men on the continent of Europe in May, June, and July, 1944. He said that the operations in North Africa and Italy had always been

considered as secondary to OVERLORD. Stalin said that he had not meant to convey the impression that he considered these operations as secondary or to belittle their significance, since they were of very real value.

Churchill said that the original force for OVERLORD would consist of nineteen American and sixteen British divisions, that being the maximum number that Britain could afford because of its manpower limitations. The additional divisions for the subsequent exploitation of OVERLORD would come in a steady stream from the United States. He said that there might be delays in the launching of OVERLORD—the great bottleneck at the moment being the shortage of landing-craft—and that pending such delays the Allied forces should not remain idle. He then reverted to the desirability of getting Turkey into the war, as he did over and over again with a persistence that was both admirable and monotonous.

Roosevelt surprised and disturbed Hopkins by mentioning the possibility of an operation across the Adriatic for a drive, aided by Tito's partisans, north-eastward into Roumania to effect a junction with the Red Army advancing southward from the region of Odessa. Hopkins thereupon scribbled a note to Admiral King: 'Who's promoting that Adriatic business that the President continually returns to?' To which King replied: 'As far as I know it is his own idea.' Certainly nothing could be farther from the plans of the U.S. Chiefs of Staff. Churchill was quick to associate himself with Roosevelt's suggestion, but Stalin asked if the continuation of operations in or from Italy would in any way effect the thirty-five divisions which he understood were earmarked for OVERLORD. Churchill replied at some length that they would not.

Stalin then expressed the opinion that it would be unwise to scatter forces in various operations throughout the Eastern Mediterranean. He said he thought that OVERLORD should be considered the basis for all operations in 1944 and that after the capture of Rome the forces used there should be sent into Southern France to provide a diversionary operation in support of OVERLORD. He even felt that it might be better to abandon the capture of Rome altogether, leaving ten divisions to hold the present line in Italy, and using the rest of the Allied force for the invasion of Southern France. He said it had been the experience of the Red Army that it was best to launch an offensive from two converging directions, forcing the enemy to move his reserves from one front to the other. Therefore, he favoured simultaneous operations in Northern and Southern France, rather than the 'scattering' of forces in the Eastern Mediterranean. He stated quite plainly, and repeated it several times, his conviction that in any case Turkey would not agree to enter the war.

Churchill said that he could not believe the Turks would be so 'mad' as to reject this opportunity to join with the United Nations under the most

favourable circumstances, but Stalin observed that there were some people who apparently preferred to remain 'mad'.

Roosevelt said that if he were to meet with President Inonu of Turkey he would, of course, do everything possible to persuade him to enter the war, but that if he were in Inonu's place he would demand so heavy a price in airplanes, tanks, and equipment that the granting of these requests would result in indefinite postponement of OVERLORD.

This first meeting ended at 7.20 p.m.—having lasted three hours and twenty minutes—and thereafter Roosevelt signed four more Congressional bills and a Proclamation and worked on his mail until dinnertime, 8.30, when he was host to Stalin, Molotov, Churchill, Eden, Sir Archibald Clark Kerr (British Ambassador in Moscow), Hopkins, Harriman, and the three interpreters. This dinner represented a major achievement by the Filipino sailors, who had moved only four hours previously into a strange kitchen, which, because of the haste with which the house had been made available, lacked most of the essential equipment, including a range. These deficiencies had been rapidly supplied and the dinner was served successfully.

Hopkins noted that Stalin was greyer than when he had seen him last in the summer of 1941 and also much dressier, now wearing a uniform with gold epaulettes each bearing a large white star fastened with a red pin. Stalin doodled and smoked during the meetings. His voice was quiet—barely audible—and he seemed to expend no effort in placing emphasis on anything as he talked to the interpreter. Harriman has said that Stalin in greeting Hopkins at Teheran displayed more open and warm cordiality than he had been known to show to any foreigner; evidently the Marshal saw in Hopkins one who had made promises and done his level best to keep them.

At dinner on the first evening Roosevelt and Stalin discussed Fairbanks, Alaska, as a suitable spot for a later meeting. Stalin again expressed himself on the subject of France, whose ruling class, he felt, was rotten to the core; he described the former Vichy Ambassador to Moscow, Bergery, as typical of the majority of French politicians. He did not consider that France could be trusted with any strategic positions outside her own borders in the postwar period. He still seemed to attach little importance to de Gaulle as a real factor in political or other matters.

The conversation turned to the subject of postwar treatment of Germany and the frontiers of Poland. Stalin said that Poland should extend to the Oder and that the Russians would help the Poles to establish their frontier thus far west, but he was not specific about Poland's eastern frontier. According to the record: 'The President then said he would be interested in the question of assuring the approaches to the Baltic Sea and had in mind some form of trusteeship with perhaps an international state in the vicinity of the

Kiel Canal to insure free navigation in both directions through the approaches. Due to some error of the Soviet translator, Marshal Stalin apparently thought that the President was referring to the question of the Baltic States. On the basis of this understanding, he replied categorically that the Baltic States had by an expression of the will of the people voted to join the Soviet Union and that this question was not therefore one for discussion. Following the clearing up of the misapprehension, he, however, expressed himself favourable in regard to the question of insuring free navigation to and from the Baltic Sea.'

The following memorandum was written on Stalin's views concerning postwar Germany:

In regard to Germany, Marshal Stalin appeared to regard all measures proposed by either the President or Churchill for the subjugation and for the control of Germany as inadequate. He on various occasions sought to induce the President or the Prime Minister to go further in expressing their views as to the stringency of the measures which should be applied to Germany. He appeared to have no faith in the possibility of the reform of the German people and spoke bitterly of the attitude of the German workers in the war against the Soviet Union. As evidence of the fundamental German devotion to legality he cited the occasion in 1907 when he was in Leipzig when 200 German workers failed to appear at an important mass meeting because there was no controller at the station platform to punch their tickets which would permit them to leave the station. He seemed to think that this mentality of discipline and obedience could not be changed.

He said that Hitler was a very able man, but not basically intelligent, lacking in culture and with a primitive approach to political and other problems. He did not share the view of the President that Hitler was mentally unbalanced and emphasized that only a very able man could accomplish what Hitler had done in solidifying the German people, whatever we thought of the methods. Although he did not specifically say so, it was apparent from his remarks that he considered that Hitler through his stupidity in attacking the Soviet Union had thrown away all the fruits of his previous victories.

As a wartime measure Marshal Stalin questioned the advisability of the unconditional surrender principle with no definition of the exact terms which would be imposed upon Germany. He felt that to leave the principle of unconditional surrender unclarified merely served to unite the German people, whereas to draw up specific terms, no matter how harsh, and tell the German people that this was what they would have to accept, would, in his opinion, hasten the day of German capitulation.

If Roosevelt made any comment on this expression of opinion on the controversial question of unconditional surrender, it was not recorded. But the subsequent record proves that he did not change his mind.

The next morning, Monday, military staff talks were held at which it was determined that it would be feasible to mount an operation against Southern France with a two-division assault and a ten-division follow-up to be launched simultaneously with OVERLORD D-Day or from two to three weeks preceding it. In the study of personnel available in the Mediterranean theatre made at this meeting appeared the note: 'Eisenhower states that 370,000 Italian troops are now co-operating with Allied Forces', which seemed a remarkable number only ten weeks after Italy's surrender and with two-thirds of Italy still in German hands.

During these talks Voroshilov asked a great many searching questions about innumerable details concerned with the actual preparations for OVERLORD. He was not interested in what the plans were, or the 'programme' for production; he wanted to know what was actually being *done*. He asked General Brooke point-blank if he attached the same importance to OVERLORD that General Marshall did. Brooke replied in the affirmative, but added that he knew how strong the German defences of Northern France were and that under certain circumstances OVERLORD could fail. Voroshilov said that the British and American forces had clearly demonstrated their superiority over the Germans in the fighting on land in North Africa and more particularly in the air over Europe, and that if the U.S. and British staffs really had the will and the desire to go through with OVERLORD it would be successful and would 'go down in history as one of our greatest victories'. He admitted the difficulties of a trans-Channel operation, as had Stalin, but said that the Russians had encountered comparable difficulties in the crossing of wide rivers and had overcome them because they 'had the will to do it'.

Marshall, whom both Stalin and Voroshilov obviously recognized as the supreme advocate of OVERLORD and therefore their friend, said that he wished to offer one comment: 'The difference between a river crossing, however wide, and a landing from the ocean is that the failure of a river crossing is a reverse while the failure of a landing operation is a catastrophe.' Marshall went on to say: 'My military education and experience in the First World War has all been based on roads, rivers, and railroads. During the last two years, however, I have been acquiring an education based on oceans, and I've had to learn all over again. Prior to the present war I never heard of any landing-craft except a rubber boat. Now I think about little else.'

Voroshilov said admiringly to Marshall: 'If you think about it, you will do it.'

While this meeting was going on Roosevelt attended to more mail. According to Harriman, Churchill sent over a message suggesting that he

and the President have lunch together preparatory to the next Plenary Session that afternoon. But Roosevelt was too conscious of the presence of the NKVD men and did not want the report to be spread that he and the Prime Minster were hatching their own schemes. Harriman conveyed Roosevelt's regrets to Churchill, who was not pleased by them and remarked that he could accept rebuffs as well as the next one—but, as Harriman told it, he said: 'I shall insist on one thing: that I be host at dinner tomorrow evening. I think I have one or two claims to precedence. To begin with, I come first both in seniority and alphabetically. In the second place, I represent the longest established of the three governments. And, in the third place, tomorrow happens to be my birthday.'

Roosevelt lunched quietly with his own household. His son Elliot had arrived that morning from Egypt, his plane having been delayed by engine trouble. After lunch the President had a short session with the Joint Chiefs of Staff, who reported their conclusions on ANVIL, the Southern France operation, and presented memoranda they had prepared for the President to discuss with Stalin for measures to be taken in anticipation of Russia's entry into the war against Japan. At 2.45 Stalin arrived. (The President's log-book indicates that Molotov was also present, but the minutes of the meeting make no mention of his being there.) Roosevelt said he wished to lend Stalin a report from a U.S. Army officer who had been with Tito in Yugoslavia and had the highest respect for the work being done there by the partisan forces. Stalin thanked the President and said he would read the report with interest and return it. Roosevelt then gave Stalin three memoranda:

(1) A request for permission for U.S. bombers from Britain to use Russian air bases for refuelling, rearmament, and emergency repair in the proposed 'shuttle bombing' of Germany.

(2) A request that planning be started at once with a view to establishing bases for upwards of 1,000 U.S. heavy bombers in the Siberian Maritime Provinces for air offensive against Japan.

(3) Requests for the exchange of information and for further preliminary planning for eventual operations against Japan.

In this memorandum Roosevelt said:

Specifically, I have in mind the following items:

(a) We would be glad to receive combat intelligence information concerning Japan.

(b) Considering that the ports for your Far Eastern submarine and destroyer force might be threatened seriously by land or air attack, do you feel it desirable that the United States should expand base facilities sufficiently to provide for these forces in U.S. bases?

(c) What direct or indirect assistance would you be able to give in the event of a U.S. attack against the Northern Kuriles?

(d) Could you indicate what ports, if any, our forces could use, and could you furnish data on these ports in regard to their naval use as well as port capacities for dispatch of cargo?

Stalin promised to study these documents. (He later agreed to the shuttle bombing not only from bases in the United Kingdom, but from Italy as well; he explained that he must defer consideration of the request relative to the Far East until after his return to Moscow.)

Roosevelt then asked Stalin if he cared to discuss the future peace of the world and Stalin said there was nothing to prevent them from discussing anything they pleased. Whereupon, Roosevelt gave Stalin an outline of his concept of an organization, based on the United Nations, for the preservation of world peace. It was to consist of three main bodies:

First an Assembly composed of all the members of the United Nations which would meet in various places at stated times for the discussion of world problems and the making of recommendations for their solution. Stalin asked if this Assembly was to be world-wide in scope, or merely European, and Roosevelt said it should be world-wide.

Second—an Executive Committee which would consist of the U.S.S.R., the U.S., the U.K., and China, together with representatives of two European nations, one South American, one Middle Eastern, one Far Eastern, and one British Dominion. This Executive Committee would deal with all non-military questions—such as economy, food, health, etc.

Stalin asked whether this committee would have the right to make decisions which would be binding on all the nations. Roosevelt was indecisive in his answer to that one. He did not believe that the Congress would permit the United States to be bound by the decision of such a body. He said that the Committee could make recommendations for settling disputes with the hope that the nations concerned would be guided thereby.

The third body, as set forth by Roosevelt, was what he termed 'The Four Policemen'—the U.S.S.R., U.S., U.K., and China. This, as its name implied, would be the enforcing agency—with power to deal immediately with any threat to the peace or any sudden emergency. The President cited the Italian attack on Ethiopia in 1935 as an example of the failure of the League of Nations to deal promptly and forcibly with an act of aggression. He said that had the Four Policemen existed at that time it would have been possible to close the Suez Canal and thereby prevent Mussolini from attacking Ethiopia.

Stalin expressed the opinion that this proposal for the Four Policemen would not be favourably received by the small nations of Europe. For one

thing he did not believe that China would be very powerful when the war ended—and, even if it were, European states would resent having China as an enforcement authority for themselves. He therefore suggested, as an alternative, that there be one committee for Europe and one for the Far East—the European committee to consist of Britain, Russia, the United States, and possibly one other European nation. The President said that this suggestion was somewhat similar to one made by Churchill for regional committees—one for Europe, one for the Far East, and one for the Americas—and Roosevelt doubted that the Congress would agree to American participation in a purely European committee which might be able to compel the involvement of American troops. He said that only a crisis such as the present one could compel the Congress to agree to such a step—that it would not have been possible to send American troops to Europe in the present war had it not been for the Japanese attack on Pearl Harbour.

Stalin said that if the President's suggestion for a world organization were carried out—particularly the Four Policemen part of it—this might require the sending of American troops overseas. Roosevelt said that he had only foreseen the sending of American naval and air forces to Europe and that any land armies needed in the event of a future threat would have to be provided by Britain and the Soviet Union.

He saw two possible kinds of threat—one minor and one major—to world peace. The minor threat might arise from a revolution or civil war in a small country, or the kind of Tacna—Arica dispute that sometimes arises between relatively small neighbouring states. This could be met by application of the quarantine method, the closing of limited frontiers and the imposition of embargoes.

The major threat would be provided by a gesture of aggression on the part of a large power; in this case the Four Policemen would send an ultimatum to the threatening nation and, if the demands were not immediately met, they would subject that nation to bombardment and, if necessary, invasion. (There seems to be no evidence of any discussion of the possibility that the offending aggressor might be one of the Four Policemen.)

Stalin talked of the immediate problem of the future treatment of Germany. He said that he had discussed the question on the previous day with Churchill and considered that the Prime Minister was too hopeful in assuming that Germany could not rise again. It was Stalin's belief that Germany would be able to recover its power completely within fifteen or twenty years unless forcibly prevented from doing so, and that therefore there must be more certain safeguards than those provided by the type of organization which the President had proposed.

Stalin said that, to provide insurance against another career of aggression by Germany, the United Nations must gain and maintain control of physical

strongpoints not only within Germany and along the borders of Germany, but also at strategic bases outside Germany. He mentioned Dakar specifically as one of such bases. He applied the same rules to the future containment of Japan, naming the islands in the vicinity of Japan as essential bases for the prevention of future aggression.

Stalin said that any organization or committee that might be set up for the preservation of peace must have the power not only to make decisions in times of emergency, but to have continued military occupation of the necessary bases against Germany and Japan.

Roosevelt said that his agreement with Marshal Stalin on this was one hundred per cent. He said that although he was fully cognizant of the present weakness of China, he had insisted that the Chinese must participate in the four-power declaration at Moscow because he was thinking far into the future and believed that it was better to have the 400 million people of China as friends rather than as possible enemies.

There was then some discussion of the ability of the Germans to convert apparently peaceable industries secretly to wartime purposes. Stalin said that the Germans had shown great skill in such deception, but Roosevelt expressed confidence that if the world organization were sufficiently strong and effective it could prevent repetition of Germany's secret rearmament.

It was now 3.30, and Stalin and Roosevelt moved over to the large conference room of the Russian Embassy, where Churchill, acting on behalf of King George VI, presented to the Marshal the 'Sword of Stalingrad'. Following this impressive ceremony, the twenty-eight participants in the conference sat down at the large round table and went to work on the Second Plenary Session. It started with a review of the morning staff session by Brooke, Marshall, and Voroshilov, and then Stalin fired the big question:

'Who will command OVERLORD?'

Roosevelt replied that this had not yet been decided. Stalin thereupon made it clear that until a supreme commander were named he could not believe in the reality of the operation. Roosevelt must have been sorely tempted at that moment to name General Marshall as supreme commander and have done with it, but he did not do so, for reasons known only to himself. He said that the decisions taken at this conference would affect the choice of the particular officer, and this probably meant that he would appoint Marshall only if the command involved *all* of Western and Southern Europe instead of OVERLORD alone.

Churchill then launched forth on a lengthy statement along familiar lines. He ranged from the Channel to Southern France to Italy to Yugoslavia to Rhodes and so to Turkey, dwelling for some time on that favourite subject. The record states that the Prime Minster 'summed up the tasks before the conference as (1) to survey the whole field of the Mediterranean, and (2) how to relieve Russia, and (3) how to help OVERLORD'.

Stalin said: 'If we are here in order to discuss military matters, among all the military questions for discussion, we, the U.S.S.R., consider OVERLORD the most important and decisive.' He said that, from the Russian point of view, Turkey, Rhodes, Yugoslavia, and even the capture of Rome, were not important. He recommended that a directive be given to the military staffs as follows:

'(1) In order that Russian help might be given from the East to the execution of OVERLORD, a date should be set and the operation should not be postponed. (2) If possible the attack in Southern France should precede OVERLORD by two months, but if that is impossible, then it should be launched simultaneously with or even a little after OVERLORD. This would be an operation in direct support of OVERLORD as contrasted with diversionary operations in Italy or the Balkans. (3) The Commander-in-chief for OVERLORD should be appointed as soon as possible. Until that is done OVERLORD cannot be considered as really in progress.' Stalin added that the appointment of the Commander-in-Chief was the business of the President and Mr. Churchill, but that it would be advantageous to have the appointment made here in Teheran.

Churchill made a final and, one must say, gallant attempt on behalf of Rhodes and Turkey as strategic points, but Roosevelt said that it seemed that he and the Prime Minister and the Marshal were agreed on the main directive to the Chiefs of Staff, which was to go ahead on the assumption that OVERLORD was the dominating operation and, while the Staffs might make recommendations for subsidiary operations in the Mediterranean area, they must be careful to consider nothing that could possibly cause a delay in OVERLORD.

Stalin thereupon said to Churchill that he would like to ask him a rather indiscreet question: Did the British really believe in OVERLORD or were they expressing their approval of it merely as a means of reassuring the Russians? The record is not quite clear at this point, but it would seem that Churchill now accepted the inevitable and said that Britain would hurl every ounce of her strength across the Channel at the Germans. Tension still existed, however, so Roosevelt observed that within an hour a very good dinner would be awaiting all of them, with Marshal Stalin as their host, and that he for one would have a large appetite for it. He suggested that the Combined Chiefs of Staff meet again in the morning and settle the matter of OVERLORD once and for all. The meeting then ended.

The official records of these meetings were written with so much circumspection that the inherent drama was largely obscured; but it was far too big to be totally disguised. One cannot read these deliberately dry and guarded accounts without the feeling that here were Titans determinating the future course of an entire planet. This was indeed the Big Three. Churchill employed all the debater's arts, the brilliant locutions and circumlocutions, of which he

was a master, and Stalin wielded his bludgeon with relentless indifference to all the dodges and feints of his practised adversary; while Roosevelt sat in the middle, by common consent the moderator, arbitrator, and final authority. His contributions to the conversations were infrequent and sometimes annoyingly irrelevant, but it appears time and again—at Teheran and at Yalta—that it was he who spoke the last word.

Some time during the Teheran Conference Roosevelt drew three circles, which represented his conception of the basis of the United Nations Organization. The centre circle was marked 'Executive Committee', the one on the right was marked '4 Policemen', and the one on the left '40 United Nations' (The General Assembly), under which came 'I.L.O.-Health-Agriculture-Food'. This, so far as I know, was the first crude outline of the U.N. structure put down by Roosevelt, who, unlike Hopkins, loved to draw charts.

The dinner on Monday evening was marked by a great deal of 'teasing' of Churchill by Stalin; I am not qualified to say whether it was intended or accepted in a spirit of good-humoured raillery, but it was evidently unremitting throughout the evening. At one point, when the question of postwar control of strategic bases was being discussed, Churchill stated that Britain did not desire to acquire any new territory, but intended to hold on to what she had and to reclaim what had been taken from her—specifically Singapore and Hong Kong—and that while she might eventually release portions of the Empire of her own free will, she could not be compelled to give up anything without a war. Stalin commented on this that Britain had fought well in the war and that he personally favoured increases in the British Empire, particularly in the area around Gibraltar which was presently the property of Franco's Spain. When Churchill asked what territorial interests Russia might have in the future Stalin was quoted as having replied: 'There is no need to speak at the present time about any Soviet desires—but when the time comes we will speak.'

During the dinner Stalin made a surprisingly frank statement of the past quality of the Red Army. According to the record: 'He said that in the winter war against Finland the Soviet Army had shown itself to be very poorly organized and had done very badly; that as a result of the Finnish War the entire Soviet Army had been reorganized; but even so, when the Germans attacked in 1941, it could not be said that the Red Army was a first-class fighting force. That during the war with Germany the Red Army had become steadily better from the point of view of operations, tactics, etc., and now he felt that it was genuinely a good army. He added that the general opinion in regard to the Red Army had been wrong, because it was not believed that the Soviet Army could reorganize and improve itself during time of war.'

Stalin had been annoyed that the afternoon conference had ended with

reference of the OVERLORD problem to the Combined Chiefs of Staff, for he could not understand why the decision should not be made there and then by Roosevelt, Churchill, and himself without interference by a mere 'military committee'. This was another evidence of the fact, noted by Hopkins on his first trip to Moscow, that there was no real authority in the Soviet Union below the top. However, when the Big Three met again before lunch the next day, Tuesday, Roosevelt asked Churchill to read Stalin the results of the Staff meeting, and when this had been done Stalin expressed great satisfaction with the decision and promised that the Red Army would undertake offensive operations concurrently with OVERLORD which would demonstrate the importance that the Russians attached to the opening, at last, of the Second Front. But—Stalin again asked—'When will the Commander-in-Chief be named?' Roosevelt said that he would need three or four days to consider the matter and to discuss it with his staff. He said that it had been decided that morning to appoint one commander for OVERLORD, another for the Mediterranean, and probably a third to command the Southern France operation temporarily during the landing phase and the advance up the Rhone Valley to the junction with the main forces in Northern France. Stalin approved this as sound military doctrine—and the military discussions at Teheran were thereby ended; but Churchill had not quit yet.

Perhaps when Churchill's own memoirs of these later years are published there will be revelation of the extent to which he was influenced in his thinking about OVERLORD by the possibility of German collapse before an invasion as a result of some such uprising against Hitler by German generals as that which was actually attempted and bungled after the invasion in July, 1944. There is no doubt that Roosevelt never took this possibility very seriously as a solution to the problems of achieving total victory. Here again he was influenced by grim memories of the results of the Armistice in 1918. Indeed, at the time of the Trident Conference he decided to issue a statement explaining that the unconditional surrender formula meant that the United Nations would never negotiate an armistice with the Nazi Government, the German High Command, or any other organization or group or individual in Germany; this statement was never issued, because, Roosevelt said, Churchill persuaded him against it. It seems evident that Stalin would have agreed with Churchill on that point, but that he certainly agreed with Roosevelt that Germany could not be defeated by anything less than the application of overwhelming armed force on the Continent itself in the west.

It is not a matter of record, but it is the testimony of some who were present at this conference that Stalin was told unofficially (and not by Roosevelt) that the President would appoint Marshall to the OVERLORD command and that Stalin made evident his conviction that no wiser or more reassuring choice could be made.

Extreme amiability prevailed throughout lunch and a short Plenary Session in the afternoon and at dinner that evening (this was Churchill's sixty-ninth birthday party; Roosevelt's gift to him was a Kashan bowl which he had purchased that day at the local U.S. Army 'PX'). During lunch the extremely important question of Russia's need for warm-water ports was brought up by Churchill, who said that his Government not only recognized the legitimacy of this requirement, but also hoped to see Russian fleets, both naval and merchant, on all the seas. Stalin remarked that the British had not felt that way in Lord Curzon's time, and Churchill replied that those were other days. Stalin smiled and said that Russia also was quite different in those days. It was Roosevelt who mentioned the possibility that Russia might have access to the port of Dairen in Manchuria—and he did so for the first time here, at Teheran, and not at Yalta (when, according to legend, he was so enfeebled as to be *non compos mentis*). Stalin immediately expressed the opinion that the Chinese would object to this proposal, but Roosevelt said he thought they would agree to having Dairen made a free port under international guarantee. It is my understanding that Roosevelt was not merely guessing about this—that he had, in fact, discussed this very point with Chiang Kai-shek in Cairo a few days previously.

While Stalin, Churchill, and Roosevelt were having lunch that day, Eden, Molotov, and Hopkins were meeting for lunch at the British Legation. The main topics of conversation were the future United Nations strategic strongpoints about the world, in which Hopkins took considerable interest, and the question of getting Turkey into the war, about which he appeared to be indifferent. Indeed, in response to a question by Molotov as to whether Turkey's entry would cause a delay in OVERLORD, Hopkins replied that it was the President's impression and that of the U.S. Chiefs of Staff that it would cause such a delay. In that case, said Molotov, Stalin would be opposed to getting Turkey into the war. Eden said it had been proposed that President Inonu be invited to meet the President and Prime Minister in Cairo a few days hence, and suggested that a Russian representative be present at these meetings.

On the subject of strategic bases, Hopkins said: 'The location of these future strongpoints and what they will require in the way of land, sea, and air forces will have to be worked out with a view as to who would be a potential future enemy. The President feels it essential to world peace that Russia, Great Britain, and the United States work out this control question in a manner that will not start each of the three powers arming against the others. The question of building up bases in the Pacific should not be a difficult one. We Americans do not want sovereignty over any of the islands that are freed from the Japanese. The United Nations may exercise some sort of protective influence over them. As regards the Philippines, when they

gain their independence we would still consider it advisable to have naval
and air bases there under United States rather than United Nations control.'

At the dinner that Tuesday evening Churchill described Roosevelt as one
who had devoted his life to the cause of the weak and helpless, one who
through his courage and foresighted action in 1933 had indeed prevented a
revolution in the United States, and had steadily since then 'guided his
country along the tumultuous stream of party friction and internal politics
amidst the violent freedoms of democracy'. Proposing a toast to Stalin,
Churchill said that the Marshal was worthy to stand with the mightiest
figures of Russian history and merited the title of 'Stalin the Great'.

In reply, according to the record, 'Marshal Stalin said that the honours
which had been paid to him really belonged to the Russian people; that it
was easy to be a hero or a great leader if one had to do with people such as
the Russians. He said that the Red Army had fought heroically, but that the
Russian people would have tolerated no other quality from their armed
forces. He said that even persons of medium courage and even cowards
became heroes in Russia. Those who do not, he said, are killed.'

It was at this dinner that Stalin made his frequently quoted statement that
without American production, the war would have been lost.

Roosevelt expressed the belief that the Teheran Conference had increased
the hopes for a better world—and by a better world he meant one in which
the ordinary citizen can be assured the opportunity for peaceful toil and the
just enjoyment of the fruits of his labours.

Hopkins also made an after-dinner speech at Teheran, telling the Russians
that he had made a long and thorough study of the British Constitution,
which is unwritten, and of the War Cabinet, whose authority and composition are not specifically defined. He said that as a result of this study he had
learned that 'the provisions of the British Constitution and the powers of
the War Cabinet are just whatever Winston Churchill wants them to be at
any given moment'. This observation was greeted with loud laughter,
particularly from the Prime Minister himself.

At lunch on Wednesday, the final day, there was long discussion of the
proposed meeting with the Turkish officials. Hopkins was firm in asserting
that before any such meeting there must be detailed agreement as to exactly
what form of military assistance should be promised the Turks if they were
to enter the war. When Churchill mentioned the requirements for landing-
craft for an assault on the islands of Rhodes in the month of March, Hopkins
was so anxious to have the record straight that he wrote out his own version
of his comments for inclusion in the minutes, as follows: 'Mr. Hopkins
again pointed out that the United States Chief of Staff had not given consideration to the detailed requirements of the Turkish Operation. The whole
of the Mediterranean was soon to come under the Combined Chiefs of

Staff—hence the resources must be examined in the light of that fact. It should be clearly understood that the American side believe that there are no landing-craft available for an attack on Rhodes—and, more important still, that even if the landing-craft were available—no decision has been reached as to whether or not the landing-craft could not be used to better advantage in some other operation. Under any circumstances it should be clearly understood that no mention can be made to President Inonu, implied or otherwise, that an amphibious landing can be made on Rhodes.'

Here was an instance of Churchill's friend, 'Lord Root of the Matter', attempting to nail down an issue so firmly that the Prime Minister would not be able to pick it up and run with it again, particularly in the conferences with the Turks, when it might suddenly assume the character of an inescapable commitment.

Following the discussion as to how to get Turkey into the war there was talk about how to get Finland out of it, but no definite conclusions appear to have been reached. During this meeting Hopkins passed a note to Roosevelt: 'Mr. President: What do you think of letting the Russians give dinner tonight—your last chance at Russian food? Harry.' To which Roosevelt replied: 'O.K. But I have to leave *early* as we sleep at the camp. F.D.R.'

During the afternoon Roosevelt had a private talk with Stalin and Molotov for the purposes of putting them in possession of certain essential facts concerning American politics. It was a cause of wonderment to the President that the Russian leaders appeared to be so inadequately informed as to conditions in the United States or the character of public opinion. They had their full quota of diplomatic representatives and the members of numerous wartime missions to furnish intelligence—in addition to which there was, presumably, the entire membership of the American Communist party. It could only be assumed that, as was so often the case with the most extensive intelligence systems, Moscow believed and trusted those agents who reported what Moscow most wanted to hear—whereas those who sent in objective and sometimes discouraging reports which approximated the truth were suspected of having been contaminated by their capitalistic environment and were transferred to less attractive posts, such as Siberia. The Russians were not the only ones who erred in this respect: American representatives in Moscow whose reports were too favourable were suspected of having gone Communist, and the State Department was traditionally on the alert against any of its Foreign Service officers who displayed the slightest tendency to become pro-British. Thus, it was always safest for those who wrote reports to take an aggressively chauvinist line toward all foreigners.

Roosevelt felt it necessary to explain to Stalin that there were six or seven million Americans of Polish extraction, and others of Lithuanian, Latvian,

Marshal Stalin, President Roosevelt and Mr. Winston Churchill,
with their chief advisers, at the Teheran Conference.

and Estonian origin who had the same rights and the same votes as anyone else and whole opinions must be respected. Stalin said that he understood this, but he subsequently suggested that some 'propaganda work' should be done among these people.

Later, Churchill and Eden arrived for the final meeting. There was a discussion of the division of the Italian Fleet on which agreement was immediate, and then one on the frontiers of Poland in which Roosevelt did not take part; it ended with evolvement of a formula much like that which was eventually adopted. There was extensive discussion of the dismemberment of Germany. Roosevelt submitted a plan for five autonomous states: (1) Prussia (reduced), (2) Hanover and North-west, (3) Saxony and Leipzig area, (4) Hesse-Darmstadt, Hesse-Kassel, and the area south of the Rhine, (5) Bavaria, Baden, and Wurtemberg—whereas the Kiel Canal and Hamburg, and the Ruhr and the Saar, to be under United Nations control. When Roosevelt offered this suggestion Churchill exclaimed: 'To use an American expression, the President has said a mouthful!' Churchill agreed that Prussia should be separated from the rest; he believed that the southern states should be detached to become part of a Danubian Confederation.

Stalin was not enthusiastic about either proposal, but said that of the two he preferred Roosevelt's. He felt that dismemberment meant dismemberment—that the Prussian officers and staffs should be eliminated but that otherwise he saw little difference between the people of one part of Germany and another. As to putting any parts of Germany in any Confederation, he said that, whatever form it might take, if there were Germans in it they would soon dominate it and the threat of a greater Germany would be revived. He said that there would always be a strong urge on the part of the Germans to unite and that the whole purpose of any international organization must be to neutralize this tendency by applying economic and other measures, including, if necessary, force. This discussion ended up nowhere; it was decided that the subject should be considered further by the European Advisory Commission in London.

It had been planned to continue the conference another day, but the weather forecasts indicated that conditions would become unfavourable for flying over the mountains to Cairo and it seemed advisable for the President to leave the following (Thursday) morning. This meant a considerable rush in preparing the official communiqué (which was one of the war's most inspiring statements) and the Declaration on Iran. The latter document was carried by Harriman from Roosevelt to Stalin to Churchill, who all signed it. Then Harriman turned it over to General Patrick J. Hurley, who took it to the Shah of Iran, who also signed it. A year later Harriman reported in a memorandum which was confirmed as to factual points by Bohlen that intensive search had failed to reveal the whereabouts of this signed document.

U

Hurley was consulted, but he could not remember where he had put it. It finally was located in a White House file.

After dinner Thursday evening Roosevelt said good-bye to Stalin. He believed in his heart that the final words of the Teheran Declaration—'We came here with hope and determination. We leave here friends in fact, in spirit, and in purpose'—were more than mere words. He had disagreed with the two men with whom he had been dealing on various important points— he had found Stalin much tougher than he had expected and at times deliberately discourteous, and Churchill's tireless advocacy of his own strategic concepts had been more than ever taxing to patience; but there was one fault in these two men which were gloriously conspicuous by its absence, and that fault was hypocrisy, for all that was great and all that was regrettable in both of them stood out in such unmistakably bold relief that no mask could be thick enough or pliable enough to cover it. Roosevelt now felt sure that, to use his own term, Stalin was 'getatable', despite his bludgeoning tactics and his attitude of cynicism toward such matters as the rights of small nations, and that when Russia could be convinced that her legitimate claims and requirements—such as the right of access to warm-water ports—were to be given full recognition, she would prove tractable and co-operative in maintaining the peace of the postwar world.

If there was any supreme peak in Roosevelt's career, I believe it might well be fixed at this moment, at the end of the Teheran Conference. It certainly represented the peak for Harry Hopkins.

Before he could leave this area Roosevelt had an engagement to fufil with the American troops of the Persian Gulf Command, and he drove from the Russian Embassy to Camp Amirabad, where he spent the night as guest of General Connolly, one of the engineer officers who had been with Hopkins in W.P.A. (The Patterson-McCormick Press evidently overlooked the opportunity to find another 'plot' in this.) On Thursday morning Roosevelt took a jeep ride around the camp and made a speech to the isolated, homesick, sun-scorched G.I.'s, who could never even know the stimulus of an air-raid alert or a sounding of G.Q. At 9.45 a.m. the President's party took off for Cairo, where a lot more White House mail, including nine more Congressional bills and a Proclamation of a 'Day of Prayer' had accumulated. On Saturday morning President Inonu and the Turkish delegation arrived, and some mad wag in Cairo circulated the report that all the Turks wore hearing devices so perfectly attuned to one another that they all went out of order at the same instant whenever mention was made of the possibility of Turkey's entering the war.

In the background of this meeting with the Turks were Churchill's talks at Adana following the Casablanca Conference, and a meeting at Cairo between Eden and Numan Menemencioglu, the Turkish Foreign Minister,

only three weeks before Teheran. The latter talks had been somewhat less than negative, which accounted for Stalin's lack of confidence in any further attempts. Roosevelt was also sceptical and Hopkins even more so, but Churchill was never discouraged. I believe that the U.S. Chiefs of Staff were actively alarmed that Turkey *might* come into the war and thereby, as General Marshall liked to put it, 'burn up our logistics right down the line'.

Roosevelt participated with Churchill in two of the meetings with the Turkish President and Foreign Minister. There was another meeting on what was known as 'the Foreign Secretaries' level', involving Numan, Eden, and Hopkins. (Laurence Steinhardt was present at all these sessions.) And, finally, after the conference appeared to have ended on a basis of 'no decision', Churchill held another meeting on his own with Inonu and Numan in an attempt to revive the subject and start all over again.

I see no need to attempt to give a detailed account of these lengthy conversations which ended just about where they began. The record is complete and available for future study by someone who may want to write on 'The Failures of the Second World War'. Suffice it to say that during the talks Roosevelt frequently betrayed a considerable amount of sympathy for the Turkish point of view, and even stated, on one occasion— and this is set forth in the solemn record—that it was quite understandable that these distinguished and amiable gentlemen should 'not want to be caught with their pants down'.

The Turks were willing to enter the war only when they could be sure they were strong enough to prevent the quick destruction of their country. The strengthening process would inevitably take time, and time was the one thing Churchill did not want to concede, for OVERLORD was now only six months away and the moment was approaching when its postponement would be impossible.

During the three days—Saturday, Sunday, Monday, December 4-6— that the Turks were in Cairo, conferences of tremendous importance, immediate and permanent, were being held by the President, Prime Minister, and the Combined Chiefs of Staff. In an earlier chapter I have expressed my belief that there was only one occasion in the entire war when Roosevelt arbitrarily overruled the unanimous decision of his own Chiefs of Staff; there is, admittedly, some question as to the accuracy of that belief, but, if it is true, then this second conference at Cairo was certainly the one occasion. Moreover, Roosevelt felt impelled to renege on his own promise to Chiang Kai-shek, made ten days previously, that the two powerful operations in South-East Asia would go forward: the land offensive in North Burma, known as TARZAN, and the amphibious moves, first against the Andaman Islands in the Bay of Bengal, known as BUCCANEER. The British, who would

have predominant responsibility for supplying the forces for BUCCANEER, were firm in opposition to it. Churchill pointed out that Stalin's sudden and voluntary statement at Teheran of Russia's intention to join in the war against Japan changed the whole strategic picture, removing the need for the establishment of air bases in China, since the bases in Eastern Siberia would be more readily accessible by way of Alaska and much more suitable for the bombing of the main industrial centres in Japan. It was undoubtedly the shipping problem, emphasized by Lewis Douglas, who was present at Cairo, which influenced Roosevelt's reluctant decision to abandon BUCCANEER altogether, or so to restrict it in scope that it became of inconsequential value. There was plenty of bitterness over this reversal, as has been testified by Stilwell's memoirs and the unpublished recollections of the U.S. Chiefs of Staff. But Roosevelt summed up his concept of the basic plan of action as follows:

'A. Accept OVERLORD and ANVIL [Southern France] as the paramount operations of 1944.

'B. Make every effort to get the additional 18-20 landing-craft for operations in Eastern Mediterranean.

'C. Let Admiral Mountbatten be told that he can keep what he has got, but is going to get nothing else; and that he must do the best he can.'

On December 5 Roosevelt and Hopkins prepared and Churchill agreed to the following message to the Generalissimo:

Conference with Stalin involves us in combined grand operations on European continent in the late spring giving fair prospect of terminating war with Germany by end of summer of 1944. These operations impose so large a requirement of heavy landing-craft as to make it impracticable to devote a sufficient number to the amphibious operation in Bay of Bengal simultaneously with launching of Tarzan to ensure success of operation.

This being the case: Would you be prepared go ahead with Tarzan as now planned, including commitment to maintain naval control of Bay of Bengal coupled with naval carrier and commando amphibious raiding operations simultaneous with launching of Tarzan? Also there is the prospect of B-29 bombing of railroad and port Bangkok.

If not, would you prefer to have Tarzan delayed until November to include heavy amphibious operation? Meanwhile concentrating all air transport on carrying supplies over the hump to air and ground forces in China.

I am influenced in this matter by the tremendous advantage to be received by China and the Pacific through the early termination of the war with Germany.

No mention was made in this message of the most important factor of all: Stalin's statement relative to Russia's entry into the war against Japan. This was deliberately omitted because of the constant apprehension that no secret was secure in Chungking—and the damage that might result from a leakage on this one was obviously inestimable.

On the same Sunday that Roosevelt made this decision which exerted so considerable an effect on relations with China—and perhaps on the whole course of the war not only in the Far East but in Europe as well—he made the momentous decision concerning the supreme command for OVERLORD. He made it against the almost impassioned advice of Hopkins and Stimson, against the known preference of both Stalin and Churchill, against his own proclaimed inclination to give to George Marshall the historic opportunity which he so greatly desired and so amply deserved.

Marshall has written me of this occasion:

> Harry Hopkins came to see me Saturday night [at Cairo] before dinner and told me the President was in some concern of mind over my appointment as Supreme Commander. I could not tell from the Hopkins statement just what the President's point of view was, and in my reply I merely endeavoured to make it clear that I would go along wholeheartedly with whatever decision the President made. He need have no fears regarding my personal reaction. I declined to state my opinion.
>
> The next day the President had me call at his Villa, either immediately before or immediately after lunch, I think the latter, where, in response to his questions, I made virtually the same reply I made to Hopkins. I recalled saying that I would not attempt to estimate my capabilities; the President would have to do that; I merely wished to make clear that whatever the decision, I would go along with it wholeheartedly; that the issue was too great for any personal feeling to be considered. I did not discuss the pros and cons of the matter. If I recall, the President stated in completing our conversation: 'I feel I could not sleep at night with you out of the country.'

Roosevelt thereupon announced his selection of Eisenhower. It was one of the most difficult and one of the loneliest decisions he ever had to make: as events proved, not only in Western Europe, but in the whole superb direction of the war, it was surely one of the wisest.

From Cairo, Roosevelt flew back to Tunis and, when he was met there by Eisenhower, said 'Well, Ike—you'd better start packing.' Eisenhower at first thought that this meant confirmation of his assignment to Washington as Acting Chief of Staff. On the subsequent flight to Malta and then to Sicily Roosevelt talked at great length to Eisenhower about the prodigious difficulties that he would confront during the next few months at his new

headquarters in London, where he would be surrounded by the majesty of the British Government and the powerful personality of Winston Churchill, who still believed, in Roosevelt's opinion, that only through failure of a frontal attack across the Channel into France could the United Nations lose the war. Eisenhower listened attentively to this advice as 'The Sacred Cow' droned over the Mediterranean waters where he had made a name for himself.

After Teheran, Hopkins cabled Molotov: 'I greatly enjoyed the conferences we held together and I hope that they may be continued. The meetings of Marshal Stalin and the President have, I am sure, done an infinite amount of good in bringing our two countries more closely together for the waging of the war and the peace. I send you my warmest regards.'

Molotov replied to this cordial message in kind, saying: 'Just like you, I cannot but express my satisfaction regarding our work together at the Teheran Conference and the possibility of continuation of this work in the future. The meeting of Premier Stalin with President Roosevelt is of the greatest importance for drawing closer together the peoples of our countries in the interests of the cause of speeding up our common victory and postwar collaboration. Best wishes.'

Of utmost significance were the reports from the American Embassy in Moscow on the Russian newspapers which indicated an almost 'revolutionary change' in the Soviet attitude toward the United States and Great Britain. It appeared that the whole propaganda machine was turned on to promote enthusiasm for the 'Historic Decisions' at Teheran which had solidified Allied unity in the common purpose to shorten the war and to make secure the peace.

On Christmas Eve, Roosevelt made a world-wide broadcast from Hyde Park. He paid tribute to Churchill, saying: 'The heartfelt prayers of all of us have been with this great citizen of the world.' (Churchill had suffered another severe attack of pneumonia in Africa.) Of Stalin, Roosevelt said: 'He is a man who combines a tremendous, relentless determination with a stalwart good humour. I believe he is truly representative of the heart and soul of Russia; and I believe that we are going to get along very well with him and the Russian people—very well indeed.'

This was the first Christmas in years that Hopkins had not spent with the Roosevelts. He and his wife and daughters were now moved into their small but cheerful house in Georgetown, and Hopkins was very happy with his new surroundings and the prospects for a better world. The President's daughter. Anna Boettiger, had come to visit the family for Christmas, and she occupied the Lincoln Study, where Hopkins had lived for three and a half years. She stayed on there, giving invaluable company and comfort and help to her father until he went to Warm Springs to die.

There now must follow a long lapse in this narrative. On New Year's Day, 1944, Hopkins was having a fine time with a gathering of friends, when suddenly he seemed to droop and said that he felt as if he had a cold coming on and had better go upstairs to bed. He was out of commission thereafter for nearly seven months. He went first to the Navy Hospital, then to Miami, and from there to the Mayo Clinic for another severe operation (which was referred to in the letter from Roosevelt that appears in the first chapter). Early in May he went to White Sulphur Springs for a long convalescence.

Some desperate appeals reached him during his illness and a large percentage of them were concerned with China. At one point T. V. Soong cabled him: 'Several years ago when you were in hospital I recall that against the injunction of your doctor you hurried from hospital when a vital international principle was at stake. Today a fateful decision is again being made . . .' On another message relayed from Soong, Hopkins wrote: 'I can't do this sort of thing out here. Tell them I'm *sick*.'

On February 2 he knew that an amphibious operation designated FLINT-LOCK was on—it was an attack on Kwajalein Atoll in the Marshall Islands—and he knew that his eighteen-year-old son Stephen, a private first class, was there with the Marines. He wrote his son the following letter:

> You can imagine how much my thoughts have been with you during the last few days and I hope that all has gone well. I am sure it has. The Japs can never withstand the force we are throwing at them in the Marshalls.
>
> David is on an aircraft carrier somewhere in that show and it may be you have already seen him.
>
> I heard from Robert a day or two ago and he is being assigned to a new theatre which will get him in the big European push whenever it comes.
>
> Louise and Diana are both well and altogether enjoying the new house.
>
> I have been laid up for the past month in the navy hospital and will probably be here for a couple of weeks more. Then I am going to take a real rest in Miami Beach for another month. It has been nothing serious, but I seem to have had more difficulty in bouncing back this time . . .
>
> Do write me if you get a moment, but I presume you will be pretty busy during the next few weeks, so I will not expect to hear from you.
>
> At any rate, you know that I wish you the best of luck.

That letter was never delivered. While Hopkins was on the train bound for Florida he received the following telegram: 'I am terribly distressed to have to tell you that Stephen was killed in action at Kwajalein. We have no details as yet other than he was buried at sea. His mother has been notified. I am

confident that when we get details we will all be even prouder of him than ever. I am thinking of you much. F.D.R.'

When the details did come in Hopkins was given cause for pride. Stephen had been killed on his first day in combat—the day before his father wrote the above letter. He was carrying ammunition to an isolated machine-gun unit. It was a routine job, of the sort that is done by thousands of soldiers every day in war, and Stephen did it until he fell with the same courage that so many other boys miraculously displayed when it was their duty to do so.

In the hospital Hopkins was visited by his old Grinnell friends, Robert and Florence Kerr, and he talked to them by the hour about his son, Stephen. He had two messages of sympathy from recent, wartime friends which touched him greatly. One was from Sir John Dill, who himself had only a few months more to live. He wrote: 'Harry, this war has hit you very hard. I know of no one who has done more by wise and courageous advice to advance our common cause. And who knows it? Some day it must be known. George Marshall and I have been talking today of the great part which you have played and are playing. So may this sorrow not weight you down too much and may you soon be fit and well to rejoice your friends and continue your great work.'

The other was a beautifully lettered scroll, forwarded by the President to Hopkins at the Mayo Clinic. It was inscribed:

Stephen Peter Hopkins
Age 18
"Your son, my lord, has paid a soldier's debt:
He only liv'd but till he was a man;
The which no sooner had his prowess confirm'd
In the unshrinking station where he fought,
But like a man he died."   SHAKESPEARE

To Harry Hopkins from Winston S. Churchill
13th February, 1944

The quotation is from the final scene of *Macbeth*.

When Hopkins moved early in May from Rochester, Minnesota, to the Army's Ashford General Hospital in White Sulphur Springs, there were the usual protests from some of the Press. 'Who entitles this representative of Rooseveltian squandermania to treatment and nursing in an Army hospital?' was one of the questions. The War Department issued a statement that Hopkins was entitled to this hospitalization as Chairman of the Munitions Assignment Board and that the Secretary of War had authorized his admission.

He was there when the forces went across the Channel into Normandy on D-Day, June 6. He told me a long time later that during the months in hospital he thought endlessly about the various problems that had arisen since 1939, and of how the bottlenecks had been broken and the desperate shortages of strategic materials converted into surpluses, and it all seemed in retrospect as if it had been easy. For production was America's game and the challenge had only to be clearly stated to be met. But, he said, there was one miracle that he could not explain: how did it happen that the United States, an unwarlike and unprepared country if there ever was one, was suddenly able to produce so large and so brilliant a group of military leaders, competent to deal with situations that had never before existed in the history of the world? Where did they come from? And what had they been doing during all those twenty years when our Navy had been used merely to pose for newsreels and our Army had been kicked around like 'a mangy old dog'?

In this connection, I looked into the 1939 edition of *Who's Who in America* and found that although Marshall, King, Arnold, Stark, and MacArthur were listed, among those *not* mentioned among the even faintly prominent of that time were: General Eisenhower, Bradley, Stilwell, Mark Clark, Patton, Patch, Hodges, Wedemeyer, Spaatz, Kenney, Eaker, and Chennault, of the Army, or Vandegrift and Howland Smith, of the Marine Corps, or Admirals Nimitz, Halsey, Spruance, Mitscher, Kinkaid, Hewitt, Sherman, and Kirk, of the Navy. Considering the list of all the commanders from Pearl Harbour on, it was extraordinary how few failed to meet the tremendous opportunities presented. There was none of the agonizing trial-and-error period through which Lincoln had to pass before he found Grant. This time, with remarkably few exceptions, the right men were assigned in the first place.

Another thought that Hopkins expressed when he had time for reflection was this: 'In trying to figure out whether we could have got across the Channel successfully in 1942 or 1943, you've got to answer the unanswerable question as to whether Eisenhower, Bradley, Spaatz, Patton, Beedle Smith, and also Montgomery and Tedder and a lot of others, could have handled the big show as they did if they hadn't had the experience fighting Germans in North Africa and Sicily?'

The debate about the Second Front will probably continue for as long as any of the immediate participants in it shall live, and after that all that will matter is that it actually happened precisely when it did and new world history was made. No one today wastes much time wondering whether William the Conqueror did the right thing in selecting the year 1066.

PART VI

1944-45—VICTORY AND DEATH

CHAPTER XXXII

THE FOURTH TERM

ON July 4, 1944, Hopkins left hospital in White Sulphur Springs and
flew back to Washington to continue his convalescence in his
Georgetown home. During the next three weeks he went to the
White House very occasionally to see the President, but he was incapable of
doing much work or catching up with the bewildering series of victories
that were being achieved all the way from Guam and Saipan in the Marianas
Group, within B-29 range of Japan itself, to the Vitebsk-Mogilev line,
which represented the last ditch for the Germans on Russian soil. (This
huge area of victory, be it said, did not include Burma and China; indeed,
the military situation in China was about to become much worse than at
any time since the Marco Polo Bridge 'incident' in 1937.)

On June 28 the Republicans had nominated Thomas E. Dewey as their
candidate for President. On July 11 Roosevelt annouced that he would run
for a fourth term if nominated by the Democratic National Convention,
which was to be held in Chicago during the week of July 19. While the
convention was in progress Roosevelt travelled to San Diego and there
embarked for Pearl Harbour to meet with Admiral Nimitz and General
MacArthur for the determining of future strategy in the war in the Pacific.
The main decision to be made there, as I understand it, was between the
Navy plan to devote the ground forces to landings on Formosa, and the
MacArthur plan to liberate the Philippines; Roosevelt ultimately decided in
favour of the latter, and there were some cynics (especially in the Navy)
who remarked in undertones that perhaps the President's choice had been
influenced by the thought that the Philippines would provide a more popular
victory in an election year.

On July 19 Churchill cabled Hopkins explaining his concern about the
forthcoming Southern France operation (ANVIL). There was continuing
debate about the wisdom of that move—and Churchill was still arguing
doggedly for the application of Anglo-American forces to the Balkans.
At this late stage, the Prime Minister may have been concerned by the
smashing Russian advances, especially those toward South-Eastern Europe.
The shattering of the Vitebsk-Mogilev line brought the Red Army well into
Poland and Lithuania and close to East Prussia; the Russians had already
entered Roumania and reached the eastern tip of Czechoslovakia, and there
appeared to be nothing that could stop them from pushing on to the Danube
and across it into Bulgaria and Yugoslavia to the borders of Greece and
Turkey. Churchill emphasized the need for another major conference,
saying that affairs were getting into a most tangled state for the Three

Great Powers—or, he added, for the Four Great Powers, if China were still included. He asked if Hopkins would accompany the President on the Pacific journey, and Hopkins replied:

> I am remaining here in Washington and not going with the President. I am able to work only two or three hours a day. Things seem to be going extremely well in the war and I think that Hitler is now really on the run. The President showed me his message to you suggesting a conference which I imagine will soon come off, and I hope to be there. I look forward to Beaverbrook's arrival, which will assure a big breeze here in Washington.

Hopkins then wrote to Sir John Dill: 'The Prime Minister sounds a little jittery, but maybe he is turning his professional manners loose on me.'

On that same day, July 20, occurred the following events: General Tojo resigned as Premier of Japan, being succeeded by General Kuniaki Koiso; a bomb planted in a conference room almost brought the life of Adolf Hitler to a timely end; and F.D.R. was renominated for a fourth term, the Democrats naming Senator Harry S. Truman as his running mate on the following day.

The British Eighth and the American Fifth Armies had been advancing steadily up the Italian Peninsula since the breakthrough at Cassino and from the Anzio beachhead and the taking of Rome on June 4, just two days before OVERLORD D-Day, a juxtaposition of events which appeared to be due to superb co-ordination of Allied planning, but which was actually largely fortuitous. The Germans had been driven back to the line from Pisa through the outskirts of Florence to Ancona, and it seemed that the Allies would soon reach the Valley of the Po. During the six weeks since the first landings in Normandy, the build-up there had gone ahead at such a phenomenal rate that it approximated a total of one and a half million men, a million and a half tons of material, and upwards of half a million vehicles—and all this had been done without benefit of a large port, the harbour at Cherbourg not yet having been cleared. On July 26 came the break through St. Lo, followed by the immortal sweep of the Third Army across the base of the Brittany Peninsula and up the Loire and across the Seine.

Hopkins wrote to the President saying that his talks with Beaverbrook had 'indicated to me how difficult it is to hold a formal economic conference with Great Britain on any single subject at this particular time. Max, himself, was quite unhappy, not so much because he did not have his way about the agreement, but because he claims he senses a good deal of hostility there. One of our present difficulties is that everybody thinks the war is over. I hope if you decide to speak on the radio from Seattle that you will scotch

this. I think the American people have no idea of the severe tests we have ahead of us, particularly in the complete defeat of Japan.'

The 'hostility' sensed by Beaverbrook was attributable to the sentiment, widely expressed in Washington at that time, that while the American forces in France were dashing ahead at a devil-may-care rate of speed and with thrilling success, the British under Field-Marshal Montgomery on the Allied left flank seemed to be 'dragging their feet'. It was reported that Eisenhower was so annoyed and worried about this that he had even appealed to the Prime Minister to visit the 21st Army Group Headquarters near Caen in Normandy to try 'to persuade Monty to get on his bicycle and start moving'. Montgomery had always been a highly controversial figure, and also a conspicuously independent one. After the Teheran Conference, the U.S. Joint Chiefs of Staff were depressed to hear that Montgomery had been named to command the ground forces in OVERLORD; although they had utmost respect for his demonstrated qualities as a superb soldier, they considered him a commander of the 'down to the last shoelace' school, and they feared that he would delay and postpone to such an extent that the one opportunity favoured as to weather for this enormous and complex operation would be lost. However, in this respect, they were pleasantly disappointed —for once Montgomery became involved in OVERLORD he was its determined champion and helped greatly in 'beefing it up' and in resisting every attempt to sabotage it—and he accepted the date set by Eisenhower and stuck to it. It is not for me to comment on the reasons for or against his subsequent delays, but I may say that I look forward with great interest to reading what the two highest living authorities, Eisenhower and Churchill, have to say about this subject. Much has been written about it already by considerably lesser authorities and the disputes between Bradley and Patton and Montgomery have been underscored and, quite possibly, overemphasized. Although these are represented as Anglo-American disputes which are said to demonstrate the hopeless differences between the two nations, it should be pointed out that at the very same time there were immeasurably more bitter and more irreconcilable feuds between two American generals in China, Stilwell and Chennault, and two other American generals who were commanding adjoining forces in the Marianas campaign and both of whom happened to bear the name of Smith. Hopkins, of course, had been deeply involved in the Stilwell-Chennault fracas, but he was glad to have no part in the distasteful battle of the Smiths, in which the adherents of these two honourable generals (one Army and one Marine Corps) hurled charges of extreme ugliness.

The Hopkins papers are very incomplete at this point, for, although he was given access to all the cables that passed through the White House to and from the President on the Pacific trip, he no longer had any real responsi-

bility for them. He was now an adviser, but not a prime factor. On June 26 he cabled Roosevelt:

> Having given considerable thought to the forthcoming conference, I feel that while it would have been advantageous for you to have gone almost anywhere for a meeting with Churchill and Uncle Joe together, it seems to me that in view of Uncle Joe's message you have nothing to gain by going to meet Churchill alone. I believe that the world would construe a conference between you and Churchill somewhere in Europe or in England as a political meeting which had left Russia out in the cold. You may well want to take up various important matters with Churchill soon, in which case, it would be much better to have him come to you instead of you going to him, and the sooner the better. As to Uncle Joe, he obviously wants to postpone his next meeting with you until after Germany collapses.

On August 6 Churchill sent Hopkins a long cable in which he explained his grief, in the midst of victory, that there still should be differences of opinion between the Allies on strategy. This was barely a week before the embarkation of the troops for the landing in Southern France, but Churchill was still attempting to prevent this operation from taking place. He said that the Riviera coast was well fortified, that Toulon and Marseilles were veritable fortresses, and that the enemy in that area was much stronger than the Allies could hope to be. This time, however, he did not urge that the ten divisions for ANVIL should be sent into the Balkans; he recommended strongly that they be dispatched around to the west coast of France to join with the OVER-LORD forces in the region of St. Nazaire. He figured that in this way they would be brought into the main campaign far more quickly, for he estimated that even if the landing in Southern France were successful there would be a long, slow, bitter fight up the Valley of the Rhone, and that it would take ninety days for these forces to effect a junction with Eisenhower's armies in the north.

Hopkins replied to Churchill that, while he had not heard from the President concerning the proposed change in ANVIL plans, he felt sure that the answer would be in the negative. He expressed his own view that 'it would be a great mistake to change the strategy now; it would delay the sure liberation of France rather than aid it. Our tactical position today, it seems to me, is precisely as it was planned and as we anticipated it when ANVIL was laid on. Furthermore, it is my belief that northern advance from Southern France would go much more quickly than you expect. There is not enough enemy strength there to stop us. The French resistance fighters will rise up and abyssiniate large numbers of Germans and also, let us hope, Laval.' It was indeed much quicker than Churchill expected. The forces

Trip China

THE WHITE HOUSE
WASHINGTON

Cairo,
December 5, 1943.

MEMORANDUM FOR:

The Prime Minister.

~~The President~~ proposes to send over ~~his~~ *my* signature the
following message to the Generalissimo tonight. Do you concur
in this action?

"Conference with Stalin involves us in combined
grand operations on European continent in late spring
giving fair prospect of terminating war with Germany
by end of summer of 1944. These operations impose so
large a requirement of heavy landing craft as to make
it impracticable to devote a sufficient number to the
amphibious operation in Bay of Bengal simultaneously
with launching of Tarzan to insure success of operation.

"This being the case: Would you be prepared go ahead
with Tarzan as now planned, including commitment to
maintain naval control of Bay of Bengal coupled with
naval carrier and commando amphibious raiding operations
simultaneous with launching of Tarzan? Also there is
the prospect of B-29 bombing of railroad and port Bangkok.

"If not, would you prefer to have Tarzan delayed until
November to include heavy amphibious operation. Meanwhile
concentrating all air transport on carrying supplies over
the hump to air and ground forces in China.

"I am influenced in this matter by the tremenduous
advantage to be received by China and the Pacific through
the early termination of the war with Germany.

FDR

I agree.

WSC

5. XII

Memorandum to the Prime Minister prepared by President Roosevelt and Harry Hopkins
regarding revised decisions on China following the Teheran Conference (*see page* 792)

under the brilliant command of General Alexander M. Patch—one of the most widely unrecognized heroes of the war—took Toulon and Marseilles far ahead of schedule, then swept northward and established contact with General Patton's Third Army near Dijon exactly four weeks after they had first hit the Riviera beaches.

It appears that there was some talk about holding the forthcoming Roosevelt-Churchill conference in Scotland, and doubtless the President would have loved that, but he agreed with Hopkins's advice and sent a radiogram naming Bermuda as a possible meeting-place. Churchill said that he had received reports of the climate there in September and suggested a return to the Quebec citadel in September, which was agreed on. Various communications passed between Hopkins and Churchill preparatory to this conference. They related largely to what was called 'Phase Two'—the period following German surrender when Lend Lease would be continued to Britain, on a somewhat different basis, to aid in the promotion of British economic recovery. There was also the usual discussion concerning the size of the delegations that each nation would send to the conference, and some understandable confusion arose among the Canadian hosts, who had to make all the arrangements for accomodations, when Roosevelt notified Mackenzie King that the American delegation would number not more than fifteen or twenty people and that the British would have a like number, whereas the lists furnished by the Chiefs of Staff showed that there would be some three hundred Americans and two hundred and twenty-five British. (The larger figures were correct.) Through all these communications Hopkins spoke as one who would, of course, be present at the conference—as he had been present at every major conference thus far in the war, including some at which he was the only American delegate—but on August 28 he sent the following cable: 'Dear Winston—Although I am now feeling much better I still must take things easy and I therefore feel that I should not run the risk of a setback in health by attempting to fight the battle of Quebec on the Plains of Abraham, where better men than I have been killed.'

Churchill replied that he was greatly depressed to hear this news.

Hopkins's excuse was hardly convincing, for he had never allowed considerations of his health to stop him from going anywhere at any time when he thought he might accomplish something. If he had ever given any thought to the importance of his own survival, he would probably have spent the entire war in bed, subsisting on liver extract and amino-acid powder. The fact of the matter was—and this was later confirmed by Hopkins to Churchill directly—that a distinct change had come about in the character of his relationship with the President. I do not know just when this was made known to Hopkins, or how it was made known, but Roosevelt's need for Hopkins's counsel and even more for his companionship

v

was no longer so great that the President was willing to defy the criticism which invariably arose in the hostile Press whenever Hopkins took Hull's place at an important conference. There was no open breach between them, as there had been irreparably between Wilson and House. There was simply an admission that while the friendship continued and Hopkins would still be useful in various ways, particularly on the domestic political front, he was no longer physically fit to share the burden of responsibility for the big decisions of the war. The trouble was that he had been out of commission too long and Roosevelt had of necessity lost confidence in his ability to stand up under the strain of a job that could never be performed on a part-time or even on a forty-eight-hour-a-week basis.

The fact that this considerable but temporary change in the Roosevelt-Hopkins relationship did not become publicly known proves that very few people were aware of it. If even an intimation of it had been passed about official Washington, there would surely have been a leak here or there, and the hostile columnists would have been overjoyed to advertise it. They might eventually have mourned the loss of Hopkins as an always convenient whipping-boy, but they could not possibly have resisted the immediate, glorious opportunity to hold festival rites over his fall from favour.

On September 1 John G. Winant sent the following letter to Hopkins from London:

You do not know how greatly your decision not to go on to the conference has been regretted by our friend here. His message to the President will have told you of his illness on arrival which is only known to a dozen people here. Tonight his temperature is back to normal and he seems on the way to a quick recovery. But each journey has taken its toll and the interval between illnesses has been constantly shortened. There is no one that I have known here who cares so much about friendly relationships between Great Britain and the United States, and few people anywhere who have been more loyal in their friendship to the President.

The conference will undoubtedly consider the planning of the war against Japan. No thoughtful person can approach the problem without remembering that Great Britain has been fighting for five years and that they are at the bottom of the barrel as regards manpower. Men from 16 to 65 are conscripted, and women from 18 to 50. The country has been on short rations for this entire period. I live on them and know what this means. The British Army is older than our Army. The British Navy is older than our merchant seamen. Only the Royal Air Force has been able to continue to recruit the youth of the country. In the Battle of Britain it saved Britain. In the intervening years its continuous operation

has done much to save life in the other services, but it has taken a frightful toll of the youth of the country.

When the war with Germany is over the war with Japan will begin for Great Britain, in spite of the early defeats at Hong Kong and Singapore, and the fighting in Burma. I have talked about this with many soldiers and sailors and airmen. I knew General Wingate well, and had something to do with his assignment to the Far East. He told me once that out of every 100 men they sent him, sixty had to carry forty. That means that you have to have a selective army if you are to fight the Japanese success-fully in tropical areas. I have talked with Admiral Cunningham, and he told me that special arrangements should be made for Navy personnel who move to the Far East. Men should have better wages than at present and both soldiers and sailors' families should be given larger family allowances if the wanted men are to continue in active service. The Royal Air Force is better positioned to move eastward, but adjustments would also have to be made in that service.

The careful planning that General Marshall has made to prepare our armies for the transition period as we move from the western theatre eastward, by educational films and in other ways, has no counterpart in the present British thinking. The whole field of psychological preparation for what for them will be the second war has been largely neglected.

It has always interested me that the plans for demobilization following the defeat of Germany have been treated with the utmost secrecy for fear of creating misunderstandings in the United States in relation to the serious intentions of Great Britain to fight a war against Japan. And yet there are many people who are now mobilized in the war against Germany who would be utterly useless in fighting a war against Japan. I have never questioned this policy, since the President is a friend of Great Britain, and even a sensible demobilization in a presidential campaign might be used against him.

All that is one side of the picture. The really gallant people of Great Britain are as anxious to join us in the fight against Japan as we are our-selves to defeat Japan, and yet for all that there has seeped into this country through military channels a belief that the British Navy is not wanted in the Pacific. I know the practical side that many of our Navy men feel that the British Navy was built for short hauls with available ports that ringed the world, and that conversion would mean clogging our navy yards and strengthening the British Navy in the postwar years. There is some truth to it all, and yet if we allow the British to limit their active participation to recapture areas that are to their selfish interests alone and not participate in smashing the war machine of Japan, if British soldiers don't cross the Atlantic to our ports and entrain for our Pacific ports in

order to move against Japan, and if we shuck the British air force in order to prove our own dominance in the air, we will create in the United States a hatred for Great Britain that will make for schisms in the postwar years that will defeat everything that men have died for in this war. Repetition of the tragedy of 1918 will be unforgivable.

I have not found more than a dozen Englishmen interested in this problem, and no one from the United States in any way concerned about it.

What are you doing about it? I hope the President is interested.

Delivery of this letter must have been rapid, for Hopkins replied on September 4:

I hasten to reply to your letter relative to the implications of the British participation in the war against Japan. First of all I want to assure you that a number of us are greatly concerned about it, and I am very hopeful that the President will land up on the right side of this problem.

I am well aware of the attitude in certain circles here, but I am convinced that they are not, in any sense, representative of public opinion. The difficulty, in matters of this kind, is that public opinion gets no opportunity to express itself and, indeed, can know nothing about it until the damage is irrevocable.

There, obviously, must be some demobilization of the British Armed Forces after the collapse of Germany, just as I have no doubt there will be some of our own. Ours will be less dramatic and, therefore, will receive far less attention. It will, no doubt, take the form, first, for practical purposes, of stopping of enlistments and inductions in the Armed Forces, but I have no doubt that hundreds of thousands of men will be quietly separated from the Armed Forces for good and sufficient reasons. It is quite easy to accelerate the discharges either simply by raising the standards as to physical fitness or age. The same will not be true in England. There is no possibility of her transferring the whole of her Armed Force either to the occupation of Germany or for the war against Japan. Such a force as England now has under arms will not be required, but I hope the British will continue their policy of playing this down, for nothing could be worse than to have any public announcement of British plans for demobilization.

We simply must find a way to have Great Britain take her full and proper place in the war against Japan. This, with the best good will in the world, is full of many difficulties—transportation, supply, etc.

You know as well as I that we do not have a chance to get a genuinely good peace unless Russia, Great Britain, and the United States can see

eye to eye, and this means far more than the narrow confines of government in the Foreign Offices. It means, so far as Great Britain and the United States are concerned, that great masses of people must approve our policies. The more I see of the problems and conflicts engendered by the kind of thing that you have written me about, the more I realize how essential it is for us to have men managing our affairs who have a deep and profound conviction not only about world peace and the harnessing of Japan and Germany, but about the bold moves which must be made if a world economy is to be developed which can provide the environment without which our goals can never be attained.

In saying all this, I would say that I hope very much that you, personally, are going to remain close to this thing in some capacity or other for the next few years. Needless to say, I believe the President is essential to it and there is little hope of accomplishing much without his re-election. This, I should tell you, I believe will take place, but I am the world's worst political guesser.

As ever, with this note I send my warmest and most affectionate regards.

Among 'the bold moves which must be made', in Hopkins's opinion, were the continuance of some form of Lend-Lease by the United States even after the cessation of hostilities, and a relaxing by Britain of the system of imperial preference which was so dear to Beaverbrook's heart and which had been something of a bone of contention ever since the drafting of the Atlantic Charter. The day before Roosevelt left for Quebec, Hopkins wrote him a note saying, 'I think it is important, in Quebec that you tell the Prime Minister how strongly you feel about knocking down some of the trade barriers to get somewhere in terms of world trade. I have a feeling that the Prime Minister thinks that that is a pet hobby of Secretary Hull's and that you may not think it of great importance. I think it is essential to our future bargaining with Great Britain that you disabuse the Prime Minister's mind of this. I rather think that he thinks that the genius of this programme in America lies with Secretary Hull, while the truth of the matter is that it is a programme that, from the beginning, has been pushed by you.'

The physical setting of the second Quebec Conference was familiar, but the surrounding atmosphere was utterly new and strange. More than nine months had passed since the last Roosevelt-Churchill meetings at Teheran and Cairo—the longest lapse since the first encounter at Argentia and in that time the whole aspect of the war and of the world had changed completely. Now the Germans were fighting on both Eastern and Western Fronts *on their own soil*. Deep in the consciousness of all the Allied leaders, military and civilian, who were old enough to have served in the First

World War, was the hope if not the conviction that the Germans would quit, as they had done in 1918, once they were forced back behind their own frontiers. It was true that they now had the Siegfried Line in the West, but these fortifications were broken near Aachen by American troops on September 15 after an assault of only two days; and there was no Siegfried Line in the East. Furthermore, the intelligence reports and estimates of German strength in the West indicated that total collapse might be imminent. There was even consideration of the possibility that the Germans might deliberately permit the Anglo-American forces to break through and surge across Germany in the hope that in this way the Reich would be spared from the awful vengeance that it had earned at the hands of the Russians.

There was, in short, a general belief among the higher authorities assembled at Quebec that German surrender could come within a matter of weeks or even days. (Roosevelt was less optimistic than most about this.) The Allies were well prepared for war to the death in Europe, but they were very ill prepared for the cataclysm of sudden total victory. It will be remembered that when the question of the future treatment of Germany had come up for discussion among the Big Three at Teheran, agreement had not been reached or even nearly approached. It had been decided to refer this explosive subject to the Russian-British-American Advisory Committee in London, and there it had remained through many long months of inconclusive conversations and 'exchanges of view' on all manner of subjects, beginning with the primary one as to which nation would occupy which zone. It was felt that some specific directive must be issued to General Eisenhower, and various proposals were made—the most famous or most notorious of them being 'The Morgenthau Plan'. The circumstances of the origination of this plan, and of its initialled approval by Roosevelt and Churchill, and of the violent repercussions when news of it was leaked to the Press, have been described in detail from various points of view by Cordell Hull, Henry L. Stimson, and Henry Morgenthau, jun., himself—and Winston Churchill will undoubtedly be heard from on this subject in due course. The Hopkins papers, while full of relevant material, tell nothing which has not already been revealed. There is no doubt that Hopkins, as a member of the President's Special Cabinet Committee, joined with Hull and Stimson in opposition to the plan, and I can confirm from my personal knowledge Stimson's statement that Roosevelt subsequently made no secret of his regret that he had ever agreed to initial the proposal. Indeed, on October 20, six weeks after the Quebec Conference, Roosevelt gave demonstration of his reaction to the episode by dismissing *all* specific planning for the treatment of Germany; he said, in a memorandum to Hull: 'I dislike making detailed plans for a country which we do not yet occupy', adding that the details were 'dependent on what we and the Allies find when we get into Germany—and we are not

there yet'. (After the first break into Germany near Aachen the Allied advance had been halted.)

Roosevelt gave evidence of the extent to which Hopkins's position had changed at that time. In a memorandum, also addressed to Hull, on the progress of the Quebec Conference, he wrote: 'We have discussed the question of the scope and scale of mutual Lend-Lease aid between the United States and the British Empire after the defeat of Germany and during the war with Japan. We have agreed that a temporary joint committee shall be set up to consider this question. Among American membership would be Stettinius, Morgenthau and Crowley.'

In neglecting to appoint Hopkins even to membership in a committee for consideration of the subject which, for more than three and a half years, had been Hopkins's particular province, Roosevelt was undoubtedly influenced by political considerations. Unpleasant suggestions had reached the President's ears to the effect that Hopkins was too thoroughly under the domination of the British, or of the Russians or the Chinese, to be a reliable representative of American interests in these important negotiations relative to postwar material and economic aid. Of course, similarly dark intimations and even worse one about Hopkins had been reaching Roosevelt ever since the earliest days of the feud with Harold Ickes in 1933, and Roosevelt had paid no heed to them; but he paid heed to them now.

I had been overseas in the European and Mediterranean theatres since early in February, 1944, so I knew very little directly of what was going on in the White House during OVERLORD and the Democratic Convention and ANVIL and the second Quebec Conference. On September 12 Hopkins sent me a message saying that the President wanted me to come back. I was in liberated Paris at the time, but I flew immediately to London, boarded a C-54 (bucket seats) of the Army Transport Command, and flew the usual route via Prestwick, Iceland, and Newfoundland to Washington. On arrival, I learned from Hopkins, Rosenman, Pa Watson, and Steve Early that there was some cause for alarm about the forthcoming political campaign. There appeared to be a considerable amount of lethargy among the voters which could result in a small registration and an even smaller turnout on election day. This had happened in the Congressional election of 1942 and had resulted in substantial Republican gains. It was obvious that if large masses of people, particularly in organized labour, were so sure the President could not lose that they would feel no need to register and vote, the President could be defeated. Dewey was travelling up and down the country making carefully planned and generally unexceptionable speeches which were well calculated to mobilize the maximum Republican vote, but at the same time to create no particular excitement. He did not attack the conduct of the war. He did not attack Roosevelt's social objectives. He repeatedly described the present

administration as a group of 'tired old men', and this was not easily refuted, for those in highest authority were unquestionably tired and were getting no younger day by day. Dewey also referred repeatedly to the recurrent wrangles and squabbles and unseemly cat-and-dog fights that broke into the public prints with disagreeable frequency. Here again he was on sure ground: there had been another final bust-up in the War Production Board which resulted in the resignation of Charles E. Wilson due to a series of Press attacks which, he said, had been instigated by Donald Nelson (Roosevelt sent Nelson to China on an apparently meaningless mission and appointed Julius Krug as Acting Chairman of W.P.B.). Later, during October, the long-suppressed enmities between Stilwell and Chiang Kai-shek and Chennault burst out in violent explosion, and Roosevelt was compelled to issue orders for the recall of Stilwell, who had become, and deservedly, a popular hero to the American people.

However, it was not what Dewey was doing or saying that provided the present cause for worry to Hopkins and the others in the White House; it was the indifferent attitude of Roosevelt himself. He seemed to feel that he had done his duty by allowing his name to be placed before the American people, and if they did not want to re-elect him that would be perfectly all right with him. As Watson put it, 'He just doesn't seem to give a damn.' Therefore, the main problem was to persuade the President to descend from his position of dignified eminence as Commander-in-Chief and get into the dusty political arena where he was still undisputed champion.

There was a great deal of extremely ugly whispering about the state of Roosevelt's health. When he had made his acceptance speech just before his departure for the Pacific tour in July a photograph had been taken in which he appeared haggard, glassy eyed, and querulous—and this photograph had been given very wide advertisement in the Press and in the pamphlets with which the Republicans were flooding the country. On his return from the Pacific trip Roosevelt had made a nation-wide broadcast from the Bremerton Navy Yard at Seattle; when he delivered this speech he wore his leg braces for, I believe, the first time since he had returned from Cairo and Teheran and he was in such pain that he had to support himself by holding on to the lectern with all the tremendous strength of his arms and hands, which made it extremely difficult for him to turn the pages of his reading copy and made the speech sound faltering and uncertain to the listeners, who were accustomed to the calm, confident, and cheerful assurance that he always conveyed. It was a significant fact that after this speech the public opinion polls indicated a sudden and ominous slump for Roosevelt and a consequent rise in Dewey's stock.

When I first went in to see the President after my return from Europe— I had not seen him for eight months previously—I was shocked by his appear-

ance. I had heard that he had lost a lot of weight, but I was unprepared for the almost ravaged appearance of his face. He had his coat off and his shirt collar seemed several sizes too large for his emaciated neck. But I soon began to suspect that the fears expressed by Hopkins, Watson, and the others were groundless. He seemed to be more full of good humor and of fight than ever. He asked me if I had listened to any of Dewey's speeches and when I said I had not yet had the pleasure, he said: 'You ought to hear him. He plays the part of the heroic racket-buster in one of those gangster movies. He talks to the people as if they were the jury and I were the villain on trial for his life.' Then Roosevelt said: 'I'm going to give a speech to Dan Tobin's boys next Saturday night and I expect to have a lot of fun with that one.' He handed me a sheet of paper, saying it was a paragraph he had dictated to Grace Tully for use in this speech. It read as follows:

> The Republican leaders have not been content to make personal attacks upon me—or my wife—or my sons—they now include my little dog, Fala. Unlike the members of my family, Fala resents this. When he learned that the Republican fiction writers had concocted a story that I had left him behind on an Aleutian Island and had sent a destroyer back to find him—at a cost to the taxpayer of two or three or twenty million dollars—his Scotch soul was furious. He has not been the same dog since. I am accustomed to hearing malicious falsehoods about myself, but I think I have a right to object to libellous statements about my dog.

When I read that I knew precisely what kind of speech he proposed to give at the dinner of the Teamsters' Union. He was certainly not going to remain on the lofty Commander-in-Chief level.

Whenever the Hearst-Patterson-McCormick Press referred to my activity as a 'ghost writer' they always spoke of my background as a Broadway playwright, and the one play invariably identified with my name was *Idiot's Delight*. It was often suggested that my function in the White House was to stud the President's speeches with wisecracks. Therefore, I was generally given credit for the famous reference to Fala—and I should like to be able to claim this credit, but I had never even heard of the rumoured episode in the Aleutian Islands until I read the paragraph quoted above. This paragraph may be said to have set the very keynote for the 1944 campaign; in a way, it was comparable to the 'Martin, Barton, and Fish' line in 1940; as someone observed at the time, 'From now on the American people will consider this as a contest of Dewey versus Fala.'

In a much earlier chapter I have said that various experts—including Judge Rosenman, who had seventeen years' experience working on Roosevelt's speeches—considered that the address to the International Brotherhood of Teamsters was the greatest campaign speech of his career. It can well be

studied as a masterpiece of political strategy and tactics. He started off: 'Well, here we are together again—after four years—and what years they have been ! I am actually four years older—which seems to annoy some people. In fact, millions of us are more than eleven years older than when we started to clear up the mess that was dumped in our laps in 1933.' In these three sentences, which were greeted with loud laughter and cheers, Roosevelt dealt with the accusation that he was an old man (and a tired and feeble one); he brought the attention right back to the 'Hoover depression' and the basic achievements of the New Deal; and, most important, he conveyed assurance to those of the people who loved him that the same F.D.R. was still with them and not floating somewhere out of sight in the stratosphere occupied solely by such mysterious Olympian figures as Churchill and Stalin.

He said further: 'There are enlightened liberal elements in the Republican party, and they have fought hard and honourably to bring the party up to date and to get it in step with the forward march of American progress. But these liberal elements are not able to drive the Old Guard Republicans from their entrenched positions. . . . Millions of Republicans all over the nation are with us . . . in our unshakeable determination to build the solid structure of peace. And they, too, will resent this campaign talk by those who first woke up to the facts of international life a few short months ago —when they began to study the polls of public opinion.' This was Roosevelt's bid for the independent Republican vote, for the support of those liberals who resented the repudiation of Wendell Willkie—and Roosevelt never neglected in his subsequent speeches to appeal to these independents who formed, in his opinion, a group large enough to hold the balance of power as between the immovable factions who were committed to vote either Republican or Democratic regardless of what was said or done in this campaign.

Roosevelt said to me at this time that, if there were fifty million people who would actually vote on election day, you could figure roughly that some twenty million of them were determined to vote Democratic and another twenty million were determined to vote Republican (give or take a few million either way) regardless of the issues or the candidates; this left ten million more or less uncommitted independents who were subject to persuasion during the course of the campaign, and it was to these that the strongest appeals must be made. I believe that it was Roosevelt's hope that this independent twenty per cent of the population, which actually held the balance of power, would increase in strength and in political consciousness and he certainly directed his own influence toward that end.

A substantial number of Negroes was included in the independent minority as Roosevelt reckoned it. It was obvious that anyone with his exceptionally positive social views would be implacably opposed to racial discrimination

and in favour of the perpetuation of such reforms as the Fair Employment Practices Commission, so that he never had to make any fabricated, hypocritical appeals to win the votes of Negroes in those parts of the country where Negroes enjoyed the same constitutional privileges as other free American citizens. Similarly, the record of his Administration spoke for itself to organized labour and frustrated the ferocious attempts of John L. Lewis to divert any substantial part of the labour vote to the Republicans.

The Teamsters speech—or 'that speech about Fala', as it was sometimes known—accomplished its objectives; it put the needed excitement into the campaign, it stimulated the overconfident Democrats with a will to rush forth and register and vote, and above all it disrupted Dewey's carefully cultivated self-assurance and caused him to start swinging wildly against the most artful dodger of them all. More and more Dewey felt impelled to appeal to the prejudices of his immediate audiences in order to get applause. He had been giving a well-rehearsed performance as a liberal crusader, albeit a soundly practical one; but now his speeches began to sound more and more like those of his running mate, John W. Bricker, whom Alice Longworth was said to have summarized as 'an honest Harding'. Dewey seemed to forget that these audiences were recruited by the local Republican machine and were therefore composed largely of people who would still have been grimly and irrevocably determined to vote against Roosevelt even if the Republican candidate had been named Tommy Manville instead of Tom Dewey. Such audiences greeted in stony silence the advocacy of any policy, such as minimum wages or social security, which smacked of the despised New Deal. In bidding for their cheers, and for their hoots and catcalls whenever Hopkins or Ickes or Frances Perkins was mentioned, Dewey ignored the great mass of undecided voters who were listening over the radio, and who, while they might be tired of the Roosevelt Administration and ready to concede that it was 'time for a change', did not want that change to involve a recession to the kind of 'normalcy' which followed the First World War.

Roosevelt never made this same mistake of addressing himself primarily to the loyal Democrats who were stuffed into the convention hall or the baseball park where he happened to be giving his speech. He knew well enough that it was easy to get roars of approval, or laughs, or shouts of 'No! No!' or 'Give it to 'em, Frank!' whenever he wanted them. His main arguments were directed into the microphone to those whose minds were not running in narrow partisan channels.

He made no major campaign speech for four weeks, although he gave one radio talk before registration week from the White House. After it became apparent that registration was heavy all over the country, it seemed to me that he never had any doubt as to victory. He mapped out a schedule well in advance:

October 21—A speech on foreign policy at a dinner in the Waldorf-Astoria Hotel in New York.

October 27 (Navy Day)—Speech on the war at Shibe Park in Philadelphia.

October 28—Speech on postwar domestic problems at Soldier Field, Chicago.

November 4—General roundup speech at Fenway Park, Boston.

November 7—The usual short election-eve Fireside Chat from Hyde Park.

This was an easy schedule and it was carried out with none of the frantic strain or epidemic of jitters that marked the final stage of the campaign against Willkie in 1940. There was no third-term issue now, no accusations of warmongering—indeed, about all that Dewey dared to say about the war was that it was rapidly drawing to a close. He made one costly blunder with a chance remark charging that insufficient supplies were being sent to General MacArthur's theatre; the public learned that he did not know what he was talking about when, on October 20, forces under MacArthur landed in the Philippines and, in the subsequent battle for Leyte Gulf, the Japanese Navy was all but obliterated.

There was, however, one serious question in this campaign: Roosevelt's health. There were innumerable baseless and incredibly malicious rumours, but there was some visible support for them—for he was now truly crippled. The frail muscles in his legs and hips had become flabby through long disuse in the months between Teheran and the Bremerton speech, during which time he had made no public appearances at which he would have to stand up—and he never wore the painful braces except on such necessary public occasions. It was now felt that he would probably never again be able to stand up and walk. Therefore, he had to make all his speeches sitting down, at a dinner table or from his automobile in the midst of some open space.

Actually, during the weeks of this campaign, he did manage to regain the use of his legs sufficiently to be able to stand up and speak from the back platform of his train for as long as half an hour. I do not know what sort of exercises he took to accomplish this, but I believe that it was largely due to the determination of Mrs. Roosevelt, who supported him in refusal to accept physical defeat, as she had done when he was first stricken in 1921.

As the campaign went along Roosevelt improved visibly in strength and resilience. He had been too long away from the people, and he knew it, and he was unmistakably glad to come home to them. On the evening of October 20 I rode with him to the train and then to New York for his foreign policy speech. Hopkins did not go on any of the campaign trips this year, because his wife was ill. When we arrived at the Bush Terminal in Brooklyn

on Saturday morning the weather was terrible, with bitter cold wind and driving, stabbing rain. Roosevelt had a fifty-mile drive ahead of him through four boroughs in an open car—the purpose, of course, being to enable millions of people to see with their own eyes that he was alive and laughing. It had not been anticipated that his physical condition would be subjected to so rigorous a test as this day imposed. I had planned to go along on this tour in one of the following cars, but when I got off the train and took a look at the weather I decided that I might as well listen to the President's progress over the radio. Roosevelt made the whole trip and ended up in a state of high exhilaration, grateful to the disagreeable elements for giving him such a fine opportunity to prove that he could take it.

An important factor in the preparation of the foreign policy speech was one Republican Senator, Joseph H. Ball, who had been appointed originally by his friend Governor Harold E. Stassen (now serving in the Navy in the Pacific) and had been a leader in the fight against isolationism on Capitol Hill. He was an important spokesman for the independent wing of the Republican party which was generally identified as 'the Willkie vote' and to which Roosevelt made repeated direct appeals. Ball made it known both publicly and in a private talk with Hopkins that he would give his support to whichever candidate took the firmest, most unequivocal position on the cardinal issues relating to the postwar world organization; the most important and controversial of these was the question as to whether the United Nations would have the authority to commit the United States to the use of armed force in emergencies without waiting for an act of Congress. Dewey ducked this question, evidently discounting Ball's political influence and feeling that he should run no risk of losing isolationist votes. But Roosevelt knew that the isolationists were unalterably opposed to him anyway, and that while Ball was personally no major figure on the political scene he happened to be expressing the sentiments of large numbers of open-minded voters who wanted a world organization equipped with teeth and guts as well as with moral principles. In his speech to the Foreign Policy Association, Roosevelt said:

The power which this nation has attained—the moral, the political, the economic, and the military power—has brought to us the responsibility, and with it the opportunity, for leadership in the community of nations. In our own best interest, and in the name of peace and humanity, this nation cannot, must not, and will not shirk that responsibility. . . .

Peace, like war, can succeed only where there is a will to enforce it, and where there is available power to enforce it.

The Council of the United Nations must have the power to act quickly and decisively to keep the peace by force, if necessary. A policeman

would not be a very effective policeman if, when he saw a felon break into a house, he had to go to the Town Hall and call a town meeting to issue a warrant before the felon could be arrested.

It is clear that, if the world organization is to have any reality at all, our representatives must be endowed in advance by the people themselves, by constitutional means through their representatives in the Congress, with authority to act.

If we do not catch the international felon when we have our hands on him, if we let him get away with his loot because the Town Council has not passed an ordinance authorizing his arrest, then we are not doing our share to prevent another World War. The people of the Nation want their Government to act, and not merely to talk, whenever and wherever there is a threat to world peace.

The references to the Town Council and the local constabulary provided another evidence—like the 'garden hose' analogy—of Roosevelt's ability to reduce an enormous and even revolutionary issue to the familiar scope of a small town. The position that he thus took seemed a highly courageous one; actually it was based on cold hard common sense and superior knowledge of the true temper of the American people. Senator Ball thereupon announced his support of Roosevelt. The isolationists howled, but the independent voters were effectively impressed.

In this foreign policy speech, Roosevelt went out of his way to speak of the action of the United States Government in granting independence to the Philippines, saying that this was another step in making good the same philosophy which animated the policy of the Good Neighbour. He then repeated a statement he had made in a speech to the Filipinos in the fall of 1942 which had attracted little or no attention at the time, but to which the President attached enormous importance: 'I like to think that the history of the Philippine Islands in the last forty-four years provides in a very real sense *a pattern for the future of other small nations and peoples of the world. It is a pattern of what men of good will look forward to in the future.*' Those italics are mine, but the emphasis was certainly Roosevelt's. In this repeated statement he was underscoring the differences between himself and his respected friend Winston Churchill on the extension of the principles of the Atlantic Charter to such areas as Burma, Malaya, the Netherlands East Indies, and Indo-China.

Roosevelt was annoyed by an editorial that appeared in *Life* magazine during this campaign. In an attempt to cleanse Dewey and the Republicans of the taint of isolationism of which Roosevelt constantly reminded the people, *Life* said that isolationism was a completely dead issue—as dead as 'locofocoism'. Roosevelt said: 'Anybody who thinks that isolationism is

dead in this country is crazy. As soon as this war is over, it may well be stronger than ever. And as for locofocoism—it isn't dead either. Harry Luce ought to spend more time reading the *Congressional Record*.' (In fact, it might be said that Roosevelt was the greatest locofoco since Andrew Jackson.)

During the preparation of the next speech to be given at Philadelphia, I suggested to Roosevelt that he might well use a quotation from Winston Churchill, who had said, in a recent House of Commons speech, that 'the United States was now at the highest pinnacle of her power and fame'. (Churchill, who well knew that his speeches were widely quoted if not always heard in the United States, often made remarks which could be construed as not unhelpful to Roosevelt's campaign for re-election.) When I made that suggestion to the President he said, very seriously: 'What Winston says may be true at the moment, but I'd hate to say it. Because we may be heading before very long for the pinnacle of our weakness.' I reproduce those words because they were burned into my memory, and my curiosity. There was no time at the moment to ask him to enlarge on that strange statement, and I never found an opportunity again to ask him just what he meant. I've always assumed that he was looking forward to the approaching moment when the reaction might set in, and isolationism again be rampant, and the American people might again tell the rest of the world to stew in its own juice.

During the latter part of October, Hopkins heard from General Marshall the amazing story of how someone, apparently in the armed services, had imparted to Dewey the fact that the United States had broken the Japanese codes before Pearl Harbour, and of Marshall's urgent message to Dewey that the revelation of this fact would be calamitous. Hopkins wrote of this:

Later that day I repeated this conversation to the President. The President was surprised at the action Marshall had taken, but expressed no criticism of that action. He merely stated that he felt confident that Governor Dewey would not, for political purposes, give secret and vital information to the enemy. His only other further comments were: 'My opponent must be pretty desperate if he is even thinking of using material like this which would be bound to react against him.' The President wondered what officer or Government official had been so faithless to his country as to give Governor Dewey the information. To the best of my knowledge the Government never discovered who gave Governor Dewey this military information.

The Navy Day speech at Philadelphia was an exuberant recitation of the record of the 'tired, quarrelsome, old men' of the Roosevelt Administration in the war. It was delivered in the wake of glorious news from MacArthur, Nimitz, and Admirals William F. Halsey and Thomas C. Kinkaid, Com-

manders of the Third and Seventh Fleets in the Pacific, and Roosevelt did not neglect to make capital of certain statements by certain Republican orators (no names mentioned, of course) to the effect that MacArthur's forces had been deliberately starved by presumably envious authorities in Washington. From Philadelphia we travelled to Chicago. In this speech Roosevelt wanted to mention the number of jobs that the United States would be able to provide for its citizens in the postwar economy. Rosenman had a considerable number of estimates as to this figure from various authoritative sources. As I remember, the highest of these estimates was slightly over fifty-seven million. When we asked Roosevelt which of these figures he wanted to use, he said: 'Oh—let's make a it good round number—sixty million.' Even Henry Wallace later conceded that he thought the President had gone much too far in setting a goal so impossible of attainment, and it is sad to think that Roosevelt did not live to see his 'good round number' exceeded in 1947.

At Soldier Field in Chicago the President's open car, with the tray of microphones laid across it, was placed in the middle of the football field, with something over a hundred thousand people in the enormous stadium surrounding it. The distances were so great that he would be in the middle of a sentence before the reverberations of the cheers or laughs provoked by the preceding sentence had come back to him. Standing by his car I had the impression that some remote sections of the gigantic crowd present could not have a very precise idea of just what it was that he was saying; however, that did not bother him as long as his words were getting through clearly over the radio. On the train going back to Washington that night, Roosevelt was strongly urged by advisers, principally Frank Walker, to schedule another speech, preferably in Cleveland, Ohio, during the forthcoming, final week of the campaign. Roosevelt refused to do so. He was in high good humour and it was plainly evident that he had no worries whatsoever as to the outcome of the election. But he was later inclined to regret this decision, for he figured that had he gone to Cleveland he might well have carried Ohio and thereby brought about the defeat of Senator Robert A. Taft, who, as it turned out, was re-elected by a very narrow margin.

During the next week Rosenman and I had some talks with various Democratic political leaders, who seemed to be greatly alarmed that Dewey was making dangerous progress in his campaign to hang the Communist label on the Roosevelt Administration. It was said that the hatred and fear of Communism were much greater than any of the emotions inspired by Nazism or Fascism. There were charges that Roosevelt had secretly begun to sell out to Uncle Joe Stalin at Teheran and that after the war he would complete the process of delivering the American free enterprise system over to Communist control. We asked if anybody were taking any part of this

November 25, 1944

Dear Bob:

I am sure you knew, when you came
back from London last summer to help in the
campaign, how great a satisfaction it was to
me. It has been more than that in the lively
months since.. It was a hard campaign but it
was a happy, fighting one, too, in which, I
know, no man ever had abler assistance. This
is just a note to say my thanks for the genius
you shared and the loyalty you gave me.

Affectionately yours,

F. D. R.

Honorable Robert Emmet Sherwood,
25 Sutton Place,
New York, N. Y.

Note from President Roosevelt to Robert E. Sherwood, written
after the Fourth Term Campaign in November, 1944.

seriously—aside from the Polish-Americans who were naturally concerned for the future independence of their homeland—and we were told that the 'Red Scare' was having an ominously positive effect in the Middle West, especially in the rural districts. Then we asked what were the farmers' principal causes for complaint at present. The reply was: 'Today the farmer for the first time in his life goes down to Main Street on Saturday night with his pockets full of money and he cannot find anything to spend it on.' We did not know how to cope with that problem, but when we reported these conversations to the President he did not seem greatly disturbed. He said in his Boston speech: 'When any political candidate stands up and says, solemnly that there is danger that the Government of the United States—your Government—could be sold out to the Communists—then I say that candidate reveals shocking lack of trust in America. He reveals a shocking lack of faith in Democracy—in the spiritual strength of our people.'

Roosevelt himself was at his most unsolemn in this speech. He poured his own brand of ridicule on his opponent. He said: 'Everybody knows that I was reluctant to run for the Presidency again this year. But since the campaign has developed I tell you frankly that I have become most anxious to win.' Merriman Smith, the United Press White House correspondent, has written that Roosevelt's attitude toward Dewey was one of 'unvarnished contempt'—and I can only add that Smith is a notoriously accurate reporter.

Hopkins later wrote: 'The President told me he meant it when he said that this was the meanest campaign of his life. He said he thought they hit him below the belt several times and that it was done quite deliberately and very viciously. He was particularly resentful about the whispering campaign which he believes was a highly organized affair.'

Travelling to Boston on this occasion evoked some painful memories for me of the trip four years previously when Roosevelt was being urged and even tearfully begged to give assurance to the mothers of America that their boys would never be sent into any foreign war. I asked the President if he would please, as a special favour, make reference to that earlier Boston campaign speech, and he did so, in these words: 'We got into this war because we were attacked by the Japanese—and because they and their Axis partners, Hitler's Germany and Mussolini's Italy, declared war on us. I am sure that any real American would have chosen, as this Government did, to fight when our own soil was made the object of a sneak attack. As for myself, under the same circumstances, I would choose to do the same thing—*again and again and again.*'

The crowd instantly recognized this allusion, for that phrase had been dinned in their ears for four years, and they roared their approval.

During the final week before election five of us in the White House put

W

$5.00 each in a pool on the President's electoral vote. The guesses were as follows: Watson—400; Rosenman—431; Hopkins—440; Early—449; Sherwood—484. (I had clear possession of the high field.) The correct figure was 432, so Rosenman, who was holding the stakes, kept them.

Hopkins cabled bulletins to Churchill and Beaverbrook before and during election day. Although describing himself as 'the world's worst political forecaster', he did not hesitate to predict that 'this will not be merely an election, it will be a census' for Roosevelt. He informed Beaverbrook that if this prediction proved wrong, 'I will underwrite the British National Debt and subscribe to the *Chicago Tribune*'.

On the afternoon of November 7 he cabled Churchill, saying: 'I have no reason for changing my opinion that it will be a Roosevelt landslide. The voting is very heavy in industrial centres. We are not likely to know definitely before 10.00 our time, which will make it pretty late even for you.' Apparently Churchill remained up most of the night to get the news. Hopkins's final bulletin consisted solely of the words: 'It's in the bag.'

There were evidences of tension at Hyde Park on election night that I could discern, for the first reports of the turnout of voters in New York City had given clear enough indication of the outcome. All that the President appeared to worry about was the size of his majority, which, naturally, he hoped would be overwhelming. It was not quite that; it was not a 'landslide' when judged by previous Roosevelt standards. But it was big enough and it produced a considerable increase in Democratic strength in Congress—which, however, proved of little value to Roosevelt in the few months that remained to him, for the conservative coalition still held the balance of power on Capitol Hill.

During this election campaign, on October 8, there had come the sudden shocking news of the death of Wendell Willkie. He had served a great purpose in times of direst peril, but that purpose was lamentably far from being completed. It was my belief in 1943 and early in 1944 that if Willkie were to win the Republican nomination Roosevelt would not run for a fourth term. I had no tangible basis for this belief, and it was a doubly hypothetical surmise, because it was evident for a long time to Roosevelt that Willkie had no chance whatever of being nominated. Greatly as the Old Guard lords of the Republican machine hated Roosevelt, they had come to hate Willkie even more, and, be it said to his eternal credit, Wilkie went out of his way to court their hatred by scorning their support.

After returning to Washington, the President, Mrs. Roosevelt, and Hopkins had a talk about the future, of which Hopkins wrote:

Mrs. Roosevelt urged the President very strongly to keep in the forefront of his mind the domestic situation, because she felt there was a real

danger of his losing American public opinion in his foreign policy if he failed to follow through on the domestic implications of his campaign promises. She particularly hoped the President would not go to Great Britain and France and receive great demonstrations abroad for the present, believing that that would not set too well with the American people.

She impressed on both of us that we must not be satisfied with merely making campaign pledges, the President being under moral obligation to see his domestic reforms through, particularly the organizing of our economic life in such a way as to give everybody a job. She emphasized that this was an overwhelming task, and she hoped neither the President nor I thought it was settled in any way by making speeches.

It has often been said that Mrs. Roosevelt acted as the President's 'eyes and ears', and so she did—but there were many others, particularly Hopkins, who helped in performing that function. There was no question of doubt, however, concerning the uniqueness of Mrs. Roosevelt's position as the keeper of and constant spokesman for her husband's conscience, and she continued to perform these duties after his death.

BEGINNINGS OF DISSENSION

IT is not improbable that one of the factors in restoring Hopkins to his former position with Roosevelt was the Morgenthau Plan episode. Roosevelt admitted that he had yielded to the importunities of an old and loyal friend when he affixed his initials to this document, and this was precisely the kind of thing against which Hopkins—who was no respecter of old friendships—was practised in protecting him. Hopkins had agreed with Stimson and Hull on the general outline for treatment of Germany, and would have been quick to detect the dangerous implications in the Morgenthau Plan, and Roosevelt realized this and was sorry that he had not taken Hopkins with him to Quebec. Of far greater importance, however, was an incident early in October in connection with a cable to Stalin which had consequences of very considerable importance. The background of this incident was as follows:

By October 1 both Finland and Bulgaria had quit the Axis and the Red Army had occupied both countries. The Russians had advanced over most of Estonia, Latvia, and Lithuania, and across Poland as far as the Vistula; they had advanced into Hungary and Yugoslavia, and had reached the frontiers of Greece and Turkey. British forces had landed in Greece. The question of control over South-eastern Europe now presented a problem of pressing urgency and Churchill was naturally so concerned about it that he felt that another Big Three conference must be held without a moment's delay. Obviously, it was difficult for Roosevelt to embark on a long journey in the midst of a political campaign, but Churchill took the unassailable position that the advancing Russians were not going to wait until the returns were in from Michigan, South Dakota, and Oregon, and he suggested that he and Eden should proceed to Moscow immediately and try to arrive at an understanding with Stalin and Molotov in respect to the delimitation of 'spheres of influence' in the Balkan area. This proposal worried Hopkins a great deal, for he believed that, if such a conference were to be held with no American representative present, it would be generally assumed that Churchill had been authorized to speak for Roosevelt—and, in fact, that this was what Churchill would undoubtedly undertake to do. Were Harriman, the Ambassador, to attend any of the meetings in the negative capacity of 'observer', the impression of American commitment to support any decisions that might be reached would be all the stronger. On the other hand, as Bohlen pointed out to Hopkins, it might well be assumed in European countries that American abstention from these conferences was a confession that the United States had 'washed its hands of European political problems'.

While Hopkins well knew that there was nothing Roosevelt could do to prevent Churchill and Stalin from discussing any subject that they pleased, whether it related to the Balkans, or all of Europe or the Far East, he believed it to be of utmost importance that Roosevelt should make it entirely clear that no decision they might reach would be considered as valid by the United States until these matters could be discussed and settled by the three nations in conference together. Of course, Hopkins was by no means sure that the meetings would result in any agreements, but just as much damage would be done if they ended up in a serious row between the British and the Russians.

On October 3 Hopkins learned that Roosevelt was dispatching a cable to Churchill in which he did in effect wash his hands of the whole matter, with the implication that he was content to let Churchill speak for the United States as well as for Great Britain. Hopkins immediately investigated and learned that this cable was already going out over the wires of the Map Room. He thereupon took one of the quick and arbitrary actions, far beyond the scope of his own authority, which had gained for him the admiration and the affection of Roosevelt ever since the beginnings of the New Deal: he gave orders to the officers on duty in the Map Room that transmission of the President's message to Stalin was to be stopped. The officers had no way of knowing that there had been any change in Hopkins's position in the White House and they complied with his order. Hopkins then went straight to Roosevelt's bedroom—the President was shaving at the time— and told him what he had done and the reasons why he had done it. Roosevelt had been thinking about other matters when that cable was drafted, and had been persuaded that the safest course for him to take was to avoid all semblance of American participation or even interest in the Moscow meetings by sending vague messages to Churchill and to Stalin merely wishing them good luck. He now listened very attentively to Hopkins and came to the conclusion that a serious mistake had almost been made. When he had finished his shaving he and Hopkins drafted a cable to Harriman, instructing him to deliver the following message to Marshal Stalin immediately:

It had been my hope that no important meeting would be held until you and Mr. Churchill and I could get together, but I understand the Prime Minister's wish to confer with you now. There is in this global war literally no question, either military or political, in which the United States is not interested. You will naturally understand this. It is my firm conviction that the solution to still unsolved questions can be found only by the three of us together. Therefore, while I appreciate the necessity for the present meeting, I choose to consider your forthcoming talks with Mr. Churchill merely as preliminary to a conference of the three of us

which can take place, so far as I am concerned, any time after our national election.

Therefore, I am suggesting that Mr. Harriman be present at your forthcoming meetings with Mr. Churchill as an observer for me, if you and Mr. Churchill approve. Of course, Mr. Harriman could not commit this Government relative to any important matters which, very naturally, may be discussed by you and the Prime Minister.

I wish to reiterate to you my complete acceptance of the assurances that we have received from you relative to the war against Japan. You will have received by now from General Deane the statement of the position taken by our Combined Chiefs of Staff on this. The war against Germany is being successfully waged by our three great countries and surely we shall have no less success joined together in crushing a nation which, I feel sure in my heart, is as great an enemy of the Soviet Union as she is of the United States.

Roosevelt then informed Harriman that he would very much have preferred to have the next conference between the Big Three. He instructed Harriman to bear in mind the important fact that there could be 'no subjects that I can anticipate that might be discussed between Stalin and the Prime Minister in which I will not be greatly concerned. It is important that I retain complete freedom of action after this conference is over'. (The italics are mine.) Roosevelt further instructed Harriman to keep Hull and himself informed throughout the conversations and to come home immediately after them to make a full report.

Stalin expressed his appreciation of the President's clarifying message, saying that he had previously been under the impression that Churchill would be authorized to speak for Roosevelt as well as for himself.

Here, then, was another occasion when Roosevelt had reason to be grateful for Hopkins's willingness to act first and ask for authority later.

Two days before this cable was sent Cordell Hull left his office in the State Department for the last time. He had told Roosevelt that he must resign. Roosevelt at first refused to accept it, but Hull was a very sick man and his life depended on the relinquishing of all the responsibilities of his office. At length Roosevelt persuaded him to postpone announcement of his resignation until after election day, for obvious reasons, and Hull did so. The question as to who should succeed him was a matter for long and prayerful consideration and discussion in the White House. James F. Byrnes was an obvious choice for the post, especially because of his high standing with the Senate which, some time within the fourth term, would be called upon to vote on United States participation in the United Nations. Hopkins opposed Byrnes on the ground that Roosevelt was going to be his own Secre-

tary of State, particularly in direct dealings with Churchill and Stalin, and Byrnes (who had once told Hopkins to 'keep the hell out of my business') was not one to conform placidly to the role of a mere mouthpiece. The name of Sumner Welles was also mentioned, and I believe that Roosevelt would have preferred him to all others; but his appointment would have been a direct affront to Hull and provocative of intense resentment on Capitol Hill. When it was finally decided that Stettinius should be promoted from Under-Secretary to the senior Cabinet post there was no doubt in anyone's mind that Hopkins was largely responsible. As the well-informed Marquis Childs wrote, 'Those of his enemies who took satisfaction in counting Hopkins out at the time of his illness after the Teheran Conference will have to guess again. His influence in the Administration is perhaps greater than it ever was.' Childs, by the way, was one of the few Washington columnists who was on friendly terms with Hopkins and who occasionally received from him some of the 'background information' that was constantly being handed out in Washington, usually through the back door and seldom from so authoritative a source. Another of Hopkins's friends in the later years was Walter Lippmann, and so were two of the most powerful of the broadcasters, Raymond Gram Swing and Walter Winchell. (Hopkins never underrated the importance of the radio audience, and neither most certainly did Roosevelt.)

Shortly after the Stettinius appointment, Hopkins noted:

Stimson asked me to have lunch with him today.

At the end of our lunch it was clear that the reason he had asked me to see him was that he wanted to know whether the President wished him to resign. He stated that he realized that he was getting along in years and that he is not as strong as he used to be and that he had been seriously considering the wisdom of resigning.

I told him that I doubted very much that the President wanted him to resign, in fact, was quite sure that he did not. I told him that, from my point of view, he was the most respected member of the Cabinet; that he had the confidence of the American people, the rank and file of the army and of General Marshall. I told him, further, that I was sure he had the President's complete confidence.

Hopkins did not overstate the case. Stimson was seventy-seven years old and his working hours were limited, and no doubt his great pride had been injured by the numerous sneering referneces to 'tired old men', but he was then as he had been throughout the past four critical years as firm and reliable a tower of strength as any President had ever been privileged to lean on. He continued to serve with unfaltering ability and distinction until after the war had ended.

Beaverbrook reported from time to time in letters to Hopkins on the situation in England. Following are some of his observations:

> Here in Britain we are passing through a strange phase in public life. For the first time, the English are not absolutely sure of themselves. They are anxious about their future. And this in some measure is due to the extent to which they have had to rely on outside assistance in the war. Without your friendship we would never have got it. We know that you came with a discerning eye. You saw the prospect of defeat and the possibility of resistance and you decided to back the resistance. But having come so far with the assistance for which you were primarily responsible, the British must very soon go forward under their own power. And it is a prospect which causes them some misgivings at present. . . .
>
> Here we are somewhat in the doldrums. The rockets come to us in London at the rate of six a day. Last Saturday morning we suffered a disaster when one fell in a suburban district, causing the heaviest death toll of any single bomb incident of the war. I do not know how much injury we shall have to sustain before the winter is over. The slogan of 'London can take it' will prevail. But there may be quite a lot to take.
>
> The Prime Minister is fully alive to the situation. He knows very well how much the public can stand before they begin to grumble and knows, too, how to suppress the grumbles when they come. His method is to set up in the people's minds a feeling of kinship with the men at the battlefront. So far he has never spoken too soon.
>
> Anyway, the rocket is to be preferred to the flying-bomb with its two warnings—first the siren and then the noise of the approaching engine. That experience was strange indeed. For while there was noise there was safety. Only when the engine cut off and silence fell did you stand in need of prayer.
>
> The political parties are squaring up for the election. In my view it should not be delayed too long. For the Government is now unable to deal with post-war issues, the limit of the capacity to compromise has been reached.

It would seem that with victory in sight—and despite the frequent reminder given by the V-2 rockets that the war was still on—the political coalition which had held together under Churchill since the beginning of Britain's darkest and finest hour was beginning to show signs of cracking. But so was the great world coalition which had been envisaged at the Atlantic Conference by Roosevelt and Churchill and realized by them in the White House within three weeks after Pearl Harbour; and the first evidences of rupture at this time were not between the Soviet Union and the Western Allies, but between Great Britain and the United States, and the main points

at issue, ironically enough, were the very principles of the Atlantic Charter itself.

One of the first public actions taken by Stettinius incurred the furious and vehemently expressed wrath of Winston Churchill. During November there were political crises in three European countries, Belgium, Italy and Greece, in all of which the Allied military forces were predominantly British. It seemed that Britain was backing the more conservative elements in these countries as opposed to the liberals or leftists who had been the most aggressive in resistance to the Germans and Fascists. The situation in Belgium was by no means clear, and perhaps it was actually no more so in Italy and Greece, but in the two latter countries it appeared that Churchill's well-known predilection for constitutional monarchy was dictating policies which were against the people's will. In Italy, King Victor Emmanuel had been dethroned in January 1944 by unanimous vote of the various party leaders, and a regency had been formed under Crown Prince Umberto. In Greece, from which the Germans had been ejected only within the past few weeks, there had been no time to set up any real Government, but some American observers believed that popular enthusiasm for the return of King George was close to non-existent. The situation in all three countries was complicated by the fact that battlefronts existed in each (in the case of Belgium, they were just beyond her frontiers), so that all were military zones of communications where law and order must be enforced by means of whatever instruments were most conveniently at hand for the purpose; but American liberal opinion had already heard too much of this explanation in connection with the various 'temporary expediency' arrangements or deals and was impatient for some proof of the establishment of democracy and application of the Four Freedoms in all liberated areas. This liberal opinion—which was feeling particularly potent after the recent election—was becoming increasingly suspicious of Churchill's apparent determination to restore the unsavoury *status quo ante* in Europe. Moreover, they were suspicious of State Department policy in these matters. When Stettinius announced his first appointments on the Assistant Secretary level anguished cries were raised that the State Department had been shaken up only to emerge more reactionary than ever. Liberals, both Democratic and Republican, who had voted and actively campaigned for Roosevelt, forgathered in consternation to ask each other: 'Who won the election, anyway?' Hopkins was given a large share of responsibility for the new appointments and suddenly found himself in the unaccustomed position of being criticized as a convert to Toryism. (I told him that he could number me among the critics.) Hopkins well knew that these protests could not be dismissed as the mere rantings of Roosevelt-haters; he knew that even though the President had just been re-elected he was going to need all the support he could get in the forthcoming battle for the peace.

At this same time, in late November, the crisis became acute in Italy. The coalition Cabinet headed by Premier Ivanoe Bonomi resigned. In the attempt to form a new Cabinet, Count Carlo Sforza was a leading spokesman of the parties to the left. Sforza was well known and greatly respected in the United States, where he had spent many years of exile, as an unflagging enemy of Fascism. He had strongly opposed the retention of the House of Savoy in the new Italy and had criticized State Department policy on numerous occasions. (The State Department's memorandum on the proposed plan for Allied Military Government in Italy, mentioned in Chapter XXIX, had provided that 'Italian political leaders in exile should have no part in the operations or administration. Their long resistance abroad, their lack of intimate contact with the people . . . largely invalidate their claim to act as trustees or spokesmen for the Italian nation'. This dictum, which would seem to have applied primarily to Sforza, was amended by Roosevelt and Hopkins to provide that such exiled leaders should have no part in the operation 'in its initial stages', with the rest of the remarks struck out.)

The British Embassy in Rome intervened in the Cabinet crisis to the extent of letting it be known that His Majesty's Government would not give its approval to any Italian Cabinet in which Sforza held a prominent post. With this, the American liberal hue and cry became really intense and it was assumed that Churchill and the British Government were making these arbitrary, anti-democratic moves with the blessing of the United States Government. Stettinius was now beginning to realize how Hull had felt under comparable fire. Roosevelt was away in Warm Springs for a rest and was not, I believe, paying a great deal of attention to the situation. On December 5 Stettinius issued a public statement saying:

> The position of this Government has consistently been that the composition of the Italian Government is purely an Italian affair except in the case of appointments where important military factors are concerned. This Government has not in any way intimated to the Italian Government that there would be any opposition on its part to Count Sforza. Since Italy is an area of combined responsibility, we have reaffirmed to both the British and Italian Governments that we expected the Italians to work out their problems of government along democratic lines without influence from outside.

He added: 'This policy would apply in an even more pronounced degree with regard to Governments of the United Nations in their liberated territories.' This last was sharply aggravating to Churchill, for it applied obviously to Belgium, and even more so to Greece, which was by now becoming the hottest spot of all. The embattled Prime Minister thereupon dispatched a cable to Roosevelt which may well have been the most violent outburst

of rage in all of their historic correspondence. Churchill said he would un-doubtedly have to make a statement to the House of Commons in view of the Stettinius statement and he would try to keep his remarks free from the 'acerbity' that the new Secretary of State had displayed in his public lan-guage. It is quite possible that Churchill would have been compelled to dis-cuss these subjects before the House even if Stettinius had said nothing, for a debate was precipitated by an amendment regretting British intervention in Greece and in other parts of liberated Europe. During this debate Churchill made several references directly and indirectly to American opinion. He said: 'Poor old England! (Perhaps I ought to say, "Poor old Britain!") We have to assume the burden of the most thankless tasks, and in undertaking them to be scoffed at, criticized and opposed from every quarter; but at least we know where we are making for, know the end of the road, know what is our objective. . . . We have not attempted to put our veto on the appoint-ment of Count Sforza. If tomorrow the Italians were to make him Prime Minister or Foreign Secretary, we have no power to stop it, except with the agreement of the Allies. All that we should have to say about it is that we do not trust the man, we do not think he is a true and trustworthy man, nor do we put the slightest confidence in any Government of which he is a dominating member. I think we should have to put a great deal of responsi-bility for what might happen on those who called him to power.' (Churchill always preferred to think of his own country as 'England' rather than 'Britain', just as he greatly preferred the word 'Empire' to 'Commonwealth'. The word 'Britain' was largely an American contrivance to avoid giving offence to the Scots, the Welsh, and the Ulstermen, if not to the actual Irish.)

Following this, relations between the White House and Downing Street were more strained than they had ever been before. Hopkins received plenty of information to indicate that his honoured friend, the Prime Minister, was in an extremely dangerous and explosive mood which might make plenty of trouble at the forthcoming Big Three Conference which was now in prospect for the end of January; and if Hopkins had lacked such information he had only to read the cables and the ample space provided between the lines of Churchill's public utterances.

The vote in the House of Commons supporting the Government position was 279 to 30 and Churchill cabled Hopkins that he could have had a much larger majority if he had chosen to apply the full force of the Government whip. However, Winant wrote to Hopkins: 'The Parliament is definitely to the Right of the country, and did not reflect, in my opinion, the extent of a troubled public opinion. Protest resolutions passed by big trade-union groups were an indication of this fact. The Conservatives in Parliament are also going to make the Polish-Russian debate scheduled for this week difficult. This is

the first time that I have felt the Government weakened following a Vote of Confidence by the Parliament. The man most hurt, in my judgment, was the Prime Minister. It is a time here when many people are discouraged by the prolongation of the war and I hope that, without surrender of principle, we can so work out our difficulties as to encourage the continuation of the Coalition Government here.'

The situation in Greece was indeed an ugly one. There had been serious fighting in the streets of Athens involving British forces and members of the resistance groups which bore the initials 'E.A.M.' and 'E.L.A.S.' It was reported that some of the rebels had marched through the streets shouting: 'Long Live Roosevelt !' American public opinion was not too well informed as to the merits of this complicated situation or the extent to which the resistance groups might be under Communist domination; all that was apparent on the surface was that British troops, engaged in the task of 'liberation', were killing Greek patriots who had been fighting the Germans, and it was even possible that the British were using American Lend-Lease weapons for this purpose.

Although there were no American troops involved in Greece, units of the Mediterranean Fleet of the U.S. Navy had been operating under British command, aiding in the transport service to Greece. This led to an incident which Hopkins described as follows:

On Saturday night, December 9, 1944, at about 7 p.m., the White House operator told me that 'John Martin' was calling me on the overseas phone. This is the name the Prime Minister uses in his telephone calls.

The connection was very bad and I could not, therefore, know what the Prime Minister was talking about. He sounded as though he was very angry and stirred up about something and wanted me to do something about it. I got the words 'Greece' and 'Halifax'. Inasmuch as it was impossible to make him understand what I was saying, I told him I would find out about it in the morning.

I then tried to get Halifax on the phone to see if he knew what it was all about, but could not reach him.

On Sunday morning I went to the Map Room and saw in the morning news summary a sentence that Admiral King had ordered Admiral Hewitt, our American Commander of the Mediterranean Fleet, not to permit any American L.S.T.s to be used to transfer supplies to Greece. King's actual cable was not available.

I went to see Admiral Leahy about this and told him that I thought Admiral Hewitt was under the command of General Wilson and that it seemed funny to me that Admiral King would issue an order directly to

Hewitt without consultation with the Joint Chiefs of Staff or the Combined Chiefs of Staff. I told Leahy that I thought King was getting into the political arena and that we would undoubtedly hear from the British about it. I told him, furthermore, that I felt that, while we should keep our troops out of Greece, and let the British do the policing, withdrawing the L.S.T.s was like walking out on a member of your family who is in trouble. Under any circumstances, we had told the British that they could use our airplanes to send their paratroopers into Greece and the action of Admiral King did not jibe with that. I told him I thought Admiral King should withdraw his order and, if Admiral King or the Joint Chiefs of Staff thought that such an order should be issued, the recommendation should be made to the President and that he should make the decision because it was in the political sphere. I told Admiral Leahy that irrespective of the merits of Admiral King's action, I thought he had gotten off base from an organization point of view. Leahy agreed with this and told me that when he saw the message he called King and told him he thought King had made a mistake, but he did not tell King to countermand the order.

While I was with Leahy he called Admiral King up and told King he was talking to me and we both felt it was a mistake and Leahy suggested to King that he withdraw the order. King readily agreed and did so. A few minutes later Lord Halifax, the British Ambassador, called me and said he had to see me urgently, and then I pasted together what the Prime Minister was talking about and this was undoubtedly it.

I met Halifax at my house at 12.30 and he had a full-blown protest which he was going to make to Stettinius, but Stettinius was out of town and his instructions were to tell it to me, which he did in no uncertain terms.

Halifax said he was sure Churchill was planning to send a very strong protest to the President and that already the British Chiefs of Staff had said they never heard of such an order and had sent instructions to Wilson to go ahead and use the ships.

I told Halifax I hoped Churchill would not send the message; that I was sure the President knew nothing about it; that the matter was all cleared up anyway, and that I knew instructions had gone to Admiral Hewitt countermanding the previous order and that I thought it would just make trouble if Churchill submitted a protest. I asked Halifax, in the light of the fact that the matter was now settled, if he would not cable Churchill and tell him I thought that any cable from him on this matter would serve no useful purpose, but merely complicate the Greek situation further. I told him that public opinion about the whole Greek business in this country was very bad and that we felt the British Government had messed the whole thing up pretty thoroughly.

Churchill expressed his warm appreciation of Hopkins's timely and effective action and said that he had cancelled the message that he had prepared for dispatch to the President. The tension was eased for a few days and Roosevelt sent friendly and soothing messages to Churchill and also to Stalin. But then, as Winant had predicted, the debate on Poland in the House of Commons caused further serious ructions. Speaking of the future Polish frontiers, Churchill said: 'All territorial changes must await the conference at the peace table after victory has been won, but to that principle there is one exception, and that exception is, changes mutually agreed.' This was an unfortunate misstatement on Churchill's part which was later corrected by Eden, but it conveyed the disturbing suggestion of 'secret agreements' among the big powers for the carving up of the small ones, and it revived the ugly accusations against which Roosevelt had been compelled to defend himself time and again ever since the Atlantic Conference. This speech was made on December 15, and the following day Hopkins cabled Churchill:

> Due to the Greek situation and your statement in Parliament about Poland public opinion has rapidly deteriorated here. I must confess I am greatly disturbed by this turn of diplomatic events which gives publicity to our various difficulties at a time when the battle is joined in Europe and in Asia and all of our energy is required for the defeat of the enemy. Although I do not know what the President or Stettinius may be compelled to say publicly, it is quite possible that one or both of them will have to proclaim their determination in unequivocal terms to do everything we can to seek a free world and a secure one.

There was plenty of indignation in Whitehall at the somewhat sanctimonious, holier-than-thou attitude which the United States was assuming toward a situation in which it was undoubtedly concerned, but for the solution of which it was taking no responsibility whatsoever. It seemed that whenever developments were favourable in any part of the world, the United States was entirely ready to share in the credit—but whenever and wherever things went wrong, the United States was quick to absolve itself of all blame. As one British observer expressed it, 'America is like an inverted Micawber, waiting for something to turn down.'

It remained for Churchill to take the one dramatic and strenuous and thoroughly characteristic action which could convert criticism into applause. With fine contempt for his advanced age (he had now passed his seventieth birthday) and for the risks both political and physical that were involved, he suddenly boarded an airplane and flew to Athens on Christmas Day, taking Eden with him. He thereby brought an end to hostilities and established a temporary regency under Archbishop Damaskinos, obtaining from King George the assurance that he would not attempt to return to the country

'unless summoned by a free and fair expression of the national will'. That ended the Greek crisis for the time being, but there were profoundly conflicting forces there which could not be suppressed permanently.

Hopkins cabled Churchill a Christmas greeting in which he said: 'No one knows better than I what a gallant role you are playing in the greatest drama in the history of the world. On this fateful Christmas, I want you to know that I am well aware of the heavy burdens that you carry. I am proud to be known and even to be attacked by some of my countrymen as your good friend.'

This was certainly a fateful Christmas. The American and British people had been given cause to forget all about political or ideological disputes by the shocking and bewildering news of the German break-through in the Ardennes and the resultant Battle of the Bulge. Three months before it had seemed that Germany might quit at any moment. Now, it seemed that a large part of the triumphant American and British forces in Holland, Belgium, and Northern France might be pushed into another Dunkirk. At the same time, the Russians had driven up the Danube Valley past Budapest and were advancing toward Vienna. To those in official Washington and London who knew that the Big Three were soon to meet again in conference to consider the long-deferred problems of the postwar world, it appeared possible for a time that the Western Allies might be in a seriously weakened condition as compared with the Russians. However, such apprehensions were very shortlived, for it soon became apparent that Hitler's bold and alarming thrust was to end in a German disaster.

Hopkins wrote the following on the genesis of the Yalta Conference:

As early as the middle of September, 1944, the President was contemplating a second conference with Stalin and Churchill. There were a variety of pressing problems which the President believed warranted such a conference, and both Churchill and Stalin were agreeable to the conference. Churchill was, indeed, insistent on it. The reasons were obvious.

By this time we had agreed upon our full-out and final assault on the German citadel, and yet there were no firm agreements as to what was to be done with Germany once she was defeated. The machinery of the European Advisory Council moved so slowly that it was quite possible to visualize the collapse of Germany without any plans or agreements having been made.

Although at Teheran Stalin had made a firm commitment in so far as Soviet participation in the war against Japan was concerned, that needed to be clarified as to precise dates and the extent of Soviet participation.

On the political side there was no agreement as to reparations against Germany; the problem of dismemberment of the Reich was hanging

fire; there was no agreement as to zones; nothing as to whether or not we were going to encourage or discourage a central German Government or, indeed, in what way the Allies were going to utilize German machinery. The policy toward war criminals was stalemated; the earmarks of trouble in Poland were already obvious—neither the eastern frontier nor the western frontier was settled. Our whole policy toward the Far East needed a thorough-going understanding, particularly so far as the Soviet Union was concerned. We knew from Teheran that the Russians wanted certain things as a condition to their declaring war on Japan or, at any rate, they said they wanted them and it was extremely important for the United States in particular, in view of our historic relationship with China, to protect China's interests in these negotiations. Things regarding the Far East had to be settled otherwise we might find the three allies going their separate ways. The place of France in European and world affairs was in an irritating state. France wanted a Zone of Occupation. She had not been given one. France wanted to be on any Control Commission governing Germany. The Allies had given her no assurances on this point. France wanted a clear-cut statement regarding the Allies' ambitions in the French Empire, particularly Indo-China. France had good reason to believe that President Roosevelt was not enthusiastic about returning Indo-China to the Empire, and were thoroughly suspicious of the Allies on this point. France wanted to have a full part in world affairs and the decision on this point, if not made at an early date, would cause endless troubles. Furthermore, there was the hang-over of the Dumbarton Oaks United Nations Conference. The voting procedure had not been settled. There seemed to be no way to settle it except by the three heads of state getting together. Indeed, all of the things I have mentioned would, in my opinion, have been hopelessly delayed without a conference.

The President, as usual, began to play with ideas about places for the conference and suggested a wide variety of locations, none of which included Russia. I told the President, as soon as the discussion started, that there was not a chance of getting Stalin out of Russia at this time in the light of the military situation on Germany's Eastern Front and that if he did not look out we would wind up with a lot of long-winded, irritating cables back and forth getting exactly nowhere, and that we might as well make up our minds first at least to go to some convenient point in Russia —preferably in the Crimea. The President was not opposed to this, but in view of the forthcoming elections, considered it to be unwise. About this time, too, it became perfectly clear that the President had to conduct a vigorous campaign for the election which made a conference prior to election out of the question. And, because he felt it to his political dis-

Stalin, Roosevelt, Churchill and Molotov lunching at Yalta—
the Prime Minister showing a strong taste for caviar.

advantage to indicate Russia as the place of the meeting, he postponed all discussion of the place until after the election was over. As soon as the election had taken place I saw Gromyko, the Russian Ambassador, and told him that we wanted to arrange the conference. Gromyko said that he knew Stalin was prepared for the conference, but that he doubted that he could leave Russia in view of the great Soviet offensive against Germany. I asked Gromyko whether there was any place in the Crimea at which it was fit to hold a conference, and he said he was sure there was, but made no further comment. A couple of weeks later the President got a message from Stalin saying he understood the President was willing to go to the Crimea and suggesting Yalta as a desirable place. This was the first indication anyone around the President had that the President would even consider a conference in Russia. All of the President's close advisers were opposed to his going to Russia; most did not like or trust the Russians anyway and could not understand why the President of the United States should cart himself all over the world to meet Stalin. This argument carried no weight with me. The all-important thing was to get the meeting. There was not a chance of getting that meeting outside of the Crimea. The President's advisers gave me a lot of acid criticism when they found out that I was the one who had talked to Gromyko about the possibility of going to the Crimea. When they descended on the President to urge him not to go the President wavered again and cooked up a lot of counter proposals, none of which made any sense. I was sure the President would wind up by going to the Crimea, the primary reason being that it was a part of the world he had never visited and his adventurous spirit was forever leading him to go to unusual places and, on his part, the election being over, he would no longer be disturbed about it for political reasons.

Churchill was none too keen about the Crimea, because he prefers a warm climate and more comfort than he thought the Crimea could afford, but he was so anxious to have the meeting that he would have gone to Moscow if necessary.

The holidays were then coming on, the President had to open the Congressional session and negotiations were then entered into and naval officers and embassy officials in Moscow hurried to the Crimea to find out if the physical conditions were such to warrant the President going to Yalta. Harriman's report was in the affirmative.

Roosevelt's State of the Union Message of January 6, 1945, was more than twice as long as usual, running to some eight thousand words; he did not deliver it in person, sending it up to the Capitol for a clerk to read out, and he was therefore not limited as to time. He gave a comprehensive survey of

x

the war—General Marshall participated in preparing the military parts of it —and dwelt at length and in a most reasonable spirit with the subject of Allied unity in general and with such problems as Greece and Poland in particular. At Hopkins's strong instigation, Roosevelt agreed to express his real friendship for France. He spoke of the 'heroic efforts of the resistance groups . . . and of all those Frenchmen throughout the world who refused to surrender after the disaster of 1940'. He said that the liberation of France 'means that her great influence will again be available in meeting the problems of peace. We fully recognize France's vital interest in a lasting solution of the German problem and the contribution which she can make in achieving international security', resuming 'her proper position of strength and leadership'. When these words were written I thought that the ashes of the Vichy policy had at last been thrown to the winds. However, as Hopkins was soon to find out, the end of the troubles with de Gaulle was not yet.

There were some disturbances in Washington during January over the dropping of Jesse Jones from the Cabinet and the appointment of Henry Wallace to succeed him as Secretary of Commerce, and over the air transport of a dog named 'Blaze' which Colonel Elliott Roosevelt had shipped from England to his wife. While the latter episode was providing happiness for some newspaper publishers, a list of officers scheduled to be promoted came to the President's desk, and on this list was the name of his son Elliott, who was recommended for brigadier-general. The President was urged to drop this name quietly before the list went to Congress for approval, but he flatly and indignantly refused to do so. He said: 'Elliott on his record has earned promotion. He did not ask that the dog be put on the plane or given high priority. And I'm not going to have him punished for something he did not do.' Roosevelt knew perfectly well what the newspapers would say about this, but he didn't give a damn.

The Fourth Inaugural was held on January 20 on the South Portico of the White House instead of at the Capitol. It was a short, simple ceremony, the brevity being due to the fact that the President was determined to stand up throughout it. (I don't think that he ever wore his braces and stood up again.) It was a bitter cold day, but Roosevelt stood there with no hat, no overcoat, wearing a lightweight suit, as he always did, with no waistcoat. His Inaugral Address lasted only about five minutes, but he worked over it with more care and more interest than he had shown in the preparation of any speech in two years. I had the feeling that he was summing up his most profound beliefs when he said: 'We have learned to be citizens of the world, members of the human community. We have learned the simple truth, as Emerson said, that "the only way to have a friend is to be one".'

Frances Perkins has written that she and Mrs. Henry Wallace were

frightened by the President's appearance—'he looked so badly'. I did not feel this at the time. In fact, I thought he seemed immeasurably better in health and strength and spirits than when I had gone to see him after my return from London four months previously. I had watched him improve steadily throughout the campaign and now, at this Inaugural, I believed he was ready for anything that the next four years might bring.

That night he celebrated his sixty-second birthday. It was ten days ahead of time, because of his imminent departure.

On the following day, Sunday, January 21, Hopkins took off for London in 'The Sacred Cow'. It had been decided that he should spend two or three days with Churchill in an attempt to promote a more amiable mood prior to the gathering at Yalta, for the tensions created during December had evidently not been entirely relaxed. Bohlen accompanied Hopkins on his trip, which was made via Bermuda and the Azores.

Hopkins wrote no notes during his short stay in London, but he reported later that his host was no less 'volcanic' than he had expected. Before leaving he sent a radio message to Roosevelt, who was by now at sea on the U.S.S. *Quincy*, reporting that the visit had been 'very satisfactory'. He quoted Churchill as saying that from all the reports he had received on present conditions at Yalta, 'We could not have found a worse place for a meeting if we had spent ten years on research'.

From London Hopkins flew to Paris, where he was taken by Ambassador Jefferson Caffery to see Foreign Minister Georges Bidault and then de Gaulle. The meeting with Bidault was most cordial, Hopkins stating that Franco-American relations were at 'a pretty low ebb' and it was high time to find out what was the cause and to correct it. Bidault recognized in Hopkins 'a devoted, loyal friend and assistant of President Roosevelt' and described himself as equally loyal and devoted to de Gaulle, but he confessed frankly that the General was at times difficult to handle. 'General de Gaulle believes that Frenchmen always try to please the man to whom they are talking. The General thinks they overdo it and he adopts a different attitude. He makes no effort to please.'

When Hopkins went to see de Gaulle he believed that by making candid admission of past differences and demonstrating a sincere desire to wipe them from the slate he could penetrate the General's austere façade. He was wrong. As Caffery reported, the General was neither 'very responsive' nor 'very conciliatory'. De Gaulle asked: 'If you really mean that you believe that relations between the United States and France are not all that they should be, why don't you do something about it?' He mentioned, for example, the failure to extend to him an invitation to attend the Crimea Conference. He conceded that the United States had helped France by arming and equipping her troops and in other material ways—'but you always seem to do it grudgingly and under pressure'.

Hopkins gave further assurances of good will, but the interview ended in the same conditions of frost with which it had started. However, Hopkins was not discouraged, and the next day in the course of a luncheon with Bidault and other Cabinet Ministers he expressed the President's cordial desire to meet de Gaulle at some French point on or near the Mediterranean, and even suggested that arrangements might be made for de Gaulle to attend the final stages of the Yalta Conference, when European political matters would come under consideration. Bidault promised to discuss these suggestions with de Gaulle and inform Hopkins of the General's reactions. Caffery reported to the State Department: 'Mr. Hopkins made an excellent impression and was very sympathetic. His stay here was very useful and timely.'

Hopkins then went on to Rome, where he was the guest of Ambassador Kirk, at whose villa near Cairo he and the President had stayed in 1943. On January 30 he was taken by Myron C. Taylor for an audience with the Pope. Hopkins told His Holiness of the President's high regard for him and appreciation for the Vatican's unfailingly sympathetic attitude toward the United States and her cause in these troubled years. He told of his recent meeting with de Gaulle and expressed his admiration for the valiant French general—an opinion to which Taylor ventured to register his dissent. The twenty-minute audience was in the Pope's library, and Taylor later said that when they left Hopkins was in a glow of exaltation, revealing a surprisingly deep religious feeling. He said that the Pope subsequently stated that he had been greatly impressed by Hopkins as a man of exceptional force of character.

From Rome, Hopkins went to Allied Force Headquarters at Caserta, near Naples, and there he was overwhelmed with hospitality by two old friends, General Ira C. Eaker and General Joseph T. McNarney. (The latter had been on the PBY flight to Archangel in July, 1941.) He was joined in Naples by Stettinius and they flew together to Malta to await the President's arrival. Hopkins by now was quite ill.

The Combined Chiefs of Staff had been meeting at Malta—and had been engaged in the most violent disagreements and disputes of the entire war. (One can read the official minutes of these meetings without suspecting that a single harsh word had been exchanged, but some of those who were present tell a much more colourful story of what went on.) The point at issue was the selection of a strategic plan for the final knockout blow against Germany. One plan was advanced by the British Chiefs, another by Eisenhower; the latter was not present at Malta, but he was volubly and vehemently represented by Beedle Smith. The arguments reached such a point that Marshall, ordinarily one of the most restrained and soft-spoken of men, announced that if the British plan were approved by the Prime Minister and

President he would recommend to Eisenhower that he had no choice but to ask to be relieved of his command. The issue was settled by the Combined Chiefs in Eisenhower's favour without need for reference to higher authority, and the plan was followed which ended three months later in junction with the Russians and Germany's surrender.

Sick as he was at Malta, Hopkins went into action on behalf of relief and rehabilitation in Europe, a subject on which he had been working for a long time. The U.S. Chiefs of Staff contended, as it was their duty to do, that American shipping in the Atlantic should be transferred to the Pacific after V.E.-Day, except that which was required to supply American forces still remaining in Europe. In putting up a fight for the retention of enough shipping to supply the needs of the civilian population of Britain and the Continent, Hopkins was not animated solely by humanitarian considerations, or the kind of 'starry-eyed, dogooder idealism' which was identified with the Santa Claus philosophy of the New Deal. He knew that there could be no recovery and no peace and no democracy in Europe if its people did not have enough to eat and the tools and materials with which to get back to work. He did not have to argue this point at any great length with Marshall and King. Their respect for Hopkins was such that they agreed to leave the arbitration of matters relating to allocation of shipping in his hands; but, as events proved, he never had a chance to exercise this authority.

On February 2 Roosevelt arrived in the Grand Harbour of Valetta on the *Quincy*, and Admiral King has told me that when he went aboard the cruiser and saw the President he was alarmed for the first time by the state of his health. King had seen him last at the Inauguration, less than two weeks before. Since then, Roosevelt had had ten days at sea, with favourable weather. Normally, no matter how tired and worn he might appear when he started off on a cruise, he emerged from it looking healthy and hearty and acting that way. It now seemed to King that instead of improvement there had been serious deterioration. But the President was as always buoyant and excited at the prospect of new adventures as he left the *Quincy* to make the rest of his journey by air.

The night of February 2-3 was a busy one at the Luqa airfield at Malta, which had been for so many years a prime target for German and Italian bombs. Transport planes were taking off at ten-minute intervals from 11.30 p.m. to dawn to carry some seven hundred people, including the President and the Prime Minister, fourteen hundred miles across the Aegean and Anatolia and the Black Sea to Saki airfield in the Crimea.

THE YALTA CONFERENCE

THE accommodations at Yalta were unexceptionable for those on the Very Important Person level and the Russians seemed eager to convince their Anglo-American guests of the warm friendliness of their hospitality. However, this was war-ravaged territory and space was so limited that, according to the records, sixteen U.S. Army colonels had to share one bedroom. Hopkins had a bedroom to himself in the Livadia Palace, where Roosevelt was staying, and he spent most of his time in it, leaving his bed only to go down to the Grand Ballroom for the full-dress meetings. He was so extremely ill that at one point Dr. McIntire wanted him to be moved to the Navy Communications ship, U.S.S. *Catoctin*, which was moored at Sevastopol, eighty miles away. (It was considered unsafe to bring the ship to Yalta because of the danger of lingering German mines, and signal corps men had laid land lines from the Livadia Palace to the ship, so that Roosevelt could have his own channels of communication.) Hopkins attended none of the big dinners at Yalta—in fact, I believe he was not permitted so much as a taste of vodka—so that his condition at least became no worse and he was able to stick it out to the end. James F. Byrnes has written: 'Members of our delegation frequently held meetings there [in Hopkins's bedroom] because Dr. McIntire insisted he remain in bed.'

Robert Hopkins was the only son at this conference, but there were three daughters, Anna Boettiger, Section Officer Sarah Churchill Oliver (of the W.A.A.F.), and Kathleen Harriman. Roosevelt's party also included James F. Byrnes, Edward J. Flynn, and Steve Early, who saw to it that this conference got much better Press coverage than had any of its predecessors, despite the fact that Roosevelt firmly refused to permit even the wire service men—'the three ghouls'—to go along with him.

The President and Prime Minister arrived at Yalta on Saturday, February 3. Stalin and his party arrived early on Sunday morning and he and Molotov came to call on Roosevelt at four o'clock that afternoon. After thanking his hosts for all the arrangements that had been made to promote the comfort and convenience of the guests, Roosevelt said that during the trip across the ocean on the *Quincy* numerous bets had been made as to whether the Americans would get to Manila before the Russians got to Berlin. Stalin laughed and said that those who had bet on Manila would win. Roosevelt remarked on the destruction that he had seen here in the Crimea, and Stalin told him that it was nothing as compared with the Ukraine, for in the Crimea the Germans had been outflanked and had been given little time to carry out planned demolition, whereas in the Ukraine they had destroyed everything

with sadistic calculation and method. Stalin then asked how things were going on the Western Front; Roosevelt told him that General Marshall would later give a detailed outline of the situation, but he could say now that a limited offensive was due to start on February 8 and another on the twelfth and that the main drive of the Anglo-American forces would begin in about a month's time. Stalin was gratified to hear this, and expressed the hope that the Allies would shortly capture the Ruhr and the Saar and thereby deprive the Germans of their only remaining sources of coal, the Russians having already captured the Silesian Basin. Roosevelt said that with the two forces now coming closer together from east and from west, he believed that it would be possible for General Eisenhower to establish direct communication with the Red Army and thereby achieve direct co-ordination of tactical operations.

Roosevelt asked Stalin how he had got along with General de Gaulle, who had visited Moscow in December. Stalin replied that he had found de Gaulle to be an uncomplicated individual and also unrealistic in his estimates of France's contribution to the winning of the war.

Roosevelt said that there had been disagreements between himself and the British over the general policy toward France and also over the question of zones of occupation in Germany. Stalin asked whether the President thought that France should have a zone of occupation and, if so, for what reason. Roosevelt evidently made a somewhat equivocal reply and Stalin and Molotov both said that this was a topic for discussion here at Yalta; they indicated that they did not view the idea with much favour.

This meeting was held in the President's study at Livadia, and a few minutes before five they moved down to the Grand Ballroom for the first formal conference. Stalin was accompanied by Vishinski, Gromyko, Gusev (the Soviet Ambassador in London), and Maisky, as well as Molotov and three Chiefs of Staff. Hopkins felt too ill to come to this meeting—which must have meant that he was very sick indeed—and ill health had prevented General Hap Arnold from coming to Yalta at all, the U.S. Army Air Forces being represented by General Laurence S. Kuter, Assistant Chief of Air Staff for Plans.

At the start of the meeting Marshal Stalin suggested that President Roosevelt should again preside. The discussion, which lasted for nearly three hours, dealt almost entirely with the military situation. General Antonov read a prepared paper giving a detailed analysis of developments on the Eastern Front and expressed the hope that the Allies would soon advance in the West and would paralyse German communications by bombing in order to prevent the shifting of troops across Germany from west to east and from Norway and Italy. Marshall reviewed the situation in the West, Portal spoke for the Air Force, and Cunningham talked of the new

German technical developments which tended to revive the U-boat threat. At one point the Prime Minister made mention of the possibility that the Allies might aid the Russian campaign on the Eastern Front by an expedition across the Adriatic into the Balkans, but this proposal does not appear to have been pursued any further.

Roosevelt was host at the dinner which followed this meeting. The Filipino mess men were on duty, but the food was strictly Russian: caviar, sturgeon, beef and macaroni, sweet cake, tea, coffee, vodka, and five kinds of wine. (In the White House the guests would have had to content themselves with one kind of California sauterne.) In his report, Bohlen stated that 'very good humour' prevailed throughout the meal, but he added a bit of conversation on the side between himself and Vishinski which sounded mildly caustic. Vishinski said that the Soviet Union would never agree to the right of the small nations to judge the acts of the Great Powers, and when Bohlen ventured the opinion that the American people were not likely to approve of any denial of the small nations' rights, Vishinski said that the American people 'should learn to obey their leaders'. Bohlen then suggested that it might be a good idea for Vishinski to visit the United States and try to tell that to the people, and Vishinski remarked that he would be glad to do so.

During the informal conversation at this dinner Churchill remarked that he was constantly being 'beaten up' as a reactionary, but that he was the only one of the three representatives present who could be thrown out of office at any time by the votes of his own people. He added that personally he gloried in this danger. This led Stalin to observe, jokingly, that evidently the Prime Minister feared the results of the forthcoming elections in Great Britain. Churchill replied that not only did he not fear them, but he was proud of the right of the British people to change their Government whenever they wished to do so. He went on to speak of the rights of the small nations and quoted a very apt proverb: 'The eagle should permit the small birds to sing and care not wherefor they sang.'

At breakfast the following morning a courier delivered to Roosevelt White House mail which had been dispatched from Washington on January 31. The courier had been five days in transit, which meant that Roosevelt was now at the extreme edge of the distance that he could travel from Washington under the ten-day limitation on his power to act on Congressional bills. (Subsequent couriers managed to make the trip in three days.) The foreign secretaries met that day for lunch with Molotov at the Koreis Villa, where Stalin and staff were staying. (Churchill was at Vorontsov Villa, twelve miles away.) At the start of this lunch Harriman announced the news that Manila had been taken, and Molotov 'immediately proposed a toast to this victory of the Allied Armies'. There followed toasts by Eden

and Stettinius to Molotov, by Molotov to Hull and to Clark Kerr, the British Ambassador, more toasts by Stettinius to his Dumbarton Oaks colleagues, Gromyko and Cadogan, by Molotov to Harriman, by Harriman to Vishinski, by Byrnes to the Red Army, by Gromyko to Byrnes, and by Maisky to the closest possible unity between the peoples, governments, and chiefs of the United Nations. It was decided that these meetings should be officially named 'The Crimean Conference'—a futile decision, as it turned out, because the conference always has and undoubtedly always will bear the name of Yalta. There does not appear to have been much more of importance discussed at the luncheon, except that Molotov made it clear that the Soviet Government expected to receive reparations in kind from Germany and hoped that the United States would furnish the Soviet Union with long-term credits. Stettinius said that he was ready to discuss these matters at any time.

The second formal meeting was held at four that afternoon and despite all the luncheon toasts the conference really got down to business. The Chiefs of Staff, with the exception of Leahy, were not present at this meeting, but Hopkins dragged himself out of bed for it and attended all the main meetings thereafter. Hopkins was too ill to write extended memoranda at Yalta as he had done at other conferences, but the precise records of his later conferences in Moscow (Chapter XXVI) throw considerable light on his attitude toward the progress made at Yalta. Byrnes has provided a lucid account of the meetings that he attended in his book, *Speaking Frankly*, and Churchill will write another. (I often wonder when, if ever, Stalin will be heard from.)

None of the momentous conferences of the Second World War has provoked more subsequent controversy than this one; Yalta has been blamed for many of the ills with which the world was afflicted in the years following the total defeat of Nazi Germany and Japan. The belief has grown that Roosevelt made various 'surrenders' to the Russians at Yalta, and the more kindly critics attribute these to the fact that he was a dying man. The complete records of the Conference, as they appear in the Hopkins papers, do not seem to substantiate this theory. Roosevelt appears to have been in full possession of all of his faculties. Only at the end of seven days of long meetings, covering a wide range of tremendous subjects, did he make a concession which, in my belief, he would not have made if he had not been tired out and anxious to end the negotiations relative to Russia's entry into the war with Japan. This will be discussed later in this chapter. Of all the 'surrenders' supposed to have been made, those most often cited and emphasized relate to the establishment of the veto power in the Security Council of the United Nations and the granting to the Soviet Union of two additional votes in the General Assembly. These two points have often been linked together under the general term, 'the voting formula', but they were entirely separate problems and the first of them was not a subject of contention at Yalta.

The principle of the veto was stated by the United States Government and the British Government in their separate 'Tentative Proposals for a General International Organization' as drafted in July, 1944, prior to the Dumbarton Oaks Conference. Throughout that conference, and the five months that followed it before Yalta, there was complete agreement that in matters which might affect world peace the veto could be exercised by any one of the four (or, if France were included, five) major powers. The arguments with the Russians that arose at Dumbarton Oaks and resulted in failure to agree on a voting formula for the Security Council were concerned not with the principle of the veto, but with the precise extent to which any power should be denied the right to vote on a dispute in which it was a participant. Various compromise proposals on this were made by Stettinius, for the United States, and Cadogan for Britain, but Gromyko, for the Soviet Union, was unbudgeable. On September 18, 1944, he had said confidently to Stettinius: 'The Russian position on voting in the Council will never be departed from.' When Stettinius expressed the fear that this unyielding attitude might break up the world organization even before it started, Gromyko said flatly that no world organization would exist in which a major power was denied the right to vote in any dispute, whether it was a participant therein or not.

It was at this same time that the question of more votes than one was raised. Stalin said, in a cable to Roosevelt: 'You, of course, know that the Ukraine and Byelorussia, which are constituent parts of the Soviet Union, are greater in population and in political importance than certain other countries which we all agree should belong to the number of initiators of the establishment of the International Organization. Therefore, I hope to have an opportunity to explain to you the political importance of this question which has been brought up by the Soviet Delegation at Dumbarton Oaks.'

On December 5, 1944, the United States Government prepared a new compromise proposal on the voting formula which was forwarded to the British and Russian Governments and which was again presented by Stettinius when this general subject first came up for discussion at Yalta. Agreement on it was reached with, it would appear, no argument at all. There certainly was no evidence on the record of opposition by Churchill, a staunch European, who was always at all these meetings a zealous and unflagging champion of the rights of small nations. Indeed, the British had been heartily in favour of the veto as a means of preventing any encroachments on their own imperial interests. The United States had favoured it as a form of insurance against the commitment by the United Nations Council of American forces to action in all sorts of possible wars in all parts of the world—and Roosevelt, with the memory of Woodrow Wilson always

alive in him, was particularly conscious of the importance of this point when the United Nations Charter would eventually be submitted for ratification by the Senate.

According to the December 5 compromise formula, the main concession to Russia provided that a major power could by its veto prevent the Council from taking action, such as application of sanctions or of war itself, against said power. What Russia yielded in this compromise was this: a major power could not by its veto prevent the Council even from considering and thereby advertising the involvement of said power in any dispute. The British and Americans at Yalta did not consider this a negligible concession, for it represented a considerable relaxing of the rigid position taken by Gromyko (in accordance, of course, with his orders from Moscow) at Dumbarton Oaks. The differences of opinion on this may be indicated by quotation of two American editorials which represented viewpoints dominated by neither Russophilia nor Russophobia. The *Providence Bulletin* said: 'It is a sizable concession on the part of the Powers who possess the military force, especially on the part of Russia, that the smaller nations can haul one up to the bar of the organization and make their charges of grievances and injustice against a Great Power.' The *Savannah News* said: 'If this compromise plan on the Council's voting procedure is allowed to stand at the San Francisco peace conference next month, the people of the United States might as well make up their minds that the new world organization will fail as miserably as did the old League. . . . The time to have a real peace organization—with teeth in it—is NOW, without fear, favour or compromise.'

It was at the fourth formal meeting on February 7 at Yalta that the Russians made their request for two or possibly three additional votes in the United Nations Assembly—and Roosevelt wanted it to be absolutely clear that they meant the Assembly and not the Council. Stalin and Molotov wanted final agreement to be reached then and there, so that the Ukraine and Byelorussia could be invited to the San Francisco Conference.

In response to this proposal Roosevelt embarked on a long speech in which he employed his familiar tactics for attempting to dodge an immediate issue by manoeuvring the conversation into the realms of irrelevancy. He mentioned the fact that certain countries are large in area, though small in population, and referred in this connection to Brazil, which he said was smaller in area than the U.S.S.R., but larger than the United States. On the other hand, there were some countries that were small in area but large in population, such as Honduras and Haiti, etc. Evidently Stalin began to betray signs of impatience and irritability as Roosevelt's vagrant remarks were translated to him, for Hopkins scribbled the following note: 'Mr. President—I think you should try to get this referred to Foreign Ministers before there is trouble. Harry.'

There is no doubt that Roosevelt had come to Yalta determined to oppose the Russian demand for the two additional votes. In fact, it is my understanding that he had previously told the Cabinet and Congressional leaders in Washington that if the Russians were to insist on this point he would demand forty-eight votes for the United States. Now, at Yalta, Churchill spoke out strongly in favour of the admission of the two republics. I do not know what his reasons were for this, but it seemed evident to the Americans present that he was influenced by British imperial considerations and especially the problem of India.

When the Foreign Secretaries' meeting considered the issue the following day, Eden supported Molotov, and Stettinius reserved his position. It was agreed, however, that only those countries which had signed the United Nations Declaration by the day on which the Yalta Conference should end would be invited to the San Francisco Conference. Subsequently, in view of the British unwillingness to join him in objecting to the two extra votes, Roosevelt decided to agree to support the Russian proposal at San Francisco, but insisted that it must be a matter for full discussion and free vote at the later conference and not a *fait accompli* at Yalta.

At the fifth formal meeting, February 8, both Stalin and Molotov expressed confidence that they could obtain the signatures of the Ukraine and Byelorussia to the United Nations Declaration while the Yalta Conference was still in session. (Presumably this involved the dispatch of one brief order to Moscow.) They felt that such signatures would entitle the two republics to invitation to the San Francisco Conference. Again Roosevelt made a bid to change the subject, whereupon Stalin said: 'I do not want to embarrass the President, but if he will explain his difficulties we will see what can be done.'

Roosevelt then said that this was a technical question, but an important one, which involved the granting to one of the Great Powers of two additional votes in the Assembly. He repeated that this was a matter which must be left for decision by all the United Nations representatives gathered at San Francisco, but he gave assurance that the United States would support the Soviet proposal. Again, Stalin proposed that the problem could be settled then and there by obtaining the signatures of the two republics—and again Roosevelt said that he did not think this would overcome the difficulty. Whereupon Stalin finally withdrew the proposal and the President expressed his appreciation of the Marshal's action in doing so.

Roosevelt proposed what he considered an 'insurance clause' for use in the event that there would be howls of protest in the Congress against American support for two additional votes for Russia in the United Nations Assembly: this was a proposal that the Soviet Union would support a demand for two additional votes for the United States in case such a demand were to be made. Stalin agreed to this, apparently without argument.

In the official records of the Yalta Conference is set down a poignant interruption by Roosevelt when Churchill was pointing out that Britain's claims to Hong Kong would be protected by the veto formula and Stalin was asking, 'Suppose that Egypt should raise the question of the return of the Suez Canal?' Roosevelt then reminded them that in the Teheran Declaration they had said: 'We recognize fully the supreme responsibility resting upon us and all the nations to make a peace which will command good will from the overwhelming masses of the peoples of the world.'

Roosevelt tried to keep the discussion on that basis, and he left Yalta believing he had been largely successful in doing so.

Stalin was at first obdurate on the subject of French participation in the control of Germany, and throughout most of the conference Roosevelt was inclined to agree with him. But, as Hopkins expressed it, 'Winston and Anthony [Eden] fought like tigers for France'. And Hopkins worked constantly from his sick bed to support them. His failure to generate any warmth in de Gaulle had not altered his conviction that France must be restored to its proper dignity, not only as its just historic due, but because stability in Europe was inconceivable without a strong and influential France.

At the second formal meeting Stalin said that he would not object to France being given a zone provided it was carved out of the British and American zones and did not affect the Russians, but he added that if this were the case then the Belgians and the Dutch and 'other states' (presumably in Eastern Europe) should also participate in the occupation of Germany; he remained adamant in opposition to the inclusion of France in the Allied Control Commission for Germany. Churchill argued stoutly that without French power, Britain alone could not undertake to contain Germany on the Western Front. Roosevelt at this time said that 'he favoured the acceptance of the French request for a zone, but that he agreed with Marshal Stalin that France should not take part in the control machinery'. Eden expressed the conviction that unless France did take such a part she would not accept responsibility for the occupation of a zone. As was usually the case when the Big Three could not come to unanimous agreement on any point, the matter was referred to the Foreign Secretaries 'for further study'.

At a meeting of the Foreign Secretaries two days later the same division occurred with Molotov and Stettinius opposed to French participation and Eden in favour of it.

At the fourth formal meeting Churchill and Stalin again argued the point. Churchill said that 'he did not wish France to be included in the present club [the Big Three] which he felt was very exclusive, at least for a while. He added, however, that he felt that the fact of permitting France to join the Control Commission would keep them quiet for a while'. Roosevelt said that 'he agreed that France should not join this body, but he was doubtful whether this would keep them quiet'.

Before the seventh formal meeting on February 10 (this was after Byrnes's departure from Yalta), Hopkins finally persuaded Roosevelt to side with Churchill on this controversial point. When at the meeting, Eden brought up the subject of France, the record states that:

> *The President* then said that he had changed his mind in regard to the question of the French participation in the Control Commission. He now agreed with the views of the Prime Minister that it would be impossible to give France an area to administer in Germany unless they were members of the Control Commission. He said he thought it would be easier to deal with the French if they were on the Commission than if they were not.
>
> *Marshal Stalin* said he had no objections and that he agreed to this.

Reading this record, it would seem that Stalin's concurrence with Roosevelt's reversal of position had come with dramatic suddenness. Such was not the case. Actually Roosevelt had previously informed Stalin privately through Harriman of his long-delayed change of mind and heart on this and Stalin had said that since this was the President's considered decision he would go along with it.

A message had reached Hopkins at Yalta from Bidault via Caffery that it was felt that nothing was to be gained by following through on Hopkins's suggestion that de Gaulle be invited to participate in the final meetings of the conference, but that de Gaulle had stated that he would be delighted to meet Roosevelt on his trip home from Yalta at any place and at any time that the President designated.

It seemed to Hopkins that the old, festering sore which had developed from the original fleabite at St. Pierre and Miquelon was at last to be healed. However, on February 14, after Roosevelt and Hopkins had left Yalta and were aboard the cruiser *Quincy* on Great Bitter Lake near Suez, a message came from Caffery stating that de Gaulle had again assumed an attitude of frigid haughtiness and announced that it was not convenient for him to go to Algiers to meet Roosevelt. When Caffery heard this he indignantly reminded Bidault of de Gaulle's previous assurance that he would be delighted to meet the President, which assurance had been duly communicated to Roosevelt through Hopkins. Bidault said in effect: 'Yes, I know he did. I have been doing everything to make him go, but he has changed his mind, and you don't know how stubborn he is.' Caffery reported that de Gaulle was in a sulky mood because the public statements issued at the end of the Yalta Conference had not paid sufficient attention to him personally. Thus he lost his last chance to establish the cordial relations with President Roosevelt which would have added so much to his own prestige with the French people.

The question of the Russian claim for reparations in kind from Germany was argued back and forth throughout the Yalta Conference. Both Churchill and Roosevelt said that public opinion in their countries was opposed to the whole concept of reparations in view of the unfortunate results of the Treaty of Versailles—and Stalin was later to confess to Hopkins that he became pretty fed up with hearing about American and British public opinion, believing that the President and Prime Minister kept on referring to it merely as a device to justify their own personal opinions and prejudices. The Russians never did succeed in understanding that public opinion could be a determining factor even with the powerful heads of state; Stalin had said to Roosevelt at Teheran that the way to overcome the moral objections of the American people to absorption of the Baltic States in the Soviet Union was to subject them to a propaganda campaign, and Vishinski had expressed precisely the same point of view in his remark to Bohlen that the American people should learn to obey their leaders.

In the final meeting at Yalta the whole question of reparations seemed to have reached a deadlock. It was decided that the matter should be referred to an Interallied Commission to be set up in Moscow, but it seemed impossible to agree on the terms of the basic directive on which this Commission would proceed. During the argument Hopkins wrote the following note and passed it to Roosevelt: 'The Russians have given in so much at this conference that I don't think we should let them down. Let the British disagree if they want to—and continue their disagreement at Moscow. Simply say it is all referred to the Reparations Commission with the minutes to show the British disagree about any mention of the 10 billion.' Roosevelt took that advice, believing he had left the door open for all sorts of deliberations in the future.

Thus, the decision on reparations was deferred, as the question of the dismemberment of Germany had been; however, unlike the question of dismemberment, it was not permitted to die of inanition, as Roosevelt undoubtedly hoped it would be. After Roosevelt's death, the Russians were arguing that he had supported their claim. They cited as their authority for this contention his statement, as Byrnes has written, that the Reparation Commission should 'take in its initial studies as a basis for discussion, the suggestion of the Soviet Government, that the total sum of reparations should be 20 billions and that 50 per cent should go to the Soviet Union'. That was the basis of the ten billion dollars claim, but a reading of the quoted statement plus a knowledge of Roosevelt's oft-proclaimed point of view would certainly suggest that he was carefully making no commitment whatsoever. I believe it can be proved that he made no commitment on any policy concerned with the post war treatment of Germany except on the matter of Allied military occupation and the principle of trial and punishment for the war criminals.

The record of Roosevelt's pertinent statements and his known character indicates very strongly his conviction that there were too many questions remaining to be answered about Germany before any blueprints could be drawn; for example—was there any fragment of truth in the hopeful reports that there was a formidable anti-Nazi and pro-democratic movement among the German people, or that there were any separatist movements in Bavaria or in any other part of the Reich? Even at this late date in the war— in February, 1945—the German territory aside from East Prussia that had been occupied by Russians, British, American or French forces was still infinitesimal, and the state of mind of the German people that might follow collapse of the Nazi Government remained a gigantic question mark.

At Yalta, Roosevelt was adhering to the basic formula of unconditional surrender; beyond that, he demanded only—to quote one of his favourite phrases—'freedom of action'. Therefore, when he said that the Reparations Commission should 'in its initial studies' take the Soviet suggestion in regard to reparations 'as a basis for discussion', it may be assumed that he meant precisely what he said and no more.

During the fourth formal meeting Roosevelt first made the proposal for a meeting of all the United Nations to be held in the United States at the earliest possible moment, perhaps even within the next four weeks, for the actual setting up of the world organization. (April 25 was eventually selected as the date and San Fransisco as the place.) While he heartily approved this suggestion 'in principle', Churchill advanced all sorts of arguments against holding such a conference in the near future. While Churchill was arguing Hopkins wrote a note to Roosevelt: 'There's something behind this talk— we do not know of its basis. Perhaps we better wait till later tonight [to find out] what is on his mind.' To which Roosevelt added: 'All this is local politics.' Whereupon Hopkins wrote: 'I'm quite sure now he is thinking about the next election in Britain.' This was a consideration with which Roosevelt could readily sympathize.

The outcome on other principal subjects considered at Yalta can be summarized as follows:

Liberated Areas—The communiqué issued on this spoke for itself. It was a heartening reaffirmation of the principles of the Atlantic Charter, all the more welcome after the unpleasant situations that had arisen in Belgium, Italy, and Greece. At the sixth formal meeting on February 9, the next to last day of the conference, Molotov offered an amendment to the communiqué: 'And in this connection support should be given to the political leaders of these countries who took an active part in the struggle against the German invaders.' Stalin pointed out, perhaps with a trace of impishness, that Churchill need have no anxiety that this Molotov amendment was designed to apply to Greece. At a later meeting of the Foreign Secretaries that same

Mr. President

The Russians have given us so much at this conference that I dont think we should let them down. Let the British disagree if they want to - and continue their disagreement at Moscow. Simply say it is all referred to the Reparation Commission with the minutes to show the British disagree about any mention of the 10 billion.

Harry

Harry Hopkins's note to the President, written during the final meeting at Yalta, suggesting a solution to the deadlock on reparations (*see page* 851).

evening, Stettinius said that the United States could not accept this amendment, since it suggested 'too much interference in the affairs of these countries and involved taking decisions on who had collaborated with the enemy, which should be left to the peoples of these countries themselves'. Eden expressed full concurrence with these views and the amendment was finally dropped.

Poland—The principles of the Liberated Areas agreement, of course, applied here, but the discussions of Poland's precise boundaries and the composition of its provisional Government seemed to have taken up more time than was devoted to any other subject in the conference. Certainly, the British and Americans left Yalta with the belief that this difficult problem had reached an honourable and equitable solution. They soon learned that they were wrong. Similarly, it was believed that the agreement reached on Yugoslavia guaranteed to that gallant, tortured country the opportunity to achieve a representative Government in accordance with truly democratic principles.

The Dardanelles—While Stalin stated his country's desire for a modification of the Montreux Convention, he did not press for an immediate agreement on this. Churchill said that the British certainly felt that the present position of Russia with her 'great interests in the Black Sea should not be dependent on the narrow exit'. He said that, since this might affect the position of Great Britain in the Mediterranean more than it would that of the United States, he suggested that it should be discussed at a later meeting of the Foreign Secretaries in London. Stalin agreed.

Iran—On this one subject the Western Allies ran into a blank wall of disagreement. Following is the text of the final discussion at the Foreign Secretaries' meeting on February 10:

Mr. *Eden* inquired whether Mr. Molotov had considered the British document on Iran.

Mr. *Molotov* stated that he had nothing to add to what he had said several days ago on the subject.

Mr. *Eden* inquired whether it would not be advisable to issue a communiqué on Iran.

Mr. *Molotov* stated that this would be inadvisable.

Mr. *Stettinius* urged that some reference be made that Iranian problems had been discussed and clarified during the Crimean Conference.

Mr. *Molotov* stated that he opposed this idea.

Mr. *Eden* suggested that it be stated that the declaration on Iran had been reaffirmed and re-examined during the present meeting.

Mr. *Molotov* opposed this suggestion.

Y

In that bit of dialogue appears the Molotov whom future Secretaries of State, Byrnes and Marshall, came to know so well.

Trusteeships—This subject had been discussed in the conferences with Anthony Eden in the White House in March, 1943 (Chapter XXIX) and Hopkins recorded at the time that it was becoming clear that Eden 'thinks very little' of the idea of trusteeships of which Roosevelt always thought so much. When Stettinius brought this subject up at the sixth formal meeting at Yalta, on February 9, it instantly became clear that Churchill thought even less of it. Stettinius reported that at a meeting of the Foreign Ministers it had been agreed that 'The five Governments which will have permanent seats on the Security Council should consult each other prior to the United Nations Conference [on] providing machinery in the World Charter for dealing with territorial trusteeship and dependent areas'. Thereupon Churchill exploded that he did not agree with one single word of this report. He said that he had not been consulted about this nor had he even heard of it previously, adding that he would never consent under any circumstances to the United Nations thrusting interfering fingers into the very life of the British Empire. He enlarged at some length and with considerable vigour on his historic assurance that as long as he was Prime Minister he would never yield one scrap of Britain's heritage. When Stettinius explained that the trusteeship principle was intended to apply to such areas as the Japanese-mandated islands in the Pacific, but not to any part of the British Empire, Churchill accepted the explanation, but stated positively that this important distinction must be made quite clear. He said that Britain had no desire for any territorial aggrandizement, and he had no objection to the trusteeship principle as applied to enemy territory. He asked Stalin how he would feel about a proposal to have the Crimea internationalized for use as a summer resort. Stalin replied that he would be glad to give the Crimea for use as a permanent meeting-place for the Three Powers.

Roosevelt told Stalin privately that he thought that Hong Kong should be given back to the Chinese or internationalized as a free port, but I do not know if he ever made that suggestion to Churchill. The decisive discussions (they are all on the record) relative to the Far East and Russia's entry into the war against Japan were conducted between Roosevelt and Stalin with Churchill not present, although he joined in signing the final written agreement which has been the subject of so much controversy since its terms were made public.

In *Where Are We Heading?* Sumner Welles has offered serious criticism of elements in this agreement. Welles saw no valid objection to the return of southern Sakhalin and the Kurile Islands to Russia, since these positions,

which the Japanese had seized, were highly important and even essential to Russian security in the Far East; nor was there objection to the internationalization of Dairen (provided it ever were truly 'internationalized') nor to the granting of permanent autonomy to Outer Mongolia. 'However,' Welles wrote, 'the restoration to Russia of the right formerly possessed by the Imperial Russian Governments to dominate Manchuria through the control of the Chinese Eastern and South Manchurian railroads, and the lease of Port Arthur as a naval base, necessarily fall into a different category. These concessions, which will make it altogether impossible for a new unified China to exercise full sovereignty within Manchuria, are all the more objectionable in view of China's absence from the conference table where they were decided.' Such criticism from Welles could hardly be dismissed as coming from one who did not know what he was talking about or who was embittered by hatred of Roosevelt. But it may be said that in writing them Welles had the considerable advantage of hindsight.

It is quite clear that Roosevelt had been prepared even before the Teheran Conference in 1943 to agree to the legitimacy of most if not all of the Soviet claims in the Far East, for they involved the restoration of possessions and privileges taken by the Japanese from the Russians in the war of 1904. It is also clear that the failure to notify the Chinese immediately of the Yalta discussions was due to fear of the security of secrets in Chungking. Stalin told Roosevelt at Yalta that he intended to start the movement of twenty-five Russian divisions across Siberia to the Far East and this operation must be conducted in utmost secrecy, and Roosevelt said that when this movement of troops had been completed (presumably within three or four months) he would send an American officer to Chungking via Moscow to inform Chiang Kai-shek of the agreements. Stalin insisted that these agreements must be put in writing and must contain the statement: 'The Heads of the three Great Powers have agreed that these claims of the Soviet Union shall be unquestionably fulfilled after Japan has been defeated.'

This, in my opinion, was the most assailable point in the entire Yalta record, and the most surprising in that it involved Roosevelt in the kind of firm commitment that usually he managed to avoid. It denied him the post-war 'freedom of action' which he valued so highly; for, if China had refused to agree to any of the Soviet claims, presumably the U.S. and Britain would have been compelled to join in enforcing them.

It must be said that in all considerations of Far Eastern matters at Yalta Roosevelt's principal concern was based on American war plans against Japan. The immensely costly operations at Iwo Jima and then at Okinawa were about to be launched, and the plans had been made for the major invasion of the Japanese home islands in the fall of 1945. MacArthur's calculations were based on the assumption that the Russians would contain

the great bulk of Japanese forces on the Asiatic mainland as they had contained the Germans in Eastern Europe. Obviously, the entry of the Soviet Union forcibly into the Japanese war by midsummer—before the major invasion—could mean the saving of countless American lives, and might even make the final invasion unnecessary. Of course, at the time of Yalta, the perfection of the atomic bomb still seemed to be only a remote possibility for the uncertain future; it was not until three months after Roosevelt's death that assurance came from Los Alamos that the long years of research and experiment on this decisive weapon had achieved success.

In spite of all of which, it is my belief that Roosevelt would not have agreed to that final firm commitment had it not been that the Yalta Conference was almost at an end and he was tired and anxious to avoid further argument. I believe that he was hopeful that, when the time came to notify the Chinese, he would be able to straighten the whole thing out with Chiang Kai-shek—but that hope, of course, was not realized.

During the discussion of the Far Eastern agreements—and there was not much discussion—Stalin said to Roosevelt that if his conditions were not met it would be very difficult to explain to the Russian people why they must go to war against Japan. (Here the Marshal was obviously using the 'public opinion' tactic which he complained of when used by Roosevelt or Churchill.) He said that the Russian people had clearly understood that they must fight the Germans to defend the very existence of their homeland, but that they could see no such threat from the Japanese. However, Stalin said, if the required political conditions were met, then it would not be difficult for him to explain to the Supreme Soviet and the people just what was their stake in the Far Eastern war.

Stalin agreed to the establishment of American air bases at Komsomolsk and Nikolaevsk in the near future, and later on Kamchatka, the delay in the latter case being due to the presence there of a Japanese Consul who could not fail to notice the presence of U.S. Air Force personnel. Stalin also agreed to the immediate institution of American-Russian military staff talks for joint planning.

It was agreed that 'in two or three months after Germany has surrendered and the war in Europe has terminated the Soviet Union shall enter the war against Japan on the side of the Allies'.

Stalin again expressed his lack of confidence in China as a world power. He said that he could not understand why the Kuomintang Government and the Communists should not maintain a united front against the Japanese. He felt that Chiang Kai-shek should assume leadership for this purpose, but that there was a need for some new leaders around the Generalissimo. He said there were some good men in the Comintern and he did not understand why they had not been brought forward. (He later restated these views more explicitly in his talks with Hopkins in Moscow.)

Roosevelt said that the new American Ambassador, General Hurley, and General Wedemeyer were much more successful than their predecessors in bringing the Communists in the North together with the Chungking Government. He said that the blame for the breach lay more with the Comintern and the Kuomintang than with the rank and file of the so-called Communists.

Stalin asked Roosevelt whether any foreign troops would be stationed in Korea. Roosevelt replied in the negative, and Stalin expressed his approval of this.

A large dinner was given by Stalin on the evening of February 8 and a smaller one (with only the principals attending) by Churchill on the last evening, February 10. The record of the principal toasts at the former dinner was as follows:

Marshal Stalin proposed a toast to the health of the Prime Minister whom he characterized as the bravest governmental figure in the world. He said that due in large measure to Mr. Churchill's courage and staunchness, England, when she stood alone, had divided the might of Hitlerite Germany at a time when the rest of Europe was falling flat on its face before Hitler. He said that Great Britain, under Mr. Churchill's leadership, had carried on the fight alone irrespective of existing or potential allies. The Marshal concluded that he knew of few examples in history where the courage of one man had been so important to the future history of the world. He drank a toast to Mr. Churchill, his fighting friend and a brave man.

The Prime Minister, in his reply, toasted Marshal Stalin as the mighty leader of a mighty country, which had taken the full shock of the German war machine, had broken its back, and had driven the tyrants from her soil. He said he knew that in peace no less than in war Marshal Stalin would continue to lead his people from success to success.

Marshal Stalin then proposed the health of the President of the United States. He said that he and Mr. Churchill in their respective countries had had relatively simple decisions. They had been fighting for their very existence against Hitlerite Germany, but there was a third man whose country had not been seriously threatened with invasion, but who had had perhaps a broader conception of national interest and even though his country was not directly imperilled had been the chief forger of the instruments which had led to the mobilization of the world against Hitler. He mentioned in this connection Lend-Lease as one of the President's most remarkable and vital achievements in the formation of the Anti-Hitler combination and in keeping the Allies in the field against Hitler.

The President, in reply to this toast, said he felt the atmosphere at this dinner was as that of a family, and it was in those words that he liked to characterize the relations that existed between our three countries. He said that great changes had occurred in the world during the last three years, and even greater changes were to come. He said that each of the leaders represented here were working in their own way for the interests of their people. He said that fifty years ago there were vast areas of the world where people had little opportunity and no hope, but much had been accomplished, although there were still great areas where people had little opportunity and little hope, and their objectives here were to give every man, woman and child on this earth the possibility of security and well-being.

In a subsequent toast to the alliance between the three great powers, *Marshal Stalin* remarked that it was not so difficult to keep unity in time of war since there was a joint aim to defeat the common enemy which was clear to everyone. He said the difficult task came after the war when diverse interests tended to divide the Allies. He said he was confident that the present alliance would meet this test also and that it was our duty to see that it would, and that our relations in peacetime should be as strong as they had been in war.

The Prime Minister then said he felt we were standing on the crest of a hill with the glories of future possibilities stretching before us. He said that in the modern world the function of leadership was to lead the people out from the forests into the broad sunlit plains of peace and happiness. He felt this prize was nearer our grasp than any time before in history and it would be a tragedy for which history would never forgive us if we let this prize slip from our grasp through inertia or carelessness.

The mood of the American delegates, including Roosevelt and Hopkins, could be described as one of supreme exultation as they left Yalta. They were confident that their British colleagues agreed with them that this had been the most encouraging conference of all, and the immediate response of the principal spokesmen for British and American public opinion added immeasurably to their sense of satisfaction with the job that had been done. As soon as Roosevelt came on board the *Quincy* on Great Bitter Lake (so ominously and perhaps so appropriately named) he received floods of messages telling of the enthusiastic response to the publication of the Yalta communiqués in the United States. One of the cables quoted Herbert Hoover as saying: 'It will offer a great hope to the world.' William L. Shirer called it 'a landmark in human history'. Raymond Gram Swing said: 'No more appropriate news could be conceived to celebrate the birth-

day of Abraham Lincoln.' Senator Barkley cabled: 'Accept my sincere felicitations upon the historic Joint Statement released today. I had it read to the Senate immediately upon release and it made a profound impression. Senator White, Minority Leader, joined me in the expressions of commendation and satisfaction on the floor of the Senate. I regard it as one of the most important steps ever taken to promote peace and happiness in the world.'

Joseph C. Harsch wrote, in the *Christian Science Monitor*: 'The Crimea Conference stands out from previous such conferences because of its mood of decision. The meetings which produced the Atlantic Charter, Casablanca, Teheran, Quebec—all these were dominated, politically, by declarative moods. They were declarations of policy, of aspirations, of intents. But they were not meetings of decision. The meeting at Yalta was plainly dominated by a desire, willingness, and determination to reach solid decisions.'

Hopkins later said to me: 'We really believed in our hearts that this was the dawn of the new day we had all been praying for and talking about for so many years. We were absolutely certain that we had won the first great victory of the peace—and, by "we" I mean *all* of us, the whole civilized human race. The Russians had proved that they could be reasonable and far-seeing and there wasn't any doubt in the minds of the President or any of us that we could live with them and get along with them peacefully for as far into the future as any of us could imagine. But I have to make one amendment to that—I think we all had in our minds the reservation that we could not foretell what the results would be if anything should happen to Stalin. We felt sure that we could count on him to be reasonable and sensible and understanding—but we never could be sure who or what might be in back of him there in the Kremlin.'

CHAPTER XXXV

THE TERRIFIC HEADACHE

SOME time after his return to the United States Hopkins wrote the following memorandum:

The last night before the Yalta conference broke up the President flabbergasted Churchill by telling him for the first time that he was going to fly to Egypt and had arranged for the King of Egypt, Ibn Saud, and Hailie Selassie to hold conferences with him aboard the cruiser in Great Bitter Lake on three successive days. There were a number of people present when the President told Churchill about this and Churchill had no adequate opportunity to ask the President what these visits were all about. Later that night he, Churchill, sought me out, greatly disturbed, and wanted to know what were the President's intentions in relation to these three sovereigns. Fortunately I could tell him I did not know, because I had asked the President the same thing. I had already made up my mind that it was, in the main, a lot of horseplay, and that the President was going to thoroughly enjoy the colourful panoply of the sovereigns of this part of the world who thought that President Roosevelt of the United States could probably cure all their troubles. I did know he intended to talk to Ibn Saud about the Palestine situation. Nothing I said, however, was comforting to Churchill, because he thought we had some deep-laid plot to undermine the British Empire in these areas.

The next day the Prime Minister told the President that he was also going into Egypt after a brief visit to Greece and see each of these sovereigns himself, and had already sent the messages asking them to remain in Egypt for conferences with him immediately after the President had left.

The public aspects of these conferences have been widely written about and I, therefore, do not intend to repeat those here. The only really important thing was the discussion the President had with Ibn Saud about Palestine, and this was short and to the point.

I am sure the President did not realize what kind of man he was going to be entertaining when he invited Ibn Saud to meet him—a man of austere dignity, great power and a born soldier and, above all, an Arabian first, last and all the time. He had spent his life fighting and enjoyed it, and his subjects all enjoy fighting and they don't like the Jews. So, when the President asked Ibn Saud to admit some more Jews into Palestine, indicating that it was such a small percentage of the total population of the Arab world, he was greatly shocked when Ibn Saud, without a smile,

said 'No.' Ibn Saud emphasized the fact that the Jews in Palestine were successful in making the countryside bloom only because American and British capital had been poured in in millions of dollars and said if those same millions had been given to the Arabs they could have done quite as well. He also said that there was a Palestine army of Jews all armed to the teeth, and he remarked that they did not seem to be fighting the Germans, but were aiming at the Arabs. He stated plainly that the Arab world would not permit a further extension beyond the commitment already made for future Jewish settlement in Palestine. He clearly inferred that the Arabs would take up arms before they would consent to that and he, as religious leader of the Arab world, must, naturally, support the Arabs in and about Palestine. The President seemed not to fully comprehend what Ibn Saud was saying to him, for he brought the question up two or three times more and each time Ibn Saud was more determined than before. I fancy Ibn Saud was fully prepared for the President's plea to which he, the President, was wholly committed publicly and privately and by conviction.

There is no doubt that Ibn Saud made a great impression on the President that the Arabs meant business. None of this had anything to do with the merits of the case. I know the conference in relation to Palestine never came to grips with the real issues, but developed into a monologue by Ibn Saud, and I gained the impression that the President was overly impressed by what Ibn Saud said. And I never could reconcile the President's statement at a Press conference later that he had learned more from Ibn Saud about Palestine in five minutes than he had learned in a lifetime —because the only thing he learned which all people well acquainted with the Palestine cause know, is that the Arabs don't want any more Jews in Palestine. They have been threatening the British for years with civil war if the lid is opened any farther and Ibn Saud merely told the President what he had undoubtedly told the British, and anybody else who wanted to ask him, many times before.

The *Quincy* remained at Great Bitter Lake from Monday until Wednesday, February 14, and then proceeded through the Suez Canal to Alexandria, where Churchill came aboard for lunch, this being the last meeting of the two Naval Persons. John G. Winant also came aboard and travelled with Roosevelt on the ship from Alexandria to Algiers.

On the first day out, the ship's newspaper, The U.S.S. *Quincy Star* issued a FLASH! FLASH! bulletin from Guam: 'Pacific fleet Commander Admiral Nimitz announces tonight that a powerful American task force is attacking military targets in and around Tokio.' This was February 15 and a great day for the United States Navy, for it was the first time that an American fleet

had attacked the Japanese home islands, and it represented the beginning of the ultimate payoff for Pearl Harbour. Roosevelt well knew what this meant: the attacking fleet, known as Task Force 58, under the command of Admirals Spruance and Mitscher, was in itself the most powerful force that had ever gone to sea; it consisted of twenty aircraft carriers, all of which had been built during the present war, escorted by some ninety battleships, cruisers, and destroyers. At this same time, as Roosevelt also knew, another huge United States fleet was moving up from the Marianas for the attack on the island of Iwo Jima which began four days later. If this piece of news from the far Pacific created excitement on the *Quincy*, I can report from the other end of the line that the news of the Yalta Conference was received without any appreciable display of emotion by those involved in Task Force 58, with which I happened to be travelling at the time on board the aircraft carrier, U.S.S. *Bennington*. Most interesting of all to the American sailors who were there within range of the Honshu coast was the statement that the United Nations Conference would be held at San Francisco, for this selection of location inspired the hope that 'Maybe now at last the Big Guys will begin to look out our way.'

During the three days between Alexandria and Algiers, Hopkins felt desperately ill and was confined to his cabin, which was inaccessible to Roosevelt. Statements were being prepared by the President and Steve Early for release to the Press at Algiers. One of these related to the curt and abrupt refusal of General de Gaulle to accept Roosevelt's invitation to a meeting. Bohlen brought Hopkins a draft of the proposed statement in which Roosevelt made no attempt to disguise his anger at de Gaulle; Hopkins sent back messages pleading with the President not to lower himself to such a petulant level, and the statement was revised.

Roosevelt, who was tired out himself, had arranged to appear before the Congress immediately after his return to Washington and deliver a speech on the Yalta Conference. (Churchill was to make his report to the House of Commons on February 27.) Roosevelt's speech must be prepared on the *Quincy* during the trip across the Atlantic, and naturally he expected Hopkins to help in its preparation, but Hopkins sent word through Bohlen that he must leave the ship at Algiers and go to Marrakech for a few days' rest and fly from there back to Washington. Although Roosevelt made no particular attempt to persuade Hopkins to change his mind about this, he was disappointed and even displeased. He was sure that Hopkins could get far better care on the *Quincy* than in Marrakech, and he apparently suspected that the desire to leave the ship was due more to boredom than anything else. It was difficult for Roosevelt to imagine anyone feeling miserable on board a ship. But Hopkins dreaded a nine-day voyage across the Atlantic during which he would probably remain confined to his cabin, with seasickness added to his

other ills. So he was glad of a chance to escape, but he had cause later to wish that he had stayed with the ship.

Rosenman had been hastily summoned from London, where the President had sent him to work on the problem of relief for Britain and the liberated countries, and he joined the *Quincy* at Algiers to aid in the preparation of the speech, but Rosenman had no knowledge of what had gone on at Yalta, aside from the announcements that he had read in the newspapers, and neither Steve Early nor Anna Boettiger nor anybody else on board knew much about the full, inside story, or just how much of it should be revealed at this time with due regard for the wishes of the Russians and the British. Thus, with Hopkins gone, Roosevelt had to do all of the real work entirely by himself.

When Hopkins left the *Quincy* to go ashore at Algiers, the President's 'good-bye' to him was not a very amiable one—a circumstance which it is sad to record, for Hopkins never saw his great friend again.

At the same time, the beloved Pa Watson lay ill in his cabin on the *Quincy*, and within two days he was dead. This was an awful blow for Roosevelt. As I have said before, he kept his personal sorrows strictly to himself: he had given no evidence to anyone of his emotions when his mother died—he had seemed to wish not even to talk about it to anyone—and it was the same after the deaths of his old friends and loyal associates, Louis Howe, Marvin McIntyre, and Missy LeHand. But he made no attempt to hide the grief caused him by the loss of Pa Watson. Indeed, the very extent to which he talked about his sadness gave alarm to those who knew him best, for it suggested that he himself was failing. The *Quincy* was not 'a happy ship' on this cruise.

Hopkins remained for four days at the beautiful Taylor villa in Marrakech where he and Roosevelt had stayed after the Casablanca Conference. On February 24 he arrived back in Washington and three days later he flew to the Mayo Clinic, where he remained until April 13. Roosevelt returned to Washington on February 28 and made his speech to the Congress on March 2. Roosevelt delivered this speech sitting down—explaining at the start, 'it makes it a lot easier for me not having to carry about ten pounds of steel around on the bottom of my legs', and so far as I know this was the only time that he ever made public reference to his physical infirmity. He was extremely casual in this speech, ad-libbing a great deal of it. He made no claims to the achievement of perfection at Yalta. He said: 'It has been a long journey. I hope you will all agree that it was a fruitful one. Speaking in all frankness, the question of whether it is entirely fruitful or not lies to a great extent in your hands. For unless you here in the halls of the American Congress--with the support of the American people—concur in the decisions reached at Yalta, and give them your active support, the meeting will not have produced lasting results.'

After this speech, disillusionment began to set in. Speaking of the voting procedure in the Security Council, Roosevelt said: 'It is not yet possible to announce the terms of it publicly, but it will be in a very short time.' There was some question as to why this could not have been announced before—and there began to be speculation as to whether there were other secret agreements as yet unrevealed. On March 5 announcement of the voting formula was made by Stettinius from Mexico, where he had gone from Yalta for the Chapultepec Conference. Press opinion on this was very much divided, most of those who criticized the veto provision interpreting it as a 'sell-out' to Stalin. The most important criticism came not from the irreconcilable isolationists, but from the 'perfectionists' who wanted the peace to be pure and unadulterated, and it was this criticism which irritated Roosevelt most acutely—perhaps because he himself was a perfectionist at heart. By the middle of March a situation had developed in Roumania which indicated that the Russians were determined to set up governments in Eastern Europe in conformance with their own interpretation of the word 'friendly' and without regard for the principles of the Atlantic Charter which had just been reaffirmed. There began to be editorial murmurings that Roumania might be providing the first test of the good faith of the Yalta agreements. However, Roumania was a Nazi satellite country, and at that stage there were few who could become greatly concerned about its fate. But Poland was another matter. Poland was not only the first European country to have been ravaged in this way—it remained always as a disturbing reminder of the cynical Molotov-Ribbentrop pact. And now it was beginning to appear evident that a complete deadlock had developed among the British, Russian, and American conferees in Moscow over the composition of the Provisional Polish Government, and that the Russians were demanding that the Lublin Government, which was entirely under their control and unrepresentative of any other Polish factions, should participate in the San Francisco Conference without further argument. Then it was announced that Molotov would not go to San Francisco, the Russian delegation there to be headed by Gromyko. Since Eden was to head the British delegation, and Stettinius the American, Molotov's abstention was generally interpreted as a blunt confession that the Soviet Government did not attach much importance to the conference. This was a very serious blasting of the high hopes which Yalta had inspired that the peoples' representatives would actually build at San Francisco the firm foundation for the permanent structure of world peace; but the structure would obviously lack one of its four cornerstones without Russia. There was now a growing feeling of uneasiness, born of the unknown and the inexplicable, regarding the true relationship between the Soviet Union and the United States, Great Britain, and other United Nations. (Hopkins, in the hospital, was 'bewildered' by these developments, as he

stated very plainly to Stalin in conversations recorded in the next chapter.) It was beginning to be feared that a monstrous fraud had been perpetrated at Yalta, with Roosevelt and Churchill as the unwitting dupes. Then, suddenly, there came a news break which made the whole situation look very much uglier.

Roosevelt had announced that the American delegation at San Francisco would be completely bipartisan—he was not going to make the mistake that Wilson had made in failing to take any Republicans to Versailles; Congress would be represented by Senators Tom Connally and Arthur Vandenberg and by Representatives Sol Bloom and Charles A. Eaton. On March 23 the President summoned members of this delegation to the White House and informed them in strictest confidence of the arrangement made at Yalta whereby the United States and Britain would support the Russian request for three votes, in return for which Russia would support the United States request for three votes if it were put forward. This important piece of information was conveyed either accidentally or through a deliberate 'leak' to the *New York Herald Tribune* and was printed on March 29. The White House and the State Department were immediately besieged by newspapermen demanding confirmation or denial of this story and the White House was compelled to issue a statement admitting that it was true. Then the Press quite naturally wanted to know why had it been kept a secret—and how many more secrets were left over from Yalta? And if Russia had been granted votes for two of her republics, would she now demand votes for all the others? Roosevelt was in Washington for only a few hours at this time, *en route* from Hyde Park to Warm Springs—Hopkins was still at the Mayo Clinic—and Stettinius had to bear the brunt of the insistent and vociferous questioning. It was plainly apparent that not even his own Assistant Secretaries in the State Department had heard of the arrangement until the news was broken in the Press. Indeed, the State Department had been conducting an 'educational' campaign intended to emphasize the absolute equality of the United Nations voting procedure which gave the little fellow exactly the same rights as the big one.

This was one of the worst all-around botches of the war and a seemingly unnecessary one. It is understandable that Roosevelt might have wanted to withhold announcement of this somewhat questionable arrangement from the original Yalta communiqué so that it would not mitigate the effect of the overall achievement; even so, it would have been far better to have included it in that communiqué and get it over with. By waiting, as Roosevelt did, to figure out a way to release it under the most favourable possible circumstances, he succeeded only in having it burst out under the worst possible circumstances. This was the aspect of it that was inexplicable—obviously it was going to be revealed anyway at San Francisco four weeks later,

and Roosevelt, of all people, had reason to know that the moment he made the facts known however confidentially to a group of delegates there was danger of leakage to the Press. It can only be said that this time he made a mistake which was thoroughly uncharacteristic of him—he underrated the intelligence of the American people—and that was the mistake that normally he left to his opponents. Actually, the greatest part of the resultant uproar was not concerned with the concession to Russia, but with the utter insulting absurdity of the American claim for three votes. All question of the United States demeaning itself by making such a demand was immediately and happily dropped. As for the Russian request, that was not considered a matter of serious importance or as a cause for any undue alarm. The *Herald Tribune*, which had produced the first eruption, expressed the healthy, intelligent attitude in an editorial: 'While an assembly "packed" by as many as sixteen Russian votes would obviously be inadmissible, a difference of two or three, one way or the other, in an international assembly of sixty or seventy members could have no possible practical significance. Even as matters stand, the United States will be able to count on the sympathetic votes of the Philippines, Cuba and others quite as surely as the United Kingdom will be able to count on those of the dominions and almost as surely as the Soviets will be able to count on White Russia and the Ukraine. To make a tortured issue out of such inconsequentialities would have been to endow them with an altogether fictitious importance.' However, substantial damage had been done, and from then on the very word 'Yalta' came to be associated in the public's mind with secret and somehow shameful agreements. When the Far Eastern discussions were finally disclosed they were viewed with intense suspicion as further evidence of devious dealings, although there had been good and sufficient reason to withhold these until Russia was ready to go into action against Japan.

It was during this last week in March that I saw Roosevelt for the last time. I had just returned from a long trip around the Pacific during which I had gone to Manila at the President's request to talk to General MacArthur in an attempt to learn something about his ideas for the future military government of Japan. It was extremely difficult for any emissary from Washington to get through to MacArthur in those days. It was reported that even generals from the War Department on inspection tours were being refused permission to enter the Philippine theatre, and those who did were as carefully chaperoned as if they were attempting to visit the Russian Front. I, however, being an obscure and relatively inoffensive civilian, encountered no difficulties and was most hospitably received. General MacArthur talked to me for nearly three hours in the temporary headquarters that he had set up in the awful, heart-rending desolation of Manila, and I came away enormously impressed with the extent of his understanding of the Orient and the breadth of his views.

On March 24 I went to see the President in his office and then walked over with him to the White House proper, where we had lunch with Anna Boettiger on the sun porch on the roof above the South Portico. I said that, while I had no idea what decisions were being made as to who would be supreme commander in the Pacific when the forces under MacArthur and those under Nimitz merged for the final assault on Japan, I believed strongly that MacArthur was the ideal choice for Military Governor of Japan after the surrender—and victory in the Pacific appeared a great deal nearer than I had imagined before I made this trip. I told the President what I had heard MacArthur say on this subject, and Roosevelt observed, rather wistfully: 'I wish that he would sometimes tell some of these things to *me*.' He then asked me to put my observations in the form of a short memorandum, and I did so as follows:

1. General MacArthur's intelligence service on the enemy and enemy-held territory is superb, due largely to the Filipino guerrilla organization which was organized and directed under his command

2. On the other hand, I was shocked by the inaccuracy of the information held by General MacArthur and his immediate entourage about the formulation of high policy in Washington. There are unmistakable evidences of an acute persecution complex at work. To hear some of the Staff officers talk one would think that the War Department, the State Department, the Joint Chiefs of Staff—and, possibly, even the White House itself—are under the domination of 'Communists and British Imperialists'. This strange misapprehension produces an obviously unhealthy state of mind, and also the most unfortunate public relations policy that I have seen in any theatre of war.

3. From the strictly military point of view, it seems to me that the operations in this theatre have been magnificent. The quality and the morale of the troops in the field are exceptionally high. I could detect no evidences of serious criticism of the co-ordination and co-operation of land, sea and air forces.

Following is a brief summary of General MacArthur's views on the future handling of Japan, which he expressed to me at considerable length and with great positiveness and eloquence:

Tracing the history of Japan, particularly in the past century, the General expressed the conviction that the 'imperial sanctity' idea is a myth fabricated by the military for their own purposes. Essential to the continuance of this myth, he said, is the legend of invincibility; the Emperor remains a god only as long as the army and navy are all-conquering. The total destruction of Japanese military power, therefore, can involve (for the Japanese civil population) destruction of the concept of Hirohito's

divinity. This will result in a spiritual vacuum and an opportunity for the introduction of new concepts. The Japanese people will have inevitable respect for as well as fear of the instruments of their own defeat. Believing that might makes right, they will conclude that we of the U.S.A. must be right. Furthermore, the prestige throughout Asia that we have established by our Philippine policy and which will be vastly increased by conquest of Japan will make us the greatest influence on the future development of Asia. If we exert that influence in an imperialistic manner, or for the sole purpose of commercial advantage, then we shall lose our golden opportunity; but if our influence and our strength are expressed in terms of essential liberalism we shall have the friendship and the co-operation of the Asiatic peoples far into the future.

It seemed to be General MacArthur's view that the Japanese civil population if treated with stern justice and strength would be more capable of eventual redemption than are the Germans.

While I was with the President that day he talked about the speech he was to give on Jefferson Day, about two weeks hence, and his speech for the opening of the San Francisco Conference. He laughed and said: 'You know Steve [Early] doesn't think I ought to open that conference—just in case it should fail. He thinks I ought to wait to see how it goes, and then, if it is a success, I can go out and make the closing address, taking all the credit for it. But I'm going to be there at the start and at the finish, too. All those people from all over the world are paying this country a great honour by coming here and I want to tell them how much we appreciate it.' For the Jefferson Day speech he asked me to look up some Jefferson quotations on the subject of science. He said: 'There aren't many people who realize it, but Jefferson was a scientist as well as a democrat, and there were some things he said that need to be repeated now, because science is going to be more important than ever in the working out of the future world.'

The Jefferson quotation that I found, and that Roosevelt used in his undelivered speech, referred to 'the brotherly spirit of science, which unites into one family all its votaries of whatever grade, and however widely dispersed throughout the different quarters of the globe'.

I did not know it at the time, but I realized later that when Roosevelt spoke of the importance of science in the future he was undoubtedly thinking of the imminence of the atomic age. He said in this last speech: 'Today we are faced with the pre-eminent fact that, if civilization is to survive, we must cultivate the science of human relationships—the ability of all peoples, of all kinds, to live together and work together in the same world, at peace.'

I wished him a happy holiday in Warm Springs, then went down to the Cabinet Room—where Hopkins, Rosenman, and I had worked so many

Mrs. Anna Boettiger (the President's daughter), Section Officer Sarah Oliver (daughter of the Prime Minister), President Roosevelt, Mr. Churchill and Harry Hopkins on board the U.S.S. *Quincy* on Great Bitter Lake after the Yalta Conference (*see page* 858).

long hours—and I wrote the memorandum on MacArthur, then walked to the Carlton Hotel and told my wife that the President was in much worse shape than I had ever seen him before. He had seemed unnaturally quiet and even querulous—never before had I found myself in the strange position of carrying on most of the conversation with him; and, while he had perked up a little at lunch under the sparkling influence of his daughter Anna, I had come away from the White House profoundly depressed. I thought it was a blessing that he could get away for a while to Warm Springs, and I was sure the trip across the country to San Francisco would do him a lot of good. The thought never occurred to me that this time he might fail to rally as he always had. I couldn't believe it when somebody told me he was dead. Like everybody else, I listened and listened to the radio, waiting for the announcement—probably in his own gaily reassuring voice—that it had all been a big mistake, that the banking crisis and the war were over and everything was going to be 'fine—grand—perfectly bully'. But when the realization finally did get through all I could think of was: 'It finally crushed him. He couldn't stand up under it any longer.' The 'it' was the awful responsibility that had been piling up and piling up for so many years. The fears and the hopes of hundreds of millions of human beings throughout the world had been bearing down on the mind of one man, until the pressure was more than mortal tissue could withstand, and then he said: 'I have a terrific headache', and then lost consciousness, and died. 'A massive cerebral haemorrhage,' said the doctors—and 'massive' was the right word.

The morning after Roosevelt's death Hopkins telephoned me from St. Mary's Hospital in Rochester, Minnesota. He just wanted to talk to somebody. There was no sadness in his tone; he talked with a kind of exaltation as though he had suddenly experienced the intimations of immortality. He said: 'You and I have got something great that we can take with us all the rest of our lives. It's a great realization. Because we know it's *true* what so many people believed about him and what made them love him. The President never let them down. That's what you and I can remember. Oh, we all know he could be exasperating, and he could seem to be temporizing and delaying, and he'd get us all worked up when we thought he was making too many concessions to expediency. But all of that was in the little things, the unimportant things—and he knew exactly how little and how unimportant they really were. But in the big things—all of the things that were of real, permanent importance—he never let the people down.'

The next afternoon, Saturday, we went to the funeral service in the East Room of the White House. I was sitting on a little gilt chair at the extreme right of the assemblage when I felt a hand squeeze my shoulder. I looked up and it was Hopkins, who had flown in from Rochester. He himself looked like death, the skin of his face a dreadful cold white with apparently no flesh

z

left under it. I believed that he now had nothing left to live for, that his life had ended with Roosevelt's.

When President Truman came into the East Room nobody stood up, and I'm sure this modest man did not even notice this discourtesy or, if he did, understood that the people present could not yet associate him with his high office; all they could think of was that the President was dead. But everybody stood up when Mrs. Roosevelt came in.

After the service Hopkins asked my wife and me to come to his house in Georgetown. He went to bed and I sat with him for a long time and listened as he talked. He didn't seem like death now. Fire was shooting out of his sharp eyes in their sunken sockets. I drastically revised my impression of earlier that afternoon that he had nothing left to live for. 'God damn it,' he said, 'now we've got to get to work on our own. This is where we've really got to begin. We've had it too easy all this time, because we knew he was there, and we had the privilege of being able to get to him. Whatever we thought was the matter with the world, whatever we felt ought to be done about it, we could take our ideas to him, and if thought there was any merit in them, or if anything that we said got him started on a train of thought of his own, then we'd see him go ahead and do it, and no matter how tremendous it might be or how idealistic he wasn't scared of it. Well—he isn't there now, and we've got to find a way to do things by ourselves.'

Hopkins talked at length of the new administration. He said: 'I'm pretty sure that Jimmy Byrnes and Henry Wallace and Harold Ickes are saying right now that they'd be President of the United States today if it weren't for me. But this time I didn't have anything to do with it. I'm certain that the President had made up his mind on Truman long before I got back to the White House last year. I think he would have preferred Bill Douglas, because he knew him better and he always liked Bill's toughness. But nobody really influential was pushing for Douglas. I think he'd gone off fishing out in Oregon or some place. And Bob Hannegan was certainly pushing for Harry Truman, and the President believed he could put him over at the Convention. So the President told him to go ahead and even put it in writing when Bob asked him to. People seemed to think that Truman was just suddenly pulled out of a hat—but that wasn't true. The President had had his eye on him for a long time. The Truman Committee record was good— he'd got himself known and liked around the country—and above all he was very popular in the Senate. That was the biggest consideration. The President wanted somebody that would help him when he went up there and asked them to ratify the peace.'

Hopkins said he was going to turn in his resignation at once, and he thought the whole Cabinet should do likewise and get out. He made exceptions of Stimson and Forrestal, who should obviously remain to the end of the war,

and he said he guessed Morgenthau ought to stay long enough to see the next bond drive through. But, he said, 'Truman has got to have his own people around him, not Roosevelt's. If we were around, we'd always be looking at him and he'd know we were thinking, "The *President* wouldn't do it that way!"' Hopkins predicted that the last one to quit the Cabinet voluntarily would be Henry Wallace.

That night we boarded the funeral train for Hyde Park. (Hopkins felt too exhausted to make this last, sad trip.) It was the same train with the same crew that we had travelled with on campaign expeditions.

In the rose garden that Sunday morning I was standing behind General Marshall and Admiral King. Across the garden was a detachment of cadets from West Point, and on the other three sides were lines of soldiers, sailors, and marines, wearing ribbons that meant Cassino, and the Persian Gulf, and the Solomons Slot, and the bocage country, and Leyte, and Medjez El Bab, and Midway and Ploesti and Iwo Jima and the Hump. In a memorial to Roosevelt in the soldiers' magazine, *Yank,* they wrote: 'He was the Commander-in-Chief, not only of our armed forces, but of our generation.'

Standing there in the rose garden I could see over the high hedge the top of a lilac bush that was just beginning to bloom, and I thought of what Walt Whitman had written eighty years ago almost to the day at the end of another war and of another President's life.

As I said near the beginning of this book, I could never really understand what was going on in Roosevelt's heavily forested interior. But, as a result of my observation of him and the time that I have had to digest that observation and the opinions of others, I am sure of one thing: although crippled physically and prey to various infections, he was spiritually the healthiest man I have ever known. He was gloriously and happily free of the various forms of psychic maladjustment which are called by such names as inhibition, complex, phobia. His mind, if not always orderly, bore no traces of paralysis and neither did his emotional constitution; and his heart was certainly in the right place. Furthermore, he was entirely conscious of these extraordinary advantages that he enjoyed, and this consciousness gave him the power to soar above circumstances which would have held other men earthbound.

CHAPTER XXXVI

THE LAST MISSION

IN his first talks with President Truman after Roosevelt's death Hopkins said that he would remain in Washington for a few weeks—he had set the date for his retirement from Government service as May 12—and would make available to the new Chief Executive every scrap of knowledge that he possessed concerning Roosevelt's unrecorded plans and hopes and apprehensions for the future—and there was, of course, a considerable amount of knowledge that only he possessed. Truman said that he was genuinely sorry to see Hopkins go, and there is no doubt that he meant just this, for he had great respect for this ardent man with whom he had been associated in the earliest days of the relief programme and, as a result of the work of the Truman Committee, he knew better than most the real nature of Hopkins's contribution to the vast organization of the United States for total war and total victory. He told Hopkins that he wanted him to stay on at his side to give the same kind of advice and counsel and assistance that he had given the late President. But Hopkins was obviously at the end of his physical rope. He said that he would require a very long rest before he could be capable of doing any real work, and that then he intended to devote himself to the sedentary occupation of writing his memoirs.

During the days before the San Francisco Conference, Hopkins wrote two short, personal memoranda. The first of them contained the following footnote:

> Stalin sent for Ambassador Harriman soon after he learned of President Roosevelt's death and told Harriman that he wanted to give some immediate assurance to the American people to indicate his, Stalin's, desire to continue on a co-operative basis with this country. Harriman promptly told him that the thing the American people would appreciate most would be to send Molotov to the San Francisco Conference. Stalin asked Harriman if he was merely speaking for himself or was he sure that our Government would support that request and said that he, Stalin, was prepared to tell Molotov to go.

> Molotov was present at the conference and indicated his reluctance to go, but Stalin told both Harriman and Molotov that Molotov would go to San Francisco. Harriman cabled this information home and the State Department prepared a cable from Truman to Stalin saying we would be glad to welcome Molotov here.

The other memorandum was inspired by an 'inside' story in Drew Pearson's column in the *Washington Post* on April 22. Pearson had written:

'Though it may get official denial the real fact is that American advance patrols on Friday, April 13th, one day after President Roosevelt's death, were in Potsdam, which is to Berlin what the Bronx is to New York City', but 'the next day withdrew from the Berlin suburbs to the River Elbe about 50 miles south. This withdrawal was ordered largely because of a previous agreement with the Russians that they were to occupy Berlin and because of their insistence that the agreement be kept.' Pearson stated that this agreement had been made at Yalta. Hopkins indignantly wrote:

This story by Drew Pearson is absolutely untrue. There was no agreement made at Yalta whatever that the Russians should enter Berlin first. Indeed, there was no discussion of that whatever. The Chiefs of Staff had agreed with the Russian Chiefs of Staff and Stalin on the general strategy which was that both of us were going to push as hard as we could.

It is equally untrue that General Bradley paused on the Elbe River at the request of the Russians so that the Russians could break through to Berlin first. Bradley did get a division well out towards Potsdam, but it far outreached itself; supplies were totally inadequate and anyone who knows anything about it knows that we would have taken Berlin had we been able to do so. This would have been a great feather in the Army's cap, but for Drew Pearson now to say that the President agreed that the Russians were to take Berlin is utter nonsense.

During those last weeks in Washington, Hopkins remained at home, most of the time in bed. Old friends and associates who came to see him included: T. V. Soong, Leon Henderson, Jean Monnet, Sam Rosenman, Anthony Eden, David Niles, Oliver Lyttleton, Frances (Mrs. Edwin M.) Watson, Morris Ernst, Grace Tully, Dr. Herbert Evatt, Isador Lubin, Colonel James Roosevelt, Laurence Steinhardt, Frank Walker, Lord Halifax, Howard Hunter, Steve Early, Felix Frankfurter, General Marshall, Bernard Baruch, Aubrey Williams, James Forrestal, Walter Lippmann, General Arnold, Edward Stettinius, John J. McCloy, Robert Lovett, Admiral Leahy, Robert E. Hannegan, General Somervell, Donald Nelson, Admiral King, James F. Byrnes, Raymond Gram Swing, Joseph E. Davies, Mrs. Eleanor Roosevelt.

On May 1 the Hamburg radio declared that Adolf Hitler was dead. On May 2 the Russians captured Berlin and hostilities in Italy ended officially following the unconditional surrender of Field-Marshal von Kesselring.

On May 4 all German forces in the Netherlands, North-West Germany, and Denmark surrendered to Field-Marshal Montgomery's 21st Army Group, and General Patch's U.S. Seventh Army, having captured Berchtesgaden, drove through the Brenner Pass and joined up with General Clark's Fifth Army.

On that day Hopkins received the following telegram from Eden, Molotov, and Stettinius in San Francisco: 'At a dinner last night we three drank a special toast to you in sincere recognition of the outstanding part you personally have played in bringing our three countries together in the common cause. We regret that you are not with us at this moment of victory. With our affectionate personal regards.'

Hopkins replied somewhat sententiously to this: 'Thanks so much for your cordial message. This day of victory over the evil forces of mankind was won by millions of Allied soldiers and sailors. It is the prelude, not only of the complete destruction of the military might of Japan, but also of the building of a sure foundation of peace in which the common people of the earth shall share the fruits of the victory.'

On May 8 Hopkins cabled Churchill: 'I want you to know that I have been thinking of you very much today', and Churchill replied: 'Your message reached me while I was sending one to you. Among all those in the grand alliance, warriors or statesmen who struck deadly blows at the enemy and brought peace nearer, you will ever hold an honoured place.' With these and other encomiums—including one from General Marshall which has been quoted in an earlier chapter—to cover the scars of the many wounds that he had received, Hopkins felt that he could now retire for ever from public life and have some fun. However, less than a week after VE-Day, it seemed that the San Francisco Conference was going on the rocks. Molotov and Eden were both headed for home. Harriman and Bohlen were on an airplane flying eastward across the continent with a sense of despair in their hearts. They asked each other whether there was any conceivable way of saving the situation. With considerable hesitancy, Bohlen suggested the possibility that President Truman might send Hopkins to Moscow to talk things out directly with Stalin and Molotov. Bohlen's hesitancy was due to the thought that Harriman, as American Ambassador in Moscow, might resent the idea of Hopkins invading his own province and taking over his duties in direct negotiation with the Soviet Government; but Harriman was enthusiastic about the suggestion and, on his arrival in Washington, went immediately with Bohlen to see Hopkins in his Georgetown house to present this suggestion to him. Both Bohlen and Harriman have told me that Hopkins's response was wonderful to behold. Although he appeared too ill even to get out of bed and walk across 'N' Street, the mere intimation of a flight to Moscow converted him into the traditional old fire horse at the sound of the alarm. But he expressed the despondent conviction that Truman would never agree to send him on this mission.

Harriman then went to the White House and presented the suggestion to the President, who said he was much interested in the idea, but would need some time to think it over. Several anxious days followed, with Hopkins

fearing that it would all come to nothing, but then Truman sent for him and asked him if he felt capable of making the long journey; Hopkins's reply was an immediate, enthusiastic affirmative.

He left Washington on May 23, less than two weeks after his retirement from Government service. On this trip, the war in Europe being over, he was accompanied by his wife, and also by Harriman and Bohlen. They flew first to Paris and then straight across Germany. When Hopkins looked down at the ruins of Berlin, he said: 'It's another Carthage.' They arrived in Moscow on the evening of May 25. The first meeting in the Kremlin was at 8.00 p.m. on May 26. Present were: Stalin, Molotov, and Pavlov, and Hopkins, Harriman, and Bohlen. The full record of this meeting follows:

After an exchange of amenities during which Marshal Stalin expressed his great pleasure on seeing Mr. Hopkins again, there was a brief conversation concerning Mr. Hopkins's flight in over Germany.

Mr. Hopkins asked Mr. Molotov if he had recovered from the battle of San Francisco.

Mr. Molotov replied that he did not recall any battles, but merely arguments at San Francisco.

Mr. Hopkins then said before he told Marshal Stalin the reason why President Truman had asked him to come to Moscow, he thought the Marshal would be interested in a brief description of President Roosevelt's state of mind just prior to his death. He said that on the way back from Yalta it had been clear to him that President Roosevelt was very tired and that his energy was on the decline. On the other hand, on the morning of his death he had done a good deal of work and had written a number of important letters relating to domestic and foreign policies. None of his doctors had expected he would have a stroke. In fact his principal doctor, Admiral McIntire, had not even been at Warm Springs. The President never regained consciousness after his stroke and had died without any suffering whatsoever. Many of those who had been closest to him had felt that his quick, easy death was really preferable to his lingering on as a hopeless invalid. Mr. Hopkins said that the President had died fully confident of the victory which was in sight.

Marshal Stalin observed that Lenin had also died of a cerebral haemorrhage following a previous stroke which had left his hand paralysed.

Mr. Hopkins said that on the trip home from Yalta the President had frequently reviewed with him the results of the Crimea Conference and that he had come away from that Conference with renewed confidence that the United States and the Soviet Union could work together in peace as they had in war. President Roosevelt on the trip home had frequently spoken of the respect and admiration he had for Marshal Stalin, and he

was looking forward to their next meeting, which the President hoped
would be in Berlin.

Marshal Stalin remarked that he recalled the toast at the Crimea Conference to their next meeting in Berlin.

Mr. Hopkins said that he recalled his first meeting with the Marshal in
July, 1941, during the troubled and anxious days of the German offensive.
He said he remembered vividly the frankness with which Marshal Stalin
had told him of the Soviet position and of the unalterable determination
of the Soviet Union to wage war against Germany until final victory was
assured. He had returned to the United States and conveyed to President
Roosevelt his own conviction that the Soviet Union would hold fast, and
President Roosevelt had thereupon initiated the programme of assistance
to the Soviet Union. At that time most people believed that a German
victory was inevitable, but President Roosevelt, in spite of all such opinions, had decided otherwise, and through his leadership he had put
through a programme of aid to Russia.

Marshal Stalin observed that at that time there had been many doubts
of the ability of the Soviet Union to keep going.

Mr. Hopkins said that although in 1941 the United States was not in
the war, President Roosevelt had already decided that Hitler was just as
much an enemy of the United States as he was of Great Britain and the
Soviet Union.

Mr. Hopkins then said that a few days ago President Truman had sent
for him and had asked him to come to Moscow to have a talk with
Marshal Stalin. There were a number of things that he and Mr. Harriman
hoped to discuss with Marshal Stalin and Mr. Molotov while he was in
Moscow, but before going into those specific questions he wished to tell
the Marshal of the real reason why the President had asked him to come,
and that was the question of the fundamental relationship between the
United States and the Soviet Union. Two months ago there had been
overwhelming sympathy among the American people for the Soviet
Union and complete support for President Roosevelt's policies which the
Marshal knew so well. This sympathy and support came primarily because of the brilliant achievements of the Soviet Union in the war and
partly from President Roosevelt's leadership and the magnificent way in
which our two countries had worked together to bring about the defeat
of Germany. The American people at that time hoped and confidently
believed that the two countries could work together in peace as well as
they had in war. Mr. Hopkins said there had always been a small minority,
the Hearsts and the McCormicks, who had been against the policy of co-
operation with the Soviet Union. These men had also been bitter political
enemies of President Roosevelt, but had never had any backing from the

American people, as was shown by the fact that against their bitter opposition President Roosevelt had been four times elected President. He said he did not intend to discuss this small minority, but to discuss the general state of American opinion and particularly the present attitude of the millions of Americans who had supported President Roosevelt's policy in regard to the Soviet Union and who believed that despite different political and economic ideology of the two countries, the United States and the Soviet Union could work together after the war in order to bring about a secure peace for humanity. He said he wished to assure the Marshal with all the earnestness at his command that this body of American public opinion who had been the constant support of the Roosevelt policies were seriously disturbed about their relations with Russia. In fact, in the last six weeks deterioration of public opinion had been so serious as to affect adversely the relations between our two countries. He said he wished to emphasize that this change had occurred in the very people who had supported to the hilt Roosevelt's policy of co-operation with the Soviet Union. He said that for the moment he was not going into the reasons why this had occurred, or the merits of the case, but merely wished to emphasize that it was a fact. The friends of Roosevelt's policy and of the Soviet Union were alarmed and worried at the present trend of events, and did not quite understand why, but it was obvious to them that if present trends continued unchecked the entire structure of world co-operation and relations with the Soviet Union which President Roosevelt and the Marshal had laboured so hard to build would be destroyed. Prior to his departure President Truman had expressed to him his great anxiety at the present situation and also his desire to continue President Roosevelt's policy of working with the Soviet Union and his intention to carry out in fact as well as in spirit all the arrangements, both formal and informal, which President Roosevelt and Marshal Stalin had worked out together. Mr. Hopkins added that, as the Marshal knew, he had not been well and he would not be in Moscow unless he had felt the situation was serious. He also said he would not have come had he not believed that the present trend could be halted and a common basis found to go forward in the future.

Mr. Hopkins said that it was not simple or easy to put a finger on the precise reasons for this deterioration, but he must emphasize that without the support of public opinion and particularly of the supporters of President Roosevelt it would be very difficult for President Truman to carry forward President Roosevelt's policy. He said that, as the Marshal was aware, the cardinal basis of President Roosevelt's policy which the American people had fully supported had been the concept that the interests of the United States were world wide and not confined to North and

South America and the Pacific Ocean, and it was this concept that had
led to the many conferences concerning the peace of the world which
President Roosevelt had had with Marshal Stalin. President Roosevelt
had believed that the Soviet Union had likewise worldwide interests and
that the two countries could work out together any political or economic
considerations at issue between them. After the Yalta Conference it looked
as though we were well on the way to reaching a basic understanding on
all questions of foreign affairs of interest to our respective countries, in
regard to the treatment of Germany, Japan and the question of setting
up a world security organization, to say nothing of the long-term interests
between the United States and the U.S.S.R. He said in a country like
ours public opinion is affected by specific incidents, and in this case the
deterioration in public opinion in regard to our relations with the Soviet
Union had been centred in our inability to carry into effect the Yalta
Agreement on Poland. There were also a train of events, each unimportant in themselves, which had grown up around the Polish question,
which contributed to the deterioration in public opinion. President Truman feels, and so does the American public, although they are not familiar
with all the details, a sense of bewilderment at our inability to solve the
Polish question.

Marshal Stalin replied that the reason for the failure on the Polish
question was that the Soviet Union desired to have a friendly Poland,
but that Great Britain wanted to revive the system of cordon sanitaire on
the Soviet borders.

Mr. Hopkins replied that neither the Government nor the people of
the United States had any such intention.

Marshal Stalin replied he was speaking only of England and said that
the British Conservatives did not desire to see a Poland friendly to the
Soviet Union.

Mr. Hopkins stated that the United States would desire a Poland friendly
to the Soviet Union, and in fact desired to see friendly countries all along
the Soviet borders.

Marshal Stalin replied if that be so we can easily come to terms in
regard to Poland.

Mr. Hopkins said that during his visit here there were a number of
specific questions that he and Mr. Harriman hoped to discuss with Marshal
Stalin and Mr. Molotov, but that the general statement he had just made
concerning public opinion in the United States was the principal cause
of anxiety at the present time. He said he had wished to state frankly and
as forcibly as he knew how to Marshal Stalin the importance that he,
personally, attached to the present trend of events, and that he felt that
the situation would get rapidly worse unless we could clear up the Polish

matter. He had therefore been glad to hear the Marshal say that he thought the question could be settled.

Marshal Stalin replied that in his opinion it was best to settle it, but not if the British Conservatives attempted to revive the *cordon sanitaire*.

Mr. Hopkins said that he had in mind the other following questions to discuss with Marshal Stalin while he was in Moscow: (1) The desire of President Truman to meet Marshal Stalin in order to discuss all of the problems arising out of the end of war in Europe and the time and place of such a meeting.

Marshal Stalin said that he had already replied to President Truman concerning the place of meeting and he had suggested the region of Berlin.

Mr. Hopkins said that that message must have come in after he had left, and Marshal Stalin instructed Mr. Molotov to give a copy to Mr. Hopkins and Ambassador Harriman.

Mr. Hopkins said the second question he desired to discuss was the setting up of the Control Council for Germany. General Eisenhower had already been appointed the American representative on the Control Council and he hoped that at an early date the Soviet representative would be named so that the Council could meet and get to work.

Marshal Stalin apparently had not heard of the appointment of General Eisenhower and stated that Marshal Zhukov would be appointed the Soviet representative on the Control Council for Germany. He implied that this appointment would be announced shortly.

Mr. Hopkins said the third question he wished to discuss was that of the Pacific War and the future relations of the United States and Soviet Union to China. He said that although he realized the answer would depend on a good many considerations, it would be most useful to the American military authorities if he could take back some idea of the approximate date of the entry of the Soviet Union into the war in the Pacific.

Marshal Stalin said he would discuss that question with his advisors and let Mr. Hopkins know.

Mr. Hopkins concluded that there was, of course, the Polish question, which he hoped to discuss here. He added that if Marshal Stalin for his part had any political questions concerning the United States which were worrying him, he would, of course, be glad to discuss them.

Marshal Stalin replied that they had, in fact, several disturbing questions on their minds in regard to the United States. He added that he was very glad that the President had sent Mr. Hopkins to Moscow and thus give him this opportunity to explore all these questions.

Mr. Hopkins stated that he would certainly not have gotten out of bed

to come to Moscow had he not believed that the future well-being of hundreds of millions of people depended on the relationship of the United States and the Soviet Union, nor would he have come had he not believed that any difficulties could be reconciled.

Marshal Stalin said he hoped that Mr. Hopkins's views would prove to be right.

Mr. Hopkins said he would stay here as long as it was necessary to accomplish what could be accomplished, although naturally he did not wish to be away too long.

Marshal Stalin said he was entirely at Mr. Hopkins's service and now that war in Europe was over he had more time at his disposal than he had, for example, a year ago.

Mr. Hopkins said he hoped the Russians would find the body of Hitler.

Marshal Stalin replied that in his opinion Hitler was not dead, but hiding somewhere. He said the Soviet doctors thought they had identified the body of Goebbels and Hitler's chauffeur, but that he, personally, even doubted if Goebbels was dead, and said the whole matter was strange and the various talks of funerals and burials struck him as being very dubious. He said he thought that Borman, Goebbels, Hitler, and probably Krebs, had escaped and were in hiding.

Mr. Hopkins said that he knew the Germans had several very large submarines, but that no trace of these had been found. He said he hoped we would track Hitler down wherever he might be.

Marshall Stalin said he also knew of those submarines which had been running back and forth between Germany and Japan, taking gold and negotiable assets from Germany to Japan. He added that this had been done with the connivance of Switzerland. He said he had ordered his intelligence service to look into the matter of these submarines, but so far they had failed to discover any trace, and therefore he thought it was possible that Hitler and company had gone in them to Japan.

Ambassador Harriman then said he wished to observe that President Truman in selecting Mr. Hopkins had chosen a man who, as the Marshal knew, had not only been very close to President Roosevelt, but personally was one of the leading proponents of the policy of co-operation with the Soviet Union. President Truman had sent him to have the kind of frank talk with Marshal Stalin that we all knew Marshal Stalin liked to have. Ambassador Harriman continued that we had, as Marshal Stalin knew, very intimate relations with Great Britain which had been developed since the American Revolution and that the Soviet Union, of course, had their special relations with Great Britain, and that although President Roosevelt had always felt that the three powers had a special responsibility, nevertheless it was obviously desirable that the United States and

the Soviet Union should talk alone on matters of special interest to them and that that was also one of the reasons for Mr. Hopkins's visit.

Marshal Stalin said he thought the Ambassador's remarks were correct and very much to the point.

Mr. Hopkins then said that at San Francisco Mr. Molotov had scored a neat trick on us by quoting President Roosevelt and Mr. Hull on the Argentine question.

Marshal Stalin and *Mr. Molotov* laughed and *Mr. Hopkins* observed that it was possible that some time in the future we might be quoting Marshal Stalin's own words to him.

Marshal Stalin then said that there was one question he wished to raise and that was the question of a peace conference to settle the European War. He said the question was ripe and, so to speak, knocking at the door.

Mr. Hopkins replied that he thought the forthcoming meeting between the President, Marshal Stalin, and the Prime Minister would be a preliminary step toward such a conference. He said he knew in general President Truman's views on the subject and would be glad while he was in Moscow to convey them to Marshal Stalin along general lines.

Marshal Stalin replied that he felt the uncertainty as to the peace conference was having a bad effect and that it would be wise to select a time and place so that proper preparations could be made. The Versailles Conference had been badly prepared and as a result many mistakes had been made. He repeated that he had already sent a message to President Truman suggesting Berlin as a place for their preliminary meeting.

(In a message received subsequently from Mr. Molotov it was explained that the reference to Berlin as a suggested place of meeting had not been in a message to President Truman, but in a reply from Mr. Molotov to Mr. Joseph Davies concerning a meeting between Marshal Stalin and the President alone.)

(*Note*. This completes the record of the first meeting.)

The second meeting, involving the same six participants as the first, was held in the Kremlin at 8.00 p.m. on May 27. Following is the record of this meeting, in full:

Mr. Hopkins said that last night the Marshal had indicated that there were a number of questions concerning the United States which were worrying him. He asked Marshal Stalin if he would perhaps care to begin with these questions.

Marshal Stalin said he would not attempt to use Soviet public opinion as a screen, but would speak of the feeling that had been created in Soviet Governmental circles as a result of recent moves on the part of the United States Government. He said these circles felt a certain alarm in regard to

the attitude of the United States Government. It was their impression that the American attitude towards the Soviet Union had perceptibly cooled once it became obvious that Germany was defeated, and that it was as though the Americans were saying that the Russians were no longer needed. He said he would give the following examples:

(1) The case of Argentina and the invitation to the San Francisco Conference. At Yalta it had been agreed that only those states which had declared war on Germany before the first of March would be invited, but at San Francisco this decision had been overturned. He said it was not understood in the Soviet Union why Argentina could not have been asked to wait three months or so before joining the world organization. He added that the action of the Conference and the attitude of the United States had raised the question of the value of agreements between the three major powers if their decisions could be overturned by the votes of such countries as Honduras and Porto Rico.

(2) The question of the Reparations Commission. At Yalta it had been agreed that the three powers would sit on this Commission in Moscow and subsequently the United States Government had insisted that France should be represented on the same basis as the Soviet Union. This he felt was an insult to the Soviet Union in view of the fact that France had concluded a separate peace with Germany and had opened the frontier to the Germans. It was true that this had been done by Pétain's Government, but nevertheless it was an action of France. To attempt to place France on the same footing as the Soviet Union looked like an attempt to humiliate the Russians.

(3) The attitude of the United States Government towards the Polish question. He said that at Yalta it had been agreed that the existing Government was to be reconstructed and that anyone with common sense could see that this meant that the present Government was to form the basis of the new. He said no other understanding of the Yalta Agreement was possible. Despite the fact that they were simple people the Russians should not be regarded as fools, which was a mistake the West frequently made, nor were they blind and could quite well see what was going on before their eyes. It is true that the Russians are patient in the interests of a common cause, but that their patience has its limits.

(4) The manner in which Lend-Lease had been curtailed. He said that if the United States was unable to supply the Soviet Union further under Lend-Lease that was one thing, but that the manner in which it had been done had been unfortunate and even brutal. For example, certain ships had been unloaded and while it was true that this order had been cancelled the whole manner in which it had been done had caused concern to the Soviet Government. If the refusal to continue Lend-Lease was designed

as pressure on the Russians in order to soften them up, then it was a
fundamental mistake. He said he must tell Mr. Hopkins frankly that if
the Russians were approached frankly on a friendly basis much could be
done, but that reprisals in any form would bring about the exact opposite
effect.

(5) The disposition of the German Navy and merchant fleet which surrendered to the Allies. Stalin said that, as we knew, certain units of the
German Army who had been fighting against the Russians had been
anxious to surrender to the Western Allies but not to the Russians, but
under the surrender terms German troops were supposed to surrender to
the army against which they had fought. He said, for example General
Eisenhower as an honest man had correctly turned over to the Soviet
Command in Czechoslovakia some 135,000 German troops who had
tried to surrender to the American Army. This was an example of fair
and honest behaviour. However, as regards to the German fleet which
had caused so much damage to Leningrad and other Soviet ports not one
had been turned over to the Russians, despite the fact the fleet had surrendered. He added that he had sent a message to the President and Prime
Minister suggesting that at least one-third of the German Navy and merchant marine thus surrendered be turned over to the Soviet Union. The
rest could be disposed of by Great Britain and the United States as they
saw fit. He added that if the Soviet Union had been entitled to a part of
the Italian fleet they certainly had more right to their fair share of the
German fleet, since they had suffered five million casualties in this war.
He said that the Soviet Government had certain information leading it
to believe that both the United States and England intended to reject
the Soviet request, and he must say that if this turned out to be true it
would be very unpleasant. The Marshal concluded by saying that he had
completed the range of his account.

Mr. Hopkins said he first of all wished to express his appreciation of
the frankness with which Marshal Stalin had exposed his worries. He
said that in so far as he and Ambassador Harriman were able they would
answer equally frankly and if on certain points they did not have full
information they would endeavour to obtain it. He said he would take
the case of the German fleet first. From conversations he had had with
Admiral King he was able to state that the United States had no desire
to retain any portion of the German fleet and merely wished to examine
the vessels for possible new inventions or technical improvements. After
that we were prepared to sink the share turned over to us. He also said
that he had always understood that the fleet was to be divided between
the United States, the Soviet Union, and Great Britain, and that in so far
as the United States was concerned there was no objection to whatever

884   THE WHITE HOUSE PAPERS

disposition the Soviet Government wished to make with its share. He
added that he thought that this matter could be definitely settled at the
forthcoming meeting of the three heads of Government.

Mr. Hopkins then said on the subject of Lend-Lease he thought it had
been clear to the Soviet Union that the end of the war with Germany
would necessitate a reconsideration of the old programme of Lend-Lease
to the Soviet Union.

Marshal Stalin said that was entirely understandable.

Mr. Hopkins continued that the history of Lend-Lease showed that
although in certain cases we had not always been able to meet every
Soviet request we had nonetheless freely accepted commitments which
we had done our best to carry out in spirit as well as in fact.

Marshal Stalin said that was undoubtedly true.

Mr. Hopkins stated that even prior to the end of the war in Europe we
had made an agreement with the Soviet Union known as Annex 3 to
Protocol I, which involved delivery of supplies which might be of use
in the Far East. He said that this grew out of recent conferences in which
Far Eastern matters had been discussed. He emphasized that this commitment was accepted in full by the United States, and we were in the process
of carrying it out. In regard to the unloading of the ships he said that that
was a technical misunderstanding and did not in any sense represent a
decision of policy on the part of the United States. That it had been the
action of one government agency involved in Lend-Lease and that it
had been countermanded promptly within twenty-four hours. He said
that no one who was responsible for Lend-Lease policy or American
Government policy had had anything to do with that mistaken order.
The only question which had to be reconsidered was the programme of
deliveries to the Soviet Union which had been based on the needs of the
war against Germany, and that it had been made clear that on the basis
of this reconsideration we would be glad to reconsider any Soviet requests and that he thought some were now being considered. He said he
wished to emphasize that he had seen no tendency on the part of those
responsible for American policy to handle the question of future Lend-
Lease to the Soviet Union in an arbitrary fashion. It was in fact a question
of law, since the basic Lend-Lease Act made it clear that materials could
only be delivered which would be useful in the process of the war. The
United States Government, however, had interpreted this in its broadest
sense and had included in addition to munitions of war foodstuffs and
other non-military items.

Marshal Stalin said this was true.

Mr. Hopkins concluded by saying that there had naturally been considerable confusion in the United States Government as to the status of

Lend-Lease towards Russia at the end of the war and that there had been varying legal interpretations, but that he wished to emphasize that the incident to which Marshal Stalin referred did not have any fundamental policy significance.

Marshal Stalin said he wished to make it clear that he fully understood the right of the United States to curtail Lend-Lease shipments to the Soviet Union under present conditions since our commitments in this respect had been freely entered into. Even two months ago it would have been quite correct for the United States to have begun to curtail shipments, but what he had in mind was the manner and form in which it was done. He felt that what was, after all, an agreement between the two Governments had been ended in a scornful and abrupt manner. He said that if proper warning had been given to the Soviet Government there would have been no feeling of the kind he had spoken of; that this warning was important to them, since their economy was based on plans. He added that they had intended to make a suitable expression of gratitude to the United States for the Lend-Lease assistance during the war, but the way in which this programme had been halted now made that impossible to do.

Mr. Hopkins replied that what disturbed him most about the Marshal's statement was the revelation that he believed that the United States would use Lend-Lease as a means of showing our displeasure with the Soviet Union. He wished to assure the Marshal that however unfortunate an impression this question had caused in the mind of the Soviet Government he must believe that there was no attempt or desire on the part of the United States to use it as a pressure weapon. He said the United States is a strong power and does not go in for those methods. Furthermore, we have no conflict of immediate interests with the Soviet Union and would have no reason to adopt such practices.

Marshal Stalin said he believed Mr. Hopkins and was fully satisfied with his statement in regard to Lend-Lease, but said he hoped Mr. Hopkins would consider how it had looked from their side.

Ambassador Harriman then suggested that he and Mr. Molotov might go into the details of the whole Lend-Lease matter together with Mr. Mikoyan the following day.

Mr. Hopkins concluded the discussions of Lend-Lease by stating that he thought it would be a great tragedy if the greatest achievement in co-operation which the Soviet Union and the United States had on the whole worked out together on the basis of Lend-Lease were to end on an unsatisfactory note. He said he wished to add that we had never believed that our Lend-Lease help had been the chief factor in the Soviet defeat of Hitler on the Eastern Front. That this had been done by the heroism and blood of the Russian Army.

Mr. Hopkins then turned to the question of the Reparations Commission. He said it was true that we had suggested France as an additional member and that the Soviet Government had indicated that if France was to be a member there were other countries with equal or better claims to be represented. He said that he had not been directly involved in this question since the Yalta Conference because of his illness, but so far as he knew our only motive was that France was to be represented on the Control Council for Germany, and it therefore appeared reasonable and logical that she should participate in the reparations discussions. He said he realized that the Soviet Union had reluctantly agreed to the participation of France in the Control Council at the Crimea Conference. In any event the situation now was that the three powers were to go ahead and begin discussions in Moscow without France. He wished to state that he also had in mind the doubts which Stalin and Molotov had in regard to the subject of reparations and how seriously they regarded this question. He wished only to say that the United States for its part considered reparations a most important and serious question which must be thrashed out in the Reparations Commission. He said he did not, of course, know, but he felt that we would probably not insist in an unyielding manner on the question of the admission of France.

Marshal Stalin replied that Poland, which had suffered even more than France, should certainly be represented if France was to be, and that Yugoslavia also deserved a place.

Mr. Hopkins then said in regard to the Argentine question, since he had not been at San Francisco he would ask Ambassador Harriman to explain that situation. He added that he had been at Yalta and he must say that the Marshal was right in regard to the decision there.

Ambassador Harriman said that he hoped that he could speak frankly on the subject of the Argentine and that Mr. Molotov would forgive him if he spoke in that fashion. He said he had not been at Mexico City and therefore was not familiar with all of the implications of certain commitments taken there. In brief, however, the situation was that we came to San Francisco with a commitment which President Roosevelt assumed at Yalta to support the admission of the Ukraine and White Russia as original members of the world organization and also with certain commitments with the South American countries in regard to Argentina. At San Francisco, at Mr. Molotov's request, Mr. Stettinius had taken up with the Latin American countries the question of their willingness to support the Crimea Decision in regard to the Ukraine and White Russia. The Latin American countries had immediately tried to connect this question with that of the admission of the Argentine. Mr. Stettinius had made it plain that he would not make any such connection and if Mr. Molotov

recalled the Latin American countries had voted solidly in support of the Yalta decision. There was, however, another step to the Ukraine and White Russia question, namely that of inviting them to the Conference, concerning which the United States had taken no commitment at Yalta. Mr. Harriman said that he, personally, felt that if Mr. Molotov had not introduced the question of an invitation to the present Polish Government we might have been successful in persuading the Latin American countries to postpone the question of Argentina, but that once Mr. Molotov had connected the question of Argentina with that of an invitation to the present Polish Government, Mr. Stettinius felt that because of the willingness of the South American countries to support the Crimea Decision and the invitation to the Ukraine and White Russia, he was committed to vote for the admission of Argentina.

Mr. Molotov said that his request for more time had not been granted.

Marshal Stalin said in any event what had been done could not be put right and that the Argentine question belonged to the past.

Mr. Hopkins then said with the Marshal's permission he would like to review the position of the United States in regard to Poland. He said first of all he wished to assure the Marshal that he had no thought or indeed any right to attempt to settle the Polish problem during his visit here in Moscow, nor was he intending to hide behind American public opinion in presenting the position of the United States.

Marshal Stalin said he was afraid that his remark concerning Soviet public opinion had cut Mr. Hopkins to the quick and that he had not meant to imply that Mr. Hopkins was hiding behind the screen of American public opinion. In fact, he knew Mr. Hopkins to be an honest and frank man.

Mr. Hopkins said that he wished to state this position as clearly and as forcibly as he knew how. He said the question of Poland *per se* was not so important as the fact that it had become a symbol of our ability to work out problems with the Soviet Union. He said that we had no special interests in Poland and no special desire to see any particular kind of government. That we would accept any government in Poland which was desired by the Polish people and was at the same time friendly to the Soviet Government. He said that the people and Government of the United States felt that this was a problem which should be worked out jointly between the United States, the Soviet Union, and Great Britain, and that we felt that the Polish people should be given the right to free elections to choose their own government and their own system and that Poland should genuinely be independent. The Government and people of the United States were disturbed because the preliminary steps towards the re-establishment of Poland appeared to have been taken unilaterally

by the Soviet Union together with the present Warsaw Government and that in fact the United States was completely excluded. He said he hoped that Stalin would believe him when he said that this feeling was a fact. Mr. Hopkins said he urged that Marshal Stalin would judge American policy by the actions of the United States Government itself and not by the attitudes and public expressions of the Hearst newspapers and the *Chicago Tribune*. He hoped that the Marshal would put his mind to the task of thinking up what diplomatic methods could be used to settle this question, keeping in mind the feeling of the American people. He said he himself was not prepared to say how it could be done, but that he felt it must be done. Poland had become a symbol in the sense that it bore a direct relation to the willingness of the United States to participate in international affairs on a world-wide basis and that our people must believe that they are joining their power with that of the Soviet Union and Great Britain in the promotion of international peace and the well being of humanity. Mr. Hopkins went on to say that he felt the overwhelming majority of the people of the United States felt that the relations between the United States and the U.S.S.R. could be worked out in a spirit of co-operation despite the differences in ideology and that with all these factors in its favour he wished to appeal to the Marshal to help to find a way to the solution of the Polish problem.

Marshal Stalin replied that he wished Mr. Hopkins would take into consideration the following factors: He said it may seem strange although it appeared to be recognized in United States circles and Churchill in his speeches also recognized it, that the Soviet Government should wish for a friendly Poland. In the course of twenty-five years the Germans had twice invaded Russia via Poland. Neither the British nor American people had experienced such German invasions which were a horrible thing to endure and the results of which were not easily forgotten. He said these German invasions were not warfare but were like the incursions of the Huns. He said that Germany had been able to do this because Poland had been regarded as a part of the *cordon sanitaire* around the Soviet Union and that previous European policy had been that Polish Governments must be hostile to Russia. In these circumstances either Poland had been too weak to oppose Germany or had let the Germans come through. Thus Poland had served as a corridor for the German attacks on Russia. He said Poland's weakness and hostility had been a great source of weakness to the Soviet Union and had permitted the Germans to do what they wished in the East and also in the West since the two were mixed together. It is therefore in Russia's vital interest that Poland should be both strong and friendly. He said there was no intention on the part of the Soviet Union to interfere in Poland's internal

affairs, that Poland would live under the parliamentary system which is like Czechoslovakia, Belgium, and Holland, and that any talk of an intention to Sovietize Poland was stupid. He said even the Polish leaders, some of whom were Communists, were against the Soviet system, since the Polish people did not desire collective farms or other aspects of the Soviet system. In this the Polish leaders were right since the Soviet system was not exportable—it must develop from within on the basis of a set of conditions which were not present in Poland. He said all the Soviet Union wanted was that Poland should not be in a position to open the gates to Germany and in order to prevent this Poland must be strong and democratic. Stalin then said that before he came to his suggestion as to the practical solution of the question he would like to comment on Mr. Hopkins's remarks concerning future United States interests in the world. He said that whether the United States wished it or not it was a world power and would have to accept world-wide interests. Not only this war but the previous war had shown that without United States intervention Germany could not have been defeated and that all the events and developments of the last thirty years had confirmed this. In fact, the United States had more reason to be a world power than any other state. For this reason he fully recognized the right of the United States as a world power to participate in the Polish question and that the Soviet interest in Poland does not in any way exclude those of England and the United States. Mr. Hopkins had spoken of Russian unilateral action in Poland and United States public opinion concerning it. It was true that Russia had taken such unilateral action but they had been compelled to. He said the Soviet Government had recognized the Warsaw Government and concluded a treaty with it at a time when their Allies did not recognize this Government. These were admittedly unilateral acts which would have been much better left undone but the fact was they had not met with any understanding on the part of their Allies. The need for these actions had arisen out of the presence of Soviet troops in Poland; it would have been impossible to have waited until such time as the Allies had come to an agreement on Poland. The logic of the war against Germany demanded that the Soviet rear be assured and the Lublin Committee had been of great assistance to the Red Army at all times and it was for this reason that these actions had been taken by the Soviet Government. He said it was contrary to the Soviet policy to set up Soviet administration on foreign soil since this would look like occupation and be resented by the local inhabitants. It was for this reason that some Polish administration had to be established in Poland and this could be done only with those who had helped the Red Army. He said he wished to emphasize that these steps had not been taken with

any desire to eliminate or exclude Russia's Allies. He must point out, however, that Soviet action in Poland had been more successful than British action in Greece and at no time had they been compelled to undertake the measures which they had done in Greece. Stalin then turned to his suggestion for the solution of the Polish problem.

Marshal Stalin said that he felt that we should examine the composition of the future Government of National Unity. He said there were eighteen or twenty ministries in the present Polish Government and that four or five of these portfolios could be given representatives of other Polish groups taken from the list submitted by Great Britain and the United States (Molotov whispered to Stalin, who then said he meant four and not five posts in the Government). He said he thought the Warsaw Poles would not accept more than four ministers from other democratic groups. He added that if this appears a suitable basis we could then proceed to consider what persons should be selected for these posts. He said of course they would have to be friendly to the U.S.S.R. and to the Allies. He added that Mikolajczyk had been suggested and he thought he was acceptable and that the question was now who else. He inquired of Mr. Hopkins whether possibly Professor Lange might be willing to join the Government.

Mr. Hopkins said he doubted whether Professor Lange, who was an American citizen, could be induced to give up his American citizenship for this purpose, but that of course was only a private opinion.

Marshal Stalin then said it might be wise to ask some of the Warsaw leaders to come to Moscow now and to hear what they had to say and to learn more of what had been decided. He added that if we are able to settle the composition of the new Government he felt that no differences remained since we were all agreed on the free and unfettered elections and that no one intended to interfere with the Polish people.

Mr. Hopkins said he would like to have some time to consider the Marshal's suggestion.

Marshal Stalin then said that there were three other questions they had not touched on:

(1) Future policy in regard to the occupation of Germany;
(2) Japan; and
(3) Meeting of the three heads of Government.

In reply to Mr. Hopkins's question *Marshal Stalin* said that he was prepared to meet at any time, but had not yet heard from the President and Prime Minister whether the Berlin area was acceptable or not.

In conclusion *Mr. Hopkins* said he felt it would be most desirable if Marshal Stalin could announce publicly as soon as possible the appointment of Marshal Zhukov as Soviet representative on the Control

Council for Germany so that that body could start its work as soon as possible.

Marshal Stalin said he was prepared to announce Marshal Zhukov's appointment either tomorrow or the next day or whenever we wanted.

It was agreed that the next meeting would take place at 6 p.m. tomorrow, May 28.

(*Note*. This completes the record of the second meeting.)

After each of these meetings Hopkins reported on them in detail by cable to Truman and the State Department, which kept the British Foreign Office fully informed as to the progress of the conversations. It will be noted that Hopkins was now most scrupulous in keeping to the formal 'channels'. He had never reported to Roosevelt in the same way—not, at any rate, since his first trip to England in January, 1941. So complete was his knowledge of Roosevelt's state of mind before he departed on each trip that he usually needed only to cable something like 'making good progress along lines we discussed' or 'having some difficulties on SLEDGEHAMMER, but will explain this when I see you'. He knew that Roosevelt did not want long reports from him in which the language was necessarily somewhat guarded, preferring to wait until Hopkins could give him a full account in characteristic terms in the privacy of the Oval Study. However, this time, the fate of the San Francisco Conference and perhaps of the whole future of world peace was at stake and the issue could not wait for Hopkins's return to Washington.

Hopkins's cabled report on the third meeting was as follows:

1. By August 8 the Soviet Army will be properly deployed on the Manchurian positions.

2. The Marshal repeated his statement made at Yalta that the Russian people must have a good reason for going to war and that depended on China's willingness to agree to the proposals made at Yalta.

3. For the first time he stated that he was willing to take these proposals up directly with Soong when he comes to Moscow. He wants to see Soong not later than July 1 and expects us to take the matter up at the same time with Chiang Kai-shek. This procedure seems from our point of view most desirable in light of Stalin's statements about the Far East which follow.

4. Stalin left no doubt in our mind that he intends to attack during August. It is therefore important that Soong come here not later than July 1. Stalin is ready to see him any time now.

5. He made categorical statement that he would do everything he could to promote unification of China under the leadership of Chiang Kai-shek. He further stated that this leadership should continue after the war, because no one else was strong enough. He specifically stated that

no Communist leader was strong enough to unify China. In spite of the reservations he expressed about him, he proposes to back the Generalissimo.

6. Stalin repeated all of his statements made at Yalta that he wanted a unified and stable China and wanted China to control all of Manchuria as part of a United China. He stated categorically that he had no territorial claims against China and mentioned specifically Manchuria and Sinkiang and that in all areas his troops entered to fight the Japanese he would respect Chinese sovereignty.

7. The Marshal stated that he would welcome representatives of the Generalissimo to be with his troops entering Manchuria in order to facilitate the organization in Manchuria of Chinese administration.

8. He agreed with America's 'Open Door' policy and went out of his way to indicate that the United States was the only power with the resources to aid China economically after the war. He observed that for many years to come Russia would have all it could do to provide for the internal economy of the Soviet Union.

9. He agreed that there should be trusteeship for Korea under the United States, China, Great Britain and the Soviet Union.

10. We were very encouraged by the conference on the Far East.

This was followed by another cable on the same meeting:

1. Japan is doomed and the Japanese know it.

2. Peace feelers are being put out by certain elements in Japan and we should therefore consider together our joint attitude and act in concert about the surrender of Japan. Stalin expressed the fear that the Japanese will try to split the allies. The following are his statements about surrender:

A. The Soviet Union prefers to go through with unconditional surrender and destroy once and for all the military might and forces of Japan. Stalin thinks this is particularly to our interest because the Japanese have a deep-seated antipathy to the United States and if the war lords, the industrial leaders and the politicians are permitted to withdraw to Japan with their armies undefeated, their navy not totally destroyed and their industrial machine partially intact, they will start at once to plan a war of revenge. Stalin made it quite clear that the Soviet Union wants to go through with unconditional surrender and all that is implied in it.

B. However, he feels that if we stick to unconditional surrender the Japs will not give up and we will have to destroy them as we did Germany.

C. The Japanese may offer to surrender and seek softer terms. While consideration of this has certain dangers as compared with (A) it nevertheless cannot be ruled out. Should the Allies depart from the announced policy of unconditional surrender and be prepared to accept a modified

surrender, Stalin visualizes imposing our will through our occupying forces and thereby gaining substantially the same results as under (A). In other words, it seemed to us that he proposes under this heading to agree to milder peace terms, but once we get into Japan to give them the works.

3. The Marshal expects that Russia will share in the actual occupation of Japan and wants an agreement with the British and us as to occupation zones.

4. He also wants an understanding between the Allies as to areas of operation in China and Manchuria.

At this same meeting in which Far Eastern matters were discussed, there was also some talk about the endless problem of postwar treatment of Germany, which was far from settlement even now, three weeks after V.E.-Day. In his report to Truman, Hopkins said:

On two occasions Stalin has emphasized the importance of planning at once for the organization of the Peace Conference in so far as it related to Europe. Apparently he is thinking about a formal conference and he emphasized that the Allies were not properly prepared at Versailles and that we should not make that mistake again. At your forthcoming meeting he will bring this up.

We reminded Stalin some days ago that he had made a speech in which he said that he did not favour the dismemberment of Germany. This appeared to be contrary to the position he took both at Teheran and Yalta. His explanation of this action on his part was that his recommendation had been turned down at Yalta and more specifically that Eden and Strang on behalf of the British had stated the dismemberment was to be accomplished only as a last resort and that Winant, who was present at the Conference at which this discussion took place in London, interposed no objection, hence Stalin states that it was his understanding that both Great Britain and the United States were opposed to dismemberment. I undertook to tell him that this was not the case; that while you had made no final decision in regard to this, the United States considered this an open question and that you would surely want to thrash it out at your next meeting. I told him that he must not assume that the United States is opposed to dismemberment because he may learn from you that just the opposite was the case. He then said that dismemberment was a matter which the three Allies must settle among themselves and that he would keep an open mind in regard to it.

He went into some detail regarding the definition of the German General Staff and stated that it would be desirable if the members of that Staff could be detained for ten to fifteen years and if a legal way could

be found to prosecute and convict the General Staff as a war criminal organization that would be all the better. The Soviets have captured certain members of the General Staff whom they consider to be war criminals and who they propose should be prosecuted as such under any circumstances. Stalin stated that the Soviets permitted no prisoner of war to go to work on farms or in factories. As to exactly what he was doing with prisoners of war he was somewhat noncommittal, but he indicated that he was bringing many of them back to White Russia and the Ukraine to work in mines and on reconstruction. He said that he did not know just how many prisoners of war they had, but he thought they had about 2,500,000 of which 1,700,000 were Germans and the balance Roumanians, Italians, Hungarians, etc. He stated that the officers were not repeat not being required to work. You can be sure that at your next meeting Stalin will have some pretty specific proposals to make about prisoners of war, and more particularly, I believe, about war criminals. He did not, as we anticipated, express any criticism of our handling of war prisoners. Stalin outlined in some detail his administrative procedure in local German communities, but I shall delay a report on that until I return home. He said he believed we should do everything to encourage them to get to work on their farms in order to provide food for themselves, and indicated that we should co-operate in getting their light consumer goods industries going. He indicated that Germany should be permitted those heavy industries required for the rehabilitation of their transportation systems, electric power, water, sewage, etc.

Although he promised that he was going to appoint Zhukov as his member of the Control Council for Germany, it has not yet been done. We shall at tonight's meeting again urge him to announce at once Zhukov's appointment.

On May 30, the fourth day in Moscow, Hopkins and his wife enjoyed some sightseeing, particularly a visit to the Russian Ballet School. When he met Stalin at the meeting at six o'clock that evening, he told his host how greatly he had enjoyed seeing this school, which was then as it has always been the veritable fountainhead of ballet art for the entire world. Hopkins noted: 'Marshal Stalin said that although he had been twenty-eight years in Moscow, he had never visited the Ballet School'—precisely like the traditional New Yorker who says: 'I've lived here all my life but I've never yet seen the Statue of Liberty.' Hopkins assured the Marshal that this was something not to be missed.

The topics discussed at this fourth meeting were the disposition of the German Fleet, arrangements for the forthcoming Potsdam Conference and Poland. Hopkins stated the basic American attitude toward the infinitely difficult Polish question in the following conversation:

Mr. Hopkins said he would like to accent once again the reasons for our concern in regard to Poland, and indeed, in regard to other countries which were geographically far from our borders. He said there were certain fundamental rights which, when impinged upon or denied, caused concern in the United States. These were cardinal elements which must be present if a parliamentary system is to be established and maintained. He said for example:

1. There must be the right of freedom of speech so that people could say what they wanted to, right of assembly, right of movement and the right to worship at any church that they desired;

2. All political parties except the Fascist party and Fascist elements who represented or could represent democratic governments should be permitted the free use, without distinction, of the Press, radio, meetings, and other facilities of political expression;

3. All citizens should have the right of public trial, defence by counsel of their own choosing, and the right of habeas corpus.

He concluded that if we could find a meeting of minds in regard to these general principles which would be the basis for future free elections then he was sure we could find ways and means to agree on procedures to carry them into effect. He then asked the Marshal if he would care to comment in a general sense or more specifically in regard to the general observations he had made concerning the fundamentals of a new Polish state.

Marshal Stalin replied that these principles of democracy are well known and would find no objection on the part of the Soviet Government. He was sure that the Polish Government, which in its declaration had outlined just such principles, would not only not oppose them, but would welcome them. He said, however, that in regard to the specific freedoms mentioned by Mr. Hopkins, they could only be applied in full in peacetime, and even then with certain limitations. He said for example the Fascist party, whose intention it was to overthrow democratic governments, could not be permitted to enjoy to the full extent these freedoms. He said secondly there were the limitations imposed by war. All states when they were threatened by war on their frontiers were not secure and had found it necessary to introduce certain restrictions. This had been done in England, France, the Soviet Union, and elsewhere, and perhaps to a lesser extent in the United States which was protected by wide oceans. It is for these reasons that only in time of peace could considerations be given to the full application of these freedoms. For example he said that in time of war no state will allow the free unrestricted use of radio transmitters which could be used to convey information to the enemy. With reference to freedom of speech certain restrictions

had to be imposed for military security. As to arrest, in England during the war individuals dangerous to the state had been arrested and tried in secret; these restrictions had been somewhat relaxed but not entirely repealed in England since the war in the Pacific was still going on.

He said, therefore, to sum up: (1) during time of war these political freedoms could not be enjoyed to the full extent, and (2) nor could they apply without reservations to Fascist parties trying to overthrow the Government.

Marshal Stalin continued that he wished to give a few examples from Russian history. He said that at the time of the revolution the Russian Communist party had proclaimed the right of freedom of religion as one of the points of their programme. The Russian Patriarch and the entire then existing church had declared the Soviet Government an anathema and had called on all church members not to pay taxes nor to obey the call to the Red Army, but to resist mobilization, not to work, etc. He said what could the Soviet Government do but to, in fact, declare war on the church which assumed that attitude. He added that the present war had wiped out this antagonism and that now the freedom of religion, as promised, could be granted to the church.

Mr. Hopkins said he thoroughly understood the Marshal's opinions. He added that when he had left the Crimea Conference President Roosevelt had thought the Polish matter was virtually settled. He had been relaxed and pleased over the situation. Mr. Hopkins said he and all the other American representatives thought the same and felt that in very short time Mr. Molotov, Mr. Harriman and Sir Archibald Clark Kerr would be able to carry out the Crimea Decision. Since that time he had been sick and out of touch with Washington and had only followed events from the Press and from personal letters which he had received from time to time. He must confess that he had been bewildered and disturbed that one thing after another seemed to occur to prevent the carrying out of the decision which all had thought was clear and sure. He said that if, with his knowledge, he had been bewildered as to the real reason for this it was easy to imagine how bewildered and concerned the masses of people in the United States were over the situation. Mr. Hopkins said that he must say that rightly or wrongly there was a strong feeling among the American people that the Soviet Union wished to dominate Poland. He added that was not his point of view but it was widely held in the United States and that friends of international collaboration were wondering how it would be possible to work things out with the Soviet Union if we could not agree on the Polish question. Mr. Hopkins added that for himself he felt very strongly that if we could find a meeting of the minds on the substance of what we wished to see in

the new Polish state we should be able to overcome the difficulties. He himself had had difficulty in understanding the immediate cause of disagreement, namely interpretation of wording such as the role of the existing government in the future Provisional Government of Poland. He concluded that he felt that the three great powers should in a short time be able to settle this matter.

Marshal Stalin replied that this was true, but it was necessary for all three Governments genuinely to wish to settle this matter. If one of them secretly did not wish to see it settled then the difficulties were real.

Mr. Hopkins replied that as far as the United States Government was concerned we had no interest in seeing anyone connected with the present Polish Government in London involved in the new Provisional Government of Poland and he did not personally believe that the British had any such idea.

After this fourth meeting, Hopkins cabled Truman that Stalin had agreed to meet with the President and Churchill in the Berlin area about July 15. In this cable, he added:

> I completed the exposition of your position relative to Poland with Stalin. The conference tonight was encouraging. It looks as though Stalin is prepared to return to and implement the Crimea decision and permit a representative group of Poles to come to Moscow to consult with the Commission. We are having what we both emphasized would be an informal exchange of views on possible candidates to come here for consultation with the tri-partite Commission at an early date. Harriman, in preparation for this exchange of views, will go over with the British Ambassador the list of candidates already submitted by us and the British.

The fifth meeting on May 31 involved a detailed discussion of names of various candidates for the Polish Government. In this, Hopkins had to rely on the information he had received from Harriman, Bohlen and the State Department. He recognized such names as Mikolajczyk or Lange, but as names of other men came up he had no direct knowledge of their political background or the precise extent of their reliability. In all of these discussions of Poland, Hopkins repeated many times that it was the desire of his Government that the Polish Government should be friendly to the Soviet Union, and Stalin agreed that this was all that he demanded. But, here again, as Roosevelt had said to Churchill, 'The Russians do not use words for the same purpose that we do': and there was apparently no way of translating the word 'friendly' from one language to the other so that it would end up meaning the same thing.

After the fifth meeting, Mr. and Mrs. Hopkins had a private dinner with Stalin at which were present some twenty of the most important men in the Soviet Union, including several members of the Politburo—Mikoyan, Beriya, Kaganovich and Shvernik and Malenkov and Voznesenski (then alternate members). George Kennan who was identified as the author of the famous 'Mr. X' article in the magazine, *Foreign Affairs*, some two years later, was also present at this dinner. After dinner Hopkins had a private conversation with Stalin, nobody else being present except the interpreter, Pavlov. Hopkins wrote the following record of this:

Last night after dinner I saw Stalin alone with Mr. Pavlov, interpreter. I told him that I wanted to impress on him as earnestly as I knew how the unfavourable effect in America caused by the detaining of the fourteen Poles within Poland and, specifically, those that were charged only with having illegal radio transmitters. I made it clear to him that I was not talking about the others charged with more serious crimes. I told him that I believed we would have no great difficulty with getting the list approved of names who might come to Moscow to consult with the Moscow Commission, if this business could be settled. I made it clear that while I did not know anything about the merits of the case, I nevertheless felt that even though the Marshal thought the offence was far more serious than it appeared to us, it was in the interest of good Russian-American relations that I hoped he would release these prisoners.

I told Marshal Stalin that if the solution of the Polish matter waited until the conference in Berlin on the 15th of July it would stir up endless trouble and probably take most of the time of the Berlin meeting. I outlined at great length the American position in regard to the Soviet Union after the war and told him that we believed the repeated assurances which he had given us that the Soviet Union also wanted to have a firm and friendly understanding with us; that we assumed that that was correct. But if that were to be accomplished I told him it had to be done in an environment that made it possible for President Truman to carry American public opinion with him.

I reminded him again of the many minority groups in America who were not sympathetic to the Soviet Union and told him very forcefully that he must believe me when I told him that our whole relationship was threatened by the impasse of Poland. I made it clear again to Stalin that Poland was only a symbol, that the United States had equal interests in all countries in this part of the world and that if we were going to act or maintain our interests on a tripartite basis, it was hopeless to do so without a strong American public opinion. I told him there was no hope of getting certain minority groups in sympathy with this position for

many years and perhaps never, and reminded him again that he should not assume that the *Chicago Tribune* or the Hearst Press had any real influence on American public opinion; that I was speaking for and on behalf of the millions of Americans who support a policy of co-operation with the Soviet Union.

I told Stalin further that I personally felt that our relations were threatened and that I frankly had many misgivings about it and with my intimate knowledge of the situation I was, frankly, bewildered with some of the things that were going on.

Stalin then said that he was unwilling to order those Poles released who were charged only with use of illegal radio sets. He stated that he had information in regard to these prisoners which was not available to us and inferred that all of them were engaged in what he called diversionist activities. He stated that he believed that Churchill had misled the United States in regard to the facts and had made the American Government believe that the statement of the Polish London Government was accurate. Just the opposite was the case.

Marshal Stalin stated that he did not intend to have the British manage the affairs of Poland and that is exactly what they want to do. Nevertheless, he stated that he believed me when I told him it was having an unfavourable effect on public opinion in America and he assumed the same was true in Great Britain, and therefore he was inclined to do everything he could to make it easy for Churchill to get out of a bad situation because if and when all the evidence is published it would look very bad for the British and he does not want to make the situation worse than it is. He stated that the men must be tried, but that they would be treated leniently and he clearly inferred that he was going to consider at once what could be done in regard to these prisoners that I was concerned with to clear the matter up.

He did not, however, indicate at any time that he was not going to have them tried. I asked him that if he was determined to go through with the trial, when the trials would be held, reminding him that so long as things were in this kind of a state it was bound to create friction between all of us.

His reply to that was he did not know, but that he would find out and let me know tomorrow. He said that we must take into consideration Russian opinion as well as American opinion; that it was the Russian forces that had liberated Poland and said that if they had not gained the victory in Poland, with such a great loss of Russian life, nobody would be talking about a new Poland. He said several times that he blamed the British for conniving with the London Poles, and each time I reminded him that we had no desire to support in any way the Polish Government in London.

He listened very attentively to everything I said in the first part of the conversation and I gained the impression that he is going to consider the move which the Soviet Union will make and that we would hear from him at an early date.

I closed the conversation by telling him that I thought the real solution lay in his releasing these men entirely so that we could clear the atmosphere not only for the immediate discussions about Poland but in preparation for the Berlin Conference.

He repeated that the men should be tried, but that he would let me know.

During the next few days, Hopkins took it easy in Moscow waiting for further orders from Truman. Voluminous cables passed back and forth between Washington, London, and Moscow containing comments on all the various Polish names mentioned. Churchill cabled Hopkins his congratulations on the splendid job that he was doing and he cabled Truman that a break in the deadlock seemed to be resulting from Hopkins's devoted efforts. In one of these cables, Churchill referred to 'The Iron Curtain' which had descended over Europe; this phrase did not come into popular currency until a long time later.

On June 6 Hopkins had his sixth and last meeting with Stalin and Molotov, with Harriman and Bohlen also present. During this, the following conversation took place:

Marshal Stalin said that he wished to thank Mr. Hopkins for his great assistance in moving forward the Polish question.

Mr. Hopkins then said he would like to raise an entirely separate question with Marshal Stalin and that relates to the impasse which had come about at the San Francisco Conference in regard to voting precedure in the security council. He said he had received an urgent message from President Truman to take this up with Marshal Stalin and to indicate the seriousness of this matter. He said it referred to the Soviet insistence that nothing could be discussed by the security council without the unanimous vote of the permanent members exclusive of those involved in a particular situation. He said that the United States Government had agreed with the Marshal that there must be unanimity among the members in regard to all questions involving enforcement action in any of its aspects, but that in the consideration of methods for the peaceful settlement of disputes, parties to the dispute, whether permanent members or not, would abstain from voting. He added that the United States thought the Yalta formula as agreed on safeguarded the freedom of discussion and the right of any member to bring before the council any situation for discussion. And that this right, which was rightly a question of the agenda, should therefore

be decided by the council by simple majority without any power having the right to veto it. He said he earnestly hoped the Marshal would see eye to eye with us and the other sponsoring powers and France who were agreed on this question.

Mr. Molotov said that the Soviet position was based squarely on the Crimea decision and that in matters involving peaceful settlement parties to dispute would not vote and that the full unanimity applied only to enforcement action. The Soviet position was that the same formula for peaceful settlement should apply in deciding whether or not the council should take up and discuss any given question. (Ensued a conversation in Russian between Mr. Molotov and Marshal Stalin from which it was clear that the Marshal had not understood the issues involved and had not had them explained to him. During this conversation Marshal Stalin remarked that he thought it was an insignificant matter and that they should accept the American position.)

Marshal Stalin then stated that he had no objection to a simple majority being applied in discussions relating to pacific settlement, but of course not to any matter involving enforcement action. He said he stressed this aspect because he knew these considerations were raised by the small nations. He had most respect for the small nations (but) it must be admitted there was a tendency among them to exploit and even to create differences between the great powers in the hope that they would obtain the backing of one or more of the great powers for their own ends. He said it was a mistake to believe that just because a nation was small it was necessarily innocent. He added that it should not be understood he would only say this in secret since he was quite prepared to tell the little nations this to their faces. He said, after all two world wars had begun over small nations.

Mr. Hopkins said he thought that possibly the difficulties at San Francisco had grown more out of misunderstanding than real differences.

Marshal Stalin continued that certain statesmen were interested in getting hold of the votes of small nations and that this was a dangerous and slippery path, since obviously the small nations would like to get great nation support.

Marshal Stalin then stated that he was prepared to accept the American position on the point at issue at San Francisco in regard to voting procedure.

Mr. Hopkins then said he had one more question to raise and he hoped Marshal Stalin would not think he was always raising troublesome questions. He said the American people through the American Red Cross were anxious to show their admiration and respect for the Polish people by sending them relief in the form of medical supplies which,

BB

unfortunately, would only be of moderate proportions. He said for this purpose American Red Cross desired to send three representatives headed by Dr. Bowers to handle the distribution of these supplies. He added that these men would, of course, refrain from any political activity and as a member of the Central Committee of the American Red Cross he was prepared to guarantee that.

Marshal Stalin said he had no objection, but it was necessary to obtain the opinion of the Polish Provisional Government, which could be done when they came to Moscow.

Mr. Hopkins then told Marshal Stalin of his plan to leave tomorrow, stopping in Berlin and going on to Frankfurt. He said he looked forward to what for him would be a pleasant spectacle, the present state of Berlin and he might even be able to find Hitler's body.

Marshal Stalin replied that he was sure that Hitler was still alive.

Mr. Hopkins then expressed to Marshal Stalin, on the part of Mrs. Hopkins and himself, their great appreciation for the many kindnesses and courtesies they had received during their stay in Moscow. He said it had been a great pleasure for them to have been here and he only wished to repeat what he had said before, that our two countries had so much in common that they could find a way to work out their problems. He added that these meetings here had left him with renewed assurances on that point.

Marshal Stalin said he fully shared Mr. Hopkins's views.

Following this last meeting, Hopkins cabled Truman: 'Marshal Stalin agrees to accept the United States position regarding voting procedure in the Council.' This was the real news that the San Francisco Conference had been saved.

Hopkins and his wife left Moscow early in the morning of June 7 and arrived in Berlin in time for lunch. The word had been passed along to the Russian military authorities there to show the distinguished travellers every consideration and these orders were obeyed to an almost embarrassing extent. The Hopkinses may have been the first American civilians to be shown into some of the Nazi holy places which were then completely under the control of the Red Army. Yielding to some of the eternal temptations of the souvenir hunter, Hopkins helped himself to several books from Hitler's private office and presented these to friends on his return.

From Berlin they flew to Frankfurt to spend a day at General Eisenhower's new headquarters, and from there to Paris. Hopkins wrote the following personal notes:

One of the difficulties in negotiating the Polish agreement in Moscow was that President Truman had sent me without discussing it in advance

with Churchill. Although, at the time of my departure, he acquainted him with my impending visit to Moscow, no British representative was present at any of my conferences with Stalin and I was in no position to deal directly with Churchill. Fortunately, Clark Kerr, the British Ambassador to Moscow, was an old friend of mine and quite in sympathy with my visit and I am sure he reported very fully to the British Foreign Office and Churchill. And, more than that, he was making recommendations to Churchill urging the British to back us up. I began to hear from Kerr that Churchill was obviously quite disturbed about the whole business but there was not very much he could say because it was probably to his political interest to get agreement on the Polish question before the British elections.

When I reached Frankfurt there was an urgent telephone message from Churchill which I answered and in which he insisted on my going to London. I stalled about this, telling him my health was not too good and that I thought I ought to get right back, but would let him know, and that under any circumstances I would not go without the approval of the President. I felt it unwise for me to go to England and see Churchill before reporting to Truman, so I gave Churchill no encouragement. Churchill wired Truman and Truman replied in the negative to Churchill. I was not acquainted with this until I got to Paris when Churchill again called me and told me the answer had come from Truman and expressed great regret at the decision and acted a little petulant about it over the telephone. I told him, however, that there was nothing I could do about it and, under any circumstances, my health was such that I felt I should not do anything but go right home.

I had several long talks with Eisenhower during the twenty-four hours Mrs. Hopkins and I spent at his country place about fifteen miles outside of Frankfurt. Amongst other things, Eisenhower told me that he and his family had always been Republicans and had voted for Roosevelt this last time.

He discussed his future at great length, repeatedly emphasizing that he did not want to go into politics. This seemed to be apropos of nothing in particular that I had said. He told me, however, that a good many people passing through raised the question of his running for President —obviously on the Republican ticket.

He seemed pretty dubious about the Allied Control Commission and was very fearful that the several governments would not give the Allied Control Commission sufficient power. I told him I was sure that the Russian Government intended to control General Zhukov completely and repeated to him the story of Vishinski being in Zhukov's ear all during our conversation in Berlin that Thursday afternoon. Eisenhower

told me the same thing had happened to him the day before. Zhukov had seemed unwilling to reply to any of his questions without first consulting Vishinski. When I saw Eisenhower on my way to Moscow he asked me to raise this question with Stalin and I did. Stalin made it very clear that Zhukov would have very little power concerning political affairs in Germany. I also told Eisenhower that I thought the British Foreign Office would write the ticket for Montgomery and that he should look forward to several departments in our government having much to do with his decisions.

As the Representative of the Allied Control Commission, Eisenhower being the good soldier that he is, of course is prepared to go through with the assignment, but he has no misapprehensions about the fact that he is almost certain to be deflated from his present outstanding position in the world.

I told Ike of Stalin's anxiety to have him come to Moscow on the 24th of June and if that was not convenient, any time before the time of the Berlin Conference or immediately after the Berlin Conference. Eisenhower told me he had been invited to Moscow sometime before but that the War Department had refused him permission to go, although he was very anxious to do so. Eisenhower thought it a mistake that he did not go when he was asked. He agreed that if he was to go to Moscow we should invite Zhukov to come to the United States. I took this matter up later with President Truman when I got back and he was all for the idea.

Ike told me during my visit that he was going to say his piece about universal military training and about a single combined military department in Washington after the war.

Eisenhower lives in a very lonely but modest home, surrounded by a great German forest and you get no impression of his having any side or pretentiousness about him. He talked at great length and freely about the strategy and tactics of the war and is quite satisfied with his whole record. He is anxious to get our troops back to their agreed occupation zones and thinks that any further delay will make trouble in Russia.

He expressed great appreciation of my getting Stalin to appoint Zhukov so promptly to the Allied Control Commission.

He has not many clear-cut views as to what the Allies should do about Germany, but treats his impending job with the Allied Control Commissions as that of a servant of the people to carry out their overall policies.

While I was there he was mixed up with very serious difficulties with the French who, against his orders, were maintaining soldiers in Italy and had refused to withdraw them. He said the French General had a technical

right to refuse, but in view of the United States request de Gaulle's position was indefensible. He said that the matter was out of his hands, however, and in the hands of the President. I saw the various dispatches later in Paris in which the French Commander in Italy had written a very abrupt and threatening note to the American Commander and had refused point-blank to remove his troops and stated that if any effort was made to move the French troops he, the French General, would consider it an unfriendly act. At the Embassy in Paris the question arose as to whether de Gaulle actually knew of this letter and had inspired it. It is unthinkable that the French General would take such high-handed action without some assurance that he would be backed up in Paris, so most of the people in the Paris Embassy seemed to think that de Gaulle knew of the action. The telegram from President Truman, which I read, had been received by de Gaulle the day before and had been answered unsatisfactorily. Truman put it right on the line that unless those troops were moved at once he would stop all Lend-Lease to the French troops. In fact, he told de Gaulle that he had ordered them stopped. In view of the fact that de Gaulle already had a public fight on with the British over the Levant, it seemed to me that he was being put in a pretty tight corner if he was going to take on the United States on the issue he had chosen. Later he backed down and the troops were removed.

Caffery, our Ambassador in France, urged Truman not to release the correspondence. There is no doubt in my mind that if the correspondence had been released at that particular moment de Gaulle's position in France would have been untenable and he would have been forced to resign. I learned later that Churchill wanted Truman to release it and so did Admiral Leahy, but Truman finally decided that he would not do so.

When I returned to Washington I urged Truman to acquaint Stalin of the French incident.

Eisenhower arranged for us to have his suite at the Raphael Hotel where he always stayed, and late Friday afternoon we flew to Paris.

Hopkins's report in the foregoing memorandum on some of Eisenhower's statements on political matters was, I believe, not entirely accurate. Eisenhower once told me (it was in London in March, 1944) that his family had always been Kansas Republicans, but that he himself had never voted in his life. He felt that since an Army officer must serve his government with full loyalty and devotion regardless of its political colouration, he should avoid all considerations of political partisanship. He conceded that there were other Army officers who felt differently about this for equally honourable reasons. Eisenhower did say to me, as he evidently said to Hopkins, that he had been opposed to the third term simply because he was naturally conservative and

a respector of tradition, but he was most emphatic in expressing his hope that Roosevelt would run for a fourth term and would be re-elected.

Hopkins arrived back in Washington on June 12 and breakfasted with Truman the next morning. The President congratulated him warmly on the extent of his accomplishment in Moscow and urged him to go to the Potsdam Conference the next month. But Hopkins knew that Byrnes would by then have succeeded Stettinius as Secretary of State, and he felt sure that his presence at Potsdam would create inevitable embarrassment, not because of any difference of opinion or ill will between the two men, but simply because of the obvious fact that both Stalin and Churchill were long accustomed to dealing with Hopkins and might therefore seem to by-pass Byrnes's authority. Truman appreciated the validity of these points and did not urge Hopkins to reconsider.

This was an extraordinary moment in Hopkins's life, for now he found himself in the thoroughly unfamiliar position of enjoying a very good Press. He was even, for a few days, something of a national hero. Of all the tributes paid to him, the one that touched him most came from a lady in Paris, Missouri, who was unknown to him—Mrs. Mary P. Blanton, wife of the editor of the *Monroe County Appeal*. She wrote: 'When I read the editorial in my husband's weekly paper this morning my impulse was to send it to you. None of us are averse to praise and "Those who stand in high places" may need a little at times. I hope your health is much improved and that you will soon be well and strong. The Middle West is proud of your work for our country.'

The editorial that Mrs. Blanton enclosed was as follows:

Palace Guard Saved the Day

Harry Hopkins is receiving much applause from newspapers and politicians who tried so hard to destroy him before Roosevelt's death. Always they sneered at him as 'the palace guard'. When a recent crisis arose between Russia on one hand and Britain and America on the other, President Truman sent Harry to Moscow to iron things out. Although in wretched health, he made the trip and did the job, thus proving the late President knew what he was doing when he kept this great American around. A lot of those who now applaud him should be apologizing to him for past slanders.

Despite Editor Blanton's admonition, I know of no instances of apologies being made to Hopkins for 'past slanders'. However, from now on the hate-drooling columnists did not pay much attention to him. They took little further interest in the White House Rasputin, probably because Hopkins's great friend, their real target, was dead. They now had nobody left to slander but the great friend's widow.

CONCLUSION

ON July 2, 1945, Hopkins finally severed his connection with the United States Government. In his letter to President Truman, he said: 'I want you to know how, along with millions of other Americans, I applaud your courageous and liberal administration of this government's domestic and foreign policy. The fact that you are surrounding yourself with competent and able men but adds to the confidence this nation has in you.' In replying, Truman paid handsome tribute to Hopkins's varied contributions to the war effort and did not overlook his earlier accomplishments as relief administrator. The President's letter ended: 'I am sure that you must feel much pride and a deep sense of accomplishment in all your great and patriotic service to our country during the last twelve years.'

Later, Hopkins realized that he had other posts—such as Chairman of the Munitions Assignment Board, member of the War Production Board, Chairman of the President's Soviet Protocol Committee, etc.—and he sent letters resigning from these as he remembered them.

Hopkins's old friend, Admiral 'Betty' Stark, wrote to him: 'Well done, thou good and faithful servant. I could nail that old Navy signal "Well Done" to every mast. There is much ahead of you, and God grant you health and a position where your splendid self may continue achievement . . . without undue strain on your health. Take care of yourself. My good wishes are ever with you—and my gratitude for all you have done for our country. We all owe you much. Keep cheerful.'

Listening to a broadcast about himself by Walter Winchell, Hopkins was so pleased that he was moved to write a letter of appreciation, which was unusual for him, mainly because he was given so few opportunities to express gratitude for kind words uttered in public. He said to Winchell: 'I don't know of anyone in semi-public life who stuck by Roosevelt as devotedly as did you. You really fought against Hitler in the days when it was none too popular and I think you deserve all the credit in the world for it. A more timid person would have backed away from that one.'

Hopkins gave up his house in Georgetown and moved to New York expecting to spend the rest of his life happily in the surroundings that he loved best. The Mayor, Fiorello LaGuardia, for whom he had tried so hard and so ineffectually to get a commission in the Army, now obtained for him appointment as impartial chairman for the New York clothing industry. This job involved a salary of $25,000 a year and not very onerous duties and Hopkins was glad to get it.

On July 4, he wrote to Winant of his decision not to go to Potsdam:

I am sorry I am not going to see you soon because I was looking forward to another visit with you. I had to stop this running around the earth at some point and this seemed as good a time as I could possibly find. While I am feeling better, I have a long way to go to be in the kind of shape I want to be in and I don't want to have to get started all over again.

I can't tell you how pleasant it has been all these years to work with you. I am sure our paths will cross frequently. At any rate I am anxious to keep in touch with you always and will let you know how things go with me.

The war in the Pacific seems to be moving as satisfactorily as we could hope but there are vital decisions still to be made.

The Germany I saw was a shambles, but I confess I am a little disquieted by suggestions I hear from some quarters that we do little or nothing to prevent the Germans from starting this business all over again. I have no confidence in them whatever, but I have a good healthy respect for their ability to hit us again in another twenty-five years.

It looks as though, if we all put our minds on it, we could throw Franco out of Spain, which would surely be a good riddance. Perhaps the House of Savoy could go along with him without anybody losing a heartbeat.

Hopkins, who had no particular record of scholarship to his credit, was surprised and delighted to receive an announcement from Oxford University that 'the Hebdomadal Council desires, subject to your consent, to submit to the Convocation of the University at an early date a proposal that the Honorary Degree of D.C.L. be conferred upon you, in recognition of your eminent services to the Allied cause'. He hastily communicated his consent and planned to go to England to receive the degree on October 25.

When the results of the British General Election were announced Hopkins said, in a letter to General Ismay: 'The news of the P.M.'s defeat is staggering. I thought the Elections would be close and that Labour might have a chance to win, but I never dreamed it would be the landslide it was. I only hope the P.M. did not take it too badly. He has been a gallant fighter and his deeds will go down in Anglo-Saxon history for all time.'

Hopkins wrote to Beaverbrook: 'I have heard from some of your men about publishing rights on anything I may want to write and I wish very much that you would put your mind on it. Specifically I am going to write at least two books and I think quite possibly three or four more. The first two are going to be a book on the war and the second book on Roosevelt as I knew him. I intend to take my time writing them and, under no circum-

stances, will the book on the war be published until the war with Japan is over. And I don't want to do any slipshod job on Roosevelt.'

Hopkins engaged an assistant, Sidney Hyman, to help in the organization of his voluminous papers preparatory to the writing of all the books that he planned. Hyman, a graduate of the University of Chicago, had been active in Midwestern political affairs before the war, in which he served with honour as an officer in the First Armoured Division in the North African and Italian campaigns. (This division was one of the few American units available for the operations known as MAGNET and GYMNAST when they were first planned at the Arcadia Conference in December, 1941.)

Hyman has written, of his first association with Hopkins in August, 1945:

I felt that H.L.H. was skidding around in his mind in search for a form he could give the book. He began everywhere and nowhere all at once. One day he would start to work on an introduction to the book, and the next day he would jump to the Yalta Conference and ask to see materials related to it. Every time the newspapers carried a story 'disclosing' a wartime secret, Hopkins would immediately re-examine his own documents as they bore on that event. It was under the prodding of current news items, for instance, that he wrote the memorandum about the conversation between F.D.R. and Ibn Saud, and between General Marshall and Governor Dewey.

When I put his papers into some rough order, he made several quick samplings of their contents and often expressed surprise at the presence of some memorandum he had written. He indicated to me that he had not only forgotten the record he made (the memoranda of his first London trip, for instance) but he had also forgotten the incident described in the record. When he went through papers that bore on his private life, he would sometimes snatch out a letter, stare at it, and snort. He made a point of the fact that all of these letters should be kept and none of them destroyed. Incidentally, he had earlier asked that I go through all his files and throw away 'irrelevant' materials. But I didn't throw away as much as one paper clip. Referring to the kind of letters he wanted saved, Hopkins said: 'This is the sort of thing I would object to having destroyed in the Roosevelt papers. The whole story of Roosevelt—and my story is part of it—is going to come out anyway in the next fifty years. I feel we will both come out with credit. And I don't see any point in trying to edit my past by destroying papers which showed precisely what I did and how I did it. I want people to know that I played politics; I also want them to know *why* I played politics.'

In his random, scattered approach to this book he quickly tired of the sampling process and at the time of his death had not gone through more

than one file drawer. In the same way that he would snort at the letters he plucked out, he would pluck books off the shelves and leaf through them. One day I saw him pick up a book put out by the W.P.A. It was an expensive printing job, with many plates and a very substantial-looking binding. He flourished the book and said to me, 'This is pure boondoggling. The people who attacked us for things like this were perfectly right. Of course, I would have been a God-damned fool to have agreed with them.' At the same time he was very proud of the guide-books put out by the W.P.A., and while he discarded several hundred novels and books on economics and politics when he moved into his Fifth Avenue house, he gave an honoured place on his library shelf to the W.P.A. series.

The paragraphs that Hopkins did get down on paper were hastily dictated and I do not believe that he ever bothered even to re-read them and work them into proper form. They were rambling and repetitious, and I have deleted some unimportant passages in the following:

I know no person in his right mind but that he believes if this nation ever had to engage in another war Great Britain would be fighting on our side, and yet, to hear some people talk about the British, you would think the British were our potential enemies. I believe that the British have saved our skins twice—once in 1914 and again in 1940. They, with the French, took the brunt of the attack in the First World War, and the Germans came within a hair's breadth of licking them both before we got into it. This time it was Britain alone that held the fort and they held that fort for us just as much as for themselves, because we would not have had a chance to have licked Hitler had Britain fallen. . . .

Many Britishers do not make it particularly easy for those of us who want to see a close-working relationship with Great Britain. When the Prime Minister said that he was not selected to be the King's Minister to liquidate the Empire, every isolationist in America cheered him. Before that, he had never been very popular with our isolationists in America. There is constant friction between our business interests and we think—and have no doubt with some good reason—that Great Britain would take an unfair advantage of us in trade around the world. It is footless to ignore the fact that the American people simply do not like the British Colonial policy. . . .

A little old-fashioned frankness on diplomatic levels would help. The wiping out of our trade barriers—and we have taken the first step in that—including reduction of our tariffs and the abolition of the British Empire preference scheme would go a long way towards accomplishing that end. The American people must realize the plain and simple truth

that the British live by trade. We are probably powerful enough, if we want to use that power, to seriously injure that trade, but I do not believe it is to our self-interest to do it. Why should we deliberately set about to make a weak Great Britain in the next hundred years unless we go on the assumption that war will be waged no more?

Two great powers such as the United States and Great Britain can afford to have minor differences. That is bound to be the case, but we cannot afford to indulge in a deliberate programme on either side which is going to force our two peoples further and further apart.

If I were to lay down the most cardinal principle of our foreign policy, it would be that we make absolutely sure that now and forever the United States and Great Britain are going to see eye to eye on major matters of world policy. It is easy to say that. It is hard to do, but it can be done and the effort is worth it.

As to our relations with the Soviet Union:

We know that we and Russia are the two most powerful nations in the world in manpower and raw materials. We know that we have been able to fight side by side with the Russians in the greatest war in all history. We know or believe that Russia's interests, so far as we can anticipate them, do not afford an opportunity for a major difference with us in foreign affairs. We believe we are mutually dependent upon each other for economic reasons. We find the Russians as individuals easy to deal with. The Russians undoubtedly like the American people. They like the United States. They trust the United States more than they trust any power in the world. I believe they not only have no wish to fight with us, but are determined to take their place in the world affairs in an international organization, and above all, they want to maintain friendly relations with us.

The great enigma about the Soviet Union in the years to come is the policy which new leaders of Russia will have toward the promotion of world-wide Communism. There is every indication that the Soviet Government today is becoming more and more nationalistic. They are going to see to it that their borders are protected from unfriendly states and I, for one, do not blame them for that.

There can be no question that the United States' permanent long-time relations with the Soviet Union are going to be seriously handicapped, not so much by our fundamental differences in ideology as between a capitalist economy and a socialist state, but between our fundamental notions of human liberty—freedom of speech, freedom of the Press and freedom of worship. The American people want not only freedom for themselves, but they want freedom throughout the world for other people as well, as they simply do not like the notion that you cannot say what you please when you want to say it.

If Russia wants a socialist state—and incidentally, anyone who thinks that the Soviet Union is moving to the right economically is, in my opinion, greatly mistaken—that is surely their own business. They are absolutely sure it is going to work better for the hundred and eighty million citizens of the Soviet Union than a capitalist economy would work. They do not think much of the way the capitalist economy worked in places like France, Belgium and Holland just before the war. They seem to have a pretty healthy respect for ours, however.

The thing the American people must look out for is that there is a minority in America who, for a variety of reasons, would just as soon have seen Russia defeated in the war and who said publicly before we got into the war that it did not make any difference which one—Russia or Germany—won. That small, vociferous minority can take advantage of every rift between ourselves and Russia to make trouble between our two countries. There are plenty of people in America who would have been perfectly willing to see our armies go right on through Germany and fight with Russia after Germany was defeated. They represent nobody but themselves and no government worth its salt in control of our country would ever permit that group to influence our official actions.

The Soviet Union is made up of a hundred and eighty million hardworking proud people. They are not an uncivilized people. They are a tenacious, determined people who think and act just like you and I do. Our Russian policy must not be dictated by people who have already made up their minds that there is no possibility of working with Russians and that our interests are bound to conflict and ultimately lead to war. From my point of view, that is an untenable position and can but lead to disaster.

France is another country whose strength and power are selfish assets to the United States. In the years to come, the French will be but a few hours from our shores. They have fought by our side ever since our Republic was founded and, indeed, joined with us in our own great Revolution. Our foreign policy towards France should not be governed by the personalities of the people who happen for the moment to be in executive power in either of our countries.

General de Gaulle has done some tremendous things for France. One thing he did was to make her people hold their heads high again and be proud they were Frenchmen, and to forget the humiliation of defeat in planning for the future. It is equally sure that General de Gaulle has not always been the easiest man to get on with in diplomatic affairs. There is no use of now trying to place the blame for the personal differences between President Roosevelt and General de Gaulle, but the important thing to the American people is not the temporary head of the Republic

of France, but the forty million Frenchmen who make up that great country. . . .

There are still plenty of people in America who think that old General Pétain was a great patriot and there are some of the old crowd in France who think like them. These people are usually scared to death because France, as, indeed, all of Europe, is moving on economic fronts to the left. It is a plain fact that the great masses of people in Europe are determined to find a new economic basis for a better life for themselves and their children. . . .

France must be sure of our friendship, not doubtful about it. France was betrayed by her military leaders, her industrialists and decadent politicians. We are the only nation in the world that can give France any economic support in this critical hour of her trial and haven't we every interest to do it?

When I speak of France I might as well be speaking of all of Western Europe, and this gets into a fundamental definition of our foreign policy in Europe and that is this: The United States first wants to do everything it can to prevent another war, hence we have an interest in every part of the world where war might break out, but even more than that, the United States' interests are not served by having any countries in Europe become totalitarism states, I don't care what label they give it.

That gets right into the question of the United States engaging in an aggressive, affirmative policy of promoting the democratic processes in Western Europe. . . . It surely is to our interest to see that the countries of Western Europe do not starve or freeze this winter, because as sure as that happens, governments are going to be overthrown and those who believe in the totalitarism system can well come into power and they are not dislodged easily. I do not see for the life of me why we should be diffident and apologetic and unaggressive about promoting the democratic process throughout the world. We do not want anything out of it for ourselves. We have no selfish interests in terms of land, but surely we do not want to see the people of the world enslaved with any more totalitarian governments. I simply think the Western world is not big enough for the kind of democracy we have and, for instance, Mr. Franco in Spain. . . .

I might say in passing here that I do not belong to the school that believes that a country like the Argentine can do as they please at our back door. I do not see why we should play ball in any way with that Fascist-dominated country.

I have had people all over the world ask me what the American interest is in places like Iraq, Iran, Poland, Greece, and so on. I give them two answers that I think are controlling in the United States. The first is

world security and the second is our interest in human freedom and justice throughout the world. I do not mean to say we do not have a proper economic interest and that we should not insist on our rights in all areas in the world for freedom of trade, but the American people in terms of a long-range foreign policy are never going to carry that as a major banner in our foreign affairs.

Nor do I see why this nation should not state unequivocally its belief in the political and economic freedom of all people throughout the world. Now, you can say that that spells the doom of all the Colonial Empires. Well, it probably does. A lot of those great Colonial States whenever they want freedom badly enough are going to get it, because none of these Colonial powers have enough soldiers to prevent them from having freedom when they really want it. You cannot dilute this business of freedom. Either you believe in it, or you don't. You can think of a hundred and one reasons why this and that Colonial country—or, for that matter, Puerto Rico—should not be free, but none of those reasons has ever made sense to me.

I am not recommending that we stir up revolutions all over the world, but I do say that the United States should not co-operate in any international enterprise that will tend to solidify for all time a political relationship which does not give actual and complete freedom to the people who want it.

If I were to indicate a country in which the United States, for the next hundred years, had the greatest interest from political and economic points of view, I would name the Republic of China. With the defeat of Japan, China will become one of the greatest land powers on earth. I do not say that she will be one of the most powerful for many years to come, but she will have regained her heritage in Manchuria and we hope that there will arise out of the welter of war a unified China.

(*Note.* This was written on August 1, 1945; Hopkins still believed that a settlement fair to China had been achieved at Yalta.)

It is ridiculous to assume China is not going to have great problems —internal political and economic problems—after this war is over. There are a great many things that need to be done in terms of human freedom in China, and I have no doubt that those things will be done. The United States, through the espousal of the 'Open Door Policy', has an absolutely clean record in China over the years. We must keep it so. China is going to depend upon us. There is no other country in the world that they can look to for economic support after this war is over. The Soviet Union is going to have all it can do to develop its own internal economy and Great Britain does not have the resources to help China to the road to anything that resembles prosperity. True, it will be a slow and painful

process and their standards of living for years to come will not resemble ours, but in many ways, with the end of this war, China will almost be our nearest neighbour. . . .

There are appalling economic differences between the masses of people in China and those who rule it. The great land reform is long overdue, but these things the Chinese people themselves will insist upon because there will be great revolutionary force at work in China to reform their economic system, and I think some of the new leaders in China, notably T. V. Soong, understand that thoroughly and are quite prepared for the kind of economic reform that must come to China.

When the results of the Potsdam Conference were announced, Hopkins was asked what he thought of them. He said: 'I don't know. It looks as if President Truman and Jimmy Byrnes did a good job—but you can't tell what the real problems are unless you're *there* and intimately involved in them and understanding all the background circumstances and the implications of what is said and what isn't said. The way the situation changes from day to day—or minute to minute—if you lose touch with it for as long as I have [one month] you're just about as ignorant of it as anybody else.' Certainly, at that time (about August 1) Hopkins had no idea that the Japanese war would end so soon, even though he did know that the Russians were about to come into it. He was eager to see Bohlen to hear his account of what went on at Potsdam.

Hopkins wrote down a few paragraphs of his views on the question of domestic policy. He said that it had been five years since he had been actively engaged in matters relating to the domestic scene, but he had talked to a great many soldiers and sailors and 'the one great question-mark in their minds is how are they going to earn a living'. He went on to say:

> We can and should have our schemes of social insurance for the old and the sick, but it would be a terrible day for America if the rest of us did not want to earn our living by work, or could not earn our living by work.
>
> These soldiers coming home simply are not going to understand our boasting about our capitalist economy if it can't deliver the goods in terms of the opportunity for work.
>
> I sense in some quarters a defeatist attitude towards this business of providing jobs for sixty million people. They think it is quixotic, or that it is radical. I can't for the life of me understand what they propose to do for the people that can't get work, but I think the other side of the picture is this: That this business of providing full employment has captured the imagination of the vast majority of the American people. They do not know just how it is going to be done, but they do not want any hesitancy

on the part of their political leaders or their industrial leaders or labour leaders to assume that it is possible.

Fortunately, in all probability for a few years after the war, apart from the adjustments that will have to be made in closing down the war plants, there will be a tremendous demand for goods and hence, a large overall employment, but the time is coming, and the planning must be made now, when the Government, industry, agriculture and labour will have to sit down together and find the way and means to assure that these opportunities shall be available.

I believe that during the war many thousands of business men have gained a healthy respect for Government and do not look at public institutions as something they wish to have no part of. After all, they know the tax structure is controlled by Government. The Government very largely controls credit. It is the biggest single business in the country. What the farmer and labourer do not want is to see Government running their affairs, but it is axiomatic that their affairs cannot be run without having a relationship to Government.

I would hate to see the backbone of full employment ever be public works for the sake of providing employment. It is a proper instrument to use when industrial employment slides off, but it surely is the line of least resistance.

On September 4 Hopkins made his last trip to Washington to receive the Distinguished Service Medal from President Truman. Secretary Stimson wrote to him: 'Your Distinguished Service Medal represented a service that was not only most distinguished and successful in crises of most far-reaching importance, but was rendered by you with a courage which was as great as it was modest. I have rejoiced in the recognition of your work which it symbolized. I share your exultation in our former trials. In the words of Virgil, *haec olim meminisse juvabit.*'

After the award of the medal, which was made in the White House garden in the presence of the Chiefs of Staff and many of Hopkins's other friends and associates, he had a private talk with Truman in which he told the President all that he knew of the negotiations with the British relative to the development of the atomic bomb. As has been recorded in earlier chapters, Hopkins had been associated with this development since the very inception of the National Defence Research Council. But he was completely out of touch with it in the final months preceding the Los Alamos test and he did not know that the bomb had become a reality until he read the dread name of Hiroshima in the headlines.

Early in October he received a letter from General Eisenhower in Berlin: 'I do not need to tell you that this job is an unholy mixture of irritations,

frustrations, and bewildering conflicts. Nevertheless, I try to keep my sense of humour and keep swinging with both hands. We have really made progress both toward the allied and the strictly national objectives, but there is much to do and in a job such as this we are particularly vulnerable to day-by-day criticism. An administrative blunder, even if local and temporary, is news; constructive progress is not dramatic.'

Eisenhower confessed in this letter that he had been thinking 'about the possibility of writing a book'. He said: 'I have even, from time to time, tried to draft a bit of narrative just to satisfy myself that I had something to say that was worth hearing. Actually I have not convinced myself of this at all and regardless of attractiveness of offers, it is the one thing on which I will have to be quite sure before I would ever consent to undertake such a job.' By this time—October—Hopkins was unable to do any real work of any kind. His health was deteriorating steadily—and, as usual, he said it was 'a touch of flu'. He was restless and unhappy and casting about for new things in which to become interested. Hyman has written:

It is my impression that on moving into his Fifth Avenue house, Hopkins seemed torn between a desire to hang on to everything he had done in the past, and at the same time to strip himself free of everything, as though he meant to get down to his own bare bones. (He commented on the fact that he was returning to New York to work among the same sort of people he had first met in New York thirty years before.) One day he asked me to contact art dealers and find out what they would be willing to pay for a great number of etchings he had had since the days of his marriage to Barbara Duncan Hopkins. An art auctioneer came over to the house one day to look at the collection and told me that their only value arose from the fact that Hopkins owned them—and that if the art concern was to make any money out of the deal, the sale would have to be advertised as 'A Harry Hopkins Auction'. I passed this information on to Hopkins, who balked at the idea of any such deal. But he asked to see the dealer. This man showed up on a day during which Hopkins had received and turned down four telephone calls from various important people. While he had earlier declared himself in no way fit to handle those calls, it was surprising to see him come down out of his bedroom to spend the whole afternoon cross-examining the art dealer on the nature of the auction business. In the first five minutes the dealer told Hopkins that the whole lot of etchings wouldn't bring more than $200. Hopkins lost interest in the sale, but he kept the dealer from two until five-thirty in the afternoon. The dealer seemed a little thinner when he left Hopkins's house. Hopkins had gouged out everything this man knew about the art auction business.

Hopkins spent less and less time at the Garment Union office—which was little enough to begin with—though he did arbitrate one case. I heard him talk of his work there and say that he found it of great interest. He was not merely content to be an impartial arbitrator, but proposed to bring about considerable changes in the structure of the garment industry.

At about this time there were two crippling strikes in the City of New York. One was an elevator strike, and the second one was a strike among coal-barge operators. He had been in bed during both strikes. But then he received word that both the elevator operators and representatives of the real estate interests were considering calling on him to arbitrate their difficulties. In watching the effect of this on Hopkins, I had a sense of a man being brought back from the dead. The dreaminess and irascibility that settled over him when he was sick were sloughed off. He got dressed, came downstairs, and spent some time on the phone barking out orders and directions. I may be quite wrong about this—but I felt that he wanted very badly to be back on active duty again. But the strike was settled without him, and Hopkins returned to his bed. A short while thereafter the same thing happened in the case of the tugboat strike, and once again he seemed to be sparked with new life when he was approached to mediate that strike.

Hopkins spent a lot of time studying catalogues and advertisements from the larger New York department stores, for he had contemplated the possibility of getting into this business ever since his association with Jesse Straus, of R. H. Macy and Company, during the days of the first Relief Programme in New York State. He also made a considerable study of modern paintings because of his wife's interest in this subject. With the advice and instruction of Monroe Wheeler, Director at the Museum of Modern Art in New York, Hopkins attacked this unfamiliar subject with the same penetrating curiosity and quick understanding that he had applied to silicosis and flood relief and grand strategy and other problems that he had been compelled to cope with in the course of his strange career. When he went to Memorial Hospital he had in his room a small Renoir, lent to him by a friend, Mrs. Barbara Wescott, and originals or reproductions of paintings by Utrillo, Picasso, Yves Tangug, Serge Ferat, Marsden Hartley and others, loaned by Wheeler.

By the middle of October Hopkins was confined to his own house and largely to his bedroom. He read the newspapers and listened to the radio and often felt the urge to express himself officially, as though he were still drafting cables for the President to send. On October 24, having read the results of elections in France, he wrote to de Gaulle:

I hasten to congratulate you on the implications of the French election. Irrespective of the merits of the various political parties concerned, the

election showed to the world the great vitality of French democracy and I think that much of the credit of this orderly outpouring of the French people to express their convictions at the polls is due to your patient and determined handling of your nation's affairs during the past dark and trying years.

France and the French people are emerging now into their own heritage, and, while I have no doubt the path ahead is going to be trying and difficult, I am as completely confident of the outcome as you have always been.

While I am no longer in the Government, I keep in close touch with affairs in Washington and I am following the fortunes of France with an ever-growing interest.

De Gaulle thanked him for his sympathy and his vision and said: 'I am happy to see that you have not lost contact with Washington, so that your country may still profit by the counsels of your great experience.'

On November 2 Hopkins wrote to the War Department on behalf of a private soldier in California, whose wife and child had been stricken with infantile paralysis. He suggested that the Department might explore the possibility of releasing this man from the Army, but he said he wished to emphasize that 'I am not requesting that anything be done for him that would not be done for any other soldier in similar circumstances'.

A few days after writing that letter Hopkins was ordered to the hospital and he remained there to die.

The Pearl Harbour Investigation had started in the Congress and Hopkins worried about it a great deal, for he knew that the main purpose of some of the Republicans and all the isolationists of both parties was to affix the blame for the Japanese attack entirely on Roosevelt. Weak and helpless as he was, Hopkins was obsessed with fears and suspicions that some of the high-ranking witnesses before the Congressional Committee would distort their testimony in order to absolve themselves from any possible share of the responsibility. His fears were groundless. He read the records of the hearings as they piled up day after day and he expressed to Hyman his particular admiration and high praise for the manner in which Admiral Stark had conducted himself before the Committee. He knew that Stark was one officer who might have grounds for resentment against Roosevelt, and who himself was one of the principal targets for criticism, but the former Chief of Naval Operations revealed his devoted loyalty and his unassailable honour under fire. There were many times when Hopkins asked the doctors to let him get out of bed and go down to Washington to give his own testimony, but he was utterly unable to do so.

He also worried a great deal about financial matters. With the arrival of

the New Year, 1946, he had been in the hospital for two months, and it was becoming more and more evident that his condition was not improving and it would be a long time before he could perform even his light duties as chairman of the clothing industry. Furthermore, he did not know when he would be able to get to work on his book, for which he had already received (and spent) advance royalties. His expenses were heavy and he was going into debt, borrowing money from friends, including Bernard Baruch.

On January 22, 1946, Hopkins wrote what I believe was the last letter of his life. It was to Winston Churchill, who was then on holiday in Miami Beach. He said:

> Only being laid up in the hospital prevented me from meeting you at the boat the other day and I do hope you will find it possible to get to New York, because it appears altogether unlikely that I could possibly be in Florida during the next month.
>
> All I can say about myself at the moment is that I am getting excellent care, while the doctors are struggling over a very bad case of cirrhosis of the liver—not due, I regret to say, from taking too much alcohol. But I must say that I dislike having the effect of a long life of congenial and useful drinking and neither deserve the reputation nor enjoy its pleasures.
>
> The newspapers indicate you and Clemmie are having a quiet and delightful time and I hope you won't let any Congressional Committee of ours bore you.
>
> Do give my love to Clemmie and Sarah, all of whom I shall hope to see before you go back, but I want to have a good talk with you over the state of world affairs, to say nothing of our private lives.

A week later Hopkins was dead. The post-mortem revealed no cirrhosis of the liver, and no cancer. He was killed by a disease known as haemo-chromatosis, the result of his inadequate digestive equipment.

Hopkins had spent so much time at death's door during the past nine years that the final act of passing through it must have been for him pretty much of a routine matter. He was generally unconscious for days before he died, but I am sure that if he had any moment of awareness of the imminence of death he did not accept it calmly, in a spirit of resignation, but did his best to fight against it, for he certainly wanted to live on with his family, whom he loved, and to know how everything was going to come out.

The day after Hopkins's death I read an editorial in the *Los Angeles Times* which recited the familiar complaint that he was 'never elected by the people to a public office' and that his activities as Presidential adviser were 'out of bounds by any constitutional concept', and it added: 'Americans need not concern themselves now whether Harry Hopkins was great or little or good

or bad; their care should be that the phenomenon of a Harry Hopkins in the White House does not recur.'

The editorial did not state just what measures should be taken to prevent such a recurrence—possibly a law providing that the President's personal friends and advisers, and even his guests at the White House, must be elected by popular vote or at least be made subject to approval by the Senate. However, I suspect that what the *Los Angeles Times* was really expressing was the hope that a phenomenon like Franklin D. Roosevelt would not recur. I believe that Roosevelt's closest friends join in that particular hope, not for the sake of his memory, which will take care of itself, but in the interests of the nation and indeed of the entire world which must never again be in the position in time of peril of placing so much reliance on the imagination and the courage and the durability of one mortal man.

I came out of my own experience of five years of Government service in wartime with alarmed awareness of the risks that we run of disastrous fallibility at the very top of our Constitutional structure. There is far too great a gap between the President and the Congress, particularly if he is, as every President should be, endowed with exceptional qualities. It is all very well to say that this gap might be closed by more efficient, businesslike methods in the White House; but the extraordinary and solitary Constitutional powers of the President remain and, in times of crises, they are going to be asserted for better or for worse.

To go back to the beginning, it may be that George Washington was too great a man for the nation's eventual good. For the Founding Fathers established the office of President with the knowledge that Washington was there to fill it. They fitted the office to his tremendous measurements. They established the triheaded system of checks and balances to ensure that no President would ever become king. But, having taken this precaution, they gave the President the supreme authority of a Commander-in-Chief in peacetime as well as in war.

In the Lincoln Memorial in Washington are the words, IN THIS TEMPLE AS IN THE HEARTS OF THE PEOPLE FOR WHOM HE SAVED THE UNION THE MEMORY OF ABRAHAM LINCOLN IS ENSHRINED FOREVER. Those are beautiful words, but they are very ominous ones. They perpetuate admission that had not this one man been born and miraculously elected, the Union would have been destroyed.

The remarkable luck that we have had in meeting major emergencies in the past should not prevent us now from giving most serious consideration to the question: Where is the guarantee that this luck will hold? Presumably it lies in the genius of the American people, but one does not need to have access to any secret documents to know how difficult it is for this genius to express itself or even to realize itself. In the fateful years of 1933 and 1940

the people needed and demanded leadership which could be given to them only by the President, the one officer of Government who is elected by all the people and whose duty it is to represent the interests of the nation as a whole rather than the purely local or special interests which are too often the predominant concerns of the Congress. There is no factor in our national life more dangerous than the people's lack of confidence in the Congress to rise above the level of picayune parochialism; the threats of Communism or Fascism are trivial as compared with this. Some Americans have looked enviously at the British parliamentary system, particularly as it demonstrated itself when, in the face of approaching disaster, the hapless, anachronistic Government of Neville Chamberlain was superseded by the vigorous and truly representative Government of Winston Churchill—a historical change which was achieved in an orderly manner, within a matter of hours, and entirely within the House of Commons whose authority and dignity continued unimpaired. However, I doubt that there are many thoughtful Americans who believe that this venerable British system or anything like it could be made to work with us. Our own problems, and they are very large ones, will be worked out in accordance with our own Constitutional system, with the President remaining in the White House and the Congress on Capitol Hill; but surely a way can be found to diminish the distance between these two points.

Roosevelt has often been blamed for widening the gap between the Executive and Legislative branches. I think he only revealed it. He brought the essential problems out into the open and gave them a much-needed airing. He was more successful than any previous President in dramatizing and personalizing the processes of government for the people. One obvious result of his influence was the enormously healthy increase in the number of votes cast in national elections. Of course, previous Presidents had not enjoyed the peculiar advantages afforded by the mechanical development of the radio, but future Presidents will have ever greater access to this means of direct communication, plus television, plus God knows how many other contrivances. This tends greatly to increase the solitary power of the President and to make him all the more indispensable in emergencies when he happens to enjoy popularity and prestige comparable to Roosevelt's.

That word 'indispensable' was flung at Roosevelt time and again in tones of wrathful scorn by his domestic enemies, and they could always sting him with it, since he could make no effective retort. There are few documents recorded in this book which interested me more than the memorandum written by Hopkins on May 28, 1939 (it appears in Chapter IV) describing a long talk with Eleanor Roosevelt: 'She thinks that the causes for which he fought are far greater than any individual person, but that if the New Deal is entirely dependent upon him, it indicates that it hasn't as strong a founda-

tion as she believes it has with the great masses of the people.' I believe that there Mrs. Roosevelt was expressing her husband's point of view as well as her own, and events proved that the survival of the New Deal reforms was not dependent on Roosevelt or on any other individual. Nevertheless, history must record the unalterable fact that in 1940 Roosevelt *was* indispensable— not because there were no other able and far-seeing and courageous states- men in the United States—but simply because he was the only one whom most of the American people re-elected, regardless of the third term tradition, and chose to follow through the gathering shadows of the Second World War.

This was a fundamental circumstance, and we may all pray that it will never recur; but as we look ahead into the dread prospects of the atomic age we can be none too sure that it will not. Our need for great men in the Presidency will continue, and our need for great men in the Congress will increase.

When I was coming to the end of the long work on this book I went to London for final checking of some of the material included, and I attended the unveiling by Mrs. Roosevelt of the statue of her husband in Grosvenor Square. That evening—April 12, 1948—The Pilgrims Society gave a dinner for Mrs. Roosevelt at which Winston Churchill expressed his solemn con- viction 'that in Roosevelt's life and by his actions he changed, he altered decisively and permanently, the social axis, the moral axis, of mankind by involving the New World inexorably and irrevocably in the fortunes of the Old. His life must therefore be regarded as one of the commanding events in human destiny.' The Former Naval Person also said of his old friend: 'The longer his life and times are studied, the more unchallengeable these affirma- tions which I have made to you tonight will become.' These were the words of a great student of history who knew whereof he spoke. I believed at the time of Roosevelt's death—and this belief has been fortified by all I have learned subsequently—that as more and more of the record is revealed, the greater his stature will become. But the story of his life is by no means ended, nor is the task to which he set himself anywhere near complete. As Hopkins said to me after the funeral service in the White House: 'Now we've got to get to work on our own. This is where we've really got to begin.'

Hopkins was able to do one job on his own—his last trip to Moscow— and after that there was too little life left in him. I believe that he went to his death with grave misgivings for the immediate future. I do not believe that he had any apprehensions as to the imminence of another war, for he could not conceive the possibility of anything so suicidal or so unnecessary. What he did fear was that there would be innumerable attempts to foul the record for partisans or for vindictive or selfish personal reasons, and that such attempts might be temporarily successful, and the people might become

mired in another age of decadent disillusionment such as that which followed the First World War, or another age of unbridled rapacity such as that which followed the Civil War. These were the real fears that Hopkins took with him into death, and it would seem that so far they have not been justified. He also took with him the knowledge that there were very few men who ever lived who were as fortunate as he in the possession of such enemies and such friends.

OPERATION CODE NAMES

ABC-1—first American-British outline of grand strategy for the war (March 1941)

ANAKIM—code name for land offensive in North Burma to drive out Japanese and reopen Burma Road and an amphibious operation in the south to recapture port of Rangoon

ANVIL—original code name for landing of American and French forces in the Toulon-Marseilles area of Southern France. Later changed for security reasons to DRAGOON.

AVALANCHE—code name for landings at the Salerno beachhead south of Naples.

BOLERO—code name given to process of building up required U.S. forces and supplies in the British Isles.

BUCCANEER—code name for briefly projected amphibious offensive against the Andaman Islands in Bay of Bengal.

DRAGOON—final code name of French-American landings in Southern France.

FLINTLOCK—code name of attack on Kwajalein Atoll in the Marshall Islands.

GYMNAST, SUPER-GYMNAST—early code names for landings in Algiers and French Morocco.

HUSKY—code name for invasion of Sicily.

JUPITER—code name for suggested landing in Norway.

LIFEBELT—code name for projected operation to seize Azores for use as a base in Battle of the Atlantic and as an airbase for ferrying bombers and transport planes. Aim of operation finally achieved by diplomatic negotiations.

LIGHTFOOT—code name for drive by Generals Alexander and Montgomery from Egypt in October 1942. Battle of El Alamein marked the beginning of this operation.

MAGNET—code name for movement of first American forces to Northern Ireland.

OVERLORD—final code name for the cross-Channel invasion.

POINTBLANK—code name of combined British-American bombing offensive of German communication and supply lines.

ROUNDUP—code name for major combined cross-Channel offensive against German-dominated Europe, to be mounted in 1943 or later. Later changed to OVERLORD.

SLEDGEHAMMER—(1) originally code name for a limited trans-Channel assault in 1942, planned originally as emergency operation in case of imminent collapse of Russian Front or internal German collapse.
(2) later used as code name for operation to seize the Cotentin Peninsula to be held as a European bridgehead until ROUNDUP could be mounted.

STRANGLE—code name of combined bombing of German communication and supply lines in Italy.

TORCH—final code name for the North Africa landings.

VELVET—code name of plan for building up a British-American air force in the Caucasus by end of 1942.

OPERATION CODE NAMES

NOTES AND INDEX

NOTES

4. The quotation of the statement made by Roosevelt to Wendell Willkie on January 19, 1941, was told many times by Willkie and this version of it has been checked with Mrs. Willkie.

6. The analogy between Hopkins's position and that of Colonel House has often been made and there were, of course, some resemblances. However, the personalities of Wilson and House, on the one hand, and of Roosevelt and Hopkins, on the other, were widely different and so consequently was the quality of the relationships.

   In connection with the quotation from Roosevelt, 'Harry is the perfect Ambassador,' etc., when Roosevelt used a relatively modern slang expression such as 'Oh, yeah?!' he would usually add 'as my boy Johnny says.' I do not know just why John Roosevelt was credited with the origination of these expressions but presumably, since he was the youngest, he was the most fecund source during the later years when I was around the White House. Near the end of his life Roosevelt picked up the expression, 'So what?' from his son John, and he loved to use it.

6–7. The quotation from Winston Churchill, 'I have been present,' etc., was in a public statement made immediately after Hopkins's death. The subsequent anecdote about 'Lord Root of the Matter' was told me by Churchill himself.

10. Quotations are made from *The Roosevelt I Knew*, by Frances Perkins (The Viking Press); 'The Morgenthau Diaries,' published in *Collier's*, September, 1947; *On Active Service in Peace and War*, by Henry L. Stimson and McGeorge Bundy (Harper & Brothers).

CHAPTER II

14. The best biographical sketches of Hopkins that I have read appeared in *Fortune* magazine (July, 1935) and *The New Yorker* (August 7 and 14, 1943), the latter a profile by Geoffrey Hellman.

CHAPTER III

40. The comment by Hopkins on Roosevelt's First Inaugural Address was quoted from a preface that he wrote for *Nothing to Fear* (Houghton Mifflin), edited by B. D. Zevin.

   Quotations from the First Inaugural and from all other speeches and official writings by Roosevelt, and from his press conferences, in this chapter are quoted from *The Public Papers and Addresses of Franklin D. Roosevelt*, edited by Samuel I. Rosenman. This same great source has been used for similar quotations up to Chapter XII.

   Quotations of Ernie Pyle were from the *Washington News*, of Walter Lippmann from the *New York Herald Tribune*, of Gerald W. Johnson from his book, *Roosevelt—Dictator or Democrat?* (Harper & Brothers); of Ernest K. Lindley from his book, *The Roosevelt Revolution* (The Viking Press).

page

55. The issue of *Time* magazine which featured Hopkins on its cover and which is quoted at various points in this chapter was dated February 19, 1934.

56. The survey of the whole relief programme from which quotations on the work of C.W.A. are made appeared in *Fortune* magazine, October, 1934.

57. The Gutzon Borglum letter to Aubrey Williams was dated December 20, 1933.

60. Hopkins's Press conference from which quotations are made was held on April 4, 1935. (Incidentally, as these notes are being written, I read that orators at the Republican Convention of 1948 are still quoting Hopkins as having said, 'The people are too damned dumb to understand.' It will be seen from the transcript of his remarks that this particular statement was directed not at the people but at the critical orators.)

73. Harold Smith, Director of the Budget during the war years, whose remarks to me are quoted in this chapter and in later chapters, kept very careful records of his many talks with President Roosevelt which will be of inestimable value to students of this era.

CHAPTER IV

78. The Hopkins notes on the Ohio situation were made in a diary which he kept spasmodically at that time. Most of his notes in this and subsequent chapters were written not in diary form but as strictly personal memoranda for his future reference; some of these were dictated, and many more were written in long-hand and never even entrusted to a secretary for copying. Once Jerome Beatty visited Hopkins in the White House and expressed the hope that he was keeping a careful diary. Hopkins replied, 'No one who keeps a diary would last long around here.' And when I first went to work in the White House, General Watson asked me if I were keeping a diary and, when I told him that I had formerly done so but had abandoned it, he advised me to keep right on abandoning it.

81. Quotations from Hugh Johson in this and subsequent chapter are from his column syndicated by the Scripps-Howard newspapers; so was the Talburt cartoon referred to.

93. The extent to which Roosevelt fostered the Hopkins candidacy for the Presidential nomination must remain among the more controversial points in this book. I can make no claims to personal knowledge on this subject. I merely present the story as I found it in the Hopkins papers supplemented by numerous interviews with various persons involved with Roosevelt and Hopkins at that time. Of course, the recollections of individuals on such matters of secret political manœuvering are apt to be coloured and confused by bias of one form or another, and I have been inevitably influenced by my own estimates of the reliability of information that I have received. Grace Tully, who has been immeasurably helpful to me in checking the accuracy of much of the material in this book, has expressed emphatic disbelief that Roosevelt ever made any attempt to 'build up' Hopkins as a Presidential candidate. She has said, 'F.D.R. and Harry both were too smart to imagine that Harry, politically unpopular and *divorced*, could possibly be nominated.' I must say that I should consider that an extremely sensible statement

page

were it not for the very substantial mass of evidence that I have found to the contrary. Miss Tully also questions the statement that Senator Robert M. La Follette could have been considered for the post of Secretary of State. She has said, 'Harry was devoted to Bob La Follette but knowing him as well as he did how could he have thought for one moment that he was not an isolationist considering his background and devotion to his father?' Here again I can only quote the statement as Hopkins wrote it in the spring of 1938 when, it must be added, the isolationist-interventionist issue had not been joined.

105. Like many other government officials, Hopkins obtained the originals of cartoons of himself and had them framed and hung on the walls of his home (when he had one). One cartoon of which he was particularly proud—and I have never been able to identify the source of it—appeared at the time of his departure from W.P.A. and appointment as Secretary of Commerce; it showed him as the man who had spent nine billion dollars of public funds without a penny of it sticking to his fingers.

112–113. The memorandum by Hopkins describing his visit to Warm Springs was written in longhand and never typed. In this memorandum, Hopkins mentioned Roosevelt's tendency to repeat the same anecdotes and reminiscences many times to the same listeners. On this, Grace Tully has written me, 'I must say he never deviated in his stories, which Missy and I heard one dozen times a year—all of them—but we loved them, provided they were spaced a bit.' Roosevelt was never one to say, 'Stop me if you've heard this.' I always felt sure that he was perfectly well aware that he had told the same story to the same audience but he went right ahead with it, regardless. It was for him a superb exercise in relaxation.

115. In reference to Hopkins's memorandum of May 28, 1939, describing a luncheon and talk with Mrs. Roosevelt at the White House: I have not questioned Mrs. Roosevelt about this or, as I have said in the Introduction, on any other points connected with the preparation of this book. My reluctance to consult so great and in many respects so final an authority on much of this material was due to my feeling that it would be embarrassing to Mrs. Roosevelt to assume any degree of responsibility, even indirectly, for any of this material.

Raymond Swing, having read proofs of this chapter, wrote to question me about my 'distaste for Harry having had political ambitions,' He said, 'I cannot as yet share your prejudice against his aspiring to be President, although I do not believe he would have made a good one, but as you wrote the passages on this question you left the impression that you knew things worse than you have included in the book. Is this so?' The answer to that is 'No.' Certainly the desire to become President of the United States is not an unworthy one, but it seemed to me that some of Hopkins' tactics were discreditable (and, indeed, so were some of those employed by Abraham Lincoln in his quest of the nomination in 1860), and I believe that Hopkins himself later regretted them. He certainly intended to make no secret of them had he lived to write his autobiography. Evidence of this is provided by remarks he made near the end of his life to Sidney Hyman, quoted in Chapter XXXVII.

CHAPTER V

129. The Elmo Roper Public Opinion Polls cited in this and other chapters appeared originally in *Fortune* magazine; the George Gallup Polls were clipped for the most part by Hopkins from the *Washington Post*.

Although it is correct to say that the Rome-Berlin-Tokyo Axis had not been formed at this time (September, 1939) and did not come into being until the Tripartite Pact of a year later, there was association of Germany, Italy and Japan in the anti-Comintern Agreement. However, the Roper Poll quoted limited its questionnaire to 'The present European war'.

132. Sir Robert Bruce-Lockhart's book, *Comes the Reckoning*, has been published in Great Britain by Putnam's, but has not at this writing appeared in the United States.

134. The famous meeting in the President's study of Roosevelt, Hull, Garner, Borah and others in the summer of 1939 was first described by Joseph Alsop and Robert Kinter in *The American White Paper* (Simon and Schuster) and again in *The Memoirs of Cordell Hull* (Macmillan).

139. The quotations from Sumner Welles on his trip to Europe in the winter of 1940 are from his book, *Time for Decision* (Harper & Brothers).

140-141. The first quotation from Winston Churchill at the end of this chapter was from his book, *Into Battle* (Cassell & Co.); the second quotation was from reports made by W. Averell Harriman of conferences in Moscow in August, 1942, at which he was present. (The speeches included in *Into Battle* were published in this country by G. P. Putnam's Sons under the title, *Blood, Sweat and Tears*.)

The Churchill war speeches appeared in *Into Battle*, covering May, 1938 to November, 1940; *Unrelenting Struggle* (Little, Brown & Company), covering 1941; *The End of the Beginning* (Little, Brown & Company), covering 1942; *Onwards to Victory* (Little, Brown & Company), covering 1943; *Dawn of Liberation* (Little, Brown & Company), covering 1944; *Victory* (Little, Brown & Company), covering 1945; and *The Secret Session Speeches of Winston Churchill* (Simon and Schuster).

CHAPTER VI

Although, as I have stated in this chapter, none of the secret cables quoted in part or summarized was included in the Hopkins papers, I have seen the full text of all those that I have mentioned and can assure the reader that I have not suppressed or glossed over any points of importance.

144. Reference is made to Edmond Taylor's book, *The Strategy of Terror* (Houghton Mifflin), which deserves to be studied as a profound discussion of psychological warfare, or 'political warfare', as it was called in England.

CHAPTER VII

Published works on which some of the material in this chapter was based included: *The Arsenal of Democracy* (Harcourt, Brace & Company), by Donald Nelson; *On Active Service in Peace and War* (Harper & Brothers), by Henry Stimson and McGeorge Bundy; *Together* (Tupper and Love, Inc.), by Katherine

Tupper Marshall; *The Battle against Isolation* (University of Chicago Press), by Walter Johnson; *Scientists against Time* (Little, Brown & Company), by James Phinney Baxter; *Atomic Energy for Military Purposes* (Princeton University Press), by Henry De Wolf Smyth.

161. The Hopkins Press conference from which quotations are made was held on May 23, 1940.

CHAPTER VIII

Quotations are made in this chapter from *Jim Farley's Story* (McGraw-Hill [Whittlesey House]) and from *You're the Boss* (The Viking Press, by Edward J. Flynn.

173–174. Missy LeHand's joke about 'The man who came to dinner' was not, of course to be taken literally, since George S. Kaufman and Moss Hart had written this highly successful comedy a year before Hopkins went to dine at the White House and remained for three and a half years.

175. My authority for the statement that 'Roosevelt considered Willkie the most formidable opponent for himself that the Republicans could have named' was Roosevelt himself. He remarked on this to me when the campaign was in its final stages that fall. I made no note of his exact words but they were, in effect, 'all the Isolationists would vote against me no matter whom the Republicans nominated. Willkie was the only one of the likely candidates who could have a good chance of cutting in on the Independent vote.'

199. In mentioning a Republican broadcast on election eve I have said that the rumours that American troops might be sent to seize the island of Martinique were 'not entirely baseless'. Special detachments had already been in training in amphibious operations for the capture of Martinique in the event of any likelihood that Germany might seek to exploit this strategic possession of the Vichy Government in the Western Hemisphere. Such American action, of course, was never taken, but it was most seriously contemplated. I doubt that Roosevelt would have hesitated to send U.S. forces to Martinique if he had considered this necessary to prevent it from falling into the hands of Hitler.

CHAPTER IX

202–203. The quotation from Marquis W. Childs was in his article, 'The President's Best Friend', in the *Saturday Evening Post*, April 19, 1941.

207–208. The original members of the Cuff Links Gang, aside from Howe, Early, and Marvin McIntyre, included Charles H. McCarthy, Thomas Lynch, Kirke L. Simpson, Stanley Prenosil and James P. Sullivan. Samuel I. Rosenman became a member during later years, and so did such old friends as Henry Morgenthau, Basil O'Connor and Henry Hooker. Added during the White House years were Hopkins, Watson, Ross McIntire, and myself. The annual meeting of this Gang was at dinner on Roosevelt's birthday and a poker game followed. The ladies who joined these gatherings (but certainly not the poker game) were Mrs. Roosevelt, Mrs. Morgenthau, Miss LeHand, Miss Tully, Marion Dickerman, Nancy Cook, Margaret Durand, and Malvina C. Thompson. It was Roosevelt's pleasant practice to give a present to each of the guests at these birthday parties.

page

These presents required a great deal of preparatory imagination and work on his part and many of them possessed historical as well as sentimental value. We generally chipped in to buy a joint gift for him in the form of old prints or rare books that we believed would add to his collections.

210. The reorganization plan, proposed originally in 1938, which in 1939 caused the Bureau of the Budget to be put into the Executive Offices, was the result of recommendations made by a committee of which Louis Brownlow was chairman and Charles E. Merriam and Luther Gulick members.

211. Many observers referred, as Harold Smith did, to Hopkins's position as that of a sort of Chief of Staff to the President. The position held after July, 1942, by Admiral William D. Leahy was that of Chief of Staff to the President in his capacity as Commander in Chief of the Armed Forces of the United States, but not as the political head of the United States Government.

218. The paragraphs quoted from Carl Sandburg were dictated by him in the White House on October 27, 1940.

219. The quotation from Hopkins on Roosevelt's speeches was in the preface that he wrote for *Nothing to Fear*, previously noted.

CHAPTER X

221. Most of the material on Roosevelt's cruise in December, 1940, was taken from the log of the *U.S.S. Tuscaloosa*.

222. Reference is made here to the motion pictures seen on shipboard. Roosevelt was very fond of movies in general, and so were both Churchill and Stalin. Roosevelt had no particular favourites, although he was greatly pleased with Darryl F. Zanuck's production, 'Wilson', in 1944. There was no question of doubt as to what was Churchill's favourite: it was 'Lady Hamilton', starring Laurence Olivier and Vivien Leigh, and produced by Alexander Korda who was rewarded with a knighthood for this dramatic tribute to British sea power. Churchill saw this picture over and over again and members of his staff, though enjoying and admiring it greatly the first two or three times, eventually wished that the Prime Minister would develop an enthusiasm for some other film. I have been told that Stalin's favourite non-Russian film was 'The Great Waltz', the Metro-Goldwyn-Mayer production based on the life and works of Johann Strauss.

The remarkable letter from Churchill to Roosevelt, dated December 7, 1940, has been quoted in part in the *Morgenthau Diaries* and the *Hull Memoirs*. I asked for Churchill's permission to quote it in full and such permission was withheld; I believe that Churchill will publish it in the second volume of his memoirs.

226. The quotation from Hopkins on the inception of Lend Lease was a personal recollection. So was the quotation from Roosevelt on the State Department deletion in his 'Arsenal of Democracy' speech.

CHAPTER XI

231. Miss LeHand was present at the conversation between Roosevelt and Hopkins mentioned at the start of this chapter and made some notes on it.

page

235. The American Embassy in London kept a complete record of Hopkins's appointments and travels during his visit to Great Britain at this time.

238. Hopkins's letters to Roosevelt on Claridge's stationery, dated January 10 and 13, 1941, were largely notes for the refreshment of his own memory when he should return to Washington and report directly to the President. He made no attempt at literary style. Miss LeHand gave these notes back to him when he returned to the White House and he never had them typed out.

242. In reference to Roosevelt's habit of going to bed at a reasonable hour: Grace Tully points out that frequently when his baskets were piled up with letters, memoranda, reports, etc., he would sit up until well after midnight with her and perhaps a relay of secretaries to get through this tiresome work. It was always amazing to me to watch him at work with these baskets: his patience seemed infinite.

250. In Hopkins's report of his lunch at Buckingham Palace is mention of 'the firing of the U.P. gun'. This was a demonstration of some sort of device; the missile became caught in the rigging of the battleship on which Churchill and Hopkins were standing and it exploded, almost ending their careers.

259. The 'note written later', in which Hopkins revealed more of Anthony Eden's views on the Far Eastern situation, was part of a memorandum written after Pearl Harbour; it is published in full in Chapter XIX.

CHAPTER XII

264-265. The 'bread-and-butter letter' from Hopkins to Churchill was dated March 19, 1941.

267. The quotations from the Roosevelt speech following the passage of Lend Lease were taken from mimeographed copies as issued to the Press. The same applies to all subsequent quotations of Roosevelt's speeches. *The Public Papers and Addresses of Franklin D. Roosevelt,* as edited by Samuel I. Rosenman, ended with the start of the third term in January, 1941. As this is written, Judge Rosenman is editing the final volume for the years 1941–1945 and these will be published by Harper & Brothers. It should be noted that the mimeographed copies of the speeches were not always ultimately accurate, for they obviously did not include Roosevelt's sometimes extensive ad-libbing; I believe that the *New York Times* was the only newspaper which invariably transcribed the Roosevelt speeches and printed them in full exactly as delivered.

272. The memorandum by Admiral Yarnell was dated January 9, 1941.

273. Although, in the plan known as A.B.C.—1, 'Subversive Activities and Propaganda' were listed as item number three in the primary measures to be taken against Germany, the United States Government had no plans for any propaganda organization or, indeed, any idea where such an organization would be put in the Administration. In July, 1941, Roosevelt authorized Colonel William J. Donovan to organize the Office of Co-ordinator of Information, but the word 'Information' applied to intelligence rather than propaganda. As part of the Donovan organization, I organized the Foreign Information Service which began to study and then carried on the operations of psychological warfare in many parts of the world

page

    outside the Western Hemisphere. In June, 1942, the Foreign Information Service became the Overseas Branch of the Office of War Information.

274. The quotation of Charles A. Beard is from his book, *President Roosevelt and the Coming of the War* 1941 (Yale University Press).

CHAPTER XIII

275–276. The memorandum from Admiral Turner to the Chief of Naval Operations was dated April 12, 1941.

    The letter from Harriman to Hopkins on 'living in a nightmare' was dated May 6.

277. Material on the President's cruise of March 19–April 1 is taken largely from the log of the *U.S.S. Potomac*.

282–287. All of the letters, memoranda, etc., from which bits are quoted in this letter were dated between the latter part of March and the early part of July.

290. Admiral Stark's letter to Hopkins relative to the Iceland Expedition was dated June 17.

CHAPTER XIV

301. The appreciation shown to Hopkins by Ambassador Winant was written by General Raymond E. Lee and dated May 27, 1941.

303–309. The letter from Stimson to Roosevelt was written June 23. The British estimate subsequently quoted was written July 1. The Davies memorandum was July 8. The Swope letter to Hopkins was also dated June 23.

312. The message from Churchill to Wavell concerning Harriman was dated June 3, and the Harriman memorandum, July 16.

318. One of the most peculiar blanks that I encountered in the Hopkins papers concerned the genesis of his first trip to Moscow. It had been my understanding that there was no mention of this between him and Roosevelt before he left Washington. His papers contained no evidence as to when or how it was decided that he would make the trip, or what instructions he received from the President. The only relevant document prior to his departure was the cable containing Roosevelt's message to Stalin, which was signed by Sumner Welles. I talked to Welles, Churchill, Ismay, Harriman, and others about this but there was no clear recollection by any of them as to how the subject had come up. It seemed to be the general impression that Hopkins had arranged it by telephone to the President from London or Chequers. Winant, however, remembered very clearly the drafting of a cable by Hopkins to the President on July 25, and a brief reply from the President telling him to go ahead. Winant had no record of these cables; in fact, he spent a long time searching for them for use in his own book, *A Letter from Grosvenor Square*. After a year and a half of search, I abandoned the hope of finding these cables, although I assumed they would turn up eventually in the Roosevelt files. In October, 1947, I suddenly learned, through John E. Masten, that both cables had been included in the millions of words of the Pearl Harbour Investigation; they had been brought out by Grace Tully from the Roosevelt

files because they happened to have bearing on the Far Eastern situation. When I learned this, I communicated the news to Winant at his home in Concord, New Hampshire. He was greatly interested and told me he would be in New York shortly and would like to look at the copies I had obtained. A few days thereafter I learned of his sudden, shocking death.

319. Concerning Churchill's week ends: Commander Thompson has pointed out to me that, although there were usually many guests at Dytchley, there were very few at Chequers who were not connected in one way or another with Churchill's official business. However, that covered a very wide range.

CHAPTER XV

324. Much of the description of Hopkins's flight to Moscow and return was given me in London in August, 1941, by Wing-Commander D. C. McKinley and Squadron-Leader C. M. Owen with whom I got in touch through the courtesy of Marshal of the Royal Air Force, Lord Tedder.

327. The description of the dinner given for Hopkins in Archangel on his arrival there was from an article by him in the *American* magazine for December, 1941, entitled 'The Inside Story of My Meeting with Stalin'. There is a later quotation from this same article in this chapter: Hopkins's remarks on Stalin, 'Not once did he repeat himself, etc.'

CHAPTER XVI

350. In this chapter is the statement that Churchill, informing the Dominion Prime Ministers of the forthcoming Atlantic Conference, had said that he had never met Roosevelt. Long after I had written this—and, indeed, when this chapter was already in type—I read the following in *The Gathering Storm*, the first volume of Churchill's tremendous work on the Second World War: 'I had met him [President Roosevelt] only once in the previous war. It was at a dinner at Gray's Inn, and I had been struck by his magnificent presence in all his health and strength.' Evidently Churchill, before he wrote this, had conducted further searches through the voluminous files of his memory.

359. In connection with the military staff talks at the Atlantic Conference mention is made of the British plan for ROUNDUP, the invasion of Normandy. I am not entirely sure if the American Chiefs of Staff had been aware of this and other long-range and extremely remote plans before they arrived at Argentia, but it is my belief that they had already been acquainted with all of them and had participated in the making of some of them.

363. When portions of this chapter were published in *Collier's* (in the United States) and in the *Sunday Express* (in Great Britain) the statement that, to the officers of the British Government, the Atlantic Charter was 'not much more than a publicity hand-out' produced a certain amount of protesting correspondence in the London *Times*. Even so, I must let my statement stand. Of course, on January 1, 1942, the terms of the Atlantic Charter were incorporated in the first Declaration of the United Nations to which His Majesty's Government solemnly subscribed, and then the Charter for the first time achieved the status of a formal State Paper.

page

365. The American destroyers which accompanied the *Prince of Wales* from New-foundland to Iceland were of course part of the regular, routine U.S. Navy escort which was by then guarding the convoy routes in the Western Atlantic.

CHAPTER XVII

367. The quotations of General Marshall on the extension of Selective Service debate, and many other quotations of him, Admiral King and General Arnold, are from *The War Reports* (J. B. Lippincott Co.) of the three Chiefs of Staff which have been published in one volume.

The *New York Times* editorial quoted was from the issue of August 13, 1941, and so also was the quotation of Senator Wheeler.

370. The Churchill cable referring to 'Mr. Sherwood' was dated September 25.

370–373. The Hopkins description of the Labour Day speech was dated September 2 and his memorandum on the 'Shoot on Sight' speech was dated September 13.

374. The message from Churchill to Hopkins described as 'one of the gloomiest' was dated August 29, and the Hopkins memorandum thereon was dated September 6.

376. The first request from Churchill to Roosevelt for help in transporting two divisions to the Middle East was dated September 1.

376–377. Roosevelt's cable to Churchill reopening the question of the transports was dated October 7. Churchill's reply was dated October 9.

377. The conversation between Hopkins and Stettinius is quoted from the latter's book, *Lend-Lease—Weapon for Victory* (Macmillan).

378. The memoranda from Hopkins to Roosevelt complaining about statements by an admiral and a general were dated November 7 and November 12.

379–380. The first note from Roosevelt to Hopkins concerning Channel Key was dated October 21, and the Hopkins note thereon, October 22. The letter from Julius F. Stone, Jr., was dated November 5, and the Roosevelt note thereon, November 15.

381. The memorandum from Admiral Stark to Secretary Hull was dated October 8.

382–383. The news story quoted from the *Washington Times-Herald* was in its issue of November 8. There would appear to be some confusion in this as to the identity of the destroyer mentioned. Although the name given is the *Kearny*, the mention of 'loss of most of her officers and crew' would indicate that the *Reuben James* was meant.

CHAPTER XVIII

387. The message from Beaverbrook to Hopkins on the eve of his departure for Russia was delivered from the British Embassy on September 22.

395–396. The memorandum written by Beaverbrook following his return from Russia was dated October 19.

396–397. Hopkins's letter to Churchill about increase of production was dated September 29.

Roosevelt's cable to Harriman congratulating him on the Moscow results was dated October 9.

397, 398. The memorandum from Marshall to Hopkins on Faymonville was dated October 10, and Hopkins' letter to Secretary Stimson was dated October 14.

400. In connection with the proposal to use an aircraft carrier to ferry planes to the Persian Gulf for the Russians: I have certainly done insufficient justice in this book to the part played by Captain Granville Conway, U.S.N., in the solution of all manner of shipping problems during the war. I believe it was he more than anyone else who worked out the system for employing tankers as transports for aircraft, which produced an enormous saving in time and in shipping, particularly on the long route round the Cape of Good Hope. Harry Hopkins had enormous respect for Conway and gratitude to him for invaluable services rendered.

401. Myron Taylor's report of his interview with Salazar was undated.

The meeting of the President's Soviet Protocol Committee, from the minutes of which quotation is made, was held on November 25, 1942.

CHAPTER XIX

408. Owen Lattimore's cable to Currie was dated August 12, 1941.

The Arnstein Report, entitled 'The Present Trucking Operations as conducted on the Burma Road and Reccomendations for their Improvement', was, I believe, undated, but was received by Hopkins some time in August.

409. The message from Major McHugh was dated August 9.

410. The message from Madame Chiang Kai-shek to Currie was received September 4.

410–412. The letter from T. V. Soong to Donovan was dated August 16; that from Soong to Roosevelt, October 24; and Soong to Hopkins, November 13.

432. The memorandum by Hopkins describing his conversation with Roosevelt following the issuance of the Roberts Report was dated January 24, 1942. It is my understanding, but I have not verified it, that Justice Roberts himself delivered the text of this Report to the President in his office in the White House. He intended to make the request to the President that the Report be made public, at least in part. Roosevelt asked the Justice to sit down while he read the entire document. When he had finished, he said that the Report must be given to the public in full and, indeed, called in Steve Early and told him to release it to the Press immediately and without change.

439. Competent authority, reviewing my manuscript, has informed me that, at the time of Pearl Harbour, General Marshall did not have facilities for communication with Honolulu by scrambler telephone. Therefore the Committee's Report, which I have quoted, must have been in error.

page
440. The letter from Secretary Knox to a member of Congress disclaiming responsibility for any catastrophe in any Shore Establishment was dated August 23, 1941. The Hopkins note thereon was in a letter to Archibald MacLeish, March 6, 1942.

CHAPTER XX

448. On the evening of the day—I believe it was New Year's Day, 1942—when Churchill returned to Washington from Ottawa, I happened to go with Hopkins into the Prime Minister's bedroom at the White House. There were quantities of New York and Washington newspapers containing the reports of the Canadian speech and the editorial comments thereon (including one in the *New York Herald Tribune* which is quoted in the next chapter). Churchill was obviously and quite naturally pleased with the favourable response and he observed that he was greatly impressed by the loyalty and patriotism of the American Press and was not accustomed to such wholehearted enthusiasm at home. Hopkins emitted one of his short, sharp, derisive laughs and said, 'Just wait ! We are still young in this war and the newspapers haven't had time to get back to normal. In a few weeks' time you'll find they will be criticizing everything.' However, Churchill continued to have a very good Press in the United States throughout the war.

449. The British suggestions for the agenda of the Arcadia Conference and the bases of grand strategies had been in a radio message from *H.M.S. Duke of York* on December 18 when Churchill and his staff were in mid-Atlantic.

449-450. Relative to the principle of 'Germany first': the German potential 'in productive power and scientific genius' was certainly demonstrated in the last year of the war in Europe with the development of the V-1 flying bombs, the V-2 rockets, jet propulsion for aircraft and the tremendously important and dangerous technical improvements in submarines. All of these came, fortunately, after the successful establishment of a Second Front in the West, and at a time when German production was being subjected to severe bombardment by the superior Allied air forces. Had Germany been given more time, the story of the war in Europe would have been a very different one.

450. My statement that 'There were not more than two occasions in the entire war' when Roosevelt overruled his Chiefs of Staff is a debatable one. The one occasion about which there can be no question of doubt was at the second Cairo Conference in December, 1943 (Chapter XXXI), and the other possible occasion was the making of the TORCH decision (Chapter XXVI). Captain T. B. Kittredge of the Historical Section of the Joint Chiefs of Staff has pointed out to me, 'It may be true that the President formally overruled them on very few occasions, but this was only because informal discussions of the President with Leahy, Marshall, King, and Arnold usually led them to know in advance the President's views. They, no doubt, frequently recognized the advantages of accepting the President's suggestions with their own interpretations, rather than of risking an overruling by presenting formally proposals they knew would not be accepted.'

The basis of the United Nations Declaration: the conditions for an association or alliance of the anti-Axis powers had been under consideration in the State, War and Navy Departments at least since January, 1941. Before the Arcadia Conference, the Secretary of State together with his staff and officers of the

page

staffs of General Marshall and Admiral Stark had prepared drafts of two documents which were submitted to the President shortly before Churchill's arrival. One of these became, with some modifications, the Declaration of the United Nations. The other was a plan for an inter-Allied war organization under a Supreme War Council; this was rejected by Roosevelt as too complicated and generally impracticable.

CHAPTER XXI

456. The quotation at the start of this chapter was from *The Memoirs of Cordell Hull* (Macmillan).

The quotations of Foreign Office cables were from memoranda prepared by the British Embassy.

457. The fact that Ira Wolfert was the sole American Press correspondent on the scene at the landings on St. Pierre and Miquelon was viewed with some suspicion in Washington, it being assumed that he had been taken into the secret purposefully by an emissary of de Gaulle's. Such was not the case. Wolfert, representing the North American Newspaper Alliance, had gone to Canada on a tip which was actually several weeks out of date. Learning that Admiral Muselier had suddenly left Ottawa for Halifax, Wolfert went there to seek him out. Muselier and his staff were living in a Halifax hotel under assumed names, but Wolfert was smart enough to find them and then to bluff them into the belief that he knew all about their projected enterprise when, actually, he knew nothing. Muselier thereupon put him under arrest, which was completely illegal but effective, and took him along under guard on the expedition in order to keep him quiet. Thus, Wolfert's exclusive story was the result of his exceptional enterprise and skill as a newspaperman plus pure accident.

463–465. The quotations of Professor William L. Langer were from his book *Our Vichy Gamble* (Knopf). This book traced the history of the Vichy policy and relations with de Gaulle and other French leaders up to the time of Darlan's assassination—which, it may be said, marked the point when the final justification for the policy ended.

CHAPTER XXII

467. Roosevelt's message to the Filipino people was printed in the form of a leaflet in English and Tagalog and delivered somehow or other to the Philippines. This was the first American propaganda leaflet in the war against Japan. Three years later the U.S. Navy was dropping quantities of leaflets on Tokyo from carrier-based aircraft. During the Arcadia Conference, the R.A.F. dropped the first American propaganda leaflets on France: these featured, of course, a picture of the State of Liberty and the assurance, 'To you who gave us Liberty we will restore Liberty.' The preparation and production of leaflets for Europe became a joint Anglo-American operation in London and, in 1944, reached the considerable total of eleven million leaflets a lay.

472. I have never been entirely clear as to the difference between GYMNAST and SUPER-GYMNAST. It is my impression that the latter included the landings in French Morocco, which were favoured by the Americans, in addition to those at Algiers.

page

489. Roosevelt's conversation with Knudsen (described in the Hopkins memorandum of January 16, 1942) must have been a particularly disagreeable one for the President who had real admiration and warm affection for Knudsen. Roosevelt loved to tell a story of how, in the spring of 1941, Knudsen had sent him a list of some twenty names of prominent businessmen for appointment to executive positions in the Office of Production Management. Needless to say, most of the important men in this agency were Republicans. Having inspected this new list, Roosevelt said to Knudsen, 'There must be some mistake here, Bill. One of the men on this list is a Democrat.' Knudsen laughed and said, 'It's all right, Mr. President—I have checked on this man and found out that last year he voted for Willkie.'

CHAPTER XXIII

498. Hopkins's cable to Churchill congratulating him on the vote in the House of Commons was dated January 29, 1942, Roosevelt's was dated January 31, and the cables from Beaverbrook to Hopkins and from Churchill to Roosevelt on this same subject were dated February 1.

499. The cable from Roosevelt to Churchill referring to Hopkins's health was dated February 11.

500. The quotation of an Anglo-American intelligence appraisal of the Russian prospects was from a memorandum to the Chief of Staff by General Raymond E. Lee on February 13. The summary of General Mason Macfarlane's report on his talks in Moscow was transmitted to Hopkins by Field Marshal Sir John Dill on February 11.

501. Roosevelt's cable to Stalin about the January-February shipments was dated February 9, and Stalin's reply, February 19.

503. The quotations of Professor Samuel Eliot Morison were from his book, *The Battle of the Atlantic*, 1939-43 (Little, Brown & Co.).

509. Roosevelt's Washington's Birthday speech of 1942 had been announced at least three weeks in advance, giving the Japanese plenty of time to get the submarine to the California coast. It had always been Steve Early's practice to build up the radio audience for the President's speeches with plenty of advance publicity and he did this extraordinary well. Now, however, the practice had to be abandoned.

Roosevelt's letter to the War Department about air-raid alarms was dated February 26.

510. The cable from Van Mook to Hopkins about the desperate situation in Java was dated February 23, and Hopkins' reply was sent the following day.

511. The letter from Soong to Hopkins, referring to Roosevelt as 'the one hope of mankind', was dated April 24.

512-513. Roosevelt's cable to Curtin in Australia was dated February 20; his cable to Churchill about the Casey appointment was dated March 22.

514-515. The cable to Churchill prepared by the Chiefs of Staff and signed by Roosevelt was dated March 7, and Roosevelt's personal message on the subject of global strategy was dated March 9. Churchill's reply was dated March 13.

page

It should have been stated in this chapter that, following Roosevelt's personal message to Churchill of March 9, some confusion prevailed over the question of command in the Pacific, and General MacArthur may have been led to believe that he was to have supreme command of the entire war in the Pacific. This was straightened out early in April in accordance with the proposals made by the United States Chiefs of Staff: MacArthur's command was limited to the southwest Pacific area, and Admiral Nimitz was given command of the remainder of the Pacific, both acting under the directions and supervision of the U.S. Joint Chiefs.

517. The quotation of Sumner Welles on the proposal to the Indian leaders was from his book, *Where Are We Heading?* (Harper & Brothers).

Chiang Kai-shek's quotation of Gandhi was included in a cable sent by the Generalissimo to Soong on April 19.

517-518. Harriman's message to the President about the alternate land route to China was dated January 31. Roosevelt's cable to Chiang Kai-shek about the ferry service was dated February 9.

518. Chiang Kai-shek's cable to Roosevelt about his observations in Burma was dated April 13.

521. Hopkins' letter to Roosevelt about Quezon was dated June 9 and Quezon's letter to Hopkins, June 19.

CHAPTER XXIV

524. The War Plans Division had considered the possibility of seizing a bridgehead in the Cherbourg or Brittany peninsulas with the SLEDGEHAMMER operation in 1942. However, the plan which Hopkins carried with him to London was, as stated, for a trans-Channel assault east of the mouth of the Seine.

I do not know the date of Marshall's memorandum to the President concerning the selection of Western Europe as the theatre for the first great Allied offensive, but this was presumably about April 1, 1942.

526. Roosevelt's cable to Churchill about the Hopkins-Marshall trip was dated April 1.

The quotation of the *Richmond News Leader* was dated April 9.

527. Hopkins's note to Lovett about the New York Giants was dated March 4 and his cable to Harriman about Aunt Bessie's lumbago, May 18.

528-529. Hopkins's notes on the first session at No. 10 Downing Street, were dated April 8. His cable to Roosevelt and his notes on the following session were dated April 9.

534. Hopkins's cable to Roosevelt about shipping losses was dated April 14.

The cable from Soong which reached Hopkins in London was delivered April 11.

535, 536, 537. Roosevelt's cable to Hopkins containing a message for Churchill about the Indian problem was dated April 11. His cable to Marshall about putting Hopkins to bed was dated April 13.

page

538. The monitoring of the Paris radio was cabled from Washington April 13.

539. The cables from Roosevelt to Hopkins and Churchill relative to supplies for the Far East were dated April 15.

543. Hopkins's cable to Roosevelt concerning Laval, and Roosevelt's reply, were both dated April 15. The reference to 'wood pussy' revived a White House joke of the 1940 campaign. Talking of misrepresentations and falsehoods made by certain Republican orators, Roosevelt wanted to say something like, 'I am now going to nail these to the barn door, just as, when I was a boy, we used to nail to the barn door the skins of small, predatory animals such as rats, weasels and wood pussies.' After considerable debate, Roosevelt decided not to use that analogy.

543-544. Leahy's report from Vichy to Washington reached Hopkins in London on April 17. Roosevelt's cable to Hopkins asking him to discuss the new French situation with Churchill was sent late that same day and reached Hopkins in Northen Ireland on the morning of April 18.

546. The letter to Hopkins from Mrs. Martum was dated April 16.

547. Roosevelt's cable to Churchill after Hopkins' return was dated April 22, and so was Hopkins' letter to Jacob Baker.

CHAPTER XXV

549. Roosevelt's cable to Churchill about the Murmansk convoys was dated April 29 and Churchill's reply to it, May 1.

550. The memorandum from Hopkins to Lewis Douglas was dated June 12.

554. The report from S. Pinkney Tuck on the attitude of Weygand was dated June 5.

554-555. Roosevelt's cable to Churchill about American bombers in Britain was dated May 19. Churchill's reply was the following day.

556-557. The letter to Hopkins from Steinhardt was dated April 24.

557. Hopkins's cable to Churchill concerning the appointment of Lord Beaverbrook as Ambassador was dated May 16.

558. The quotation concerning the production lag on landing craft was from *Industrial Mobilization for War* (U.S. Government Printing Office).

572-573. The note from Colonel Walker to Hopkins was dated May 31, as were the notes written by Hopkins about the meeting of the President with Marshall and King and Roosevelt's cable to Churchill about the Molotov visit.

580-581. The note from General Burns on his meeting with Molotov was dated June 3, as was Hopkins' note on his reply to this. The subsequent message from Burns was dated June 4.

582. Hopkins's letter to Winant about the Molotov visit was dated June 12.

CHAPTER XXVI

586. The quotation of Churchill by General Arnold appeared in the latter's report on his conversations in London. There were protracted arguments between the R.A.F. and the U.S.A.A.F. over heavy bombing tactics, the Americans favouring daylight 'precision' bombing and the British adhering to night-time 'saturation' bombing. In pursuance of their policy, the Americans suffered heavy losses, but the ratio was reduced as the strength of American fighter escorts (which had considerably longer range than the Spitfires and Hurricanes) was increased at United Kingdom bases. Later in the war, of course, the combined air forces with their different tactics maintained a round-the-clock bombardment of Germany. At dawn, as the last Lancasters were returning from their missions, the first Flying Fortresses were taking off.

596–597. Hopkins's note on the telephone calls from Churchill, Arnold, and Harriman, was dated May 30, 1942. The reference in this to 'the battle in Africa going well' is interesting in view of subsequent developments.

587. The letter from Mountbatten to Roosevelt was dated June 15.

589. The cable from Roosevelt to Stalin relative to the situation in the North Pacific was dated June 17.

590. Churchill's cable to Roosevelt speaking of 'a complete decision' in Libya was dated June 1.

The quotation of Molotov's speech at an Extraordinary Session of the Supreme Soviet was from *The Year of Stalingrad* (Knopf), by Alexander Werth.

591. The Roosevelt message to Marshall and King relative to a possible German breakthrough in Russia was dated June 20.

593. The quotation of Stimson in this and the following chapter was from his book, *On Active Service in Peace and War* (Harper & Brothers).

595. The quotation of Churchill about General Marshall's 'mass production of divisions' was from a letter to me in response to the questionnaire mentioned in the Introduction.

596. Hopkins's note on the last day of Churchill's visit was dated June 25.

The Churchill cable to Hopkins referring to 'Tube Alloys' was dated February 27, 1943.

599–600. The Stilwell cable reporting his conversation with Chiang Kai-shek relative to the diverted bombers was dated June 27, and Roosevelt's cable to the Generalissimo was sent the same day.

601. Roosevelt's cable to Stalin thanking him for authorizing the transfer of bombers was dated July 9.

Roosevelt's cable to Churchill reluctantly agreeing on the Murmansk convoys was dated July 15, as was his cable announcing the imminent departure of Marshall, King, and Hopkins for London.

602. The quotation of Arthur Krock was in the *New York Times*, April 17, while Hopkins and Marshall were in London discussing the plans for ROUNDUP.

page

603. Hopkins's cable to Churchill expressing delight at the vote in the House of Commons was dated July 2, as was Churchill's reply.

608. Hopkins's cable to Roosevelt about Churchill throwing the British Constitution at him was dated July 20.

610, 611, 612. Roosevelt's cable to Hopkins, Marshall and King giving his views on various alternative operations was dated July 23. His next cable on this subject was dated July 24. His final cable referring to Hopkins's wedding was dated July 25.

612. At the end of July, after Hopkins had left Washington for his honeymoon, the Joint Chiefs of Staff unanimously recommended against the North African landings, but the President summoned them to the White House to inform them that the decision to undertake the TORCH operation as early as possible must be carried out. He insisted that preparations for the landings must be pushed forward rapidly and vigorously.

613-614. The material on the yacht, *My Kay IV*, was taken from a report made on this strange episode by the F.B.I.

CHAPTER XXVI

616. Roosevelt's cable to Churchill before the latter's departure for Moscow was dated July 29, 1942.

618. Roosevelt's cable to Churchill in Moscow was dated August 14.

620. Harriman's reply to Stalin's *aide-mémoire* was dated August 15.

622. Roosevelt's cable to Stalin after the meetings had been concluded was dated August 18.
    Roosevelt's message to the Chiefs of Staff expressing anxiety about the Southwest Pacific was dated October 24. At this time there was considerable controversy between General Arnold on the one hand, and Admiral King and General MacArthur on the other as to the allocation of air forces. Arnold was arguing for concentration of air power in the United Kingdom for the air offensive against Germany. King argued that there was risk of disaster in the Pacific unless adequate forces were sent there.

625. Roosevelt's cable to Churchill relative to the Persian railway was dated September 15.

627. Churchill's reply to Roosevelt about 'the whole burden' of TORCH was dated September 1.

628. The operation known as LIGHTFOOT—the British drive from Egypt towards Tripoli and Tunisia—had been in process of planning since the meetings in London in July. Therefore, Churchill's reference to it in his September 22 cable to Roosevelt was merely confirmation of the fact that it was going forward and and that it had been given its code name.

page

634. Hopkins's reply to Harriman relative to unloading ships in Scotland was dated October 27.

635. Hopkins's cable to Churchill stating that messages had been forwarded to the President was dated September 22, as was his telegram to Roosevelt reporting on a conversation with the Chiefs of Staff.

636. Roosevelt's cable to Churchill from the train between California and Texas was dated September 26.

638. Roosevelt's cable to Stalin relative to the air force in the Caucasus and other measures for aid was dated October 8.

639. Roosevelt's cable to Churchill about the Russians not using 'speech for the same purposes that we do' was dated October 27.

   General Burns's memorandum to Hopkins on Russia was dated December 1.

643. Churchill's cable to Roosevelt about the message to Pétain was dated November 2.

644. The quotation of Eisenhower relative to the day of the TORCH decision was from *My Three Years with Eisenhower* (Simon and Schuster), by Harry Butcher.

645. The quotations of Murphy's report on his meeting with Darlan early in the morning of November 8 were from Professor Langer's book, *Our Vichy Gamble*.

646. Roosevelt's cable to Churchill about his troubles with Giraud was dated November 11.

647. Stalin's message to Churchill relative to the Darlan deal was received in Washington on December 2.

650. Roosevelt's message to Eisenhower relative to Darlan was dated November 16.

651. There was no question of doubt that Churchill was fully informed of all stages of the negotiations with Darlan by Admiral Sir Andrew Cunningham who participated in these with General Mark Clark and, indeed, strongly urged to Clark and Eisenhower the importance of reaching agreement with Darlan, not only to stop resistance to the landings near Oran and Casablanca, but also to get the support of Boisson in West Africa, of Esteva in Tunis, and possibly also to get the French fleet to leave Toulon and join the Allies. Churchill in turn urged Roosevelt to approve these arrangements. However, the British Foreign Office subsequently made few efforts to prevent all the blame from being placed on the Americans.

653. Churchill's cable to Roosevelt about the possible abandonment of ROUNDUP was dated November 24 and Roosevelt's reply was dated November 25.

656. Roosevelt's message to Stalin about the Solomons was dated November 25.

657. Hopkins' memorandum on the arrival of Madame Chiang Kai-shek was dated November 25.

CHAPTER XXVII

676. Despite the cancellation of de Gaulle's projected visit to Washington, an exchange of messages continued between de Gaulle and Giraud (through Admiral Stark and General Eisenhower) in an effort to find means of achieving unification and co-ordination of the anti-Vichy French factions. It was agreed that General Georges Catroux, representing de Gaulle, should proceed at once to Algiers, with the possibility that he would take over the Governorship and civil administration of North Africa. Then came news of the imprisonment of de Gaulle adherents in Algeria following the assassination of Darlan, and after that the revelation that Peyrouton was being imported from South America. De Gaulle was understandably angered by these developments and his negotiations with Giraud were broken off a few days before the start of the Casablanca Conference. These factors should be borne in mind in considering de Gaulle's resentment when he was suddenly, arbitrarily summoned to proceed to a conference of which he had not previously been informed. He could hardly be blamed for expressing 'no pleasure' when Eden handed him the message from Churchill on January 17, 1943.

678. Captain T. B. Kittredge, USN, who has been so helpful to me in so many ways in the preparation of this book, has furnished me with a footnote on the de Gaulle relationship. He is particularly expert on this subject since he was Admiral Stark's principal aide in London in the handling of the extremely delicate liaison with de Gaulle and his associates. He has written me the following record:

On 16 December, 1942, Stark spent the evening with de Gaulle as he (Stark) was leaving the next day for Washington and expected de Gaulle to be arriving there a week later. In a long and friendly conversation, de Gaulle pointed out that (a) nothing in his past experience qualified him to act as political and military leader of the French in continuing the war against Germany after defeatist sentiments had led nearly all French leaders to expect a quick German victory in 1940. (b) He had been unable to persuade French leaders whom he wanted to serve on the French national committee (Reynaud, Herriot, Jeanneney, Louis Marin—even Leon Blum) to leave France by underground channels to go to London. Hence de Gaulle was surrounded by Frenchmen who happened to be available in London, whom he had not known before, and of whose trustworthiness he was not certain. (c) He was convinced that French representation in Allied higher political and military councils was essential, in conducting the war against Germany, in liberating the Allied countries, and in re-establishing national governments and a new international order in Europe. (d) He was also convinced that French culture, intelligence and capacities of leadership were so widely diffused in France that when any elite or governing class failed France, through decadence or defeatism, new individuals were always projected upward out of the French masses, to give enlightened and inspired leadership to 'eternal France'; that this had been true through the centuries, from the time of Charlemagne to that of Hitler. (e) Thus de Gaulle referred to the rise of the Capetian royal house, to Joan of Arc, to Henri IV, to the revolutionary leaders (1789–93), to Napoleon, finally to Poincaré and Clemenceau; de Gaulle added—'perhaps this time I am one of those thrust into leadership by circumstances, and by the failure of the other leaders.'

Admiral Stark was much impressed by this historical and philosophical analysis and suggested that de Gaulle, on meeting Roosevelt (a great student of French history and politics) should attempt to make the President understand his concepts.

This de Gaulle attempted at Casablanca; but later told Admiral Stark that he had hardly ever been permitted to finish a sentence. The President was determined to make de Gaulle understand and accept the attitude of the Roosevelt administration toward France; and did not seem interested in, or to have any patience with, de Gaulle's views, perhaps expressed in his usual cold, standoffish and brusque manner.

According to Kittredge, de Gaulle was later informed that Roosevelt had told the Joan of Arc and Clemenceau story to General Vargas in Brazil, and de Gaulle was so deeply offended 'he never wanted again to meet the President.'

682. References to the *Queen Elizabeth* and *Queen Mary*: early in 1941 it was considered that each of these ships could carry a maximum of 4,000 troops; early in 1942 this capacity had been increased to 7,000; by 1944 each of them was carrying nearly 16,000 troops on every eastbound voyage from New York to the Clyde.

689. Although there was no record of it in the Hopkins papers, I believe that at Casablanca General Marshall and Admiral King again proposed that, if the British were not prepared to undertake the cross-Channel operation in 1943, United States forces should be diverted to the war against Japan, rather than to the Mediterranean for 'eccentric operations', or to the United Kingdom where they might remain out of combat for a year or more.

693. Expressions of views by Stalin on the subject of unconditional surrender will be found in Chapters XXXI and XXXVI.

CHAPTER XXIX

695. Hopkins's article in the *American* magazine, 'You and Your Family Will Be Mobilized', appeared in the November, 1942, issue.

697. The quotation of Roosevelt by Donald Nelson appeared in the latter's book, *Arsenal of Democracy*.
    Stalin's cable to Roosevelt and Churchill acknowledging their message from Casablanca was dated January 30, 1943.

698. Churchill's cable to Hopkins referring to Eisenhower's message about postponement of HUSKY was dated February 13. The cable from Eisenhower to the Combined Chiefs of Staff had been sent February 11.

700. Hopkins's first cable to Churchill about the latter's illness was dated February 18 and Churchill's reply was the following day.

702. Stalin's message to Churchill about the bombing of Germany was received in Washington March 18.

703. Harriman's cable to Hopkins about Admiral Standley's statement was dated March 14.

page

Hopkins's memorandum on Madame Chiang Kai-shek at the White House was dated February 27.

704. Hopkins's memorandum on the meeting with Roosevelt and Welles before Eden's arrival was dated March 10, as was the memorandum from Winant to the President on the forthcoming visit.

716. Hopkins's cable to Churchill on the proposed award for General MacArthur was dated March 29.

717. Adolf Berle's memorandum on the President's constitutional powers was dated March 25.

720. Hopkins's copy of Roosevelt's cable to Churchill on the removal of Fascists in Italy bore no date.

CHAPTER XXX

723. Churchill's cable suggesting another meeting with Marshall and Hopkins, and Hopkins's reply to it, were both dated April 9.

725. In reference to Churchill's statement that the Second World War had just passed the Gettysburg phase: the Battle of Gettysburg was fought some twenty-one months before the end of the Civil War, and Churchill's speech to the Congress was a little less than two years before the end of the war in Europe.

During the lunch in the White House at which there were forty-eight guests, whose names are listed in the text of this chapter, Army or Navy photographers took several feet of motion picture film of the hats that were piled on the shelves outside of General Watson's office and this 'shot' was used most effectively in 'The True Glory', the great motion picture record of victory in Europe which was directed by Carol Reed, for the British, and Captain Garson Kanin, for the U.S. Army.

726. The quotations from General Stilwell are from his book *The Stilwell Papers* (Wm. Sloane Associates). Churchill wrote me, in response to my questionnaire, that he had 'a great respect and liking for General Stilwell and was very sorry when he was recalled'.

730 The profile of Hopkins by Geoffrey T. Hellman was published in *The New Yorker* in the issues of August 7 and 14, 1943.

733 Harriman's letter to Roosevelt describing his session with Churchill was dated July 5.

735. Hopkins's memorandum on the meeting in the President's bedroom concerning China was dated July 15.

740. The Hopkins's memorandum on the new regime in Italy was dated September 22. Churchill's cable about the propaganda to Italy was dated August 2.

741. The Roosevelt-Churchill cable to Stalin from Quebec was dated August 10.

The reports by General Smith and Brigadier Strong on their first encounters with Castellano were cabled from AFHQ in Algiers to the War Department on August 20.

page

743. The Roosevelt-Churchill cable to Stalin relative to the Azores was dated August 16.

744. The War Department document entitled 'Russia's Position' was dated August 10.

746. The article by Walter Trohan likening Hopkins to Rasputin appeared in the *Chicago Sunday Tribune*, August 29.

747. The Hopkins letter to Captain Donald Duncan was dated September 10.

749. The letter to Hopkins from the lady in Colorado was dated September 2 and Hopkins's reply, September 7.

749. Hopkins's cable to Brendan Bracken (through Winant) was dated October 15. Bracken's reply was dated October 21.

750. Hopkins's letter to Beaverbrook about the latter's return to the government was dated September 27.

750-51. Winant's cable to Hopkins about the difficulties of his position was dated October 16, and Hopkins's letter in reply was dated October 25.

CHAPTER XXXI

757. The letter in which Hopkins described as 'amazing' the story involving him in a 'plot' against General Marshall was dated October 2.

758. The Stimson letter to Roosevelt about postponing the date when Marshall should take over command was dated September 16.

Churchill's cable to Hopkins expressing concern about all the newspaper talk was dated September 26.

Hopkins's cable to Churchill about the newspaper hullabaloo was dated October 2. Roosevelt's cable to Churchill on the same subject was dated October 4.

759. Hopkins's notes on a telephone conversation with Churchill relative to the Dodecanese were dated October 7. On October 12, General Marshall's aide, Colonel Frank McCarthy, wrote to Hopkins about cautioning the Prime Minister relative to statements over the telephone.

761-762. Churchill's cable to Hopkins about the five Senators was dated October 14. Hopkins's replies were dated October 14 and 15. Churchill's statement in the House of Commons was reported in the *New York Times*, October 19.

763. The memorandum from the Joint Chiefs to the President on board the *U.S.S Iowa* was dated November 17.

763-764. Hopkins's memorandum on the torpedo episode was undated, but the episode was confirmed in the ship's log.

765-766. The letter to Hopkins signed by forty-three Press correspondents at Cairo was dated November 26.

page

777. The memorandum on Stalin's views concerning postwar Germany was written presumably by Bohlen and dated Novemember 28.

787. In reference to Hopkins's after-dinner speech about the British Constitution: Hopkins said to me in the fall of 1944 that it was his observation that Churchill was able to exercise considerably more authority than he actually possessed as Prime Minister because of the dominant force of his tremendous personality.

CHAPTER XXXII

802. Hopkins's cable to Churchill stating that he was not accompanying Roosevelt on the Pacific trip was dated July 20, 1944.

Hopkins's letter to Roosevelt about his talks with Beaverbrook was dated August 5.

804. Hopkins's cable to Churchill concerning proposed changes in ANVIL was dated August 7.

The ANVIL forces were under the over-all command of General Jacob L. Devers and included the American Seventh Army, under General Patch, and the French First Army, under General Jean de Lattre de Tassigny. Devers was then serving under Field Marshal Sir Henry Maitland Wilson as Deputy Supreme Allied Commander in the Mediterranean theatre. After General Patch's Seventh Army had joined up with the forces under Eisenhower in Northern France, Devers went to that theatre to take command of the Sixth U.S. Army Group.

805. Roosevelt's message naming Bermuda was received at the White House August 8, and Churchill's cable naming Quebec, August 10.

Hopkins's cable to Churchill saying that he was not going to Quebec was dated August 28.

809. Hopkins's memorandum to Roosevelt about trade barriers just before the Quebec Conference was dated September 8.

811. Roosevelt's memorandum to Hull on progress at Quebec was dated September 16.

820. The Hopkins memorandum on the Marshall-Dewey incident was written some time in October, 1945. Reference is made to this in a quotation from Sidney Hyman which appears in Chapter XXXVII.

When Roosevelt gave his speech at Shibe Park in Philadelphia on October 27, Postmaster General Frank C. Walker was sitting next to him. Walker has told me that, at one point, he saw the President ruffling back through the pages of his reading copy, while going right on talking. Now and then, Roosevelt would glance down at one of these earlier pages but proceed with the delivery of text that he was not even looking at. After the speech, Walker asked Roosevelt what he was doing, and the President explained that there was some point he had made early in the speech that had gone over so well he thought he would like to make it again. This was another demonstration of Roosevelt's amazing assurance and command of the situation when delivering a speech.

page

While we were on the train en route to Chicago on October 28, 1944, Sam Rosenman and I were discussing with Roosevelt various industrial improvements which would follow the war and help to achieve the goal of sixty million jobs. One of them was 'streamlined railroad trains capable of greatly increased speed', but Roosevelt refused to include that in his speech, saying, 'Trains go too fast as it is.' I have read several times that Roosevelt loved speed, and it would have been in his nature to do so; but it was my observation that he liked to travel at a moderate pace in all vehicles except his own wheelchair.

822. Hopkins's pre-election cable to Beaverbrook was dated November 6.

822–823. Hopkins's memorandum on his talk with the President and Mrs. Roosevelt after the election was dated November 10.

CHAPTER XXXIII

825. Roosevelt's cable to Harriman containing a message for Stalin was dated October 4, 1944.

827. The quotation of Marquis Childs was from the *Washington Post*, December 4. Hopkins's memorandum on his lunch with Stimson was dated December 12.

828. Beaverbrook's letter to Hopkins on the situation in England was dated October 23.

831. Winant's letter to Hopkins about the vote in the House of Commons was dated December 11.

832. Hopkins's memorandum on the telephone call from 'John Martin' and subsequent developments was dated December 12.

835. Hopkins's memorandum on the genesis of the Yalta Conference was written some time in October, 1945. It represented his final attempt to get to work on the writing of his own memoirs of the war years.

CHAPTER XXXIV

845. The quotations of James F. Byrnes on the Yalta Conference were from his book *Speaking Frankly* (Harper & Brothers).

846. Stalin's cable to Roosevelt mentioning (I believe for the first time) the additional votes for the Ukraine and Byelorussia was dated September 7, 1944.

859. In reference to the quotation of Hopkins made by me at the end of this chapter on the subject of relations with the Soviet Union: further expression of his views on this may be found in Chapter XXXVII.

CHAPTER XXXV

860. Hopkins's memorandum on the meetings of Roosevelt with the three kings was written by him at the same time in October, 1945, when he wrote of the genesis of the Yalta conference.

CHAPTER XXXVI

872–873. Hopkins's memorandum on Harriman's conversation with Stalin after Roosevelt's death was dated April 23, 1945, as was the memorandum on the Drew Pearson column.

891–892, 897. Hopkins's cable to Truman reporting on his third meeting with Stalin was dated May 29. The subsequent cable on the same meeting was dated May 30. His reports on the fourth meeting were also dated May 30.

892, 898. Hopkins's memorandum on his after-dinner conversation with Stalin was dated June 1.

900. Churchill's cable of congratulations to Hopkins in Moscow was dated June 2.

902. Hopkins's final cable to Truman from Moscow was dated June 6.

903. Hopkins's memorandum on his meeting with Eisenhower was dated June 13.

906. The letter to Hopkins from Mrs. Mary P. Blanton was dated June 21.

CHAPTER XXXVII

907. President Truman's letter to Hopkins was dated July 3, 1945.
Admiral Stark's letter to Hopkins was dated July 5, 1945.
Hopkins's letter to Winchell was dated June 18, 1945.

908. The letter stating that Oxford University wished to confer the Honorary Degree of D.C.L. on Hopkins came from Douglas Veale and was dated June 19, 1945.
Hopkins's letter to General Ismay was dated July 28, 1945.
Hopkins's letter to Beaverbrook was dated July 6, 1945.

916. Stimson's letter to Hopkins was dated September 14, 1945.
General Eisenhower's letter to Hopkins was dated October 3, 1945.

Following is the full text of the War Department citation of Hopkins for the Distinguished Service Medal which was read aloud by President Truman in the Rose Garden of the White House on September 4, 1945:

Mr. Harry L. Hopkins performed services of outstanding value to the United States of America from December, 1941, to July, 1945. As Special Adviser to the President during critical months of World War II, he assumed tasks of utmost urgency and far-reaching consequences, lightening the burden of the Commander-in-Chief. He gave great assistance to the armed forces in their relationships with the Chief Executive, attacking with piercing understanding the tremendous problems incident to the vast military operations throughout the world. As Chairman of the Munitions Assignment Board, he channeled material to all Allied forces with a skill measurable in terms of the steady successes which have been achieved in crushing Germany and closing with Japan in the final struggle. As Chairman of the President's Soviet Protocol Committee, he determined supply quotas to be dispatched to Russia, accomplishing this mission with statesmanshiplike skill. At major conferences of world powers he threw his every effort toward the speedy solution of weighty problems. With deep appreciation of the armed forces' needs and broad understanding of the Commander-in-Chief's over-all policy, with exceptional ability to weld our Allies to the common purpose of victory over aggression, Mr. Hopkins made a selfless, courageous and objective contribution to the war effort.

INDEX

A

ABC—1 (war plan), 273, 925, 935
A.B.D.A. Area, 469, 470–1, 474–6, 478–80, 497, 504, 510, 514
Aberdeen News (So. Dak.), 91
Acheson, Dean, 196
Advisory Committee on Allotments, 69–70
Agar, Herbert, xiii, xv, 303
Aime, Adah, xiii, 14, 17, 34
Aimwell, H.M.S., 692
Air Ferry Command, 534, 669
Air Force, U.S. Army, 554, 555, 856, 945
Akron Times Press, 82–3
Alexander, A. V., 540
Alexander, Gen. Sir Harold, 615–16, 625, 628, 655, 674, 688
Alexander, John G., 133
Alison, Lt. John R., 324, 329
Allied Control Commission, 849, 879, 903–4
Alsop, Joseph V., 100, 175, 267–8, 726, 735
America First Committee, 131, 168, 227, 383
American Commonwealth, The, 17–18
American Booksellers Association, 203–4
American Magazine, 344–5, 695, 749, 949
American Public Welfare Association, 46 f.
American Youth Congress, 139–40
ANAKIM, operation, 672, 688, 728, 766–8, 925
Anderson, Sir John, 313
Anglo-Soviet Alliance, 559, 590
Antonov, Gen. A. I., 843
ANVIL, operation, 743, 801, 804, 925, 952
Appleby, Paul, xiii, 22
Arauca, S.S., 277
ARCADIA conferences (Wash., 1942), 446–91, 940
  staff talks at, 448, 449–82
  United Nations' declaration at, 450–5
Archangel, Russia, 326–7, 348, 937
Argentia, *see* Atlantic Conference
Argentina, 881 f., 886–7
Army and Navy Journal, 756–7
Army and Navy Register, 77, 757
Arnim, Col. Gen. Dietloff von, 723
Arnold, Gen. H. H., xi, 317, 358, 476 ff., 523, 554, 585–7, 671–2, 678–9, 756, 945
Arnstein, Daniel, 101, 289–90, 408–9

Arsenal of Democracy, 160–1, 949
"Arsenal of democracy" speech, 224–6
Ashford General Hospital, 8, 796
Associated Powers, *see* United Nations
Association for Improving the Condition of the Poor, 23–7
Astor, Lady, 260
Atlantic Charter, 360–4, 390, 512, 829, 852, 937
Atlantic Conference, 317, 332, 353–366, 937
  discussion of Japan at, 354–6
  See also Atlantic Charter
Atlantic Monthly, 288–9
Atlantic Ocean patrol, 291–2, 309–11
Atomic bomb, 156–7, 596, 665, 700–1, 856, 916
Attlee, Clement, 362, 450, 532, 542
Auchinleck, Gen. Sir Claude, 490, 528, 530, 590, 599
Augusta, U.S.S., 353
Austin, Warren, 437–8
AVALANCHE, operation, 741, 925
Azores Islands, 727, 744

B

B-17 Flying Fortress, 270, 310
B-24 Liberator, 310, 387
Bachelder, Toinette, 214, 265–6
Backer, George, 200
Badoglio, Marshal Pietro, 738 ff., 748
Bailey, Josiah, 106
Baillieu, Sir Clive, 302
Baker, Jacob, 52, 547
Balfour, Harold, 387, 424–5
Ball, Joseph H., 817 f.
Baltimore Sun, 90, 206
Bane, Frank, xiii, 46–7, 51, 52
Bankhead, William B., 178
Barclay, Edwin, 692
Barkley, Alben W., 96, 178, 438, 859
Barnes, Joseph, 632
Barrows, Roberta, 195
Barton, Bruce, 190
Baruch, Bernard M., xiii, 9, 95, 109, 111, 280, 282, 285, 488, 695, 696, 920
Bataan Peninsula, 500, 510, 514, 542
Bate, Fred, 166
Batt, William L., 108, 387
Battle of the Atlantic, 311, 316, 317, 381–4, 502–4, 598, 602, 743

Battle of Britain, 177, 220
Battle of the Bulge, 835
Battle of the Coral Sea, 546
Battle of the Java Sea, 510
Battle of Midway, 583, 584, 585
Baxter, James Phinney, 932
Beard, Charles A., 274, 936
Beardall, Capt. John R., 430
Béarn (Fr. carrier), 146, 221
Beatty, Jerome, 930
Beaverbrook, Lord, xii, xiii, 247–9, 253, 287, 312, 364, 369, 443–4, 470, 477 *f.*, 483 *f.*, 508, 614, 724, 750, 802–3, 828, 908
   and Atlantic Charter, 360–2
   mission to Moscow, 387–93
   and Second Front, 305, 395–6, 557–8, 731–3
Belgium, 143, 829
Bellairs, Adm. R. M., 272
Benes, Eduard, 252, 320
Benson, B. M., 16
Benson, Lt.-Col. Rex, 284
Berle, Adolf A., Jr., 44, 296–7
   on Presidential powers, 296–7
Berlin, Irving, 298
Berlin Diary, 100
Bernhardt, Prince (Netherlands), 302
Berry, Capt. Robert W., xii
Bethesda, Md., 192
Bevin, Ernest, 312, 532
Bidault, Georges, 839–40, 850
Biddle, Anthony D., 285
Biggers, John D., 109, 282
Bismarck (Ger. battleship), 291, 294–6
Bissell, Gen. Clayton L., 678
Blanton, Mary P., 906
Blitzkrieg, 127, 142–4, 169, 275
Bloom, Sol, 284, 437–8, 571, 865
Board of Child Welfare, 25
Board of Economic Warfare, 736
Boettiger, Anna, xiii, 631, 794, 842, 867, 869
Boettiger, John, 771
Bohlen, Charles E., xi, 769, 824, 839, 844, 874–5, 916
Boisson, Pierre, 647, 687
BOLERO, operation, 523 *f.*, 559, 573–4, 593, 595, 597, 603 *f.*, 607, 654, 688, 925
Bonomi, Ivanoe, 830
Bookman, Clarence M., 52
Borah, William E., 67, 116, 134
Borglum, Gutzon, 57–60
Boston Herald, 166

Bottlenecks, production, 280, 287
Bracken, Brendan, xii, 235, 239, 243, 262, 295, 352, 373–4, 749–51
Bradley, Dwight, 16
Bradley, Gen. Omar N., 803, 873
Brady, Dorothy, 195, 214
Brains Trust, 44, 183
Brandeis, Louis D., 93
Braun, Fr. Leopold, 395
Brenner Pass conference, 299
Bricker, John W., 815
Briggs, Dr. Lyman J., 156
Brooke, Gen. Sir Alan, 528, 541, 755, 778
Broun, Heywood, 101, 108
Brown, Prentiss M., 612
Brown, Adm. Wilson, 741, 764
Browning, Albert J., 12
Brownlow, Louis, xii, 51, 52, 932
Bruere, Henry, 24, 31
Bryand, G. J. D., 326
Bryce, James, 17–18
BUCCANEER, operation, 791–2, 925
Buckingham Palace, 243, 250–2, 935
Budd, Ralph, 159
Budget, *see* Bureau of the Budget
Bullitt, William C., 113, 144, 151, 286
Bureau of the Budget, 49, 210–11, 278, 934
Bureau of Standards, 156–7
Burke, Edward R., 158
Burma, 289–90, 408–9, 728, 767
Burns, Gen. James H., xiii, 161–2, 278, 283, 310, 384, 387, 580–1
   memorandum on Soviet relations, 639–42
Burritt, Bailey B., 26, 27
Bush, Dr. Vannevar, xiii, 155–7, 181, 701
Butcher, Harry, 673, 948
Byrnes, James F., 65, 177, 264, 487, 488, 632, 736, 826–7, 842, 845, 851, 870, 915, 953

C

CADOGAN, Sir Alexander, 258, 354 *f.*, 846
Caffery, Jefferson, 839, 850 *f.*, 905
Cairo Conference, first, 765–70
   second, 790–3, 941
Callaghan, Adm. Daniel, 192, 221, 652
Calvert, George A., Jr., 382–3
Cambon, Roger, 676
Campaigns, second term, 81–8
   third term, *see* Third term
   fourth term, 801 *f.*, 811–22

Canaday, Ward, 285
Carmona, Gen. Antonio, 643
Carruthers, Roy, 115
Casablanca Conference, 671-91, 949
  journey to, 666-70
Casey, Richard G., 284, 285, 513
Cash and Carry law, 127, 144, 220
Castellano, Gen. G., 741-2
Catalina, *see* PBY
Catoctin, U.S.S., 842
Catroux, Gen. Georges, 728, 948
Caucasus, projected air force in, 635-9
Cazalet, Maj. Victor, 302
Cerf, Bennètt, 624
Chamberlain, Neville, 111-12, 142, 238
Chaney, Gen. James E., 313, 315, 387
Channel Key, Fla., 379-80
Chatel, Yves, 643
Chennault, Gen. Claire L., 632, 658, 678-9,
  725 *ff.*, 735-6, 803, 812
Chequers, 241, 253, 255, 260-1, 310, 318-
  21, 534 *ff.*, 609, 937
Cherwell, Lord, xiii, 242, 319, 350, 354
Chiang Kai-shek, 347, 408 *ff.*, 471, 517,
  518-19, 539, 578, 599-600, 632, 726-7,
  735-6, 766-7, 856, 891-2
  See also China
Chiang Kai-shek, Mme., 347, 410, 599,
  642-3, 657-8, 703-4, 736, 766
Chicago, Ill., 15
Chicago Daily News, 105, 164, 166
Chicago Sunday Tribune, 951
Chicago Tribune, 82, 188, 206, 746-7
Chiefs of Staff, *see* Combined Chiefs; Joint
  Chiefs
Childs, Marquis, xiii, 202-3, 827, 933, 953
China, 289-90, 332-4, 534, 713-15, 766-9,
  854-5, 914-15, 925
  See also Lend Lease
Christadora House, 21-3
Christian Science Monitor, 859
Churchill, Mary, 742
Churchill, Randolph, 671, 681
Churchill, Winston, xi, xii, 6-7, 128-9,
  140-1, 203-4, 233, 286-7, 369-70,
  443, 516-17, 651-2, 697 *ff.*, 733-5,
  739, 778-9, 801 *ff.*, 861, 874, 902-3,
  920, 934, 940-1, 949-50
  aversion to Second Front, 262, 592-6,
    742-3, 762-3, 770, 782-3
  conference with Stalin, 615-22
  and destroyer transfer, 175-6, 222
  dispute over Italy, 829-31
  during Blitzkrieg, 142-51
  and Greek crisis, 829, 831-5

Churchill, Winston—*Continued*
  and Hess flight to Scotland, 293-4
  relationship with Roosevelt, 351-2,
    364-5, 446-8
  speeches, 112, 145, 261-2, 305-6, 460-1,
    498-9, 602, 745-6, 923, 932, 951
  and supreme command, 758-62
  talks with Hopkins, 238-47, 255-6, 260-
    1, 310-21, 528-45, 608-12, 840
  See also Conferences
Churchill, Mrs. Winston, 243, 320, 491
Ciano, Galeazzo, 445, 742
Cincinnati Times Star, 105
City of Cleveland, S.S., 614
Civil Affairs Division (Army), 722
Civil Works Administration, 52-63
Claggett, Gen. Henry B., 411
Clapper, Raymond, 3-4, 91, 105, 234
Claridge's Hotel, 236-8, 247-9, 254-5,
  321, 352, 608-9
Clark, Bennett C., 101, 188
Clark, Delbert, 65-6
Clark, Grenville, xiii, 157-8, 164
Clark, Gen. Mark, 609, 648, 651 *f.*
Clark Field, 433
Claunch, Mr., 206
Clinchy, Rev. Russell, 612
Coast Farmer, S.S., 509
Code names, *see* War plans
Codes, Japanese, breaking of, 426, 430, 819
Cohen, Benjamin V., xiii, 175
Combined Chiefs of Staff, 423, 484, 504,
  510, 521, 591 *ff.*, 658, 671-2, 739, 761,
  769, 783 *ff.*, 840-1
  organization of, 480-2
  preliminary talks, 271-3, 358-9
  and unity of command, 469-70
    See also Conferences: ARCADIA;
      Casablanca; Second Cairo; TRI-
      DENT
Combined Food Board, 583
Combined Production and Resources
  Board, 578, 658
Comes the Reckoning, 130, 932
Commandos, 532, 541, 623
Commerce Department, 108-9, 120
  Bureau of Standards, 156-7
Committee to Defend America by Aiding
  the Allies, 167-9
Commons, Dr. John R., 51
Communism (U.S.), 131, 139-40, 236,
  303, 788
Compton, Karl T., 155
Conant, James B., xiii, 155, 168, 270, 701,
  745

Cone, Howard M., 666
Conferences
  ARCADIA (Wash., 1942), 446–91, 940
  Atlantic, 317, 332, 353–66, 937
  Cairo, first, 765–70
    second, 790–3, 941
  Casablanca, 671–91, 949
  Dumbarton Oaks, 846 f.
  Moscow (1941), 388–98
  Quebec, first, 740–45
    second, 809–11
  San Francisco, 864–5, 874, 900–2
  Teheran, 770–90
  TRIDENT (Wash., 1943), 724–9
  Yalta, see Yalta Conference
Connally, Tom, 437–8, 569, 571, 865
Connolly, Gen. Donald H., 83, 85, 98, 790
Conventions, Democratic (1940), 177–9
  Republican (1940), 174
Conway, Carle C., 109
Conway, Capt. Granville, xiii, 939
Cook, Nancy, 933
Cooke, Capt. C. M., 272
Coonley, Howard, 108
Corcoran, Thomas J., 47
Cornell, Douglas B., 221
Corregidor, 502, 513
Cotentin Peninsula, 524, 525
Coughlin, Fr. Charles E., 83, 130, 167–8
Council Bluffs, Neb., 15
Cowles, Gardner, 632
Cox, Oscar, xiii, 227, 278, 283, 286, 287,
  722
Coy, Wayne, xiii
Craig, Col. H. A., 526
Craig, Gen. Malin, 89
Cranborne, Lord, 261
Cresswell, Lt.-Col. Harry I. T., 424
Crete, 275, 301, 314, 378
Crim, Howell G., 206
Crimea Conference, see Yalta Conference
Cripps, Sir Stafford, 305, 332, 529, 535–6
Cross, Samuel H., xiii, 559–61, 564–72,
  575–80
Cudahy, E. A., 108
Cuff Links Gang, 933–4
Cunningham, Adm. Sir Andrew, 648,
  674, 688, 807, 843–4, 947
Currie, Lauchlin, 208, 283, 286, 408ff.
Curtin, John, 512–13

D

Daily Oklahoman, 81–2
Daily Worker, 234, 303

Damaskinos, Archbishop, 835
Danckwerts, Adm. V. H., 272
Daniels, Jonathan, 208
Darlan, Adm. Jean, 146 f., 296, 473–4, 461–
  2, 553, 659–60, 683–4
  North African deal with, 644–53, 672,
    677–8
Davenport, Russell W., 187, 284
Davey, Martin, 78–9
Davies, Joseph E., xiii, 49, 562, 729, 747,
  881
  memorandum on Russia, 306–9
Davis, Chester C., xiii, 21–2, 159
Davis, Elmer, 166, 442, 649
Davis, James J., 105
Declaration of the United Nations, 450–5,
  940–1
De Gaulle, Gen. Charles, 146, 627, 646,
  654, 659–60, 719, 729, 776, 839–46,
  843, 850, 862, 905, 912, 918–19, 948–9
  at Casablanca Conference, 675–9, 682–
    90
  and St. Pierre-Miquelon affair, 456–66
Delabrooke, 116–17
Delano, Fred, 200
Delano, Laura, 5
Democratic National Committee, 69, 217
Denyer, James, 255
Des Moines Register, 166
Destroyers, transfer of, 175–7
De Valera, Eamon, 231
Devers, Gen. Jacob L., 952
Dewey, Thomas E., 87, 152, 175, 187, 195,
  633
  Presidential candidacy (1944), 801, 811–
    13, 815ff., 818–19
Dickerman, Marion, 933
Dickinson, Lester J., 82
Dies, Martin, 102
Dietrich, Dr. Otto, 397
Dill, F.M., Sir John, 256, 316, 359, 482,
  528, 688, 763, 796, 802
Division of Applications and Information,
  69
Doolittle raid on Tokyo, 546
Donovan, William J., 230, 258, 283, 410,
  935
Douglas, Lewis, xi, 44, 56, 550–1
Douglas, William O., 487, 488, 870
Dowding, Air Marshal Sir Hugh, 147
Draft, see Selective Service
DRAGOON, operation, see ANVIL
Dreyfus, Louis G., 771
Duke of York, H.M.S., 541
Dumbarton Oaks Conference, 846f.

Duncan, Barbara, *see* Hopkins, Barbara
Duncan, Capt. Donald, 747
Dunkirk, 143
Durand, Margaret, 933
Durno, George E., 222, 685
Dykstra, Clarence, xiii
Dytchley, 241–3, 293–4, 937

E

EAKER, Gen. Ira C., 554, 840
Earle, George, 94
Early, Stephen T., xiii, 207, 293, 448, 572, 608, 737, 749, 842, 868, 933, 942
Eaton, Charles A., 437–8, 865
Eberstadt, Ferdinand, 696
Eccles, Marriner S., 302
Eden, Anthony, xii, 258–9, 428, 443, 454, 531, 658, 848 f., 853
    visit to Washington (1943), 704–19
Edison, Charles, 137
Edmonds, T. S., 52
Egypt, 598–9
    See also Middle East
Eisenhower, Gen. Dwight D., 450, 608–9, 615, 628, 644, 659–62, 686 f., 698, 748, 755 f., 803, 816, 840–1, 879, 883, 903–6, 916–17
    North African problems, 654–52, 659–60, 673–5
    and supreme command, xi f., 765, 793
Elizabeth, Queen (Eng.), 116, 149, 250–2
Elliott, Dr. Harriet, 159
Embick, Gen. S. D., 272, 302
Emergency Relief and Construction Act, 46
Emerson, Dr. Haven, 28
Emmons, Gen. Delos C., 271
Engel, Albert J., 284
Enterprise, U.S.S., 68, 656
Ernst, Morris, xiii, 9
Escort vessel shortage, 682, 688, 743
Essary, Helen, 88
Esteva, Adm. Jean Pierre, 647, 648
Eusterman, Dr. George B., 112, 119
Evatt, Dr. Herbert, xiii, 511, 520, 521
Ewings, Oscar R., 285
Executive Office reorganization, 208–11

F

FALA, 5, 215, 813
Farley, James A., 32, 45, 69, 85–6, 95, 96, 109, 116, 137, 165, 172–3, 227, 933
    antipathy to third term, 171–2
    at *1940* convention, 177–8, 179

Farm Resettlement Administration, 71
Faymonville, Col. Philip R., xiii, 387, 397, 501
Federal Arts Programme, 57–61
Federal Bureau of Investigation, 249–50, 270, 277, 613–14, 946
Federal Emergency Relief Administration, 44–49, 53, 56
Feis, Herbert, xiii
Fields, William, xiv
Fight For Freedom Committee, 169, 292, 303
Finland, 125, 139, 575–6, 707–8
Fireside Chats, 42–43, 224–6, 552–3
Fish, Hamilton, 189–90, 437
Fisher, Dorsey, 321
FLINTLOCK, operation, 796, 925
Flying Fortress (B-17), 270, 310
Flynn, Edward J., 173, 178, 186, 842, 933
Foley, Edward H., 227
Folks, Homer, 31
Folsom, M. B., 109
Ford, Henry, 281
Foreign Policy Association speech, 817–18
Forrestal, James, xii, 165, 208, 273, 283, 303, 870–1
Forster, Rudolph, 208
Fortune magazine, 16, 56–7, 62, 929
Forum magazine, 92
Four Freedoms, 231, 266, 362, 453, 829
Four Power Declaration, 742
Fourth term campaign, 801 f., 811–22
Fox, Lt.-Comm. George, 113, 208
France, 688–9, 838, 882, 886, 904–5
    and Allied Control Commission, 849–50
    destruction of Navy, 150
    fall of, 142–50, 302
        See also Free French; Vichy Government
Francis, Clarence, 108
Frank, Jerome, xiii
Frankfurter, Felix, xiii, 94, 108, 231, 757
Franklin D. Roosevelt Library, Inc., 172, 183
Franklin D. Roosevelt Memorial Foundation, 206
Free French forces, 452 f., 456–66, 540, 627, 676, 683–4
Freeman, Air Marshal Sir W., 350, 354
French Committee of National Liberation, 719, 742
Frontier on the Potomac, 208
Fruehauf, Roy, 612, 614
Fulton, Comm. James R., xiii, 526, 537–8, 608

G

GALLUP POlls, 87, 102–3, 191, 198–9, 933
Gamelin, Gen. Maurice, 142
Gandhi, Mohandas K., 517
Gannett, Lewis, 86
Garner, John N., 95, 134, 171–2, 227
Gathering Storm, The, 739, 937
Gauss, Clarence E., 632
George VI, King (Eng.), 116, 233, 243, 250–2, 543
George II, King (Greece), 829, 834
George, Walter, 284
Georges, Gen. Alphonse, 29
Germany, 112, 125
  invasion of Soviet Union, 302–10
  postwar plans for, 708–10, 711–13, 789, 809–11, 893–4
  See also Hitler, Adolf
Gerow, Gen. L. T., 272
Ghormley, Adm. R. L., 271, 272, 290, 313
Ghost writing, *see* Speeches, preparation of
G.I. Bill of Rights, 737
Gifford, Walter S., 46
Gilbert, Richard V., xiii
Gill, Corrington, 52, 93, 103
Gillette, Guy M., 105
Giraud, Gen. Henri H., 646–9, 652, 659, 675, 677f., 679–81, 684, 687ff., 719, 729, 948
Girdler, Tom M., 193
Gneisenau (Ger. cruiser), 291, 506
Goebbels, Joseph P., 114, 130, 154, 241, 322, 391, 880
Goering, Hermann, 154, 545
Goldberg, Dr. Jacob A., xiii, 28
Goldschmidt, Mr. and Mrs. A. E., xiii
Golikov, Gen. Filipp I., 322
Gompers, Samuel, 51
Gordon, Max, 101, 289
Graham, Philip, xiii
Grandi, Count Dino, 742
Grayson, Adm. Cary T., 89
Greater East Asia Co-Prosperity Sphere, 271
Greece, 275–6, 829, 831–5
Greengrass, Barney, 183
Grenwell, Lt.-Col. S. A., 425–6
Greer, U.S.S., 371
Gregory, Nicholas, 161
Grigg, Sir James, 540
Grinnell, Iowa, 15–17, 110
Grinnell College, 15–21
Gromyko, Andrei, xiv, 837, 846f., 864
Gross, Ethel, *see* Hopkins, Ethel

Gruber, Gen. W. R., 600
Guadalcanal, 622–3, 652
Gulick, Luther, 934
GYMNAST, operation, 472–4, 478–9, 515, 525, 545, 559, 588, 593, 604, 610–12, 925, 942
  See also TORCH

H

HAAKON VII, King (Norway), 252
Hackmeister, Louise, 380, 741
Halifax, Lord, xiii, 237–8, 246, 310, 451, 520–1, 557, 833
Hall, James Norman, 284, 413
Hall, Wilfred H., 254
Halsey, Adm. William F., 819
Hamilton, Duke of, 294
Handy, Gen. T. T., 644
Hankey, Lord, 312
Hannegan, Robert, xiii
Harkness, Richard L., 231
Harriman, Kathleen, 319, 321, 842
Harriman, W. Averell, xi, 108f., 276, 428, 517, 527, 658–9, 679–80, 702–3, 733–4, 751f., 776, 824–6, 874–5
  as Lend Lease expediter, 268, 285f., 444–5, 634
  Moscow missions, 386–97, 616–21, 624–5
  on religion in Soviet Union, 393–5
  trip to Middle East, 301, 312
Harrington, Col. Francis C., 76, 104
Harris, Air Marshal Arthur T., 302
Harris, Rev. F. B., 447
Harsch, Joseph C., 859
Hart, Moss, 174, 933
Hart, Adm. T. C., 470, 480, 497, 499, 504
Harvey, Major A. L., 387
Hassett, William D., xiii, 206, 207
Hastings, Neb., 15
Head, Frances, xiii
Heidrich, Reinhardt, 590
Heiss, Maj. G. K., 283
Helfrich, Adm. Conrad, 499, 504
Hellman, Geoffrey T., 730, 929, 950
Hemingway, Ernest, 222
Hemisphere Defence Plans, No. 1, 292
  No. 2, 292–3
Henderson, Leon, xii, 158, 287, 629
Henry-Haye, Gaston, 459
Hermann, Mr., 161
Hermes, H.M.S., 530
Herriot, Édouard, 146
Hertz, John M., 115, 289

Hess, Rudolph, 294, 374, 392
Hewitt, Adm. H. K., 832–3
Hillman, Sidney, 158, 287, 310
Hillquit, Morris, 25
Hirohito, Emperor, 867
Hitler, Adolf, 38, 64, 97, 114, 154, 183, 240, 296 f., 305, 343, 358, 369–70, 397, 565–6, 693, 777, 880, 902
    wish for negotiated peace, 127–8, 306–9, 370–1, 375
Hobbs, Franklin W., 108
Hobcaw Barony, 111
Hodson, William, 31, 152–3
Hoey, Jane, xii
Holland, 142–3
Hollis, Gen. Sir Leslie, xiii, 350
Home Fleet, see Royal Navy
Hood, H.M.S., 295
Hooker, Henry, 933
Hoover, Herbert, 30, 38–9, 45–6, 253–4, 633, 858
Hoover, J. Edgar, 250, 270
Hopkins, Adah, see Aime, Adah
Hopkins, Anna P., 14–16, 19
Hopkins, Barbara, 34–5, 37, 48, 88, 92
Hopkins, David, ix, xiii, 24, 120, 795
Hopkins, David A., 14–16, 18–19
Hopkins, Diana, 37, 93, 104, 114, 116 f., 119–20, 252, 353, 533, 794
Hopkins, Ethel, xiii, 24, 34–5
Hopkins, Harry L., 25–6, 49–50, 89–91, 99–103, 107–8, 247–50, 257–8, 291–2, 302–3, 373–6, 397–8, 506–8, 907–8, 917–18, 954
    background, 14–16
    and C.W.A., 52–63
    early welfare work, 21–30
    education, 16–21
    as F.E.R.A. administrator, 44–49
    feud with Ickes, 69–72, 79–80
    on future domestic policy, 915–16
    on future foreign relations, 910–15
    grasp of war problems, 6, 12–13
    illness, 7–9, 15–16, 92, 94, 110–12, 117–20, 141, 320, 325, 348, 350, 384, 499–500, 526–7, 537–8, 746, 795–7, 841, 842, 862–3, 919–20
    missions to England, 231–63, 310–21, 527–44, 608–12, 839
    missions to Russia, 317–19, 324–49, 875–902, 936
    and Pearl Harbour, 430–3, 435–9
    and preparation of speeches, 196, 198, 212–18, 296–7, 370–3

Hopkins, Harry L.—Continued
    Presidential ambitions, 90–7, 172–3, 930–1
    as Sec. of Commerce, 11, 102–11, 115, 120, 179–83
    speeches, 19–21, 83–5, 109, 319–23
    and third term, 115–16, 172–3, 177–9
    value to Roosevelt, 3–9, 202–3, 211–12, 805–6, 824–6
    and W.P.A., 68–72, 76–7
Hopkins, John E., 14, 118–19, 125
Hopkins, Lewis, xiii, 14, 19, 32–4, 63, 65, 80, 110, 118–19
Hopkins, Louise, ix, 104, 596–7, 612–14, 667, 695, 748, 794 f., 875, 894, 898
Hopkins, Robert, xiii, 24, 117, 671, 681, 685, 765, 770, 842
Hopkins, Rome, 14
Hopkins, Stephen, 24, 117, 384–5, 795–6
Hormel, Jay, 131
House, Col. Edward M., 6, 234, 929
Houston, U.S.S., 64, 79–80, 510
Howe, Louis M., 32, 44, 933
Howe, Quincy, 132
Hughes, Charles Evans, 94
Hull, Cordell, 94 f., 134, 171 f., 185, 268–9, 285, 290, 371 f., 433, 436 ff., 582, 658, 712 ff., 752–3, 810–11, 826
    talks with Japanese envoys, 426–7, 435
    and Vichy policy, 453, 458–66, 645, 647, 675–6
Hump, the, 518, 534
Hunter, Howard, xiii, 52, 97
Hurja, Mrs. Emil, 286
Hurley, Gen. Patrick J., 789, 857
HUSKY, operation, 671, 674, 689, 714, 720, 728, 925
Hutchins, Robert M., 51, 131, 264
Hyde Park, 64, 94, 101, 174, 198–200
Hyman, Sidney, x, xiii f., 909–10, 917–18

I

IBN SAUD, King (Saudi Arabia), 285, 860–1
Iceland, 290–1, 304
Ickes, Harold L., xiii, 44, 51 ff., 81, 92 f., 165, 171, 175,178, 181, 277, 723, 870
    feud with Hopkins, 69–71, 79–80, 202
    and Relief Programme, 68–72
Illustrious, H.M.S., 244
Imperial Preference plan, 361–2, 809
Independent Committee, 186
India, 516–17, 529–30
Indian Ocean, 530, 539, 541

Industrial Mobilization for War, 944
Industrial Mobilization Plan, 280
Ingram, Adm. Jonas, 669
Inonu, Ismet, 697, 776, 786, 788, 790
Interventionists, 135
Invasions, *see* War plans
Iowa, U.S.S., 762–5
Iran, 853
Ismay, Gen. Sir Hastings, xii, 147, 242, 313, 352, 908
Isolationism, 125–40, 167–8, 171, 227, 264, 274, 281, 303, 384
  factions in, 128–35
Italy, 829–31
  surrender of, 737–42, 745, 748

J

JACKSON, Robert H., 95, 277
Jacob, Gen. E. J. C., 661
Japan, 133, 258–9, 271, 309, 316, 318–19, 332–4, 773, 779–80, 807–9
  pre-Pearl Harbour negotiations, 422–35
  U.S. messages to, 354–8
Jewett, Frank B., 155
Johnson, Gerald W., 74, 929
Johnson, Herschel V., xiii, 236–8, 247, 257*f*.
Johnson, Hiram, 108, 437–8, 753
Johnson, Hugh S., 44, 81, 89, 90, 108, 166, 522
Johnson, Dr. Kenneth, 112
Johnson, Louis A., 95, 137, 162, 529
Johnson, Walter, 933
Johnson, Wayne, 287
Joint Board Estimate, 413–23, 438, 488
Joint Chiefs of Staff, xii, 423, 541, 572–3, 594, 597, 615, 622–3, 671, 762–3, 776, 779, 803, 840–1, 938, 940, 946–7
  See also Combined Chiefs of Staff
Jones, Jesse H., 302, 488*f*., 736, 838
Journal (Knoxville, Tenn.), 346
Juliana, Princess (Netherlands), 302
JUPITER, operation, 559, 628, 653, 925

K

KANIN, Garson, 950
Kansas City Times, 86
Kaufman, George S., 105, 174, 933
Kearney, Neb., 15
Kearney, U.S.S., 382, 938
Kelley, Frances, xii
Kelly, Edward J., 173, 178–9

Kennan, George, 898
Kennedy, Joseph P., 92, 113, 151–2, 192, 231, 239
Kenney, Gen. George C., 623
Kent, Frank R., 100–1
Kerr, Sir Archibald C., 639, 776, 903
Kerr, Florence, 19, 110, 796
Kerr, Robert, xii, 14, 19, 110, 746
Kesselring, F. M. Albert, 873
Kimmel, Adm. Husband E., 429–30, 433, 482
King, Adm. Ernest J., xi, 165, 365, 473*ff*., 546, 563, 567–9, 585, 611, 671, 679, 756, 764–5, 775, 832–3, 841
King, Mackenzie, 457, 596, 805
King George V, H.M.S., 245, 549
Kingsbury, Dr. John A., xiii, 23–7, 31, 34*f*.
Kinkaid, Adm. Thomas C., 819
Kintner, Robert, 100, 267–8
Kirk, Capt. A. G., 272
Kirk, Alexander C., 769–70, 840
Kirkpatrick, Ivone, 294
Kittredge, Capt. T. B., xii, 940, 948
Knollys, Lord, 527
Knowlson, James S., 288–9
Knox, Frank, 163–5, 227, 265, 284, 290, 293, 372, 435–6, 440, 509, 613, 940
Knudsen, William S., 158, 162, 224, 488–90, 942
Koenig, Gen. Joseph-Pierre, 590
Koiso, Gen. Kuniaki, 802
Konoye, Prince Fumimaro, 363, 381, 423
Korea, 877
Kozlov, Gen. D. T., 570
Krock, Arthur, 100–1, 194–5, 602–3
Krug, Julius, 812
Kung, H. H., 347
Kung, Madame, 736
Kuniholm, Berbel E., 290
Kuomintang (China), 409, 735*f*., 856–7
Kurusu, Saburo, 426, 435
Kuter, Gen. Laurence S., 843

L

LA FOLLETTE, Robert M., 94, 131, 931
La Guardia, Fiorello, xiii, 186, 283, 302, 352, 907
  desire for Army service, 720–2
Lamont, Thomas W., xiii
Land, Adm. Emory S., 282, 284*ff*., 478
Landing craft shortage, 558, 582, 587
Landon, Alfred M., 81
Lange, Oscar, 890, 897
Langer, William, 78

Langer, William L., xiii, 461, 463, 465, 627, 941, 947
Langley, U.S.S., 510
Langner, Lawrence, 156
Lansing State Journal, 105
Lascelles, Sir Alan, 250
Lasker, Albert, 193
Latta, Maurice, 208
Lattimore, Owen, 408, 642
Laval, Pierre, 540, 543–5, 673, 675
Layton, Lord, xiii
League of Nations Association, 166
Leahy, Adm. William D., xii, 296, 463–4, 504–5, 543–5, 615, 668, 759, 832–4, 934
Leathers, Lord, xiii, 532f.
Lee, Gen. Raymond E., 313, 315–16, 424, 942
Leger, Alexis, 676
LeHand, Marguerite, 112–13, 172, 173–4, 191, 205, 231, 265, 286, 293, 933f.
Lemaigre-Dubreuil, Jacques, 646
Lend Lease, 51, 226–7, 253–4, 857
  administration of, 267–70, 272, 278–90, 313, 378–9
  to China, 407, 410–14
  to Great Britain, 443–4, 511–12, 805, 809
  inception of, 223–41, 934
  passage of, 227–8, 261, 264–5
  to Soviet Union, 396–7, 398–400, 548–50, 555–6, 572, 574–5, 578–81, 632, 634–9, 882–3, 884–5
  speeches on, 223–6, 261–2, 265–7
  to Turkey, 557
Leopold, King (Belgium), 143, 251–2, 271
Lewellin, Col. J. I., 261
Lewis, Fulton, 614
Lewis, John L., 131, 193, 723, 815
Libby, Comm. R. E., 608
Liberty League, 80
Lidice, Czechoslovakia, 590
Life magazine, 818
LIFEBELT, operation, 727, 925
LIGHTFOOT, operation, 628, 925, 946
Lindbergh, Col. Charles A., 131, 154–5, 168, 286, 292
Lindemann, F. A., see Cherwell, Lord
Lindley, Ernest K., 44, 929
Lippmann, Walter, xiii, 67–8, 827, 929
Literary Digest, 86–7
Litvinov, Maxim, 334, 391, 452–3, 562f., 575, 577, 589, 710–11, 730
Lloyd George, David, 140
Lockhart, Sir Robert Bruce, xiii, 132, 628, 932

London, H.M.S., 387–8
Long, Breckenridge, 286
Long, Huey, 74, 78
Los Angeles Times, 105, 920–1
Lothian, Lord, 220, 223–4
Loudon, Alexander, 521
Lovett, Robert A., 165, 283ff., 527
Low Countries, 142, 144
Lozovski, S. A., 347
Lubin, Isador, xiii, 216, 280, 284ff., 722
Luce, Henry R., 168, 819
Lynch, Thomas, 933
Lyttelton, Oliver, xiii, 508, 531, 583, 586, 658

M

MACARTHUR, Gen. Douglas, 407, 436, 467, 502, 509–10, 514, 563, 588, 598, 623, 716, 756, 801, 855–6, 943
  views on future of Japan, 866–8
McCarthy, Charles H., 205, 933
McCarthy, Col. Frank, 608, 951
McCarthy, Leighton, 297
McCloy, John J., xi, 161–2, 166, 719
McClure, Gen. Robert A., 537, 545
McClure, Robert S., xiii, 52
McComas, Lt. Anthony, 261
McCormack, John, 437
McCrea, Adm. John, xiii, 669f., 680, 762f.
Macfarlane, Gen. Mason, 500–1, 942
McHugh, Major, 409
McIntire, Adm. Ross T., xiii, 7–8, 116–17, 120, 206, 208, 217, 221–2, 262, 668ff., 691–2, 764, 842, 875, 933
McIntyre, Marvin, 93, 183, 206, 207–8, 933
McKinley, D. C., xiii, 324–6, 348–9, 937
MacLeish, Archibald, xiii, 215, 649
Macmillan, Harold, 673, 688, 721
McMorris, Adm. C. H., 428–9
McMullin, Russell, 380
McNarney, Gen. J. T., 272, 324, 331, 840
McNary, Charles, 437–8
McNutt, Paul, 94
Macready, Gen. G. N., 387, 483–4
McReynolds, William H., 159
Macy, Jesse, 17–18
Macy, Louise, see Hopkins, Louise
Madagascar, 553
"Magic" (code breaker), 426, 430, 445, 819
Maginot Line, 138, 144
MAGNET, operation, 472, 474, 476–7, 925
Maisky, I. M., 319, 321, 703, 711–2, 730

Malta, 841
Maritime Commission, U.S., 400
Markham, Gen. Edward, 89
Marks, Eva, xiv
Marshall, Gen. George C., 12, 76–7, 165–6, 270, 281, 317, 367–8, 409, 413, 436, 438, 497, 537, 445–6, 588, 595, 598–600, 601–2, 644, 655, 660–1, 686–7, 735, 807, 819
    advocacy of Second Front, 524–5, 528, 531, 538*ff*., 567, 610–11, 667–8, 671–2, 778
    regard for Hopkins, 3, 98–9, 796
    and Supreme Command decision, xi-xii, 615, 755–62, 765, 782, 793
    on unity of command, 469–70
    See also Chiefs of Staff; Conferences; War plans
Marshall, Mrs. George C., 545, 755, 758
Martin, J. M., 243, 350
Martin, Joseph W., Jr., 133, 187, 189–90, 373, 437, 614
Martinique, 146, 199, 221, 295, 933
Massigli, René, 729
Mast, Gen. Charles, 646
Masten, John E., xiv, 936
Mathews, William H., 24–5, 29
Matsuoka, Yosuke, 333, 358
Matthews, H. Freeman, 532, 545
May, Stacy, 287
Mayo Clinic, 92, 97, 111, 112, 117–20, 795, 863, 865
Means Test, 53
Mellon, Andrew, 33
Memphis, U.S.S., 669–70, 691–2
Menemencioglu, Numan, 790
Merriam, Charles E., xiii, 934
Michelier, Adm. François, 644
Middle East, 301, 312, 376–7, 598–9, 604J
Mikolajczyk, Stanislaw, 890, 897
Milbank Fund, 26, 35
Miles, Gen. Sherman, 272
Military government, 719–22
Miller, Dr. James A., xiii, 27–8, 29
Miller, Malcolm, 103
Millis, Walter, 132
Missenden, Sir Eustace, 236
Mitchel, John Purroy, 23, 25
Mitchell, Lucy, xiii
Moir, Phyllis, xiii
Moley, Raymond, 44
Molotov, V. M., 330, 332–4, 549–50, 559, 590–1, 618, 794, 842–3, 844–5, 852–3, 853–4, 864, 875, 885–7
    talks with Roosevelt, 560–81, 584f.

Monnet, Jean, xiii, 224, 232–3, 288, 302, 675–6, 719, 729
Montgomery, F.M. Sir Bernard, 625, **628**, 674, 803, 904
Mook, H. J. van, 510
Mooney, James D., 108, 131
Morgan, Gen. Sir Frederick, 359
Morgenthau, Henry, Jr., xiii, 10, 44, 116, 163, 183, 265, 488, 757, 871, 933
Morgenthau Plan, 810–11, 824
Morison, Samuel E., 271, 503, 644, 942
Morocco, Sultan of, 643, 687
Morris, Gen. E. L., 272
Morrison, Herbert, 352
Morrow, Dwight, 38
Morrow, Mrs. Dwight W., 168
Morton, Sir Desmond, 242
Moscow Conferences (1941), 388–97
Mountbatten, Lord Louis, 532, 542, 559, 587–8, 686, 742, 768
Munitions Assignment Board, 482–6, 521, 796
Murmansk, Russia, 548–9, 565, 568, 581, 601, 634–8, 656
Murray, Philip, 386
Murphy, Frank, 94, 95, 101–2, 108, 386
Murphy, Grace, xiii, xiv
Murphy, Robert, 464, 645–7, 649, 672*ff*., 681, 683, 687, 721
Murrow, Edward R., xiii, 166, 237
Muselier, Adm. Emile, 456–8, 459, 941
Mussolini, Benito, 80, 130, 143, 173, 189, 213, 240, 299, 737–8, 742
'My Day,' 97, 116
My Kay IV (yacht), 612–14, 946
My Three Years with Eisenhower, 947

N

NASH, Walter, 521
Nathan, Robert, xiii, 287
National Conference of Social Work, 47
National Defence Advisory Commission, 158–9
National Defence Research Council, 156–7, 163, 270
National Emergency Council, 53–4, 65
National Geographic magazine, 309–10, 311
National Health Centre, 192
National Resources Planning Board, 731
Nation's Health, 28
Naval Appropriations Bill (1940), 175–6
Naval Medical Centre, 262
Navy Department, 137–8, 216, 380–1, 400
Navy Hospital, 384–5, 456, 491, 496, 795

Nehru, Jawaharlal, 529
Nelson, Donald M., 53, 108, 159*ff.*, 377,
    583–4, 655–6, 949
  and War Production Board, 487–9,
    696–7, 812
Neutrality Law, 125*ff.*, 134, 138, 167, 235*f*
  amendment of, 376, 381, 384
New Deal, x–xi, 42, 44, 64–5, 75, 88–9,
    922–3
New York Herald Tribune, 86, 108, 166,
    196, 206, 460, 522, 865*f.*
New York Times, 65–6, 146, 194, 206, 368–
    9, 457–8, 602
New York Tuberculosis Association, 26–9
New Yorker, The, 730, 929, 950
Niles, David K., xiii, 103, 109, 209, 757
Nimitz, Adm. Chester W., 563, 716, 726,
    801, 819, 861, 867, 943
NKVD (Russian secret police), 771, 779
Noble, Edward J., 110–11, 159
Noguès, Gen. Auguste, 611, 644*ff.*, 687*f.*
Nollen, Dr. John, xiii
Nomura, Kichisaburo, 356–7, 426*f.*, 430,
    435
Non-Partisan Committee for Peace
  through Revision of the Neutrality
  Law, 166–7
Normandie, S.S., 440, 505, 518
Norris, George W., 186
North African theatre, 643–53
North Carolina, U.S.S., 541, 544
Norway, 142

O

O'BRIEN, Sam, 16
O'Connor, Basil, 933
Office of Civilian Defence, 721
Office of Price Administration, 629
Office of Production Management, 377
Office of War Information, 72, 632, 738,
    935–6
Office of War Mobilization, 736
Oldendorf, Adm. Jesse B., 668
Oliphant, Herman, 227
On Active Service in Peace and War, xiv,
    945
One World, 632
Operations, *see* War plans
Oran, Algeria, 150
Osawatamie Speech, 41–2
Ottawa Agreements, 361–2, 809
Oumansky, Constantine A., 321, 393–5,
    562
Our Vichy Gamble, 461, 463, 465, 947

OVERLORD, operation, xi–xii, 359, 525,
    727*f.*, 742–3, 755*ff.*, 765, 770, 774–8,
    782–6, 802–3, 925, 935
Owen, C. M., 325, 937

P

P-40 (fighter plane), 329–30
Pacific War Council, 514–15, 520–2, 523,
    558, 596
Paley, William S., 302
Palmer, A. Mitchell, 131
Parker, Dorothy, 303
Patch, Gen. Alexander M., 805, 852
Patterson, Eleanor M., 9
Patterson, Robert P., xiii, 158, 164–5, 273,
    289, 489–90
Patton, Gen. George S., 615, 646, 663*f.*,
    674, 681, 686, 803
Paulus, Field Marshal Friedrich, 692
PBY (patrol bomber), 296, 317, 324–6,
    348–9
Pearl Harbour, 426, 428–9, 431, 801, 939
Pearson, Drew, 872–3
Pepper, Claude E., 93
Perkins, Frances, xiv, 10, 44, 838–9
Perry, Albert, 255
Pershing, Gen. John J., 756, 758
Persian Gulf Command, 548, 790
Pétain, Henri, 144*ff.*, 463, 504–5, 643–4,
    648, 677*f.*, 683–4, 772, 913
Peter II, King (Yugoslavia), 277
Peyrouton, Marcel, 672–6
Philadelphia Inquirer, 231
Philip, André, 729
Philippine Islands, 467, 786–7, 816, 818,
    866, 941
Phony War, 125–41, 154
Pius XII, Pope, 386, 840
Plans, war, *see* War plans
Pleven, René, 676
Ploesti, bombing of, 728
Poland, 125, 706*ff.*, 834, 853, 878–9, 887–
    90, 894–900
Polangin, Frederick, xiii, 109
POINTBLANK, operation, 743, 925
Poletti, Charles, 722
Politburo, 621, 898
Poniatowski, Count, 679–80
Port Everglades, Fla., 277
Portal, Air Marshal Sir Charles, 256, 313,
    316, 352, 479, 542, 544, 843
Potomac (Pres. yacht), 117, 174, 277, 936
Pound, Adm. Sir Dudley, 256, 313, 316,
    350, 354, 476–7, 541

Pratt, Gen. Henry C., 668
Prenosil, Stanley, 933
Prettyman, CPO Arthur, 215
Price, Byron, 572
Price control, 551-2, 629-30, 631-2
Prince of Wales, H.M.S., 295, 348, 350-5, 362, 365, 428, 446, 497, 938
Pringle, Henry, 215
Prinz Eugen (Ger. cruiser), 291, 295, 506, 567
Proclamations, Limited Emergency, 135
  Unlimited National Emergency, 296-8
Providence Bulletin, 847
Psychological Warfare Division, 502, 627-8
Public Papers and Addresses of Franklin D. Roosevelt, The, 929, 935
Public Works Administration, 52, 69-71
Public Works fund, 51, 70-2
Punjabi, H.M.S., 549
Purvis, Arthur B., 283, 302, 374
Pyle, Ernie, 62, 929

Q

QUEBEC Conferences, first, 740-5
  second, 809-11
Queen Elizabeth, S.S., 682, 949
Queen Mary, S.S., 682, 949
Quezon, Manuel, 521
Quincy, U.S.S., 839, 841, 850, 858, 861-3

R

RAMSEY, Capt. DeWitt, 272
Ranger, U.S.S., 539
Rankin, Jeannette, 499
Rayburn, Sam, 437-8
Reciprocal trade, 136
Reconstruction Finance Corporation, 46
Red Cross, 25-6
Reed, Carol, 950
Reed, Stanley, 103
Reichers, Lt. L. T., 387
Reilly, Michael F., 771
Relief, unemployment, 41-77
Rennell, Lord, 721-2
Reorganization Bill, 209-11
Republican National Committee, 55
Repulse, H.M.S., 428, 446
Reuben James, U.S.S., 383, 938
Reynaud, Paul, 145-7
Reynolds, Quentin, xiii, 319-20, 387

Reynolds, Thomas F., 221, 223
Ribbentrop, Joachim von, 569
Richardson, Seth W., 430-2
Richberg, Donald, 65
Richelieu (Fr. battleship), 670
Riom trials, 504-5
Rivers, Dr. Andrew B., 8
Robert, Adm. Georges, 456, 462
Roberts, Owen J., 427, 939
Roberts Commission, 427, 430-3, 496, 939
Robin Moor. S.S., 296, 299
Rommel, Gen. Erwin, 275, 473, 490, 496, 504-5, 590, 595, 598-9
Roosevelt, Anna, *see* Boettiger, Anna
Roosevelt, Eleanor, xiv, 30, 48, 78, 94, 97, 172, 199, 203-5, 215, 298, 440, 667, 687, 822-3, 870, 922-3, 931
  and Diana Hopkins, 104, 116
  on third term, 115-16
Roosevelt, Elliott, 185, 192, 670 *f.*, 680 *ff.*, 765, 770, 779, 838
Roosevelt, Franklin D., 3-9, 79-80, 112-13, 156-7, 159-60, 378-80, 386, 400, 506-9, 513-17, 949
  as administrator, 73-4, 159-60
  and Atlantic patrol, 291-3, 309-10, 311
  and Caucasian air force, 635-9
  complexity of, 10, 298-9
  death of, 869-71
  decision to aid Britain, 150-3
  and Executive reorganization, 209-11
  health, 668 *ff.*, 691-2, 812-13, 816-17, 841, 863
  and isolationism, 125-40
  New York governorship, 29-33
  and Pearl Harbour, 430-9
  political philosophy, 74-5
  relations with Churchill, 364-5, 446-8
  and social legislation, 11, 29 *ff.*, 44, 46, 736
  and Supreme Court fight, 89, 170
  third term, *see* Third term
  and unconditional surrender, 690, 692-4, 699, 738, 785, 852
  White House staff, 205-11
  See also Speeches, F. D. Roosevelt
Roosevelt, Franklin D., Jr., xiv, 365, 585, 671, 765
Roosevelt, James, 93, 97
Roosevelt, Mrs. James, Sr., 200, 251, 386-7
Roosevelt, John, 192, 929
Roosevelt, Theodore, 22, 164, 189
  Osawatamie Speech, 41-2

Roosevelt: Dictator or Democrat? 74–5, 929
Roosevelt I Knew, The, xiv
Roosevelt Revolution, The, 44, 929
Roper, Daniel C., 95
Roper, Elmo, xiv
Roper Polls, 87, 103, 129, 199, 932
Rosenman, Dorothy, 198
Rosenman, Samuel I., xii, 9, 204, 504–5,
    757, 813, 820, 822, 929, 936
  and preparation of speeches, 179, 183–4,
    196–7, 212–17, 296–7, 372–3, 737, 863
Ross, Harold, 730
ROUNDUP, operation, 359, 525 f., 559,
    595, 604–5, 607, 609, 612, 615, 617,
    653, 672, 925, 937
  See also OVERLORD
Rowe, James, Jr., 208, 287
Rowlands, Sir Archibald, 387
Royal Navy, 149 f., 152, 530, 806–7
  Home Fleet, 142, 148, 245, 539–40, 568,
    573
Rumania, 571, 864
Rumelt, Ruthjane, 195
Ruml, Beardsley, xiv
Russia, *see* Soviet Union

S

ST. PIERRE and Miquelon, 456–66, 941
Salazar, Dr. A. de O., 401, 744
Salter, Sir Arthur, 284
Samrock, Victor, xiv
San Francisco Chronicle, 166
San Francisco Conference, 864–66, 874,
    900–2
Sandburg, Carl, 135, 199, 218, 246, 934
Sargent, Sir Orme, 258
Savannah News, 847
Scapa Flow, Scot., 245, 348–9
Scharnhorst (Ger. cruiser), 291, 318, 506
Schuirmann, Capt. R. E., 423
Schulz, Comm. L. R., 430–2, 434–5
Scott, Adm. Norman, 652
Searles, Mr., 206
Second Front, 532–3, 538–9, 547, 557–8,
    565–7, 581–3, 633, 671 f., 697–8, 773–
    4, 785, 940
  dispute over, 240, 262, 395–6, 530–1,
    540–3, 572–5, 578–80, 587–97, 609–
    12, 615–17, 619–20, 762–3, 782–3
  planning for, 523–6, 731–3, 742–3

Second World War, 118, 125
  See also Blitzkrieg; Conferences;
    Phony War; Theatres of War;
    War plans
Secret Service, 682–3, 771
Selective Service, 133, 157–8, 163, 175, 190
  extension of, 367–9, 939
Serbia, 708
Sevastopol, siege of, 590
Sforza, Count Carlo, 830–1
Shangri-la, 72, 213, 624, 724, 737
Sheil, Bishop Bernard, xiv
Sherman, Adm. Forrest, xiv
Sherwood, Madeline, 198, 200
Sherwood, Robert E., 49–50, 72, 168,
    183–4, 191, 204, 370, 933
  and preparation of speeches, 212–18,
    296–7, 737–8, 868
Shirer, William L., 97, 166, 858
Sholis, Victor, xiii, 109
Short, Dewey, 747
Short, Gen. Walter C., 428–9, 439, 482
Sicily, invasion of, 671–2
Sikorski, Wladyslaw, 394, 701
Simone, Sam, xiii
Simpson, Kirke L., 933
Sinclair, Sir Archibald, 312, 540
Sioux City, Iowa, 14
Sioux City Journal, 91, 347
SLEDGEHAMMER, operation, 525, 541,
    558, 559, 593, 603–7, 609–11, 616–17,
    925, 943
Slessor, Air Commo. J. C., 272
Smith, Alfred E., 11, 29–30, 81, 95, 386
Smith, Harold, xiii, 73, 160, 210–11, 488,
    930
Smith, Merriman, 631, 821
Smith, Sir Reginald D., 289–90
Smith, Gen. Walter Bedell, 608, 653, 661,
    701, 741–2, 840
Smith-Connally Anti-Strike Bill, 736
Smuts, Jan Christiaan, 574
Smyth, Henry D., 933
Social Justice, 167–8
Socialist party, 25, 107
Somervell, Gen. Brehon B., 77, 586, 757
Soong, T. V., 410–12, 517 ff., 534, 642,
    704, 735, 741, 795, 891
Southampton, H.M.S., 244
South-East Asia Command, 742 f., 768
South-West Pacific theatre, 597, 601, 604,
    622–3, 630, 654, 656, 678–9
Soviet Protocol Committee, 401–2

Soviet Union, 125, 133, 139, 259, 264, 300, 311, 386, 452-4, 500-1, 639-42, 706, 729-30, 744-5
  German invasion of, 302-9
  and German reparations, 851, 882
  religion in, 393-5
  and war against Japan, 774, 835-6, 854-6, 891-3
  See also Lend Lease
Spaatz, Gen. Carl, 554, 608
Spalding, Gen. George R., 278
Spalding, Gen. Sidney P., 278
Speaking Frankly, 845, 953
Speeches, F. D. Roosevelt, 508-9, 929, 935, 942, 952
  Boston (1940), 191-3
  Brooklyn (1940), 193-5
  Charlottesville (1940), 145
  Cleveland (1940), 195-7
  on Communism, 139-40, 821
  Fireside Chats, 42-3, 224-6, 552-3
  first Albany Inaugural (1929), 11
  first inaugural (1933), 40
  Labour Day (1941), 370-3
  on Lend Lease (1941), 224-6, 265-7
  Madison Square Garden (1940), 189-90
  Navy Day (1941), 383
  Pan-American Day (1941), 292-3, 296-8
  Pearl Harbour (1941), 441-2
  preparation of, 50, 184, 195-6, 212-19, 265-6, 296-7, 320, 665-6, 819, 862-3
  on price control (1942), 552-3
  State of the Union (1942), 468-9
  State of the Union (1943), 665-6
  Teamsters' Union (1944), 217, 813-15
Spellman, Cardinal Francis J., 190
Spending to Save, 86
Spokane, Wash., 18
Stabilization Act, 631-2
Staff talks, *see* Combined Chiefs of Staff
Stalin, Joseph, 6, 140-1, 145, 291, 307-9, 317-18, 549-50, 600-1, 647, 668, 729-30, 745, 804, 872-3, 949
  on Russian Air Force, 338-9
  on Russian strategy, 335-41
  and Second Front, 343-4, 533, 616-20, 656, 697-8, 702, 729-30
  on supplies to Russia, 329-30, 337-8, 340-1 389, 391, 501, 637-9
  talks with Hopkins, 328-31, 334-45, 875-902
  See also Conferences: Moscow,, Teheran; Yalta
Standley, Adm. William H., 387, 501, 549, 637f., 702-3, 729

Stark, Adm. Harold R., xiv, 165, 176, 271-3, 290-1, 302, 354, 413, 427, 431-2, 435-6, 438-9, 449, 608, 907, 919, 948-9
  war estimate by, 380-1
Starling, Col. Edward W., 192
Stassen, Harold E., 817
State Department, 114-15, 136, 216, 226, 278, 299, 373, 433, 562f., 627, 647, 673-4, 678, 738-9, 769, 829-30, 865
  Foreign Service, 64, 114-15, 752
  and military government, 719-20
Steiner, Dr. E. A., xiii, 18, 21, 34
Steinhardt, Laurence A., xi, 299, 327-8, 332-4, 347, 501, 556-7
Stephenson, Sir William, xiv, 270
Stettinius, Edward R., Jr., xiv, 108-9, 158, 285, 377-8, 384, 388, 752f., 846
  as Sec. of State, 827, 829-31, 844-5, 848, 854, 865
Stevens, Robert T., xiv, 162-3
Stilwell, Gen. Joseph W., 518, 599-600, 728, 742, 755, 766ff., 950
  disputes in China, 632, 657-8, 725-7, 735-6, 803, 812
Stilwell Papers, The, 950
Stimson, Henry L., xii, xiv, 13, 163-6, 268, 367, 399, 466, 509, 597, 722, 758, 827, 870-1, 917, 945
  on German-Russian war, 303-4
  on supreme command, 762
  See also War Department
Stitt, Adm. Edward R., 120
Stokes, Thomas L., 96
Stone, Julius F., 52, 379
Strang, William, 715
Strategy, *see* War plans
Strategy of Terror, The, 932
Straus, Jesse I., 31, 34, 918
Strong, Gen. George V., 270, 271, 554
Strong, Brig. K. W. D., 741-2
Suckley, Margaret, 5
Sullivan, James P., 933
Sulzberger, Cyrus L., 765
SUPER-GYMNAST, operation, 472-4, 478-9, 941
  See also GYMNAST
Supply Priorities Allocation Board, 377
Supreme command controversy, xi-xii, 755-62, 882-3, 793
Supreme Court packing issue, 89, 170
Survey Graphic, 23
Swing, Raymond G., ix, xiv, 166, 827, 858-9, 931, 939
Swope, Herbert Bayard, xiv, 5, 23, 306

T

TABER, John W., 267, 522
Taft, Robert A., 134, 152, 175 ƒ., 820
Talmadge, Eugene, 78
Taranto, Italy, 220
Task Force, 58, 861
Tass News Agency, 502
Tassigny, Gen. J. de L. de, 952
Taylor, Edmond, 144, 932
Taylor, Myron C., xiv, 386, 400–1, 840
Teamsters' Union speech, 217, 813–15
Tedder, Air Marshal Lord, 674, 688, 937
Teheran Conference, 770–90
Teheran Declaration, 789–90
Temporary Emergency Relief Adminis-
    tration, 31–33
Tennessee Valley Authority, 174
Terrell, George B., 55
Texas, *U.S.S.*, 628
Thank You, Mr. President, 631
Theatres of war, *see* A.B.D.A. Area;
    North African; South-West Pacific;
    War plans
Third term, 94, 115–16, 163, 169
    campaign for, 186–201
    Chicago convention, 177–9
    as issue, 170–3
Thompson, Comm. Charles, xiv, 242,
    261, 350, 546, 608, 937
Thompson, Dorothy, xiv, 87–8, 196, 199,
    319–20
Thompson, Malvina C., 933
Thorp, Willard L., 115
Thors, Thor, 290
Time for Decision, The, 932
Time magazine, 55–6, 538
Times, London, 539
Times-Union (Jacksonville, Fla.), 346–7
Timoshenko, Marshal S. K., 570
Tirpitz (Ger. battleship), 291, 542, 637
Tizard, Sir Henry, 270
Together, 545
Togo, Shigenori, 426
Tojo, Gen. Hideki, 381, 423, 802
TORCH, operation, 472–3, 615, 617–18,
    620ƒ., 625–8, 633ƒƒ., 642–5, 653–4,
    925, 940, 946
Tovey, Adm. Sir John, 350, 352
Towers, Adm. John H., 555
Treasury Department, 163, 227
Tree, Ronald, 241
TRIDENT conference (Wash., 1943),
    724–9
Tripartite Treaty, 271

Trippe, Juan, 287
Trohan, Walter, 746–7, 951
Truman, Harry S., xiv, 6, 51, 207, 802,
    870–1, 872, 874 ƒƒ., 891, 902–3, 905–6,
    907, 915 ƒ., 954
Tuck, S. Pinkney, 554
Tugwell, Rexford G., xiv, 44, 65, 71
Tully, Grace, xii, 191, 195, 205–6, 213 ƒ.,
    216, 296–7, 380, 437, 607, 741, 813,
    931, 935 ƒ.
Tunis, Bey of, 643
Turkey, 556–7, 653 ƒƒ., 680, 774 ƒƒ., 786 ƒƒ.,
    790–1
Turner, Adm. R. K., 272, 275–6, 302
Tuscaloosa, *U.S.S.*, 221–3, 934
Tydings, Millard E., 105, 613

U

UMBERTO, Prince (It.), 829
Unconditional surrender doctrine, 690,
    692–4, 899, 738, 777–8, 785, 852, 892
Unemployment relief, 41–77
United Nations, 471, 546, 552, 576, 623,
    704–5, 817
    additional Russian votes, 846–8, 865–6
    Declaration of, 450–4, 940–1
    organization, 715–16, 718, 780–2, 784,
        852
    veto principle, 846–7, 864, 900–2
    See also San Francisco Conference
U.S.S.R., *see* Soviet Union

V

VANDENBURG, Arthur H., 105–7, 152, 865
Vandenburg, Col. Hoyt S., 608
Van Meter, Mary, 103
Vargas, Getulio, 692, 949
Vatican, 386, 401
Veale, Douglas, 954
VELVET, operation, 637, 925
Versailles, Ky., 115
Vichy Government, 459–66, 504–5, 543–5,
    552–4, 569, 618, 643–7, 649–50, 672–8
Vickery, Adm. H. L., 283, 286, 310, 714
Victor Emmanuel, King (It.), 738ƒƒ., 748,
    829
Victory Programme (production), 486–7
Vigerie, Gen. d'Astier de la, 659
Villard, Oswald G., 168
Vishinski, Andrei, 766, 844, 903–4
Volstead Act, 43
Voroshilov, Marshal K. E., 778
Vyshinski, *see* Vishinski, Andrei

W

WADSWORTH, James W., 158

Wainwright, Gen. Jonathan M., 514, 542

Wald, Lillian, 24

Walker, Frank C., xii, 32, 53–5, 65, 79, 172, 302, 386, 820, 852
  and Relief Programme, 69–72

Walker, Col. K. M., 572

Wall Street Journal, 346

Wallace, Henry A., 44, 94, 141, 170, 227, 358, 377, 437–8, 488–9, 736–7, 820, 838, 870*f.*
  Vice-Presidential nomination, 178–9

Waltman, Franklyn, 90

War agency policy, 159–60

War Department, 97–9, 114, 137, 202, 216, 227, 303–4, 380, 397–8, 436, 700–1, 919

War plans, ABC, 1, 273, 925, 935
  ANAKIM, 672, 688, 728, 766–8, 925
  ANVIL, 743, 801, 804, 925, 952
  AVALANCHE, 741, 925
  BOLERO, 523*f.*, 559, 573–4, 593, 595, 597, 603*f.*, 607, 654, 688, 925
  BUCCANEER, 791–2, 925
  DRAGOON, *see* ANVIL
  FLINTLOCK, 796, 925
  GYMNAST, 472–4, 478–9, 515, 525, 545, 559, 588, 593, 604, 610–12, 925, 942. *See also* TORCH
  Hemisphere Defence Plans, 292–3
  HUSKY, 671, 674, 689, 714, 720, 728, 925
  Joint Board Estimate, 413–23, 438, 488
  JUPITER, 559, 628, 653, 925
  LIFEBELT, 725, 925
  LIGHTFOOT, 628, 925, 946
  MAGNET, 472, 474, 476–7, 925
  OVERLORD, xi–xii, 359, 525, 727*f.*, 742–3, 755*ff.*, 765, 770, 774–8, 782–6, 802–3, 925
  POINTBLANK, 743, 925
  RAINBOW, 449
  ROUNDUP, 359, 525*f.*, 559, 595, 604–5, 607, 609, 612, 615, 617, 653, 672, 925, 937. *See also* OVERLORD
  SLEDGEHAMMER, 525, 541, 558, 559, 593, 603–7, 609–11, 616–17, 925, 943
  SUPER-GYMNAST, 472–4, 478–9, 941
  See also GYMNAST

Hemisphere Defence Plans—*continued*
  TORCH, 472–3, 615, 617–18, 620*f.*, 625–8, 633*ff.*, 642–5, 653–4, 925, 940, 946
  VELVET, 637, 925

War Plans Division, 524

War Production Board, 487–9, 696–7, 812

War Reports, The, 938

War Shipping Administration, 550–1

Warburg, James P., 628

Wardlaw-Milne, Sir John, 602

Warm Springs, Ga., 5, 65, 112–13, 931

Warren, Joseph, 135

Washington, U.S.S., 540

Washington News, 62

Washington Post, 44–5, 61, 90, 872–3

Washington Times, 88

Washington Times-Herald, 382–3

Wasp, U.S.S., 540

Watson, Gen. Edwin M., 80, 88, 182–3, 192, 196, 206–7, 221, 249, 764, 812, 863, 930

Watson, Mrs. Edwin M., xiv, 873

Wavell, Gen. Sir Archibald, 221–2, 256, 275, 312, 470–1, 480, 510, 725–6

Wedemeyer, Gen. A. C., 526, 537, 760, 857

Weinberg, Sidney J., 109

Weir, Ernest T., 193

Welles, Sumner, xiv, 136–7, 139, 282, 294, 296–7, 318, 321–2, 407, 438, 517, 673–4, 704–5, 752, 827, 854–5, 932, 943
  See also Atlantic Conference

Werth, Alexander, 702, 945

Wescott, Barbara, 918

Westbrook, Col. Lawrence, xiii, 76, 87, 88

Weygand, Gen. Maxime, 142–3, 146, 147, 240, 463, 554

Wheeler, Burton K., 133, 227–8, 368

Wheeler, Monroe, 918

Whelan, Alex. A., xiv

Where Are We Heading? 360–1, 854–5, 943

White, E. B., 730–1

White, Wallace, 106, 108, 859

White, William A., 167–9

White Committees, 49, 167–9

White House, 173–4, 202–18
  cuisine, 214
  furnishings, 204–5
  staff, 205–12

Wilbur, Gen. William H., 683–4, 686

Wilhelmina, Queen (Holland), 251

Williams, Aubrey, xii*f.*, 50–2, 57, 93, 103, 107
Williams, Dr. Frankwood E., 34
Williams, Dr. Linsley R., 28
Williams, Pierce, 52
Willkie, Wendell, 4, 50, 88, 152, 164, 169, 234–5, 263, 288, 487, 672, 822, 929
  and destroyer transfer, 176
  presidential candidacy, 174–5, 177, 184–91, 198–9, 200–1, 932
  visit to England, 251, 253–4, 260
  world trip, 632–4
Willkie, Mrs. Wendell, xiv, 929
Wilson, Gen. Arthur R., xiv, 97–9
Wilson, Sir Charles, 387
Wilson, Charles E., 696–7, 812
Wilson, Sir Henry Maitland, 760–1, 832–3, 952
Wilson, Mrs. Howard, 87
Wilson, Woodrow, 16–17, 22, 43, 225, 263, 361, 694, 753, 846–7, 865
Wilson, Mrs. Woodrow, 441
Winant, John G., xii, 258, 262, 312, 321, 350, 352, 402–3, 427–8, 443, 532, 582–3, 704, 831–2, 908, 936
  problems as Ambassador, 269, 750–2
  on war against Japan, 806–8
Winchell, Walter, 827, 907
Windsor, Duke of, 221
Winner, Percy, 628
Wolfert, Ira, xiv, 457–8, 941
Wood, Sir Kingsley, 313
Wood, Gen. Robert E., 108, 131, 383

Woodin, William H., 44
Woodring, Harry H., 137
Woodrow Wilson League, 16
Woodward, Ellen, xiii, 52, 103
Woollcott, Alexander, 199
Woolton, Lord, 312
Work Relief Bill, 67–9, 75–6
Work Relief Programme, 65–7, 78–9
Works Progress Administration, 49, 69–72, 75–7, 79, 83–6, 96, 103–4
World War II, *see* Second World War
Wrong, Hume, 521

Y

YAKOVLEV, General, 331, 346
Yalta Conference, 842–58
  Foreign Secretaries' meetings, 844–5, 848, 849, 852–3
  genesis of, 835–7, 953
  reparations talks, 851
  United Nations talks, 846–9
Yarnell, Adm. Harry E., 272, 378, 935
Year of Stalingrad, The, 702, 945
Yeaton, Maj. Ivan, 328, 331, 397–8
Yorktown, U.S.S., 68
Young, Philip, 278, 285, 287

Z

ZHUKOV, Marshal G. K., 879, 890–1, 894, 903–4, 913–14